D1554028

Making Sense
of the
New Testament

Making Sense
of the
New Testament

TIMELY INSIGHTS &
TIMELESS MESSAGES

Richard Neitzel Holzapfel
and Thomas A. Wayment

DESERET
BOOK

Salt Lake City, Utah

© 2010 Richard Neitzel Holzapfel and Thomas A. Wayment

All rights reserved. No part of this book may be reproduced in any form or by any means with-out permission in writing from the publisher, Deseret Book Company, P. O. Box 30178, Salt Lake City, Utah 84130. This work is not an official publication of The Church of Jesus Christ of Latter-day Saints. The views expressed herein are the responsibility of the author and do not necessarily represent the position of the Church or of Deseret Book Company.

DESERET BOOK is a registered trademark of Deseret Book Company.

Visit us at DeseretBook.com

Library of Congress Cataloging-in-Publication Data
Holzapfel, Richard Neitzel.
   Making sense of the New Testament : timely insights and timeless messages / Richard Neitzel Holzapfel and Thomas A. Wayment.
        p. cm.
   Includes bibliographical references and index.
   ISBN 978-1-60641-668-6 (hardbound : alk. paper)
   1. Bible. N.T.—Criticism, interpretation, etc. 2. The Church of Jesus Christ of Latter-day Saints—Doctrines. I. Wayment, Thomas A. II. Title.
   BS2361.3.H66 2010
   225.7'7—dc22   2010011484

Printed in the United States of America
Publishers Printing, Salt Lake City, UT

10   9   8   7   6   5   4   3   2   1

For my companion in the Lord's vineyard
Sister Jeni Broberg Holzapfel
Alabama Birmingham Mission, 2010–2013
—Richard Neitzel Holzapfel

To Shelby, for asking questions and helping me
appreciate the depth of the message
—Thomas A. Wayment

CONTENTS

CONTENTS

ACKNOWLEDGMENTS

Ultimately, we alone are responsible for the content of this book. Nevertheless, we appreciate the many friends, colleagues, and commentators who have shared their ideas through conversation, conferences, or written articles and books. It has been a wonderful journey for us to visit the New Testament again.

We spent most of our long days and some rather long nights carefully reading the New Testament and important secondary literature; writing several drafts of each section; reviewing each others' work; and reviewing and considering comments by thoughtful outside readers. But this was not enough to bring this project to a successful conclusion. There were some expenses to cover student help, provide review stipends, and purchase expensive academic New Testament books. The resources to do so were provided by kind donors, to whom we express gratitude.

We thank our colleagues Frank Judd Jr. and Gaye Strathearn, whose careful reading of the manuscript made the finished product much better and more thoughtful, and Richard Draper for providing important feedback on the book of Revelation. We also thank our New Testament students at BYU during the past few years; they helped us reach further into the text of the New Testament to find answers to today's challenges and not just respond to today's concerns with yesterday's answers.

Joany Pinegar, administrative assistant at the Religious Studies Center (BYU), took care of the budget and coordinated the hiring and supervising of most of our student employees. Emily Broadbent, Nicholas K. Brown,

Acknowledgments

Alan Taylor Farnes, Berit Green, Chris Keneipp, Laurie Mildenhall, Kipp Muir, Vanessa Rothfels, Stephanie Sant, Samuel Smith, and Rachel Taylor, our research assistants, checked sources and text for accuracy and completeness, an arduous task given the number of scripture citations. Additionally, several of them carefully reviewed the 1979 Latter-day Saint edition of the Bible to ensure that we had taken full advantage of excerpts from the Joseph Smith Translation, alternative translations from the Greek, explanations of idioms and difficult constructions, and alternate words to clarify the meaning of archaic expressions noted in the footnotes of the standard works.

We appreciate the continued interest of Deseret Book Company in our work. We thank especially Cory Maxwell, Suzanne Brady, Shauna Gibby, and Rachael Ward for their contributions to the publication of this volume.

Introduction

THE "GOOD NEWS" IS STILL GOOD NEWS

One may rightfully wonder why another commentary on the New Testament is necessary or even helpful in light of the many works that have already been written on this remarkable book of scripture. At the turn of the twentieth century, Elder James E. Talmage wrote *Jesus the Christ*, one of the most influential books on the life of the Savior that has been written for the Church. Later, Elder Bruce R. McConkie wrote a series of volumes on the life of Jesus Christ and an in-depth commentary on the text of the New Testament. The testimonies of Elder Talmage and Elder McConkie, as apostolic witnesses of Jesus Christ, will continue to bless the lives of the Saints for generations to come.

Interestingly, both apostles drew upon scholarship, primarily Protestant, available to them in their day to help them tell the story of Jesus Christ. In this they followed the Lord's direction: "Seek ye out of the best books words of wisdom; seek learning, even by study and also by faith" (D&C 88:118) and "become acquainted with all good books, and with languages, tongues, and people" (D&C 90:15).

We too have taken advantage of scholarship, viewing it through the lens of the Restoration. One of our intentions is to bridge the gap between recent advances in New Testament studies and earlier interpretations of the late nineteenth and twentieth centuries. Just as those studies benefited from earlier efforts, so we stand on their shoulders in order to see farther. Perhaps a future generation will do the same with our current efforts to understand the world of the New Testament. New archaeological and textual

1

discoveries as well as the way the text is interpreted allow us to appreciate more fully the cultural and historical setting of this important spiritual witness of Jesus Christ.

In drawing from the larger field of current New Testament scholarship, we follow the direction of the Prophet Joseph Smith when he taught, "One of the grand fundamental principles of 'Mormonism' is to receive truth, let it come from whence it may" (*History of the Church*, 5:499). On another occasion he said, "We should gather all the good and true principles in the world and treasure them up, or we shall not come out true Mormons" (*Teachings of the Prophet Joseph Smith*, 316). The works we consulted are listed in a bibliography at the end of the commentary to assist the reader who wishes to study further.

In following the text of the New Testament, our commentary begins with the Gospels, which are divided into stories in a way that we think will be the most helpful to the reader. In the next chapter we focus on the book of Acts. Luke's account is divided into individual units that we feel provide an opportunity for the reader to best understand the basic story line. Finally, we examine each of the remaining books of the New Testament (the Pauline Epistles, general Epistles, and the book of Revelation) in the order they appear in our current New Testament. We begin with a brief introduction to each book, discussing dating, authorship, and historical context. Each book is then divided into smaller sections in order to highlight how the various authors sought to share their testimonies of Jesus Christ and teach his basic doctrines to the Saints in the first century. This arrangement allows the reader to approach the text with a sense of the problems and issues that each author was addressing.

Rather than being reasoned discourses on doctrine, many of the letters in the New Testament represent responses by Church leaders to particular concerns over conditions in a specific place or with a specific individual or group. In this way they resemble modern general conference talks, which address issues of our day but which are aimed at the broader audience of the worldwide Church. Unlike the New Testament epistles, general conference talks do not deal with the problems of a specific stake, much less a specific ward within that stake.

It is often easier to understand and apply the message of a general conference talk than it is to understand and apply the message of a New Testament epistle. We are conversant with the modern historical setting whereas we are less familiar with the setting and circumstance of a message written nearly two thousand years ago. Hence, not knowing the historical context, we may struggle to grasp the full meaning of Paul's letter to the Saints in Corinth, for example. Nevertheless, there are clues in the epistles that can help us reconstruct the setting with some reasonable approximation.

Looking at the New Testament book by book, as we do in this commentary, allows us to gain unique insights as we see how faith affected the lives of men and women who knew Jesus during his mortal ministry or following his Resurrection. This approach helps us as long as we do not lose sight of the larger, comprehensive, saving message of the good news. Also, focusing on individual authors may cause us to slip into favoring some New Testament authors over others. Therefore, we encourage the reader to review the entire New Testament, not just favorite books within it.

Because this commentary is tied to the New Testament text, some subjects are not treated exhaustively in a single entry. This practice reflects the text to which it is linked, where, for example, the writers of the Gospels report the acts of the Atonement, such as the dramatic events of Gethsemane and Golgotha, but do not extensively interpret the Atonement itself. Other New Testament authors, especially Paul, provide several different ways of interpreting, understanding, and applying the Atonement. For instance, Paul speaks of God redeeming us, literally buying us back (Galatians 4:5); he also speaks of Jesus' acting as a substitute on our behalf (Galatians 3:13). In Romans, Paul speaks of our joint suffering with Christ (Romans 8:17), and elsewhere he tells of Jesus' being offered in sacrifice for our sins (Romans 3:23–25, 28). Of course, no metaphor is complete, but each represents a part of a larger picture, and in this example we see the interpretation of the event separated from the historical report.

We recognize that other authors may have emphasized certain words, phrases, or stories that we do not. We also recognize that, inevitably, other commentators will naturally arrive at different conclusions from ours on certain points. Nevertheless, Latter-day Saint authors share a belief in the essential historical truths of the New Testament: "For I delivered unto you first of all that which I also received, how that *Christ died for our sins* according to the scriptures; and that *he was buried*, and that *he rose again the third day* according to the scriptures" (1 Corinthians 15:3–4; emphasis added). In this we are united in a single witness of the New Testament's most important message—the redemption and resurrection that comes through Jesus Christ, the Redeemer and Savior of the world.

We acknowledge that other approaches to the study of the New Testament help the Saints apply the scriptures to their lives by making the stories and teachings of the New Testament relevant and meaningful. We have been blessed by such efforts, especially those that have provided a selection of inspired quotations from Church leaders. General Authorities of The Church of Jesus Christ of Latter-day Saints, particularly those we sustain as prophets, seers, and revelators, have a special and unique commission from the Lord to provide authoritative doctrinal and application insights for the Saints. We happily defer to them in that divinely appointed role. Therefore, we focus our attention on the text of the New Testament itself, believing that we can learn something from the New Testament writings that will make us better disciples and help us be better prepared to apply the scriptures in our lives as we listen to a prophet's voice.

Although the New Testament disciples may not have anticipated that we would read their words in modern translations or seek to apply them in our day, they nevertheless knew they were preserving an important witness. John explicitly states, "But these are written, that ye might believe that Jesus is the Christ, the Son of God; and that believing ye might have life through his name" (John 20:31). In the end, the several authors of the New Testament had a testimony that Jesus Christ is the author of salvation and that their accounts of his life and teachings would provide the inspiration necessary to embrace his gospel and keep his commandments and thus find the fulness of life God intended for his sons and daughters.

This volume attempts to anticipate questions that readers might have regarding the stories preserved in this ancient record by engaging the Greek and English translations of the New Testament directly, providing brief historical context, and focusing our Restoration perspective on the New Testament by using the tools and resources available to us today. We know we cannot always be certain of the past—the New Testament does not contain all the detail necessary to provide a complete picture of Jesus, Peter, or Paul. Therefore, we have exercised caution and have attempted to be judicious in presenting historical, cultural, and linguistic insights by using such words as *likely, possible,* and *probable* in order to provide the reader with a wider variety of options to consider.

We have included at the end of the volume a glossary of terms, in which particular words and historical issues are discussed in greater detail. Each term in the glossary appears in bold type in the text. We have not used footnotes or endnotes; where documentation has seemed desirable, we have included such information parenthetically within the text.

As Elder McConkie did, so we have incorporated into our analysis many passages from the Joseph Smith Translation of the Bible, including some that are not found in the Latter-day Saint edition of the King James Version. Recent advances in research in the Joseph Smith Translation have provided us a clearer picture of what the Prophet left to the Church in his translation of the Bible. The source of our quotations from that translation is an accessible resource that reflects the most current discoveries regarding the text of the Joseph Smith Translation: Thomas A. Wayment, ed., *The Complete Joseph Smith Translation of the New Testament: A Side-by-Side Comparison with the King James Version* (Salt Lake City: Deseret Book, 2005).

The New Testament may be compared to a diamond. First, just as diamonds are created through extreme heat and pressure, so the New Testament is the product of remarkable sacrifice, both in time and in financial resources. Given the historic reality of the first century, it is a miracle that we can read and study the New Testament today. Second, a diamond's true beauty is measured by how near it comes to ideal proportions, which are based on a mathematical formula. The cut of a diamond causes it to reflect light, so each facet is important to the total effect. The same is true of the New Testament. The primary message is enhanced as we draw deeply from all of its books rather than from just a few of our favorite ones.

We hope our approach will make the meaning of the New Testament more accessible by providing the reader the timely insights and the timeless messages contained in this amazing book of scripture. We believe with all our hearts and minds that the "good news" proclaimed by the authors of the New Testament is still good news.

1

THE GOSPELS

The Beginning of the Gospel of Jesus Christ
MATTHEW 1:1; MARK 1:1; LUKE 1:1–4; JOHN 1:1–18

The first words that each of the four evangelists put down on papyrus as they endeavored to distill the **gospel** of **Jesus Christ** for future readers reveal something of the way in which they saw the story as well as how they felt about some of the issues contemporary to their day. Matthew and Luke began their accounts similarly, telling the birth story of Jesus, and Joseph's and Mary's struggles associated with those miraculous events. John, on the other hand, chose to look back into premortality and record a testimony of Jesus prior to his life on earth. Mark skipped those preliminary details and focused immediately on Jesus' mortal ministry, beginning with the ministry of John the Baptist and then on to the events of the Savior's early ministry.

Mark was the first evangelist to write his Gospel account and to have his record survive the ravages of time. Paul's writings preceded his, but it appears that Mark set the stage for the later evangelists. He began auspiciously: "The beginning of the gospel of Jesus Christ, the **Son of God**," (Mark 1:1; emphasis added) informing the reader that Mark's focus was not purely historical. He set out to define the gospel through the story of Jesus Christ. Several important issues arise from this, the earliest gospel verse. Mark already knew that the message of Jesus had come to be called a gospel and not a biography or narrative; and he knew the name *Jesus* had become inextricably connected with the title *Christ*, or "Anointed One." The title

7

expresses a position of faith as the author identifies with all who have come to accept Jesus as the Christ and who seek to know the gospel message he taught.

Invariably, once a story has been told, questions arise from what was not told and as outsiders begin to challenge the story as it has been told. Mark had the privilege of starting that conversation, and Matthew and Luke had the challenge of continuing it in light of what appears to have been growing prejudice and controversy. When Matthew and Luke wrote, they entered what was an already lively conversation, and as a result of that conversation, they shaped their accounts to help answer some of the troubling questions being raised about Jesus: namely the question of his parentage and lineage, the challenge of explaining his ministry using Old Testament prophecies, providing an explanation of why he was rejected among his own people, as well as other significant issues of the late first century A.D. Matthew began his record by drawing clearly on the Old Testament, using concepts such as a "register of the genealogy" (Nehemiah 7:5) to testify that Jesus was a **son of David** *and* a son of Abraham. From his position of faith, Matthew reached out to his audience to see in Jesus one who was of the seed of Abraham (as all Jews were) and that he was of the ancient Davidic line that held the promises.

Luke was more transparent in explaining his reason for writing when he told his audience that he had relied on written sources for guidance: "Forasmuch as many have taken in hand to set forth in order a declaration of those things which are most surely believed among us, even as they delivered them unto us, which from the beginning were eyewitnesses, and ministers of the word; it seemed good to me also, having had perfect understanding of all things from the very first, to write unto thee in order, most excellent Theophilus, that thou mightest know the certainty of those things, wherein thou hast been instructed" (Luke 1:1–4). By the time Luke wrote, it seems that even the order of the story was in question, and Luke revealed his corrective tendency in saying he had a "perfect understanding" to "write . . . in order," that is to put the story in its proper sequence. Luke converted to Christianity years after the death of Jesus (Acts 16:10 is the first instance where Luke inserts himself into Paul's story) and therefore tells the reader that he was a receiver of the tradition that had been passed down through faithful channels and that he was not an eyewitness to the events. He had great faith in the authority of the eyewitnesses, whom we assume were likely the **apostles**, and the accuracy of the story as they passed it on. In Luke's Gospel, based on his opening lines, we expect to see an author who will pay attention to the order of the stories from Jesus' life.

In many instances, John's Gospel and its opening lines are more difficult to interpret and to discover their intent. John begins his Gospel with a hymn about Christ that looks back into the premortal realm and forward to John the Baptist, who would be witness to the Lord's mission. It incorporates technical terminology that was derived from Hellenistic Jews of the day (for example, *logos*, "divine reason," or "word"). The hymn is also poetic, and its symmetry can still be seen in four stanzas (John 1:1–2, 3–5, 10–12, and 14–16, with the exception of v. 15). That hymn, which has been included by the author of the fourth Gospel, draws upon the teachings of John the Baptist by placing them in what appears to be a new context. John the Baptist is he of whom it is said, "There was a man sent from God, whose name was John. The same came for a witness, to bear witness of the Light, that all men through him might believe. He was not that Light, but was sent to bear witness of that Light" (John 1:6–8). Moreover, "John bare witness of him, and cried, saying, This was he of whom I spake, He that cometh after me is preferred before me: for he was before me" (John 1:15). From these passages, it is apparent that the author felt close to John the Baptist and valued his testimony of who Jesus Christ was and is. The remarkable degree of verbatim language shared by John's opening verses and Doctrine and Covenants 93, together with the first-person wording ("I"), may suggest that the revelation recorded in Doctrine and Covenants 93 includes information from the author of the Gospel or, perhaps, that the revelation can be interpreted to mean that John the Baptist was the author of some of the wording of the hymn.

John 1:18 seems to make a claim that is contradictory to both the Old Testament and the Restoration: "No man hath seen God at any time; the only begotten Son, which is in the bosom of the Father, he hath declared him." This was changed in the Joseph Smith Translation to read, "And no man hath seen God at any time; except he hath borne record of the Son, for except it is through him no man can be saved" (JST, John 1:19). Certainly Joseph's experience in the Sacred Grove makes it abundantly clear that God does reveal himself. This verse in the King James Version, which appears to so definitively state that no man can see God, has an important textual variant that demonstrates that others also saw the apparent contradiction with passages from the Old Testament (Isaiah 6:1). In the Freer Codex of the fourth or fifth century, as well as in some Old **Latin** manuscripts, the verse reads, "No man hath seen God at any time *except* the Only Begotten Son" (emphasis added). This rendering of the verse could be interpreted, as in the Joseph Smith Translation, to mean that no man has seen God unless he has also seen the **Son of God**. It is difficult to know whether this reading is original, but it testifies that seeing God was not impossible, for seeing God meant seeing the Son. Unlike this particular variant, most textual variants were likely the result of careless copying and scribal mistakes. Only a few of the variants that survive can be ascribed to malicious scribal intent.

Genealogies of Jesus
MATTHEW 1:2–17; LUKE 3:23–38

A pressing textual difficulty facing New Testament scholars is why both Matthew and Luke recorded two different genealogies of Joseph, **Jesus'** stepfather. If the two authors wrote in two very different locales, then it is possible to understand that both were recording the traditions that they had received, but if there was any contact between the two, of which there is considerable evidence, then the question is more difficult to answer. Despite modern attempts to harmonize the two genealogies, making one the genealogy of Joseph and the other of Mary, or those of Joseph's two fathers through the practice of **levirate marriage**, there is really no ancient evidence to support those claims.

More important than harmonizing the accounts is being able to understand the purpose behind the two genealogies. Matthew's genealogy presents a stylized, and not literal in every case, father-to-son relationship that builds on the shoulders of patriarchs, kings, and commoners, including four **Gentile** women. Having established what appears to be a royal genealogy, Matthew then states, "Now the birth of Jesus Christ was on this wise" (Matthew 1:18), suggesting that in spite of the prestigious genealogy just outlined, Jesus was born in humble circumstances, and that Joseph was Jesus' stepfather rather than literal father as one might assume after reading the genealogy. Matthew's purpose, which can be glimpsed in the genealogy, may have been to point out that Jesus (the Messiah) came in an unexpected and surprising way that was perhaps not anticipated by his countrymen.

Luke, on the other hand, appears more interested in a literal genealogy, but even here the genealogy is focused on tracing Joseph's lineage back to Adam, and hence to the father of all mankind, including **Gentiles**. Luke is also more explicit in pointing out Joseph's role as stepfather to Jesus: "And Jesus himself began to be about thirty years of age, being (*as was supposed*) the son of Joseph" (Luke 3:23; emphasis added). Perhaps Luke's interest surfaces here also, where a more universal outlook is portrayed by tracing Joseph's genealogy back to a time before the covenant was made with Abraham.

Zacharias and Elisabeth

Luke 1:5–25

Following Luke's introduction, which emphasizes the accounts of the eyewitnesses who preceded Luke and places the stories of **Jesus** in order, Luke preserves the only historical account of the birth of John the Baptist and a brief glimpse into the time when the revelation concerning John's birth was given in the Jerusalem **temple**. The reader is immediately given a wider perspective on history and how the story of Jesus' saving mission began before the last week of his life: The story of salvation stretches back to include the lives of those who became his witnesses.

The first four verses of the Gospel of Luke serve as an introduction to this account, and the fifth verse shifts into a narrative detailing Zacharias's service in the temple, using terminology from the Old Testament. The story is also personal, suggesting that Luke was acquainted with witnesses who knew the family well. He relates that Zacharias was of the "course of Abia" (Luke 1:5), the eighth course or "lot" and not the high priest (1 Chronicles 24:1–18). In doing so, Luke is not aggrandizing the parents of John the Baptist. Instead, he relates that Zacharias was an ordinary priest who served faithfully and who was "righteous before God, walking in *all* the commandments and ordinances of the Lord blameless" (Luke 1:6; emphasis added). In other words, the Lord blessed this couple because of how they lived and not simply because of their lineage.

The phrase "well stricken in years" (Luke 1:7) could be rendered more accurately, "both of them were getting on in years." The phrase itself has no specific period of life in mind, but the added reference that Elisabeth was "barren" may hint that she was past childbearing age. These facts, combined with the note that she hid herself for the first five months of the pregnancy, suggest that she hoped to avoid the embarrassment associated with the uncertainty of the early months of a pregnancy. These details show Luke's great interest in telling the story accurately and with great attention to the human component of the story.

Following ancient precedent as recorded in Daniel 10:15 and also in Alma 30:50, Zacharias was struck dumb for asking a sign of the angel, who is named Gabriel (harking back to the Old Testament; Daniel 8:16). In showing what preceded Zacharias's miraculous vision in the temple, Luke's purpose seems to be to draw the reader's attention to a new dispensation that would begin with John the Baptist.

Luke understood well how the temple functioned and that Zacharias needed to enter into the temple proper, where he would stand near to the Holy of Holies and offer incense. Having been chosen by lot to officiate in this manner, he was alone that day. But Luke was not interested solely in the sacrificial practice or method but rather on the announcement that came. Details such as which side of the altar the angel appeared upon (Zacharias's right or the angel's right?) or where Zacharias was standing are not important for Luke. Rather, it is the revelation that matters, and the discourse of the angel is intended to cause action. As a result of

in former times and recorded in the **Jewish scriptures** (Old Testament) were about to be fulfilled (Luke 1:64–79). The fulfillment would come in the most unexpected way—through the birth of two babies, John and **Jesus**.

Zacharias, whose name means "Yahweh remembers," proclaimed that God had remembered his **covenant** promises to Abraham (Luke 1:69–75). This song of praise, known as the **Benedictus** (**Latin**, "blessed"), contains references to several **messianic** prophecies, including Isaiah 9:2; 40:3; Malachi 4:2. Specifically, Zacharias said that his son, John, would prepare the way (Luke 1:76) for the second, unnamed child, who was identified as the "horn of salvation" (Luke 1:69), the one sent to redeem, that is, to ransom, humanity (Luke 1:68). Some scholars believe that the Benedictus preserves an early Jewish-Christian hymn (Luke 1:68–79).

The story ends with Luke's observation, "And the child grew, and waxed strong in spirit, and was in the deserts till the day of his shewing unto Israel" (Luke 1:80), without explaining when and why John left the village of his birth to live in the wilderness.

The Taxation by Caesar Augustus (Octavian)
LUKE 2:1–7

The well-known account of the taxation by Caesar Augustus of "all the world" (Luke 2:1) and Joseph and Mary's subsequent visit to Bethlehem demonstrates Luke's interest in the history of God's work. When he tells of the taxation under the Syrian governor Cyrenius, Luke is certainly not relating events for the sole purpose of recounting history. Luke lived in a world where Publius Nigidius announced to the senate at the birth of Augustus, "the ruler of the world has been born" (Suetonius, *Lives of the Caesars* 2.94) and where the emperor assumed that he had the power to carry out a taxation or census of the entire world. But the Old Testament writers had taught about the dangers of carrying out a census in order to assess whether Israel had enough strong men to follow God's will, thus relying on their physical ability and not the Lord's power to deliver (2 Samuel 24:1–10). Luke's narration of the census or taxation thus underlines the fact that the Lord had forbidden such practices in the past and reveals Luke's interest in contrasting the two types of kingship: pride and humility.

The actual taxation may have been either a registration of inhabitants (*apographe*, "census") or a taxation of personal property (*apotimesis*, "census"). Luke indicates by his choice of words that a registration of inhabitants was called for and took place under Quirinius, who was governor of Syria in A.D. 6. The difficulty in connecting **Jesus'** birth, which we are told took place in the days of Herod (37–4 B.C.), and the trip to Bethlehem, which Luke places in A.D. 6, is obvious. This discrepancy could well be a product of the eyewitness sources that Luke knew and popular memory that had connected the two events many years after they had taken place.

As the story unfolds, Augustus presumes to have the power to carry out a registration of all the inhabitants of the **Roman Empire**. In sharp contrast to this ruler's arrogance, the true King was born in lowly circumstances, a king who knew his people and did not need to rely on the power of his arm to count his subjects. Joseph and Mary followed the custom of the day and went up to Bethlehem, a journey highlighted in Luke 1:39–56 that would result in the reversal that Luke had foreshadowed in the previous chapter.

The taxation or census that took Joseph and Mary from Nazareth, a modest settlement widely believed to be between two hundred and four hundred people in size, to Bethlehem, fifty miles away, was necessary because Joseph "was of the house and lineage of David" (Luke 2:4) and was required to go to the place of his family's origin for the census. This explains why the family resided in Nazareth but were in Bethlehem for the birth of Jesus. In the Gospel of Matthew the family is said to be in Bethlehem at the time of the birth (Matthew 2:1), but this information could simply reflect the differing details from the writers' respective sources. If the census was indeed a registration of individuals, then it is likely that the family would have been required to return to their place of origin. An early papyrus fragment, Papyrus London 3.904, describes a similar situation in which a Roman official in Egypt required citizens to return from wherever they might be living to their places of origin and confirms what was probably a similar practice elsewhere (Hunt and Edgar, *Select Papyri*, 109).

Additionally, Luke's account of Mary's visit to her relative Elisabeth in the hill country of **Judea** seems to be more understandable if she was already a resident of Bethlehem, which is only a short distance from the hill country of Judea.

The Shepherds and Wise Men Adore Jesus
MATTHEW 2:1–12; LUKE 2:8–18

Despite a heartfelt interest to know more about the Wise Men, we have no credible extrabiblical records documenting their visits. Matthew and Luke are the lone recorders of many of the events that occurred during the days and weeks immediately following **Jesus'** birth. Each evangelist had a distinct purpose in telling the story that surpassed historical interest alone; the stories of the shepherds and Wise Men tell us something of the way the evangelists understood Jesus' mission as well as preserve important historical data.

Matthew's first subtle suggestion in the story of the days and weeks following Jesus' birth is that the heralded King of the Jews was born in Bethlehem and that the newly born King had a royal genealogy that could be traced back to David and the patriarchs before him (Matthew 1). Matthew adds irony to the story by describing how this new King is opposed by another king—King Herod—who has no lineal claim to the throne (Matthew 2). In this tumultuous environment an unspecified number of "magi" (translated as "wise men"; Greek *magoi*, "wise men, magicians, or sorcerers") arrived in Jerusalem seeking the new King, irrespective of the reigning king, whom they ask concerning the birth and location of the **Messiah**, suggesting they were unfamiliar with the prophecies (JST, Matthew 2:2).

Certainly Matthew did not hold Herod in high esteem, and each piece of the early story reveals additional negative details of the first man who would seek to slay Jesus. Matthew was apparently not interested in the origin of the Magi; rather, his inclusion of their story seems aimed primarily at demonstrating the reality that the "king" of the Jews had completely missed the birth of the true King of the Jews. Matthew tells us that Herod was so uninformed of the traditions about the Messiah that he called "chief **priests** and **scribes**" (Matthew 2:4) to tell him the prophesied birthplace of the Messiah (Micah 5:2).

For Matthew, the story of the Magi seems to demonstrate that those who should have been aware of the signs of the Savior's birth were completely unaware, whereas those signs were so profound that men sought him from the eastern countries (a rather vague description of everything east of Jerusalem). We are left to wonder how foreigners could have seen the signs and yet those same signs were not noticed by many nearby.

Unlike Matthew, Luke does not appear to have such a controversial bent in his narrative. Certainly neither Matthew nor Luke told a comprehensive story of Jesus' birth; each drew upon stories that had been passed down and perhaps they even selectively left out stories that could have been included. In Luke's case, the first persons to visit the newly born king are shepherds, undoubtedly Jewish, on the very night of the Savior's birth. Luke was careful to use setting to develop his story, and in the birth account he informs us that Jesus was born in a stable or manger. It is unlikely that the family would stay in those circumstances any longer than necessary; and according to Luke, the shepherds visited the family while the babe was still "in a manger" (Luke 2:16), reinforcing the idea that they were the first to visit Jesus. Matthew informs us that when the Wise Men visited they found the family living in a "house" (Matthew 2:11), evidently after a period of time had passed. Luke's purpose seems to be to show that the humble and lowly in Israel came to know Jesus and recognized the signs of his coming while Matthew makes the point that strangers recognized Jesus while the covenant people mostly did not.

The fact that the shepherds found the baby in a manger indicates that they must have visited within a few days of the birth, perhaps even within a few hours. Because the family was living in a house when the Wise Men came, it would seem that they visited the family after the shepherds did, although we cannot be certain how much later. Matthew does not record all that the Wise Men said to Herod, but Herod's determination to slay all infants under two years old seems to be a response to the times given to him by the Wise Men.

The locations where Joseph and Mary stayed while in Bethlehem are unclear from our surviving sources. Matthew indicates they were in a house, but he does not specify who owned that house. Because Matthew may imply that the family lived in Bethlehem and did not travel there (Matthew 1:18–2:1), the reader could assume that they stayed in their own house or the house of one of their parents. Luke, on the other hand, states that the family stayed in an "inn," a word that is translated from the Greek *katalymati*, meaning "a room, a guestroom, or inn." The base meaning of the word could imply that Joseph and Mary were familiar with the family who owned this particular "room."

The Circumcision and Naming of Jesus
MATTHEW 1:25; LUKE 2:21

The naming of **Jesus**, which is mentioned only in passing in Matthew, is of particular concern to Luke, who relates that Joseph and Mary followed the customs of the law of Moses in having Jesus circumcised on his eighth day of life and in giving him the name that the angel had revealed (Luke 2:21). The **circumcision** of Jesus signaled the beginning of the end of an ancient ordinance. For **Gentiles**, who had previously been required to be circumcised to become proselytes, the practice was discontinued soon after Jesus' Resurrection (Acts 15:1–11), being replaced with **baptism** and the giving of the gift of the **Holy Ghost**. A subtle subtext of the story is that Joseph and Mary were careful and obedient in their observance of the law of Moses, which would be required until the law was later fulfilled by Jesus himself. They were not associated with any of the popular movements of the day that had either abandoned the **covenants** of Israel or had declared the **temple** to be corrupt and had moved away from Jerusalem in expectation of God's punishment. In giving Jesus a name, Joseph complied with the direction and commandment given to him before the child was even born; and with the naming, Joseph reaffirmed his acceptance of the calling to be

Jesus' mortal guardian. This action, which both evangelists relate, could also have served to respond to continuing accusations that Jesus' birth was illegitimate.

The Flight to Egypt, Herod Slays Infants in and near Bethlehem
MATTHEW 2:1–23

Matthew's account highlights that **Pax Romana** (Roman peace) was based on violent and cruel suppression of anyone thought to threaten Roman authority. Jesus' first years were anything but peaceful—revealing the brutal nature of Roman power, especially as exercised by its client kings. In this case, the client king was Herod the Great.

Nevertheless, continuing the theme of fulfillment, Matthew relates how God protected his anointed Son, even as an infant. First, the Magi, "being warned of God in a dream" (Matthew 2:12), left Bethlehem without reporting back to King Herod, the chief **priests**, and elders in Jerusalem what they had discovered about the child. Second, God sent an angel to warn Joseph to flee into Egypt to avoid Herod's wrath over being deceived by the Magi and over his possible fear of there being a new king. Finally, Joseph was directed in a dream to return to the land of Israel after Herod is dead (Matthew 2:20). In this section, all that happened had been anticipated by the prophets, which Matthew clearly points out (Matthew 2:15, 17–18, 23).

Josephus, a first-century Jewish historiographer, depicts Herod's reign, especially during his final years, as comparable to other political leaders of the period. These rulers, including the Roman emperors, were often paranoid, thinking that someone was in the shadows ready to seize power. In most cases, they ruthlessly eliminated anyone they suspected as a threat, real or imagined. Even though Josephus did not record Herod's slaughter of the children in and around Bethlehem, given the other things Josephus chose to highlight about his reign, there is nothing extraordinary about Matthew's depiction of this event.

Throughout this section of Matthew, dreams and visions play a prominent role. Unlike the Magi and Joseph, however, Pilate later does not respond appropriately to a dream, this one received by his wife (Matthew 27:19). Matthew may have intended some comparison between Joseph who was sold into Egypt and Joseph the husband of Mary, both of whom saw visions (Genesis 37, 39–41).

Though fragmentary, the record does provide some important clues to the early years of Jesus' life to help the reader understand the progression of the story and the struggles faced by the family of Jesus. First, the family consisted of only three people: Joseph, Mary, and Jesus. Second, the Magi arrived some time after Jesus was born—when they appeared in Bethlehem, the little family lived in a "house" and Jesus was a "child" (Matthew 2:11), no longer a baby. Third, Matthew may have been establishing an archetype of a new Moses (for example, Exodus 4:19 records that the Lord told Moses to return to Egypt "for all the men are dead which sought thy life"). Finally, Matthew reveals that Jesus' enemies at his birth came from the same class as his enemies at his death: **Caesar's** representatives (Herod and Pilate) and the chief **priests** (Matthew 26:3–4; Acts 4:27). The angel's words emphasized that Herod was not Jesus' only enemy: "For *they* are dead which sought the young child's life" (Matthew 2:20; emphasis added).

The record is silent about when and how long the little family stayed in Egypt. Eventually, Joseph returned to the land of Israel and moved to Nazareth, a small, obscure town off the main road in southern **Galilee** (Matthew 2:21–23). Because we know that Herod died in about 4 B.C., **Jesus** must have been born sometime before that date, highlighting the problematic nature of the current calendar system.

Passover in Jerusalem When Jesus Was Twelve Years of Age
LUKE 2:41–52

Luke is the only New Testament author to provide any details of **Jesus'** life between his birth and the beginning of his public ministry. The subject of Jesus' early and undocumented life was of great interest to the

23

pseudonymous writers of the Apocrypha; the fact that Luke shows interest in this period of Jesus' life could suggest that by the time Luke wrote, the apocryphal tradition was beginning to take hold and the evangelist was attempting to set matters straight. These apocryphal sources rely on far-flung legends and cannot be trusted to reconstruct the story of Jesus' life with any degree of accuracy. Luke's story, however, seems to answer, in part, an important question that no other author asked: At what point in Jesus' life was he prepared to begin the work of the Father?

After the birth narratives, the record tells us that in obedience to the law Joseph and Mary traveled yearly to Jerusalem to participate in the **Passover** (Luke 2:41), one of the great Jewish pilgrimage feasts. Jesus was with them until the end of the feast. When they left Jerusalem to return to Nazareth, Joseph and Mary noticed that Jesus was missing and found him in the temple conversing with the elders. Luke calls him a "child," not a young man or a man and thus not yet independent. For Luke, then, this story demonstrates the young Jesus' growing awareness of his true identity when he declares, "How is it that ye sought me? wist ye not that I must be about my Father's business?" (Luke 2:49).

Following an emphasis that is evident elsewhere in the Gospel of Luke, the evangelist seems interested not only in the doctrines arising out of the events in Jesus' life but also in the historical details associated with those events. In this case, Luke was careful to note the number of days that Jesus was missing from the party that had begun its return to Nazareth. Depending on how the days were reckoned, it is possible that Jesus might have been gone as little as two days (if reckoned following Jewish custom) or as long as five (if Luke intended the reader to add the references together). Perhaps more important, though, is not how long Jesus was missing but rather the place where Joseph and Mary found him. If Joseph and Mary had ties to Bethlehem, located near Jerusalem, they might have sought him there, at least initially. When they did find him, he was in the **temple**, "both hearing them [the doctors], and asking them questions" (Luke 2:46). Interestingly, the Joseph Smith Translation interprets verse 46 in this way: "They found him in the temple, sitting in the midst of the doctors, and they were hearing him, and asking him questions" (JST, Luke 2:46).

Luke, however, does not include much about the subject matter of that conversation. Instead, he shows us this early part of Jesus' life through Mary's perspective. Jesus' answer, "How is it that ye sought me? wist ye not that I must be about my Father's business?" (Luke 2:49) is placed in the context of a slight misstatement on Mary's part. She said to Jesus, "Son, why hast thou thus dealt with us? behold, thy father and I have sought thee sorrowing" (Luke 2:48). As the boy's mother, Mary likely expressed not only her own fears and worries but also those of Joseph, who was Jesus' stepfather. Certainly Luke did not relate the story to show disrespect to Jesus' mother and Joseph but rather to affirm Jesus' awareness of his true identity, calling, and ministry. In fact, the story concludes with the comment that Jesus took that awareness home with him to Nazareth where he "was subject unto them: but his mother kept all these sayings in her heart" (Luke 2:51).

The phrase—"wist ye not that I must be about my Father's business?"—as translated in the King James Version represents one possible meaning of Jesus' response to Joseph and Mary. Because he was sitting in the temple, and because the phrase can also be translated, "I must attend to my Father's house," it is also possible to make the interpretation that his attention had shifted from being a child in the house of Joseph and Mary to being a teacher in his Father's house. The statement therefore looks forward to a new calling. The Joseph Smith Translation of verse 46 also seems to signal that **Jesus** had progressed to a point that he had already begun teaching and that he had learned what was necessary for him to teach publicly.

The Beginning of the Ministry of John the Baptist
MATTHEW 3:1–12; MARK 1:1–8; LUKE 3:1–18; JOHN 1:19–34

In one of the few points of convergence between the four evangelists, John the Baptist's ministry is interpreted in each Gospel in its historical setting as forming the beginning of **Jesus'** mortal ministry. Of the four evangelists, John added details that give the fourth Gospel not only a unique perspective on those events but also a unique *eyewitness* perspective as he establishes the presence of the unnamed **disciple** (that is, John himself) at important events in Jesus' ministry. Mark is the most abrupt in his approach. The first verse of the Gospel of Mark introduces the subject of "the beginning of the gospel of Jesus **Christ**, the **Son of God**," and the second verse introduces John the Baptist: "Behold, I send my messenger before thy face, which shall prepare thy way before thee" (Mark 1:2)—signaling to the reader that the "beginning of the gospel of Jesus Christ" begins with the story of the ministry of John the Baptist. In comparing the accounts, it is interesting to note that two Gospel authors passed over the story of Jesus' birth (Mark and John), only two provided a genealogical introduction (Matthew and Luke), and one (John) looked back at Jesus in premortality, but all four of them introduced Jesus' ministry by introducing John the Baptist.

One of the historical reasons for this approach may have been the enormous popularity of John's message. Matthew, in particular, points out that Judeans were intrigued by the new prophet who dressed like Elijah (2 Kings 1:8): "Then went out to him Jerusalem, and all Judaea, and all the region round about Jordan" (Matthew 3:5). The evangelists were also aware that prior to Jesus' **baptism** a dispute had already arisen between John and the Pharisees and **Sadducees** (Matthew 3:7), prefiguring Jesus' rivalry with these same groups.

Each author brought his own unique viewpoint to the story. Mark, author of the Gospel that is believed to be the earliest of the four accounts, looked back on John's ministry as a distant observer (see Acts 12:25, where Mark enters the narrative as a companion to Paul and Barnabas years after Jesus' death and Resurrection). He seems to have become a follower of Jesus after the Resurrection and therefore at a time when Christianity had already begun. Mark began his testimony by detailing the fulfillment of scripture (Isaiah 40:3) and describing the Lord's new prophetic messenger (Mark 1:2–6). In Mark's account there is no mention of any hostility toward John the Baptist, as there is in Matthew's, but rather toward them "of Jerusalem" who went out to meet him, "confessing their sins" (Mark 1:5).

Matthew added to the story by recounting John's open hostility toward the Pharisees and Sadducees who had come to see him (Matthew

3:7–10). In fact, the description of his negative response is longer than the introduction of John. This follows Matthew's overall intent to underline the important fact that the Jews had missed the coming of their **Messiah**. (Remember that only the Gospel of Matthew reports that foreigners are the first to worship the young child Jesus.)

Luke followed the approaches of Matthew and Mark in many respects; however, he is the one who placed the commencement of John the Baptist's ministry in a specific historical context: "Now in the fifteenth year of the reign of Tiberius **Caesar**, Pontius Pilate being governor of Judaea, and Herod [Antipas] being tetrarch of **Galilee**" (Luke 3:1). Luke placed the baptism of Christ during the time when governors (here, Pilate) began ruling **Judea** and the sons of Herod—Philip and Antipas—were ruling portions of their father's former kingdom. Lysanias, who ruled Abilene, is also mentioned, perhaps to include those regions where the gospel spread in its early years, or to include the current rulers of Herod's former domains. The "fifteenth year of the reign of Tiberius," which could have been calculated from the death of Augustus (A.D. 14), or from the time the Roman senate granted Tiberius power (A.D. 12). Luke (3:2) also mentioned Annas (A.D. 6–15) and Caiaphas (A.D. 18–36). Including these historical figures is consistent with Luke's apparent interest in showing how the life of Jesus shaped and changed human history. He began his story of Jesus' life by telling of a census under Augustus, and now he sees John's ministry as an important point in Tiberius's reign, as well as for the **Roman Empire** in general.

John's testimony of John the Baptist was different from the others. The story begins with an explanation of who John the Baptist was and how he interpreted his own role in light of Jesus' impending ministry (John 1:19–23). There is a slight break in sense between John 1:19 and 1:20. The Levites asked John a rather simple question: "Who art thou?" (John 1:19), which seems to imply very little, but John saw in it a question of whether his own calling was that of **Messiah**. He responded forcefully: "And he confessed, and denied not; but confessed, I am not the Christ" (John 1:20). The wording of the phrase is rather cumbersome in Greek, but the Joseph Smith Translation makes it clear: "And he confessed, and denied not that he was Elias; but confessed, saying; I am not the Christ" (JST, John 1:21). The author seems to want to clarify and emphasize who John the Baptist was. Some thought that he was the Messiah, and recording his own testimony to the contrary was one important way to reach out to those who continued to view him as the fulfillment of prophecy and not the precursor.

John also recounts that the **priests** and Levites asked the Baptist whether or not he was Elias (the Greek spelling of the Hebrew *Elijah*) or "that prophet" (perhaps meaning that prophet like unto Moses—Christ—whose coming was promised; Deuteronomy 18:15–18; 1 Nephi 22:20). Following the logic of the account, the interrogators also asked how John could baptize if he were not Elijah [Elias], or the prophet like unto Moses (Christ), implying that they expected them to baptize but not John. These questions and answers served the purpose of establishing a better understanding of the fundamental relationship between the Messiah and the forerunner, clarifying what had become confused over time. The evangelists certainly understood that John bore testimony of Jesus, but the force with which they emphasized that idea implies that others were less certain.

According to John, the place where these events occurred was in "Bethabara" (John 1:28), a place name which is confirmed in the Book of Mormon (1 Nephi 10:9). Most ancient Greek manuscripts of the Gospel of John, however, place the events in Bethany instead of Bethabara. Some critics have seen in this an opportunity to criticize the Book of Mormon for using a lesser known and attested version of the story. The fallacy with this criticism is that a city or place named Bethany "beyond Jordan" is otherwise unattested, whereas Bethabara, "the crossing," is mentioned in the **Talmud**. There is no apparent reason why **scribes** would prefer one place name over the other, and there is no obvious symbolic reason for choosing one name over the other. Rather, this appears to be a simple case of corruption in the text, where Bethabara is as likely to be original as Bethany. With the added witness of the Book of Mormon, however, Bethabara stands out as the correct reading.

The Baptism of Jesus and the Beginning of His Ministry

MATTHEW 3:13–17; MARK 1:9–11; LUKE 3:21–22; JOHN 1:32–34

One of the few historical facts that most scholars agree on is that **Jesus** of Nazareth appeared at the Jordan River and was baptized by John sometime around A.D. 26–27.

Traditionally, the **baptism** is associated with a site on the east bank of the River Jordan southwest of Amman, Jordan, just north of the Dead Sea. Interestingly, there are only a few verses about the baptism, and John does not even mention the baptism itself. Here Jesus is identified as God's "beloved son" by a heavenly voice (Matthew 3:17; Mark 1:11; Luke 3:22; see also Psalm 2:7; Isaiah 42:1; Matthew 12:18) before going into the wilderness where **Satan** would challenge that declaration. The descent of the Holy Spirit is another key element of the story—Jesus is enveloped by the Spirit, fulfilling the **Messianic** prophecy of Isaiah (Isaiah 61:1). The apostle Peter also emphasizes this point in one of the earliest post-**Pentecost** speeches (Acts 10:37–38).

Perhaps John's most important additions to this part of the story are found in the verses about Jesus' baptism, following the interrogation of the Baptist by the priests and Levites. For reasons that are no longer clear, in the King James Version, John the Baptist seems not to know Jesus by sight (John 1:31, 33), even though Luke relates that their mothers were relatives (Luke 1:36). But the Joseph Smith Translation makes it clear that the Baptist *did* know Jesus when he saw him (JST, John 1:29–33). Through a vision, John the Baptist was prepared to recognize and baptize the "Lamb of God"; when the Lamb came, he would be given a sign—the sign of the Holy Spirit descending like a dove and abiding with that person (John 1:29–33). The sign was for John—to confirm to him that he had baptized the Messiah and to enable him to "manifest [him] to Israel" (JST, John 1:30). The physical sign completed John's witness.

In addition to Jesus' own knowledge of who he was and what his mission was to be, when the time came for his mission to begin, it was likely divine communication with his beloved Father and a profound commit-ment to obeying his will that motivated Jesus to leave his family and a relatively peaceful life to begin his public ministry, a ministry that would provoke the fear and hatred of powerful leaders in the region and make the Roman emperor's own representative—Pilate—agree to his execu-tion. Leaving Nazareth to begin a journey that would ultimately lead to Gethsemane and Golgotha, Jesus first went to John to fulfill God's promise to bless the nations of the world through Abraham's seed (Genesis 12:1–3) Nothing remained the same in Jesus' life and the story of Israel after the pivotal event of his baptism.

Matthew 3:16–17 and Luke 3:21–22 record material that Matthew and Luke share but which is not found in the Gospel of Mark. It is possible that both Matthew and Luke used an external source when writing their Gospels, but it is also possible that they drew upon the Gospel of Mark as a source and then drew upon the other Gospel (Matthew drawing upon Luke, or vice versa, depending on which was written first) as a second source; three sections in the Gospel of Mark are preserved nowhere in Matthew and Luke: Mark 1:1; 3:19–21; 4:26–29; 7:31–37; 8:22–26; 14:51–52; 16:14–18. Because Luke so explicitly mentions that he used sources when writing (1:1–3), it is possible that he drew on both Matthew and Mark.

Jesus' Temptations
MATTHEW 4:1–11; MARK 1:12–13; LUKE 4:1–13

The author of Hebrews observed, "For we have not an high priest which cannot be touched with the feeling of our infirmities; but was in all points tempted like as we are, yet without sin" (Hebrews 4:15). The **Synoptic** accounts of **Jesus'** temptation in the wilderness emphasize this point—confronted by evil, Jesus did not yield.

Both Matthew and Luke, using unique material—non-Markan tradi-tions or sources (we do not have to assume a single oral or written source), inform us that Satan came to Jesus at the end of the forty-day fast. Though the order of the temptations is preserved differently in Matthew and in

Luke, the point of the narrative seems to be to highlight Satan's challenge to the baptismal declaration: "This is my beloved Son, in whom I am well pleased" (Matthew 3:17).

A strong theme in the Gospels is Jesus' determination to do the will of the Father instead of seeking an alternative way to fulfill his mission. The temptation narrative prepares us for his responses to the options for escape presented to Jesus by well-meaning **disciples** such as Peter (Matthew 16:22–23), by his enemies (Matthew 27:42), and uttered by himself during his struggles in Gethsemane (Matthew 26:39, 42). Without fail, he proved true to his divine mission.

John Is Imprisoned
MATTHEW 4:12; MARK 1:14; LUKE 3:19–20

Traditionally identified as occurring at the beginning of Jesus' Galilean ministry, John's imprisonment marks the transition between the rise of **Jesus** and the fading of John the Baptist, who had prophesied, "He must increase, but I must decrease" (John 3:30). Fortunately, we have another source that provides information regarding John's ministry, including his arrest. The Jewish historian Josephus wrote that John the Baptist was "a good man and had urged the Jews—if inclined to exercise virtue, to practice justice toward one another and piety toward God—to join in **baptism**." Additionally, he noted, "Herod [Antipas], fearing that John's great influence over the people might result in some form of insurrection (for it seemed that they did everything by his counsel), thought it much better to put him to death. . . . So the prisoner, because of Herod's suspicion, was sent to Machaerus, the stronghold previously mentioned" (*Antiquities* 18:116–19). John's arrest and imprisonment were a warning to Jesus. Certainly, Jesus understood the implication—he too could be arrested.

Jesus' Ministry Prior to Gathering His Disciples
MATTHEW 4:12–17; 23–25; LUKE 4:14–15

It would have been natural for many at the time to see **Jesus** as John the Baptist's successor: "Now when Jesus had heard that John was cast into prison, he departed into **Galilee**. . . . From that time Jesus began to preach, and to say, **Repent**: for the kingdom of heaven is at hand" (Matthew 4:12, 17). Most scholars agree that Jesus was known for teaching and healing. Josephus noted, "At this time there appeared Jesus, a wise man. For he was a doer of amazing deeds, a teacher of persons who receive truth with plea-sure. He won over many Jews and many of the Greeks" (*Antiquities* 18:63).

Both Matthew and Luke highlight this early period, identifying what Jesus taught and where he preached. Of particular interest is Matthew's note that Jesus "came and dwelt in Capernaum" (*Kefar Nahum*, or "village of Nahum"), moving from the family's traditional residence to a rather large town located on the northwest shore of the Sea of Galilee, a town that is widely accepted as having had between one thousand to fifteen hundred inhabitants (Matthew 4:13).

Early Disciples
MATTHEW 4:18–22; MARK 1:14–20; LUKE 5:4–11; JOHN 1:35–51

One of the distinguishing aspects of **Jesus'** ministry was the calling of **disciples** to follow him. Mark emphasized their response: "And *straightway* they forsook their nets, and followed him" (Mark 1:18; emphasis added).

Matthew and Luke echoed Mark's narrative, but John's Gospel provides additional information regarding the first disciples (John 1:35–51). First, John indicates that some of Jesus' earliest followers were closely associated with John the Baptist and some were even his disciples before they came to believe in Jesus (John 1:35–37). Second, at the very beginning, John said, some believed Jesus was the **Christ** (John used the Greek rendering of Messiah, "*Messias*," for the first time in this section; John 1:41). Third, Jesus was identified as "Rabbi" (John 1:38, 49). Later Jewish sources introduce us to officials known as "Rabbis," apparently ordained teachers who met certain requirements, including age and education. However, it does not appear that there were any such officials in the early part of the first century. Rabbi, therefore, should be understood as an honorific title given to any "teacher" without specific qualifications. Fourth, Andrew, Peter, and possibly Philip were from Bethsaida (John 1:44), a fishing village located on the north shore of the Sea of **Galilee**, near where the northern part of the Jordan River enters the sea and within the political boundary of Herod Philip's tetrarchy. Fifth, the early **disciples** believed Jesus fulfilled **messianic** prophecies found in the **Law (Torah)** and the **Prophets** (*Nevi'im*), two of the threefold divisions of Jewish scripture (John 1:45). Sixth, Jesus gave Simon a new name, Cephas (an **Aramaic** word that is roughly the equivalent to the Greek *Petros*, "Peter"), meaning "rock" or "stone" (John 1:42). Interestingly, even though the Lord here gives him the Aramaic name *Cephas*, it is translated as the Greek *Peter* in the other 161 times it is used in the New Testament. Finally, John tells us something about this society where people were judged in part by their place of origin. In this case, Nathanael used Nazareth, the small Jewish village where Jesus was "brought up" (Luke 4:16), as a lens through which to judge Jesus' worth (John 1:46).

Those who first heard these accounts, even before they were recorded in the Gospels, may have been surprised that when Jesus called men to follow him, they did so, often immediately (Mark 1:16–20). Imagine meeting someone at the store, at school, or at work. When he asks you to follow him, you leave everything behind—the world you knew well—for an uncertain future! The commanding presence of the mortal Jesus was remembered and described again and again by his disciples.

Jesus' Ministry in Nazareth
LUKE 4:16–30

Only Luke preserves a story about **Jesus'** appearance in Nazareth following his **baptism**. As in earlier accounts (Luke 2:41–42, for example), Luke portrays Jesus' family, and Jesus himself, as observant Jews (loyal to

God, the **Torah**, the **temple**, and the chosen people). In this case, Jesus "went into the **synagogue** on the **sabbath** day, and stood up for to read" (Luke 4:16). One can only imagine the local gossip about **him**. After years of living a rather quiet and obscure life in Nazareth, Jesus had suddenly left his home and family to visit John the Baptist. Unlike many who were baptized by John, Jesus did not return home to continue his occupation and the life he was accustomed to, but instead preached the "good news" throughout **Galilee** and beyond.

After a period of time, Jesus "returned in the power of the Spirit into Galilee" (Luke 4:14), eventually making his way back to the small village where his mother, brothers, and sisters lived (it is thought that Joseph had passed away by this time). There must have been heightened expectations when he arrived. What could he report about John the Baptist? What had Jesus been doing since he left Nazareth? Were the stories about him true? Could he heal? What caused the change that took Jesus permanently from his work, family, and village?

When Jesus entered the synagogue on this particular Sabbath "there was delivered unto him" a copy of the record of Isaiah (Luke 4:17). A scroll dating from 125–100 B.C. was found at the Dead Sea, providing a window into Jesus' world. It is a beautiful scroll (the longest complete scroll of the **Dead Sea Scrolls**, measuring about twenty feet long), made of animal skins, written upon in black ink in the recognizable squared Hebrew script. Individual sections were sewn together to form the scroll. Natural oils from fingers and hands have darkened sections of the scroll, providing some idea about which sections were read most often.

Whether or not there was an established reading calendar that pre-scribed the weekly readings, as is common today in Jewish worship services, is unknown. If, on the other hand, Jesus chose this specific text, it must have taken several minutes to carefully unroll the scroll to the exact spot—heightening the sense of expectation.

Traditionally, many assume that the text was read in Hebrew before the reader provided commentary in **Aramaic**, the language of the day. Whether Jesus read in Hebrew or an **Aramaic** translation of Isaiah, known as a **Targum**, is not essential to an appreciation of the story.

34

The passage Jesus read was **messianic** (Luke 4:18–19); note the phrase, "because he hath *anointed* me to preach the gospel" (Luke 4:18; emphasis added)—*Messiah* means "the anointed one." When Jesus returned the scroll to the synagogue official, the "eyes of all them that were in the synagogue were fastened on him" (Luke 4:20). Then Jesus boldly declared, "This day is this scripture fulfilled in your ears" (Luke 4:21), causing the people to marvel. But the mood changed when Jesus declared, "No prophet is accepted in his own country" (Luke 4:24). Luke records that, now angered, those assembled in the synagogue became a mob and attempted to kill Jesus, but "he passing though the midst of them went his way" unharmed (Luke 4:30).

The Wedding at Cana
JOHN 2:1–11

Without the modern chapter and verse divisions of the King James Version, John's continuation of the story of Jesus talking to Nathanael of Cana (John 1:47–2:2) is more obvious. John 2:1 relates that "the third day there was a marriage in Cana of **Galilee**," connecting the conversion of Andrew, Philip, Nathanael, and the unnamed **disciple** (John 1:35–51) with what followed in Cana. In fact, by counting back three days in the story, it appears that John the author was counting forward from the decisive moment when John the Baptist was questioned concerning his mission and ministry (John 1:19–28). On the day following that inquiry ("The next day"; John 1:29), **Jesus** was baptized, and on the "day following" (John 1:43), Philip reported to Nathanael that he had found the person of whom Moses prophesied (Deuteronomy 18:15–18). On that same day, if counted inclusively, **Jesus** attended a wedding in Cana. Although the tradition that first marriages, or marriages of "virgins," occur on Wednesday was recorded after the New Testament was written, it may reflect a practice that had been in place for some time (*Ketuboth* 1.1). If it were the case that the marriage in Cana took place on a Wednesday, and the reconstruction of time proposed above is what John intended to convey to his readers, then Jesus would have been baptized on Tuesday, the day before the wedding.

35

But more important, John was connecting the accounts of the earliest disciples through a series of events and **miracles** that brought them to **Christ**. The chronology of the story seems to support this objective. John 2:2 reports, "And both Jesus was called, and his disciples, to the marriage," noting for the first time that not only had Jesus identified disciples (John does not mention a number) but they were so identifiable as to be invited to a wedding as a group. With this reference, the evangelist has effectively shown the call of the disciples as taking place on the day of Jesus' **baptism**. Perhaps John was providing evidence that baptism was a requirement for all of the **disciples** who were later ordained as apostles. Indeed, when the new apostle was called after the death of Judas, it was required that he be chosen from those who had been followers of Jesus from the time of his baptism (Acts 1:21–22).

In the account of the wedding at Cana, when the party ran out of wine, Jesus' mother went to him with the guests' complaint: "They have no wine" (John 2:3). John 2:5 makes it clear that Mary hoped for something from Jesus—perhaps a miracle—when she directed the servants, "Whatsoever he saith unto you, do it." John hints that she had knowledge that would lead her to hope that Jesus could remedy the awkward situation. Jesus' response to this request, "Woman, what have I to do with thee? mine hour is not yet come" (John 2:4), seems abrupt to us, but in the Joseph Smith Translation this verse shows his true respect for his mother. The form of address here translated as "woman" is sometimes used as a normal word of address, although determining the degree of politeness or abruptness is difficult. Perhaps more important, we note that this was the way that Jesus commonly addressed women, and the Greek translation that we have of his actual words seems intended to relay respect (John 4:21; 8:10; 20:13; 19:26; Matthew 15:28).

The focus of this story is the actual creation of or turning water into wine. John emphasized such details as the number of stone pots and the number of gallons of wine produced. This is where the heart of the story lies. The stone pots were on hand for "the purifying of the Jews" (John 2:6), as Mark recorded, "For the **Pharisees**, and all the Jews, except they wash their hands oft, eat not, holding the tradition of the elders. And when they come from the market, except they wash, they eat not" (Mark 7:3–4). The pots were made of stone because the law of Moses declared that earthen vessels could be defiled (Leviticus 11:29–33). The pots contained a significant volume of liquid; in fact, each pot contained two or three "firkins" (a "firkin" is an old English unit of measurement and is not used elsewhere in the Gospels) equaling roughly eighteen to twenty-four gallons of liquid. The total volume may have been nearly 150 gallons of wine. This amount is staggering and would not have gone unnoticed by an ancient reader familiar with the volume of "two or three firkins" (John 2:6).

From John's account of Jesus creating wine in old containers we may draw a figurative lesson using the themes of discipleship and new wine. The symbolism is rich and recalls Jesus' teaching that "no man putteth new wine into old bottles: else the new wine doth burst the bottles, and the wine is spilled, and the bottles will be marred: but new wine must be put into new bottles" (Mark 2:22). As his new disciples looked on, Jesus literally placed new wine—in fact, excellent wine—into old jars. Underlying this physical gesture is the fact that the gospel of Jesus Christ, symbolized by the wine, would come through the newly called disciples and not through the old "stone jars" of the law. In the end, the new wine of the gospel would rupture the old "containers." John added this conclusion to the event: "This beginning of miracles did Jesus in Cana of Galilee, and manifested forth his glory; and his disciples believed on him" (John 2:11), to which the Joseph Smith Translation adds the insight "and the faith of his disciples was strengthened in him" (JST, John 2:11).

The Ministry at Capernaum
MARK 1:21–28; LUKE 4:31–37; JOHN 2:12

Jesus was a teacher and a healer, both of which caused the people to be astonished, amazed—or angry. In this section, we first note the Sabbath controversies that caused constant disagreement between Jesus and his antagonists: What actions were permissible on the Sabbath?

The Gospels agree that **Jesus** observed the rites of the Jewish religion, and his ministry in Capernaum began in the **synagogue** on the **Sabbath** day. The fifth-century limestone synagogue visible today in Capernaum stands on a basalt foundation that is likely the remains of that first-century synagogue.

Mark's unique contribution is the details of a particular day in the life of Jesus. The day began in the synagogue in Capernaum (Mark 1:21) and continued in the house of Simon and Andrew (Mark 1:29). In the evening Jesus healed the sick (Mark 1:32) and then he arose early the next morning to pray alone (Mark 1:35). This twenty-four-hour account illustrated for later followers what a day in the life of Jesus may have included.

Raising the Widow's Son at Nain
LUKE 7:11–17

The raising of a widow's only son at Nain is the first of **Jesus' miracles** wherein he brought the dead back to life. This particular miracle had a powerful effect on all who witnessed it. Some reacted with fear (Greek, *phobos,* "fear" or "fright"), some glorified God—all of which was reported to John the Baptist by his own **disciples** (Luke 7:16–18). Luke does not relate the details of the widow's family or the names of individuals, but rather seems more interested in the implications of Jesus' actions: The people said, "That a great prophet is risen up among us; and, *That God hath visited his people*" (Luke 7:16; emphasis added).

Simon Peter's Mother-in-Law
MATTHEW 8:14–15; MARK 1:29–31; LUKE 4:38–39

Mark and Luke both report another incident, the healing of Simon Peter's mother-in-law on the **Sabbath**. It is a rather remarkable story, with details that must have come directly from an eyewitness. **Jesus** entered the multigenerational home of Peter, seemingly located just a few yards from the **synagogue**. (Archeologists have uncovered the ruins of a first-century home in Capernaum that may be part of the dwelling compound where

Jesus healed this woman.) Perhaps like the angels who ministered to Jesus in the wilderness (Mark 1:13), this woman ministered to Jesus after being freed from her fever.

Early Miracles in Galilee

MATTHEW 4:23–25; 8:14–15; MARK 1:7–12, 32–45;
LUKE 4:40–44

Often the Gospels narrate stories where **Jesus'** teachings and **miracles** were met with opposition and open hostility. The hostility of the later ministry, however, was different from that of the early Galilean ministry. When Jesus taught near Capernaum, his fame became so far-reaching that it "went throughout all Syria. . . . And there followed him great multitudes of people from **Galilee**, and from Decapolis, and from Jerusalem, and from Judaea, and from beyond Jordan" (Matthew 4:24–25). Before the organization of the Quorum of the Twelve Apostles, Jesus preached to accepting crowds (with the exception of Nazareth). His early ministry was more characterized by healing miracles than the teachings that generated so much controversy later in his life.

Mark's statement that "Simon [Peter] and they that were with him followed after [Jesus]" is probably an indication that Peter's entire household and extended family came to know Jesus through those early miracles (Mark 1:36). Mark also reports that there were teachings during those early months (Mark 1:39), but he focused more on the miracles. Showing that Peter's life was indeed touched by a miracle during the early ministry, Luke relates, as mentioned earlier, that Peter's mother-in-law was healed prior to the calling of the Twelve. Matthew places this miracle much later (Matthew 8:14–15), but it seems that the messages of all three evangelists converge on a single point concerning the early Galilean ministry—Jesus began his ministry by healing the sick.

One detail that is preserved here in Matthew's account may help explain some of the hostility that Jesus encountered in Jerusalem much later in his ministry. As word of the **miracles** spread, his fame became so great that even those in **Judea** and "beyond Jordan" had heard of him (Matthew 4:25). Only one other individual's ministry was associated with the Jordan River valley—John the Baptist—and Matthew may have included this detail to explain that as Jesus' fame grew, the hostility that was aimed at John the Baptist eventually came to be directed at Jesus, who began to attract listeners in the regions where John taught and even among his followers (John 1:35–42).

Jesus Teaches from a Boat on the Sea of Galilee
LUKE 5:1–3

The account found in Luke 5:1–3 corroborates the idea that we do not have a record of everything that **Jesus** said or taught. In this case Luke informs us only that Jesus spoke to a group from a boat on the lake of Gennesaret (a freshwater lake in **Galilee** known by various names, including the Sea of Galilee and the Sea of Tiberias). Even when the evangelists preserve a sermon, reading that sermon out loud takes only minutes, so it is most likely only a synopsis of what Jesus said on that occasion.

The Cleansing of the Temple
JOHN 2:13–25

After turning water into wine at Cana, **Jesus** traveled to Jerusalem for **Passover**, as was the custom of his family. For the Gospel of John, this event provided an opportunity to highlight a miracle and to foreshadow the fulfillment of prophecy. In the miracle at Cana (John 2:1–11), Jesus had placed new wine in stone jars, symbolic of the rejection that his teachings (the new wine) would receive from the Jews (the stone jars). The story of the cleansing of the **temple** provides another example of rejection.

After entering the temple complex in an area referred to as the Court of the **Gentiles**, pilgrims to the Passover feast would have been confronted with at least two types of vendors—those who sold sacrificial animals and who may have accepted only Tyrian shekels, and those who would, for a fee, exchange money embossed with pagan symbols for Tyrian shekels. John refers to the presence of "sheep, and . . . oxen" (John 2:15), which would be quite surprising within the walls of the **temple** complex, given Jewish concerns for purity.

But John told this story for reasons other than historical interest. At the beginning of his ministry, Jesus had found **disciples** among those who had seen the miracles he had performed and among the followers of John the Baptist, and had at the same time acquired enemies among the Jewish leaders. For John, the focus of the controversy seems to be the temple itself, highlighting that the conspiracy to kill Jesus centered there from the very beginning. Unfortunately, Jesus' attempted reform of the temple did not lead to lasting change, and a generation later, Simon, a Jewish leader, found the practice of selling animals in the inner courts unchanged (*Kerithoth* 1.7).

Several hints in the account reveal how this event was remembered many years after Jesus' death. In the opening lines, John refers to the event as the "Jews' passover" (John 2:13), whereas during the life of Jesus it was simply known as the Passover, thus signaling a distancing between Christianity and Judaism at the time the author wrote. At the end of the account, John relates that the disciples did not fully understand the importance of the event at the time it occurred: "But he spake of the temple of his body. When therefore he was risen from the dead, his disciples remembered that he had said this unto them; and they believed the scripture, and the word which Jesus had said" (John 2:21–22).

The **Synoptic** authors place the cleansing of the temple as a conclusion to Jesus' triumphal entry into Jerusalem, which helps explain the virulent loathing the Jewish leaders felt for him. It may be that the Synoptic authors are correct in their placement of the story. The act of turning over the tables of the money changers would definitely have been detrimental to commerce, and the money involved would have been substantial. This was really an act against the state and impurity in the temple.

Nicodemus

JOHN 3:1–21

John contrasts light and darkness at the beginning of his Gospel: "And the light shineth in darkness; and the darkness comprehended it not" (John 1:5). This theme may continue in this story because Nicodemus "came to **Jesus** by night" (3:2), and when **Jesus** tells him that he must be "born again" (3:3), this senior Jewish leader fails to comprehend him (3:9).

Jesus commands men and women to become as little children (Mark 9:36–37). In this case, he says we need to become infants—a radical call to the kind of fundamental changes Jesus demanded of his **disciples**. Continuing the theme found in John 3:3 (see also 3:22; 4:1–2), Jesus tells Nicodemus that seeing and entering into the kingdom of heaven comes only by the **baptism** of water and the baptism of the Spirit. Additionally, **Jesus** informs him, being born again—being born from above (Greek, *anothen*, "from above," translated as "again") or being born of the Spirit—comes from God. Like the wind (the Greek word means both "spirit" and "wind"), the Spirit cannot be seen, but it can be heard and felt, and its effects can be observed. One can be physically baptized into the **Church**, but unless one is baptized by the Spirit (which comes from God) one cannot enter into the kingdom of heaven. Jesus says both are necessary. In the early Church, some members believed that if they received the baptism of water, they did not need to worry about the spiritual birth (1 Corinthians 10:1–13). Today, many Christians believe that the baptism of water is not necessary. Yet Jesus is clear—one must receive both in order not only to "see," but also to "enter into the kingdom of God" (John 3:3, 5). The first baptism is necessary to become part of the visible community of the Saints on earth, and the second is necessary to become part of the heavenly community of Saints. Another important part of the story is that Jesus introduces us to a new way of knowing—coming from God, or coming from heaven (3:10–13).

Finally, John highlights how this **Pharisee**, a ruler of the Jews and a Judean, disappears into the night as this story ends, yet, perhaps at least partially converted, reappears to defend Jesus to the Pharisees (7:50), and later comes to Jesus' burial place with costly herbs and spices (19:39).

Jesus Baptizes in Aenon near Salim and Appeals to John's Followers
JOHN 3:22–36

The author notes that **Jesus** and his **disciples** arrived in **Judea** where they baptized following the pattern set by John the Baptist. Ironically, some of the Baptist's followers assumed that John's work would continue for some time; they may even have believed that his ministry would continue to the end of time. They did not know he was about to be arrested and executed—ending his preaching, teaching, and baptizing. The book of Acts records there was a subsequent ministry that perpetuated the memory of John independent of Jesus **Christ** (Acts 19:3–4).

At this time, jealousy had surfaced about Jesus' fame. When his followers asked John about Jesus' success, the Baptist attempted to place his own ministry in the context of the larger work of God, particularly the coming of the **Messiah**, describing himself as the best man at a wedding. Jehovah had often been portrayed in the Old Testament as the bridegroom who would take his bride (Israel) to himself (see, for example, Isaiah 62:5). John, as would any loyal best man, celebrated the coming of the bridegroom—the coming of Jesus: "He must increase but I must decrease" (John 3:30).

The last lines in this section (3:31–36) may in fact be the author's conclusion instead of a continuation of John's response. Like Mormon, when he edited the stories and sermons for the Book of Mormon and then interjected himself into the story (for example, Helaman 12:1), our author has likely pulled together some primary sources about the event recorded here, but has also taken an opportunity to make an observation about the significance of the story.

Jesus Departs from Judea

MATTHEW 4:12, 17; MARK 1:14–15; LUKE 4:14–15;
JOHN 4:1–3, 43–45

Details of **Jesus'** early ministry remain unclear, both because some of those who wrote about them were not eyewitness to the early weeks and months of the mortal ministry and because there was little emphasis placed on Jesus' physical movements throughout **Judea** and **Galilee**. The gospel authors tended to favor recounting his teachings. Shortly after the **baptism** of Jesus, and indeed after the temptations in Judea, Jesus returned to Galilee. Matthew relates the move in a cause-and-effect manner: "Now when Jesus had heard that John was cast into prison, he departed into Galilee" (Matthew 4:12). Exactly why John's arrest would have caused Jesus to go to Galilee is unclear, but the implications of Matthew 14, which details the arrest and death of John, are that the arrest and beheading took place in Galilee, although Josephus places the execution at Machaerus. Therefore, Jesus would have been traveling to the epicenter of the opposition and not away from it.

For Matthew, Mark, and Luke, although less pronounced in Matthew, there is a direct connection between the beginning of Jesus' ministry and the ending of John's. According to Luke, the departure to Galilee was not done in fear, but "Jesus returned in the power of the Spirit into Galilee" (Luke 4:14). Jesus likely saw the ending of John's life as the beginning of his own public ministry and perhaps also as the beginning of the end of his own life.

Drawing upon another version of the story, John narrates that Jesus departed into Galilee because "the **Pharisees** had heard that Jesus made and baptized more disciples than John" (John 4:1). Thus, the reason for the departure into Galilee was to avoid the opposition of the Pharisees and to teach to more accepting crowds. The story is interrupted, however, with an insertion that directly contradicts the Gospel. It says, "(Though Jesus himself baptized not, but his disciples,)" (4:2). This assertion counters what John says in 3:22 and 4:1 and was changed in the Joseph Smith Translation to harmonize the accounts. Although the text of this passage (4:2) is not in dispute, it raises the question of why John would so easily contradict what has been said elsewhere. There is, of course, no doctrinal reason why Jesus could not have baptized those who followed him (and indeed JST John 4:3 indicates that he did perform some baptisms), but perhaps the practice could have led to claims of superiority based on who performed an ordinance (1 Corinthians 1:12). Because the fourth Gospel has clearly been edited in other instances (John 21:24–25), it is possible that this passage, which corrects the earlier statements, is a later addition inserted to answer the needs of the second-century Church.

Samaria and the Woman at the Well
JOHN 4:4–42

In a surprising move, **Jesus** talks with a **Samaritan** woman at Jacob's well, located near modern-day Nablus in the West Bank (Palestine), on his way to Jerusalem. Traditionally, women gathered at the village well in the morning and late afternoon—to avoid the heat of the day, and not only to obtain water but also to socialize. However, this unnamed woman came at the "sixth hour" (John 4:6); in other words, she came in the heat of the day at twelve noon. She might have made her daily pilgrimage to the well at this time to avoid the other women from the village who would have naturally ostracized her (the reason will soon be revealed).

In this setting, she meets a Jewish man. Though modern readers might not be surprised, the **disciples** were (4:27), and understanding some first-century cultural sensitivities will help us to know why.

First, the Samaritans and the Jews had been antagonistic neighbors since the time when the Jews returned from their Babylonian exile in the fifth century B.C. The Samaritans were descendants of Abraham, but Israel had intermarried with the foreign people who had colonized the region after the fall of Israel in the eighth century B.C. (2 Kings 17:24; Ezra 4:2, 10). Since that time, they had been known as Samaritans.

The Samaritans volunteered to assist the Jews to rebuild the **temple** in Jerusalem but were rebuffed because of their intermarrying with non-Israelites (Ezra 4:1–3). As a result, the Samaritans opposed Jewish efforts to reestablish worship in Jerusalem and eventually established their own temple on Mount Gerizim near Jacob's well, perhaps even altering their own version of the **Torah** to justify their actions.

In the following years, animosity between the two peoples included acts of violence, killings, and the destruction of the Samaritan temple by the Hasmoneans in 109 B.C. The Samaritans never forgot or forgave the Jews for this act.

Even Roman efforts to establish **Pax Romana** in the region did not stop the bloodshed. Jewish pilgrims making their way from **Galilee** to Jerusalem through **Samaria** (which separated the two Jewish regions) were sometimes attacked, beaten, and killed. As a result many pilgrims traveled the longer route down through the Jordan River Valley to Jericho. From Jericho travelers made their way up to Jerusalem—the setting of the story of the good Samaritan, one of Jesus' most beloved **parables** (Luke 10:30–35). Jesus took this longer route on his last journey to Jerusalem at **Passover** in A.D. 30.

On the other hand, as a minority religion and population at the time, Samaritans were often despised, hated, and abused themselves, victims of a spiral of violence. Another important first-century sensitivity focused on inter-gender relations. Because observant Jewish men and women did not allow themselves to be alone with someone of the opposite gender who was not their spouse or a family member, they carefully avoided such circumstances. If they did find themselves in such an awkward situation, they avoided talking with each other and quickly separated. In this story, Jesus finds himself alone with the woman—a female who was not his wife, mother, aunt, or daughter. Adding to the sensitivity of the situation, this particular woman was a despised Samaritan and, as we find out through Jesus' own questioning, also a woman of questionable reputation.

One last surprise awaits us. Jesus not only remains and talks with her but also asks the Samaritan woman to give him a drink. This is all the more remarkable because it was believed that touching an earthenware cup or leather bucket from a Samaritan would make a Jew unclean—even more so because a Samaritan woman was considered by Jews to be unclean from birth—perpetually in the state of menses.

In this particular encounter, Jesus talks about living water—not from a pool or well but from a moving river, a source of water considered to be significantly purer and more desirable than even the water from the one-hundred-foot-deep well dug by the great patriarch Jacob and where Jesus encountered the woman.

Though she does not at first understand Jesus' teachings, the woman eventually comes to believe that Jesus is the long-promised **Messiah**. In fact, for the first time in the Gospel of John, Jesus announces that he is the Messiah, and it is to this unlikely woman that he does so (John 4:25–26).

Leaving her pot behind, the Samaritan woman runs to tell the people of the village that she has found the true Messiah and that he is at Jacob's well. In a remarkable act of faith (or perhaps initial curiosity), the villagers venture out to see and hear for themselves (4:30, 39–42).

Before there were chapters and verses in the Bible, a practice established as late as the sixteenth century, this story did not begin with a new chapter but was part of a continuing story found in the preceding chapter. The story seems purposefully connected to the story of Jesus and Nicodemus, allowing people to compare and contrast the two incidents. The first story was about a Jewish male leader who came under cover of darkness to visit with Jesus and left in darkness, failing to grasp what Jesus said about being born again. The second story was about a marginalized woman (in two ways—she was a Samaritan and living with a man to whom she was not married). She came to Jesus at noonday and though, as did Nicodemus, she struggled to understand what Jesus was saying about the living water, she eventually recognized Jesus as the promised Messiah.

The Setting for the Sermon on the Mount
Matthew 5:1–2; Luke 6:17–19

In the verses preceding the Sermon on the Mount, Matthew recounts that **Jesus'** fame had begun to spread beyond **Galilee** into Syria and

Decapolis while Luke records the calling of the **disciples** and the healing of a great multitude. Whereas Matthew's account is more sparing on details, Luke answers two very important questions. First, the "disciples" mentioned in Matthew 5:1 refer to the Twelve Apostles of the ministry and, second, the reason Jesus sought to escape the crowds was that they had thronged him following the healing of the multitude. That the Sermon on the Mount and the Sermon on the Plain were originally the same discourse seems to be implied as both Matthew and Luke drew upon and expanded the same story found in the Gospel of Mark (3:13).

The setting for the sermon delineates the first division of an inner group of followers (the disciples) and an outer group ("the people"; Matthew 7:28) and thus prefigures at least two reactions toward Jesus. Interpreted in this way, the sermon outlined the way to becoming a disciple but, importantly, did not exclude that revelation from anyone who was interested in hearing. The mount where the sermon took place cannot be identified, although the hill near Tabgah has been a popular suggestion. The mountain or hill may be a symbolic designation, indicating a new revelation similar to that given to Moses and others on Sinai (Exodus 24:9–11). The Sermon on the Mount opens the concept of discipleship to all who will listen and obey.

The Beatitudes

MATTHEW 5:3–12; LUKE 6:20–26

The gospel is not simply good advice but is "good news," and that is what Jesus announces at the beginning of the Sermon on the Mount in what has become known as the Beatitudes. Matthew and Luke share four of the Beatitudes (Matthew 5:3, 4, 6, 11–12; compare Luke 6:20, 21–23).

The title comes from the **Latin,** *beatus,* which means "blessed," revealing the enduring influence of the Latin Vulgate Bible translated by Jerome in the fourth century A.D. The Old Testament contains similar announcements (see, for example, Psalm 1:1–2; Proverbs 8:32). The New Testament contains as many as forty similar announcements, including twenty-eight in Matthew and Luke and another seven in Revelation. However, those found here are the most famous and well known. Whether there are eight, nine, or ten beatitudes depends on how one divides this text.

Each one begins, "Blessed" (Greek, *makarios*). Although we are most familiar and therefore more comfortable with the English translation, "blessed," it may not capture the nuance of what **Jesus** intended in his proclamations. Jesus likely spoke **Aramaic** as his primary language, and what he was remembered to have said on this occasion was later translated into Greek. Therefore, the Greek word chosen by the authors represents their attempt to capture Jesus' original meaning.

"Blessed" naturally ties Jesus' statements to a liturgical (cultic) formula that does not seem to work well here, so another English word may be preferred. Translators who have been interested in getting beyond the Latin Vulgate have proposed other possible English translations for *makarios*, including "congratulations, fortunate, happy," and "wonderful news."

If one believes God bestows rewards on people despite their actions, then congratulations works: "Congratulations, you just won the sweepstakes!" Nevertheless, this rendering seems to fall flat. A better translation may be happy or wonderful news because Jesus is announcing the consequence of actions already taken. The opposite is also true: The merciless will not receive mercy.

What is lost on most readers, because we have become so familiar with them, is that these were shocking announcements. Commentators have noticed that the Beatitudes contain counterintuitive teachings—ones not obtained by observing how things are done in the world. The merciful do not always receive mercy nor do those who mourn always obtain comfort. Yet, Jesus announces the opposite. Through revelation Jesus knows that God will make things right—his justice demands it. Additionally, it is clear that these blessings cannot be disconnected from Jesus himself and his saving acts in our behalf. The direct context of Jesus' announcement is most likely Isaiah 61:1–7. Jesus announces that he fulfills Old Testament prophecy as he declares what he intends to do for those who believe God sent him. As a result of what Jesus did, those who act appropriately will receive the kingdom of heaven (Matthew 5:3), shall be comforted (5:4), shall inherit the earth (5:5), shall be filled (5:6), shall obtain mercy (5:7), shall see God (5:8), and will be called the children of God (5:9). Therefore, they should be happy at the wonderful news Jesus announces.

The first and the last beatitudes contain the present-tense form of the verb and those in between contain the future-tense forms. The Beatitudes end in the second person "Blessed are ye," personalizing the teachings (5:11). This section ends with "Rejoice, and be exceeding glad: for *great is your reward in heaven*" (5:12; emphasis added). Note the reward is not heaven itself but a reward received after you enter heaven. This possibly highlights the difference between salvation and exaltation. Both the Book of Mormon (3 Nephi 12:2–12) and the Joseph Smith Translation provide additional insights to the Beatitudes by emphasizing the connection between believing Jesus and the promised blessings.

The Salt of the Earth
MATTHEW 5:13–16; MARK 9:50; LUKE 8:16–18; 11:33–36; 14:34–35

Salt had many uses in the ancient world, but perhaps two uses stand out. Leviticus 2:13 directs the use of salt as an additive to **sacrifice** (see also Numbers 18:19, "**covenant** of salt"), and from writings external to the Bible, we learn that it was also used as a preservative. These two ideas seem to stand behind the Lord's direction: "Ye are the salt of the earth: but if the salt have lost his savour, wherewith shall it be salted? it is thenceforth good for nothing, but to be cast out, and to be trodden under foot of men" (Matthew 5:13). Although not specified in the direction, the teaching seems to imply that the **disciples** would become the salt of the sacrifice and therefore part of the larger offering of worthy lives on behalf of the world, or as a preservative for the world in general. The ambiguity may also have been intentional as the disciples fulfilled both roles.

The debate over whether or not salt can chemically lose its savor is probably reaching beyond the original focus of the saying as the disciples were not encouraged to consider this possibility nor were they being threatened with it. Instead, the direction of the saying is implied in the phrase,

"Ye are the salt of the earth." For a first-century audience, the phrase is a stark contrast to popular claims that the **Pharisees** or **Sadducees** were the salt of the earth or that even the law of Moses or the people of Israel were the salt of the earth. Instead, the disciples were the salt, and they were to savor the earth, not Israel alone. This saying of Jesus is the first recorded that implies and foresees a **Gentile** mission beyond the boundaries of Israel. Whether the disciples immediately understood the implications of what was being asked is not stated, but Luke's fondness for repeating the saying from Jesus' later teachings may indicate that he, writing in the period of the worldwide Gentile mission, understood it that way.

The purpose of being the salt of the earth, or of placing one's candle (oil lamp) on a lamp stand, was to "glorify your Father which is in heaven" (Matthew 5:16). Jesus understood the continued work of the Father for his newly identified disciples. Their work, like his own, would glorify the Father by spreading the gospel to the earth.

The Law Is Fulfilled

MATTHEW 5:17–20

Matthew's Gospel states, "Think not that I am come to destroy the law, or the prophets: I am not come to destroy, but to fulfil" (5:17). The translation "fulfil" can become a point of possible confusion because it implies many different things ranging from "done away with" to "completing." The verb (*pleroō*) indicates the filling up or completion of something that has already begun. In other words, a prophecy can be fulfilled in this sense; a missing piece can be added to complete the puzzle. As an extended meaning, the verb can also imply that something has ended because the final part has been added. In this sense, it appears that **Jesus** was declaring his own message and saving ministry—a message that completed the law and the prophets. They without him could not be considered whole, complete, or fulfilled.

For many, the completion of the law has signaled its end when in reality much of the law is still in effect. The commandments delivered on Sinai are still valid, as are many others. Jesus appears to have realized that some would interpret his statement as a negative appraisal of the law. He endorsed the law saying, "Whosoever therefore shall break one of these least commandments, and shall teach men so, he shall be called the least in the kingdom of heaven: but whosoever shall do and teach them, the same shall be called great in the kingdom of heaven" (5:19). The prophets and **apostles** of the second half of the New Testament struggled to help their followers understand which parts of the law had ended with the Resurrection of Jesus Christ because common practice and long-held traditions sometimes conflicted with revelation. But in the end the revelations received by the apostles clarified that many of the physical and outward requirements were to end and a spiritual counterpart was to replace them.

The Five Laws
MATTHEW 5:21–48; LUKE 6:27–36

Jesus' teachings on the fulfillment of the law and the directive to be or to become the salt of the earth beg the question of how the **disciples** should move forward. They certainly had shown faith in Jesus, but the change he envisioned for them is not expressed until Matthew 5:21–48. In a way, the two sayings preceding this section form an introduction to what might be called the higher law.

The law of Moses is popularly characterized as a lengthy list of commandments that require strict obedience and sometimes unquestioned acceptance. To see the rather stark difference in Jesus' teachings, one only needs to compare how often he spoke of new or different commandments in reference to his own teachings. At the heart of Jesus' teachings are the commandments of the Old Testament as well as new directions on how to live them by following the Spirit. At the beginning of the Sermon on the Mount, the Lord specifically mentioned five commandments that were reinterpreted in a consistent way. Those five commandments are the following: thou shalt not kill, thou shalt not commit adultery, thou shalt not forswear thyself (Leviticus 19:12; Exodus 20:1–15), an eye for an eye (Deuteronomy 19:21), and love thy neighbor (Leviticus 19:18).

Public Forms of Worship and the Lord's Prayer
MATTHEW 6:1–18; LUKE 11:2–4

Second **Temple** Judaism was not a monolithic religion as the **Dead Sea Scrolls** and the New Testament demonstrate. Within the diversity of common Judaism, various groups often criticized each other. The **Pharisees, Sadducees,** Essenes, and other such groups, including the **priests, elders, scribes** and the common people, generally believed their interpretations and practices represented the "correct" way to live the **Torah** commandments. In an effort to define their boundaries or self-understanding, Jewish groups often censured other Jews for not believing or practicing as they did. Understanding this inter-Jewish dialogue (debate) is necessary to appreciate this section—a section where **Jesus** is critical of some practices operating within the common Judaism of his day.

These practices represented, and still represent, the obligation of every Jew—donating money (**alms** giving), praying, and fasting. Jesus does not question these practices but criticizes wrong-headed motives involved in such practices in the first century. He certainly expected his **disciples** to help the poor, pray to the Father, and fast when necessary.

First, Jesus warns the disciples that giving alms is about the covenantal obligation Israel has to God because he delivered them from bondage to become his people, rather than a means of publicly promoting one's self (Matthew 6:1–5).

The Greek word translated "alms" here is one of those interesting words that can be translated in different ways. For example, it is the same word used earlier in the Sermon on the Mount: "For I say unto you, That except your *righteousness* shall exceed the righteousness of the scribes and Pharisees, ye shall in no case enter into the kingdom of heaven" (Matthew 5:20; emphasis added).

"Righteousness" or "acts of religious devotion" are good alternative translations, but even better may be "**covenant** obligation," instead of "alms" as rendered in the King James Version.

The public display of giving money looked more like the common non-Jewish practice of patronage—a system that bound clients (*cliens*) to patrons (*patronus*). Patronage centered on the public acknowledgment of inequality between the patron and the client—a public display of social status in which the patron provided money or services to the client (individual, extended family, group, city, or in the case of the emperor—the empire) and in return, the client gave back to his or her patron deference (generally through public greetings each morning), political support, or some other means of service to the patron.

Second, Jesus is remembered to have commanded his followers, "When thou prayest, enter into thy closet, and when thou hast shut thy door, pray to thy Father which is in secret" (Matthew 6:6). He continued by explicitly criticizing a non-Jewish practice—complicated and wordy prayers: "Use not vain repetitions, as the heathen [**Gentiles**] do: for they think that they shall be heard for their much speaking" (Matthew 6:7). Rather, the Father "knoweth what things ye have need of, before ye ask him" (Matthew 6:8). From inscriptions and writings, abundant evidence exists of such vain repetitions practiced among Gentiles. One did not always know which god or goddess needed placating and it was hoped that by using some magical formula repeated over and over again, the petitioner might receive what he or she wanted or needed or avoid some imagined judgment. From the literary sources, one gets the feeling that there was always a certain sense of doubt and frustration in such attempts as one could not be certain which god was listening, if the right formula was being used, and more intimidatingly, if the god or goddess was even interested in the petitioner in the first place.

The Gospels tell us that Jesus prayed (Matthew 14:23; 26:39; Luke 3:21; 5:16; 6:12; 9:18, 28–29; 11:1) and that he taught the disciples to pray as he prayed (Matthew 6:1–18; Luke 11:2–4). Following the warnings on public almsgiving and vain and repetitious prayer, Jesus provided a simple payer as a model.

Matthew and Luke preserve two forms of the prayer that is now known appropriately as the Lord's Prayer. The difference between the two forms found in Matthew and Luke may suggest different traditions that preserved the core material, but adapted the surrounding material to meet specific liturgical needs—the Lord's Prayer was most likely prayed as the use of the first person plural strongly hints. Or, because Jesus does not suggest that we should always use the same words in our prayers (he himself did not), perhaps these prayers represent various versions of prayers uttered by Jesus.

This prayer also highlights an important insight about Jesus' own prayers. Both Matthew and Luke use the Greek vocative *pater* (Father), which most likely represents the **Aramaic** *abba*, and therefore reveals Jesus' distinctive use of *abba* (Father), a very tender expression, in contrast to what Jesus' contemporaries would have said when they invoked the Father—Lord or *Adonai*.

Similar language is found in Jesus' prayer in Gethsemane (Matthew 26:39, 42; Luke 22:42, 46). Interestingly, the same language is found in Mark (Mark 14:36, 38; see also John 12:28 for the use of *pater*). This is all the more surprising because Mark and John do not contain the Lord's Prayer. That echoes exist in Mark and John most likely indicates how important the Lord's Prayer was to the early disciples.

One of the most important aspects of the prayer, picked up by both Matthew and Luke, is Jesus' insistence on forgiveness. First, one should ask the Father to forgive him or her. Jesus taught that our actions are not set in stone forever but that we can be forgiven. We should ask often with the assurance that God will freely offer forgiveness as often as we ask for it. Second, Jesus provides in his prayer the condition upon which forgiveness is granted—we must forgive others: "And forgive us our debts, as we forgive our debtors" (Matthew 6:12; compare Luke 11:4 where he uses "sins" instead of "debts"). The topic will surface again in Matthew 18.

This section ends with Jesus' discussion regarding fasting, the third standard Jewish practice (Matthew 6:16–18). Again, Jesus does not challenge the practice, though he will tell the disciples that while he is present, they should not fast (Matthew 9:14–15). Jesus is more interested in why a person fasts and therefore pleads with us to fast to God in private instead of making a public display of discomfort, which often diverts us from God to a specific audience of people.

Finally, Jesus emphasizes that seeking a public reward or recognition by donating money, praying, and fasting is wrong. Yet, he says that those who do these things in private will be rewarded (Matthew 6:4, 6, 18).

Treasure in Earth
MATTHEW 6:19–34; LUKE 11:34–36; 12:22–34; 16:9–13

The subject of earthly wealth is addressed in several of the Lord's discourses, and in those contexts there is often the warning to be careful with riches. Such is the case with a significant section of the Sermon on the Mount (Matthew 6:19–34), although Luke records the same materials in a variety of different settings. The focus of these teachings on riches is quite clear: when considered in an eternal perspective, riches have very little value in comparison to righteousness. The word used to describe riches, "mammon," is a simple transliteration of the **Aramaic** word for money. For reasons that are not entirely clear, the evangelists remembered that specific word even when they could have used a Greek word to translate it. The preservation of Aramaic words in the sermon also attests that it was originally spoken in Aramaic.

In the Sermon on the Mount, **Jesus** addresses the legitimate concerns of temporal welfare when one takes, "no thought for your life, what ye shall eat; neither for the body, what ye shall put on" (Luke 12:22). If followed literally, this teaching could lead to an ascetic ideal, where worldly concerns are completely neglected. Jesus taught that if we seek first the kingdom of God, he will provide in a timely way, much as he cares for the ravens, which are fed and sustained through God's benevolence. This saying should not be interpreted to mean that a person needs to put aside all concerns for food, shelter, and clothing, but rather that the exclusive pursuit of those things can lead a person to overlook weightier matters.

Luke's version of these sayings demonstrates that Jesus returned to the subject of treasure in heaven on a number of occasions. In one pointed instance, at the conclusion of a parable where Jesus used the model of shrewd investments, he said ironically, "And I say unto you, Make to yourselves friends of the mammon of unrighteousness" (Luke 16:9). Without context, this saying seems to contradict Jesus' earlier teachings to avoid making friends with mammon. But within the context of the parable, the saying serves to emphasize the idea that those of the "mammon" look out for their own even when catastrophe occurs (Luke 16:9).

Judgment

MATTHEW 7:1–5; LUKE 6:37–39; 41–42

Matthew's account of **Jesus'** teaching on judging others, "Judge not, that ye be not judged" (7:1), is followed by principles of judgment, suggesting that "judge not" was not to be interpreted in absolute terms. Rather, as the ensuing verses relate, there are certain principles involved in judging, but the opportunity to judge is not reserved for God only. At the heart of the matter are hypocritical judgments, where a person has a log (KJV, "beam") protruding from his or her eye and then attempts to dislodge a splinter (KJV, "mote") from another person's eye. This hyperbole underlines how important righteous judgment is, which the Joseph Smith Translation also highlights when it teaches, "Judge not unrighteously, that ye be not judged: but judge righteous judgment" (JST, Matthew 7:1).

The subject matter of the proceeding lines makes it clear that the **disciples** would be required to render sacred judgment regarding wicked persons who appear to be externally righteous and pretenders who seem to do mighty works in the name of the Lord. That the language of the mote and beam is told in hyperbolic fashion may also reveal that "judge not" was part of the overall hyperbole.

Luke's version of the saying is interpreted in light of forgiveness so that "judge not, and ye shall not be judged" is followed by "forgive, and ye shall be forgiven" (6:37). To those who give abundantly of their means, following the paring of opposites of forgiving and being forgiven, Jesus promised an abundant return couched in merchandizing terminology: a "good measure, pressed down, and shaken together, and running over" (6:38). Such an abundant portion would likely be awarded at the same time that those who forgave received forgiveness and those who did not condemn escaped condemnation. In other words, the promise seems to presuppose the Final Judgment.

Sacred Things
Matthew 7:6–12; Luke 11:9–13

Jesus' instructions on handling the sacred things of God are recorded in two slightly different versions. Matthew remembered the odd relationships that Jesus spoke of—pearls and swine, and dogs receiving holy things—and Luke remembered the context of a father being asked a favor from a son, perhaps alluding to the father-and-son relationship that is fundamental to human existence.

Pigs are certainly an odd choice of animal to caricature, given that they are deemed unclean in the law of Moses. That pigs would somehow become enraged at being given pearls is also a striking image; and the normally docile domestic pigs envisioned here turning again to attack a giving hand is also at odds with normal behavior. But those very images bespeak the threat involved in revealing sacred truths out of context and out of place. Those who are normally docile might act as do the pigs in Jesus' metaphor.

Luke's account focuses on giving and not on the behavior of those who receive. Both Matthew and Luke record the saying, "If ye then, being evil, know how to give good gifts unto your children: how much more shall your heavenly Father give the Holy Spirit to them that ask him?" (Luke 11:13), with one small difference—the means of giving. In Matthew, the Father will give good things to those who ask, whereas Luke records that the Father will give the Holy Spirit to those who ask. Luke's saying seems to be informed from the time after Jesus had ascended to heaven as John taught: "But this spake he of the Spirit, which they that believe on him should receive: for the **Holy Ghost** was not yet given; because that Jesus was not yet glorified" (John 7:39). In contrast to Luke's account, Matthew's appears to look forward, whereas Luke's may represent a later version of the saying at a time when Christians had realized that Jesus was speaking of the Holy Spirit.

The Way
MATTHEW 7:13–14; LUKE 13:23–24

This short saying, both a part of the Sermon on the Mount and a later discourse, envisions rigorous requirements for entrance into the kingdom of God. In **Jesus'** day, many Jews, particularly Pharisaic Jews, focused their attention on rigorous obedience to the commandments as the means of attaining salvation. At times the focus tended to shift toward rigor and away from principle. In a day when such an attitude was prevalent, Jesus drew upon that line of reasoning to teach his followers about the rigors of following the Lord. What is profound in this teaching is the context rather than the actual words spoken. Given the day and age, one would expect this saying to be delivered in the context of enumerating specific commandments. Instead, Jesus describes the paths and who will follow them. But one must turn to the Savior: "I am the way, the truth, and the life: no man cometh unto the Father, but by me" (John 14:6). That is, Jesus stands at the entrance to that narrow path and will sustain his followers on their journey.

Luke may have preserved another context for this story when an interested observer asked whether only a few could be saved. To that question, which is certainly the natural question arising among a people who were chosen and who also emphasized rigorous obedience, Jesus said, "Strive to enter in at the strait gate: for many, I say unto you, will seek to enter in, and shall not be able" (Luke 13:24). Here the challenge of entrance is emphasized rather than the importance of maintaining one's position on the path. The discovery of the path and the resulting discovery of faith in Jesus that is described in these passages led some outside of Christianity and eventually Christians themselves to refer to Christianity itself as "The Way" (Acts 9:2).

Opposition from Within

MATTHEW 7:15–27; LUKE 6:43–49; 13:25–30

Jesus ends the Sermon on the Mount with a solemn caution—a warning against false prophets "which come to you in sheep's clothing, but inwardly they are ravening wolves" (Matthew 7:15). The Old Testament also warns about false prophets (Deuteronomy 18:22), which is reflected in Jesus' teaching on the same matter: "Wherefore by their fruits ye shall know them" (Matthew 7:20).

Nevertheless, Jesus has something more in mind than simply looking at a tree and deciding if the fruit looks delicious or not. The fruit must nourish those who eat it because "not every one that saith unto me, Lord, Lord, shall enter into the kingdom of heaven" (Matthew 7:21). In fact Jesus warned, "Many will say to me in that day, Lord, Lord, have we not prophesied in thy name? and in thy name have cast out devils? And in thy name done many wonderful works?" (7:22).

Only by *hearing* and *doing* what Jesus says are we like the "wise man, which built his house upon a rock" (7:24). The opposite is also true; anyone who hears Jesus but does not do what he says is called a "foolish man, which built his house upon the sand" (7:26).

This would be particularly true after Jesus' death when his words and deeds circulated in an oral form. Members of the early **Church** must have been aware that false teachings—stories and sayings attributed to Jesus that were not in harmony with the established traditions about **Jesus** already accepted and guarded by the **apostles**—could also circulate. Living witnesses who could attest to the things Jesus said and did were therefore extremely important. However, once those stories and teachings were written down we should not suppose that this ended the role of such witnesses because they still could say, "We saw, we heard." Nevertheless, the written record—the Gospels—did provide a measure of security as the voices of the witnesses fell silent in death. These writings helped ensure that what Jesus said, including his warning about hungry wolves, could be heard and acted upon.

Jesus Teaches with Authority

MATTHEW 7:28–29

Many commentators have observed that Matthew portrays **Jesus** as a new Moses or a prophet like unto Moses (Deuteronomy 18:15, 18). For example, not unlike Moses, who went to a mountain and returned to teach the people, Jesus, in the Sermon on the Mount, went to a mountain and delivered his teachings to the people. Further, many scholars have suggested that the Gospel of Matthew was modeled on the five books of Moses (**Torah** or Pentateuch)—that is, they are divided into five separate teaching blocks. The first block, which began at Matthew 5:1 ends here: "And it came to pass, when Jesus had ended these sayings, the people were astonished at his doctrine" (Matthew 7:28). Similar statements divide the remaining blocks (13:53; 19:1; 26:1).

Matthew notes that at the conclusion of the sermon, "the people were astonished . . . for he taught them as one having authority, and not as the **scribes**" (Matthew 7:28–29). This immediately reminds us of Mark's early observation that what Jesus said and did, he said and did (Greek, *kat' exousian*) "with authority" (Mark 1:27). Matthew picks up that same theme here.

A major issue confronting Second **Temple** Judaism was the question of who had the authority to interpret Torah once the gift of prophecy had faded. A variety of groups, including the **Pharisees, Essenes, priests, elders**, and **scribes**, attempted to fill the vacuum and claimed that right. Certainly, many people who met Jesus may have thought at first that he was simply one more voice claiming authority to interpret scripture. Jesus is, after all, identified as a teacher, the most common title associated with him throughout the Gospels. Even Josephus recalled that Jesus was "a teacher of the people" (*Antiquities* 18.63). He seems to have accepted this identification gladly and taught using the same types of material (aphorisms, metaphors, maxims, **parables**, wisdom sayings) that other teachers did at the time. Nevertheless, Jesus left those who followed him, those who heard him, and those who opposed him to struggle to communicate what they observed with their eyes and heard with their ears.

Throughout the Gospels, Jesus is remembered as saying, "I say unto you" (Matthew 5:20) in contrast to prophets who said, "Thus saith the Lord" (see, for example, Exodus 4:22). Additionally, and more significantly, Jesus often said, *"For verily I say unto you"* (Matthew 5:18, 26; 6:2, 5, 16; emphasis added). In the King James Version, "for verily" is often the translation of the word found in Hebrew and **Aramaic**, "amen." *Amen* was generally used as a declaration of strong, solemn affirmation of what someone has said (see, for example, Deuteronomy 27:15; Nehemiah 8:6). Today, one thinks of *amen* as what is said at the end of prayers; however, Jesus uses it in a different way—he uses "amen" to endorse what he himself has said! He also says it before he declares something.

In making an unprecedented claim to being anointed by God (Isaiah 61:1), Jesus separated himself from all other contemporary parallels, including the scribes. Remember that immediately before these verses, Jesus said that a person must hear him and do what he says so that his house will be built upon a rock foundation that will withstand the rains, wind, and floods (Matthew 7:24–25).

Such a claim to authority, given his lack of formal training and the fact that Jesus did not quote dead sages, definitely impressed people—they were in fact "astonished," not only by what he taught but also by the audacity of his claim to be divinely endowed with authority to teach. Many of his teachings still surprise us—especially if we do not attempt to create a politically correct Jesus who doesn't say anything about divorce or wealth or who doesn't ask us to become as little children or who doesn't chide us as he did Martha. We may forget that people were not only astonished but also offended by what he said and did (see, for example, Mark 3:1–6, especially 6).

The Healing of a Man with Leprosy
MATTHEW 8:1–4; MARK 1:40–45; LUKE 5:12–16

This brief episode and its retelling suggest that Matthew and Luke relied on Mark for some details of the story. Certainly, the **disciples** themselves began to immediately retell this incident in the wake of the healing, even later that day as they gathered. They most likely continued to do so on numerous occasions thereafter. In its various oral versions the story took shape, reflecting the essential elements of the healing (often identified as its core). In this case, a man afflicted with **leprosy** was touched by **Jesus** and healed.

In antiquity the word *leprosy* denoted a wide variety of skin diseases, including Hansen's disease, or modern-day leprosy, as recent discoveries have demonstrated. The Greek term *lepi* means "fish scales." This identifies the primary external symptom of this highly communicable disease that appears after bacteria attack the nervous and upper respiratory systems of the victim. A progressive disease, leprosy can and often does permanently damage the eyes, limbs (through the loss of sensation), and nerves.

Mark records Jesus' inward feelings as the man knelt before him, pleading that Jesus save him: "And Jesus [was] moved with compassion" (Greek, *splanchnistheis*, "deeply moved") (1:41). In response to the man's faith, Jesus touched the afflicted man, an act that made Jesus ritually impure, possibly affirming Jesus' ultimate replacement of the Mosaic law since he is the instrument by which the man is healed.

Leviticus 13–14 delineates a range of skin diseases using the Hebrew word *tsara'at* ("to strike"), translated in the Greek **Septuagint (LXX)** as *lepra*, which eventually provided us the English word *leprosy*. Traditionally, those afflicted were cast out of the community. A rather complex ritual outlined in Leviticus 14 stipulates how a person whose symptoms had disappeared or who had been healed could be pronounced clean and returned to full fellowship within the community.

Interestingly, Jesus commands the man to "go thy way, shew thyself to the priest, and offer for thy cleansing those things which Moses commanded" (Mark 1:44), demonstrating how the "good news" was preached in the context of Second **Temple** Judaism. However, unlike the priest who simply confirmed that the person was clean, Jesus cleanses the man by touching him. The section ends with Luke's notation: "But so much the more went there a fame abroad of him: and great multitudes came together to hear, and to be healed by him of their infirmities" (Luke 5:15).

The Healing of the Centurion's Servant/ Nobleman's Son
MATTHEW 8:5–13; LUKE 7:1–10; JOHN 4:46–54

Another non-Markan story found in both Matthew and Luke and which may have a parallel in John is a remarkable account of the healing of a centurion's servant from a distance by **Jesus**. There is significant diversity in the first part of the story but remarkable (nearly word for word) agreement in the main section of the story. Matthew emphasizes the *faith* of the centurion while Luke emphasizes the *worthiness* of the centurion. The story could possibly have foreshadowed in the minds of both Matthew and Luke the expansion of the gospel to the **Gentiles**.

What certainly impressed the **disciples** was the respect, faith, and confidence this Gentile official had in Jesus. Jesus also recognized this, declaring, "Verily I say unto you, I have not found so great faith, no, not in Israel" (Matthew 8:10).

John's account coincides in at least ten points with the story recorded in Matthew and Luke and therefore likely represents another version of this tradition. In this account, **Jesus** is in Cana, where earlier he turned the water into wine (John 4:46). Interestingly, most of the narrative in John is set in **Judea**, principally in Jerusalem. Only a few incidents are set in **Galilee**, and this is one of them. The "royal official" (possibly an official of Herod Antipas) from Capernaum meets Jesus and explains his plight: his son is sick, near death. **Jesus** tells him, "Go thy way; thy son liveth." On his return to Capernaum, the royal official's servants (slaves) meet him and inform him that his son has recovered. The official asks them when the son began to feel better. They say the fever left him yesterday afternoon at 1:00 P.M. The man knew that was the time Jesus had promised his son would live. He believed, along with his household. This was the second "sign" Jesus manifested in Galilee (John 4:46–54).

Unlike the accounts in Matthew and Luke, John has Jesus warning the people, saying, "Except ye see signs and wonders, ye will not believe" (4:48).

It seems that the people were much more interested in the "signs" instead of where the signs are to lead them—to Jesus himself.

The Son of Man Has Nowhere to Lay His Head
MATTHEW 8:18–22; LUKE 9:57–62

This event, which both Matthew and Luke record in similar language and order, may ultimately derive from a source that predates the Gospels. The lament "Foxes have holes, and birds of the air have nests; but the **Son of man** hath not where to lay his head" (Luke 9:58; see also Matthew 8:20) is nearly verbatim in each account and appears to have been remembered more precisely than the other details of the story. Perhaps this convergence in the accounts demonstrates how impressive these words were to the Gospel authors.

The words function differently in both accounts, coming during the early part of the ministry in Matthew, but later in Luke's account, immediately after Luke noted, "And it came to pass, when the time was come that he should be received up, he stedfastly set his face to go to Jerusalem" (9:51). So for Matthew the lament appears to describe a lack of physical comforts, whereas for Luke it may look toward the **temple**, which should have been a place of peace and refuge for Jesus but through corruption had become a den of thieves. When Jesus decried the lack of a place to lay his head, he may have had in mind the loss of the temple.

The second part of the story shows a contrast between two types of discipleship. Jesus, who was willing to give up all comforts to do the will of the Father, stands in stark contrast to the **disciple** who asked for time to bury his father. Both parts of the story show how even genuine concerns such as physical comforts and family ties can become obstacles to discipleship. That Jesus would so strongly answer, "Let the dead bury their dead" (Matthew 8:22), seems harsh but may have reference to the tradition of a second burial, where family members would gather up the bones of the deceased about a year after a person had died and then place those bones in an ossuary. The practice of reburying deceased ancestors was commonplace, and

Jesus' seemingly strong answer may reflect his condemnation of an unnecessary practice that would prevent a person from accepting the call to discipleship. In such a scenario, one ought to follow first and then attend to the matter later. It remains equally possible that Jesus intentionally used strong language to emphasize the importance of following him while he was yet alive, particularly given the context in which Luke placed the account—just prior to Jesus' betrayal and crucifixion.

Calming the Storm on the Sea of Galilee
MATTHEW 8:23–27; MARK 4:35–41; LUKE 8:22–25

This great **miracle**, which occurred on the Sea of **Galilee**, was witnessed by the **disciples** and a handful of other followers (Mark 4:36). The force of the storm left the disciples with little hope that they would survive the capsizing of their boat, and the evangelists seem to hint that their intent in waiting to call upon the Lord for salvation was to protect Jesus or at least not to bother him until it became absolutely necessary. Their request that Jesus save them represents both a symbolic and literal plea—to spare them from drowning *and* to redeem their souls. Perhaps this was one small way God helped them see in Jesus a Savior.

But the story also has significant theological overtones. The disciples' request was met with a rebuke even though their plea appears to be an evidence of genuine belief and understanding. They needed help, and they asked for help when it became apparent that they could not save themselves, but their plea earned for them Jesus' rebuke: "Why are ye so fearful? how is it that ye have no faith?" (Mark 4:40). Little did the disciples know at the moment that drowning in the Sea of Galilee would not constitute an atonement for mankind; or at least the Gospels do not record anything in Jesus' teachings that would have alerted them to know the full scope of his mission. Had they known that Jesus could not die in that way, they may have realized they would survive the storm. Perhaps there is also something implied in their request that is not apparent in their words. All three evangelists record that the disciples said, "What manner of man is this, that even the wind and the sea obey him?" (Mark 4:41). Their summary of the event indicates the disciples had not yet gained an understanding that Jesus was not simply a man.

Jesus Casts Out Devils That Enter Swine
MATTHEW 8:28–34; MARK 5:1–20; LUKE 8:26–40

Both Mark and Luke record this **miracle** as having taken place in Gadara in Decapolis, whereas Matthew places this event in the otherwise unknown city of Gergesa. Although there is some textual variation among the different place names as later Christian **scribes** attempted to harmonize the texts of the Gospels, both Gadara and Gergesa present difficulties. Some manuscripts of Mark record a third possibility, Gerasa (modern Jerash, in Jordan), as the site of the miracle. The city of Jerash lies nearly thirty miles from the Sea of **Galilee**, thus making that city an unlikely candidate. Gadara (modern Um Qeis) lies about five miles from the Sea of Galilee, and its "country" probably did extend to the sea, thus making it possible that the miracle took place in the land lying between the sea and the city. The reading "Gergesenes" is probably a third-century conjecture based on unknown sources, although the village of Kursi has been venerated as the location of the miracle and may have some connection to this ancient conjecture. Because of the presence of pigs and pig farmers in the story, it is important to be precise in the location of the city. Assuming that the city was part of the Decapolis, its inhabitants would have been mainly Greeks, whereas a Galilean city would have been inhabited primarily by Jews, and the presence of pigs would be more difficult to explain.

Although all three Gospel authors seem to overlook the issue of financial loss in the story, an underlying subtext of this story is that someone (perhaps a **Gentile** but possibly a Jew) suffered a significant financial setback through the suicide of a herd of pigs. Those who tended the pigs, and who also lost at least a portion of their income, reported the event. These details may explain the cold reception **Jesus** received after performing such a mighty miracle.

This particular miracle is one of the most complex in the New Testament, both because of the discussion between Jesus and the man possessed by legions of evil spirits and because of the ensuing action of the pigs in the story. As Mark records, the man cried in a loud voice, telling Jesus, "I adjure thee by God, that thou torment me not" (5:7). Mark then notes that the man possessed had said this because "he (Jesus) said unto him, Come out of the man, thou unclean spirit" (5:8). That the evil spirits would even attempt to adjure or entreat Jesus after having been commanded to depart is noteworthy.

According to Matthew, after hearing the spirits' desperate plea, Jesus replied simply, "Go" (8:32) or "Get out," but all three accounts leave ambiguous whether Jesus intended to grant their request. Even though the spirits asked to possess the pigs, it is not clear from the account that Jesus complied with their request. Rather, it seems very unlikely that Jesus would even entertain such a request, particularly in light of the fact that he had commanded the spirits to depart.

If Jesus did not grant the spirits their desire to inhabit the bodies of the swine, we are left to wonder what it was that compelled them to stampede down a steep place and into the sea. In any event, the man was restored to health, and eventually the inhabitants came out to see what had happened. Before arriving at the scene, they received a report of Jesus' action from those who had lost their employment. This theme seems to run through the entire story—that loss of income or employment can color a person's likelihood of accepting the gospel. This miracle took place prior to the calling of the Twelve **Apostles** and may have signaled to them that such a loss should not keep them from acting on their faith.

Following this tumultuous event, Luke sadly notes, "Then the whole multitude of the country of the Gadarenes round about besought him to depart from them; for they were taken with great fear" (Luke 8:37).

The Healing at Capernaum

MATTHEW 9:1–8; MARK 2:1–12; LUKE 5:17–26

The Gospels often focus on **Jesus'** healings—some thirteen such stories are found in Mark alone. In this section, a crowd gathers to hear Jesus teach at a house in Capernaum, possibly his own home and thus encouraging a figurative interpretation of Matthew 8:20. Unable to enter, four men take a man suffering with palsy on a stretcher to the rooftop so they can lower him down by ropes to get Jesus' attention. They do so, but Jesus says something totally unexpected: "Son, thy sins be forgiven thee" (Mark 2:5). As the story unfolds, it becomes clear that he is concerned not only about the man's physical condition but about a damaged human spirit—and he is going to fix it.

We do not know what Jesus knew about this particular man. However, unlike the previous healing stories mentioned in Mark, Jesus chose to focus on the man's guilt, not his physical disabilities.

Some of those present were offended. "Why doth this man thus speak blasphemies? who can forgive sins but God only?" (Mark 2:7) Luke says **Pharisees** were present, some of them visiting from Jerusalem (Luke 5:17). As they question Jesus' authority in their hearts, he asks them if it is easier to say, "Thy sins be forgiven thee" or "Arise, and take up thy bed, and walk" (Mark 2:9). Obviously it is easier to say "Thy sins be forgiven thee," because no one would or could know if the man's sins were forgiven. Really, anyone could say it! Of course, it is much more difficult to tell someone who is paralyzed to stand up and walk because if you do not have the power to make it happen, everyone present would know within moments.

In this setting, Jesus announces his authority: "But that ye may know that the **Son of man** hath power on earth to forgive sins, (he saith to the sick of the palsy,) I say unto thee, Arise, and take up thy bed, and go thy way into thine house" (Mark 2:10–11; emphasis added).

The man "immediately" rose up, took the stretcher, and walked home. Those present were amazed. Mark adds what some scholars call the choral effect: "We never saw it on this fashion" (Mark 2:12), which in modern

English might mean, "We never saw anything like this before!" Matthew notes, "They marvelled and glorified God, which had given such power unto men [tois anthrōpois]" (Matthew 9:8). Jesus' authority is an important part of the story (see Matthew 9:6, 8, where the KJV uses "power" for the Greek word exousian, which is better translated as "authority").

Another important element in the story is Jesus' identification with the "Son of man." Only the theme of the kingdom of God (heaven) is more dominant in the Gospels than Jesus' declarations that he is the "Son of man." In total, Jesus' association with the "Son of man" appears some eighty-two times in the Gospels. In every case, with only one exception (John 12:34), it is Jesus who uses it—no one else addresses him or identifies him with the phrase.

The Greek phrase ho huios tou anthrōpou (the son of the man) does not appear in any contemporary Greek source and is universally assumed to be the direct translation of the Hebrew or **Aramaic** idiom ben 'adam (Hebrew) or bar a'nasa (Aramaic). Jesus, who was profoundly aware of whose Son he was and of his divine mission, may well have been inspired to use the term "Son of man" in this way and then provide an innovative interpretation of the phrase. Apparently, no one during this period associated the "Son of man" with any **messianic** office. Notice also that no one initially takes offense at his using the term; only later, when it is combined with a citation from Psalm 110:1, does a high priest object. Most likely, even the **disciples** may not have understood its significance until after Jesus' death and resurrection, eventually making it a title (moving from "the son of the man" to "Son of Man"). Remember, the Gospel authors' first attempt was to remember what Jesus said and then interpret what he said in light of his suffering, death, and resurrection.

There is no consensus within New Testament scholarship about what Jesus may have meant by the phrase "Son of man." Jesus likely understood his own mission through the lens of Daniel 7:13–14, where suffering was followed by vindication. Prophecies of his Passion (the traditional identification of Jesus' suffering, death, and resurrection; Acts 1:3) were articulated as such (Mark 8:31; 9:12; 10:33).

In the end, this story provides a condensed outline of Jesus' ministry.

He came to teach, heal, and forgive but was charged with blasphemy (Mark 14:62–64). Nevertheless, in a remarkable moment, Jesus was vindicated when the Father raised *him* from the dead (Acts 2:22–24). Mark's audience was surely aware of the resurrection symbolism in 2:9 (arise), 11 (arise), and 12 (arose).

Matthew the Tax Collector
MATTHEW 9:9–13; MARK 2:13–17; LUKE 5:27–32

The Gospel of Mark highlights how **Jesus** continually "astonished" and "amazed" people by what he taught and how he healed (see, for example, 1:22, 27). This section reveals another way Jesus surprised people—this time by calling Levi, son of Alphaeus, to follow him. Levi is identified as Matthew in the Gospel of Matthew, another possible reason why this particular Gospel was associated with Matthew; it is the only Gospel that mentions Matthew.

Levi was a **publican** (a toll and tax collector), a member of Herod Antipas's royal bureaucracy. There had always been ill feeling between peasants, common laborers (including fishermen), and members of the bureaucracy, especially those individuals sent to bully and in some cases illegally seize goods and coins as part of their efforts to collect revenue to maintain Antipas' lifestyle, to keep his government in business, and to pay tribute to **Rome**.

Adding to the general disgust for such individuals was the fact that it had not been many years since Herod the Great ruled a larger area that included **Galilee, Samaria, Judea,** and Perea, as king of the Jews. After his death in 4 B.C., Herod's kingdom was divided among his sons. Archelaus was given Judea, Herod Antipas was given Galilee and Perea, and Herod Philip was given his father's northeast districts—modern day Golan Heights. Eventually, the Romans took direct control of Judea, leaving Antipas and Philip in power in the north. The Jordan River and the Sea of Galilee divided their territories, with Capernaum (Antipas's territory) and Bethsaida (Philip's territory) serving as important border towns at their frontiers.

Antipas established an extension of his royal bureaucracy in Capernaum, including a tollbooth with supporting personnel such as soldiers, toll and tax collectors, and others who supported the regime in various ways. Additionally, there was a host of individuals, including prostitutes, who could always be found where soldiers and royal bureaucrats were located. Their presence in a Jewish town such as Capernaum was a daily reminder that Israel was an occupied land. Most Jews knew all they wanted to know about tolls, taxes, absentee landlords, kings, and kingdoms. Additionally, they could remember the day when passing between Bethsaida and Capernaum did not necessitate paying any toll.

Those working for Antipas, as did Levi, were generally despised, hated, and in some cases forced from the **synagogue** (excommunicated). They worked for the client ruler of **Rome** and as a result encountered the animosity of the people on a daily basis.

Levi must have been impressed and surprised when Jesus called him—there was no accusation that Levi had robbed Jesus or any resentment for his chosen occupation, only the call to "follow" (Mark 2:14). In an instant, he left the employ of Antipas, who thought *he* was the king of the Jews, to become Jesus' **disciple**—the true King of Israel (Mark 8:29; Luke 5:27–28).

Some time after Levi's call, Jesus hosted a dinner at "his house" in Capernaum where a number of Antipas's employees had gathered (Luke says it was Levi's home; see Luke 5:29; Matthew is less clear). Mark also says there were "sinners" present on this occasion (2:15). What he meant by "sinners" is much debated, but at least the group may have included non-**Torah** observant Jews (those who would have no problem socializing with toll collectors) and other marginalized Jews. Note Mark's reference to "many," suggesting that a rather large group of people was in attendance (2:15).

A group of **scribes** and **Pharisees** was offended because they believed that an observant Jew would not dine with such corrupt individuals. Although table fellowship was an important Pharisaic concern, the Pharisees were also, at this period, vigorously nationalistic, rejecting not only Roman control but also condemning anyone suspected of cooperating with pagan and local leaders who supported the occupation.

The disciples did not respond to their questions, but Jesus did: "They that are whole have no need of the physician, but they that are sick: I came not to call the righteous, but sinners to **repentance**" (2:17). Of course, Jesus meant to be ironic, because all are sick and all need a physician, including the scribes and Pharisees who raised the question in the first place. This was the heart of the matter—no one should look at another person to judge him or her but to see individuals as God sees them—deserving of Jesus' healing touch.

It is worth noting that the other disciples could have been as surprised as anyone when Jesus called Levi. Certainly Peter, Andrew, James, and John had no love for a member of the local royal bureaucracy. Had Levi hounded them for tolls and taxes in the past? If so, his call was all the more personal, adding another dimension to the kind of discipleship Jesus demanded.

The Question about Fasting
MATTHEW 9:14–17; MARK 2:18–22; LUKE 5:33–39

Often identified as mini **parables**, this section contains three comparisons (fasting and feasting, new and old cloth, and new and old wine skins).

This story also shows an important difference between the mission of John the Baptist and the mission of **Jesus**. John is portrayed as physically rigorous in his obedience and attire: He dresses in camel hair, eats honey and locusts, and grew up in the desert (Luke 1:80). Jesus, on the other hand, lives in a house (see Mark 2:1, where the Greek *en oiko* means "at home" and Matthew 9:1, where Capernaum is identified as "his own city"), was a frequent dinner guest (Luke 7:36, for example), owns an expensive coat (John 19:23), and in one pejorative but revealing comment was identified as a glutton and winebibber (Matthew 11:19; Luke 7:34)—suggesting that he was known for attending banquets (for example, see John 2:1–3, where Jesus attends a wedding feast and provides the best wine for the guests).

Additionally, John's message was one of anticipation—God's wrath is about to be poured out upon the wicked (Matthew 3:7) and someone is coming—someone greater than himself (Mark 1:7). Although Jesus does not negate a final judgment (John 5: 21), he nevertheless speaks of a postponement—a time when the "good news" is preached (Mark 1:15). The "good news" is nothing more or less than a time of great celebration because God is offering inexhaustible, amazing, absolute, and unfathomable goodness through his Son at that very moment—not in the future, but right then (Acts 10:39).

The kingdom Jesus proclaimed may not look like what anyone expected—no fasting and an invitation to all to join a great and sumptuous banquet (Matthew 22:9–10). Jesus understood and remarked portentously, "No man also having drunk old wine straightway desireth new: for he saith, The old is better" (Luke 5:39). Some were too much invested in the old way God had worked through the **Law**, the **temple**, and the **priesthood**, to accept Jesus' new vision.

Jesus does not say that the old was necessarily bad (Matthew 5:17)— fasting and mourning, anticipation and expectation had their place while the night lasted, but now that the dawn had come, what was done at night was no longer appropriate (another night is coming soon enough and there will be plenty of time to fast and mourn; Mark 2:20).

The issue that brought this topic to the forefront was fasting—if John's **disciples** (and the **Pharisees**) fasted frequently (Matthew 9:14; Luke 5:33), why didn't Jesus' disciples fast regularly as well? Note that issues related to eating practices (table fellowship) were among the constant criticisms leveled at Jesus and his disciples; for example, they ate with **publicans** and sinners (Mark 2:16); ate with unwashed [defiled] hands (7:2); and picked and ate grain on the **Sabbath** (2:23).

Fasting was an important Jewish tradition and the Jews often fasted to remember national and personal calamities (for example, the destruction of the first temple in 586 B.C.). There were regular fast days, and some Pharisees may have fasted twice a week (Luke 18:12). Jesus has already given warnings about fasting in the Sermon on the Mount (Matthew 6:16) and said there were circumstances when it might be necessary, but given his declaration in this story, that would be in the future (Mark 9:29) because he specifically says that you don't fast at wedding feasts (you mourn and fast at funerals).

By the first century, the wedding feast (banquet) was a well-known image from the Old Testament—the Lord (the bridegroom) will take Israel (his bride) in an everlasting **covenant** and celebrate a new world (see, for example, Isaiah 49:18; 54:1–8; 62:4–6; Hosea 2:19–20). The occasion, like those celebrated in everyday life, is observed with much cheerfulness and joyfulness; it is a time of feasting, not fasting. The sense of celebration may allude to the **Messianic** promise Jesus quoted when he preached in Nazareth, "The Spirit of the Lord God is upon me; because the Lord hath anointed me to preach good tidings. . . . To appoint unto them that mourn in Zion, to give unto them beauty for ashes, the oil of joy for mourning, the garment of praise for the spirit of heaviness" (Isaiah 61:1, 3).

This section also reveals one of Jesus' characteristic teaching styles—the contrasting of pairs; see, for example, the strait and narrow way (Matthew 7:14; Luke 13:23–24); the wise and foolish builders (Matthew 7:24–27; Luke 6:47–49); two sons (Luke 15:11–32); the wise and foolish virgins (Matthew 25:1–13); the young prodigal and his obdurate older brother (Luke 15:11–32); the publican and the Pharisee (Luke 18:9–14).

As with all analogies, one cannot push this one too far, because in the comparison of the old and the new cloth, one needs to find an old cloth to repair an old garment, not a new piece. The point of this analogy and that of the wine skin is that the old and the new do not mix well.

Matthew and Luke follow Mark but include a few differences, reminding us that 95 percent of Mark is found in either Matthew or Luke. A close comparison between Mark and Matthew in this section demonstrates an undisputable literary dependence on Mark (almost word for word).

The Raising of Jairus's Daughter
MATTHEW 9:18–19, 23–26; MARK 5:21–24, 35–43;
LUKE 8:41–42, 49–56

Between the beginning and the end of the story of the healing of Jairus's daughter, Mark includes a brief account of an unnamed woman who suffered from "an issue of blood." The two stories are interrelated and share common features: Each has to do with a woman—one older with a longstanding illness and one younger who had actually died. Furthermore, under Jewish law, both women were impure and coming into contact with either would make a person ritually unclean. The older woman had been bleeding for twelve years, and the young woman was twelve years of age—about the age when she would be engaged—ready for marriage. In one story, the older woman touches **Jesus** and in the second story, Jesus touches the young woman.

Mark breaks off the account of Jairus at a critical point only to return to the story when some people arrive to inform Jairus that his daughter has died, making it no longer necessary for Jesus to come to the house.

Mark seems to rely upon Peter as his primary eyewitness (for the tradition that Mark served as Peter's translator, see Irenaeus, *Against Heresies* 3.1.1). The inclusion of relatively obscure names (not public names such as Pilate, Herod, Peter), as is the case in this story, suggests that the named individual (Jairus, in this instance) may be the eyewitness who first told the story. Frequent retelling of the story would have naturally established the core material or relevant details. Additionally, often these accounts, which contain the name of an obscure individual, also contain vivid details not generally found in similar stories that feature unnamed individuals. In this story, an example would be the note "and commanded that something should be given her to eat" (Mark 5:43).

How was it possible to preserve such details? First, the event was not only unique (one did not witness such a **miracle** every day), but as it is in this story, the healing mentioned was of such personal significance to Jairus himself—it was his daughter, after all, and it would understandably deeply affect him.

This story also illustrates a phenomenon in the Gospels—the dropping of the names in later Gospel accounts. In this case, Matthew drops Jairus's name, though Luke retains the name. Interestingly, no unnamed person in Mark is identified with a name in Matthew and Luke, unless it was a well known individual. Later, apocryphal New Testament texts did supply names for those unnamed in the Gospels. Most scholars agree that this tendency of the apocryphal gospels provides no historically reliable information but is simply an effort to fill in information not provided by the Gospels.

Another interesting point is found by comparing the accounts of Luke and Matthew. Luke indicates that Peter, James, John, and the parents entered the home with Jesus. When Jesus said to them, "Weep not; she is not dead, but sleepeth," Luke adds, "and *they* laughed him to scorn," indicating that the **disciples** and/or parents were the ones who laughed inappropriately (Luke 8:52–53; emphasis added). Matthew smoothes out this reading (even adding some information about professional mourners who were already at the home—minstrels): "And when Jesus came into the ruler's house, and saw the minstrels and the people making a noise, He said unto them, Give place: for the maid is not dead, but sleepeth. *And they laughed him to scorn*" (Matthew 9:23–24; emphasis added). Although it is impossible to know whether Matthew or Luke was written first, this demonstrates how different oral versions of the story were eventually recorded.

Of course, this account, just as the story of the woman with an issue of blood, is about faith. Matthew and Luke may have expected their readers to consider an earlier story—the story of the healing of the centurion's servant (Matthew 8:5–13; Luke 7:1–10). The soldier in the earlier story did not need Jesus to come to his home—his faith was sufficient—whereas the Jewish **synagogue** leader needed Jesus to come to his home.

A Woman Touches Jesus' Garment and Is Healed
MATTHEW 9:20–22; MARK 5:25–34; LUKE 8:43–48

The poignant story of the woman with an issue of blood (hemorrhaging) reminds us that **Jesus**' reputation was growing and as a result, people were seeking him out (Mark 5:25–34).

Under the law of Moses, certain genital discharges made a man or a woman ritually impure (unclean). Women naturally fell under this ruling during their menses (Leviticus 15:19–24). However, given the realities of the first century when women married at puberty and were either pregnant or nursing most of their lives, this was not a regular experience for most women. Additionally, abnormal female discharges of blood (Leviticus 15:25–30) also made a woman ritually impure.

In order to be considered cleansed, women were obligated to undergo a ritual purification process at the end of their cycle. Until that ritual was complete, however, such women were prohibited from participating socially and religiously in several important and fundamental ways. The woman mentioned here had been perpetually unclean for twelve years—basically, socially dead. Her condition would have certainly prevented her from marriage or would have been a cause for divorce if she were already married. Significant and constant physical suffering and perpetual ostracism caused this woman to do the unthinkable—to reach out and touch another human being.

In a narrow, crowded lane in Capernaum, Jesus is moving toward Jairus's house when the woman reaches from behind him and touches the tassels of his clothes ("hem of his garment" in Matthew 9:20). Religious symbols based on the **Torah** (Numbers 15:38; Deuteronomy 22:12), these fringes were sacred markings that provided a reminder to keep the commandments and most likely would have meant something to Matthew's Jewish audience (Mark does not mention them for his basically **Gentile** audience in **Rome**, where the fringes would have had little meaning). The presence of the fringes also reminds the reader that Jesus was a Jew and dressed like his peers, even wearing tassels on his robes. Later, it was difficult for Jews to distinguish between tradition and gospel with respect to clothing and diet (Acts 10:14).

In this story, **Jesus** asks the **disciples**, "Who touched me?" Because of the close quarters of the crowd, his disciples must have been stunned, saying, "Master, the multitude throng thee and press thee, and sayest thou, Who touched me?" (Luke 8:45) Nevertheless, Jesus knows that someone has not just accidentally touched him because he has felt "virtue" (Greek, *dynamis*, "power") leaving him (Luke 8:46). The woman confesses humbly that it was she, but Jesus commends her: "Daughter, thy faith hath made thee whole; go in peace" (Mark 5:34). She was thus rewarded for having acted in the hope that Jesus had the power to meet her need, providing all of us with yet another powerful example of the efficacy of faith.

Matthew significantly edits the material to only seventy-two words in English. This is another example where Matthew is looking for space to include his unique material (such as the Sermon on the Mount). Luke, on the other hand, preserves much of Mark's account but omits Mark's detailed elaboration on the suffering the woman had endured, for she "had suffered many things of many physicians, and had spent all that she had, and was nothing bettered, but rather grew worse" (Mark 5:26). Luke clearly edited Mark's description to say that she had "spent all her living upon physicians, neither could be healed of any" (Luke 8:43), omitting the implication that the physicians had somehow been ineffectual in their treatments. Some have used this softening of the text as evidence that the person referred to by Paul as "Luke, the beloved physician" (Colossians 4:14) is the author of the Gospel of Luke.

The Blind Are Healed
MATTHEW 9:27–31; 20:29–34; MARK 10:46–52; LUKE 18:35–43

Although Matthew records this healing in two different versions, which differ in detail from Mark, it is nearly certain that these four accounts actually report the same original event. Mark's account still preserves the name of the blind man, "Bartimaeus, the son of Timaeus" (Mark 10:46), likely because the man was still alive to be a witness to the healing.

The focus of all four stories is the declaration of the blind man, "Thou **son of David**," which he may have uttered in the weeks leading up to Jesus' triumphal entry. Such a declaration foreshadows what **Jesus** had come to do in Jerusalem. Matthew remembered that Jesus asked the men (Matthew is the only author to report two men instead of one) that they "see that no man know it" (Matthew 9:30). This detail is absent in the second version of the healing.

That Matthew reported the story twice in nearly identical language attests to its importance for early Christians. All four accounts show how those who were healed from various illnesses formed the base of Jesus' followers as well as becoming missionaries of the word.

First Accusation of Healing by the Power of the Prince of Devils
MATTHEW 9:32–34; LUKE 11:14–15

The first accusation of healing by the power of **Satan** is mentioned almost in passing in Matthew and Luke. The account is not found in Mark, but its purpose in Matthew and Luke is quite clear. After **Jesus** had cast out a devil in a man, which was confirmed by the fact that the man could speak after the healing, the "multitudes" marveled at Jesus. Matthew's reference to the multitudes believing is actually the focus of the **Pharisees'** concern and not the actual healing. As Matthew constructs the story, the Pharisees responded not directly to Jesus but rather to those who assumed that Jesus healed by the power of God. The Jewish leaders are portrayed here as hard-hearted and of limited scope, worried more about the popularity of Jesus than the power of God to heal. This particular **miracle** is part of a larger narrative that develops the theme that the Pharisees and others would eventually reject Jesus because of their bias and limited perspective.

Matthew 9:34 is missing from some ancient manuscripts of Matthew, and it is more than likely that **scribes** removed this verse because it has a strong similarity to Matthew 12:24, and they might reasonably have assumed that it had inadvertently been repeated here. Luke 11:15 attests that this verse was part of the story early on and not a later addition.

Jesus Preaches in Unnamed Galilean Cities
MATTHEW 9:35–38; MARK 6:6; LUKE 8:1–3

In a short transitional section, Mark tells us that **Jesus** "went round about the villages [of **Galilee**], teaching" (6:6). It is clear that he did not remain in Capernaum but left the fishing community to teach in other towns and villages. However, we should not assume that Jesus was some type of itinerate teacher or Cynic philosopher. As noted earlier, Jesus lived in Capernaum and may have lived in his own house. Additionally, we have no evidence that Cynic philosophers traveled in the company of women.

Matthew expands the narrative by informing us that Jesus proclaimed "the gospel of the kingdom" and healed "every sickness and every disease among the people" (9:35). Additionally, he says Jesus was "moved with compassion" because the people were like "sheep having no shepherd" (9:36). Finally, Matthew records Jesus' words: "The harvest truly is plenteous, but the labourers are few; Pray ye therefore the Lord of the harvest, that he will send forth labourers into his harvest" (9:37–38). This is one of the few times, besides the Lord's Prayer, when Jesus instructs his **disciples** exactly what to pray for.

Luke follows Matthew but provides also some helpful additions to the story, including specific identification of those who were with Jesus as he went round about the cities and villages in Galilee. First, "the twelve were with him" (Luke 8:1). This is not surprising, because the Twelve play a significant role in Jesus' ministry, with Peter, James, and John at the center of the group, and with Peter as spokesman.

What is surprising is the second group Luke identifies as traveling with Jesus, "certain women" (8:2). Our mental picture of Jesus walking the dusty roads and pathways in Galilee with only a group of male disciples has to change. The tradition is too strong to doubt that Luke has eyewitness information about the presence of these women. In fact, some scholars suggest that the women specifically named were the eyewitnesses.

Luke not only mentions "certain women" but names some of them, including Mary Magdalene (Mary of Magdala/Migdal); Joanna, wife of Chuza (Herod's steward); Susannah; and many others "which ministered [*diēkonoun*] unto him of their substance" (8:2–3).

Since Jews living in the first century did not have last names, methods to distinguish individuals who shared a common first name were developed, including designating a person by their relationship to another (for example, Joanna, wife of Chuza, or Simon bar Jonah) or place of birth or residence (for example, Mary of Magdala/Migdal, or Jesus of Nazareth). Luke therefore, provides important information about two of the women in this group—Mary and Joanna. Mary was from Magdala or Migdal, an important fishing town located between Tiberias and Capernaum. Joanna was married to a member of the Herodian royal bureaucracy, Herod Antipas's household manager, Chuza.

Luke also tells us something about these women's efforts—not only did they travel with Jesus but they also provided important resources, most likely domestic service and money. They would have also provided, as did the men who traveled with Jesus, a network of family and friends in the various cities and towns they visited.

Later, we discover that Jesus visited Chorazin and Bethsaida, towns very close to Capernaum, where he may have spent a significant amount of time, given the strong condemnation they receive (Matthew 11:21–24). Other towns and villages in Galilee would have also been visited.

Jesus' mission to Israel included a specific call to individuals to become disciples; some accepted the call and others did not. Additionally, some of those called joined him on his travels and others remained at home. Nevertheless, the Gospels inform us that women also traveled with Jesus and not just to Jerusalem for his final **Passover** (Mark 15:40–41).

The Calling of the Twelve
MATTHEW 10:1–4; MARK 3:13–19; LUKE 6:12–16

Mark indicates that **Jesus** "ordained twelve" male **disciples** to receive special training and a commission to represent him (Mark 3:14). The Gospels describe them in various ways; for example, Matthew sometimes speaks of the "twelve disciples" (Matthew 10:1; 11:1; 20:17); Luke says "twelve" (Luke 9:12); whereas Mark and Matthew have the "disciples." The **Synoptics** also identify them as "**apostles**" (see, for example, Matthew 10:2; Mark 6:30; Luke 9:10).

Although we cannot always be certain who is included by a certain term, a disciple generally represents anyone who believes in Jesus, whether he or she stays home or joins his traveling company. An apostle is anyone Jesus commissions or "sends" on a mission, since the word *apostle* was a common Greek secular word (Greek, *apostolos*, "one sent") that was used regularly in non-New Testament documents for anyone who was "sent" or commissioned by someone else on his or her behalf; for example, a slave "sent" to represent his master was an *apostolos*. However, at some point, the word was appropriated by the early **Church** and resignified in light of Jesus' calling of twelve disciples. The Twelve is a specific group numbering twelve individuals Jesus chose at this time to receive specific and sometimes private instruction from him before he sent them on missions. Translators and commentators sometimes capitalized the term, *Twelve*, since it designates a specific group (1 Corinthians 15:5). The term could also be used to simply refer to the group, even if twelve individuals were not present (see, for example, 1 Corinthians 15:5, as noted above, where Judas is obviously absent).

As a result, the Gospels may reveal various circles of Jesus' followers. First, an outer circle of those who believed in Jesus—identified broadly as disciples. Second, an inner circle of those disciples whom Jesus "sent" or commissioned—identified as apostles (more than twelve—including individuals such as Paul). Finally, the inner circle of those especially commissioned by Jesus—identified as the Twelve.

Therefore, the Twelve were also by definition apostles because they were "sent" by Jesus *and* were likewise disciples, that is, "followers" of Jesus. In the Restoration the term *apostle* eventually became rather specifically identified to refer exclusively to an office in the priesthood. But even then, ordination to the office of apostle did not necessarily make one a member of the Twelve. There are numerous examples of men ordained as apostles who never served in the Twelve in both the nineteenth and twentieth centuries (for example, Oliver Cowdery, Hyrum Smith, and Alvin R. Dyer).

Interestingly, the Gospels only mention the specific callings of six of the Twelve (Simon [Peter], Andrew, James, John, Levi [Matthew], and Philip), although the names of all are given in the Gospels. Of the Twelve, it is likely that Peter, James, and John constituted an inner circle with Peter as spokesman. Some scholars have suggested that the inner circle of three implied Davidic connections (see 2 Samuel 23:8–23, where David has three especially loyal bodyguards, "mighty men with David").

There are four lists of the Twelve in the New Testament (Mark 3:16–19; Matthew 10:2–4; Luke 6:14–16; Acts 1:13). Even though John does not provide a list of the Twelve, there are specific references to the group (John 6:67, 70, 71; 20:24) and many more implicit references. The various lists do not entirely agree on membership in the Twelve; however, it is reasonable to assume that through the years lists might have changed due to the death or apostasy (as in the case of Judas Iscariot) of members of the original Twelve. In every instance, Simon Peter is listed first, suggesting his prominent role. Often, the order of names in a list in antiquity suggests social status. On the other side, Judas is always listed last, perhaps because he was the final disciple called—or because he betrayed Jesus.

The Twelve included members of various family groups such as Simon and Andrew (brothers) and James and John (brothers and possibly Jesus' cousins). Each of the members of the Twelve was drawn from various social and occupational groups, including fishermen (Simon, Andrew, James, and John) and at least one member of Antipas's royal bureaucracy (Levi [Matthew]). All appear to have been from **Galilee**, but one exception has been identified: Judas. Some have suggested that he may have come from Kerioth (Hebrew, *'ish qeriyyot*, "man of Kerioth"), a village in **Judea** south of Hebron (Joshua 15:25). However, there is ample evidence that some families continued to be associated with the place of origin of a relative who lived several generations earlier. This seems most likely in this case, especially because the identification was preserved in Hebrew instead of Aramaic. Therefore, it may be assumed that all of the original Twelve lived in Galilee when Jesus called them.

There has been some speculation regarding Simon, identified as the "Canaanite" in Mark (3:18) and the zealot in Luke (6:15; *ho zelōtes*). By the time the Jewish War broke out in A.D. 66, a specific revolutionary political party had developed, identified by Josephus as **Zealots**. However, there is no information to suggest that such a political revolutionary party existed earlier, during the ministry of Jesus.

Mark may have transliterated the Aramaic (*qan'an*) so as to avoid any suggestion that Jesus had called a member of this Jewish group to the Twelve since he was writing about the time of the Jewish revolt. Most likely, the nickname zealot should be understood in the way Paul uses the term to describe himself—one who had zeal for the **Torah**, the **temple**, and the Lord (Acts 21:20; 22:3). Even though he could have done so, it seems unlikely that Jesus recruited a militant revolutionary to join the Twelve.

Commentators have wrestled with the question of why Jesus called the Twelve. Most likely the call reminded Israel of its origins (the twelve sons of Jacob) and at the same time signaled the long anticipated restoration of Israel—envisioned in the new **covenant** Jesus initiated (Ezekiel 37:15–22). Matthew and Luke add that the Twelve will sit on thrones to judge Israel (Matthew 19:28; Luke 22:30), highlighting an eschatological identification. Most interestingly, Jesus did not call eleven others to serve with him so as to constitute the Twelve, but he called Twelve to represent him.

Mark and Matthew point out that Jesus gave them power or "authority" (Matthew 10:1; Luke 9:1)—these "twelve *Jesus sent forth*" (Matthew 10:5; emphasis added). There is a sense of urgency in this mission. Jesus offered Israel reconciliation, but if rejected they would experience judgment (Matthew 10:15). However, the judgment would not come by God sending down fire from heaven, but rather by destruction and dispersion at the hands of the **Roman Empire**. This was Israel's last chance to accept God's peace (Matthew 10:13) before the Jewish War (A.D. 66–70) would sweep across the land of Israel.

On a similar note, the message of warning that the **disciples** carried with them was certainly based on the Old Testament, and it may have been that they carried with them for the first time the words of Jesus. This mission may have necessitated the need to write down Jesus' words, thus creating what would likely become the beginning of the later written Gospels.

The Mission of the Twelve Apostles

MATTHEW 10:5–42; MARK 6:7–13; LUKE 9:1–6; 12:2–9, 11–12, 49–53; 14:25–28

It appears that Matthew greatly expanded Mark's original description of the mission of the Twelve **Apostles** during **Jesus'** ministry, whereas Luke recorded details from that mission in several different contexts. Following Mark's brief narrative, Matthew recorded very specific instructions for the newly called apostles, who were to visit the "lost sheep of the house of Israel" (10:6). Those lost sheep are interpreted as the lost within Israel and not in the modern context of the ten tribes that were carried away into Assyria in the eighth century B.C. Luke adds that they were to go "through the towns" or, following the Greek *kata tas komas*, "village to village." There were roughly two hundred such villages in **Galilee** at the time of the Jewish revolt, all within walking distance of a day or two from the region of Capernaum.

The **disciples** were instructed to teach their message to those who had been lost in Israel, teach that the kingdom was at hand, provide saving ordinances, use their **priesthood** to perform **miracles**, and travel without extra money or food. When their message was rejected, the disciples were directed to dust off their feet as a testimony against their inhospitable hosts. The cultural context of this action was the first-century requirement that a host was obligated to open his home to travelers and provide food, a place to sleep, and water for the washing of feet. Failure to provide water was taken as an insult. Here, the disciples were being purposely insulted by not being given water and were therefore required to dust off their own feet. These early instructions have both positive and negative connotations. The instructions speak positively of the organization of Jesus' disciples into a quorum of apostles who now had the priesthood and who had been trained to the extent that they were prepared to represent Jesus to all Israel. They were trusted, even to the point that they were given power to judge, foreshadowing their role in the Final Judgment (Matthew 19:28).

Jesus warned the disciples before they departed, "Behold, I send you forth as sheep in the midst of wolves: be ye therefore wise as serpents, and harmless as doves. But beware of men: for they will deliver you up to the councils, and they will scourge you in their **synagogues**; and ye shall be brought before governors and kings for my sake, for a testimony against them and the Gentiles. But when they deliver you up, take no thought how or what ye shall speak: for it shall be given you in that same hour what ye shall speak" (Matthew 10:16–19).

For Matthew, the calling of the disciples and their first mission was a focal point of the gospel. He dedicated an entire chapter to the mission, whereas Mark described it in seven verses and Luke separated the story. As the opposition to Jesus escalated, so did Jesus' care for the Twelve, whom he trained and established as a living, functioning body prior to his death and resurrection.

In the mission discourse, Jesus warned his disciples that acceptance of the gospel message would divide households and set family members against one another. Furthermore, Jesus taught that whoever should "confess me before men" (Matthew 10:32) would be accepted of the Father. The idea of confessing Jesus foreshadows later Christian centuries and is somewhat unusual so early in the ministry. As John notes, the confession of Jesus became an early sticking point between Christians and Jews, and even though some believed in Jesus, they were afraid to "confess him" because it might jeopardize their standing in the synagogues (John 12:42). In these instances, the confession of Jesus related to accepting Jesus as the **Messiah** or Jesus as the **Christ** rather than something akin to the later Christian creeds.

Another startling image is Jesus' mention of taking up a cross and following after him, which is the earliest reference to the cross in Jesus' teachings, and is certainly a foreshadowing of what would happen to him (Matthew 10:34; Luke 9:23). Even during the first mission of the Twelve, Jesus was already foreshadowing the cross as the purposeful conclusion of his mission. The symbolic meaning of the cross eventually became a staple of Christianity, but in Roman times it was a vehicle of crucifixion. The disciples were committing their lives as Jesus had already committed his to that end. As Matthew taught, Jesus already had a clear vision of the end and focus of his life.

Follow-Up Mission in the Cities of the Apostolic Mission
MATTHEW 11:1; LUKE 10:1

Matthew 11:1 ends the block of teachings preserved in 10:5–42, traditionally identified as the Missionary Discourse. In this verse we discover the use of a rather rare verb in Matthew: "And when **Jesus** had made an end of *commanding* his twelve **disciples**" (11:1; emphasis added). The verb *diatassein* can be translated in a number of ways ("to teach," "to instruct," or "to command"). The King James Version translations seem to fit the context, because Jesus' directives to the Twelve are more of a "command" than simply some general teachings or instructions that could have been given to anyone or any group.

Following the command, Jesus begins again "to teach and to preach" in the villages and towns of **Galilee**. This verse does not identify exactly which "cities" were involved, but the Gospels reveal Jesus' activities in Nain, Cana, Nazareth, Chorazin, and Bethsaida. However, there may have been a much larger number of potential towns and villages. Josephus says there were some 204 hamlets, villages, and towns in Galilee (*Life*, 235), numbering from a few dozen inhabitants to as many as twelve thousand (in Tiberias).

Luke indicates that Jesus appointed "other seventy, and sent them two and two before his face into every city and place, whither he himself would come" (10:1). In the context of the circles of Jesus' followers, the seventy would be disciples and **apostles** (those "sent" by Jesus). However, Luke distinguishes them from the Twelve.

John the Baptist Sends Followers to Jesus
MATTHEW 11:2–6; LUKE 7:18–23

John's delegation to **Jesus** is depicted as occurring quite late in the Baptist's ministry even though John's arrest occurred much earlier (Matthew 4:12; Mark 1:14; Luke 3:20). It may be that John languished in prison for some time under Herod Antipas (Matthew 14:1–12). John's question to Jesus that was communicated via two of his **disciples** was, "Art thou he that should come, or do we look for another?" (Matthew 11:3). The text seems to incongruously imply that John sought the answer to the question, thus suggesting the unlikelihood that John may have lost sight of what he had known previously. Luke made this connection even more explicit by recording a delegation that reported the works of Jesus to John, which in turn caused John to ask Jesus whether he was "he that should come?" (Luke 7:18–19).

The source of this story raises interesting questions. There is no record that the two disciples, or indeed even any of the disciples John sent on that day, were converted as a result of the testimony that Jesus bore to them. Even though the question is simple enough, it appears that Matthew and Luke have left the intent of the question ambiguous, which may suggest that the source for this interchange was an oral report. The simple question "Art thou he that should come, or do we look for another?" can be interpreted in a variety of ways. First, it could signal that John had lost faith in Jesus and shortly before his death was seeking confirmation of what he had once known. Second, it could indicate that John sought an answer to this question so that his disciples could hear the answer and thus begin following Jesus, the traditional Latter-day Saint interpretation. Third, it may represent a question that was being considered among the followers of John and that John told them to go and ask Jesus themselves.

As Acts records, John's teachings were perpetuated independently of

Jesus' teachings and gospel message (19:1–5), thus making it likely that the last two possibilities were what John intended. There is solid evidence that John had disciples who did not convert to the teachings of Jesus. The modern-day Mandeans, a baptismal sect struggling to survive in southern Iraq with diminishing numbers, may have ties to a very ancient group of followers of John the Baptist. That Jesus would reach out to hesitant followers of John is in line with the other gospel accounts of his ministry.

Jesus' Testimony of John
MATTHEW 11:7–19; LUKE 7:24–35; 16:16–17

At the departure of John's followers, **Jesus** took the opportunity to comment on John's ministry in a way that is both accusatory and challenging, thus suggesting that some in the audience may have doubted John. The fact that both Matthew and Luke included this story independently of Mark shows that even in the later decades of the first century there were concerns about John's followers and exactly what John had come to do. The story was not included for purely historical reasons, and the polemics and sharp rebukes of this interchange have not been softened.

One of the underlying concerns in this passage can be seen in Jesus' questions to the crowd: "What went ye out into the wilderness to see? A reed shaken with the wind? But what went ye out for to see? A man clothed in soft raiment? behold, they that wear soft clothing are in kings' houses. But what went ye out for to see? A prophet? yea, I say unto you, and more than a prophet" (Matthew 11:7–9). Jesus is certainly contrasting John with the popular ideology of his day. The image of a reed being shaken by the wind may refer to the reeds growing along the banks of the River Jordan, but it is also possible that there is a veiled reference to kingship. Herod Antipas used the image of a reed on coinage in Jesus' day, and the reference to soft clothing and kings' houses may further encourage that connection. Certainly Jesus was drawing attention to John's coarse clothing and rigorous ways as opposed to the luxury and opulence that some hoped for in the coming of the Messiah.

In furtherance of this argument, Jesus comments on John in a way that may leave questions in the mind of the reader. He said, "Among them that are born of women there hath not risen a greater than John the Baptist: notwithstanding he that is least in the kingdom of heaven is greater than he" (Matthew 11:11). The passage has been interpreted in a number of ways. First, the sentence may indicate that John had certainly achieved greatness, but the gospel message would exalt a person beyond what John had achieved. Second, the sentence may be interpreted to mean that even though John was great, Jesus' followers would be greater than John, even so much that the least Christian would be greater than John. Third, the word translated as "least" (*mikroteros*) may also be interpreted as "youngest" thus indicating that Jesus intended the comment to be understood as a self reflection. This way of interpreting the passage would indicate that Jesus was teaching that despite John being older and therefore of greater standing in society, Jesus was greater. The Prophet Joseph Smith offered commentary on this verse that seems to accord with elements of the above possibilities: "He that is least in the Kingdom is greater than he? who did Jesus have reference to? Jesus was looked upon as having the least claim in all gods kingdom—He that is considered the least among you, is greater than John! that is myself" (Ehat and Cook, *Words of Joseph Smith*, 160.)

The passage concludes by Jesus addressing some of the popular criticisms of his teaching and life. Some felt that Jesus should have been more ascetic or pious in his mannerisms. The popular claim was that John fasted, which earned him the illogical appellation of having "a devil" (Matthew 11:18). Jesus, on the other hand, "came eating and drinking," which earned him the appellation of being a glutton and winebibber (Matthew 11:19). The actions that are the bases of these accusations are not specifically mentioned, but perhaps Jesus' attendance at the wedding in Cana or feasting with his **disciples** on occasion made some think less of him because he did not follow the preconceived notions of an ascetic prophet. Both Matthew and Luke report that Jesus was accused of associating with "sinners" (Matthew 11:19; Luke 7:34). This reference might serve to point out the inherent ambiguity in the term, because *sinner* could refer to **Gentiles**, the blatantly wicked, or even those who did not accept Pharisaic or Sadducean interpretations of the law of Moses.

Jesus' Disciples Pluck Wheat on the Sabbath
MATTHEW 12:1–9; MARK 2:23–28; LUKE 6:1–11

This section reveals the escalating antagonism toward **Jesus** as it highlights another **Sabbath**-day controversy. Along with the story of Jesus healing the man with a withered hand (Matthew 12:10–13), this account is best understood within the context of first-century Judaism.

In the wake of the Babylonian exile and increasingly so during the Syrian occupation of their land in the post-exilic period, Jews set themselves apart from those around them in various ways, including a strict Sabbath day observance. The Sabbath had become a boundary marker and was one of the foundational building blocks of a radical nationalism that supported armed resistance to occupying forces. Jesus knew that such a vision of the kingdom of God would only and eventually bring about destruction and scattering and would also inevitably divide Jews from others at the very time God was ready to invite all people to share the covenantal blessings originally given to Israel.

Jesus taught that the Sabbath is a gift from God—he does not suggest that Jews should refrain from Sabbath observance—but he does reject the increasingly rigid interpretation and elaboration that some Jewish groups applied to the Sabbath. In the end, doing good and saving life were much more at the heart of the kingdom of God than any boundary markers.

The accounts of Luke and Matthew appear to be dependent on Mark's account, except that Matthew has added a significant element to the story—the noteworthy precedent of the priests profaning the temple when performing circumcisions on the Sabbath day (Matthew 12:5–7). Both Matthew and Luke, however, omit the problematic reference to Abiathar. At the time of the incident mentioned, Ahimelech was the high priest, not his son Abiathar.

Another interesting point to the story is that Jesus may have originally said something like, "The sabbath was made for man, and not man for the sabbath," with the idea that man is lord even of the Sabbath, referring to Adam's dominion over the creation (Genesis 1:26–31).

Jesus Heals a Man with a Withered Hand
MATTHEW 12:10–15; MARK 3:1–6; LUKE 6:6–11

This account follows an earlier **Sabbath** controversy when **Jesus' disciples** plucked grain on the Sabbath (Mark 2:23–28). *Shabbat* means "rest" or "cessation," and that is exactly what Jesus will do in this story: He will provide a man with an emaciated hand a cessation from his disability. However, healing on the Sabbath and in the **synagogue** was a double offense, according to some of the self-proclaimed interpreters of the law.

Matthew and Luke follow Mark. However, Matthew deletes material in two places (all of Mark 3:3, most of 3:4, and half of 3:5), but adds that the **Pharisees** asked Jesus, "Is it lawful to heal on the sabbath days?" and Jesus' challenge (Jesus often responds to a question by asking a question), "What man shall there be among you, that shall have one sheep, and if it fall into a pit on the sabbath day, will he not lay hold on it, and lift it out?" (Matthew 12:10–11). Jesus then observed that they should not have a problem with saving a human, who is infinitely more valuable than a sheep, on the Sabbath (Matthew 12:12). Most likely, the Pharisees would have countered that the man's life, unlike the sheep's, was not in immediate danger and therefore, the man could have waited until after the Sabbath to be healed. However, they were not interested in answering Jesus because they were looking for an opportunity to accuse him (Mark 3:2).

Both Matthew and Luke often seem to delete Mark's observations dealing with Jesus' feeling, and that is exactly what they do here: They edit Mark's comments that Jesus was angry (Mark 3:5). Mark indicates that Jesus is angry because of the "hardness of their hearts" (3:5). Paradoxically, Old Testament prophets often condemned ancient Israel for hard-heartedness because they broke the law; here Jesus condemns them for missing the point of the Sabbath law, not for breaking it.

Ironically, the story ends when the Pharisees and the **Herodians** conspire to "destroy" Jesus. According to Mark and Matthew, this forces Jesus to retire with the disciples (Mark 3:7; Matthew 12:15).

Why the Pharisees would conspire with the Herodians has raised some interesting responses. Traditionally, the Herodians have been identified as a political group who supported Herodian aspirations to reestablish King Herod's dynastic rule over "greater" Israel and may have included members of the Herodian family itself (see Bible Dictionary, "Herodians"). If this is the case, then the Pharisees, who were generally at odds with Herodian claims, decided they needed the political power of the Herodians to destroy Jesus because they had no power to do so. After all, it was Herod Antipas who had arrested and subsequently killed John.

Another option is that the Herodians could be identified as Essenes, *Herodians* being a pejorative nickname because King Herod had protected them during his reign. A much more conservative group even than the Pharisees, the Essenes would have been a natural ally for a strict and conservative interpretation of Sabbath-day observance.

Isaiah's Servant Song
MATTHEW 12:16–21

Matthew provides an interpretation of **Jesus'** healing ministry, suggesting that it fulfilled a prophecy found in Isaiah; he then quotes the verses (Isaiah 42:1–4), making this the longest Old Testament citation in the Gospels (Matthew 12:18–21). A comparison between Matthew's version and the Old Testament version reveals a rather free translation of the material. This is not just because the New Testament was written in Greek and the Old Testament was written in Hebrew but also because the authors were anxious to transmit a text interpreted in light of Jesus' mission.

Generally in antiquity the servant mentioned in Isaiah 40–50 had been understood to represent Israel, so it is rather unexpected that the servant is identified as Jesus here. The servant (Greek, *pais*, can also be translated as "son") is chosen, beloved, and highly favored. After the Spirit falls upon him, reminding us of Jesus' **baptism**, he announces and executes justice on the entire world (12:18).

It has been suggested by some analysts that the servant is pictured not as a Davidic warrior **Messiah** but rather as a Messiah who achieves victory through compassion ("a bruised reed shall he not break")—a very different vision of the Messiah than many first-century Jews held.

Jesus Is Accused of Healing by the Power of Beelzebub

MATTHEW 12:22–30; MARK 3:20–27; LUKE 11:14–20

Both Matthew and Luke contextualize this story differently than Mark by mentioning a specific instance of healing that preceded the accusation that **Jesus** healed by the power of Beelzebub. In this way the response of the **Pharisees** is interpreted as a reaction against Jesus' power to perform **miracles** and the ensuing faith of the people who believe in Jesus as the "son of David." To an extent, their accounts contrast the faith of the people with the hard-heartedness of the **Pharisees** and **scribes**. But Mark mentioned a more official inquiry into Jesus' miracles, where the **scribes** traveled from Jerusalem to **Galilee** to make the official accusation that Jesus healed by the power of **Satan**. Their accusation was likely based on Leviticus 20:27, which makes relying on the power of spirits an offense punishable by stoning. Therefore, in Mark's account the response to Jesus falls in line with other legal maneuvers to thwart the work of Jesus.

The King James Version spells the name *Beelzebub*. The name is probably built upon the roots *Ba'al* and *Zebub*, which mean "Lord of the flies" or "the Prince of devils" (2 Kings 1:2–3). Both origins for the name are possible, and the Gospel authors seem to point to the latter because of the interpretation of the term they provided. With either spelling, it is certain that Jesus' antagonists were attempting to characterize his healing power as deriving from a dark and wicked source.

Jesus' response reveals a subtle but powerful rebuke to their thinking. Jesus warned that if Satan were to cast out his own in order to deceive, then such a policy would result in the ruin of Satan's kingdom. In that case, by leaving Jesus alone the Pharisees could be certain that Jesus' ministry would come to naught. If Jesus did not cast out **demons** by the power of Satan, "then the kingdom of God is come unto you" (Matthew 12:27–28). If it were that Jesus healed by the power of God, then the scribes and Pharisees would be found to fight against the power of God.

Matthew and Luke, by connecting the story to a healing, may have intended to draw the reader's attention to a sublime truth that Jesus taught: "Or else how can one enter into a strong man's house, and spoil his goods, except he first bind the strong man? and then he will spoil his house" (Matthew 12:29). The story begins in Matthew and Luke with Jesus binding a strong man—Satan—and spoiling his house. For those who were seeking a testimony of Jesus' power to heal, the story contains a powerful witness that Jesus had power over the spirits in a very real way.

Blasphemy against the Holy Ghost
MATTHEW 12:31–37; MARK 3:28–30; LUKE 12:10

Mark's original story is expanded significantly by Matthew, perhaps because of the latter's perspective that the hostility to **Jesus** had continued to escalate. The result of that escalation in anger directed at Jesus was the shift to teaching in **parables**. In Mark, the teaching on committing blasphemy against the Spirit lacks some of the accusatory follow-up that Matthew's account contains. John completely passed over this story—perhaps a result of his understanding that "the **Holy Ghost** was not yet given; because that Jesus was not yet glorified" (John 7:39). Without the full administration of the Spirit, it is difficult to imagine that anyone would have the capacity to blaspheme the Spirit.

Another matter that arises from the various accounts is what Jesus said concerning the consequence of committing blasphemy against the Holy Ghost. It is easy to use modern terminology in this discussion, but the revelation of the kingdoms of glory postdates this particular teaching, and the statement concerning an unpardonable sin must be placed in the context

96

of salvation and damnation rather than into outer darkness, as might be implied if this were a modern statement.

Mark records, "But he that shall blaspheme against the Holy Ghost hath never forgiveness, but is in danger of eternal damnation" (Mark 3:29), whereas Matthew recorded, "But whosoever speaketh against the Holy Ghost, it shall not be forgiven him, neither in this world, neither in the world to come" (Matthew 12:32). Mark's rendition of the saying appears to have a very specific offense in mind when he mentions blasphemy, while Matthew seems to have a more general sin in mind, which he mentions as carrying consequences both in this world and in the world to come. The saying is contextualized in both Gospels in terms of speaking against the **Son of man**. Given that context, it appears that Mark's version looks forward to an eternal punishment whereas Matthew's version considers present implications also. The difference in wording may reflect something of the time when these two Gospels were written, with Matthew's account reflecting issues facing the followers of Jesus when he wrote. Paul seems also to be aware of such a problem: "No man speaking by the Spirit of God calleth Jesus accursed" (1 Corinthians 12:3).

The original setting of the story—of slandering or speaking against the Son of Man—should remain the focus of this teaching as the two deeds are compared and contrasted. Against the backdrop of an unpardonable sin, speaking against the Son of Man is certainly a much less egregious act.

Jesus' Mother and Brothers Seek Him
Matthew 12:46–50; Mark 3:31–35; Luke 8:19–21

Both Matthew and Mark record this saying in connection with **Jesus'** teaching on blasphemy, while Luke recorded it immediately after Jesus' teaching on lighting a candlestick and placing it under a bed. These two different contexts could possibly suggest that when Jesus' family visits him they resemble those who speak against the **Son of man** or are similar to those who hide their light before men. Such an association may be easily dismissed, but John relates that Jesus' brothers were at times antagonistic to his teachings (John 7:1–7). While this information is not explicitly found in the **Synoptics**, the connection presented here could potentially imply that meaning.

This particular saying also conveys Jesus' teachings on what the kingdom should become: a family unit that follows "the will of my Father which is in heaven" (Matthew 12:50). The contrast with sectarian forms of religion in his day is stark where orthopraxy, or strict attention to action, dominated the religious landscape. That Jesus could speak of a community of brothers and sisters is a surprising turn of events and underscores how such terminology has become fundamental to the Church today.

Why Jesus Taught in Parables

MATTHEW 13:1–2, 10–17, 34–35; MARK 4:1–2, 10–13, 33–34;
LUKE 8:4, 9–10; 10:23–24

The **Synoptic** Gospels portray Jesus' ministry as a series of increasingly antagonistic encounters until the point when Jesus alters his public teaching style because, "hearing ye shall hear, and shall not understand; and seeing ye shall see, and shall not perceive: For this people's heart is waxed gross, and their ears are dull of hearing, and their eyes they have closed; lest at any time they should see with their eyes, and hear with their ears, and should understand with their heart, and should be converted, and I should heal them" (Matthew 13:14–15). This reference to Isaiah 6:9–10 suggests a reason Jesus withheld the truth from his antagonistic listeners.

Another aspect of the change in teaching style to speaking in **parables** is that Jesus' public discourses began to focus on loss and restoration, or on other sheep instead of on the sheep within his hearing. That loss and eventual restoration is described in the seven parables of Matthew 13, and the Prophet Joseph Smith's statement helps shed light on one of the important truths that was being withheld: "In my mind [the parables of Matthew 13] affords us as clear an understanding, upon the important subject of the gathering, as any thing recorded in the bible" (*Messenger and Advocate*, Dec. 1835, 225).

The Parable of the Sower
MATTHEW 13:3–9, 18–23; MARK 4:3–9, 14–20;
LUKE 8:5–8, 11–15

All three **Synoptic** evangelists record this parable in nearly identical language and order, with the explanation following shortly after the parable is given. The parable of the sower, following Jesus' interpretation had an immediate context rather than an exclusive premillennial context. Jesus interpreted it in terms of how different people receive the word of God.

The parable envisions several levels of reception. First, there are those who do not understand the word, who are eventually led astray as a result of the shallowness of their comprehension (Matthew 13:19). Second, there are those who externally accept the word of God but who do not internalize it (Mark 4:16–17). Third, there are some who apparently accept the word but who are not prepared to nourish it and are overcome by their own ill-prepared souls. These broad categories help describe the various levels of commitment and acceptance the **disciples** would encounter, but in contrast to those who rejected their message, there are others who would receive them, "and bring forth fruit, some thirtyfold, some sixty, and some an hundred" (Mark 4:20).

Even though both sides are represented in the parable—acceptance and rejection—the parable and interpretation focus on the issue of rejection. This emphasis may indicate Jesus' understanding or anticipation of what the disciples would encounter. His own teachings had been met with mixed acceptance, and it would be no surprise if the disciples were similarly rebuffed.

The Candle under a Bushel
MARK 4:21–25; LUKE 8:16–18

The joining of the references to the candle and the bushel and subsequent application of the principle taught in both Mark and Luke in different forms helps solidify this connection as originating with **Jesus**. Whereas the order of events and sayings is often attributable to the evangelists, in this instance it appears that both might have followed an earlier oral or written source.

The teaching is very similar to that of the candle and bushel in the Sermon on the Mount (Matthew 5:15) and in its longer form may represent a later version of the saying that Jesus used to teach a similar concept. The ensuing application teaches that all actions shall be revealed, and therefore one should be transparent in doing as well as in being. Eventually, hidden or secret actions will be brought forward in judgment, and those who have not been transparent in who they really are will suffer under the weight of the knowledge that they were inwardly or privately something other than what they had presented themselves to be. Jesus consistently rejected such hypocrisy.

The Wheat and the Tares
MATTHEW 13:24–30, 36–43; MARK 4:26–29

Of all of Jesus' parables, this is the only one where his **disciples** asked for an interpretation. In the context of Matthew 13, the parables take on a forward-looking interpretation, to the time when the kingdom would be wrested from the Jews. For the disciples and those listening to this parable, there were immediate consequences to the opposition that they faced. Eventually, and time would reveal that it would come soon, the kingdom would be taken from the Jews because of their intense nationalistic mentality. Opposition to Jesus and his disciples became a barometer for the end of the Jewish state. This parable is introduced using a passive form of the Greek verb (*ōmoiōthō*) that indicates either a general truth or something that is already happening (that is, reflects the reception Jesus was then receiving); at other times parables are introduced using a future tense of the verb, which indicates events that would occur after Jesus' death.

Because of the notion of noxious weeds growing up among the tender wheat, the parable of the wheat and tares may foreshadow the fall of the kingdom in parallel to the fall of the state. The focus of the parable was not the devastating effect that these weeds would immediately have; they were, after all, permitted to remain until the harvest. Up to this point in Matthew and Mark, very little has been implied concerning the disciples' role in Jesus' mission (Matthew 8:23–27; but following this parable in Mark 4:35–41). But here the disciples intuitively asked for an interpretation of the parable, which they supposed had application in their own day and age. The more forward-looking parables were not interpreted by the Lord, but parables that had immediate application were—one voluntarily by Jesus and one by him at the request of the disciples (see D&C 86:1–11, where the Lord applies the parable to events taking place during the Restoration).

The Mustard Seed
MATTHEW 13:31–32; MARK 4:30–32; LUKE 13:18–19

Traditionally known as one of the three "**parables** of growth," this parable deals with the kingdom of God, comparing it to a mustard seed. **Jesus** says, "Whereunto shall we liken the kingdom of God?" (Mark 4:30). Those present would instantly have recalled Isaiah's famous words: "To whom then will ye liken God? or what likeness will ye compare unto him?" (Isaiah 40:18). Isaiah's message was that the God of Israel is able to restore and save Israel after a time of tribulation—and in this respect, no one is his equal. Jesus' message was similar: God will save (provide shelter) to those who accept his message: "The time is fulfilled, and the kingdom of God is at hand: **repent** ye, and believe the gospel" (Mark 1:15).

Anciently, mustard was cultivated both in gardens and fields for the oil produced from its seed and for spice. Black mustard was generally planted in Galilee and was the smallest seed cultivated at the time, but could grow to a height of between eight and ten feet. Wild mustard can in certain regions be considered a nuisance—overrunning a garden or orchard. However, Jesus does not seem to concern himself whether it would be planted on purpose or simply appear as a noxious plant. The point he was making was the vast difference between the size of the seed and what it grows to be.

Similarly, the kingdom begins small, but when it grows, it becomes large—big enough so that the birds of the air [and small animals] might nest in it (Ezekiel 17:23; 31:6; Daniel 4:11–12, 21).

The Leaven
MATTHEW 13:33; LUKE 13:20–21

Likening the kingdom of heaven [kingdom of God in Luke] to leaven (a substance that produces fermentation in the making of bread), **Jesus** draws on another familiar illustration from his world. Jews used leaven, except at **Passover**, in making bread.

Because it breaks down organic matter through the fermentation process, leaven was often used as a symbol of something evil or unclean (Matthew 16:6; 1 Corinthians 5:6–8). In this parable, however, leaven is an agent that produces enough bread to feed large numbers of people. Similar to the mustard seed, the leaven is initially obscure but produces a great outcome. In this dispensation, the Prophet Joseph Smith elaborated on this concept by declaring that "The Church of the Latter-day Saints has taken its rise from a little leaven that was put into three witnesses. . . . It is fast leavening the lump, and will soon leaven the whole" (*History of the Church*, 2:270).

Why Jesus used leaven in this way is unknown. Perhaps this story represents a "gospel reversal" or paradox—something totally unexpected. The kingdom message was heard by tax collectors and sinners, those people marginalized by some Jewish groups who thought they were evil and therefore unclean.

The phrase "the kingdom of heaven is like" is unique in Second **Temple** Judaism and may have captured the attention of those who heard him because Jesus is remembered to have used it often.

The Treasure in a Field
MATTHEW 13:44

The first of three **parables** found only in Matthew, the parable of the treasure hidden in the field describes the complete surprise and joy of discovering the most valuable thing in the world. To obtain the treasure, the person who discovers it "selleth all that he hath, and buyeth that field" (Matthew 13:44). Pushed too far, the actions of the person may appear to be unethical. Note, however, the person is not a thief. He found the treasure, reburied it, and then purchased the field. We must remember that this is a metaphor ("like") and not an exact literal description of things. Its intent is to emphasize the importance of accepting the salvation **Jesus** offers through embracing the coming kingdom of God—*no* **sacrifice** is too great to obtain it.

The Pearl of Great Price
MATTHEW 13:45–46

In the twin to the parable of the treasure hidden in the field (Matthew 13:44), **Jesus** emphasizes again the great value of accepting his work through the coming kingdom. Pearls in antiquity, as today, were highly prized. It is reported that Julius **Caesar** gave a pearl worth six million sesterces ($400,000) to Servilia, Marcus Brutus's mother (Suetonius, *The Deified Julius*, 1.50, in *The Lives of the Caesars*) and that Cleopatra owned a set of pearls worth sixty million sesterces ($4 million) and actually dissolved and drank one of them (Pliny, *Natural History*, 9.68).

A difference between this parable and the earlier one is that the merchant sought out the treasured item rather than merely stumbling across it or finding it accidentally.

The Net Cast into the Sea

MATTHEW 13:47–50

The final of three unique **parables** found in Matthew, the parable of the net cast into the sea, compares ("like") the kingdom of God to a dragnet, which, when pulled back to shore, is found to be full of fish (Matthew 13:47). This is an image taken from daily life around the Sea of **Galilee**. After hauling in his catch, the fisherman separates the good and bad (Greek, *sapra*, can be translated as "rotten" or "worthless," but in this case means unclean) fish on shore. The unclean fish are those Jews could not eat—those without fins (Leviticus 11:10; Deuteronomy 14:10)—which are necessarily discarded.

The emphasis is on a day of judgment, when the righteous and unrighteous will be separated. In its imagery of the good being separated from the bad, this parable reminds us of the parable of the wheat and tares (13:24–30). **Jesus** saw history moving in a straight line with a specific conclusion. In this case, for the Jews living in Galilee and **Judea**, the end was very near (the Jewish War, A.D. 66–70) and hence, the urgency to "**repent** . . . and believe the gospel" (Mark 1:15). The parable obviously also looks forward to the Final Judgment when Jesus will separate the faithful from unrepentant sinners.

The Householder

MATTHEW 13:51–52

Jesus asks the **disciples** if they have understood the **parables** he has just told. Unlike the people (Matthew 13:13), they respond, yes! (13:51). He then provides one final parable, the final of seven recorded in this section, what might be called the parable of the householder. We cannot be certain who "every **scribe**" is, but Jesus is the model for the **disciples** and therefore is the "householder, which bringeth forth out of his treasure things new and old" (13:52); that is, from the old **covenant** and also from the new covenant. It is obvious from his ability to freely quote from it that Jesus was well grounded in Hebrew scripture (Matthew 4:3–11); yet people were astonished at what he said—there was always something new and fresh about his vision of the kingdom. The disciples are enjoined to do the same in their teachings.

The Prophet Joseph Smith explained the householder in terms of "the Book of Mormon coming forth out of the treasure of the heart. Also the covenants given to the Latter-day Saints, also the translation of the Bible— thus bringing forth out of the heart things new and old" (*History of the Church*, 2:272).

Matthew 13:1–52 concludes, "And it came to pass, that when Jesus had finished these parables, he departed thence" (13:53), signaling the end of the second of five teaching blocks Matthew has created (again, reminding his audience of the Pentateuch, or the five books of Moses).

The Second Rejection in Nazareth
MATTHEW 13:53–58; MARK 6:1–6

The third of five teaching blocks (Matthew 13:1–58) Matthew has created begins with **Jesus** entering the **synagogue** in Nazareth, though neither Mark nor Matthew mentions it by name, only by *patris*, meaning native town, region, or country.

Matthew takes his material from Mark (6:1–6), making some stylistic changes but also making some significant content changes, at least eight of them. These include deleting the reference to the **Sabbath** day; identifying Jesus as the "son of the carpenter," instead of as "the carpenter"; and by stating that Mary is his mother, instead of identifying him as the "son of Mary." Finally, and more importantly, Matthew says that Jesus "did not do many mighty works there because of their unbelief" (Matthew 13:58), replacing Mark's comment that "he could there do no mighty work, save that he laid his hands upon a few sick folk, and healed them" (Mark 6:5).

In this section we see Matthew's editorial work most clearly as he improves Mark's style and, more important, eliminates any false implication that might have been drawn from Mark's language (for example, to be identified as the "son of Mary" would likely imply illegitimacy because it avoids the more powerful and literal title, **"son of God"**).

The material is important because it provides information about Jesus' family. First, it appears that Joseph is dead as he is conspicuously absent from the narrative. Jesus had four brothers with well-attested Jewish nationalistic names (suggesting the kind of religious context of Jesus' childhood) and at least two sisters. Only here are his brothers named in the **Synoptic** gospels.

Jesus (Mark) and Joseph (Matthew) are identified as *tekton*, which means "builder," and given the geographical setting of Nazareth most likely includes working with stone and/or wood. It may be that Luke intentionally left out the mention of Jesus working at a trade because it would have been considered degrading (compare Mark 6:3 and Luke 4:22). Traditionally, the eldest son would have taken over his father's business, but in this case, since Jesus had left Nazareth, the next oldest son, James, would have been in charge of the business and the family. In an honor/shame society built on the Mosaic directive, "Honour thy father and thy mother" (Exodus 20:12), Jesus' departure from Nazareth and the seeming abandonment of his family may have been interpreted as scandalous by some in his day—contributing to the reason the family, including extended family members and friends, were offended.

In this story Jesus gives the now-famous maxim, "A prophet is not without honour, but in his own country, and among his own kin, and in his own house [family]" (Mark 6:4). Interestingly, the people of Nazareth do not deny that Jesus was a doer of miraculous things or that he taught astonishing things, but they are nevertheless "offended at him" (Mark 6:3). The Greek verb *skandalizō* implies an on-going action—they were finding him to be a stumbling block. Additionally, the people of Nazareth confirm that Jesus was not taught, leaving the reader to assume that what he knew came from God. Some of Jesus' family members most likely were present, including James and Jude, who later become **disciples** of Jesus themselves. However, at this point they remain bewildered, perhaps even somewhat irritated by Jesus. They not only did not understand him but rejected him. The rejection is complete as the sky darkens over Jesus' ministry and immediately precedes the unleashing of a violent storm in the next section when John is killed.

Report on the Death of John the Baptist
MATTHEW 14:3–12; MARK 6:17–29

This section contains an account of the capricious Herod Antipas arresting John the Baptist. Josephus emphasized the political aspect of the story, indicating that Antipas detained John based simply on the suspicion that he might be a threat to the stability of Antipas's reign. The Gospels, on the other hand, focus on the religious or moral aspects of the sad account, indicating that Antipas incarcerated John because the Baptist criticized Antipas's marriage to his brother's wife (Mark 6:17–19).

Various first-century sources emphasize John's popularity and that he baptized and called for a national reform (**repentance**). Antipas was conflicted—on the one hand he could not refrain from listening to John (Mark 6:20), but on the other hand he felt threatened by the Baptist.

The story also shows the brutal exercise of power when Antipas executes John without a trial (Mark 6:27). Josephus adds some interesting details, including the name of Herodias's daughter—Salome—and the place of execution—Machaerus, a Herodian fortress overlooking the Dead Sea, located today in the Hashemite Kingdom of Jordan about an hour's drive southwest from Amman (Josephus, *Antiquities* 18:119). The Gospels reveal that an executioner's ax ended the Baptist's life and that his **disciples** took the decapitated body (apparently without its head) and buried it (Mark 6:29).

The presentation of John's head on a platter reminded those in the court of Antipas's power over life and death. News quickly spread throughout **Galilee** and must have had a sobering effect on **Jesus**' followers—a warning of what could happen to one who was seen as John's successor.

Herod and Jesus
Matthew 14:1–2; Mark 6:14–16; Luke 9:7–9

Mark informs us that **Jesus'** growing fame finally reached the court of Herod Antipas in Tiberias (6:14). Discussions of Jesus' activities would have been part of the court gossip. Additionally, Antipas's spies would have reported anyone who was preaching, "The time is fulfilled, and the kingdom of God is at hand" (Mark 1:15), though Antipas does not seem to have been overly concerned about whether **Jesus** had a political agenda. Additional information might have come to him through Joanna, the wife of one of his officials, who had become one of Jesus' female followers (Luke 8:1–3).

There was some confusion among the members of Antipas's court as to the identity of Jesus. Some thought Jesus was Elijah (2 Kings 2:11; compare Malachi 3:1; 4:5), others thought he was one of the prophets (Deuteronomy 18:15). Antipas had his own irrational idea: "It is John, whom I beheaded; he is risen from the dead" (Mark 6:16). Nevertheless, Antipas wanted to meet Jesus (Luke 23:8).

Commentators often note that Mark's account of the death of John (Mark 6:17–29) is purposefully sandwiched between the report of Jesus sending the Twelve on their missions (6:7–13) and their return from those missions (6:30). If so, these same scholars posit, Mark's point was to emphasize the real cost of discipleship—foreshadowing Jesus' death and the persecution that would impact his followers afterward.

The Feeding of the Five Thousand
Matthew 14:13–21; Mark 6:30–44; Luke 9:10–17; John 6:1–14

After hearing that John the Baptist had been beheaded, **Jesus** "departed thence by ship into a desert place apart," possibly to mourn the loss of his friend and associate, and also perhaps because of the implications John's death had for his own ministry (Matthew 14:13). Luke records that the place where he sought solitude was near the city of Bethsaida (Luke

thousand, one of the few accounts from **Jesus'** ministry that is found in all four Gospels. But unlike the **Synoptic** authors, John included material that detailed a controversy surrounding what the feeding **miracle** implied about Jesus.

The story contains surprisingly few textual variations (except for verses 22–24), attesting both to its coherency in its original form (**scribes** did not feel the need to offer corrections as they frequently did in other stories) and impact from early on (the story as it appears in the Gospel of John was firmly fixed at a very early date). The story is also rife with symbolism and harks back to the beginning of the Gospel where the terms *light*, *life*, and *truth* also appear in proximity. The Gospel of John begins with the incarnation of Jesus, and the Bread of Life discourse teaches the importance and necessity of that incarnation.

After Jesus had fed the five thousand on "the day following" (John 6:22), he departed across the Sea of **Galilee**, where he was met by a multitude who had followed him because of the earlier feeding miracle. For reasons that are not entirely clear, Jesus took the opportunity to explain the important symbolism of the miracle as well as offer commentary that would cause many of his **disciples** to go "back" or go back home and cease following Jesus (6:66). Some of the teachings of this discourse are considered part of the hard or difficult sayings of the Lord.

That Jesus intentionally drew a parallel to Moses (6:40–48) is interesting because the confusion that initiated some of the discussion hinged on whether Jesus was a deliverer of the Moses type (6:15). Jesus rejected that interpretation of his ministry and departed from the crowd who thought in that way. Later, when he commented on his role in giving manna to the children of Israel, it was to show them that there was both a literal and symbolic meaning to that act.

John 6:54 uses the verb *trogō*, "eat" or "chew," which is often used to describe the way animals eat but not the way humans eat. It carries with it the symbolism of consuming completely rather than eating in haste or lightly. Jesus' flesh was to be "chewed," or deliberately consumed and digested, thus showing how important death and resurrection were to Jesus' mission and the salvation of mankind. This was at least part of the focus of the Bread of

Life discourse that was not understood by those who wanted to come and make Jesus king.

Some ancient manuscripts record that Jesus taught these things while he was in the **synagogue** in Capernaum on the **Sabbath**.

The sermon ends with certain disciples questioning Jesus for teaching, "an hard saying" (6:60). Those same disciples also quit following Jesus, even though the dispute mentioned at the beginning of the chapter implies that the questions arose among members of the multitude who had experienced the feeding of the five thousand. The implication here is that just as the multitude had misunderstood Jesus on a fundamental level, so that same misunderstanding had begun to affect some of Jesus' "disciples." John then introduces the contrast to these erstwhile disciples, "Then said Jesus unto the twelve," thus showing that Twelve had not been affected by a **messianic** misunderstanding. To further clarify the matter, John also records Peter's testimony: "Lord, to whom shall we go? thou hast the words of eternal life. And we believe and are sure that thou art that **Christ**, the Son of the living God" (6:67–69).

John concludes the account by including a reference to the revelation that one of the Twelve would betray Jesus. In this instance, John referred to him as "Judas Iscariot the son of Simon" (6:71).

Jesus Teaches Again in Galilee
JOHN 7:1

Many scholars have seen in this reference the evidence of textual loss in the Gospel of John. In John 5:1, **Jesus** travels to Jerusalem; in John 6:1, Jesus is suddenly in **Galilee** crossing the sea; and then in John 7:1, it appears that Jesus has returned to Galilee recently because of the opposition he faced in Jerusalem. Of course, these shifts in location can be explained by unmentioned trips that took place between the chapters, but the wording of John 7:1 seems to follow most closely Jesus' movements in John 5:1. Perhaps the current chapters have been placed out of order because of some ancient mix-up, or perhaps a chapter or more has been lost. John noted that Jesus had returned to Galilee because of the opposition he faced in Jerusalem, which also served to point out the opposition of Jesus' brothers who challenged him to go to Jerusalem and declare his intentions (John 7:3–5).

Jesus' Return to Gennesaret
MATTHEW 14:34–36; MARK 6:53–56

Both Matthew and Mark record in broad terms a return to the land of Gennesaret, which may refer to any region around the Sea of **Galilee**, which is also known as the Sea of Gennesaret (Luke 5:1). No ancient city with this name has been identified. **Jesus** is greeted with open acceptance, and the people throng him to touch the hem of his garments. The word translated as "hem" refers to the tassels at the borders of Jesus' robe that are mandated in Numbers 15:37–41 (Hebrew, *tzitziyot*).

What Comes Out of a Man Defiles
MATTHEW 15:1–20; MARK 7:1–23

At conflict in this passage is the oral tradition of the Jerusalem **Pharisees** in contrast to the teachings of **Jesus,** or more specifically the practice of the **disciples**. Mark introduces the incident by noting that the **Pharisees** had seen Jesus' disciples eat with unwashed hands (7:2). Matthew does not include this specific reference, thus giving Jesus' response to the Pharisees broader context. Matthew 15:2 mentions specifically the oral tradition (*paradosin*, "handed on") and, like Mark, provides a scriptural rebuttal of that oral law, teaching us that Jesus held that the oral tradition should be subject to the written law and not vice versa.

In the interchange, a specific instance of the oral tradition was questioned, that of making Corban vows. The **Aramaic** word *Corban* indicates a "gift" and was in use in the second century A.D. as a way of removing something from secular usage and symbolically dedicating it to the **temple**. The item dedicated could have been kept at home, but through dedicating it to the temple, the ritual purity of the temple was transferred to a family's home. The intent of such vows is not a controversial matter, but Jesus challenged a particular type of Corban vow where property or income was dedicated to the temple, and thus one could avoid sharing an inheritance or properly taking care of one's parents (Matthew 15:5; Mark 7:11). These texts are our only witnesses to this practice in the early first century, and come from a time when many Jews were still very skeptical about the Pharisaic oral tradition.

The point of focus in the parable is captured in the teaching, "There is nothing from without a man, that entering into him can defile him: but the things which come out of him, those are they that defile the man" (Mark 7:15). Purity, as defined by the Pharisees, was an external condition determined by surroundings, food, and people. Jesus taught instead that purity is an inner quality that emanates to a person's surroundings. These teachings should not be taken out of context to imply that external things, such as substances, cannot be unclean, but only that being pure because one's surroundings are pure is a faulty presupposition.

This story also reveals how Matthew borrowed from Mark when writing his own Gospel. In this incident, where there is a significant degree of verbal similarity, it is seems likely that Matthew used the Gospel of Mark as his source. The reason for thinking this way is that Matthew abbreviated the discussion of the tradition of washing hands (Mark 7:3–4) and removed wording that might imply all Pharisees or Jews are represented in this story (Mark 7:1, 3). Matthew may have felt that his audience (Jews) was already aware of hand-washing traditions. The disciples' concern that the Pharisees might have been offended at what Jesus had said is unique to Matthew and may be an example of the author reaching out to any Pharisees who were interested in the gospel message. Mark's audience may not have included Jews from Jerusalem who would have been offended at such a castigation of Pharisaic ideals.

The Gentile Woman's Daughter
MATTHEW 15:21–28; MARK 7:24–30

Neither Matthew nor Mark provides an explanation of why **Jesus** departed from **Galilee** into the regions of Tyre and Sidon. Previous to this journey, Jesus had remained mostly in predominantly Jewish cities, and it may be that he left Galilee because of increasing hostility. While in the region, he was met by a "Syrophenician" woman (Mark 7:26) who was of Greek descent. She pleaded (KJV, "besought") with Jesus to heal her daughter, a request that Jesus at first rebuffed. Jesus taught that it was not appropriate (KJV, "meet") to take bread from the children of the kingdom and give it to "dogs" (Mark 7:27) and by implication to her. This stunning rebuke to her request seems at least initially intended to drive the woman away (the **disciples** had asked for this favor in Matthew 15:23). Showing remarkable faith, the woman accepted the rebuke and offered a counter: "Yet the dogs under the table eat of the children's crumbs" (Mark 7:28). In response to her faith, Jesus healed her daughter. The story may have served to teach the disciples about the faith of those living outside Galilee and **Judea**, thus hinting at a future successful **Gentile** mission.

Healings
MATTHEW 15:29–31; MARK 7:31–37

What is treated with brevity in Matthew receives greater attention in Mark. Instead of placing these **miracles** near the Sea of **Galilee**, Mark details that **Jesus** actually traveled to Tyre and Sidon by way of the Decapolis, a grouping of ten cities where Greco-Roman civilization thrived surrounded by eastern religions and traditions (Mark 7:31).

In recording the miracles that Jesus performed in Tyre and Sidon, Mark specifically focuses on a single healing where Jesus took a man aside from the multitude "and put his fingers into his ears, and he spit, and touched his tongue" (7:33). This ministration was accompanied by Jesus saying, "Ephphatha, that is, Be opened" (7:34). Rarely do the Gospel authors preserve the actual **Aramaic** words that Jesus spoke but instead present the reader with a Greek translation of his words. In a few instances the actual words are preserved, most likely to emphasize the memory of the early **disciples** who heard him speak in that way and the importance those words had in the early **Church** (Mark 5:41; 15:34). It is not clear why Jesus healed the man in such a dramatic fashion, and ancient parallels do not confirm that this was a common practice of the day. Perhaps the healing held symbolic gestures, but in a simple way, Jesus touched each part of the man that needed healing. Both Matthew and Mark emphasize that this event was part of Jesus' fulfillment of the prophecy of Isaiah 61:1, which became an important text for early Christians (Luke 7:21–22).

Jesus Feeds the Four Thousand
MATTHEW 15:32–39; MARK 8:1–9

The account of the feeding of the four thousand is in almost all particulars the same as the story of the feeding of the five thousand. What is surprising is that after witnessing the feeding of the five thousand, the **disciples** would yet ask, "From whence can a man satisfy these men with bread here in the wilderness?" (Mark 8:4). The previous lesson had not yet been cemented in their hearts, and **Jesus** again showed that he had the power to feed the multitude. With its obvious sacramental imagery, the second feeding **miracle** may serve to foreshadow the weekly renewal of the ordinance after Jesus had died.

Pharisees and Sadducees Ask for a Sign
MATTHEW 16:1–4; MARK 8:10–13; LUKE 12:54–57

Commentators have noted the great irony in this account. On the heels of an amazing **miracle**, the feeding of the four thousand (Matthew 15:32–38), the **Pharisees** and **Sadducees** ask **Jesus** to provide them a "sign from heaven" (Matthew 16:1). We may be surprised to find the Pharisees and Sadducees working together because they were unlikely allies, but it may be that the Jerusalem authorities had finally listened to the Pharisees' warnings about Jesus and had sent a delegation to **Galilee** to see for themselves what Jesus was doing and claiming. The Pharisees allied themselves earlier with the **Herodians** (Mark 3:6), so it should be no surprise that they might do the same with the Sadducees, the two groups having found a common enemy in Jesus. These doubters being unwilling to demonstrate faith as Jesus required, he identifies them as "a wicked and adulterous generation" (Matthew 16:4).

Interestingly, both groups may have acknowledged that Jesus did in fact perform miracles. However, they sought a sign from heaven to validate the miracles that they came through God's power. Jesus refuses to provide such. In Matthew, Jesus offers what appears to be a well-known adage: "When it is evening, ye say, It will be fair weather: for the sky is red. And in the morning, It will be foul weather to day: for the sky is red and lowring" (Matthew 16:2–3), indicating that though they can read the weather, they are unable to read the signs of the times. Jesus also reminds them of the sign of Jonah previously given (Matthew 12:39–40) and then simply walks away, leaving them to stand there alone, without his providing any further acknowledgment of their request.

Jesus Teaches the Disciples about the Pharisees
MATTHEW 16:5–12; MARK 8:14–21; LUKE 12:1

Following his encounter with a group of **Pharisees** and **Sadducees** who attempted to challenge and test him (as **Satan** had done in the wilderness), **Jesus** meets with his **disciples** alone and warns them sternly, "Take heed, beware of the leaven of the Pharisees, and the leaven of Herod" (Mark 8:15). The disciples are unaware of the meaning of the warning and wonder if Jesus is referring to the fact that they have forgotten to bring more than one loaf of bread. Mark notes, "And when Jesus knew it, he saith unto them. Why reason ye, because ye have no bread? perceive ye not yet, neither understand? have ye your heart yet hardened?" (Mark 8:17). Matthew edits Mark to read, "O ye of little faith, why reason ye among yourselves, because ye had brought no bread?" (Matthew 16:8), softening Mark's stark portrait of the disciples with a much milder observation. The Greek *oligopistoi* ("little faith") suggests that though they are indeed fallible, they nevertheless can complete the mission God assigned them since he requires only a "little faith" (Matthew 17:20). This is not the first time Matthew has provided a more sympathetic portrayal of the disciples than Mark has (see, for example, Matthew 8:26 and Mark 4:40).

Jesus' warning against the Pharisees and against Herod ("Sadducees" in Matthew) most likely refers to the counter vision of the kingdom they offered Israel. The nationalistic Pharisees' vision of the kingdom was one of armed resistance against Roman occupation, seeking to create an Israel independent from other nations. The Herodians' vision of the kingdom focused on the renewal of King Herod's united kingdom under one king of the Jews—a descendant of Herod the Great.

Both visions were fundamentally flawed in their notions of a "kingdom." While the Pharisees' and Herodians' visions dictated armed resistance and a ruler by right of ancestry, Jesus' vision of the kingdom of God (heaven) would be centered in human compassion, suffering, and the selfless sacrifice of God's unique Son—a kingdom that would invite all to join the bounteous banquet offered by God.

The Healing at Bethsaida
MARK 8:22–26

Only Mark reports this occurrence, perhaps because **Jesus'** first attempt to heal the man might be interpreted as unsuccessful, prompting Matthew and Luke to exclude it. The healing is in fact a two-step process where Jesus first "spit on his eyes, and put his hands upon him" (8:23). After the first effort, the man's sight was only partially restored and he was able to see "men as trees, walking" (8:24), whereupon Jesus laid hands on him again and restored his full sight. The story may have a figurative interpretation that goes beyond the physical aspect of the healing. After the second effort, the man saw more than his surroundings, observing "every man clearly"

(8:25). Interestingly, Mark notes that Jesus led the man out of the town and therefore away from the people, but when Jesus healed him fully, he was able to see every man clearly. Perhaps the story was intended to teach the difference between physical and spiritual sight.

"Whom Say Men That I Am?"
MATTHEW 16:13–20; MARK 8:27–30; LUKE 9:18–22

The location of this event is not provided in Luke, likely because the specific designation of Caesarea Philippi would not be so important to Christians living distantly from the land of Israel. Instead, Luke moves immediately to the testimony of Peter, who says in reply to Jesus' inquiry, "But whom say ye that I am?" by declaring, thou art "the **Christ** of God," (Luke 9:20; **Aramaic** "the **Messiah** of God"). Matthew provides significant additional details to the account that are not found in Mark and Luke, partly because of the pivotal nature of this story and because he appears to have known more about the interaction, implied by the vividness of the testimony.

Up to this point in the Gospels, the **Son of man** sayings had allowed Jesus a way to openly declare his Messianic identity while at the same time veiling the full scope of his ministry from those who might oppose him. The Son of man sayings are certainly transparent enough that Jesus' followers would have understood the intent, but Matthew makes the point of demonstrating that at Caesarea Philippi Jesus specifically confirmed his identity by demanding of his disciples, "Whom do men say that I the Son of man am?" (Matthew 16:13).

The enigmatic answers convey a wide range of possibilities, none of which capture the full **messianic** implications of Jesus' ministry: "Some say that thou art John the Baptist: some, Elias; and others, Jeremias, or one of the prophets" (16:14). Elias should be understood to be Elijah, which the Greek renders as *Elias*, and the mention of Jeremiah can only be understood comparatively, that is as a great prophet and probably not as Jeremiah himself returned to life.

Jesus then asked, "But whom say ye that I am?" (16:15), and Peter testified of his own witness: "Thou art the Christ, the Son of the living God" (16:16). In response, Jesus acknowledged Peter's testimony and taught him further: "Blessed art thou, Simon Bar-Jona: for flesh and blood hath not revealed it unto thee, but my Father which is in heaven" (16:17). The antecedent of "it" in 16:17 is Peter's testimony of the preceding verse. Using that distinction, Jesus then taught Peter, "upon this rock I will build my **church**" (16:18)—that is, upon the rock of testimony or personal revelation regarding Jesus (see footnote 18*a* for an enlightening explanation of the Greek text).

These verses, which are unique to Matthew, emphasize the powerful role of revelation in the building up of the "church." However, the verses are not intended to diminish Peter's role in leading that church, because to him were promised the keys of that church: "And I will give unto thee the keys of the kingdom of heaven: and whatsoever thou shalt bind on earth shall be bound in heaven: and whatsoever thou shalt loose on earth shall be loosed in heaven" (16:19). Peter was thus promised that he would preside over the "church" holding the keys of the **priesthood**, thus making him uniquely authorized, together with the other members of the Quorum of the Twelve **Apostles**.

The mention of the "church" in these verses is also unique to the Gospel of Matthew and seems to envision a gathering of Saints rather than the fully functioning and revealed church of the modern era. The Greek *ekklēsia*, "body" or "assembly," may have been mentioned because it envisions a civic gathering of people and not necessarily a body of like-minded believers who have a canonized body of literature to guide them, thus emphasizing the need for personal testimony and revelation in governing that early assembly of Saints.

Jesus Rebukes Peter

MATTHEW 16:21–23; MARK 8:31–33

Matthew and Mark report this story in almost identical fashion, and the focal point of the interchange between **Jesus** and Peter is a misunderstanding regarding the scope of Jesus' mission. Peter had previously borne testimony of Jesus (Mark 8:29), but that testimony apparently did not entail a complete understanding. When Jesus began openly discussing the conclusion of his ministry, stating that he would be put to death and he would go to Jerusalem for that purpose, Peter attempted to dissuade him from doing so, apparently not understanding that the death of the Savior was a necessary event in the fulfillment of Jesus' true mission. Jesus rebuked him sharply, censuring him for being concerned about the things "that be of men" (Matthew 16:23).

Jesus' allusion to his "suffer[ing] many things of the elders and chief **priests** and **scribes**" (Matthew 16:21) does not specifically pinpoint them as culpable in his death but rather as instruments of his suffering.

On Taking Up a Cross

MATTHEW 16:24–28; MARK 8:34–38; 9:1; LUKE 9:23–27

The **Synoptics** provide five specific commands regarding discipleship in this section: one must deny oneself, take up one's cross, follow **Jesus**, lose one's life, and be not ashamed of Jesus. Matthew and Luke depend on Mark but make slight adjustments in these sayings. For example, Matthew continues his account, modifying Mark's account slightly to emphasize that these instructions were directed to the **disciples** themselves, after Jesus rebuked Peter, "*Then said Jesus unto his disciples*, If any man will come after me, let him deny himself, and take up his cross" (Matthew 16:24; emphasis added).

This call to "come after me" should most likely be tied to Jesus' previous command to Peter: "Get thee behind me" (Mark 8:33). To "get thee behind me" may imply not only a physical place but also the worthy attitude of a disciple—that is, one who follows Jesus must also accept God's divine will. In this case, God willed Jesus' suffering and death.

Jesus intensifies what it means to follow him, reminding us that we do not always understand what is in store for us when we join the **Church**, just as the disciples did not know the cost of discipleship when Jesus first called them to follow him. He does so here with one of the most powerful metaphors possible, given the first-century historical context. He said they must take up a cross. This would almost certainly have reminded the disciples of **Rome's** extreme method of execution—crucifixion—a punishment that they would know about because they had witnessed it. Note that Jesus says they must take up their *own* crosses, not Jesus' cross. Perhaps Matthew has envisioned potential suffering and martyrdom (not merely personal burdens such as physical sicknesses or disabilities, financial setbacks, or even difficult and challenging relatives). Luke, however, nuances the statement to reflect personal sacrifice in daily living out Jesus' teachings (Greek, *kath hemeran*) as disciples (Luke 9:23). The saying may also be related to Jesus' invitation to "take my yoke upon you" (Matthew 11:29).

The similarity in statements found in the Synoptics about losing one's life hinges on "for my sake" (Mark reads, "for my sake and the gospel's" [8:35]) and therefore emphasizes that Jesus is not simply asking us to give up things (see Matthew 16:25, for example). Doing so, as it has been observed, would not make us disciples, but would only make our lives truly empty. Self-humiliation and self-denial is as wrong-headed as seeking self-esteem, self-interest, and self-fulfillment. Jesus stresses that one should focus on his life-giving mission without reference to self, either in the positive or the negative sense.

When Jesus asks, "For what shall a man give in exchange for his soul?" (Mark 8:37) he reminds us that a life is invaluable (see Psalm 49, especially 6–8). Some commentators have seen an indirect indictment against human trafficking—a ubiquitous institution in antiquity and one that continues to grow in modern times—in this saying, but that might be going too far.

Jesus' five commands do not adequately or completely describe discipleship and would not have been seen by Jesus or the first-century Saints as some type of list that needed to be checked off, though Jesus expected that those who followed him would do as he instructed. They are in one sense distinctive aspects of what being a disciple of Jesus means—a radical call to follow him in an ongoing journey.

In the end, though there are many things worth living for, Jesus says there are also things worth dying for. Nevertheless, Jesus says that for his disciples there is everything to gain and nothing to lose when we accept and follow him, reminding us of the rather well-known aphorism, "He is no fool who gives what he cannot keep to gain what he cannot lose" (Elliot, *Through Gates of Splendor*, 172).

John 12:25 (compare with Mark 8:35) and Matthew 10:32–33/Luke 12:8–9 (compare with Mark 8:38) suggest that Jesus taught these points on more than one occasion and in various contexts. Given his changing audiences, it would be unlikely that Jesus said some things only once during his ministry.

This section ends with a cryptic prophecy: "Verily, I say unto you, That there be some of them that stand here, which shall not taste of death, till they have seen the kingdom of God come with power" (Mark 9:1). Some suggested interpretations of this saying include reference to Jesus' powerful healings, including casting out evil spirits; the Transfiguration; the rending of the **temple** veil; the acknowledgment of the Roman centurion; the Resurrection (as vindication); the Pentecostal empowering of the disciples; or the Second Coming. Some might think of Jesus' later statement found in Mark: "Verily I say unto you, that this generation shall not pass, till all these things be done" (13:30). Whatever Jesus specifically meant, he certainly knew that some of those present would witness or experience the coming kingdom before death overtook them. Again, Jesus' statement here, "Verily, I say unto you" (or "Amen, I say to you"), reminds us of his sweeping claim of authority—he does not appeal to the authority of another, not even to the **scriptures**, but to himself.

The Mount of Transfiguration
MATTHEW 17:1–13; MARK 9:2–13; LUKE 9:28–36

Matthew, Mark, and Luke all record a miraculous experience had by Peter, James, and John when Jesus took them to an unidentified mountain some six months before his death. Peter and John most likely refer to this event in their own writings (2 Peter 1:16–19; John 1:14,17:5). On the mount, Jesus was transfigured before them (Mark 9:2). Our current English word *transfiguration* derives from the fourth-century Latin Vulgate (*transfiguratus*), not the Greek *metamorphōsis*.

From a human point of view, Jesus was a somewhat usual first-century Jew who spoke a Galilean dialect of **Aramaic** and dressed in the common fashion of his day. He was probably not much taller or shorter than the average man of the period. The length of his hair and beard (if he had one) would not have set him apart. In other words, Jesus probably looked like many others. His common appearance was foreseen by Isaiah: "He hath no form nor comeliness; and when we shall see him, there is no beauty that we should desire him" (Isaiah 53:2). However, the Transfiguration revealed that he was in fact not only a descendant of Abraham and David, but God's own Beloved Son—different from all other human beings.

Mark informs us that "Elias" (the Greek form of the Hebrew name Elijah) and Moses appeared to Jesus, Peter, James, and John; but they spoke only with Jesus (Mark 9:4). The Joseph Smith Translation adds that John the Baptist was present without removing Elijah from the story. The presence of Elijah on the mount in addition to John the Baptist is confirmed by the fact that the Joseph Smith Translation does not change the accounts of Matthew and Luke to indicate that Elias referred to John the Baptist. Shortly thereafter, "there was a cloud that overshadowed them: and a voice came out of the cloud, saying, This is my beloved Son: hear him" (9:7). Interestingly, this is one of the very few places where God the Father's voice is heard in the New Testament. The focus of the Gospels centers on Jesus; even in this instance God is speaking about Jesus. One study demonstrates that the Father is the subject of less than .02 percent of Mark's

Gospel. This profound declaration is the focus of the written accounts. The Transfiguration answers once and for all, at least from God's perspective, who had the right and authority to interpret Jewish scripture, a question that became a central issue of debate in Second **Temple** Judaism. Following the end of the Old Testament period, when no new prophets arose in Israel, various individuals attempted to fill the void by claiming exclusive privilege to interpret the **Torah**. One group in particular—the **Pharisees**—fought vigorously to gain public approval for their interpretation of the Law and prophets (Josephus, *Antiquities* 17.41). Mark's Gospel provides incident after incident where Jesus challenges these individuals and groups, claiming for himself that right (Mark 1:27; 3:1–3; 7:1–13; 10:2–12; 12:18–27, 28–34, 35–38). God settled the question when he said, "This is my beloved Son: *hear him*" (Mark 9:7; emphasis added). They were to listen to and obey Jesus, not the **Sadducees**, Pharisees, **scribes**, or any other group or person. When Mark concludes, "And suddenly, when [Peter, James, and John] had looked round about, they saw no man any more, save Jesus only" (Mark 9:8), he seems to be signaling the end of the days of Old Testament prophets and the beginning of the days of the **Son of God**.

Matthew follows Mark's account very closely, more so than Luke. Nevertheless, Matthew edits and arranges his material to suit his purposes. Many commentators assume that on this occasion, Moses and Elijah passed along the "keys of the kingdom," as promised to Peter a few days earlier (Matthew 16:19).

Luke, on the other hand, provides additional information about Moses and Elijah. He informs his audience that Moses and Elijah also "appeared in glory" with Jesus (Luke 9:31). Additionally, Luke reports a conversation among Moses, Elijah, and Jesus. The Greek text indicates they communicated with Jesus about his exodus (Greek, *exodos*), not simply about his death, as the King James Version suggests by its choice of the word *decease*. The Greek word literally means "the way out" or "departure." Most likely, Luke intended his audience to understand that Moses and Elijah spoke to Jesus about his death, his mission in Jerusalem, and ultimately his Resurrection and **Ascension** as steps in his "departure" to the Father.

Jesus Heals a Boy Possessed
MATTHEW 17:14–21; MARK 9:14–29; LUKE 9:37–42; 17:4–6

Unlike Matthew and Luke, Mark preserves an extended account of the healing of a young boy following the seminal experiences on the Mount of Transfiguration. All three **Synoptic** evangelists place this story immediately after **Jesus** came down from the mount, which when considered in light of the verbal similarities in the stories, makes it certain that Mark's extended account detailed the same story as the one recorded in Matthew and Luke.

When a man asked Jesus if he were able to heal the man's son, Jesus offered an abrupt rebuke: "O faithless generation, how long shall I be with you? how long shall I suffer you? bring him unto me." (Mark 9:19). The man also informed Jesus that his **disciples** had not been able to heal the boy, which is the only recorded instance of their inability to effect a healing in the New Testament. Coming as this failure does so late in the Gospels and immediately after the sealing powers had been given to some of the disciples, it contextualizes the story and makes more poignant their inability to heal the afflicted boy.

The story is also unique in the vivid description of the boy's condition, which contains details that could possibly be consistent with epilepsy, although both Jesus and the crowd summarized the malady as a spirit possession. That the Lord would rebuke that generation because the disciples could not heal the boy breaks the sense of the story because it was the disciples who were not able, rather than the multitude. However, the account moves on to relate that it was the faith of the father in addition to Jesus' own ability to perform a **miracle** that brought about the healing. For that reason, the rebuke is appropriate because it reminds the reader that a healing is a two-part endeavor and depends on both the person giving the blessing and the person receiving it (here, depicted as the father, "have pity on us and help us" [9:22]).

Two events make this miracle particularly memorable. First, the father, after responding to Jesus' inquiry of faith, said, "I believe; help thou mine unbelief" (9:24). The Greek text can be interpreted as "aid my unbelief" or "assist me in my unbelief," which indicates the man intended something such as, "I believe in some things, but this thing is too overwhelming. Help me to believe it is possible." Second, Jesus, at the conclusion of the miracle informed the disciples, "This kind can come forth by nothing, but by prayer and fasting" (9:29). The verb *fasting* is not preserved in many ancient texts, which may reflect a later scribal deletion. In its original form, Jesus appears to have told the disciples that their preparation could have been strengthened through intense prayer. The request to fast, if original, offers the perplexing challenge of waiting to fast before a blessing is given, which because of the immediacy of this blessing and many others would create an unduly long waiting period.

Jesus Prophesies of His Death and Resurrection
MATTHEW 17:22–23; MARK 9:30–32; LUKE 9:43–45

Matthew and Luke follow Mark (with some variations) as **Jesus** provides the second of three Passion and Resurrection prophecies. Each prophecy builds upon the others, moving from indirect speech and general description to very specific details climaxing in the final prophecy.

The first prophecy follows immediately after Peter testifies that Jesus is the **Christ** (Mark 8:29–33). This second prophecy comes on the heels of the Mount of Transfiguration experience and just shortly after the gathering at Caesarea Philippi: "For he taught his **disciples**, and said unto them, The **Son of man** is delivered into the hands of men, and they shall kill him; and after that he is killed, he shall rise the third day. But they understood not that saying, and were afraid to ask him" (Mark 9:31–32). The final prophecy was given as Jesus made his way to Jerusalem for the last time (Mark 10:32–34).

Just as in the first and final prophecies, the second Passion prophecy refers not only to the possibility and probability of Jesus' being killed but to the divine necessity of Christ's suffering and death—it is God who delivers (Greek, *paradidōmi*) Jesus into the hands of men (Romans 8:32). Additionally, here Jesus uses the active voice, "shall kill him," instead of the passive, "be killed," as he did in the first prophecy. Most interestingly, Jesus does not simply rely on quoting Old Testament prophecies but provides new prophecies about his death in these statements.

The death of John the Baptist, like the fate of earlier prophets and increasing hostilities and confrontations between Jesus and Jewish leaders, had created a situation that made Jesus' death a probability. But such a scenario contradicted the Jewish expectations of the **Messiah's** victory in Jerusalem. In this context, following the first prophecy, Peter rebuked **Jesus** for suggesting that his mission would end in rejection in Jerusalem. However, in this case, the disciples did not know what to say, were most likely recalling Jesus' chastisement of Peter, and were "afraid to ask him." Fear begins to take hold of the disciples on many levels—a major theme that develops as the events unfold.

A Question about Taxation
MATTHEW 17:24–27

Matthew here related one of two questions put to **Jesus** regarding the legitimacy of paying taxes. The tax specifically mentioned in this story was the half-shekel tax levied on all Jewish men to support the Jewish **temple**. The **Mishnah**, which was composed several generations after the event depicted here, stipulated that the temple tax was to be collected annually in Adar (around February/March) and was to be paid by all adult males over twenty years of age. That Matthew was referring to the temple tax and not a Roman tax is made certain by the Greek text which reads *didrachma*, referring to the half-shekel tax.

Because the question came in **Galilee**, and the question implies that Jesus might not pay the tax, there is a possibility that some people in Galilee may have questioned the legitimacy of the temple tax. Jesus' response, which compares the kings of the earth and the children of the kingdom, may suggest a critique of what temple worship had become in his day. Others suggest that Peter, rather than Jesus, is approached because teachers of the law may have been exempted from paying the tax, although evidence for this suggestion is late and difficult to corroborate in the first century.

Who Is Greater?
MATTHEW 18:1–6; MARK 9:33–37; LUKE 9:46–48

The origin and context of this saying differs in all three **Synoptic** accounts. In Luke, the **disciples** argued (Greek, *dialogismos*) amongst themselves, while in Matthew the disciples asked **Jesus** openly who was the greatest in the kingdom. Mark's account states that the disciples had a discussion about greatness in the kingdom but that they were possibly embarrassed to tell Jesus what they had been discussing. The text suggests, however, that the discussion had simply become who among the disciples would be judged by the Lord the greatest in the kingdom—a point that Luke makes specifically (9:46). But the question need not imply that the disciples were arguing who in the Twelve was greatest, a point that Matthew and Mark contribute to the story. Indeed, the question might have been about whether John the Baptist or Jesus was greater, or whether one of the prophets was greater than the others, or perhaps any number of comparisons. Jesus settled the dispute, whatever it was, by declaring, "If any man desire to be first, the same shall be last of all, and servant of all" (Mark 9:35). The account in Matthew has Jesus responding to the dispute by calling a little child to him and setting him in the midst of the group, perhaps subtly chastising his disciples for their immaturity: "Whosoever therefore shall humble himself as this little child, the same is greatest in the kingdom of heaven" (18:4).

Woe to Those Who Offend
MATTHEW 18:7–11; MARK 9:42–50; LUKE 14:34–35; 17:1–2

The woe pronounced upon those who offend little children is qualified in the Gospels: "But whoso shall offend one of these little ones *which believe in me*" (Matthew 18:6; emphasis added). Both Mark and Matthew then add

131

three analogies that teach the same principle—that offending or abusing little children is akin to committing an unforgivable sin. The analogies employed have echoes in the Sermon on the Mount (Matthew 5:29–30) and represent a favorite metaphor in **Jesus'** teachings.

Mark included as an ending a rather enigmatic reference: "Salt is good: but if the salt have lost his saltness, wherewith will ye season it? Have salt in yourselves, and have peace one with another" (Mark 9:50). The purpose of the saying can be captured either in Paul's statement to the Corinthians where he said, "Let your speech be alway with grace, seasoned with salt, that ye may know how ye ought to answer every man" (Colossians 4:6) or in an early patristic reference where Ignatius encouraged Christians to "be salted in Jesus" (*Magnesians* 10.2). It is likely that **Jesus** intended that our actions and words be savored with salt, that is, brought into subjection so that they become a holy offering to the Lord, or that **Christ** may act as a curative force in our lives. It is interesting to note that in prescribing religious rituals for the children of Israel, the Lord made the use of salt an integral component in the sacrifice of animals (Leviticus 2:13).

The Other Healer
MATTHEW 10:42; MARK 9:38–41; LUKE 9:49–50

In this story, which Matthew passes over almost completely, the **disciples** encounter someone who was healing in the name of **Jesus**. The situation bothered the disciples and they forbade the man from healing in Jesus' name. Jesus taught them a greater principle, "For he that is not against us is on our part" (Mark 9:40). The identity of the man remains uncertain, and Luke repeats Mark's account nearly verbatim. Certainly the events behind the story were more complex than described here, but Mark and Luke pass it on in the context of the disciples learning to accept outsiders into the fold.

The Parable of the Lost Sheep
MATTHEW 18:12–14; LUKE 15:1–7

Matthew and Luke preserve one of **Jesus'** many memorable stories, the parable of the lost sheep. Luke, as was his custom, joins the parable with the lost coin (Luke 15:8–10). This pairing of **parables** was a literary device that Gospel writers often used in reporting Jesus' teachings.

Following his statement, "For the **Son of man** is come to save that which was lost" (Matthew 18:11), Jesus tells an astonishing, even shocking story of a man who leaves ninety-nine sheep to look for just one.

The Old Testament basis of such a story is obvious, beginning with the blessing of Joseph: "But his bow abode in strength, and the arms of his hands were made strong by the hands of the mighty God of Jacob; (*from thence is the shepherd, the stone of Israel:*) even by the God of thy father, who shall help thee; and by the Almighty, who shall bless thee with blessings of heaven above" (Genesis 49:24–25; emphasis added; see also Psalm 23:1; 28:9; 68:7; 74:1; 77:20; 78:53; 79:13; 80:1; 100:3; Isaiah 40:10–11; 49:9–10; Jeremiah 13:17, 20; 23:3; 31:10; 50:17; Ezekiel 34:1–31; Micah 2:12; 4:6–8; 5:4; 7:14; Zechariah 10:2–3; 11:7, 15–17; 13:7).

However, the nomadic days of Israel were long gone by the beginning of the first century A.D. By that time, shepherds were part of the class of people cut off from the community, as were sinners, toll and tax collectors, sailors, camel drivers, gamblers, dyers—often despised and marginalized. This fact adds to the surprising nature of the story since Jesus characterizes himself as a shepherd (John 10:11, 14; 1 Peter 5:2).

Jesus often used the analogy of sheep and shepherds in his teaching and made an extensive declaration on his being "the good shepherd" who, unlike the hireling, would not abandon his flock but rather give his life for his sheep (John 10:1–16). Matthew records that Jesus said, "I am not sent but unto the lost sheep of the house of Israel" (15:24); commanded the **disciples** to go to the "lost sheep" (Matthew 10:6; 15:24); quoted from Zechariah 13:7 (Mark 14:27 and Matthew 26:31); told the disciples, "Fear not, little flock; for it is your Father's good pleasure to give you the kingdom" (Luke 12:32;

see also Doctrine and Covenants 35:27). Finally, Jesus is portrayed as being "moved with compassion . . . [for the crowds in **Galilee**], because they fainted, and were scattered abroad, *as sheep having no shepherd*" (Matthew 9:36; emphasis added).

The Greek text of Matthew says the man left the ninety and nine "on the mountains" ("wilderness," literally "desert" in Luke), not as it is mistranslated in the King James Version: "doth he not leave the ninety and nine, *and goeth into the mountains*, and seeketh that which is gone astray?" (Matthew 18:12; emphasis added). This parable is, therefore, shocking in two ways: first, the shepherd leaves ninety and nine to search for one, and second, he leaves the ninety and nine in the mountains, not safely in the sheepfold!

The parable was given as a continued response to criticism that Jesus consorted with tax collectors and sinners (Matthew 9:11–12), made explicit in Luke where the audience is composed of antagonistic opponents (Luke 15:2–3).

The ending in each account is rejoicing. One is reminded of Jesus' response to John's disciples: "Go and shew John again those things which ye do hear and see: The blind receive their sight, and the lame walk, the **lepers** are cleansed, and the deaf hear, the dead are raised up, and the poor have the gospel preached to them" (Matthew 11:4–5). The "good news" is preached, therefore there is much joy (attested to in both Matthew 18:13 and Luke 15:7).

The ninety and nine likely represent Jewish leaders who oppose Jesus, including **Pharisees**, **Sadducees**, and **scribes** (lost in the mountains or deserts, a group who does not recognize that they need a doctor, thinking they are not sick; compare Matthew 9:12). Jesus says their "righteousness" (Matthew 5:20) did not make the man (Matthew 18:13) or heaven rejoice more (Luke 15:7)—therefore, this is a bold criticism of their self-righteousness.

The Parable of the Lost Coin
LUKE 15:8–10

This parable has doctrinal affinities with the parable of the pearl of great price (Matthew 13:45–46), and even though the terminology is different, the ideas taught in each are quite similar. Perhaps Luke's version represents a later retelling of the earlier parable in Matthew, where **Jesus** sought to convey a similar idea to a different audience. The nuance of Luke's version is that the woman who finds the coin celebrates with her friends upon finding it, whereas the merchant who buys the pearl of great value is willing to give up everything simply to possess it.

The Parable of the Prodigal Sons
LUKE 15:11–32

Unfortunately, the modern popular title of this parable often obscures the fact that both sons in this parable are prodigal. The difference between the two is the moment of their lack of faith, the first son being shortsighted in spending his inheritance and the second son being hard-hearted toward his brother who **repents**. Neither son behaves well, and the reader is left with the realization that neither son should be commended for exemplary behavior (see Holland, "The Other Prodigal," 62–64).

The depiction of the first son's journey is characterized by terms associated with a **Gentile** city but not a Jewish city. The boy travels and joins himself to a "citizen of that country" and is given the job of feeding swine (Luke 15:15). Both the job and the description of the man's citizenship are characteristic of a Roman period city where people could obtain citizenship. Jews living in **Judea** were not typically Roman citizens. At the depth of his realization that he had sinned, the first boy grew humble and sought **repentance** for his sins (15:18).

The second son is a more complex figure who broods over the younger brother's return and the very idea that his father would so easily forgive the foolish boy and even celebrate his return. In fact, the son who was dead but now lives, an allusion to the Resurrection, is not even greeted by the older brother, who "was angry, and would not go in: therefore came his father out, and intreated him" (15:28). The entreaty includes the comforting reminder, "Son, thou art ever with me, and all that I have is thine" (15:31). The phrase can equally be interpreted, "Son, you are always with me and what I have left is yours." With the second son ending on a note of hard-heartedness, it is difficult to interpret the final phrase positively, although it appears that the father is reminding him that his inheritance has not been squandered and that he can find safety in his financial stability.

At the core of this story of two brothers is the story of a forgiving father who forgives two types of poor behavior: sin and hard-heartedness. The paradox of this story is the father who shortens the distance between his sons when he runs to greet the returning son and goes outside to bring his angry older son back into his house. The two types of behavior may characterize **Gentile** and Jewish attitudes towards obedience to God's commandments. In fact, it is the father who is anxious to forgive: "His father saw him, and had compassion, *and ran, and fell on his neck, and kissed him*" (15:20; emphasis added). In antiquity a rich man did not run to greet anyone, and the servants would have been in charge of that function. It may be that the parable intentionally highlights the father's actions even though interpretations have focused on the sons.

Reproving a Brother
MATTHEW 18:15–22; LUKE 17:3

In this story that is unique to Matthew, the question of how often the faithful are required to forgive is addressed. The question implies the formation of a community of Saints and lays the foundation for the practice of excommunication. In fact, **Jesus** explicitly references "the **church**" (Matthew 18:17). The **disciples** are to attend to admitting and excommunicating using the keys of the **priesthood**: "Whatsoever ye shall bind on earth shall be bound in heaven: and whatsoever ye shall loose on earth shall be loosed in

heaven" (18:18). This verse is also the earliest reference in the Gospels to
the fact that the entire quorum held the power to seal.

Peter sought for a specific clarification, asking Jesus how often he should
forgive a brother. The answer to that question was likely of great interest to
Christians living many years after Jesus' death, and here Peter shows fore-
sight in asking it. Jesus taught that he should forgive "until seventy times
seven" (18:22). The large number (490) implies that Peter should continue
to forgive without limit, even though the Lord had taught him that some
must be "loosed" or excommunicated from the kingdom.

Unprofitable Servants
Luke 17:7–10

This short saying is unique to Luke's Gospel and poses the important
question of whether servants/slaves should be thanked when they simply
perform an action that they are commanded to do. Likewise, should the
faithful be rewarded for doing what the Lord has commanded them to do or
what they have promised to do? The answer is that the Lord blesses us, but
the Lord encourages us here to do more than just our duty.

The Parable of the Unmerciful Servant
Matthew 18:23–35

Following **Jesus'** teachings on reconciling with one's brother, the parable of the unmerciful servant offers context to the abstract teaching:
"Lord, how oft shall my brother sin against me, and I forgive him? till seven
times? Jesus saith unto him, I say not unto thee, Until seven times: but,
Until seventy times seven" (Matthew 18:21–22). The parable goes on to tell
of a servant who has been forgiven the debt of an almost incomprehensible
amount of money. Josephus recorded that the tax for Judah as a whole was
600 talents (*Antiquities* 17.320). The amount of 10,000 talents is simply unfathomable as a literal amount. The forgiven servant then pursues a debtor
who owes him only a hundred denarii, the equivalent of 1/60 of one talent

or 1/600,000 of the amount he had been forgiven (1 talent was equivalent to roughly 6,000 drachma. The Roman denarius was roughly equivalent to the Greek drachma at the time of Jesus). The point of the story is that if we desire to be forgiven of our sins, we are obligated to forgive those who have trespassed against us, as reflected in the Lord's Prayer: "And forgive us our debts, as we forgive our debtors" (Matthew 6:12).

Jesus and the Feast of Tabernacles

JOHN 7:2–9

As the **Feast** of Tabernacles approached, **Jesus** faced a dilemma: a group of Jerusalem Jews was intent on killing him, and Jesus was intent on attending the feast in Jerusalem. Thus, as John frames the story, Jesus could either stay in **Galilee** and miss the feast or travel to Jerusalem and risk his life. The King James Version's peculiar wording "in Jewry" simply translates the Greek "in **Judea**."

This story formally introduces Jesus' siblings into the story, and for the first time the Gospel of John uses "brethren" to indicate Jesus' younger half-brothers (James; Joses, a shortened form of Joseph; Juda; and Simon; Mark 6:3). His half-brothers, upon recognizing the dilemma, taunted Jesus to attend the feast: "Depart hence, and go into Judaea, that thy **disciples** also may see the works that thou doest" (John 7:3). The intimate knowledge of Jesus' plans and challenges certainly implies a viewpoint from within the circle of his family; and, therefore, "brethren" here should not be interpreted in the sense of merely a disciple or follower.

Jesus responded to his half-brothers' challenge: "My time is not yet come: but your time is alway ready" (7:6). The Greek wording, *ho kairos ho emos* can simply indicate "my time" but it may also look forward in purpose, and can be translated as "my right time." The Greek *kairos* "time" carries with it the idea of Jesus' death or the end of his time in mortality. It was not a simple matter of convenience that he spoke of but, rather, the appropriate time for the end of his life had not yet arrived. Thus, Jesus was telling his brothers that he did not intend to travel to Jerusalem and end his life prematurely, but instead would go when the time was right and not as a result of his siblings' challenge. That he did go to the festival demonstrates that he desired to go and worship and not to prove his brothers right or wrong in their accusations (7:10).

Jesus Departs from Galilee
MATTHEW 19:1; LUKE 9:51

Matthew provides the third statement (7:28; 13:53; 26:1) about **Jesus** finishing a discourse: "And it came to pass, that when Jesus had finished these sayings" (Matthew 19:1), indicating that Jesus has ended his fourth of five discourses. Matthew then notes that Jesus "departed from **Galilee**, and came into the coasts of **Judea** beyond Jordan" (19:1). The geographical focus of the story moves, therefore, away from Galilee to the land of his birth and **baptism**. Luke says Jesus "set his face to go to Jerusalem" and at the same time immediately encounters opposition and rejection, foreshadowing what will happen in the Holy City. All in all, this represents an important transition in the story as the tension continues to build.

Jesus Sends Missionaries to Samaria
LUKE 9:52–56

The Gospels do not clearly indicate at what moment the full scope of **Jesus'** ministry became clear to him or even at what point he revealed that information to his **disciples**. Various points in each of the Gospels can be used to demonstrate that he had that knowledge (see, for example, Matthew 16:21). For Luke, the moment when the full end of the ministry became distinguishable from the beginning occurred when he "set his face to go to Jerusalem" (Luke 9:51). At that moment, Jesus' ministry was clearly conjoined with the purpose for which he had come to earth. Exactly how Jesus conveyed this idea in mortality is not clear, although Luke interpreted it as a change in his visage.

Despite earlier successes in **Samaria** (John 4:39–42), this time the disciples were not welcomed because the **Samaritans** were able to likewise discern a change in Jesus. Following the Greek wording, the implication is that the Samaritans, when they understood that Jesus' ministry was inextricably linked with Jerusalem and the Jews, would no longer entertain the notion that he had come for them and would potentially divorce himself of his Jewish heritage or more likely his Jewish messianism.

James and John interpret this rejection in apocalyptic terms, possibly because of the instruction they had received for their earlier mission (Matthew 10:14–15). At the outset of the first apostolic mission, Jesus had equated the cities that rejected the disciples with Sodom and Gomorrah.

That the rejection in Samaria was physical, meaning they would offer him no shelter and food for the night, is clear from Luke's conclusion to the story: "And they went to another village" (Luke 9:56).

The Calling of the Seventy

LUKE 10:1

Luke provides an interesting note: "After these things the Lord appointed other seventy also, and *sent* them two and two" (10:1; emphasis added). He sent [Greek, *apostellō*] these **disciples** as "**apostles**," that is, they were commissioned by him to perform a duty in his name. The mission was to proclaim the gospel in all the cities (10:2–12).

Commentators have seen in this second mission of the seventy a foreshadowing of the second phase of the mission agenda outlined in Acts by Luke (Acts 10:1–11:18; 11:19–26), that of taking the gospel to the Gentiles. Nameless, these disciples were sent to unknown cities, suggesting that although the story of the seventy was known, it was nevertheless a reminiscent found only in Luke's special sources (Luke 1:1–4) with no equivalence in the other Gospels. Such singly attested stories imply that the collection of stories about **Jesus**, which included written as well as oral accounts, was much larger than what any one author could draw upon as he produced his account. Additionally, this demonstrates that Matthew, Mark, Luke, and

John were selective in their choices of what to include in their individual accounts.

The Mission of the Seventy
LUKE 10:2–12

In an interesting twist, **Jesus** does what he asks the **disciples** to pray for: "Pray ye therefore the Lord of the harvest, that he would send forth labourers into his harvest" (Luke 10:2). He sends the seventy (10:1) and gives instructions to them, reminding us of his directives to the Twelve (9:1–6). Jesus expects that they will be recipients of first-century Jewish hospitality and instructs them not to carry "purse, nor scrip, nor shoes" and remain in a home "eating and drinking such things as they give" (10:4, 7). As "**apostles**," that is those "sent" by Jesus, they are to heal the sick and proclaim the "good news," the "kingdom of God is come nigh unto you," as he had (10:9).

Luke provides the Lord's additional instruction: "But into whatsoever city ye enter, and they receive you not, go your ways out into the streets of the same, and say, Even the very dust of your city, which cleaveth on us, we do wipe off against you" (10:10–11). A similar command was given to the Twelve (Luke 9:5). Scholars have been fascinated by the reference to broad streets (Greek, *plateias*) used here and in other places (Matthew 6:5; Luke 13:26; 14:21). Usually, such streets were found only in large cities, such as Tiberias and Sepphoris, not in the rural villages and towns such as Capernaum, Bethsaida, and Chorazin that play such a prominent role in Jesus' activities as noted immediately after this section (Luke 10:13–16). This may hint that Jesus was more familiar with an urban setting (not just the villages and towns in **Galilee**) than the Gospels explicitly reveal. Had Jesus spent time in Sepphoris, he would have experienced Greek language and culture, but the silence of the Gospels on this matter is convincing given that they do not report Jesus ever speaking Greek.

Jesus Upbraids Capernaum, Bethsaida, and Chorazin
MATTHEW 11:20–24; LUKE 10:13–16

Nothing has prepared us for the woes pronounced against Capernaum, Bethsaida, and Chorazin. First, the only reference to Chorazin and Bethsaida in Matthew is here (both Mark and John mention Bethsaida, however). Second, although a similar warning appeared earlier in Matthew, it was directed to unnamed towns (Luke 10:15). Finally, **Jesus'** own town, Capernaum, seems to have welcomed him (see, for example, Matthew 4:13; 8:5). The shock of the pronouncements only emphasizes the fragmentary record we have of Jesus' activities in these towns. Located in the northwest quadrant of the Sea of **Galilee**, they are the closest towns to each other (Bethsaida is eight miles northeast of Capernaum, and Chorazin is about two miles northwest and up the hill from Capernaum), which suggests that they most likely witnessed a number of events in Jesus' mission that have not been preserved in the Gospels.

Some New Testament scholars have suggested that Jesus may have pronounced judgment against these towns as he left Galilee for the last time on his way to Jerusalem. Certainly, Jesus must have been disappointed by the lack of response to his mission. He had taught and healed with power and authority. Yet Capernaum, Bethsaida, and Chorazin did not respond appropriately to Jesus' call to repent and believe, even though they accepted and witnessed mighty deeds. Specifically, Jesus says the fate of Capernaum is to be like unto that of Babylon (Isaiah 13:13, 15).

Such woes are found throughout the Old Testament (see, for example, Numbers 21:29; Amos 1:1–2:2; Isaiah 10:5; 13–23; Jeremiah 13:27; Ezekiel 25–32; Obadiah 1:1–21). What is shocking in this instance is that Tyre, Sidon, and Sodom were representatives of wickedness and evil in the Hebrew Bible, but here, in what is best described as another gospel reversal, Jesus says they will fare better on Judgment Day than will the Jewish towns where he preached and healed. Luke notes that Tyre later responded because **disciples** could be found there (Acts 21:3–4).

142

In the context of the Old Testament pronouncements, these judgments against Capernaum, Bethsaida, and Chorazin should not be seen as set in stone. If the inhabitants repent, they would be saved (see, for example, Jonah 3).

The Seventy Return
LUKE 10:17–20

The mission of the seventy drew to a close only after **Jesus** had purposefully made his way to Jerusalem to accomplish his atoning **sacrifice**. The good news reported in the return of the seventy intersects Jesus' movements toward Jerusalem and likewise foreshadows the **priesthood** power the seventy would bear in hostile circumstances. That lesson was made clear to them when Jesus taught, "Notwithstanding in this rejoice not, that the spirits are subject unto you; but rather rejoice, because your names are written in heaven" (Luke 10:20). Their hope was for a heavenly reward, though Jesus had also assured them, "Behold, I give unto you power to tread on serpents and scorpions, and over all the power of the enemy: and nothing shall by any means hurt you" (10:19).

Jesus Gives Thanks
MATTHEW 11:25–30; LUKE 10:21–22

Only the first three verses of Matthew's account have a parallel in the Gospel of Luke, but in those parallel verses the two accounts are nearly identical. The wording is so similar, in fact, as to suggest that one of these authors might have borrowed from the other or that both borrowed from an external source. The strength of this tradition may reveal a point of emphasis or importance.

In the prayer, the standard invocation "Lord" is coupled with the irregular "Father," which later became popular among Christians. In Matthew and Luke, "these things" refers to the destruction of the wicked (Matthew) and the fact that the **disciples'** names have been written in heaven (Luke).

Luke appears to have preserved the original order of the story, and the revelation to "babes" would then logically refer to the seventy, whereas it is unclear who the "babes" would be in Matthew's account. Matthew, however, clearly contextualized the verses in another way by including **Jesus'** proclamation, "Come unto me, all ye that labour and are heavy laden, and I will give you rest" (Matthew 11:28). That promised rest looks forward to a heavenly rest, just as was promised to the seventy in Luke.

The Joseph Smith Translation picked up on the change in Matthew's context and reconstructed the setting of the story by adding, "And at that time there came a voice out of heaven; and Jesus answered . . ." (JST, Matthew 11:25). In the King James Version, verse 25 begins abruptly with an answer but no question, thus suggesting that a question at one time preceded this story.

The Parable of the Good Samaritan
LUKE 10:25–37

The lawyer (Greek, *nomikos*, "a person trained in law") who initiated the discussion that set the stage for the parable of the good **Samaritan** may not be an exact equivalent to a modern-day lawyer. Luke indicates the "lawyer" was "tempting" Jesus, which might mean "baiting" the Lord when he asked, "What shall I do to inherit eternal life?" Perhaps he was trying to entrap or embarrass Jesus. A more charitable supposition would be that the man simply had an academic interest in matters of doctrine. In either case, the discussion between Jesus and the lawyer eventually focuses on the definition of "neighbor," to which the parable was given in answer.

As previously noted, Jewish attitudes toward Samaritans were formed largely as a result of Jewish disdain for ethnic mixing, in this case intermarriage between Israelites and non-Israelites. Josephus offers another reason why there were such strained relations between the two groups: the Samaritans were a people that accepted Jews who could not live up to the strictures of the law of Moses and were thus a community of sinners (*Antiquities* 11.340–47). The Romans held a more open view toward the Samaritans but also recognized that their religion was a mixture of foreign customs and religious practices (Dionysus, *Antiquitates Romanae* 1.60.2–3). Whether these historians are representative of their Jewish and Roman contemporaries is not certain, but Jesus' use of a Samaritan in his parable suggests that at least the Jews generally thought the Samaritans were a loathsome people. The "two pence" the Samaritan man paid would have been equivalent to about two days' pay for a common laborer. That Jesus suggested there is an open door for salvation, one through which the Samaritans might also enter, would have likely been the most startling teaching of this parable, which declares the Samaritans were their neighbors and that as such Jews should love them. Later interpreters saw a parallel between the Samaritan and Jesus, seeing in the rescuer a type of **Christ**, whose **Atonement** was the ultimate act of charity.

Mary and Martha
Luke 10:38–42

Contrary to ancient stereotypes, Martha "received" **Jesus** "into her house" (Luke 10:38). In providing this hospitality, Martha complained to Jesus that Mary was of no assistance and that Mary's role should have been to help serve (Greek, *diakonian*, "serve" or "administer"). That is, Mary should have acted as a servant or **deacon** (the English word is derived from the Greek word for servant) instead of as a **disciple** and listener. Jesus, however, taught Martha that the greater role was that of disciple: "But one thing is needful: and Mary hath chosen that good part, which shall not be taken away from her" (10:42), even though Jesus taught elsewhere that "whosoever will be chief among you, let him be your servant" (Matthew 20:27). Here the issue was not seeking for greatness but rather the relative merits of two things: the opportunity to learn at the feet of the Lord or the necessity of attending to household chores.

The Friend at Midnight
LUKE 11:5–8

In conjunction with the revelation of the Lord's Prayer in the Gospel of Luke, there is an interpretive analogy that helps reveal **Jesus'** intent. In the Lord's Prayer it reads, "Give us day by day our daily bread" (Luke 11:3), which may have raised concerns about long-term preparedness and perspective. Living life day-to-day requires adjustment coupled with faith and hope. In this context, Jesus was teaching that when a friend asks for aid, it is given on the basis of, "Though he will not rise and give him, because he is his friend, yet because of his importunity he will rise and give him as many as he needeth." (11:8). The analogy implies that prayers and petitions are answered on the basis of need, which also suggests that Matthew's wording of the Lord's Prayer is closer to the original when it says, "Give us this day our daily bread" (Matthew 6:11). Luke's wording suggests that it is appropriate to ask in advance for our daily bread, while Matthew's wording has us asking each day anew, a perspective that is also addressed in the story of the friend at midnight. Further, it is possible that the two accounts represent two different versions of the Lord's Prayer that **Jesus** spoke during his lifetime.

Keep the Word
LUKE 11:27–28

Given the first-century realities in which women were generally valued for bearing and caring for children, we should not be surprised by the cry from the crowd: "Blessed is the womb that bare thee, and the paps which thou has sucked" (Luke 11:27). **Jesus'** response to this woman reminds us of what he said about family earlier (Luke 8:21). In this instance Jesus challenges her understanding of what constitutes true blessedness: "Yea rather, blessed are they that hear the word of God, and keep it" (11:28). Although this is a unique saying preserved only by Luke, it reinforces what we already know about Mary from the opening chapter of Luke. Mary was

146

characterized by Elisabeth as being "blessed . . . among women." However, it was not only because she was to give birth to the Son of God (as great an honor as that is) but also because Mary "believed" such a thing were possible (Luke 1:44–45). Jesus requires hearing, believing, and doing.

Coveting
LUKE 12:13–21

As **Jesus** finishes speaking to an "innumerable multitude of people" (Luke 12:1–12), an unnamed individual in the group approaches Jesus asking him to become a third party in a dispute between the man and his brother over the division of their inheritance. This passage speaks to us today as much as any. Families are often embroiled in such quarrels when parents and grandparents die and estates are settled. As greed enters into the hearts of those involved, good feelings are often extinguished. Tragically, family members become adversaries. In this case, Jesus refuses to be drawn into a family argument and warns the man, "Take heed, and beware of covetousness" (12:15). Following a brief transition, Jesus then tells a parable about a rich man who tore down his barns to build bigger ones to house an abundant harvest, only to discover that his life would end that very night; God tells him, "Thou fool, this night thy soul shall be required of thee: then whose shall those things be, which thou hast provided?" (12:20). An earlier aphorism is made concrete in this parable: "For what is a man advantaged, if he gain the whole world, and lose himself, or be cast away?" (9:25).

It is often noted by commentators that riches and poverty are two of Luke's principal themes (1:51–53; 3:10–14; 4:14–30; 6:24; 8:14; 12:13–21; 14:12–14; 16:1–12, 19–31; 19:1–10). The parable, therefore, is another warning to the rich who do not share their abundance, reminding us that Jesus challenged everyone—rich and poor, old and young, men and women, Jews and **Gentiles**, religious and nonreligious—to consider their motives in all things and repent and believe the good news.

The Parable of the Barren Fig Tree
LUKE 13:1–5

Although **Jesus** offered peace to those he met, he nevertheless talked about future judgment (both immediate judgment resulting from the approaching Jewish War, A.D. 66–70, and an ultimate Final Judgment at the end of time). Certainly, this is one of the common threads that is woven through his preaching of the "good news" as remembered by his **disciples**. Here, Jesus refers to two historical incidents that must have been well known to his audience but for which we have no contemporary source beside these references: first, Pilate's slaughter of a group of Galileans at the **temple**, and second, the death of eighteen people when the Siloam tower fell on them. That calamities happen unexpectedly even to those who should not be considered the most wicked only heightens the need to respond to Jesus' call to **repent** immediately, that is, with a sense of urgency.

Jesus says that the fate of those who died in these tragedies is analogous to the fate of the unrepentant: Both perish. In Jesus' message about the coming kingdom of God, exclusion from it has a horrifying result: The individual will perish (Greek, *apoleisthe*, "to be lost"; "to be ruined"; "to be destroyed"). Numerous **parables** and stories reflect this message, including the parable of the prodigal son (Luke 15:11–32) and the story of Zacchaeus (Luke 19:2–10).

As has been noted, the Greek word *metanoeō* behind the King James Version's "repent" means "to change one's mind." Even though implicit is the idea that one does so with a sense of regret for the ideas held previously, the term is not as strong as the one Jesus most likely used in **Aramaic**. Most scholars agree that the more radical Aramaic *tub*, "to go back and return," was likely on Jesus' lips. Therefore Jesus was calling Israel to return to God, who promised them safety and protection.

A Woman Is Healed on the Sabbath
LUKE 13:10–17

Just as with other healing **miracles** Jesus performed on the **Sabbath**, this miracle was interpreted by some, including "the ruler of the synagogue," as an act of work. Jesus was chastised by the man: "There are six days in which men ought to work; in them therefore come and be healed, and not on the sabbath day" (Luke 13:14). The position of ruler of a local **synagogue** (Greek, *archisynagogos*) is attested in inscriptions and appears to have been a temporary appointment, with some evidence suggesting that it could be held by several people at one time. In other instances Jesus faced widespread opposition, but here the challenge came from a local leader who would have likely had a close relationship with the member of the community who had been healed.

To defend his actions, Jesus drew the analogy that a person must "loose" his or her animals to get water on the Sabbath; therefore, this woman could legitimately be "loosed" from her affliction on the Sabbath (13:15–16).

Jesus Turns toward Jerusalem
LUKE 13:22

Following his previous mention that **Jesus** had set his face to go to Jerusalem, Luke returns to the theme of the journey to Jerusalem, reminding the reader of the divine purpose of the mission.

Jesus Comments on Herod Antipas
LUKE 13:31–33

Only Luke preserves **Jesus'** comment regarding Herod Antipas. After being warned by friendly **Pharisees** that the Galilean ruler would kill him (13:31), Jesus responded, "Go ye, and tell that fox, Behold, I cast out devils, and I do cures to day and to morrow, and the third day I shall be perfected" (13:32). Jesus further attests that he will not die in **Galilee** but will instead suffer the historical fate of Israel's prophets—he must (Greek, *dei me*) "perish" in Jerusalem (13:33).

Although Jesus knew it was God's divine will that he would die in the Holy City, he nevertheless recognized that Antipas posed a threat. In fact, one reason for establishing his mission center in Capernaum may have been that its location on the border between Antipas's and Philip's territories afforded Jesus an option to quietly and quickly cross the frontier (both across the lake and the Jordan River just north of Capernaum) in case Antipas should pose too great a threat. When considering what happened to John the Baptist, such precaution does not imply any kind of paranoia on Jesus' part.

Luke refers to "eyewitnesses" at the beginning of his narrative (Luke 1:2). That such a story may have come from one of them suggests that the saying had profound meaning in light of his Resurrection, since it indicates that Jesus knew that on the third day he would be perfected (13:32).

When Jesus refers to Antipas as a fox (Greek, *alopex*), scholars generally assume that in this figure of speech Jesus has reference to Antipas's reputation for being cunning. That he succeeded in ruling from 4 B.C. until A.D. 39 suggests the appropriateness of such a portrayal. He would eventually meet Jesus, not in his own jurisdiction, but in Jerusalem: "And when Herod saw Jesus, he was exceeding glad: for he was desirous to see him of a long season" (Luke 23:8).

Counting the Costs of Discipleship
LUKE 14:28–33

Coming late in the ministry, this parable is attached to a specific application: "So likewise, whosoever he be of you that forsaketh not all that he hath, he cannot be my **disciple**" (Luke 14:33). Interpreting forsaking all that one has as the cost of discipleship may reflect the historical situation of the **apostles** but may also be taught here to extend the requirement spiritually to all of **Jesus'** followers. Asking his listeners to count the cost or to have forethought encouraged his followers to realize, first, that some disciples had already done so and, second, that all may spiritually be called upon to do so. This saying seems to contradict Jesus' earlier teaching, "For my yoke is easy, and my burden is light" and may indicate why Matthew did not include it (Matthew 11:30). This invitation to permit Jesus to help carry our load also stands in contrast to Jesus' counsel to "let the dead bury their dead: but go thou and preach the kingdom of God" (Luke 9:60). The difference in the two sayings is a matter of urgency and not rashness. Teaching the kingdom is the most urgent matter, but Jesus acted carefully.

The Parable of the Unjust Steward
LUKE 16:1–8

This parable may be the most difficult of **Jesus' parables** to interpret because it seems to justify unjust behavior and reward cheating one's master. The parable provides some contextual clues that help one interpret it. The amounts owed to the rich man are enormous for a private estate (a hundred measures of oil and a hundred measures of wheat). These numbers appear to imply that the steward envisioned in the parable was a tax collector, a **publican**. When he mentions, "I cannot dig" (Luke 16:3), however, one is led to think that a vast rural estate is being referred to. Given these two clues, it appears there is a veiled reference to Herod Antipas and perhaps also to Philip, both of whom collected taxes and who likewise managed vast estates.

The reward then, or the commendation, may contain a veiled reference to Herodian or even Roman taxation policies which the "children of light" (16:8) could learn from. It is highly doubtful that Jesus intended to recommend the unjust nature of the steward's acts. Instead, the emphasis is on shrewd business practices. Matthew included another of Jesus' teachings that sounds a similar warning: "Behold, I send you forth as sheep in the midst of wolves: be ye therefore wise as serpents, and harmless as doves" (Matthew 10:16). The stewards of this world, who are often willing to break laws and violate principles, are at times more perseverant in pursuing their worldly goals than are the children of light in seeking the kingdom of heaven.

Lazarus and the Rich Man
LUKE 16:19–31

This uniquely Lukan parable draws upon several stereotypes that were popular in **Galilee**, namely that the rich oppress the poor and that the poor are beloved of God. In the parable, the rich man passes away and is sent to "**hell**," here described as a place of suffering (Luke 16:23). Lazarus, on the other hand, is carried out of his poverty into "Abraham's bosom" (16:22), a place where his mortal suffering ended. Aside from the rich man's indifference to Lazarus's hunger, no sins or even good deeds are mentioned for either the rich man or Lazarus, thus shifting the focus away from what they had done to merit such punishments or blessings and toward how they act once they have been assigned to their respective destinies.

The rich man in his torment in the flames pleads with Abraham to permit Lazarus to descend from his now-favored situation and at least cool his parched tongue. When that is denied him, the rich man then asks that someone be sent to warn his family members to not follow his selfish example. The statement in the King James Version, "have mercy on me, and send Lazarus" (16:24), is a command, much as the rich man would command a servant. The rich man is informed that his brothers already have the teachings of Moses and the prophets, implying that a scriptural witness is equal to a heavenly witness such as Lazarus (16:29). In either case, they would not accept the message.

There are several interesting features of this parable. First, Lazarus is the only named person in all of **Jesus' parables**, and he is very poor, perhaps providing a glimpse into the financial status of Jesus' close friend by that name (John 11:5). Second, because no sins are mentioned and the rich man seems to personify popular attitudes of the rich, it may be that this parable was intended to rebuke the upper echelons in the socioeconomic situation then prevailing in rural Galilee, where powerful landowners oppressed the poor. Finally, the parable provides a glimpse into the world of the spirits, where the concept of a division between the wicked and the righteous is taught for the first time in the New Testament.

Ten Men with Leprosy
LUKE 17:11–19

In another unique Lukan contribution, we learn **Jesus** continued his journey to Jerusalem for one final visit (covered in Luke 9:51 through 19:27). He and the **disciples** likely traveled near **Samaria**, although Luke is inexact on this point, perhaps because he is not as familiar with the exact geographical boundaries of **Galilee**, Samaria, and **Judea** as are Matthew, Mark, and John. This may be another internal clue to authorship if Luke was not a disciple in Galilee or Judea.

On the road, Jesus met ten desperate men who had been outcast from their families and friends and were in every way untouchables. Afflicted with **leprosy** (Hansen's disease) or some other skin affliction that made them ritually unclean according to the **Law** (both the Jewish and **Samaritan** Pentateuch emphasize this point), they were required to live outside the towns and cities and away from others (Numbers 5:2–3). Whenever such outcasts encountered other people, the law required them to shout, "Unclean, unclean!" (Leviticus 13:45). If by some **miracle** they were cured, the law provided a means by which a priest could pronounce them clean, allowing them to return to fellowship within the community.

In this story, according to social custom and the dictates of the law, the men stand at an appropriate distance from Jesus and the disciples. Bound together by a common disease and a common fate, they cry out in unison, "Jesus, Master, have mercy on us" (Luke 17:13). Only found in Luke, *epistata* is translated as "Master." Jesus' disciples always use it, except in this instance (see, for example, 5:5, 8:24, 45; 9:33).

Luke informs us that the men were healed on their way after Jesus commanded them to "shew yourselves unto the **priests**" (17:14). This is not the first mention of Jesus healing those afflicted with leprosy (Luke 5:12–16;

7:22). It may be of interest to note that Luke tends to humanize people in such instances. Instead of identifying these men as **lepers**, Luke says, literally, "ten men that were lepers" (17:12), just as he had once identified a man not as a paralytic but as a man who was paralyzed (5:18).

As the men depart they are healed, but one of them, "when he saw that he was healed, turned back, and with a loud voice glorified God, *and fell down on his face at his feet*, giving him thanks" (17:15–16; emphasis added). In other instances, people often fell at Jesus' feet to plead for mercy (see, for example, 8:41); in this case the man has already been healed, but still falls to the ground as an act of worshipful, unrestrained gratitude.

Luke adds, "and he was a Samaritan" (17:16), reminding us of the parable of the good Samaritan, given earlier, where the Samaritan not only saw the wounded man (as did the priest and Levite), but also acted (Luke 10:30–35) as this Samaritan also saw and acted.

When the man fell at Jesus' feet, Jesus asked three questions and made a very telling statement: "Were there not ten cleansed? but where are the nine? There are not found that returned to give glory to God, save this stranger?" (17:17–18). In response to the healed man's faith and gratitude, Jesus literally tells him, "Your faith has saved you," (author's translation) instead of the inexact King James Version rendering, "thy faith hath made thee whole" (17:19). In an instant, we learn that the other nine men received what they requested—departing from the scene healed and happy. However, this stranger, who praised God and showed gratitude, received more than he could have imagined or expected—salvation in addition to being healed.

The Unjust Judge

LUKE 18:1–8

Also known as the parable of the importunate widow, the theme of the unjust judge treats a favorite theme of the Gospel of Luke—prayer. The King James Version's "to this end" printed in italics to indicate that it is not represented in the Greek text of Luke is an attempt to emphasize the focus of interpretation, "that men ought always to pray, and not to faint" (18:1). The final verse associates the interpretation of this parable with the discourse on the Second Coming at the end of chapter 17. This context helps demonstrate the need for prayer even when the matter seems lost or the judge seems unwilling to hear. In the context of **Jesus**' return to earth, it may be suggestive of events yet to come, but also soon to be applicable to the **disciples** who would be brought before councils and judges.

Perea

MATTHEW 19:1–2; MARK 10:1

The Perean ministry in the country near the Jordan just northeast of Jerusalem placed **Jesus** only a short distance from the place where his ministry would come to an end. The mention of Perea and Jesus' approach to Jerusalem seems situated so that Jesus could time the triumphal entry into Jerusalem.

The Feast of Tabernacles

JOHN 7:10–13

Earlier, during the **Feast** of Tabernacles (Festival of Booths), **Jesus** went to Jerusalem "not openly, but as it were in secret" (John 7:10). John has already informed us of the reason: "the Jews sought to kill him" (7:1). Here again we must remember that all the actors in this story are Jews, both ethnically and religiously. Most likely, we should understand that the term "Jews," which can be translated as "Judeans," refers to the Jewish leadership in **Judea**.

These verses once again point out the division Jesus caused among the people and among their leaders, an important theme in John's Gospel. The two possible options are starkly contrasted: he is either "a good man" or he "deceiveth the people" (7:12). Of course, the latter charge reminds us of Deuteronomy where Moses warns Israel about false prophets and teachers who give "signs" and perform "wonders" to deceive the people.

The **law** commands that they "shall be put to death" (Deuteronomy 13:5). Additionally, John adds that the people were afraid of their leaders in Judea and therefore were careful in what they said about Jesus (John 7:13).

This short section reveals the importance of the decisions we make about Jesus and prepares us for the rather lengthy discourse that follows (7:14–52).

Discourse on Jesus' Mission

JOHN 7:14–30

The events depicted here occur in the "middle of" the Feast of Tabernacles, providing eyewitness type evidence to begin the account. This subtle detail alerts the reader that witnessing will be an important part of the story. To begin, some Jews marveled how **Jesus** could so readily read and comment on scripture, "having never learned?" (7:15). The question was not simply one of academic training but also of who Jesus' teacher had been. Jesus responded to the latter by saying, "My doctrine is not mine, but his that sent me" (7:16). Jesus then discussed the law of witnesses.

Alluding to prior confrontations, Jesus mentions a plot to take his life, a plot that may have had its origins in the first cleansing of the **temple** (John 2:13–17). That event, coupled with the healing in John 5, were the only controversial events from the mortal ministry that would have led to a plot to kill Jesus. Jesus singled out one of the two: "I have done one work, and ye all marvel" (7:21). The reference to one specific event almost certainly refers to the **Sabbath** as the following verse makes clear when it refers to other acts performed on the Sabbath.

The argument here is not simply whether Jesus' act of healing violated the Sabbath but rather what God intended by the commandment to keep the Sabbath day holy. Avoiding work, even the smallest act (John 5:10), was the interpretation favored by Jews, but Jesus taught that it was a day for doing good. If the **priests** were permitted to break the prohibition against work to perform the ordinance of **circumcision**, for example, then Jesus' act of healing was therefore acceptable.

The debate then shifts to the question of the **Messiah's** origins, which some thought precluded Jesus from being the Messiah **(Christ)** because he was from Nazareth and not of heavenly origin as popular thinking taught. The tradition is summed up in the phrase, "Howbeit we know this man whence he is: but when Christ cometh, no man knoweth whence he is" (7:27). To conclude, Jesus testified of his mission from the Father ("he that sent me").

Because of the blasphemous nature of what he had taught, the Jews sought to arrest him, both confirming Jesus' earlier prediction that they had plotted to kill him and indicating that his teachings had further infuriated them. But when they sought to take him, "no man laid hands on him" (7:30). It is not clear whether this meant no one was able to lay hands on him, or that he simply avoided their attempt to arrest him, or something else entirely.

The final portion of the story recasts Jesus as the hidden Messiah. He would be with them for a short while and then would become hidden to them. They did not understand his meaning, and even though their very words depict the hidden Messiah, they did not seem to comprehend that he was exactly what they had sought.

The Spirit Testifies
JOHN 7:37–53

The "last day" of the feast refers to the Feast of Tabernacles mentioned at the beginning of the chapter. The Feast of Tabernacles, which recalled the time of Israel's wanderings in the wilderness, celebrated also the waters that would flow from Jerusalem to heal the Dead Sea (Zechariah 13:1; 14:8; Ezekiel 47:1–2). Thus, while teaching, most likely in the courtyard of the **temple**, **Jesus** indicated that he was the source of the water that would flow from that spot and heal the world, thus giving the Old Testament prophecies a symbolic interpretation: "If any man thirst, let him come unto me, and drink. He that believeth on me, as the scripture hath said, out of his belly shall flow rivers of living water" (John 7:37–38; see Exodus 17:6; Numbers 20:11).

The verse following this statement has been one of the most difficult in the New Testament to interpret. Following what he had just said, that new and living water would flow from him from the Temple Mount, verse 39 offers an explanatory interjection intended to clarify the meaning of the preceding verses. In its most literal sense, the verse serves to contrast the lifeless and dry teachings of contemporary Judaism with the Spirit-filled gospel of Jesus **Christ**. In the day in which these words were spoken, the Spirit came through obedience to the law of Moses, but John saw that a fuller endowment of the Spirit awaited those who would "believe on him" (7:39). The verse may not have been intended to indicate that there was a withholding of the Spirit in that day, but rather a contrast in the two laws: that of Moses compared to that of Jesus.

Many of those who heard Jesus teach these things responded by declaring their faith that Jesus had come to fulfill the prophecy of the coming of a prophet similar to Moses, spoken of in Deuteronomy 18:15–18. Others thought that he was the **Messiah (Christ)**; still others, who recognized that there were no prophecies of a Messiah who would come from **Galilee** (Nazareth is in **Galilee**, and Jesus was thought to come from Nazareth), thought that he could not be the Messiah. Ironically, some argued that the prophecy of Micah 5:2 indicated that the Messiah would be born in Bethlehem. Unfortunately, the stories of Jesus' birth were not widespread, or at least not among the Jews of Jerusalem, and therefore they stumbled over their own limited understanding, which John chose to include as a contrast to the clear vision of Jesus expressed in his testimony at the Feast of Tabernacles.

A more official response is also included as a contrast to Jesus' testimony, thus solidifying John's understanding that rigid interpretation of the written word kept people from accepting the living witness. After the "chief **priests** and **Pharisees**" (7:45) had sent officers, probably the wardens of the temple, to arrest Jesus, they came back without having fulfilled their duty. They testified how powerful the living witness was: "Never man spake like this man" (7:46), to which the Pharisees offered a blistering criticism of written versus living testimony: "But this people who knoweth not the law are cursed" (7:49), implying that had they known the law, or more literally the prophecies of the Old Testament, they would not have been confused by a living witness. In this heated confrontation, Nicodemus cautioned that they should proceed with moderation (7:50–51; see Deuteronomy 1:16). John seems to say that the matter was not fully resolved, and even though it appears from the narrative that the debate was one against many, the concluding verse implies the division among the Pharisees was more pronounced: "And every man went unto his own house" (7:53). This story, which preserves a private discussion among leading Pharisees at the time of Jesus, may have been passed down to the author of the Gospel of John by Nicodemus, who appears in several instances to be the only named link between Jesus and the Pharisees (John 3:1).

The Woman Taken in Adultery
JOHN 8:1–11

The story of the woman taken in adultery has a long and complicated textual history that cannot easily be resolved. In the earliest manuscript copies of the Gospel of John, the story is missing. Two early papyrus codices, papyri 66 and 75 (both early third century A.D.) and the fourth-century bibles Sinaiticus and Vaticanus do not preserve this story. Literally dozens of other later manuscripts also omit this important story from the Gospel of John. From this evidence, it would appear that the story was not part of the Gospel of John in its original form.

However, Codex Bezae (fifth century A.D.), as well as dozens of other manuscripts, contains the story in its current position in the Gospel of John. The reasoning is that since the oldest two copies omit the story while later ones are mixed, the story must have been inserted later, probably in the third century. However, the Syriac *Didascalia Apostolorum* (Codex Sangermanensis) makes reference to the story, and Papias (Eusebius, *Church History* 3.39) may also have made reference to it in the early second century, thus preserving an equally early reference to the independent existence of the story as well as a potentially earlier record of it.

From the surviving evidence, it is probable that the story is indeed ancient, probably originating in the late first century, but it is not connected to the Gospel of John until later, probably the middle of the third century. That a tradition could survive independently of one of the Gospels attests to its popularity and the likelihood that it represents an event from the life of **Jesus**, recorded by a now-unknown author. The Book of Mormon attests to a similar phenomenon where additional **scriptures** were added much later to make the record more complete (3 Nephi 23:7–13).

The story itself hinges on a narrow interpretation of one of Jesus' teachings. The Old Testament directs that those guilty of adultery should be put to death (Leviticus 20:10), which had implications regarding Jesus' teaching on what constituted adultery: "That whosoever shall put away his wife, saving for the cause of fornication, causeth her to commit adultery: and whosoever shall marry her that is divorced committeth adultery" (Matthew 5:32). Therefore, Jesus' interrogators appear to be asking regarding the relative weight of Jesus' teachings in regard to the law of Moses. Their question was whether he would accept the implications of his earlier teachings, that a remarried divorcee, which had been called an adulterous relationship in some instances, should be stoned according to the law of Moses stipulations. This may also clarify why no male partner is mentioned in the story.

The trap the **Pharisees** laid for Jesus was intended to turn Jesus' followers, or the public generally, against Jesus because he had proclaimed his word as greater than the law of Moses (assuming, of course, that he would recommend that the woman be stoned to death). The legal consequences of stoning the woman would have been far greater than anything Jesus could have said.

Upon seeing that the woman's accusers had departed, Jesus said to her, "Neither do I condemn thee: go, and sin no more" (John 8:11). These final words may hold a clue to why the story dropped out of the New Testament, because Jesus seems to forgive too quickly. The statement, however, likely indicates simply that because the witnesses to the crime had departed, neither Jesus nor anyone else was in a position to condemn the woman.

The Light of the World
JOHN 8:12–59

The **Feast** of Tabernacles (Leviticus 23:33–43) featured four gigantic oil lamps in the Court of the Women in the **temple** during the first century A.D. so large, as later witnesses report, that they cast light across the entire temple complex and into the adjoining neighborhoods. Adding dramatically to the symbolism of the celebration (reminding Israel that the Lord's presence was with them during their journey as a pillar of fire), the people danced with torches in their hands as they worshiped the Lord in the evening. In this context **Jesus** says that he is the ultimate fulfillment of the festival: "I am the light of the world" (John 8:12).

Another controversy immediately ensues when the **Pharisees** reject Jesus' testimony (witness). Using the context of **covenant** renewal, an important feature of the celebration, Jesus says, "It is also written in your law, that the testimony of two men is true" (8:17). He then declares that he and the Father are witnesses of the things Jesus says and does. When the obtuse Pharisees ask where his Father is, Jesus says, "Ye neither know me, nor my Father" (8:19)—a forceful condemnation of those who were doctors and the presumed interpreters of the law.

John then provides specific eyewitness insight: "These words spake Jesus in the treasury, as he taught in the temple" (8:20). Additionally, the author reminds us that Jesus' "hour was not yet come," so the officials are unable to arrest him (8:20).

Jesus continues revealing himself when he says that he is from above and that he is preparing to go back to the Father. His enemies wonder if he is contemplating suicide (8:22), demonstrating further that they are in complete darkness (John 1:5). Jesus provides a sign: "When ye have lifted up the **Son of man**, then shall ye know that I am he, and that I do nothing of myself; but as my Father hath taught me, I speak these things" (8:28).

Turning to those who believe, Jesus says, "And ye shall know the truth, and the truth shall make you free" (8:32). The Jewish leaders respond, "We be Abraham's seed, and were never in bondage to any man" (8:33).

Ironically, Israel's history had witnessed periods of bondage on numerous occasions, and most recently the Jews were subject to **Rome's** political, economic, and military occupation.

John points out one of the charges against Jesus by the Jewish leadership: "Say we not well that thou art a **Samaritan**, and hast a devil?" (8:48). Jesus repudiates the charge of being possessed by a **demon**: "I have not a devil; but I honour my Father, and ye do dishonour me. And I seek not mine own glory: there is one that seeketh and judgeth" (8:49–50).

This section ends with Jesus' statement, "Verily [amen], verily [amen], I say unto you, If a man keep my sayings, he shall never see death" (8:51), reminding us of what he said earlier: "If ye continue in my word" (8:31), true freedom (freedom from death) is the gift of him who is the ultimate truth. Just as **Satan** introduced sin, bondage, and death (8:44), Jesus promises to end sin, bondage, and death through his own suffering, death, and resurrection.

A Blind Man Is Healed

JOHN 9:1–41

This story is another **miracle** account of giving sight to someone blind, one of many found in the Gospels (Matthew 9:27–31; 20:29–34; Mark 8:22–26; 10:46–52; Luke 18:35–42). However, there are some unique and distinctive features in this account that would cause the **disciples** to especially remember it, even though such healings occurred often in **Jesus'** ministry.

First of all, it must be remembered that Mark and Luke each recount eighteen miracles; Matthew recounts twenty; and John recounts only seven miracles. The fact that this is one of those seven stories points to its significance: "*Since the world began* was it not heard that any man opened the eyes of one that was born blind" (John 9:32; emphasis added). Of course, such selectivity also allows the author to spend more time explaining the significance of the miracle. Additionally, this miracle follows on the heels of Jesus' declaration, "I am the light of the world" (8:12)—a claim Jesus repeats in 9:5. The story begins with a question by the disciples based on a common understanding that sin and illness are somehow connected (notice that the **Pharisees** share this understanding; 9:34). When Jesus rejects this speculation, he immediately reaches out to bring "light" to the man. Interestingly, the man has not asked Jesus to heal him—Jesus simply performs this miracle as an affirmation that "the works of God should be made manifest in him" (9:3).

The author provides a clue to his audience when he interprets the Hebrew word *Siloam* (9:7). Additionally, John explains Jewish practice on several occasions, indicating the likelihood that his audience was **Gentile**.

Following the healing, a controversy arises among the people as to whether this man who was healed was the same man who was blind (9:8–10). Additionally, the healing was on the **Sabbath**, providing the **Pharisees** yet another opportunity to question Jesus' commitment to God and the **Torah**. Confusion continues when some of the Pharisees declare, "This man is not of God, because he keepeth not the sabbath day. Others said, How can a man that is a sinner do such miracles?" (9:16). As before, Jesus' action produces "a division among" the people—one of the themes that runs through the entire Gospel narrative.

The reported interrogation of both the parents and the man by Jewish authorities is full of irony and even sarcasm. When the Pharisees asked a second time how he was healed, the man goaded them: "*I have told you already*, and ye did not hear: wherefore would ye hear it again? will ye also be his disciples?" (9:27; emphasis added). Later, Jesus found the man and began to lead him to spiritual insight. This results in recognition and worship (9:35–38), thereby revealing the main doctrinal point of the story—blindness is not based on whether a person can or cannot see with their eyes, but whether or not they recognize God's work in their midst.

The Parable of the Good Shepherd
JOHN 10:1–21

The sheepfold mentioned here is probably the type of enclosure where stones were piled up to create an artificial enclosure where the sheep would remain. The enclosure would have been fairly rudimentary, with a small wooden gate. Such walls could be easily scaled, and briars may have been grown on them to keep out unwanted visitors, but more than likely to keep the sheep in. Someone who entered the enclosure by scaling the wall would indeed be a thief.

In contrast to someone who would climb the wall, **Jesus** refers to the shepherd who knew the sheep by name and who was able to call his sheep from amidst the other sheep. This parable implies that there were several flocks of sheep within the enclosure and that the shepherd was able to call his sheep from among them. Following custom, the ancient shepherd went before the sheep to lead them.

The situation described in the parable is straightforward, and it is likely the application was what eluded Jesus' listeners: "but they understood not what things they were which he spake unto them" (10:6). To remedy the misunderstanding, Jesus interpreted this parable. He taught them that he is "the door of the sheep" (10:7), which in other ancient manuscripts reads, "the shepherd of the sheep." The change from shepherd to door, which is both confusing and unexpected, is probably an ancient scribal mistake when the word *door* from verse 9 was transposed into verse 7.

Furthermore, Jesus explained that he was the door to the sheepfold and the shepherd, thus making it obvious that the sheep were the followers of the Lord. What Jesus taught, "All that ever came before me are thieves and robbers: but the sheep did not hear them" (10:8), should be interpreted in terms of **messianic** pretenders of Jesus' day and age but not in reference to the prophets. The prophets did not scale the wall but came through the gate, thus authorizing them as shepherds. Jesus seems to say this very thing in different words: "I am the door: by me if any man enter in, he shall be saved, and shall go in and out, and find pasture" (10:9).

More importantly, however, Jesus took the opportunity to teach how he was the door by which the sheep enter and exit the sheepfold. To teach that principle, Jesus revealed his upcoming death as an act of giving his life for his followers (10:11). Hired sheepherders flee when they see the wolf approaching, but Jesus, who it is implied can see the wolf coming, does not flee from fate, suggesting that by this point in the ministry he had pondered those very points.

To further draw on the analogy of shepherding, Jesus teaches that as a shepherd he cannot be killed. Someone might rightly ask what would happen if someone were to kill such a well-intentioned shepherd and scatter the flock, but Jesus makes it very clear that no one can kill him (10:18). Rather, he would lay down his life, giving it up freely for the preservation and salvation of his sheep. To demonstrate that he saw the wolf from afar, Jesus here attempts to stave off the disillusionment that some may have felt when the shepherd was taken from their midst.

To further reinforce the idea in their minds, Jesus taught that the Father had given him the commandment to lay down his life and take it up again, thus linking his temporary departure with the permanence and staying power of the Father. The teaching that he would lay down his life and take it up again appears to have been given in the context of alleviating future worry rather than making a doctrinal statement about the power of the Resurrection.

Within these teachings, Jesus referred to the Nephites when he taught of other sheep who must also hear his voice (10:16). Certainly there are other sheep as well, and the phrase would have been interpreted in the context of Diaspora Jews, or Jews living abroad, as well as perhaps the **Gentiles** and **Samaritans**. However, a fold is a portion of a flock and does not distinguish specifically any group, such as the Nephites, without further prophetic guidance. The fold envisions a small gathering when the followers of the Lord become "one fold, and one shepherd" (10:16). Jesus taught that there were other folds "which are not of this fold" (10:16). Those folds would one day be gathered into a single fold (see also 3 Nephi 15:21–22).

Why the Jews would assume that Jesus had "a devil" after hearing him teach these things is no longer clear. It may have been that the teachings were so out of the ordinary that the Pharisees concluded that Jesus was deluded or irrational in his thinking. Some responded to this way of thinking by referring to the **miracle** of John 9 that indicated he was not "mad" (John 10:20–21).

The Question about Divorce
MATTHEW 19:3–12; MARK 10:2–12

This discussion revived the classic conversation between the two most prominent schools of thought in **Jesus'** day. Both Hillel and Shammai and their followers had debated the very issue under consideration in this account. Both schools sought to interpret the counsel given in Deuteronomy: "When a man hath taken a wife, and married her, and it come to pass that she find no favour in his eyes, because he hath found some uncleanness in her: then let him write her a bill of divorcement, and give it in her hand, and send her out of his house" (Deuteronomy 24:1). The question was whether a couple could divorce for "every cause" (Matthew 19:3). Mark omitted this phrase, which reflects the debate of the first century (Mark 10:2). The omission of this crucial phrase may indicate that he was not familiar with the debates and circumstances of first-century **Galilee** and **Judea**.

Logically, the account moves from the initial question to the **scriptures**, which plainly permit divorce. The underlying assumption, based on Moses' teachings, was that divorce was permissible, but Jesus' contemporaries sought clarification on *when* it was permissible. Jesus' rejoinder draws upon the biblical precedent of Genesis (Genesis 1:27; 2:24) and teaches that Moses did not command or encourage divorce but rather permitted or allowed it based on the "hardness of your heart" (Mark 10:5). Therefore, Jesus' interpretation seems to follow the more conservative interpretation of Shammai with some significant differences.

Rather than broadly permitting divorce, Jesus taught that there was one case where it was allowed. But even in that instance he gave some guidance. Matthew and Mark each preserve a slightly different version of the saying, which further makes it difficult to interpret. According to Mark, the **disciples** asked Jesus for further clarification, to which Jesus responded, "Whosoever shall put away his wife, and marry another, committeth adultery against her. And if a woman shall put away her husband, and be married to another, she committeth adultery" (10:11–12). Mark's wording could imply that *any* remarriage after divorce is considered adulterous against the first spouse, or in other words, people may divorce but not remarry. Matthew's wording paints a slightly different picture: "Whosoever shall put away his wife, except it be for fornication, and shall marry another, committeth adultery: and whoso marrieth her which is put away doth commit adultery" (Matthew 19:9). Matthew's account sanctions divorce in cases of *porneia*, a Greek term that indicates sexual misconduct and is here translated as fornication.

The question is whether Jesus permitted divorce as a result of fornication or whether he forbade it entirely. Most scholars argue that Mark's version is closer to the original, whereas Matthew's appears to reflect a growing awareness that in cases of fornication (adultery), divorce is warranted. In a modern context, prophets and apostles have noted that divorce is permissible when it is based on issues of abuse, infidelity, and other compelling reasons.

The disciples asked regarding this teaching specifically, "If the case of the man be so with his wife, it is not good to marry" (Matthew 19:10). Jesus' response, which is considered one of his most difficult teachings and is only recorded in Matthew reads, "All men cannot receive this saying, save they to whom it is given. For there are some eunuchs, which were so born from their mother's womb: and there are some eunuchs, which were made eunuchs of men: and there be eunuchs, which have made themselves eunuchs for the kingdom of heaven's sake. He that is able to receive it, let him receive it" (19:11–12). Matthew's context appears to offer the most ancient interpretation of this saying. Jesus responded to the limited view expressed in the disciples' question by using a metaphor, saying that at times some are asked to act like eunuchs for the kingdom of heaven's sake. He drew upon two standard views of eunuchs, that some were made that way because of their employment and others were eunuchs by birth. The statement may also have reference to the fulfillment of the promise made to eunuchs in Isaiah 56:3–5.

Suffer the Little Children
MATTHEW 19:13–15; MARK 10:13–16; LUKE 18:15–17

In a world where the infant mortality rate was alarmingly high, it is not surprising that mothers, sisters, and grandmothers would take young children ("infants" in Luke 18:15–17) to **Jesus** so he would "put his hands on them, and pray" (Matthew 19:13). When the **disciples** chided them, Jesus was "much displeased" (Mark 10:13–14).

Matthew and Luke follow Mark in this remarkable story of reversal—a child represents those who will be welcomed into Jesus' kingdom. This recalls the earlier discussion regarding who will be the greatest in the kingdom (Mark 9:33–37). Additionally, it emphasizes Jesus' theme of the child-like trust the disciples must have in the Father. Here Jesus used a child as the example. He did not expect the disciples to act childishly but was emphasizing their total dependence upon God. This short account ends tenderly: "And he took them up in his arms, put his hands upon them, and blessed them" (10:16).

The Rich Young Ruler
MATTHEW 19:16–26; MARK 10:17–27; LUKE 18:18–27

The suggestion that the young man who came to question **Jesus** regarding obedience was a rich young ruler is actually a collective title based on all three Gospel accounts. Only Luke refers to him as a ruler, while Matthew supplies the idea that he was young, and all three Gospels indicate that he was wealthy. The question personifies a literalist interpretation of the law where acts of obedience are the way to achieve eternal life. Following the question, "What shall I do that I may inherit eternal life?" (Mark 10:17), Jesus responds by citing some of the Ten Commandments. The list of commandments differs in the three accounts, but they all appear to derive from Exodus 20 except for Mark's statement, "Defraud not," which may have been shaped through oral memory of Jesus' teachings (Mark 10:19).

Jesus taught the young man how to be perfect: "If thou wilt be perfect, go and sell that thou hast, and give to the poor, and thou shalt have treasure in heaven: and come and follow me" (Matthew 19:21). The word translated here as "perfect" (Greek, *teleios*, "complete" or "whole") is the same word used in Matthew 5:48, "Be ye therefore perfect."

Only Mark notes, "Then Jesus beholding him loved him" (Mark 10:21). Because of that love, and the fact that the young man went away sorrowful, Jesus remarks to his **disciples**, "For it is easier for a camel to go through a needle's eye, than for a rich man to enter into the kingdom of God" (Luke 18:25). Contextually, from the disciples' reaction, it appears that they found the statement shocking and not easily understood because they knew of no such gate in the city wall. Matthew reports that they were "exceedingly amazed" (Matthew 19:25), and Mark records that "they were astonished out of measure" (Mark 10:26), while Luke notes, "And they that heard it said, Who then can be saved?" (Luke 18:26). If salvation were as difficult (or seemingly impossible) to achieve as the act of literally pressing a camel through the eye of a needle, is salvation even possible? Jesus seems to have understood their confusion and adds, "With men it is impossible, but not with God: for with God all things are possible" (Mark 10:27).

The Twelve to Rule Israel
MATTHEW 19:27–30; MARK 10:28–31; LUKE 18:28–30; 22:28–30

This short and almost passing reference records the **disciples'** reflections on the account of the rich young man that preceded this event. If heaven was so difficult to enter, then what implications did that have for the Twelve? Concern is clearly evident in Peter's question: "Behold, we have forsaken all, and followed thee; what shall we have therefore?" (Matthew 19:27).

Jesus promised Peter three things as a result of his obedience. First, he assured Peter and all his other followers, "Ye which have followed me, in the regeneration when the **Son of man** shall sit in the throne of his glory" (Matthew 19:28). Second, he promised the Twelve specifically that "Ye also shall sit upon twelve thrones, judging the twelve tribes of Israel" (Matthew 19:28). And third, Jesus promised all who follow him, "And every one that hath forsaken houses, or brethren, or sisters, or father, or mother, or wife, or children, or lands, for my name's sake, shall receive an hundredfold, and shall inherit everlasting life" (Matthew 19:29). The promise to judge the tribes of Israel follows the more general promise that "ye which have followed me," possibly indicating that Jesus would exclude Judas, who would not follow him to the end.

In Mark, similar promises are made with the exception that the prophecy that the Twelve would judge Israel is missing. Luke follows the text of Mark in its particulars in 18:28–30, but he also follows the text of Matthew (19:27–30; Luke 22:28–30). Luke may have been aware of the fact that Jesus repeated the promise that the Twelve would judge Israel on a separate occasion (Luke 18:28–30; 22:28–30).

The Parable of the Laborers in the Vineyard
MATTHEW 20:1–16

This parable directly follows the discussion of the rich young man and Peter's question regarding the state of the **disciples** in the hereafter. Some, therefore, may see in this parable a warning concerning how the first shall be last and the last shall be first. However, because the parable contains many different groups, rather than only two as one would expect if it were a warning to Peter and the other disciples, the parable seems to expand the discussion of who will be saved to include those who work a twelve-hour day all the way down to a one-hour day.

The wage the laborers earn in this parable, a denarius translated here as "penny," is notoriously difficult to interpret in modern terms. It is frequently cited as the normal pay for a day's wage for a laborer, but that definition usually spans hundreds of years of evidence when people were actually paid a denarius for a day's wage. The denarius began to be significantly devalued in the second half of the first century but had already been devalued in the beginning of the first. Basing the value of the denarius on prices known from Egypt in a previous century cannot tell us much concerning its value in **Judea** in the same time period. The **rabbis** of later generations agreed that it was common for a day laborer to earn this wage, but they do not tell us whether it was a miserly wage. The existing evidence suggests that such a wage was at the poverty level, perhaps barely enough to sustain life for a small family.

Jesus describes four groups of people who work in the vineyard, each group working successively less than the first but all receiving the same pay. That the focus of the parable involves perceptions about salvation is made obvious from the way in which the pay is distributed at the end. Those who had worked the longest were paid at the end, giving them the likely impression that they would earn more based on their longer workday. However, at the end of the day they were paid the same wage as the other workers: "And when they had received it, they murmured against the goodman of the house" (Matthew 20:11), thinking that they should have been paid more.

The parable returns to the issue of the wage, teaching the disciples that the wage was the same for all men and women even though there was a difference in time spent working in the vineyard. This may suggest that there are many different jobs in the kingdom, some of which seem to garner greater prestige than others. Another interpretation might be that the essential thing is not at what point we commit but that the commitment is made. At the end of the day, the wage is the same.

The Feast of Dedication
JOHN 10:22–39

The author states, "And it was at Jerusalem the feast of the **dedication** [*Hanukkah*], and it was winter. And **Jesus** walked in the **temple** in Solomon's porch" (John 10:22–23).

Providing an accurate picture, John tells us that Jesus is in Jerusalem in December (the previous story was set in late September or early October, when the Feast of Tabernacles was held) and that it was now winter. Naturally, Jesus spent time in the eastern part of the temple complex

(Solomon's porch) where he could find protection from the winter weather. At 2,700 feet above sea level, Jerusalem is susceptible to wintertime strong winds, cold rain, and even occasional snowfall.

In this setting, Jewish leaders ask Jesus, "How long dost thou make us to doubt?" (10:24). In reality, the Greek idiom recorded here is difficult to translate. Certainly, the King James Version is an adequate translation, but others are also possible reflecting a range from suspense to a genuine desire to have Jesus tell them plainly (Greek, *parrēsia*) what he thinks about himself.

For the Jewish leaders, the question seems to revolve around whether or not Jesus claims to be the long expected **Messiah**—the true king of Israel. However, Jesus has something greater in mind; he is in reality the very **Son of God**. When he tells the Jewish leaders that he and the Father "are one" [Greek, *hen*], they react violently taking "up stones again to stone him" (10:31). This section prepares us for Jesus' interrogation before the high priest and the Sanhedrin in the **Synoptic** Passion Narratives.

Jesus responds, "Many good works [Greek, *erga*] have I shewed you from my Father; for which of those works do ye stone me?" (10:32). Here we are to assume that the "good works" are not limited to **miracles**. The Jewish leaders respond that they will not stone him for the works he has performed but for "blasphemy"—because he has made himself like God (10:33). This is the only place in John were such a charge is offered (Matthew 26:65; Mark 14:64). Actually, the Jewish leaders misunderstand Jesus because he does not say that he and the Father are one person, as the Greek *hen* (neuter, not masculine) reveals. What Jesus has in mind is that he and the Father are engaged in the same work, making it impossible to distinguish between Jesus' good works and God's good works. *Good* (Greek, *kalos*) reminds us that Jesus is the "Good Shepherd" who brings abundant life (10:1–10). All the issues debated earlier about his claims (John 2–10) are answered here (10:30, 38).

Because Jesus offers life as God gives life (5:21; 10:28) and judges as God judges (5:22; 9:39), he is, therefore, much more than the traditionally accepted Jewish Messiah—a mere mortal anointed by God's Spirit. The scripture citation from Palm 82:6 reveals that Jesus' claim is not of his own invention. The prime purpose of this section is to reveal Jesus' relationship with God, who Jesus is, and what authority he has received from the Father. Scholars have noted the various details found here and the parallels found in Jesus' prayer recorded in John 17. In the end, "they sought again to take him: but he escaped out of their hand" (10:39), emphasizing that his "hour" has not yet come.

John's Followers Believe
JOHN 10:40–42

Jesus retired again to Bethany (John 1:28; KJV, "Bethabara"), thus symbolizing an end to the public ministry in the same place where it had begun. Also pointing in this direction is the testimony given: "All things that John spake of this man were true. And many believed on him there" (John 10:41–42). Unlike in the **Synoptic** authors, the transition from following John the Baptist to believing in Jesus as the **Messiah** proceeds much more smoothly in the Gospel of John (see footnotes to Matthew 11:1–6).

Lazarus Dies
JOHN 11:1–7

John's intent with these verses seems to be twofold: first, that **Jesus** waited intentionally for Lazarus to die (John 11:6); and second, that he dearly loved Mary, Martha, and Lazarus (11:5). After waiting for Lazarus to die, Jesus tells his **disciples** that they are returning to **Judea** (11:7). From these few verses, it appears that Jesus was shaping this event for the training of the disciples, who interpreted going to Judea as a sure sign that they would die (11:16). Although Thomas was correct to think of a trip to Judea as a death sentence, the story of the raising of Lazarus also teaches that love will overcome the fear of death (1 John 4:18).

Lazarus Is Raised

JOHN 11:8–53

The raising of Lazarus is probably the one **miracle** in which **Jesus** healed a close personal friend (he also healed Peter's mother-in-law); therefore, the dynamics of this story differ from those in which there was a controversy over method and the law of Moses. The trip to Bethany begins with Thomas's expressed concern that traveling to **Judea** was a dangerous proposition. Perhaps the suggestion was that if Lazarus was only ill then such a trip was not necessary: "Then said his **disciples**, Lord, if he sleep, he shall do well" (11:12). Although no one in the account had informed Jesus that Lazarus had died, he was aware of that fact before they traveled there: "Then said Jesus unto them plainly, Lazarus is dead" (11:14). The story then shifts to becoming a teaching experience for the Twelve: "And I am glad for your sakes that I was not there, to the intent ye may believe" (11:15). When they arrive in Bethany, the group of those who will grow in faith is expanded to include Martha and Mary, who seemingly complain to Jesus about his tardiness in arriving to help. Speaking for both, Martha says, "If thou hadst been here, my brother had not died" (11:21; see also 11:32).

There appears to have been an assumption that raising someone from death after four days is too great a thing to ask from Jesus. Whether four days has any symbolic meaning is difficult to know, but it appears in the account as a practical concern: "Lord, by this time he stinketh: for he hath been dead four days" (11:39). Could Jesus really heal a person whose body had begun to decompose? This appears to be the focus of the miracle for those who knew Lazarus well. For the disciples, the focus appears to be whether they should travel to Jerusalem when their lives were in danger.

When Lazarus was brought back from the dead, the description of him shows that his body had already been prepared for burial, "bound hand and foot with graveclothes: and his face was bound about with a napkin. Jesus saith unto them, Loose him, and let him go" (11:44). That Jesus would say "let him go" highlights his power in contrast to death's inability to hold Lazarus back.

The raising of Lazarus touched off a conspiracy to kill Jesus because "If we let him thus alone, all men will believe on him: and the Romans shall come and take away both our place and nation" (11:48). Apparently the raising of Lazarus was so well advertised that many people came to believe on Jesus because of it. As a result, Caiaphas and others began to feel concern that such a large gathering of followers would attract the attention of **Rome**, which would in turn take away any degree of political autonomy they enjoyed. Caiaphas may have voiced a literal concern when he said, "Ye know nothing at all, nor consider that it is expedient for us, that one man should die for the people, and that the whole nation perish not" (11:49–50). Caiaphas invoked a principle quite similar to what Nephi concluded when killing Laban, although Caiaphas's may have been based on the faulty assumption that Jesus and his followers intended to rise against Rome. Hence his concern seems to have been self-preservation and not the faith of the people. The account of Caiaphas's private conversation, which John interpreted in a symbolic manner, most likely came to the author's attention via Nicodemus, the only named member of that council who had shown any positive interest in Jesus.

The raising of Lazarus also introduces another significant theme, namely Martha's testimony, which is similar in many respects to Peter's testimony at Caesarea Philippi. Here, Martha says, "Yea, Lord: I believe that thou art the **Christ**, the **Son of God**, which should come into the world" (11:27). In Matthew, it is Peter who represents the crowning testimony of Christ, but in John it is Martha who expresses the most profound testimony of the living Jesus. John, the author, also adds a powerful testimony after Jesus' Resurrection (John 20:31).

On Being Great

MATTHEW 20:20–28; MARK 10:35–45; LUKE 22:24–27

The three accounts of this story in the **Synoptic** Gospels seem to indicate differing levels of interest or perceptions of importance. Luke preserves only a highly condensed form of the story, while Matthew and Mark present it in some detail. Matthew relates that the mother of James and John asked **Jesus** to grant her two sons the privilege to "sit, the one on thy right hand, and the other on the left, in thy kingdom" (Matthew 20:21), whereas Mark relates that James and John had asked Jesus directly to do them a favor: "Master, we would that thou shouldest do for us whatsoever we shall desire" (Mark 10:35). The favor they asked is the same asked by their mother in Matthew 20:21. Perhaps the origin of this story has ties to Jesus granting John the Beloved the ability to live until the Savior's Second Coming, a fragmentary account of which is preserved in John 21:23: "Then went this saying abroad among the brethren, that that **disciple** should not die: yet Jesus said not unto him, He shall not die; but, If I will that he tarry till I come, what is that to thee?"

What follows in the account is a strong rebuke of James and John, revealing that the request almost certainly was made by them rather than by their mother. As part of that rebuke, Jesus also reveals details of his coming days that demonstrate his knowledge of the pain he would soon experience. The two disciples' acknowledgement that they could indeed suffer the things that Jesus would suffer resulted in disagreement among the disciples.

Luke chose to include only the final part of this exchange, detailing Jesus' teachings of how the chief among the disciples should be the servant of all. As elsewhere in Jesus' teachings, the least is extolled as the greatest. The interchange between Jesus and his disciples also presents an interesting teaching on Jesus' role in judgment: "To sit on my right hand, and on my left, *is not mine to give*, but it shall be given to them for whom it is prepared of my Father" (Matthew 20:23; emphasis added).

Two Blind Men Are Healed

MATTHEW 20:29–34; MARK 10:46–52; LUKE 18:35–43

See Matthew 9:27–31 for commentary.

Zacchaeus

LUKE 19:1–10

The Gospel of Luke contains a significant amount of unique material; this account is another in a long list of such distinctive stories. It provides another example where a non-prominent person is named in the narrative, suggesting that Zacchaeus may be the primary eyewitness source of the story itself. It contains one of the most vivid descriptions of an event in all the New Testament and supplies a counterbalance to the story of the young rich ruler in the previous chapter (18:15–30). In fact, that earlier account sets up the reader to expect a similar outcome. However, the exact opposite of what is expected happens in this story—another gospel reversal.

The focus of the narrative remains **Jesus**, who "entered and passed through Jericho" (19:1). However, Luke tells us about a man—a man named Zacchaeus, a chief **publican** (Greek, *architelōnēs*, the only extant use of this term in Greek literature), who is rich (19:2). Zacchaeus (Hebrew, *Zakkai*) is most likely the short form of Zachariah. Luke informs us that Zacchaeus is a descendant of Abraham (19:9), even though the crowd considered him a "sinner" (19:7).

Because he is short in stature, Zacchaeus runs to climb a tree (disregarding social convention, because rich men did not run or climb trees) so he can see Jesus as he passes by on his way to Jerusalem. Interestingly, the type of tree, sycamore (fig), is identified, suggesting an eyewitness recollection. When he looks up and sees Zacchaeus above him, Jesus breaks a rule of common etiquette by inviting himself to dinner at Zacchaeus's home (19:5). After the crowd complains, Zacchaeus stands and says, "Behold, Lord, the half of my goods I give to the poor; and if I have taken any thing from any man by false accusation, I restore him fourfold" (19:8). Commentators are divided on how to interpret this statement. Even though the Greek is generally understood to mean that Zacchaeus has decided at that moment that he will divide half his goods and restore what was not rightfully collected, it can be read to indicate that Zacchaeus has been doing this all along.

No matter how one understands Zacchaeus's declaration, Jesus informs him, "*This day* is salvation come to this house" (19:9; emphasis added). Luke's report here focuses on the present availability of salvation, though he uses the same expression in detailing a later event, when Jesus says to one of the men being crucified alongside him, indicating a *future* event, "*To day* shalt thou be with me in paradise" (23:43; emphasis added). However, the emphasis is the here and now in most cases in Luke. For example, "For unto to you is born *this day* in the city of David a Saviour" (2:11; emphasis added); "*This day* is this scripture fulfilled in your ears" (4:21; emphasis added). Notice also that Jesus says to Zacchaeus, "make haste, and come down; for *to day* I must abide at thy house" (19:5; emphasis added).

This is the second **miracle** to occur at or near Jericho. The first was the healing of the blind man (notice the emphasis on "seeing" in both accounts) just before this incident (18:35–43). The second miracle is that a rich man is declared saved, which is just as miraculous if not more so than the first, given what Jesus said earlier about the effect of riches (Luke 18:24).

The story ends with a summary of Jesus' mission: "For the **Son of man** is come to seek and to save that which was lost" (19:10). His **parables**, actions, and his death in Jerusalem emphasize this point.

That such a story was remembered is not hard to imagine since it would have had tremendous personal significance for Zacchaeus and was likely the most remarkable event in his life. As a participant, Zacchaeus, most likely told the story often, beginning immediately after he met Jesus in Jericho. It also highlights a frequent occurrence in the Gospels that Jesus was often an invited guest in private homes.

Jesus Travels to Ephraim

JOHN 11:54

Similar to Matthew and Mark's reference to **Jesus'** removal to Perea (Mark 10:1), John detailed a similar move to Ephraim. The ancient city of Ephraim appears to have been near Bethel (Josephus, *War* 4.551) and was in the Judean hill country. The modern village of Et-Taiyibeh should likely be identified as ancient Ephraim.

Jerusalem at Passover
JOHN 11:55–57; 12:1

In preparation for **Jesus'** final **Passover** pilgrimage to Jerusalem, John announces on a menacing note and with three legal terms, "Now both the chief **priests** and the **Pharisees** had given a *commandment* [give orders], that, if any man knew where he were, he should *shew it* [report], that they might *take* [arrest] him" (John 11:57; emphasis added). Chapter 12 follows the trajectory when it continues, "Then Jesus six days before the passover came to Bethany," just a few miles from Jerusalem (12:1). This is the beginning of the end of the accounts (John 3:16), linking the decision to kill Jesus (11:53) with the upcoming feast of the Passover where Jesus, as the Lamb of God (John 1:29, 36), will suffer and die. The narrative is full of irony and paradox. John has carefully prepared the reader for this moment, when Jesus' hour has come (John 2:4). Of course, the Passover, when the Pascal lambs were ritually slaughtered for **temple sacrifice**, provided the perfect symbolic backdrop for these events. Even though Jewish leaders had attempted to kill him before, Jesus chose the time and place to lay down his life (John 10:17–18).

Conspiracy to Kill Lazarus
JOHN 12:9–11

John concludes three events he has just narrated—the raising of Lazarus (John 11:1–44); the plot to kill **Jesus** (11:45–54); and Jesus' anointing at Bethany (11:55–12:9)—in three short verses. The main device John uses here is linking the raising of Lazarus and the decision to kill Lazarus.

As noted earlier, the Jewish leadership in **Judea** is afraid that Jesus' increasingly popular ministry (both in **Galilee** and **Judea**) will draw "all men" to him (11:48). They seem to envision uncontrollable large crowds in the Holy City at the upcoming **Passover** (a kind of "Independence Day" celebration), heightened **Messianic** expectations with political overtones, and Jesus' continuing challenge to their leaders, which might produce a situation that could lead to further Roman intervention—replacing them as guardians of Second **Temple** Judaism, destroying Jerusalem (some commentators interpret "this place" as the temple), and "taking away [our] nation."

John informs us that their worst fears are coming true: "By reason of [Lazarus] many of the Jews went away [from them], and believed on Jesus" (12:11). Killing the living witness of Jesus' last **miracle** [sign] in his public ministry seems to be another desperate solution to their problem.

Prophetic Preparation for the Triumphal Entry
MATTHEW 21:1–6; MARK 11:1–6; LUKE 19:28–34

The **Synoptic** Gospels report this story in nearly verbatim fashion and may have intentionally drawn a parallel to the temptation stories where the Spirit led **Jesus**. In these accounts, the Spirit again goes before Jesus to prepare the way of his atoning **sacrifice**. The triumphal entry entailed riding a donkey from Bethany to the east through the Kidron Valley to the west and on to the Temple Mount. Jesus instructed his **disciples** to seek out an animal, the owner of which having been prepared to relinquish it. The account includes one mix-up of the biblical text that implies two animals: "And straightway ye shall find an ass tied, and a colt with her: loose them" (Matthew 21:2), whereas Mark and Luke mention only a single animal. A later **scribe** seems to have misread **Septuagint (LXX)** Zechariah 9:9 as implying the presence of two donkeys. The Joseph Smith Translation corrects Matthew's account so that there is reference to only one donkey. It is important to note that Jesus directed his disciples' actions, thus initiating the prophetic fulfillment of Zechariah 9:9.

The Triumphal Entry

MATTHEW 21:7–11; MARK 11:7–11; LUKE 19:35–40;
JOHN 12:12–18

When the **disciples** returned with the donkey, Matthew records, "and they set him thereon" (Matthew 21:7) while Mark notes, "and he sat upon him" (Mark 11:7). Mark is probably correct that **Jesus** mounted the donkey as an act that worked towards the fulfillment of prophecy (see "Prophetic Preparation to the Triumphal Entry," above). The Joseph Smith Translation harmonizes Matthew to the other accounts.

Once Jesus was within sight of the city, a crowd began laying their clothing on the ground in front of Jesus and literally strewing the way with palm fronds. Their actions indicate their anticipation that Jesus would be proclaimed **Messiah** upon his entry into the city. Moreover, such tributes and ceremony were reserved for the enthronement of a king or the triumphal entry of **Caesar** or a conquering general, although they would have ridden a horse. When the crowd began singing Psalm 118:26 (Matthew 21:9), it demonstrated their faith in Jesus as their Deliverer and Savior. The psalm itself was sung at **Passover** and celebrated the deliverance of Israel. This psalm of thanksgiving had a cultic or liturgical setting and continues on to describe a **sacrifice** of thanksgiving, thus providing a fitting metaphor for Jesus' entry into the city to offer sacrifice.

There is some discrepancy in what the crowds sing and what the multitude declares. Jesus is proclaimed by some as the "**Son of David**" (Matthew 21:9), but the multitude wonders whether he is the "prophet of Nazareth in **Galilee**" (Matthew 21:11). Perhaps the evangelists frame the story in this way to prepare the reader to see why Jesus was not proclaimed as **Messiah** and why the jubilant crowds did not continue to press for a public declaration of Jesus as the Messiah. Mark may have signaled a similar sentiment when he concludes the account by saying, "and now the eventide was come, he went out unto Bethany with the twelve" (Mark 11:11). In other words, the crowds dispersed and left Jesus alone with the Twelve rather than a multitude of believers.

Pharisees Disapprove

LUKE 19:39–40; JOHN 12:19

John summarizes the material found in John 11–12 when the **Pharisees** conclude that they are powerless to stop the crowds from following **Jesus**, "behold, the world [Greek, *kosmos*] is gone after him" (John 12:19). Luke informs us that the Pharisees even complain directly to Jesus about his popularity, demanding that he silence the enthusiastic crowds that have greeted him at Jerusalem (Luke 19:39). Jesus responds, "I tell you that, if these should hold their peace, the stones would immediately cry out" (19:40).

Jesus Weeps over Jerusalem

LUKE 19:41–44

Luke has already reported **Jesus**' earlier lament: "O Jerusalem, Jerusalem, which killest the prophets . . . how often would I have gathered thy children together . . . Behold, your house is left unto you desolate" (Luke 13:34–35). Earlier, Jeremiah, in another setting, also lamented that Jerusalem would not listen to the Lord (Jeremiah 11–20) before its destruction by the Babylonians. Here, Jesus again reflects on Jerusalem's fate. False militant **Messianic** expectations, Herodian political intrigue seeking to restore Herod the Great's kingdom, increasing violent resistance to Roman authority, and other dangerous activities are spreading among the people. Jesus' counter-vision of the kingdom of God offers the Jews the only viable solution to their increasingly precarious situation. However, rejection and misunderstanding of Jesus' offer, "the things which belong unto thy peace!" (Luke 19:42), will certainly result in only one frightful conclusion—the destruction of Jerusalem and its **temple**.

Jesus' prophecies found here (19:43–44) are fulfilled in every detail as outlined in Josephus' vivid portrayal of the Jewish War (A.D. 66–70), especially the Roman siege of Jerusalem by Titus. His account is a shocking and horrifying reminder of how war affects a population. Continuing on this theme, Jesus will later tell the daughters of Jerusalem not to weep for him, but for themselves and their families (23:28–31).

Greeks Wish to See Jesus

JOHN 12:20–22

Commentators are divided on the significance of these verses: "And there were certain Greeks among them that came up to worship at the feast: the same came therefore to Philip, which was of Bethsaida of **Galilee**, and desired him, saying, Sir, we would see **Jesus**. Philip cometh and telleth Andrew: and again Andrew and Philip tell Jesus" (John 12:20–22).

These Greeks (Greek, *hellēnes*) are not the Greek-speaking Jews (Greek, *Hellēnistai*) mentioned as "Grecians" in the King James Version (Acts 6:1; 9:29; 11:20). The presence of non-Jews, even if they are **proselytes** or God-fearers, further emphasizes, "the world [Greek, *kosmos*] has gone after him" (John 12:19). Although we cannot be certain of exactly who these Greeks are, it should not be forgotten that Herod's **temple** complex, the largest platform in antiquity, was not only a Jewish religious sanctuary but also an international destination. People from around the known world came to visit (as tourists), pray, worship, and offer **sacrifices** at Jerusalem (even as non-Jews). In a polytheistic world, many people had no problem worshipping at the national shrines of another people. Interestingly, John does not tell us whether or not Jesus met with them. However, they may have been present when Jesus said that he would draw "all men" unto him (12:32).

Of note is the prominent place Philip and Andrew (both with Greek names) have in this little section. Andrew was among the first to "come and see" (John 1:39), and Philip invited Nathanael to "come and see" (1:46). That the **Gentiles** "would see Jesus" may connect the stories (12:21). Others speculate that Andrew and Philip appear here because of their role in the later Gentile mission (Acts 8:5, 26). Nevertheless, their appearance at the end of the story recalls their presence at the beginning of the story as not only early **disciples** but also as faithful and longsuffering disciples of Jesus.

It may also be that the visit of these Greeks necessitated a translation of Jesus' words (Mark 7:26). If so, these events may represent an account of the origins of the Greek-speaking mission and gospel tradition.

Jesus Is Sent by the Father
JOHN 12:23–50

John continues his account after the Greeks arrive on the scene (John 12:20–22). However, it is a rather odd transition because **Jesus** does nothing about their request to meet him. Instead, he immediately launches into a long discourse about a variety of subjects, including a seed, death, the hour, servant, and being sent by the Father.

It has been observed that Jesus' declaration, "The hour is come, that the **Son of man** should be glorified" (12:23) brings us to the moment the gospel has anticipated. Earlier, we learn that Jesus' "hour is not yet come" (John 2:4) and "his hour was not yet come" (7:30). Finally, "the hour is come." Jesus follows this announcement by providing several teachings that directly relate to his suffering and death. He says that a seed must die if it is to yield fruit thereafter. Additionally, Jesus informs those listening, "He that loveth his life shall lose it; and he that hateth his life in this world shall keep it unto life eternal" (12:25). It has been observed that this statement is one of the best-documented sayings of Jesus (Matthew 10:39; 16:25; Mark 8:35–36; Luke 9:24; 17:33).

Another focus in this section is a rather direct statement: "And I, if I be lifted up from the earth, will draw all men unto me. This he said, signifying what death he should die" (John 12:32–33). In this saying, Jesus reveals more fully how God will accomplish his will—how he will save his creation.

John also reveals that we should never picture the Jewish leadership in **Judea** as a monolithic block: "Nevertheless among the chief rulers also many believed on him" (12:42; compare Acts 6:7). Finally, **Jesus** talks about being sent of the Father: "Jesus cried and said, He that believeth on me, believeth not on me, but on him that sent me" (12:44).

Since chapter 12 is the conclusion to Jesus' public ministry it contains the transition between the first part of the book (1:19–12:50) and the last part of the book (13:1–20:31). Known today by commentators as the "Book of Signs," this first part of the Gospel of John highlights Jesus' remarkable deeds, identified as "signs" (often translated in the KJV as "**miracles**"; see 2:11; 4:54; 6:2,14; 12:18, for example).

Some scholars argue that the statement "And *many other signs* truly did Jesus in the presence of his **disciples**, *which were not written in this book*" (20:30; emphasis added) actually was the concluding statement in chapter 20. Because the word *signs* occurs sixteen times in the first part of the Gospel of John and is not used again (except in 20:30), this might be a reasonable supposition.

Jesus Cleanses the Temple
MATTHEW 21:12–16; MARK 11:15–19; LUKE 19:45–48

See John 2:13–25.

Jesus Curses the Barren Fig Tree
MATTHEW 21:17–22; MARK 11:12–14, 20–26; LUKE 13:6–9

The cursing of the fig tree took place on the day after the triumphal entry (Mark 11:12) as **Jesus** reentered the city to teach. When he found no fruit on the tree, he cursed it and caused it to whither. Given the context of the saying—**Passover**—one would not expect to find ripe figs but only a budding or recently budded tree. Mark notes, "for the time of figs was not yet" (Mark 11:13), or more literally, "for it was not the right time for figs." This recognition sets up a symbolic interpretation of the event with the realization that it was also not the right time for several events: the proclamation of Jesus as the **Messiah**, the acceptance of Jesus into the city by the Jewish leaders, and the glorification of the Son through his Resurrection.

Luke provides a parable rather than a narrative description of these events, and his account may reflect an earlier teaching on the same subject. In that parable, the owner of the fig tree is permitted to keep the tree as long as it is nourished and fertilized. This foreshadowing may indicate what would have happened if it had been the "right time."

Mark relates that the **miracle** occurred over two days, so that the **disciples** passed by the next day and remembered that Jesus had cursed it. Matthew, on the other hand, reported that the fig tree was cursed and withered on the same day (Matthew 21:12–20). It is likely that Matthew condensed his record in order to move on to other matters.

Priests Challenge Jesus

MARK 11:27–33; LUKE 20:1–8

In a series of events, including the triumphal entry into Jerusalem and the cleansing of the **temple, Jesus** directly challenges the authority of the Jewish leadership in Jerusalem. Mark tells us that in response, the chief **priests, scribes,** and elders demand that Jesus answer two questions: "By what authority doest thou these things? and who gave thee this authority to do these things?" (Mark 11:28). In an honor/shame society such as that of first-century Judaism, this is a significant challenge.

Obviously, Mark believes that his readers will understand the irony of the moment as they remember that Jesus "taught them as one that had authority, and not as the scribes" and that "with authority commandeth he even the unclean spirits, and they do obey him" (Mark 1:22, 27). Further, they will recall the storm on the lake in **Galilee:** "What manner of man is this, that even the wind and the sea obey him?" (Mark 4:41).

Additionally, this section contrasts Jesus' (and John's) authority with these groups. The priests' authority is based on hereditary descent. The scribes' authority is based on education and training. The authority of the elders is based on social and economic considerations. Jesus, on the other hand, does not claim any authority based on their claims, at least implicitly (he is a descendant of David), but says that his authority comes from heaven, that is, from his Father. The section ends, affirming this authority when he refuses to respond to their questions (11:33).

In the center of the confrontation, Jesus responds to them in an ingenious way (pitting his wisdom—derived from God—against their human wisdom), promising that if they will answer, he will answer their questions: "The **baptism** of John, was it from heaven, or of men?" (11:30). As they reasoned among themselves, they realized that any answer they might give would be problematic. For example, if they acknowledged that John was a prophet, Jesus would ask them why they did not believe him. If they said he was not a prophet, the people (who accepted John) would have been angry with them. Herod Antipas was concerned also about John's influence with the people, so this paints a realistic dilemma. When they found themselves between the proverbial rock and a hard spot, they answered, "We cannot tell" (11:33). The Jewish leaders are silenced; they are shamed by Jesus.

Luke follows Mark, but he also introduces new material. For example, he provides the setting of the story: "And it came to pass, that on one of those days, as he taught the people in the temple, and preached the gospel, the chief priests and the scribes came upon him with the elders" (Luke 20:1). In this way, Luke stresses that the Jewish leadership was not only concerned about Jesus' entry into Jerusalem and the cleansing of the temple but also questioned his authority to teach. Therefore, they question Jesus' entire ministry. Luke also adds explicitly what Mark only implicitly acknowledges about the leaders' concern over what the people think: "But and if we say, Of men; all the people will stone us: for they be persuaded that John was a prophet" (Luke 20:6). The threat of violence is real. Later, during the Jewish War (A.D. 66–70), many Jewish leaders, especially the chief priests, were murdered by their own people as power struggles ensued in Jerusalem over control of the city and the Temple Mount.

Prophecy of Death and Resurrection
Matthew 20:17–19; Mark 10:32–34; Luke 18:31–34

A third prophecy recorded in Mark, followed by both Matthew and Luke with variations, is made as **Jesus** and his **disciples** begin their journey for the final **Passover** feast together in the Holy City. In a most dramatic way Mark reports Jesus' action as he moves toward Jerusalem, where Jesus says that he will die: "And they were in the way going up to Jerusalem; and Jesus went before them: and they were amazed; and as they followed, they were afraid" (Mark 10:32).

Jesus specifically tells the disciples, in this third Passion prophecy, that the **Gentiles** will kill him (Mark 10:34). Matthew, Mark, and Luke know and affirm that it was the Romans who crucified Jesus. Since our sources are fragmentary, we cannot be certain, but it appears that Herod Antipas could execute an individual by beheading, as was the case with John the Baptist; the chief **priests** could execute an individual by stoning, as was the case with Stephen; but only the Romans could execute an individual by crucifixion. If this was the political reality at the time, Jesus implies here that he will be crucified.

The prophecy continues as it turns to Christ's Resurrection. Mark says that Jesus will rise after three days. However, Matthew and Luke are more precise, indicating that he will rise on the third day, thus reflecting more accurately the roughly two days and two nights spent in the tomb. Both Mark and Luke say he will rise again, while Matthew provides the more doctrinally·correct "he shall be raised" (Matthew 17:23; the King James Version is not as clear as the Greek text), indicating that it was God who raised Jesus (Acts 2:24; Galatians 1:1).

The Parable of the Two Sons
MATTHEW 21:28–32

Here we have a uniquely Matthean addition to the accounts of the parable of the two sons, or the parable of two imperfect children (Matthew 21:28–32). This parable is the first of three that deal with the Jewish leaders' failure to **repent** and believe (21:28–32, 33–44; 22:1–14). **Jesus** has just silenced the Jewish leaders (21:23–27) and begins, "But what think ye?" drawing them out so they must be prepared to respond. Jesus continued, "A certain man had two sons [Greek, *tekna*]; and he came to the first, and said, Son, go work to day in my vineyard. He answered and said, I will not:

but afterward he repented, and went" (21:28–29). Everyone listening would have recognized that the vineyard is Israel. In context, the man making the request represents John the Baptist, although others have seen him as representing God. Jesus continued, "And he came to the second, and said likewise. And he answered and said, I go, sir; and went not" (21:30).

Jesus traps the Jewish leaders when he asks them, "Whether of them twain did the will of his father?" When they naturally respond, "The first" (21:31), Jesus immediately applies the parable to the current situation: "Verily I say unto you, That the **publicans** and harlots go into the kingdom of God before you" (21:31). Jesus compares the publicans and harlots to the first son—initially rejecting God's call to work in the vineyard when John asked Israel to repent, but having come to themselves, repenting. The second son, the one who said deceitfully that he would work in the vineyard but did not, represents the Jewish leaders who listened to John the Baptist, but "repented not" (21:32). The contrast between the first son who "changed his mind" (repented) and the second son who would not change his mind (repent) is obvious.

The Parable of the Wicked Husbandmen
Matthew 21:33–46; Mark 12:1–12; Luke 20:9–20

In the second of three **parables** directed to the Jewish leadership in Jerusalem, **Jesus** talks about a man who planted a vineyard, dug a winepress (KJV, "winefat"), and built a [watch] tower (Mark 12:1). Such agricultural pursuits were ubiquitous in the Holy Land. The man then "let it out to husbandmen, and went into a far country" (12:1). The economic realities of the first century, where absentee landlords allowed tenant farmers to work their land, makes this story relevant to those listening to Jesus at the time. At the harvest, the man sent a slave to receive the owner's contracted share of the crops, but the husbandmen "caught him, and beat him, and sent him away empty" (12:3). The man sent another slave who received the same treatment. When the man sent an additional slave, the husbandmen "killed" him (12:5). Finally, the landlord sent his "well beloved" son whom he hopes "they will reverence" (12:6). Instead, the husbandmen, who may have assumed the owner was dead and that the son wanted his inheritance, not just his share of the harvest, said, "This is the heir; come, let us kill him, and the inheritance shall be ours" (12:7). One of the shocking details in the parable is that the husbandmen shame the son by throwing his body outside the vineyard for carrion birds and wild dogs to feed on. Jesus then asks, "What shall therefore the lord of the vineyard do?" Answering his own question, he responds, "he will come and destroy the husbandmen, and will give the vineyard unto others" (12:9).

The parable is full of allusions, including a possible reference to Isaiah 5, where Israel is God's vineyard, prophets are portrayed as the "slaves [servants] of the Lord" (Jeremiah 7:25, 25:4; Amos 3:7), and the winepress and tower are associated with the **temple** and the altar of **sacrifice**.

The point of the parable was not difficult to discern. First, and most important, Jesus knew that his mission would end, as it had for a number of Old Testament prophets, as well as John the Baptist, with rejection and death. Second, the husbandmen not only have failed to manage the vineyard properly, beaten and stoned the owner's representatives, and killed his son—the heir—but have also fraudulently claimed that they are the rightful owners of the vineyard. Third, when the husbandmen rejected the son, they actually rejected the father. According to Mark, the Jewish leaders understood it and "sought to lay hold" on [and kill?] Jesus (Mark 12:12). Because they feared that arresting Jesus on the spot might incite a riot at the feast, they decided to leave Jesus alone. What did others, including the **disciples**, think of the parable? Most likely, they pictured God as tirelessly, and not without cost, seeking to save his rebellious people—continuing to send prophets, and ultimately his son, to save them before it is too late.

In comparing Matthew's and Luke's accounts with Mark's, it becomes clear that the main points, including sequence and structure, are consistent in the various accounts. However, many of the nonessential details reflect an oral tradition that allowed some variation. For example, Matthew identifies the man as the landowner. In Mark, the man wants only his share of the fruit, but in Matthew the owner wants all the fruit. Nevertheless, it seems clear that the climax of the parable remains the sending of the son by the father. In some places Mark most likely presents the earliest form of the story—going directly back to Jesus. In one such example, Matthew and Luke record that the husbandmen first cast the son out of the vineyard before killing him, reversing Mark's order. This most certainly reflects a post-Passion arrangement since Jesus was killed outside the city walls.

Jesus continues by citing the book of Psalms (Psalm 118:22–23) about the builders (the **scribes** were known as "**Torah** Builders" in the first century) who rejected a stone (Hebrew, *'eben*), most likely a play on words because the Hebrew for "son" is *ben*. The stone, however, became the keystone (KJV, "head of the corner") as the Greek (*kephalēn gōnias*) implies, not the cornerstone.

The Parable of the King's Son
MATTHEW 22:1–14; LUKE 14:15–24

Both Matthew and Luke record another parable of **Jesus**, the parable of the king's son or the parable of the wedding banquet. The relationship between Matthew and Luke is debated because the language varies so much. It might be important to consider that Jesus may have given several **parables** on this theme at different times, which may explain the differences between Matthew and Luke. Given his many different audiences, it would seem strange if Jesus taught any given parable only once during his ministry. In Matthew, this parable is the last of three parables directed toward the Jewish leadership in Jerusalem. Matthew provides a brief introduction before relating the parable itself. He then preserves Jesus' commentary or explanation of the parable.

It should be remembered that in an honor/shame society such as first-century Judaism, certain obligations were considered paramount. Attending a wedding banquet was one of those social obligations. Adding to this, Jesus says it was a king who invited people to attend, making the social obligation even stronger. What is clear from this parable is that those invited guests (chief **priests**, **scribes**, and elders) refused to attend and that those not originally invited (**publicans** and sinners) do attend. This is another example of gospel reversal, where those attending the banquet are the most unlikely guests. However, the parable provides a twist to the story: "And when the king came in to see the guests, he saw there a man which had not on a wedding garment: and he saith unto him, Friend, how camest thou in hither not having a wedding garment? And he was speechless. Then said the king to the servants, Bind him hand and foot, and take him away, and cast him into outer darkness; there shall be weeping and gnashing of teeth" (Matthew 22:11–13). As several commentators have noted, the invitation to attend is open to all, but that does not mean there are no requirements for the guests who choose to attend.

On Paying Tribute to Caesar
MATTHEW 22:15–22; MARK 12:13–17; LUKE 20:21–26

The entanglement envisioned in this account is tied to the assumption, "we know that thou art true, and carest for no man" (Mark 12:14). Matthew and Mark use the Greek *melei*, "care for," to translate **Jesus'** words, whereas Luke translates the phrase using Greek *lambaneis prosōpon*, or "to show favoritism" toward something. At the heart of their question seems to be a desire to flatter Jesus by saying that he does not respect persons and therefore should be able to settle the age-old dispute concerning the validity of what are always interpreted as onerous taxation policies. Jesus certainly cared for people, but they attempted to draw him in by suggesting that he would not shrink from commenting on Roman taxation policies.

The coin in question was a silver Greek denarius. Jesus drew attention to the image on the denarius, which would have borne the image of Augustus or Tiberius, and recommended that they give **Caesar** his due and to God what is his. In effect, Jesus did not answer their question about the fairness of taxation but rather enjoined them to show deference where it is due. The question was designed to create dissension among Jesus' followers by getting him to either speak against taxation, a position highly popular but full of anti-Roman rhetoric, or on behalf of the practice, which would have been very unpopular with the masses. He did neither but simply answered the question of what to do when a person finds a coin belonging to Caesar. It is doubtful that there would have been any legal ramifications of speaking either for or against taxation, but the popular appeal of condemning taxation, which included Roman, Herodian (land and tolls), and Jewish (the **temple** tax), would have been enormous.

Seven Husbands

MATTHEW 22:23–33; MARK 12:18–27; LUKE 20:27–38

This question probably made little sense outside of **Judea** and **Galilee**, where a unique interpretation of Old Testament marriage law was in question, and it was probably asked by **Sadducees** to discredit those who believed in the resurrection. **Jesus** was almost certainly not the first to respond to this question.

The debate hinges on a unique view of the levirate law (Deuteronomy 25:5–10) where the brother-in-law was required to marry his deceased brother's spouse and raise children in his brother's name. The Sadducees contrived a scenario where a woman was forced to marry seven brothers in turn, having no children with any of them. This impossibly complex scenario is then implied as a way of discrediting the resurrection because no one, not even God, would be able to say whose spouse the woman should be in the hereafter. There are certainly a number of fallacious assumptions that Jesus' could have responded to, but instead he answered, "For when they shall rise from the dead, they neither marry, nor are given in marriage; but are as the angels which are in heaven" (Mark 12:25).

Such an elusive answer does little to explain how Jesus would teach the doctrine of eternal marriage. The saying was delivered in the context of a controversy, and it must be noted that **Jesus'** answer may reflect the context of controversy. In other words, when he spoke of marriage in that context, his answer may have had relevance only for those who were asking. Jesus went on to refute the idea that there would be no resurrection with a rather technical argument. He taught them that God declared his own name by using the names of three deceased individuals. Jesus then said that God was a living God, or is the true and living God, implying that Abraham, Isaac, and Jacob, those who were deceased, were by implication living: "God spake unto him [Moses], saying, I am the God of Abraham, and the God of Isaac, and the God of Jacob? He is not the God of the dead, but the God of the living: ye therefore do greatly err" (Mark 12:26–27; see also 1 Thessalonians 1:9).

The Great Commandment
MATTHEW 22:34–40; MARK 12:28–34; LUKE 10:25–37

The Ten Commandments were seen by religious Jews as an appropriate summary of the **Torah**. In this episode, one of the **scribes** asks **Jesus**, "Which is the first commandment of all?" (Mark 12:28). It is important to note that this teacher of the law was impressed with Jesus; instead of asking a question to trap him, this man was sincere, as his follow-up statements reveal. In response to the question, Jesus quotes the quintessential Jewish prayer—the *Shema* ("Hear, O Israel; The Lord our God is one lord: and thou shalt love the Lord thy God with all thy heart, and with all thy soul, and with all thy mind, and with all thy strength") found in the Torah (Deuteronomy 6:4–6). Jesus declares that this contains the "first commandment" then adds, "And the second is like unto it, namely this, Thou shalt love thy neighbour as thyself," also quoted from the Torah (Leviticus 19:18). He continues, "There is none other commandment greater than these" (Mark 12:31). The scribe responds, "Well, Master, thou hast said the truth" (12:32). The questioner goes further by observing that these two commandments are "more than all whole burnt offerings and **sacrifices**" (12:33), reminding us of earlier prophetic warnings about focusing on rituals without worrying about sin (see, for example, Psalm 51:16–17; Isaiah 1:10–17). Jesus approves of his assessment and insight: "And when Jesus saw that he answered discreetly [wisely], he said unto him, Thou art not far from the kingdom" (12:34). Mark states, "And no man after that durst ask him any question" (12:34), signaling the end of debates between Jesus and his enemies.

194

Two Pharisees Are Silenced
Matthew 22:41–46; Mark 12:35–37; Luke 20:41–44

In a remarkable passage demonstrating **Jesus'** unique ability to interpret the scriptures, he asks why the teachers of the **Law** say that the **Messiah** is the **Son of David** (Mark 12:35). He then quotes a passage from the book of Psalms: "The Lord said unto my Lord, Sit thou at my right hand, until I make thine enemies thy footstool" (Psalm 110:1). This passage from Psalms was important in early Christianity (1 Corinthians 15:25–27; Ephesians 1:20–23; 1 Peter 3:21–22). Jesus indicates that Jewish expectation that the Messiah would simply be a descendant of David was fundamentally flawed. Although Jesus was born of the seed of David (Romans 1:3), he nevertheless is David's Lord, since David calls him "My Lord." Mark concludes, "And the common people heard him gladly" (Mark 12:37); in other words, "the large crowd listened to him with delight" (NIV, Mark 12:37).

The Widow's Mite
Mark 12:41–44; Luke 21:1–4

Jesus' teaching in the **temple** ends with a final incident in the Court of the Women, where thirteen trumpet-shaped chests, or receptacles, were located to facilitate the collecting of the temple tax and other free-will offerings (KJV, "treasury"). Mark notes, "And Jesus sat over against the treasury, and beheld how the people cast money into the treasury: and many that were rich cast in much. And there came a certain poor widow, and she threw in two mites, which make a farthing" (12:41–42). Jesus gathered his **disciples** to reflect upon what he had seen: "Verily I say unto you, That this poor widow hath cast more in, than all they which have cast into the treasury: for all they did cast in of their abundance; but she of her want did cast in all that she had, even all her living" (12:43–44). Many New Testament scholars assume that Jesus implied that she gave her living for that day—not her life.

This is not the first time we have encountered a widow in Luke's

195

Gospel (2:36–38; 4:25–26; 7:11–17; 18:1–8; and 20:47). Jesus was obviously concerned about them, and Luke was intrigued by Jesus' attention to this most vulnerable member of ancient society.

The significance of the story about two copper coins (Greek, *lepta*), the smallest coins in circulation at the time, is difficult to discern. Some have estimated that it would take at least 128 leptons to make a denarius (a Roman silver coin)—what some have suggested was a typical daily wage for a common laborer, or perhaps even less. Since this is all she had that day, the woman's poverty is further emphasized. The identification of the woman as a widow connects the story with Jesus' condemnation of the teachers of the law (**scribes**) who "devour widows' houses" (Mark 12:40). Interpretation has ranged from condemning a system that would take the last coins from a poor widow to highlighting the personal piety of an exemplary woman who is willing to give her all to God. This range of possibilities not only challenges our ability to understand exactly what Jesus meant but also how the disciples (and those who first heard it retold or read to them) understood the incident.

A Denunciation of Hypocrisy
Matthew 23:1–36; Mark 12:38–40; Luke 11:37–54; 18:9–14; 20:45–47

Matthew and Luke expand greatly on Mark's account of **Jesus'** criticism of some of the religious opinion makers of the day: "Beware of the **scribes**, which love to go in long clothing, and love salutations in the marketplaces, and the chief seats in the **synagogues**, and the uppermost rooms at feasts: which devour widows' houses, and for a pretence make long prayers: these shall receive greater damnation" (Mark 12:38–40). In Matthew, Jesus' condemnation, which includes certain **Pharisees**, is three-pronged. First, "they say, and do not" (Matthew 23:3). Second, "they bind heavy burdens" (23:4). Finally, "But all their works they do for to be seen of men" (23:5). Matthew follows with the famous "woe" passages (23:13–33). Many scholars believe that these woes were addressed to those not present—a literary form

196

identified as an apostrophe. Jesus' words are rooted in the Old Testament where the woe formula is also utilized (Isaiah 45:9–10; Jeremiah 13:27; 48:46; Ezekiel 16:23).

The significance of Matthew's use of the word *hypocrites* (Matthew 23:13) is often interpreted in light of what the Greek word (*hypokritēs*) means, "the act of playing a part on a stage." This is generally associated with wearing a theater mask. Since Jesus most likely spoke these sayings in **Aramaic**, an analysis of the Greek may not be as helpful as one might hope. Matthew certainly attempted to capture the nuance of Jesus' original Aramaic word, providing his Greek-speaking readers a translation that would give them understanding of what Jesus said in the original context. Hypocrisy does, at its root, reveal a concern about what others think instead of what God thinks of the individual—a form of idolatry.

Primarily, Jesus argues that these hypocrites "shut up the kingdom of heaven" against themselves and others—an even greater sin (Matthew 23:13). The remaining woes center around various features of first-century worship, and in most cases Jesus does not necessarily condemn the specific practice but rather the exaggerated practice or the practice of certain traditions and commandments in lieu of living the more important purposes of the law. For example, Jesus speaks about the use of phylacteries, placing fringes on clothing, the payment of tithes and offerings, straining out bugs from drinking water, cleaning cups before drinking, and erecting monuments to the prophets. In and of themselves, there is nothing wrong with these behaviors—in fact, Jesus likely wore phylacteries and placed fringes on his own clothing (Mark 6:56). However, Jesus is interested in "the weightier matters of the law," which bring about true **repentance**, true worship, and true trust in God.

Jesus Laments over Jerusalem
MATTHEW 23:37–39; LUKE 13:34–35

Matthew and Luke preserve **Jesus'** lamentation over the Holy City: "O Jerusalem, Jerusalem, thou that killest the prophets, and stonest them which are sent unto thee" (Matthew 23:37). Luke places this lamentation much earlier in the account than Matthew, who has placed it here during the last visit to the city itself. Jesus will return only when he is arrested, tried, and executed. Jesus recognizes that the political, economic, and religious agendas of leaders of the day were leading Israel on a collision course with **Rome** because the Jewish leaders had rejected both the Messenger and the message: "Behold, your house is left unto you desolate" (23:38). In August A.D. 70, Jesus' prophecy was fulfilled when Titus destroyed the **temple** in Jerusalem.

Signs of the Second Coming
MATTHEW 24:1–51; MARK 13:1–37; LUKE 12:35–48; 17:20–37; 21:5–38

The Olivet Discourse, delivered in the final week of **Jesus'** life, so named because it was given on the Mount of Olives, is the only sermon devoted exclusively to discussing events that would shortly befall the **disciples** as well as events that would not be fulfilled for quite some time. The original discourse appears to have arisen over a question about the **temple**, particularly its magnificence, with the implied understanding that the temple's grandeur was in stark contrast to the wickedness of its leaders (Mark 13:1).

The discourse can be divided into four distinct sections: events related to the **apostles'** day (Mark 13:1–13); events associated with the abomination of desolation in the **last days** (13:14–23); signs of the Second Coming (13:24–31); and a parable encouraging obedience in spite of what appears to be a delay in the Lord's return (13:32–37). Matthew and Luke follow closely the order in which Mark preserves the discourse with some minor variations. Joseph Smith–Matthew in the Pearl of Great Price preserves the Joseph Smith Translation of Matthew 23:39–24:1–51, although the Joseph Smith–Matthew changes are not noted in their entirety in the footnotes or at the back of the Latter-day Saint edition of the Bible.

The discourse reveals the fulfillment of the prophecies of Daniel. The following parallel themes can be found in the discourse: the destruction of the temple (Daniel 9:26), rumors of war (Daniel 9:26; 11:44), persecution that would follow God's people (Daniel 7:25; 11:33; 12:1), the abomination of desolation (Daniel 8:13; 9:27; 11:31; 12:11), and the coming of the **Son of man** (Daniel 7:13). These themes reveal that the book of Daniel was on Jesus' mind while he delivered this discourse, but the Olivet Discourse is more than a running commentary on Daniel. The Joseph Smith Translation adds a second reference to the abomination of desolation that will occur in the last days (JST, Matthew 1:32).

The discourse is filled with both predictive and descriptive signs, or in other words, signs that help followers *predict* the timing of the return of the Lord and signs that *describe* conditions generally but are not intended to describe the precise timing of that event. For example, some of the predictive signs are the abomination of desolation (Mark 13:14), seeing the Son of man coming in the clouds (Mark 13:26), and the sign of the Son of man that will appear in the heavens (Joseph Smith–Matthew 1:36). The descriptive signs are, for example, rumors of war (Mark 13:7), the gospel being preached among all nations (Mark 13:10), suffering affliction (Mark 13:19), and the stars falling from heaven (Mark 13:25). In comparing the two types of signs, it is apparent that descriptive signs dominate the discourse.

The conclusion of the Olivet Discourse also signals the Lord's chosen point of emphasis—being prepared in the season of his return. Although all three accounts of the discourse provide slightly different conclusions, they point to a similar theme. In Joseph Smith–Matthew, for example, Jesus teaches the parable of the fig tree, which is interpreted in the following manner: "When its branches are yet tender, and it begins to put forth leaves, you know that summer is nigh at hand" (Joseph Smith–Matthew 1:38). Following Jesus' own interpretation, he taught the disciples that they would know the season of his return (summer), but not the precise day and time, thus signaling how the sermon should be interpreted.

One interesting facet of this discourse is that it preserves traces of Matthew's own hand as he addresses the reader: "whoso readeth, let him understand" (24:15). These editorial insertions signal points of emphasis that Matthew wished to pass on. They also show how post-Easter experiences influenced the way the Gospel authors looked at the events and sayings from Jesus' life. In this particular instance, Matthew stresses to the reader the importance of understanding the abomination of desolation, possibly because he had, by the time of his writing, already seen the devastation of the destruction of the **temple** in A.D. 70.

The Parable of the Ten Virgins
MATTHEW 25:1–13

This parable divides Jesus' followers into two distinct classes—wise and foolish. All ten virgins are invited guests who share the same familiarity with the bridegroom. Their punishment comes as a result of their lack of preparation when the time for the wedding comes.

In a real sense, the parable simplifies the process of salvation by making the punishment of the five unwise virgins a result of not having oil at a specific place and time. In actuality, they may have always had oil in their lamps but had not brought it on this one occasion; or they may have frequently been forgetful and this parable was intended to criticize a certain class of individuals. And though the parable points to the Second Coming, the five virgins who call "Lord, Lord" evoke an identical statement given in the context of the Last Judgment.

In all probability, this parable was intended to teach the need for preparedness and consistency in discipleship. It seems more applicable in all of its details to the situation that would soon face the **disciples** rather than being a discussion of what is required to successfully achieve exaltation.

The Parable of the Talents/Pounds
MATTHEW 25:14–30; LUKE 19:11–27

Although some of the details in these two stories differ slightly, they certainly draw upon the same historical source. It is possible that **Jesus** told the parable on a number of occasions and that the two evangelists reflect different versions of the same parable. However, the structure and similarity of purpose reveals a shared intent.

In Luke, it is a "certain nobleman" who distributes "ten pounds" (Greek, *minas*) to ten of his servants (Luke 19:12–13). One *minas* was the equivalent of 100 denarii, or about three and a half months of pay for a day laborer. That each was given "ten pounds" shows the sum was reasonably high but not fantastic or incredible. In Matthew, however, the sums are enormous (Matthew 25:15). A talent is equivalent to roughly 6,000 denarii, thus making a single talent the equivalent of a lifetime of pay for a day laborer. Five talents of real wealth is an enormous sum. The varying amounts in the **parables** may reflect the natural tendency over time to inflate numbers to emphasize a message.

The story, despite the mention of money, has as its focus the delay in the Lord's return at the last day. In both versions, the central message is on behavior while the Lord delays his coming. In Luke, the purpose is stated explicitly: "He added and spake a parable, because he was nigh to Jerusalem, and because they thought that the kingdom of God should immediately appear" and implicitly, "his citizens hated him, and sent a message after him, saying, We will not have this man to reign over us" (Luke 19:11, 14). Matthew added, "After a long time the lord of those servants cometh, and reckoneth with them" (Matthew 25:19). The question being addressed is how Jesus' followers will act after his departure.

Handling large sums of money, whether they are enormous (Matthew) or simply large (Luke), raises the question of avarice and greed. The servants had an opportunity to follow the master (Jesus) or seek other ways of spending, investing, or wasting the money given to them. When the rewards are handed out in the parable, it is apparent that Luke agrees with Matthew that there was originally an unequal distribution of wealth because one was rewarded with ten cities, one with five, and one with nothing. Keeping with the monetary setting of the story, Luke records that the faithful servants were each given "cities" to rule over, while Matthew writes that "I will make thee ruler over many things: enter thou into the joy of thy lord" (Matthew 25:21).

Rewards in heaven are differentiated in Luke's account (19:17–18), which may reflect a variant version of Jesus' teaching but more likely reflects a corruption of what was originally intended. Following Jesus' teachings elsewhere, the same reward is offered equally to all faithful servants (Matthew 20:1–16).

The Parable of the Sheep and Goats
MATTHEW 25:31–46

The parable of the sheep and goats is unique to Matthew although it certainly advances a theme that is consistently emphasized in the Gospel of Luke, namely a concern for the poor and needy. This parable also follows the telling of two other **parables** that emphasize the theme of sins of omission. **Jesus** here challenges his disciples to reinterpret judgment within the framework of a rigid comparison to the law and instead encourages them to see that the division between the "nations" will be made based on how they cared for the stranger, the hungry, thirsty, naked, sick, and socially marginalized. This new way of looking at the Final Judgment would have been surprising to many of Jesus' peers.

The de-emphasis of belief and instead a refocus on charitable actions sets up the beginning of the book of Acts, which details the beginning of the law of consecration and the early **Church's** concern to physically care for the widows. These early efforts may reflect a literal application of Jesus' teachings in Matthew 25.

Prophecy of the Crucifixion
MATTHEW 26:1–2

Matthew has carefully constructed his Gospel narrative around five separate speeches (possibly reminding us of the five books of Moses). This transition represents the end of the final section: "And it came to pass, when **Jesus** had finished all these sayings" (Matthew 26:1). Matthew informs us that Jesus has finished his public teaching; the rest of Matthew's account will focus on Jesus' suffering, death, and resurrection. In this context Jesus announces to his **disciples**, "Ye know that after two days is the feast of the **passover**, and the **Son of man** is betrayed to be crucified"

(26:2). Note a similar context found in Mark when the Passover is introduced to the reader. Mark highlights the action of **Jesus'** enemies: "The chief **priests** and the **scribes** sought how they might take him by craft, and put him to death" (Mark 14:1).

It has long been recognized that one historical fact regarding Jesus that virtually every New Testament scholar (believer and nonbeliever) accepts as true is that Jesus of Nazareth was crucified at Passover in Jerusalem.

Caiaphas's Palace

MATTHEW 26:3–5; MARK 14:1–2

Jesus' enemies, "the chief **priests**, and the **scribes**, and the elders of the people" (Matthew 26:3), gathered at Caiaphas's palace to secretly plan Jesus' arrest and execution. Traditionally located on the site of the modern Catholic Church, St. Peter's in Gallicantu (located on the eastern slope on Mount Zion just outside the Old City walls), Caiaphas's home was most likely composed of a large compound with an assembly and dining hall, ritual baths (Hebrew, *miqva'ot*), courtyards, and gates. Israeli archaeologists have uncovered such homes in what is now the northwest section (Jewish Quarter) of the Old City, near St. Peter's in Gallicantu revealing the splendor and opulence of the wealthy high priestly families in the first century A.D.

Nothing in the text suggests that the entire Sanhedrin met in this late night session; rather it was most likely an ad hoc committee that "sought how they might take him by craft, and put him to death" (Mark 14:1). In the end, they decided to wait until after the **Passover** feast to arrest Jesus because they feared the people's reaction (14:2). The compact with **Rome** required that these Jewish leaders maintain a stable peace—to allow taxes, tolls, and trade to flow uninterrupted. Passover was not the time to risk an uproar among the people.

Hostility between the rulers and the people often lay just below the surface. The common people thought the Jewish leaders were collaborators. Additionally, there was the usual distrust between the wealthy, powerful elite and the common people; the Gospels portray the common people as generally sympathetic with Jesus' ministry. Certainly, there were wide ranges of opinions about him. Some would have seen him as simply a wise teacher; others would have believed that he was a powerful healer. Some believed that he was the long expected **Messiah**, even a political king. Probably most saw him as a defender of the poor, outcast, and marginal members of society. He challenged the social, political, economic, and religious leaders and as a result found support among the people.

The Feast with Simon the Pharisee
MATTHEW 26:6; MARK 14:3; LUKE 7:36

This passing reference to a meal at the house of Simon the **leper** (also a Pharisee, according to Luke) may have been included to provide a setting for the anointing of **Jesus** in Bethany (Mark 14:3). The frequency of the name Simon, even in the New Testament, argues against making any firm declarations about the specific identity of this Simon. That Jesus would dine at the home of someone who had formerly been declared unclean is certainly within his character as it has been described elsewhere in the Gospels, although it was probably surprising to those who interpreted the law more rigidly (Mark 2:16).

The Anointing of Jesus
MATTHEW 26:7–13; MARK 14:4–9; LUKE 7:37–50; JOHN 12:1–9

John places this event six days before **Passover** (John 12:1) and later contextualizes this reference by indicating its place on the day before the triumphal entry (12:12). The **Synoptic** Gospels set the event in the home of Simon the **leper**, which John omits, likely because he reports that the anointing took place in Bethany with Martha, Mary, and Lazarus being present there (12:2), although it is possible that two separate events are being narrated.

When Mary anointed **Jesus'** feet, she used "a pound of spikenard

[nard], very costly" (12:3), which was kept in an alabaster jar (Matthew 26:7), again focusing attention on the cost of the perfume. Nard, or spike-nard, was used to anoint the dead, most likely out of respect and to show honor as well as the more pragmatic concern of countering the odors associated with decomposition. Mary, however, anointed Jesus' feet while he was alive in an act that foreshadowed his death. On the afternoon of the crucifixion, the women who would have anointed his body with nard were unable to because of the approach of the **Sabbath** (Mark 16:1). Here, Mary has the opportunity to anoint Jesus while there is still time.

The account also serves to introduce Judas Iscariot, and for Matthew and Mark, this is the first significant negative action ascribed to Judas, who complained about the cost of the perfume, indicating that it could have been sold for a large sum, about 300 denarii, or about a year's wages, for someone of the working class, and the proceeds given to the poor. In Luke only, where the reference to Judas is omitted in place of the **Pharisees**, the Lord pauses to teach Simon the Pharisee a parable about forgiveness. Luke thus ties the Pharisees' unforgiving attitude to the concept of the parable—that they ought to love him who forgave them. Luke's report of Simon calling the woman (Mary) a sinner may be more hyperbole than a literal statement of Mary of Bethany's former status.

Judas's Conspiracy

MATTHEW 26:14–16; MARK 14:10–11; LUKE 22:3–6

In the Gospels, the Jewish leaders are shown to be somewhat fearful that arresting **Jesus** will cause a disturbance. However, the timing of their move against Jesus changes when one of his closest associates volunteers to help them get Jesus alone—away from the crowds: "And Judas Iscariot, one of the twelve, went unto the chief **priests**, to betray him unto them [literally, "he might hand him over to them"]. And when they heard it, they were glad, and promised to give him money. And he sought how he might conveniently betray him" (Mark 14:10–11).

Judas is identified as both the "indispensable and dispensable" actor in the events surrounding Jesus' arrest and death. Much ink has been spilled attempting to explain why Judas decided to "hand over" Jesus to his enemies. During the first century, speculation had already seized on several propositions. This continued during the next few centuries as people tried to make sense of what Judas had done. One of the earliest efforts to answer the "why" question is found in Matthew, who suggests that it was simply a matter of greed and seems to edit Mark's account in two significant ways at this point as a means to reveal the motive. First, Matthew reports that Judas asked for money instead of its being offered to him by the chief **priests** as in Mark (Matthew 26:15). Second, the undetermined sum offered to Judas in Mark 14:11 becomes "thirty pieces of silver" in Matthew (26:15), an obvious allusion to Zechariah 11:12–13, as Matthew states himself (27:9). Many scholars believe that the coinage mentioned (Greek, *argyria*, "silver") is the Tyrian shekel—the highest grade of silver coin in circulation at the time. Thirty shekels are estimated to have been worth the typical wages for one hundred and twenty days of labor.

Luke takes us in another direction in his effort to identify the why: "Then entered **Satan** into Judas surnamed Iscariot, being of the number of the twelve" (Luke 22:3). Luke's audience has waited for Satan's return since the wilderness temptation: "And when the devil had ended all the temptation, he departed from him *for a season*" (Luke 4:13; emphasis added). Finally, John combines both themes (John 12:4–6; 13:2). The emphasis throughout the New Testament about Jesus being "handed over" is an important theme, divided into three separate but related categories that sometimes intermingle in the accounts. Throughout the New Testament Gospels, Jesus is handed over by humans, himself, and by God. In this section, human activity is directly involved in handing Jesus over. Although we think of Judas as a betrayer, from the Greek (*paradidōmi*), which means "to give over, hand over, deliver up," he is never specifically called a betrayer in the Greek text. The King James Version rendering, "betrayed," obscures the broader context—Jesus is "handed over" on a number of occasions to others (men, chief priests, and sinners). First, Judas hands him over to the arresting party, who in turn hands him over to the ad hoc committee that met at Caiaphas's palace for the late-night hearing. This group hands Jesus over to Pilate, who then hands him over to the death squad. Interestingly, Jesus tells Pilate, "Therefore *he that delivered me* unto thee hath the greater sin" (John 19:11; emphasis added). Apparently everyone in the chain is responsible, but someone, perhaps Caiaphas, is more culpable than all, although Judas and Satan could equally be implicated in the statement.

Some scholars have argued that this story was embarrassing to the early **Church** and therefore must be historically accurate because no one would have made it up!

The First Day of Unleavened Bread
MATTHEW 26:17–19; MARK 14:12–16; LUKE 22:7–13

The combination of the Feast of Unleavened Bread (Nisan 15–21) and the **Passover** (Nisan 14–15) had become so prevalent that mention of one implied the other. **Jesus** and his **disciples** were actually at dinner on the night when the Passover lambs were sacrificed in the **temple**. In the evening, near dusk, the meal would commence. Mark notes, probably because of some relationship to or special knowledge of the location where the dinner took place, that they ate in "a large upper room furnished and prepared" (Mark 14:15). Because of the size of the group and the nature of a Passover meal, there would likely have been many others in the room to help prepare and serve the meal. They too would have heard Jesus say that the time of his departure had come (Matthew 26:18).

The Passover Meal
MATTHEW 26:20; MARK 14:17; LUKE 22:13–14; JOHN 13:1–2

According to the **Synoptics**, **Jesus** ate a traditional **Passover** meal in the evening at the beginning of 14 Nisan. The Jews reckoned the beginning of the day at sundown. John places the meal "before the feast of the passover" (John 13:1). It is not clear when the discrepancy in the accounts arose or why established tradition would be altered. Whether Jesus' final meal with his **disciples** was a Passover (the Synoptic view) celebration or other (the Gospel of John) is no longer clear, and 1 Corinthians 11:23, which refers to the events of that night, does not clarify the matter either. The room in which they ate the **Last Supper** possibly survives to this day and can be visited in downtown Jerusalem. If the *Coenaculum* is indeed the place of the Last Supper, then it raises the intriguing possibility that it was held in the home of a Jerusalem priestly family, given its location so near the **temple** and in the downtown district.

The Prophecy of Betrayal
MATTHEW 26:21–24; MARK 14:18–21; LUKE 22:21–23; JOHN 13:18–22

Similar to the three earlier prophecies about his death (Mark 8:31; 9:31; 10:33–34), **Jesus** offers the **disciples** three more prophecies this evening, all dealing with those closest to him (Judas, the Twelve, and Peter). The first is mentioned here: "Verily I say unto you, One of you which eateth with me shall betray me" (Mark 14:18). Mark implicitly (John explicitly) refers to a passage in Psalms: "Yea, mine own familiar friend, in whom I trusted, which did eat of my bread, hath lifted up his heel against me" (Psalm 41:9). Here Jesus applies the Old Testament prophecy to an immediate event. He will do the same regarding the second prophecy—about the Twelve being scattered in the evening (Mark 14:27).

Matthew and Luke follow Mark with some variation, but John provides additional material not found in the **Synoptic** accounts. For example, Jesus tells the disciples why he has informed them of this heinous sin in advance: "Now I tell you before it come, that, when it is come to pass, ye may believe that I am he" (John 13:19).

All four accounts reveal the Twelve's concern about themselves: "And they began to be sorrowful, and to say unto him one by one, Is it I? and another said, Is it I?" (Mark 14:19).

Judas Is Identified

MATTHEW 26:25; JOHN 13:23–30

No reader is surprised that Judas is the one who hands **Jesus** over to his enemies, as he has been identified as such from the start. When Jesus called the Twelve at the beginning of his ministry, Judas was branded as the one who "betrayed him" (Mark 3:19) and is identified thereafter in the narrative as such. Mark's comments are, of course, reflective—written decades after the events. Nevertheless, this is striking since Judas was among those whom Jesus personally called to be among his closest **disciples.**

No one who gathered for the **Last Supper**, except Jesus and Judas, knew about the conspiracy to arrest Jesus and Judas's part in it. That is why they are all surprised by Jesus' announcement that one of them will hand him over. Apparently, the Beloved disciple and Peter are told during the meal (see below). Most likely, the rest of the Twelve did not learn about Judas's collaboration with the chief **priests** until he entered Gethsemane with the arresting party.

Matthew adds to Mark's account, one of his sources, a unique story—a private conversation between Jesus and Judas following the announcement that one of the Twelve would hand him over (Matthew 26:24). According to Matthew, Judas asked Jesus, "Master, is it I? He said unto him, Thou hast said" (26:25). This exchange highlights Judas's hypocrisy in a matter-of-fact way. Additionally, many commentators have noticed that Judas uses the outsider term (in Matthew's Gospel) "Master" (Greek, "*rabbi*"). This outsider usage is emphasized by Jesus' condemnation of the practice (Matthew 23:7–8). In the Gospel of Matthew the disciples use the insider term "Lord" when addressing Jesus. Judas' choice of greetings suggests that he has already defected.

John provides additional insights about this scene when he introduces the beloved disciple for the first time in his narrative. This disciple will continue to play a significant role through the end of the story (John 19:26–27; 20:2–10; 21:7, 20–23). John, the Beloved disciple, and Judas are compared in this section—they are in fact, disciples at polar ends of the spectrum.

John notes that "Simon Peter therefore beckoned [nodded] to him, that he should ask who it should be of whom he spake. He then lying on Jesus' breast saith unto him, Lord, who is it?" (13:24–25). Jesus tells the beloved disciple that the one to whom he gives the sop (an ancient Middle Eastern practice of using bread as a spoon to dip into a bowl when eating) is the person who would hand him over. Jesus then gives the sop to Judas—the intimacy of the act (personally feeding Judas) again emphasizes the magnitude of Judas's treachery.

Although it is not his purpose, John tells us something about the dinner arrangement that night. As was the custom in such settings (free men and women reclined, whereas slaves sat or stood to eat), Jesus and the Twelve would have used cushions to recline on their left sides at low tables, leaving the right hand free for eating. These low tables, arranged in the shape of a "U" (known as a Triclinium), allowed those serving access to the tables. Most likely, Jesus was positioned at the head of one of the tables with the Beloved disciple reclining on one side—Jesus' right side, so he could lean into Jesus' chest. Judas may have been reclining on the other side—Jesus' left side. As the Twelve's treasurer, he held the "bag," and Judas may have had a position of honor next to Jesus this night—though we cannot be certain. Nevertheless, Judas had to be close enough so that Jesus could personally feed him. The other disciples must have reclined along the sides of the other tables. The only other individual specifically mentioned is Peter, who was most likely positioned some distance from Jesus since he had to "nod" to the Beloved disciple. This reconstruction is tentative because the text is not explicit.

John's account continues when Jesus speaks directly to Judas and sends him on his way (ironically, Judas obeys Jesus in this instance): "Then said Jesus unto him, That thou doest, do quickly" (John 13:27). John reflects, "Now no man at the table knew for what intent he spake this unto him. For some of them thought, because Judas had the bag, that Jesus had said unto him, Buy those things that we have need of against the feast; or, that he should give something to the poor. He then having received the sop went immediately out: and it was night" (13:28–30).

In what can only be seen as a powerful literary device, John ominously notes, "It was night." Night is a symbolic metaphor with a variety of applications in John's Gospel. In the end, Judas disappears into the darkness, both physically and spiritually. His eventual suicide can only be understood in the context of such a descent into a personal darkness where there is no more light left in his world (Matthew 27:3–10).

The Sacrament Is Instituted
MATTHEW 26:26–29; MARK 14:22–25; LUKE 22:15–20

The earliest account of the institution of the sacrament of the Lord's Supper is found in Paul's letter to the Corinthians (1 Corinthians 11:23–25), written in about A.D. 50–51, a decade and a half before the first Gospel (Mark) was prepared. Together with the Corinthian material, the **Synoptic** Gospel accounts of this event provide an opportunity to consider a specific moment in **Jesus**' life—when Jesus blessed bread and wine. Yet, as commentators have often noted, we must be careful not to make too much of the specific wording in the Greek text because Jesus spoke **Aramaic**, not Greek. The words Jesus spoke to his **disciples** the "same night in which he was [handed over]" have already been translated (1 Corinthians 11:23).

Neither the Corinthian Saints nor the original recipients of the Gospels had to wait to read Paul, Matthew, Mark, and Luke to know about the sacrament—they participated in breaking bread and drinking wine on a regular basis as part of their gatherings in the local house-churches where they lived (see, for example, 1 Corinthians 11:26–34).

Mark, the earliest Gospel account of the institution of the sacrament, reports that "Jesus took bread, and blessed, and brake it, and gave to them, and said, Take, eat: this is my body. And he took the cup, and when he had given thanks, he gave it to them: and they all drank of it" (Mark 14:22–23). Mark then adds, "And he said unto them, This is my blood of the new testament [**covenant**], which is shed for many" (14:24). This last statement alludes to Jesus' taking symbols of the old covenant (whether or not this is a **Passover** dinner or pre-Passover dinner), established at Mount Sinai, and investing them with new meaning as he institutes the new covenant (as promised in Jeremiah 31:31). This usage explains why Christians call the Hebrew Bible the Old Testament (old covenant) and the Christian writings the New Testament (new covenant).

We have two distinct forms of the sacramental prayer—one in Paul and Luke (Paul's sometime traveling companion) and another in Mark and Matthew. Some scholars argue that the first forms (Paul and Luke) fit the meal setting of the story whereas the second forms (Mark and Matthew) fit a liturgical (ordinance) setting of the house-churches. Whatever one's conclusions are about the differences preserved in these four separate accounts, there is a stable core material found in them all. Additionally, each preserves the kind of variety expected in an oral retelling of the story of when Jesus sat with his disciples and instituted the sacrament.

Jesus' words emphasize his unshaken faith that his immediate future actions (suffering and death) will have a specific result in the lives of his disciples and that beyond betrayal, denial, desertion, and death there will be a glorious and wonderful conclusion to his "giving himself over" to the chief **priests**, to men, and to sinners (Mark 8:31; 9:31; 14:41).

The accounts are full of ironies, including the fact that Jesus came to save sinners but will only be able to do so by being handed over to them. Additionally, although blood was the ultimate pollutant according to the **Law**, Jesus taught that his blood is the ultimate agent of forgiveness, redemption, and cleansing. However, it is clear that Jesus does not teach that his blood is itself the agent but that shedding of his blood acts as the catalyst for a cosmic reversal. Finally, even as Jesus is promising to give his life for his disciples and others, Judas is on his way to hand over Jesus' life to his enemies as he has promised.

In the end, Jesus promises (vows) that he will drink no more wine with the disciples until he "drink[s] it new in the kingdom of God" (Mark 14:25). This last saying provides us one final clue that Jesus knew he was about to die—he was face-to-face with death, and this was a farewell meal, the last one he would share with his disciples until after he comes into his Father's kingdom.

The silence regarding the institution of the sacrament in the Gospel of John is deafening. Although commentators have attempted to explain with a variety of opinions about why it is missing, almost all of them agree that sacramental imagery is found throughout John's Gospel (see John 6, for example).

Peter's Protest
JOHN 13:2–12

As a prelude to the washing of feet, the author provides a look into the mind and heart of the devil and **Jesus**. First, we learn that Jesus' enemy is at work again—this time putting something evil into Judas's heart (13:2). Second, we learn that Jesus, "knowing that the Father had given all things into his hands, and that he was come from God, and went to God," is about to act also (John 13:3). Only then does John begin to describe the remarkable and striking (given the social customs of the day) act of service Jesus performs for his **disciples** when he "riseth from supper, and laid aside his garments; and took a towel, and girded himself. After that he poureth water into a bason, and began to wash the disciples' feet, and to wipe them with the towel wherewith he was girded" (13:4–5).

We do not think about washing our own feet—we do it daily, and therefore it has become mundane, a task accomplished without much thought, something to get done before we begin the day. However, washing someone else's feet (not our own little children's, but another adult's) is a rather different experience. We need to remember that in antiquity, people walked in dusty lanes, wearing sandals, and without regular access to a shower. Foot washing, then as now, is generally the duty of the person himself or herself, a part of personal hygiene. One should not imagine that this occurred on a regular basis, let alone on a daily basis, in the small hamlets and villages of **Galilee** or **Judea** where obtaining water was a major undertaking. When visiting family or friends, social convention (as an act of hospitality) suggested that the host would provide water and a towel so the visitor could wash his or her feet after a journey (Luke 7:44; compare 1 Samuel 25:41). In more wealthy homes, a slave (but certainly not the host) might perform this degrading service.

So it is with shock and surprise that we see Jesus seemingly demeaning himself in performing the duty of a slave (Philippians 2:5–11). Note that the same verb (Greek, *tithēmi*) used to describe Jesus' act of laying aside his garments here is the same one used elsewhere by Jesus to describe laying down his life (John 10:15, 7–18; compare 10:11; 13:37–38; 15:13). Just as Peter had reacted negatively to Jesus' prophecy about being rejected and killed in Jerusalem (Jesus' ultimate act of service for humanity), he again does so here: "Peter saith unto him, Thou shalt never wash my feet" (13:8). Jesus then reveals the significance of the foot washing, "If I wash thee not, thou hast no part with me" (13:8), before Peter will consent. Again, just as emphatically as he had rejected Jesus' service, the impetuous Peter now wants even more: "Lord, not my feet only, but also my hands and my head" (13:9). Jesus corrects Peter's understanding, saying, "He that is washed needeth not save to wash his feet, but is clean every whit" (13:10). John concludes, "So after he had washed their feet, and had taken his garments, and was set down again, he said unto them, Know ye what I have done to you?" (13:12).

Jesus Is an Example
JOHN 13:13–17

Jesus here teaches the **disciples** the literal meaning of the ordinance of the washing of feet. He, as the "Master," serves all, thus demonstrating in a physical way how the greatest of all came to serve. The word translated here is *didaskalos*, or "teacher." Jesus did not place any symbolic interpretation on this ordinance that he performed for the disciples, but rather he taught its simple reminder: "The servant is not greater than his lord; neither he that is sent greater than he that sent him" (John 13:16; see also D&C 88:139–141).

A New Commandment
JOHN 13:31–35

The new commandment given to the **disciples** as they eat their last supper with **Jesus** summarizes the heart of his ministry. However, the new commandment, "That ye love one another" (John 13:34), is really an old commandment: "But thou shalt love thy neighbour as thyself" (Leviticus 19:18). Here there is a slight difference in emphasis. The new commandment encourages love of one another, whereas the Old Testament encourages the love of one's neighbor and is more inclusive yet open to interpretation (Luke 10:29). It may be that Jesus was expressing the simple truth that if this one commandment were to be observed, then God's kingdom on earth would sooner be realized.

Jesus Comforts the Disciples
JOHN 14:1–15

In this discourse, **Jesus** pauses to teach his **disciples** "the way, the truth, and the life" (John 14:6). The discourse begins with Jesus informing the disciples, "In my Father's house are many mansions," (14:2) following a translation that appears to have been heavily influenced by Renaissance tradition. From the Greek translations, Jesus appears to have said something more akin to "in my Father's house there are many rooms" (Greek, *monai*, or "rooms"), indicating close dwelling conditions and not separate dwellings. Jesus follows that teaching by telling the disciples that, "whither I go ye know, and the way ye know" (14:4).

These statements appear to have piqued the disciples' interest, and Thomas asks for clarification, whereas Philip says, "Shew us the Father, and it sufficeth us" (14:8). As Jesus maintained a focus on how he is the way, the truth, and the life, he broadened the lesson by saying, "I am in the Father, and the Father in me" (14:10). Furthermore, Jesus taught them concerning his role in answering their prayers, "And whatsoever ye shall ask in my name, that will I do, that the Father may be glorified in the Son" (14:13).

The preliminary discussion recorded in these verses eventually leads Jesus to discuss the role of the Second Comforter, and to describe a personal visit of the Father and Son (14:23), thus revealing in a literal way how Jesus is "the way, the truth, and the life" (14:6).

Another Comforter

JOHN 14:16–31

Jesus speaks of another comforter: "And I will pray the Father, and he shall give you another Comforter [Greek, *paraklētos*], that he may abide with you for ever" (John 14:16). The Greek noun used in the King James Version for "Comforter" actually allows a variety of possible English translations, all of them reasonable. As a result, various translations have provided different nouns in addition to "Comforter" (Tyndale/KJV), including "Advocate" (NRSV/TNIV) and "Counselor" (NIV/RSV). To bypass such translation issues, scholars often identify the Comforter as "Paraclete," believing that the original Greek-speaking audience would most likely have understood the various nuances of the word that one does not obtain with a single English noun translation. *Paraclete* is even used in one modern English translation (NJB). The use of "another" (Greek, *allos*) to modify Comforter suggests that there is more than one Comforter. Jesus himself is identified as the Paraclete (LDS usage, "Second Comforter") in 1 John: "We have an advocate [Greek, *paraklētos*] with the Father, Jesus **Christ** the righteous" (2:1). This means that the Comforter is not a name but a description of what Jesus and the **Holy Ghost** do, that is, their function.

Jesus also promises, "I will not leave you comfortless [Greek, *orphanous*]" (John 14:18). John's use of *orphanous* (orphans) reveals an interesting facet of Jesus' relationship to the **disciples**—Jesus addresses them as "little children" (13:33). His departure will not abrogate his relationship to them—he will not abandon them or leave them as orphans when he departs.

To prepare them for the shock of his death, Jesus warns them not to fall into despair and disillusionment. He says, "Yet a little while, and the world seeth me no more; but ye see me: because I live, ye shall live also" (14:19). Further, Jesus promises that he will also come to his disciples: "I will love him, and will manifest myself to him" (14:21). This is particularly fulfilled in the post-Resurrection appearances shortly after his death but is not limited to that brief time period (20:14–18; 21:1–14). Jesus adds to his teaching about his continuing presence among the disciples, "If a man love me, he will keep my words: and my Father will love him, and we will come unto him, and make our abode with him" (14:23).

Jesus adds, "But the Comforter, which is the Holy Ghost, whom the Father will send in my name, he shall teach you all things, and bring all things to your remembrance, whatsoever I have said unto you" (14:26), a powerful reminder that the disciples are to remember what he has said and done.

Jesus offers additional comfort to the disciples: "Peace I leave with you, my peace I give unto you: not as the world giveth, give I unto you. Let not your heart be troubled, neither let it be afraid. Ye have heard how I said unto you, I go away, and come again unto you. If ye loved me, ye would rejoice, because I said, I go unto the Father: for my Father is greater than I. And now I have told you before it come to pass, that, when it is come to pass, ye might believe" (14:27–29).

This section ends when Jesus says, "Arise, let us go hence" (14:31). These five words constitute one of the most challenging phrases in the Gospel of John. As one continues reading, it seems that Jesus does not depart with his disciples at this point but continues to speak to them through 17:1. This has led some scholars to suggest that the material that follows was added later as an alternative ending to Jesus' farewell discourses. Traditionally, many people (including Latter-day Saints) assume that Jesus did depart at this point and continued talking with the disciples on his way to and in Gethsemane ("garden" in John). This is not without problems since John writes, "When Jesus had spoken these words, he went forth [out] with his disciples over the brook Cedron, where was a garden, into which he entered, and his disciples" (18:1), suggesting that at this point Jesus and the Twelve left the upper room (a reasonable interpretation). Another proposal is to rearrange the material to what appears to be the original order. This suggestion argues that the farewell discourses were displaced at some point in their transmission and what is needed is such a rearrangement to get them back in the right place. However, this proposal causes more interpretive problems than it solves. The first solution, noted above, creates its own problems, too.

The True Vine
JOHN 15:1–8

As a precursor to the revelation that the **disciples** would soon face persecution, **Jesus** taught them that he was in control of the process of purging, under the direction of the Father acting as the "husbandman" (John 15:1–2). Knowing this, they need not fear the process of pruning and receiving nourishment through the vine.

Love One Another
JOHN 15:9–17

It is well known that love plays a significant and particular role in the writings of John, including this profound insight: "For God so loved the world, that he gave his only begotten Son" (John 3:16). John also records the new commandment **Jesus** gave his **disciples**: "A new commandment I give unto you, That ye love one another; as I have loved you, that ye also love one another" (13:34). He adds a strong and compelling yet difficult-to-live saying of Jesus: "By this shall all men know that ye are my disciples, if ye have love one to another" (13:35).

These themes continue (and in some cases are restated) in this section: "As the Father hath loved me, so have I loved you: continue ye in my love. If ye keep my commandments, ye shall abide in my love; even as I have kept my Father's commandments, and abide in his love. . . . This is my commandment, That ye love one another, as I have loved you" (15:9–10, 12). For Jesus, the test of discipleship is to live in love and loyalty with the one who has shown his love and loyalty to us in ways beyond what any of us at this point can fully comprehend.

Jesus reveals how he will show his love (Gethsemane and Golgotha are obviously in view): "Greater love hath no man than this, that a man lay down his life for his friends [Greek, *philos*]" (15:13). This is the most exact declaration on how to love as **Jesus** loved in the **scriptures**. In case they did not know, Jesus tells them, "Ye are my friends" (15:14). The word translated "friends" derives from the Greek verb to love (*phileō*), suggesting that to be Jesus' friend is the same as being loved by Jesus. Therefore, as has been suggested, the English noun *friend* does not adequately express what John attempted to convey by his use of the Greek.

Jesus reminds the disciples that their place as friends came by his initiative, not by their own decision: "Ye have not chosen me, but I have chosen you, and ordained you, that ye should go and bring forth fruit, and that your fruit should remain: that whatsoever ye shall ask of the Father in my name, he may give it you" (15:16).

Finally, Jesus repeats himself: "These things I command you, that ye love one another" (15:17). What is most striking about this command, along with those noted earlier, is that they are given by him who has demonstrated what love looks and acts like in its most profound manifestation.

Hatred of the World
JOHN 15:18–27

In one of **Jesus'** most powerful prophecies regarding the fate of the **disciples**, he clearly associates his own fate with that of the disciples. On the eve of his arrest and crucifixion, these words may have seemed strange given the context that the disciples were not hated, and that the Gospels do not report any previous significant persecution having been directed at the disciples independently of Jesus. But the death of Jesus would lead to the persecution of the disciples, much in the same way that the death of John the Baptist led to increased persecution of Jesus. The persecution that Jesus here speaks of would also serve as a test to the promised witness they would receive (John 14:15–27).

The Old Testament allusion to Psalm 109:3 in John 15:25 places their experiences in the context of the fulfillment of scripture. The promise that the "Comforter" would also bear witness to these things and the disciples would also witness to their experiences follows the law of witnesses discussed in John 5.

Warning to the Apostles
JOHN 16:1–6

Before his death, **Jesus** warned the **disciples** about a specific form of persecution that they would encounter, namely religious persecution from their own countrymen: "They shall put you out of the **synagogues**: yea, the time cometh, that whosoever killeth you will think that he doeth God service" (John 16:2). The sentiment that killing the wicked is a form of service to God is expressed in at least one instance in the **Mishnah** (Sanhedrin 9.6). These warnings were given to the disciples so they would not be "offended" or, more literally, "scandalized" (Greek, *skandalizō*, "to feel shock" or "to give up the faith") by what would befall them.

The Comforter
JOHN 16:7–16

To address the scandal of **Jesus'** death, the Gospel of John here preserves an account of the remedy—the coming of the Comforter or Paraclete (Greek, *paraklētos*). The ministry of the Comforter, or Holy Spirit, is outlined in detail in these verses, where the Spirit's primary role is to "reprove" (Greek, *elenxō*, "to rebuke" or "to try"). The Spirit's primary mission is to try mankind to see if they will sin out of lack of faith (John 16:9), to test their faith during Jesus' absence (16:10), and to judge mankind to the extent that mankind has followed "the prince of this world" (16:11).

In contrast to his ministry of trying and proving mankind, the Spirit will "guide you into all truth" (16:13), he will "shew you things to come" (16:13), he will glorify **Jesus** (16:14), and he shall show the **disciples** the things of God (16:15). It is likely for these latter reasons that the Spirit is here called the Paraclete ("helper" or "one who makes intercession"). Certainly the Spirit's role in trying the hearts of mankind could be interpreted as an act of helping mankind progress, but his role as revealer and teacher will offer more immediate help in Jesus' absence.

220

Opposition

JOHN 16:17–30

Jesus here describes openly the sorrow and joy the **disciples** will experience after his death. He is fully cognizant of what his death will mean to the disciples and encourages them to remain steadfast in the hope that joy will return to them. Jesus compared his departure to the birth of a child, which is brought forth in pain, but that pain turns to joy when the healthy child arrives (16:21). The point of focus for the disciples is Jesus' departure and not simply self-concern that they will struggle and face adversity. It is certain that they loved him dearly, and seeing him again would remedy their sorrow.

This discourse began with the disciples asking a question, a theme to which Jesus returned when he said, "And in that day ye shall ask me nothing. Verily, verily, I say unto you, Whatsoever ye shall ask the Father in my name, he will give it you" (16:23). The statement, "ye shall ask me nothing" (Greek, *erōtaō*, "to ask a question") is being compared to a plea or petition, "ye shall ask the Father in my name" (Greek, *aiteō*, "to request" or "to ask"). The difference in the choice of verbs is apparently meant to convey that in the future the disciples would no longer ask questions about the meaning of words and phrases: "These things have I spoken unto you in proverbs" (16:25). Rather, they would petition the Father to do his will because they would fully understand that will.

Toward the end of this short interchange, the disciples grasp Jesus' role as the intermediary and messenger of the Father's will. The full scope of the ministry now comes into perspective for them, namely that Jesus had come to earth to glorify the Father and do his will. When the disciples express that belief, Jesus warns them that difficult times lie ahead and they will flee from him, a clear allusion to their flight at the moment of the arrest. This abrupt departure among friends is remedied in the promise, "I will see you again, and your heart shall rejoice, and your joy no man taketh from you" (16:22). The joy he speaks of here is in contrast to the fleeting joy they now have, which will be shortly torn from them. The joy that Jesus promised was enduring and could not be taken from them. It is also connected to his return visit.

The Flock to Be Scattered
MATTHEW 26:31–32; MARK 14:27–28; JOHN 16:31–33

In the second of three prophecies, all associated with his closest **disciples** (the Twelve) given on this last night, **Jesus** reveals another shocking truth: "All ye shall be offended because of me this night: for it is written, I will smite [hit or slay] the shepherd, and the sheep shall be scattered" (Mark 14:27). Just as in his earlier prophecy about being handed over, Jesus again cites the **Jewish scriptures** as a context for his own prophecy. Jesus explicitly refers to Zechariah's prophecy: "Awake, O sword, against my shepherd, and against the man that is my fellow, saith the Lord of hosts: smite the shepherd, and the sheep shall be scattered" (Zechariah 13:7). Additionally, Jesus reshapes the passage to say, "I will smite" instead of "smite the shepherd" as found in Zechariah, suggesting that God is in control and that it is his will that Jesus die. Finally, Jesus is adamant; no one disciple will escape this night, for all will be offended (from the Greek, *skandalizō*, "to fall away, to be shocked, to be offended, to stumble"). Nevertheless, their desertion will not end their fellowship with Jesus, as he adds, "But after that I am risen, *I will go before you* into **Galilee**" (Mark 14:28; emphasis added), either ahead of the disciples or at the head of the disciples (the Greek is not precise).

Although Matthew follows Mark, with a few variations such as the addition "of the flock" to "the sheep of the flock shall be scattered abroad" (Matthew 26:31), John provides a different version with a different focus: "Behold, the hour cometh, yea, is now come, that ye shall be scattered, every man to his own, and shall leave me alone: and yet I am not alone, because the Father is with me" (John 16:32).

The Great Intercessory Prayer

JOHN 17:1–26

Jesus' great Intercessory Prayer, or great High Priestly Prayer, is the final discourse in the Gospel of John and functionally takes the place of Jesus' prayer in Gethsemane, although it was given while the **disciples** listened. The prayer can be outlined in the following manner: Jesus prays for the glorification of the Father and the Son (John 17:1–5); he then prays for the disciples (17:6–11); after which he prays that the disciples will be protected and sanctified of the Father (17:11–19); and finally, he prays for those who will come to know Jesus through the testimony of the disciples (17:20–26).

Each verse contains reminiscences of earlier experiences and teachings, thus making this concluding prayer a summary of the gospel message. In parts of the prayer, Jesus speaks in the past tense: "I have finished the work which thou gavest me to do" (17:4), and "Now I am no more in the world" (17:11). In these verses and elsewhere, Jesus has become the divine intermediary, standing on the earth although one with heaven and pleading the cause of the disciples and those who should come after them. This chapter offers a physical realization of how prayer works as the Lord acts as a mediator for the disciples.

The theme of stewardship also runs through this prayer, when Jesus accounts for the fulfillment of the work he had been given, for having trained stewards who would follow him, and for having lost one of those that were given to him. In this regard, the Intercessory Prayer may function as a model of Final Judgment.

The Mount of Olives

MATTHEW 26:30; MARK 14:26; LUKE 22:39; JOHN 18:1

After concluding their dinner with a hymn, generally assumed to be the Hallel sung both at the beginning (Psalms 113–14) and the end of the **Passover** meal (Psalms 115–18), **Jesus** led his **disciples** to the Mount of

Olives (Mark 14:26). Both Luke and John fail to report this in their accounts of the **Last Supper**. The Hallel ends on a sobering note: "The stone which the builders refused is become the head stone of the corner. This is the Lord's doing; it is marvellous in our eyes. This is the day which the Lord hath made; we will rejoice and be glad in it. Save now, I beseech thee, O Lord: O Lord, I beseech thee, send now prosperity. Blessed be he that cometh in the name of the Lord: we have blessed you out of the house of the Lord. God is the Lord, which hath shewed us light: bind the **sacrifice** with cords, even unto the horns of the altar. Thou art my God, and I will praise thee: thou art my God, I will exalt thee. O give thanks unto the Lord; for he is good: for his mercy endureth for ever" (Psalm 118:22–29).

Luke makes an important addition to Mark's account: "And he came out, and went, *as he was wont*, to the mount of Olives; and his disciples also followed him" (Luke 22:39; emphasis added), helping to explain how Judas knew where Jesus would be this night.

When You Are Converted
LUKE 22:31–32

The Gospels do not definitively tell the reader how strong the **disciples'** testimonies were when **Jesus** was taken from them. In this passage, Peter is warned of upcoming trials, using the analogy of how wheat is sifted from the husk or chaff. Jesus then tells Peter, "when thou art converted" (Luke 22:32), indicating that the process of conversion was not yet complete. The Greek verb translated as "converted" is *epistrephō* and means literally "to turn around" or "to turn back." It is not entirely certain that Jesus had Peter's conversion in mind, but more likely his turning back after the three denials. Jesus encouraged Peter to "turn back" and strengthen the brethren after Peter had denied him. Luke places this saying immediately before the predictions that Peter would deny Jesus.

Before the Cock Crows

MATTHEW 26:33–35; MARK 14:29–31; LUKE 22:33–34;
JOHN 13:36–38

This is the third of three prophecies directed to the closest of his **disciples** (the Twelve), given by **Jesus** on this last night. The first two were directed to the general group of disciples and were supported by citations from the Hebrew Bible. However, in this final prophecy, Jesus speaks directly to Peter without any scriptural context.

Jesus has just told his disciples that all of them would be offended this night, and as a result, they would all desert him (Mark 14:27). Just as he has done on several occasions, Peter protests, and he disputes Jesus' prophecies (Mark 8:31–32). Mark recalls, "But Peter said unto him, *Although all shall be offended, yet will not I*" (14:29; emphasis added). One can only wonder what James, John, and the others thought when Peter seemed to have separated himself from them, claiming that he alone would remain faithful this night. Following Peter's bravado, Jesus tells him, "Verily I say unto thee, That this day, even in this night, before the cock crow twice, thou shalt deny me thrice" (14:30). Again, Peter protests: "If I should die with thee, I will not deny thee in any wise" (14:31).

The question is whether Jesus' three prophecies will come true this night or if the disciples' own prophecies (they will not desert, betray, or deny Jesus) will come true. In effect, they claim they know themselves better than Jesus knows them.

President Spencer W. Kimball asks a very good question about what Jesus intended in the verse. Interestingly, he does not answer his own question and in fact states, "I do not pretend to know what Peter's mental reactions were nor what compelled him to say what he did that terrible night" (*Peter, My Brother*, 5). Focusing on only one of the raised possibilities, President Kimball does not disclose what else he might have to say regarding this particular incident. In the end, we are left to carefully consider the Gospel accounts. Some thoughtful scholars have argued for an alternative understanding, namely that Peter may have been commanded or encouraged to deny the Lord, a reading that is based on a particular interpretation of one isolated verse. Nevertheless, the broader context suggests that the simplest reading is the best reading: Jesus prophesied this night that one of the Twelve would hand him over to his enemies, that all of them would be offended and scattered, and that Peter in particular would deny him.

Reckoned among the Transgressors
LUKE 22:35–38

These enigmatic verses that are found only in Luke represent **Jesus'** teaching concerning the days when the **disciples** would need swords. It appears that Luke's account may only preserve a portion of the original, and likely these verses should be placed in the larger context of Jesus' teachings in John 15–16, where he also taught the disciples of future persecutions. The scripture quotation derives from Isaiah 53:12.

Jesus' Prayer in Gethsemane
MATTHEW 26:36–46; MARK 14:32–42; LUKE 22:40–46; JOHN 18:1

At some point **Jesus** and the **disciples** go "to a place which was named Gethsemane" (Mark 14:32). John describes the location as across the "brook Cedron, where was a garden" (John 18:1). The name *Gat-shemana* means "oil press" and is traditionally located in the lower part of the Mount of Olives, across the Kidron Valley from the city walls. Today one can visit the "Cave of Gethsemane," which Byzantine Christians believed was the place where the disciples waited for Jesus as he prayed. The Church of All Nations, located nearby, is the place where many Christians believe Jesus prayed on that fateful night—a rock by the altar is identified as the exact spot. Although some olive trees located here are very old, none of them dates from the time of Jesus (the Mount of Olives was denuded by Titus's army during the siege of Jerusalem in A.D. 70). However, the gnarled trees provide the visitor an opportunity to remember Jesus' prayer in an olive orchard at the beginning of the Passion Narrative (from Gethsemane to the Grave).

The Passion Narrative or account of the **Atonement** is the longest continuous account in any of the Gospels—detailing Jesus' last twenty-four hours. Mark, more than any of the other Gospel accounts, portrays Jesus' agony in Gethsemane in clear and moving language revealing the reality of his suffering and the severity of his struggles. Most scholars agree that this story reveals something about what happened to Jesus because no one in the ancient world would have described a Greek hero or a Jewish martyr as suffering and trembling because of pain. It truly is a unique account from beginning to the end.

It is generally recognized that Mark's concise portrayal contains five sets of doublets. The consistent use of these structural doublets, in some cases using nearly exact words, serves to highlight and intensify the description of the events.

Since the date of **Passover** is determined by the cycles of the moon (Jews observed a lunar calendar), we know that a full moon shone this night. Its light would have filtered through the olive orchard as the group entered from the main road leading up and across the Mount of Olives. Once in the grove, Jesus "saith to his disciples, Sit ye here, while I shall pray. And he taketh with him Peter and James and John, and began to be sore amazed, and to be very heavy; and saith unto them, My soul is exceeding sorrowful unto death: tarry ye here, and watch. And he went forward a little, and fell on the ground, and prayed that, if it were possible, the hour might pass from him" (Mark 14:32–35).

As he had done at the raising of the daughter of Jairus and on the Mount of Transfiguration, Jesus takes Peter, James, and John apart from the other disciples to pray. Mark provides a word picture (contrary to many modern depictions of the scene) of Jesus in Gethsemane: "And he went forward a little, and fell on the ground"; that is, he threw himself face down, prostrate, to pray. This Jewish attitude of supplication is one of utter and complete submission to God, emphasizing Jesus' sincere and earnest desire to be heard.

227

Mark continues, "And he said, Abba, Father, all things are possible unto thee; take away this cup from me: nevertheless not what I will, but what thou wilt" (14:36). The name Jesus uses in his prayer, "Abba" (Father), heightens the pathos of this tragic scene. *Abba* is the Hebrew/ **Aramaic** word for "Father," not Dad, Daddy, or Papa. Jesus was remembered as addressing God with the familiar and intimate address of a child to a father. Traditionally, Jews in the first century addressed God with something like, "O Lord, King of the Universe" or "Lord God, Maker of Heaven and Earth," a much more formal address (Matthew 11:25). What is striking about Mark's account is that *Abba* meant nothing in Greek—it is simply four Greek letters (alpha, beta, beta, alpha). Yet, the early **Church** remembered Jesus' original Aramaic word in transliteration (see Galatians 4:6, for example). Mark does not tell us why Jesus prayed, "Take away this cup from me." First, Jesus anticipates the judgment or wrath of God, represented by the "cup" (Psalm 75:8; Isaiah 51:17, 22; Jeremiah 25:15; 49:12; Lamentations 4:21). Second, he who knew God as "Abba" from the beginning did not want to be cut off from his presence, to be "God forsaken" (Mark 15:34). In this, we see that Jesus experienced an actual and difficult test. Commentators have suggested that Jesus' final decision to accept God's will is all the more impressive because he chose intentionally and thoughtfully to submit his will to that of the Father's, as noted in the last part of his prayer: "Nevertheless *not what I will*, but what thou wilt" (14:36; emphasis added). "Nevertheless" may also suggest that Jesus may not have been sure that it was God's will for him to die at that time. Mark portrays Jesus as coming to this realization during three separate prayers (compare 2 Corinthians 12:8).

Mark adds, "And he cometh, and findeth them sleeping, and saith unto Peter, Simon, sleepest thou? couldest not thou watch one hour? Watch ye and pray, lest ye enter into temptation. The spirit truly is ready, but the flesh is weak" (Mark 14:37–38). Jesus' use of the name Simon may indicate that he was not yet the rock (Peter). Here again, the context may suggest a reflection on the disciples' weakness, but also a personal reflection on the difficulty of the task ahead.

The account turns as we watch the disciples begin their descent into

maim the high priest's servant, making him ineligible for temple service. Only Luke relates that Jesus healed Malchus's wound (Luke 22:51). Jesus' act of healing Malchus's ear symbolically ends the use of violence as a form of retribution, the so-called *lex talionis*, or law of retribution—"eye for an eye" (Leviticus 24:19–21).

The Disciples Flee

MATTHEW 26:56; MARK 14:50

At the conclusion of the arrest narrative, Mark states, "And they all forsook him, and fled" (Mark 14:50). Matthew, as he has done before with Mark's narrative, makes explicit what Mark implicitly states: "Then *all the* **disciples** forsook him, and fled" (Matthew 26:56; emphasis added). The second prophecy associated with Zechariah 13:7 given by **Jesus** during the **Last Supper** (Mark 14:27) has now been fulfilled, and only one of the three prophecies remains unfulfilled—Peter's thrice denial.

The situation in Gethsemane changed quickly. At first, the disciples stand firm in opposition to Jesus' arrest (even one of them strikes out at a member of the arresting party), but finally they all desert him and flee. Mark's account emphasizes their complete abandonment of Jesus: "And *they all forsook him*, and fled" (Mark 14:50; emphasis added). It is natural to wonder, What had happened? What had changed? Why did the disciples, who stood firm at first, give up hope and flee? The disciples believed that Jesus was the long-promised **Messiah**, yet this story may convey a shift in their understanding of a Messiah who would physically deliver them to a Messiah who would save them from their sins. As Jesus attempted to correct their vision, the disciples often resisted. We cannot be certain if they thought their vision would end up being correct nevertheless. We can only speculate that the triumphal entry sparked hope—maybe Jesus was, after all, the kingly warrior-Messiah they prayed for, dreamed about, and sang about. The cleansing of the **temple** would certainly have raised that hope because that was exactly what they expected the Messiah to be and do. Yet Jesus kept telling them that his mission would end in rejection, suffering, and death. Perhaps his refusal to fight and his willingness to place himself in the hands of his enemies in Gethsemane convinced them that Jesus did not plan to appear in power on the Mount of Olives as expected. Instead, he departed from the lower portions of the famous mount in no better condition than a common criminal.

Jesus Is Arrested
MATTHEW 26:55–57; MARK 14:46–52; LUKE 22:52–54; JOHN 18:1–3, 12–13

The Gospels report that the arresting party carried with them "swords and staves" (Matthew 26:55) and came "with lanterns and torches and weapons" (John 18:3). John records the only reference to **Pharisees** in the trial scenes, "having received a band of men and officers from the chief **priests** and Pharisees" (John 18:3), thus suggesting that Pharisee involvement was not as significant as Sadducee involvement.

Mark adds the unique detail of an unnamed **disciple** who became caught up in the melee and fled on foot naked (Mark 14:51–52). Mark's interest in relating the story of this unnamed disciple/follower may show that the author was familiar with him and his story but that his audience was not familiar with him personally; hence, the name has been dropped. The story also vividly demonstrates why the disciples "forsook him, and fled" (Mark 14:50), namely because they were also in danger.

John provides a context for Judas's betrayal here when he mentions the location of the place of arrest: "He went forth with his disciples over the brook Cedron, where was a garden, into the which he entered, and his disciples" (John 18:1). At the **Last Supper, Jesus** had apparently not signaled the location where they would go afterwards, but "Judas also, which betrayed him, knew the place: for Jesus ofttimes resorted thither with his disciples" (John 18:2). No specific site is referenced here, but the point where Jesus was arrested appears to be within view of the temple, which sat across the Kidron brook in the direction they had traveled from.

The Hearing before the Chief Priests

MATTHEW 26:57–68; MARK 14:53–65; LUKE 22:54, 63–71;
JOHN 18:12–15, 19–24

That Caiaphas did not personally venture out to arrest **Jesus** is made explicit in the scenes that follow where Jesus is led to the high priest. John mentions that the arresting party took Jesus to Annas first, probably at his private residence, and that Caiaphas directed the proceedings (John 18:13). The **scribes** and elders "were assembled" (Matthew 26:57), implying that there was a conspiracy already at work and that whatever might happen in the hearing, Jesus' fate was already sealed.

The proceedings eventually consider one of Jesus' teachings more closely, one that he had spoken in the context of cleansing the **temple**: "I will destroy this temple that is made with hands, and within three days I will build another made without hands" (Mark 14:58). Some manu-scripts read, "I will *raise* another made without hands," which is probably a later scribal emendation to make the connection to the Resurrection more explicit, although it is possible that even here Jesus foreshadowed his Resurrection quite openly. From Jesus' opening words, the reader is given the impression that Jesus is focused on the culmination of his mission while Caiaphas is interested in attempting to kill Jesus, thus inadvertently also bringing about Jesus' mission.

Caiaphas eventually asked, "Art thou the **Christ**, the Son of the Blessed? And Jesus said, I am: and ye shall see the **Son of man** sitting on the right hand of power, and coming in the clouds of heaven. Then the high priest rent his clothes, and saith, What need we any further witnesses?" (Mark 14:61–63). Caiaphas's actions and summary statement indicate that he has interpreted the saying to be blasphemous. At the time of Jesus, the **Sadducees**, in particular, came to understand that it was their particular duty to defend the honor of God to the point that even pronouncing God's name was defined as blasphemy. Later evidence relates that Jesus' statement would not have been interpreted as blasphemous (Sanhedrin 7.5), although the Sadducees were particularly strict in their interpretations (Josephus,

Antiquities 13.297–98). In this interchange, the two words, "I am" (Greek, *egō eimi*) are the focus of the debate, and it is unclear whether Matthew's, "Thou hast said" (Matthew 26:64) or Mark's "I am" (Mark 14:62) is closest to the original.

Because the hearing is not depicted as a formal trial, the Gospel authors do not bother detailing the potential violations of Jewish law and practice. Instead, for them this was a lynch mob, who "spit in his face, and buffeted him; and others smote him with the palms of their hands" (Matthew 26:67). Why they blindfolded Jesus to begin with is unclear (Luke 22:64), unless it was to further secure his submission.

John added to the account that "Simon Peter followed Jesus, and so did another disciple: that disciple was known unto the high priest, and went in with Jesus into the palace of the high priest" (John 18:15). Traditionally, it has been assumed that the "other disciple" mentioned here was John, the author of the fourth Gospel. It could also be possible that the unnamed disciple, whom the other Gospel authors do not mention, was Judas Iscariot. The Gospel of Matthew relates that Judas was at the hearing: "And when they had bound him, they led him away, and delivered him to Pontius Pilate the governor. *Then Judas,* which had betrayed him, *when he saw that he was condemned . . .*" (Matthew 27:2–3; emphasis added). That same unnamed disciple was also a friend of the high priest, thus making him an associate of Jesus' foremost enemy.

Peter's Denial
MATTHEW 26:69–75; MARK 14:66–72; LUKE 22:55–62;
JOHN 18:15–18, 25–27

Peter's denial stands in sharp contrast to other passages in the New Testament: "But whosoever shall deny me before men, him will I also deny before my Father which is in heaven" (Matthew 10:33), and thus attests to the lasting power of this account. Formally, the account describes Peter's attempt to save himself from punishment in light of his association with **Jesus**. As the reader knows, Peter's life is important to the continuation of Jesus' work. The interchange took place in the "palace" (Greek, *aulē;* Matthew 26:69). The reference to the palace is probably intended to indicate the large courtyard of a Roman period home where Jesus was being interrogated inside the home as Peter stood "without" (Matthew 26:69). The events are described in great detail, including references to Peter's accent (Mark 14:70), to the place where Peter stood on a "porch" (Matthew 26:71), and to "Peter warming himself" (Mark 14:67).

It is impossible to know exactly what Peter felt on the night of the denial and how he interpreted Jesus' words to him when the Lord prophesied Peter's denial. However, Peter's actions on that night seem to indicate that he understood his denial in a negative way, or in a way that was detrimental to his discipleship and not as a fulfillment of duty. All three Synoptic Gospels indicate that he wept after having denied the Lord.

Soldiers Mock Jesus

MATTHEW 26:67–68; MARK 14:65; LUKE 22:63–65; JOHN 18:22

Mark provides the details of an incident at Caiaphas's palace during **Jesus'** hearing before the Jewish leaders following his arrest: "And some began to spit on him, and to cover his face, and to buffet him, and to say unto him, *Prophesy:* and the servants did strike him with the palms of their hands" (Mark 14:65; emphasis added).

The violent episode is full of irony on a variety of levels. First, it fulfills Isaiah's **messianic** prophecy: "I gave my back to the smiters, and my cheeks to them that plucked off the hair: I hid not my face from shame and spitting" (Isaiah 50:6). Second, Jesus' earlier Passion prophecy is also fulfilled in the episode: "Behold, we go up to Jerusalem; and the **Son of man** shall be delivered unto the chief **priests**, and unto the **scribes**; and they shall condemn him to death, and shall deliver him to the **Gentiles:** and *they shall mock him,* and shall scourge him, and shall spit upon him, and shall kill him: and the third day he shall rise again" (Mark 10:33–34; emphasis added). Finally, Jesus' prophecies made hours earlier regarding his closest **disciples** (the Twelve) have only recently been fulfilled or were being fulfilled at the very moment his enemies were demanding that he prophesy.

Matthew's account omits Mark's use of the word *some* in his own narrative: "Then did they spit in his face, and buffeted him; and others smote him with the palms of their hands" (Matthew 26:67), suggesting the Jewish leaders themselves spit and hit Jesus. If this is correct, they are cruel indeed, doing things that Pilate and Herod Antipas are not reported to have done. Additionally, Matthew describes the chief priests' taunting and sarcastic address to Jesus: "Prophesy unto us, thou **Christ**, Who is he that smote thee?" (26:68). Jesus is an example here of his teachings: "But I say unto you, That ye resist not evil: but whosoever shall smite thee on thy right cheek, turn to him the other also" (5:39).

Luke adds, "And many other things blasphemously spake they against him" (Luke 22:65). Interestingly, there is an additional reference to Jesus being struck in John: "And when he had thus spoken, one of the officers which stood by struck Jesus with the palm of his hand, saying, Answerest thou the high priest so?" (John 18:22). The relationship between these two incidents is uncertain, but nothing in the record suggests that the two events are mutually exclusive.

The Transfer to Pilate
MATTHEW 27:2; MARK 15:1; LUKE 23:1; JOHN 18:28

Mark reports, "And straightway in the morning the chief **priests** held a consultation with the elders and **scribes** and the whole council, and bound **Jesus**, and carried him away, and delivered him to Pilate" (Mark 15:1). The theme of handing Jesus over continues (KJV, "delivered") as the Jewish leaders take Jesus to Pilate. Matthew provides additional details about Pilate: "And when they had bound him, they led him away, and *delivered* him to Pontius Pilate the governor (Matthew 27:2; emphasis added). Mark identifies Pilate with the general term "governor" (Greek, *hegemoni*), although early sources such as Josephus and Tacitus use the term *procurator*, and the discovery of an inscription in Caesarea Maratima in 1961 identifies Pilate as "prefect" or military governor.

Luke references a "whole multitude" (Luke 23:1). John reports, "Then led they Jesus from Caiaphas unto the hall of judgment: and it was early; and they themselves went not into the judgment hall, lest they should be defiled; but that they might eat the **passover**" (John 18:28). The location of the meeting where Pilate met Jesus is the "hall of judgment" (Greek, *praitorion*), most likely in the Herodian palace. Although we cannot be sure of the precise time when Jesus met Pilate, the identification that it was early may suggest that Jesus was brought to Pilate about 6:00 A.M.

John points out one of the extreme ironies in the story when he informs us that the Jewish leaders would not enter the hall of judgment because they did not want to defile themselves for the Passover feast, yet were participating in judicial murder.

The Hearing before Pilate
MATTHEW 27:11–14; MARK 15:1–5; LUKE 23:1–6;
JOHN 18:28–38

Mark records, "And straightway in the morning the chief **priests** held a consultation with the elders and **scribes** and the whole council" (Mark 15:1), which is intended to return the focus of the account back to **Jesus** after having reported Peter's denials. Mark's "consultation" should not be interpreted as a second council, but rather a sweeping reference to the council held the previous night. The Gospels also mention that the visit was "in the morning" (Mark 15:1) "and it was early" (John 18:28). The reference to the time of day may be to infer that the hearing of Jesus was rushed to avoid attracting the followers of the triumphal entry. In this way, Mark and John note that the trial occurred before many people could become aware of the proceedings.

The function of the accounts is in part to describe Pilate's involvement in the execution of Jesus, of which Pilate is uniquely in charge. Pilate is described in terms that represent the historical situation accurately. Pilate handled the matter personally and considered a distinct legal charge: "We found this fellow perverting the nation, and forbidding to give tribute to **Caesar,** saying that he himself is **Christ** a King" (Luke 23:2). As Luke reports the events, the hearing before Pilate became a discussion where Jesus' accusers were present (Luke 23:5). Their continued accusations eventually lead to the discovery that Jesus is from **Galilee** and therefore Pilate becomes interested in seeking to answer the question of jurisdiction. If Jesus were indeed a Galilean, then Herod Antipas might accept the responsibility to try him.

John's unique contributions are several. First, John mentions that the hearing took place in the "hall of judgment" (John 18:28, 33), which would typically describe the private palace or residence of the governor (Greek, *praitōrion*) and would not likely refer to the Antonia Fortress. Second, Jesus' accusers are not present for the entire interrogation. Pilate appears more in control and less manipulated by Jesus' accusers, and at one point Pilate threatens to dismiss the case and send it back to them for trial (John 18:31). Jesus also bore testimony to Pilate concerning his message of truth, which had irritated his Jewish audience during the ministry but which is now said openly to Pilate. The Gospel of John's section on witnesses may underlie this account where Jesus said, "If I bear witness of myself, my witness is not true" (John 5:31). Pilate had not seen the **miracles** or heard the teachings of Jesus, and this singular witness was all that Pilate had to guide him in judgment.

Judas's Death

MATTHEW 27:3–10

When Judas went to the chief **priests** and elders to return the thirty pieces of silver, Matthew records that "he cast down the pieces of silver in the **temple**" (Matthew 27:5). The word here translated as "temple" is *naos*, whereas the usual Greek word is *hieron*. The change from the usual word may be to indicate the location where the exchange took place, which may also indicate that Matthew was attempting to convey that the money was thrown down near the sacrificial altar and not simply in the courtyard of the temple, thus defiling the temple with money used to purchase blood (27:6).

There are two traditions concerning Judas's death in the New Testament. The account in Acts 1:18 differs slightly from Matthew's, which is harmonized in Joseph Smith Translation Matthew 27:5: "and [Judas] hanged himself on a tree. And straightway he fell down, and his bowels gushed out, and he died." It is likely that various accounts of Judas's final moments circulated in early Christianity.

The purchase of the field and the burial of Judas is framed following Zechariah 11:13: "And the Lord said unto me, Cast it unto the potter: a goodly price that I was prised at of them. And I took the thirty pieces of silver, and cast them to the potter in the house of the Lord."

The Hearing before Herod
LUKE 23:7–10

Only Luke provides a narrative about **Jesus** meeting Herod Antipas in Jerusalem at **Passover**: "And as soon as [Pilate] knew that he belonged unto Herod's jurisdiction, he sent him to Herod [Antipas], who himself also was at Jerusalem at that time" (Luke 23:7). Just as other Jews, Antipas came to the Holy City to celebrate the Passover, one of the pilgrimage feasts required of every Jewish male. We cannot know where Antipas stayed during such visits. Wherever the meeting was held, Luke informs us that Antipas was anxious to meet Jesus: "And when Herod saw Jesus, he was exceeding glad: for he was desirous to see him of a long season, because he had heard many things of him; and he hoped to have seen some **miracle** done by him" (23:8).

That Antipas "was exceeding glad" underscores what Luke had reported earlier: "Now Herod the tetrarch heard of all that was done by [Jesus]: and he was perplexed, because that it was said of some, that John [the Baptist] was risen from the dead; And of some, that Elias [Elijah] had appeared; and of others, that one of the old prophets was risen again. And

Herod said, John have I beheaded: but who is this, of whom I hear such things? And he desired to see him" (9:7–9).

Luke continues, "Then he questioned with him in many words; but [Jesus] answered him nothing. And the chief **priests** and **scribes** stood and vehemently accused him" (23:9–10).

Herod and Men Mock Jesus
LUKE 23:11–12

Antipas decides to punish **Jesus** for not responding to his questions or demonstrating some great **miracle**: "And Herod with his men of war set him at nought, and mocked him, and arrayed him in a gorgeous robe, and sent him again to Pilate" (23:11). Luke shows how the action of Jesus' enemies (three specific acts—setting him at nought [treating him with contempt]; mocking him; and putting on an elegant robe to ridicule him as the pretended King of the Jews) actually fulfills Jesus' prophecies (9:22; 18:32). However, Luke knows this is not an end of the taunting and mocking (22:63; 23:36).

Luke adds one more detail: "And the same day Pilate and Herod were made friends together: for before they were at enmity between themselves" (23:12). Since Luke is interested in healings (he describes them in detail), some commentators have argued that this is another Lucan story about healings—this time the healing of a relationship. Others have suggested that Luke cites this incident to emphasize that reconciliation promised by God through Jesus has already begun. Both interpretations are interesting, but Luke may simply have wanted to record one of the many stories about Jesus he found—a typical insight that Luke often provides (1:66; 2:50; 3:15; 8:29; 9:14; 16:14; 21:1).

The Return to Pilate
MATTHEW 27:15–26; MARK 15:6–15; LUKE 23:13–23

Except for the brief interlude with Herod Antipas, recounted only in Luke, **Jesus** remained in Pilate's custody from about 6:00 A.M. until he handed Jesus over to the executioners around 9:00 A.M. on Friday. The **Synoptic** accounts of this period cover a wide range of activities, but one of the most important is the reaction of the crowd during Jesus' interrogation by Pilate.

Mark reports, "And Pilate answered and said again unto them, What will ye then that I shall do unto him whom ye call the King of the Jews? And they cried out again, Crucify him. . . . And they cried out the more exceedingly, Crucify him" (Mark 15:12–14). Mark makes it clear that the crowd is only doing the work for the Jewish leaders: "But the chief **priests** moved the people" (Mark 15:11). Matthew provides the same narrative but adds that Pilate's wife told him, "Have thou nothing to do with that just man: for I have suffered many things this day in a dream because of him" (Matthew 27:19). Dreams and visions are an important theme in the Gospel of Matthew (Joseph's visions in particular: see Matthew 1:20; 2:13, 19; and the Wise Men: see 2:12). Additionally, Matthew also notes, "But the chief priests and elders persuaded the multitude that they should ask Barabbas, and destroy Jesus" (Matthew 27:20). The crowd affirms, "Let him be crucified" (Matthew 27:22). Again Pilate attempts to release Jesus, but the crowd cries out, "Let him be crucified" (Matthew 27:23). In fear of a riot, Pilate washes his hands "before the multitude, saying, I am innocent of the blood of this just person: see ye to it. Then answered all the people, and said, His blood be on us, and on our children" (Matthew 27:24–25).

The cries to crucify Jesus have echoed down through the centuries. However, what is often forgotten is that Matthew (a Jew) is writing about Jews (Jesus included) for a Jewish audience. Perhaps Matthew and his original audience would have understood the doctrinal implication of the crowd's cry, "His blood be on us, and on our children," as **atonement** ("to cover") language. Although they did not understand what they were saying, that is exactly what was going to happen: Jesus' blood would cover the people as a powerful symbol of purification and cleansing.

Barabbas Is Released

MATTHEW 27:15–21, 26; MARK 15:6–15; LUKE 23:18–25; JOHN 18:39–40

Some manuscripts of the Gospel of Matthew record that Barabbas's common name was **Jesus**, so an almost perfect parallelism seems to develop where the Jesus who took lives is freed while the Jesus who gives life is condemned (Mark 15:7). The practice of releasing prisoners at the **Passover** celebration, the *privilegium paschale*, is not known from external sources, and the Gospels do not explicitly state that this was an ongoing practice, but perhaps more of a remedy for Pilate's decreasing popularity. The practice of releasing prisoners for political reasons is suggested in a number of ancient sources and fits the practice described in the Gospels (*Pesahim* 8.6; Josephus, *Antiquities* 17.205; 20.215).

Functionally, the story of the release of Barabbas serves to shift blame away from Pilate and toward the crowd that cried out for the release of Barabbas, although Pilate certainly is not absolved of guilt: "For he knew that for envy they had delivered him" (Matthew 27:18). This focus on Jewish involvement suggests that there were lingering tensions and sensitive feelings regarding the release of a murderer instead of Jesus. Historically, it is important to note as well that Pilate remained in control of the proceedings and did not relinquish control of the trial to a subordinate, a detail that is confirmed in the accounts.

Matthew alone adds the detail of Pilate's wife's dream. The knowledge of the dream suggests that the story is being told in retrospect after Matthew had time to reflect on the events. Whether Pilate was historically the puppet of the Jewish ruling elite is not known, but in the matter of Jesus' death, the Gospels are unanimous that he bowed to pressure, or as Mark observed, was "willing to content the people" (Mark 15:15).

Pilate Washes His Hands

MATTHEW 27:24–25; LUKE 23:22; JOHN 19:4

Matthew's interest in providing this detail is certainly not to recount the ritual practice of hand washing, either in Roman or Jewish terms. The literary purpose of these verses is to shift blame away from Pilate and toward the crowd that would say, "His blood be on us, and on our children" (Matthew 27:25). The irony of the passage is that if taken literally, it offers a glimpse of chilling hard-heartedness. But if taken symbolically, it serves as an unconscious request for the Atonement to wash them clean.

Some debate exists over whether Pilate adopted the Jewish practice of washing of hands, or whether there was a practice in a Roman cult that he mimicked. From Matthew's language, it is apparent that Deuteronomy 21:6–7 provides the textual background for the construction of these verses: "And all the elders of that city, that are next unto the slain man, *shall wash their hands* over the heifer that is beheaded in the valley: and they shall answer and say, *Our hands have not shed this blood*, neither have our eyes seen it" (emphasis added). It may be also that there is some hint of the Roman practice of *lustratio* as well. In the Gospels, the incident serves to emphasize Pilate's attempt to absolve himself from any guilt associated with killing Jesus.

Jesus Is Scourged and Mocked

MATTHEW 27:27–31; MARK 15:15–20; JOHN 19:1–12

Scourging or flogging was a common and legal but brutal form of punishment inflicted by Romans. Its main purpose was to make the prisoner suffer terribly even before his crucifixion. In some cases, those administering the flogging killed the criminal. Generally, the victim was stripped naked and bound to a pillar, then soundly beaten by two soldiers, positioned to access the entire back, buttocks, and legs. The Jews limited the number of stripes to a maximum of forty (thirty-nine in case of a miscount), but the Romans did not. **Jesus** survives the scourging, only to be executed.

The account continues: The "soldiers led [Jesus] away into the hall, called the Praetorium; and they call together the whole band. And they clothed him with purple, and platted a crown of thorns, and put it about his head, and began to salute him, Hail, King of the Jews! And they smote him on the head with a reed, and did spit upon him, and bowing their knees worshipped him. And when they had mocked him, they took off the purple from him, and put his own clothes on him, and led him out to crucify him" (Mark 15:16–20). The text does not necessarily support the long-held tradition that a thorny crown was used purposely to pierce Jesus' head as added torture (we cannot even be sure what plant is referred to in this passage). If such a thorny plant as we picture was used, the thorns could have been placed outward so the crown represented the rays of divinity that surrounded the head of the emperor or ruler on coins. It seems that all of the objects (cape/robe, thorns/crown, reed/scepter) used by the soldiers in this scene were props used in a cruel parody.

It is generally assumed that Pilate utilized soldiers that came from auxiliary troops recruited from the region, including **Samaria**. Most likely, many of them were apathetic toward Jews at best and rabidly anti-Jewish at worst. This mocking of Jesus could be seen as fulfilling three purposes: first, to ridicule Jesus; second, to ridicule the Jews in general; and third, to ridicule the Jewish leaders in particular.

Matthew identifies the Praetorium as the "common hall" (27:27). He adds "and they stripped him" before clothing him in a "scarlet robe" (27:28), amending Mark's "purple" (Mark 15:17). In other words, the soldiers used one of their own capes—obviously they would not have had access to the emperor's purple robe. Matthew says that the soldiers put "a reed in his right hand" (adding to the parody of the scene) and that it was with that reed they later "smote" him (27:29–30).

John provides some additional insights. For example, he says that the soldiers "smote him with their hands" (John 19:3). Additionally, John notes that "Pilate therefore went forth again, and saith unto them, Behold, I bring him forth to you, that ye may know that I find no fault in him. Then came Jesus forth, wearing the crown of thorns, and the purple robe. And Pilate saith unto them, Behold the man!" (19:4–5). John portrays Pilate as superstitious (19:8). Additionally, Pilate wants to release Jesus; however, he succumbs to pressure when charged: "If thou let this man go, thou art not **Caesar's** friend: whosoever maketh himself a king speaketh against Caesar" (19:12).

Golgotha
MATTHEW 27:32–34; MARK 15:20–23; LUKE 23:26–31; JOHN 19:13–17

As the soldiers took **Jesus** and the other two men to the place of execution, Mark states that "they compel one Simon a Cyrenian, who passed by, coming out of the country, the father of Alexander and Rufus, to bear his cross" (Mark 15:21). Both Matthew and Luke delete the reference to the two sons in their accounts (scholars assume Mark's Roman audience knew them; compare Romans 16:13). Since none of these three men is a public figure in the Gospels, one or more of them may have been the original eyewitnesses to the story, and their names were thus preserved in Mark's account. That one, if not all of them, had become followers of Jesus is not beyond the realm of possibility. An ossuary that may be Alexander's has been found and is now housed at Hebrew University on Mount Scopus (next to the Brigham Young University Center for Near Eastern Studies in Jerusalem).

The four Gospels each identify the location of Jesus' execution; "Golgotha" (Mark 15:22); "Golgotha" (Matthew 27:33); "Calvary" (Luke 23:33); "Golgotha" (John 19:17). Mark, Matthew, and John interpret the Hebrew name *Golgotha* as being the "place of a skull" (Mark 15:22; Matthew 27:33; John 19:17). The visual image of a "green hill" is not based on the text. Rather, it is a notion popularized in a beautiful and reverential hymn written in the nineteenth century by Cecil Frances Alexander: the terrain surrounding the city of Jerusalem is in fact stony and hard. Mark's account does not give directions to the place of execution but merely states that he was brought "unto the place Golgotha" (15:22). There are two sites associated with this event, two of which are extremely popular destinations for tourists and pilgrims today (the Church of the Holy Sepulchre, now within the Old City walls, and the Garden Tomb on Nablus Road). Protestants and Latter-day Saints are attracted to the Garden Tomb, discovered in 1883, where visitors see two side-by-side caves, which combine with fissures in the rock to resemble a gigantic skull, especially when viewed from the top of the Old City's walls. However, the Joseph Smith Translation says that it was the "place of burial," not "place of a skull" (JST, Matthew 27:33).

The Crucifixion
MATTHEW 27:25–44; MARK 15:24–33; LUKE 23:32–43; JOHN 19:18–22

Although we cannot know exactly what was in the minds of those who first heard the Gospels read or the earlier accounts of Jesus' execution, we do know that their mental image of how Jesus died was not like those of the paintings, movies, and sculpture to which we are exposed—and which often have aspects that definitely fall under the heading of artistic license. They knew what happened because they had, in many instances, witnessed firsthand a crucifixion.

Crucifixion was a brutal, gruesome, and vicious mode of execution—even some Roman writers thought it was barbaric—and of course, by law, no Roman citizen could be executed in this manner. Although Rome did not invent it, they used it effectively to punish the most dangerous enemies of the Empire—slaves and political prisoners. The individual died either from suffocation, exhaustion, exposure, shock from the terrible pain, or a combination of these. It was a public punishment meant to dehumanize the victim (who had been stripped of all clothing) and served to warn others what would happen if they challenged Rome's authority.

The Gospels further indicate that Pilate ordered Jesus' execution at the behest of the Jewish leaders (the crowd who called for Jesus' crucifixion did so because the chief priests and elders asked them to do so; see Mark 15:11). Josephus makes the same point: "When Pilate, upon hearing him accused by men of the highest standing amongst us, had condemned him to be crucified" (*Antiquities* 18:64; see also Tacitus, *Annals* 15.44).

That this was a Roman action has rarely been disputed. The identification of the two other men executed at the same time provides additional support for this conclusion. They are described as "thieves" (Greek, *lēstai*) in Matthew 27:38 (Luke describes them as "malefactors" [Greek, *kakourgoi*] in 23:33). In this verse, however, the King James Version is wrong in its translation of *lestai* as "thieves." They were robbers, like the man Pilate released: "Now Barabbas was a robber [*lēstēs*]" (John 18:40). Luke describes Barabbas, "who for a certain sedition made in the city, and for murder, was cast into prison" (Luke 23:19). Mark adds, "And there was one named Barabbas, which lay bound with them that had made insurrection with him, who had committed murder in the insurrection" (Mark 15:7). Matthew notes that Barabbas was "a notable prisoner" (Matthew 27:16). One wonders if the two men executed with **Jesus** were among "them that had made insurrection."

The difference between "thief" and "robber" is significant and provides a clue that explains why Pilate executed the two men with Jesus. Generally, someone who acts alone, steals secretly, and does so without violence is identified as a thief (Greek, *kleptai*)—they are tried and punished with some monetary fine. The King James Version gets it right in Matthew 6: "Lay not up for yourselves treasure upon earth, where moth and rust doth corrupt, and where thieves [*kleptai*] break through and steal" (6:19).

On the other hand, a robber is someone who may act in groups and who uses deadly violence—such criminals were generally captured and executed by the military without a formal trial. Notice what **Jesus** said to the armed arresting party who came to Gethsemane: "Are ye come out as against a thief [*lēstēn*]?" (Matthew 26:55). Here again, the King James Version gets it wrong; "against a robber" would have been a better translation. The context is political. The differences between thieves and robbers have caused many scholars to use "bandits" or "brigands" to describe robbers. Ironically, unlike the robbers operating in **Judea** and **Galilee**, Jesus had not robbed, plundered, collected arms, raised militant followers, or murdered anyone. Yet he was executed as though he had done so.

Given what we know about these events, we cannot be certain exactly why Pilate ordered Jesus to be executed. Some have argued that he was killed because others believed he was the king of the Jews. Still others argue that Pilate executed Jesus as a precautionary measure, just as Herod Antipas had done to John. Whatever motive(s) brought about his death, Jesus was executed by crucifixion, a Roman punishment, most likely in April A.D. 30.

The Soldiers Cast Lots
MATTHEW 27:35; MARK 15:24; LUKE 23:34; JOHN 19:23–24

The **Synoptic** evangelists saw in these events a fulfillment of Old Testament prophecy (Psalm 22:18), while John's account appears to rely on an eyewitness perspective recording very specific details about **Jesus'** clothing. Although there does not appear to be a significant doctrinal purpose to these verses or even a particular emphasis, they do show how careful the evangelists were in preserving details of Jesus' final hours.

The Sign on the Cross
MATTHEW 27:37; MARK 15:26; LUKE 23:38; JOHN 19:19–22

There is little variation in the Gospel accounts of the superscription on the cross. The superscription indicated the criminal charges for which the person was being crucified, thus the Greek, **Latin**, and Hebrew (**Aramaic**) inscription "The king of the Jews" indicates that **Jesus** was formally condemned for having claimed to be the king of the Jews and interestingly not for claiming to be the Jewish **Messiah**. No such words can be traced to Jesus, and the superscription offers a sublime irony of the crucified Creator and Lord. John notes that there was concern by the "chief **priests**" that the superscription should be changed to read, "He said, I am King of the Jews" (John 19:21). The superscription would likely have been recorded somewhere on the cross for onlookers to see and to act as a deterrent to any would-be criminals.

John Is Charged to Take Care of Jesus' Mother
JOHN 19:25–27

The most natural interpretation of the Greek text of John 19:25 is that there were four women standing by the cross: **Jesus'** mother; his mother's sister; Mary, the wife of Cleophas; and Mary Magdalene. Two of these women are introduced to the narrative for the first time in this scene, which shows Jesus' deep and abiding love for his mother.

Jesus' declaration, "Woman, behold thy son!" might be taken to refer to a request of sorts by Jesus wherein he asked his mother to care for Jesus' **disciple**, "whom he loved" (John 19:26), although the verse could equally intend that Jesus asked his mother to look at him, her son. In the latter instance, the shocking conclusion of Simeon's prophecy is brought full circle: "Yea, a sword shall pierce through thy own soul also" (Luke 2:35). Jesus' dying request was that John, the disciple whom Jesus loved, care for his mother despite the fact that Jesus had brothers still living (Acts 1:14). This story is the one place in John's Gospel account of the **Atonement** in which earthly concerns intersect Jesus' divine mission.

Jesus' Last Words
MATTHEW 27:46; MARK 15:34; LUKE 23:34, 43, 46; JOHN 19:26–28, 30

The Gospels record seven sayings that **Jesus** uttered from the cross before he died (no one Gospel preserves all of these seven sayings). However, we should not necessarily assume that this is all he said while he hung on the cross.

Mark, the earliest source, records Jesus' words both in **Aramaic** (transliterated) and Greek (translated): "Eloi, Eloi, lama sabachthani? which is, being interpreted, My God, my God, why hast thou forsaken me? (Mark 15:34). Mark does not suggest that these were Jesus' last words: "And Jesus cried with a loud voice, and gave up the ghost" (15:37). Matthew, as he does throughout the Passion narrative, closely follows Mark: "Eli, Eli, lama sabachthani? that is to say, My God, my God, why hast thou forsaken me?" (Matthew 27:46). Matthew's *Eli* is the Hebrew form for "my God," but the rest of the saying appears to be Aramaic. This saying is based on Psalm 22:1.

Luke provides three separate statements from the cross. First, Luke states, "Then said Jesus, Father, forgive them; for they know not what they do" (23:34; compare JST, 23:35). Second, when Jesus responded to one of the robbers' request to him, Jesus said, "Verily I say unto thee, To day shalt thou be with me in paradise" (23:43). Finally, Luke says that just before Jesus died, he said, "Father, into thy hands I commend my spirit" (23:46). John adds three statements: First, "When Jesus therefore saw his mother, and the disciple standing by, whom he loved, he saith unto his mother, Woman, behold thy son! Then saith he to the disciple, Behold thy mother!" (John 19:26–27). Second, "After this, Jesus knowing that all things were now accomplished, that the **scriptures** might be fulfilled, saith, I thirst" (19:28). And third, "When Jesus therefore had received the vinegar, he said, *It is finished*: and he bowed his head, and gave up the ghost" (19:30; emphasis added).

The Death of Jesus
MATTHEW 27:45–50; MARK 15:33–37; LUKE 23:46; JOHN 19:28–30

Some vivid details of the crucifixion emerge from **Jesus'** last moments in mortality. An onlooker put a sponge on a "reed," indicating that the cross was out of reach and thus above the head but not too far (Mark 15:36). The timing of the event is noted in detail, and Jesus' very words are preserved in **Aramaic**. The vividness of the detail in these accounts not only suggests an increased interest in documenting the story precisely but also documents the testimonies of living apostles who bear witness of events foretold by Old Testament prophets.

Mark, followed by Matthew and Luke, indicates that around noon, "the sixth hour," there was darkness over the land and that for three hours

Jesus hung in darkness though still alive (15:33). Around 3:00 P.M., or the "ninth hour," Jesus called upon the Father, "Eloi, Eloi, lama sabachthani?" (15:34), and shortly afterward he died. Jesus' death is described in very human terms, with anguish, human suffering, and a plea for help marking the account.

The onlookers to the crucifixion serve the purpose of documenting what Jesus might have felt without having Jesus directly declare his thoughts. The onlookers think that in calling for the Father he actually called for Elijah (15:35), and they tried to give him "a spunge full of vinegar" to quench his thirst (15:36). Vinegar here is a sour wine (Greek, *oxos*) that was commonly mixed with water and drunk at mealtimes. The purpose of the offering seems to be to ease Jesus' sufferings. Even Jesus' final evocation was made "with a loud voice," suggesting pain and agony (15:34). Some interpreted that shout to be a desperate call for help (15:35).

John's description of Jesus' dying moments is more austere, recalling the willing sacrificial victim and an omnipotent Lord who gives away his life rather than having it taken from him. John noted: "After this, Jesus knowing that all things were now accomplished, that the scripture might be fulfilled, saith, I thirst" (John 19:28). The reference to scripture in this verse may grammatically be taken in the larger sense to refer to Jesus' life and death as a fulfillment of Messianic prophecy ("all things were now accomplished" rather than in reference to Jesus' statement, "I thirst"). If John intended to draw attention to the fulfillment of Jesus' saying "I thirst," then he likely had in mind Psalm 69:21, which mentions being given gall or poison to drink (KJV, "vinegar"). John, just as in the **Synoptics**, describes Jesus being given a weak wine rather than anything noxious or poisonous.

Jesus' Side Is Pierced
JOHN 19:31–34

One of John's unique contributions to the record is found in these verses that speak of the day before the beginning of **Passover**, because it was the day of preparation, the day when the paschal lambs were sacrificed.

John's insight "for that **sabbath** day was an high day" has caused no small difficulty for interpreters (John 19:31). John does not, however, mention the paschal lambs in his account of the **Last Supper**. The high day mentioned in this verse is one of seven additional Sabbaths that were held according to date rather than by day of the week: The seven high Sabbaths were Passover (first and seventh days), **Pentecost**, *Rosh Hashanah, Yom Kippur*, **Atonement**, and Tabernacles (Leviticus 23). There are two ways to interpret this information. First, the traditional interpretation is that the Sabbath of the week that **Jesus** died was also a high day and thus the two coincided. Second, some commentators have interpreted the verse to mean that there were two Sabbaths the week Jesus died and that John referred to the first of the two, thus meaning that Jesus was crucified earlier in the week. Although the second possibility is innovative, tradition unanimously supports the day of the crucifixion as Friday.

At issue in these verses is the Roman practice of leaving crucified individuals on the cross for several days even after they were dead and the Jewish practice of burying their dead within twenty-four hours, so the Jews "besought Pilate that their legs might be broken, and that they might be taken away" (John 19:31; see Deuteronomy 21:23). The breaking of the victims' legs expedited their deaths, and this was seen as a favor that Pilate should grant so the Sabbath would not be violated. That Jesus' bones were not broken is significant as will be shown later (John 19:31–33).

Whether for symbolic reasons or historical interest, John includes the detail of Jesus' side being pierced: "And forthwith came there out blood and water" (19:34). The symbolism of blood and water is prevalent throughout the Gospel, and here John connects the symbols to the Atonement to give them eternal importance (John 1:13; 2:9; 3:5; 4:13; 6:53–56).

The Veil of the Temple Is Rent
Matthew 27:51–53; Mark 15:38; Luke 23:45

One immediate result of the death of **Jesus** is the rending of the veil that partitioned off the Holy of Holies, thus permitting all to see into those sacred precincts. This event symbolically marks the beginning of the **Gentile** mission and foreshadows the gospel being taken to all nations. Matthew clearly associates events that occurred after the Resurrection with the death of Jesus, emphasizing the doctrinal focus of these verses.

The Scriptures Are Fulfilled
JOHN 19:35–37

This short testimony is given from the perspective of the beloved **disciple** who addresses the reader directly, bearing witness that **Jesus** "fulfilled" the types and shadows of the Old Testament. The first fulfillment was that the paschal lambs should not have any bones broken, which is expressed in Exodus 12:46 and Numbers 9:12. The second fulfillment refers to an exact scriptural and prophetic passage found in Zechariah 12:10. In John, the living witnesses are passed over in favor of prophetic witnesses.

Watchers near the Cross
MATTHEW 27:54–56; MARK 15:39–41; LUKE 23:47–49

The focus of this incident is the testimony or witness of the centurion, who should not be identified with the centurion of Matthew 8:5–13 but rather as a leader of 100 men or auxiliary troops. Prior to the Jewish war of A.D. 66, the Romans used auxiliary troops, which would mean in all likelihood the centurion here was not from **Rome** but rather had been promoted through the ranks and was of local origin. His testimony follows Jewish thinking: "Truly this man was the **Son of God**" (Mark 15:39), although Luke presents a more cosmopolitan declaration: "Certainly this was a righteous man" (Luke 23:47).

Among those gathered at the cross were Mary Magdalene, Mary the mother of James the less and of Joses, and Salome. These women witnessed not only the death of Jesus but also the attending earthquake (Matthew 27:56; Mark 15:40). The identity of James the less or younger is complicated by the fact that there are so many individuals with the same name. "The less" is a comparative term indicating "of a younger age" or "of less stature" and is made in comparison to another James, most likely James of Zebedee and brother of John. The most likely candidate is James son of Alphaeus, although he is referred to by that title only at the end of the Gospels and not earlier during the ministry (Mark 16:1). The title may also be a much later appellation that reflects the time of the writing of the Gospels and may not have been in actual usage in Jesus' day. One would expect the **disciples** to bear witness to this unique moment, but their absence is not surprising, given the criminal accusations against Jesus and the contorted charges that he had planned to throw down the **temple**.

Jesus' Burial
MATTHEW 27:57–61; MARK 15:42–47; LUKE 23:50–56; JOHN 19:38–42

By the time the evangelists wrote, not all of the details of **Jesus'** burial had been pressed into a single, unified picture. All four accounts witness to Joseph of Arimathaea's (There is a lively discussion concerning the location of ancient Arimathaea, and it is likely that it was a Judean city and not located in **Galilee**) involvement, but there are some variations in the accounts concerning his standing among the Jews and his ownership of the tomb wherein Jesus was laid. Matthew and John report that Joseph was a "**disciple**" of Jesus (Matthew 27:57; John 19:38). Luke refers to him as a counselor (Greek, *bouleutēs hyparchōn*, "leader of the council," and used in the Gospels to refer to a member of the Sanhedrin) and someone who "waited for the kingdom of God" (Luke 23:51). This agrees with what Mark reports, except that Mark interprets "counselor" to mean a member of the council that convened to decide Jesus' fate and therefore a member of the governing elite. Certainly these four accounts can be rectified one with another, but in the years between the death of Jesus and the writing of the Gospels, it is surprising that the account comes to us in at least three different forms. We might surmise that Joseph, together with Nicodemus (John 19:38–39), knew of the death of Jesus because of their associations with the

Jewish governing elite and that they also knew how to go about retrieving the body of Jesus. This act may have put Joseph and Nicodemus at risk by identifying them as followers of Jesus, but from the accounts it would appear that they were not **disciples** in the same sense that Peter and others were, but in the more general sense of interested and concerned followers.

Only John seems interested in the exact location of the tomb, and he provides only vague locational clues, indicating that the site had not yet become a pilgrimage site: "Now in the place where he was crucified there was a garden; and in the garden a new sepulchre, wherein was never man yet laid" (John 19:41). The others simply describe the tomb without providing any directional clues. Matthew indicates that it was Joseph's own tomb (Matthew 27:60), while Mark and Luke appear to draw upon the same source, which indicated simply that it was a new tomb.

Great attention to detail can be found in the manner in which Jesus' body was prepared for burial and on what day the crucifixion took place. Matthew notes, "When the even was come" (Matthew 27:57), while Luke points to a need to hurry to prepare the body before the **Sabbath** day began: "And that day was the preparation, and the sabbath drew on" (Luke 23:54). John notes with even greater urgency, "There laid they Jesus therefore because of the Jews' preparation day; for the sepulchre was nigh at hand" (John 19:42). John also indicates that they chose a nearby sepulchre so they would be able to bury Jesus before sundown, or the beginning of the Jewish Sabbath.

The preparation of Jesus' body for burial is also of special concern as each evangelist made a point of mentioning some detail of how his body was cared for. Mary Magdalene, the other Mary (probably the mother of James and John), and Mary the mother of Joses were present on that day as well, likely to help Joseph of Arimathaea prepare the body for burial. Because of time constraints the task was not completed before the beginning of the Sabbath, and they would return to the tomb to finish their task on Sunday morning, when the Sabbath was formally ended ("And they returned, and prepared spices and ointments; and rested the sabbath day according to the commandment" [Luke 23:56]). On Friday, they were only able to wrap the body "in a clean linen cloth" (Matthew 27:59), and wash the body in spice-infused water using "a mixture of myrrh and aloes, about an hundred pound weight," which is a remarkable amount, and thus emphasizes that this was a royal burial of their king (John 19:39). When their preparations were done, or ended because the Sabbath was beginning, they "rolled a stone unto the door of the sepulchre" (Mark 15:46).

The Tomb Is Sealed
MATTHEW 27:62–66

Matthew includes the only **Synoptic** reference to Pharisaic involvement in **Jesus**' death and burial and thus demonstrates how over time the burden of guilt slowly shifted from the **Sadducees**, who were largely responsible for the death of Jesus, to the **Pharisees**, who were his primary antagonists in mortality. It is not unlikely that Pharisees were involved in the death of Jesus at some level, but the responsible parties, those who had the power to carry out the act, were the Romans and the Sadducees. Matthew's short report also provides evidence that knowledge of Jesus' prophecy concerning his resurrection from the dead had become widespread, so much so that people seemed to be looking for it (27:64). Matthew's description of the stone that sealed the sepulchre uses the terminology of sealing a letter, and may indicate simply a well-fitted stone rather than a haphazard blocking of the entrance (27:66).

Women Disciples Visit the Tomb
MATTHEW 28:1–2; LUKE 24:1–2

Matthew alone records the detail of the earthquake at **Jesus**' Resurrection and explains that "the angel of the Lord descended from heaven, and came and rolled back the stone from the door, and sat upon it" (Matthew 28:2). Luke reports simply that Mary and Mary Magdalene "found the stone rolled away from the sepulchre" (Luke 24:2), but he does not indicate how the stone came to be moved. The purpose of their visit can be seen in Luke's account: "bringing the spices which they had prepared"

(Luke 24:1) so they could finish anointing Jesus' body. Both Matthew and Luke note that it was the day after the **Sabbath**, Matthew making certain that it was clearly not on Saturday evening, but clearly on Sunday morning (Matthew 28:1).

Peter and Another Disciple Go to the Tomb
LUKE 24:12, 24; JOHN 20:3–10

The story of Peter's visit to the empty tomb is told in detail in the Gospel of John because it was also attested to by the unnamed **disciple** believed to be the author of the Gospel. The details in John's account are much more vivid, indeed indicating an eyewitness source: "And the napkin, that was about his head, not lying with the linen clothes, but wrapped together in a place by itself" (John 20:7). The purpose behind retelling this event is unclear unless the authors were interested in enumerating the many witnesses to the empty tomb. It is important also that even though the Gospels were written after **Jesus'** death, they show no interest in pointing out the location of the tomb as a pilgrimage site. This may be due to the fact that the Romans had taken over Jerusalem by A.D. 70.

John indicates that the two disciples, after seeing the empty tomb, "went away again unto their own home" (20:10). Their home, as far as the Gospel has reported it up to this point, was in **Galilee**, and this phrase should most likely be translated as, "to their own place of lodging" (Greek, *autous*), perhaps an inn or other place of temporary residence—unless, of course, John intended to imply that the disciples were prepared to return to Galilee (their home).

Mary Magdalene Witnesses the Resurrected Lord
JOHN 20:11–17

The eyewitness nature of John's Gospel continues into Mary Magdalene's encounter with the resurrected Lord, where she sees "two angels in white sitting, the one at the head, and the other at the feet, where the body of **Jesus** had lain" (John 20:12). Mary was already familiar with the tomb, having seen the place when the body was placed in it and therefore she already knew in which direction Jesus' body lay.

Mary was not surprised at seeing "two angels" (20:12) but rather openly speaks with them concerning the body of Jesus. Her grief resulted from her assumption that "they have taken away my Lord" (20:13). "They" must in this instance refer to those men who were responsible for crucifying Jesus and not the **disciples**.

Perhaps the most remarkable turn of events in this account is that Mary saw Jesus but did not recognize him, possibly because of his rather ordinary appearance or because through her grief she did not pause long enough to make a proper identification. Even Jesus' voice did not initially tear Mary from her grief, but when he spoke her name, she immediately recognized him: "Jesus saith unto her, Mary. She turned herself, and saith unto him, Rabboni; which is to say, Master" (20:16). The instant she turned and saw the resurrected Lord, she became the first mortal to witness the resurrected Lord. She became the first of many witnesses. Her comment shows a familiarity that defines a disciple-teacher relationship. She referred to him as "teacher" using the **Aramaic** *Rabboni* (transliterated into Greek by the Gospel authors), a word derived from the more familiar *rabbi*.

According to the King James Version, Jesus then said to Mary, "Touch me not" (20:17), a phrase that can also be translated as "do not hold me back" (Greek, *mē mou aptou*). The Joseph Smith Translation offers an interesting change to this verse, "hold me not" (JST, John 20:17), suggesting with the Greek that she had touched him or embraced him. Jesus then carefully reminded Mary that there was a gulf between them even though he was tangible and physically present. He said to her, "I am not yet ascended to my Father: but go to my brethren, and say unto them, I ascend unto my Father, and your Father; and to my God, and your God" (20:17). Jesus' words reveal a special relationship with God that is distinct from that of Mary or the disciples. His instructions to Mary also made her a messenger to the disciples.

Disciples Disbelieve Reports of Jesus' Resurrection
MARK 16:10–11; LUKE 24:9–11; JOHN 20:18

Mark and Luke agree that the **disciples** had doubts concerning the truthfulness of the reports that **Jesus** had been resurrected. Perhaps they had counted the number of days incorrectly, or perhaps they simply doubted the physical fulfillment of Jesus' prophecies concerning the Resurrection. Whatever the cause, the disciples needed a more literal witness than a secondhand report. They acted as Thomas did in the Gospel of John, and in a way they represent all those who know the prophecies but refuse to believe the witness of others.

The Two Marys
MATTHEW 28:1; MARK 16:1–4; LUKE 23:55; 24:3, 10; JOHN 20:1–2

The list of women who visited the empty tomb includes mostly named followers—Mary Magdalene, the other Mary, Mary the mother of James, Salome, and Joanna. Although Mark specifies Mary Magdalene and Mary the mother of James, Matthew refers to Mary Magdalene and the "other" Mary, perhaps because she had passed away by the time he wrote or she was so familiar to his audience that they needed no further indication as to her identity. That "other" Mary may have been the mother of James and John, **Jesus' disciples**, and it may be that she was Mary, the wife of Cleophas (John 19:25). Only Mark clearly indicates the purpose for which these women came to the tomb; they "had bought sweet spices, that they might come and anoint him" (Mark 16:1).

"He Is Risen"
MATTHEW 28:2–8; MARK 16:5–8; LUKE 24:4–8

Whether the announcement came from one angel (Matthew and Mark) or two angels (Luke; JST, Matthew 28:2; JST, Mark 16:5), the angel appears to have waited in the tomb to make the stunning announcement, which echoed the beginning of Matthew's Gospel: "Fear not" (Matthew 1:20). The two injunctions form the beginning and end, with the added instruction that the women followers of **Jesus** should not fear because "he is risen" (Matthew 28:6). Mark refers not to an angelic herald, but "a young man" (Mark 16:5). The message that the women **disciples** are to convey is that "he goeth before you into **Galilee**; there shall ye see him: lo, I have told you" (Matthew 28:7).

The Women Meet Jesus
MATTHEW 28:9–10; MARK 16:9

Jesus met the women while on their way to testify of the empty tomb, which following the Gospel of John, constitutes the second appearance of the resurrected Lord (John 20:11–17). Mark 16:9 alludes to an earlier event involving Mary Magdalene that is detailed only in Luke 8:2, possibly in an effort to hint at the great love she felt for Jesus.

Officials Bribe Soldiers
MATTHEW 28:11–15

This incident appears to be included in the Gospel of Matthew to counter rumors that were circulating wherein the soldiers had claimed that the sepulchre had been robbed. In desperate times, rumors and counter-rumors abound, and despite the number of times that **Jesus** appeared and the number of different people, men and women, who had seen him, there appears to have been a persistent rumor that the **disciples** had taken the body of Jesus. The simple fact that guards had been sent to the tomb, and that they had remained until the third day, indicates a widespread knowledge of the prophecy that Jesus would rise on the third day. Because he was executed as a criminal, it is likely that guards would have been stationed at the tomb until the body was safely entombed, but no contemporary account records guards standing watch for so long, thus suggesting that Jesus' entombment was treated differently because of the animosity felt toward him. But even after going to great lengths to stop grave robbing, the "elders" were unable to stop the story of the Resurrection from spreading. Matthew also reports that the elders were afraid that knowledge of Jesus' disappearance would reach Pilate, a concern that they had voiced earlier (John 11:48).

Two Disciples
MARK 16:12–13; LUKE 24:13–35

This particular incident finds greater focus in Luke than anywhere else, probably because Luke, or the churches to which he wrote, had a special knowledge or relationship with Cleopas and his companion who visited with the Lord while on the road to Emmaus. The unnamed companion who traveled with Cleopas could certainly have been his spouse, but perhaps also another unnamed **disciple** with whom the reader would not be familiar.

The account focuses on retelling an event rather than in moving the story of **Jesus'** Resurrection toward a doctrinal position. The incident also encapsulates the beginning of the gospel message itself, replete with misunderstanding and clarification. As Luke relates, Cleopas and his traveling companion encounter a man on their journey to Emmaus. The stranger, Luke tells us, is the resurrected Lord, but the two disciples do not recognize him because "their eyes were holden that they should not know him" (Luke 24:15–16). When asked by Jesus why they were sad, Cleopas provides a summary of all that had transpired in Jerusalem, revealing their dashed hopes. "And they said unto him, Concerning Jesus of Nazareth, which was a prophet mighty in deed and word before God and all the people: And how the chief **priests** and our rulers delivered him to be condemned to death, and have crucified him. *But we trusted* that it had been he which should have redeemed Israel: and beside all this, to day is the third day since these things were done. Yea, and certain women also of our company made us astonished, which were early at the sepulchre; and when they found not his body, they came, saying, that they had also seen a vision of angels, which said that he was alive. And certain of them which were with us went to the sepulchre, and found it even so as the women had said: but him they saw not" (Luke 24:19–24; emphasis added).

Realizing that his account could not end with an empty tomb, Luke adds, "The Lord is risen indeed, and hath appeared to Simon" (Luke 24:34). Without specifically framing the story as a discourse, Luke ends with the proclamation of the good news that Jesus is risen from the dead (3 Nephi 27:13–15).

Jesus Appears to His Disciples
MARK 16:14; LUKE 24:36–49; JOHN 20:19–23

The post-Resurrection appearances of **Jesus** to his **disciples** serve several important functions. From the three accounts of the first visit, it is clear that the disciples were initially afraid. Jesus said upon seeing them, "Peace be unto you" (Luke 24:36; John 20:19, 21). Luke describes the disciples' fear in specific detail, although he connects their fear with the concern that they were seeing a spirit: "But they were terrified and affrighted, and supposed that they had seen a spirit. And he said unto them, Why are ye troubled? and why do thoughts arise in your hearts?" (Luke 24:37–38). Mark, on the other hand, relates that the disciples were skeptical of the reports circulated by the women who had seen the risen Lord, whereas John records that they were afraid for their lives. Whatever the specific reason for their fear, those volatile days between the death and Resurrection of Jesus must have been difficult for them as they wondered what, if anything, they should do. All seemed lost.

A second matter that is woven into these accounts and the ones that follow it is the emphasis upon the idea that Jesus' resurrected body was physical in nature. Such emphasis on that subject raises the question of whether the evangelists were attempting to settle concerns that had arisen years later concerning the physical nature of the Resurrection. In Luke, the resurrected Jesus eats "broiled fish, and of an honeycomb" (Luke 24:42). John reports immediately after this first visit, an appearance where Thomas was able to touch Jesus' hands and side, but even in the first appearance there is emphasis placed on the physical resurrection, "And when he had so said, *he shewed unto them his hands and his side.* Then were the disciples glad, when they saw the Lord" (John 20:20; emphasis added).

Finally, the disciples received instruction on that first visit. In Luke, he "opened . . . their understanding, that they might understand the **scriptures**, and said unto them, Thus it is written, and thus it behoved **Christ** to suffer, and to rise from the dead the third day" (Luke 24:45–46). The scripture that he opened to them is Hosea 6:2, which was now interpreted in reference to his Resurrection. But the instruction they received does not appear to have been limited to a single clarification of Hosea. John adds, "And when he had said this, he breathed on them, and saith unto them, Receive ye the **Holy Ghost**" (John 20:22), thus providing clarification to John 7:39, which refers to the Spirit being limited during the mortal ministry.

The disciples were also instructed to teach the gospel of the remission of sins, to "remit" sins and in some instances to "retain" sins (John 20:23). Luke associates that Spirit-filled meeting with a promise of an even greater spiritual endowment: "And, behold, I send the promise of my Father upon you: but tarry ye in the city of Jerusalem, until ye be endued with power from on high" (Luke 24:49). The endowment of power (Greek, *enduō*, "to clothe" or "to take on") was promised to them at that meeting, an event that is further explained in D&C 95:8–10. These verses contain the only clear reference in the New Testament Gospels to an endowment of power.

Thomas Disbelieves
JOHN 20:24–25

This short passage records a tradition where the **disciple** Thomas resists believing the testimony of the other ten disciples because he seeks a literal, physical witness that the Resurrection is real. There may have been many reasons for preserving this incident, which affected only one of the disciples, but it also serves to demonstrate unlike any other account that **Jesus'** resurrected body was tangible and fleshly, as his mortal body had been. After this event the Gospel of John records how Thomas touches his body and then later how Jesus eats a meal with the disciples on the Sea of **Galilee**, each event confirming the physical nature of Jesus' body.

Jesus Appears Again to His Disciples
JOHN 20:26–29

The second appearance of **Jesus** to his **disciples** eight days later, that is, on the Sunday following the Resurrection, emphasizes the physical quality of Jesus' resurrected body. In this instance, Thomas is permitted to touch Jesus' body where it had been wounded previously although no mention is made by Jesus of the wounds. John records, "Reach hither thy finger, and behold my hands; and reach hither thy hand, and thrust it into my side: and be not faithless, but believing" (20:27). Jesus then commends those who would believe in his Resurrection through testimony rather than through physical manifestations (20:29).

John's Closing Testimony
JOHN 20:30–31

Unlike the other Gospel authors, John closes his account by bearing testimony and revealing his purpose in writing: "But these are written, that ye might believe that **Jesus** is the **Christ**, the **Son of God**; and that believing ye might have life through his name" (John 20:31). From the structure of the Gospel and the inclusion of a final testimony at the end of chapter 20, it appears that John had originally intended to end the book at this point. The final chapter (21) appears to have been added later as a postscript to answer questions or settle a growing dispute.

The Disciples in Galilee
JOHN 21:1–19

The appearance of **Jesus** at the Sea of **Galilee**, called his "third," indicates that the author is counting only the visits of Jesus to his **disciples** and
not the visit to Mary Magdalene (John 20:19–30). John records that this
particular visit included only seven of the eleven remaining Apostles: Peter,
Thomas, Nathanael, James, John, and two unnamed Apostles. And though
there may be some symbolic interpretation of the number seven in this account, the author makes no mention of it.

The focus of the story is the apostles' return to their former occupation of fishing. Moreover, they appear in this description to be lacking direction until Peter tells the others, "I go a fishing" (21:3). Without a clear
manifestation of what they should be doing, Peter returns to what he had
done previous to meeting Jesus and what probably seemed to be his duty.
It may also be that the disciples were hungry and needed to eat. As they
proceeded, Jesus appeared to the seven and revealed to them what they
should be doing.

When Jesus appears to the **apostles**, they do not immediately recognize him, but when he speaks to them, John is able to recognize his voice:
"Therefore that disciple whom Jesus loved saith unto Peter, It is the Lord"
(21:7). Prior to the Lord's visit, the disciples had not been successful in their
quest to catch fish, but following the Lord's instructions they were able to
catch fish in abundance. Two important points can be seen in this interchange. First, the disciples recognize Jesus not by seeing him, but by his
voice, which inspires them to change their ways. Second, when they follow
the Lord, their temporal endeavors are rewarded.

"Now when Simon Peter heard that it was the Lord, he girt his fisher's
coat unto him, (for he was naked,) and did cast himself into the sea" (21:7).
This verse reads as though Peter dressed before jumping into the water, thus
increasing the likelihood that he would drown. However, it is more likely
that he was fishing in his undergarments rather than being fully dressed.
When he saw the Lord, he reached for his fisher's coat and brought it with

him as he swam to shore. The "fisher's coat" that the author has in mind here appears to be some type of coat that would shed water.

When Peter and the others reached the shore, they saw that Jesus already had fish and bread (21:9), but he asked that they "bring of the fish which ye have now caught" (21:10) and join them with his catch. The full focus of the story now comes into view as the Lord teaches the seven that they should bring their abundant catch and join it with the catch he had already made. Their catch would be much greater than his, but the purpose was to bring them together. To make this point clear, Jesus directed Peter to feed his sheep.

There certainly may be some symbolic interpretation of Jesus' thrice-repeated directive to "feed my lambs" and indeed the verbs of loving and knowing as well as the noun for sheep vary in the story. However, such a symbolic interpretation may miss the simple need for variety in the communication and the fact that they spoke **Aramaic** and that the Greek is simply a translation of what was said. The three directives to Peter build upon one another, and the first asks a relative question: "Simon, son of Jonas, lovest thou me more than *these?*" (21:15; emphasis added). "These" in this verse grammatically refers to the fishes, but possibly the disciples as well. That Peter had returned to his former occupation raises the question of which he loved more, the Lord or the world. The second inquiry removes the comparative element of the question and asks simply, "Simon, son of Jonas, lovest thou me?" (21:16). Finally, Jesus asks a third time, "Simon, son of Jonas, lovest thou me?" (21:17), which hurt Peter: "Peter was grieved because he said unto him the third time, Lovest thou me?" (21:17). There are likely more complex reasons the Lord asked the same question three times, but the thrice-repeated affirmation immediately reminds the reader of the three denials. In front of six of the other disciples, Peter was able to testify three times to what he had previously denied three times.

To confirm Peter's faith and ability to stand facing adversity, again hinting at the earlier denials, Jesus prophesied of Peter's impending death: "Verily, verily, I say unto thee, When thou wast young, thou girdedst thyself, and walkedst whither thou wouldest: but when thou shalt be old, thou shalt stretch forth thy hands, and another shall gird thee, and carry thee whither thou wouldest not" (21:18). Tradition holds that Peter was crucified upside down under the reign of Nero (Eusebius, *Ecclesiastical History* 2.25.5; 3.1.2–3). The verb translated as "gird" (Greek, *zōnnymi*, "to tie up or on") most likely refers to the act of having one's arms tied to a crossbeam prior to being crucified. If Peter were to truly feed the sheep, then it would lead to his death just as it had led to Jesus' death on a cross. They, Peter and Jesus, would share essentially the same fate, giving literal meaning to Jesus' closing injunction, "Follow me" (21:19).

Peter Inquires Concerning the Fate of John the Beloved
JOHN 21:20–22

These three verses seem to have been included as a way of leading into the discussion of John's death and the controversy surrounding it. They report no new information, but rather reveal Peter's interest in self-preservation. His fate having just been revealed to him, Peter inquired concerning John, about whom there was an underlying understanding that he would not die: "**Jesus** saith unto him, If I will that he tarry till I come, what is that to thee? follow thou me" (John 21:22). The presupposition is that the reader would know the tradition surrounding John's fate and would be able to understand the contrast between living forever and the revelation that Peter would die as had been recounted immediately preceding these verses (21:18).

Testimony about John
JOHN 21:23–25

These final verses of the Gospel of John were certainly added after the Gospel was originally written, with the intent to offer a clarification concerning one of **Jesus'** teachings. While the saying might allow for the possibility that John the Beloved would not face death, this addition to the Gospel proposes a small clarification: "Then went this saying abroad among the brethren, that that **disciple** should not die: *yet Jesus said not unto him,*

He shall not die; but, If I will that he tarry till I come, what is that to thee?" (John 21:23; emphasis added). Unfortunately, there is no record of the original saying in the Gospel of John; however, it is fortunate that latter-day revelation offers clarification on this matter (D&C 7:1–4; compare Luke 9:27).

The final two verses reveal the hand of the editor who added these clarifying verses: "and *we* know that his testimony is true" (21:24; emphasis added). The editor then adds in the first-person singular that there are many other matters that could be discussed: "I suppose that even the world itself could not contain the books that should be written. Amen" (21:25). Certainly this editor had praiseworthy intentions and seems to be telling Christians that they should not lose faith despite what may appear to be John's death or departure. The time of writing of this addition should probably be placed at the beginning of the second century A.D. when the accounts of John the Beloved begin to grow more legendary (Tertullian, *Prescription against Heresies*, 36).

The Great Commission
MATTHEW 28:16–20; MARK 16:15–18

The **disciples'** retirement to a mountain recalls other mountain settings where **Jesus** taught the disciples (Matthew 5:1; 17:1). From the language of the King James Version, it appears that Jesus had commanded the disciples to meet him in an appointed location. However, the words translated as "where Jesus had appointed them" could equally be translated as "where Jesus instructed them" (Greek, *ou etaxato autois ho Iēsous*). The hill, instead of being simply a meeting place, was a place of instruction for the future mission and for those who may have "doubted" the reality of the resurrected Lord (Matthew 28:17). Matthew does not give expression to their doubts, but only that those doubts were resolved on the mountain when he appeared to them.

When Jesus gave the disciples "all power" on the mountain, it must be read in context of other passages where **priesthood** power is mentioned (Matthew 10:8; 16:19; 18:18) and thus truly was a commission and recognition that the disciples were now the leading authorities on the earth.

The command to "go ye therefore, and teach all nations" (Matthew 28:19) ends Jesus' earlier instruction that they "go not into the way of the **Gentiles**, and into any city of the **Samaritans** enter ye not" (Matthew 10:5) and was necessary for the disciples so that they would understand that the ministry would no longer be in Israel only.

The final verse, "Teaching them to observe all things whatsoever I have commanded you: and, lo, I am with you alway, even unto the end of the world. Amen," offers an interesting perspective on what the Gospel of Matthew has presented (Matthew 28:20). The words of Jesus, although they rarely present specific commands, have now become the gospel: "all things . . . I have commanded you." They leave no doubt that Jesus' life and teachings constitute a new law and way of life.

Matthew follows Mark in almost all particulars, adding further reflection on the power of the priesthood that they would use: "They shall take up serpents; and if they drink any deadly thing, it shall not hurt them: they shall lay hands on the sick, and they shall recover" (Mark 16:18).

Jesus' Ascension and Proclamation
MARK 16:19–20; LUKE 24:50–53

The Gospel of Mark closes with a rather short summary statement indicating knowledge of an extended ministry after the Resurrection: "And they went forth, and preached every where, the Lord working with them" (Mark 16:20). Luke likewise documents a ministry after the Resurrection, "And he led them out as far as to Bethany" (Luke 24:50). As an added note, Luke prepares the reader to transition immediately into the book of Acts by adding, "And were continually in the **temple**, praising and blessing God" (Luke 24:53). The **disciples** must have tarried in the courtyards of the temple teaching and participating in the daily public prayers. At that time the temple was devoted wholly to administering the ordinances of the Mosaic law, and in Acts, Luke frequently places preaching and healing events in the temple (Acts 3:1–11).

271

2

THE ACTS OF THE APOSTLES

Luke, the author of Acts, divided his two-part work (Luke–Acts) into distinct halves—Jesus' mortal ministry and the ministry "through the **Holy Ghost**" (Acts 1:2)—and covers the history of the **Church** from roughly A.D. 30 to A.D. 60/62, with little information from A.D. 37 to A.D. 46. This two-part division may also have been determined in part because of the practical consideration of the length of a papyrus or parchment roll.

The Savior's Post-Resurrection Ministry
ACTS 1:1–14

Luke begins by addressing Theophilus, perhaps a symbolic name (Greek, *theophilos*, "lover of God"), or possibly even a wealthy patron who had commissioned Luke to write the Gospel.

Luke's sources now shift from being comparative, in constant dialogue with the other written Gospels, to being the sole witness for many of the events he describes in Acts. In doing so, Luke became, whether by official call or through happenstance, the first Church historian, with an emphasis on Paul and an almost complete neglect of Roman history unless it informs Christian history (for example, he passes over the assassination of the Emperor Caligula in A.D. 41). The sources he drew upon were incomplete for the forty-day ministry, regarding which Luke says that Jesus, "being assembled together with them, commanded them that they should not depart from Jerusalem, but wait for the promise of the Father, which, saith he, ye

272

have heard of me" (1:4). The Lord revealed in this dispensation what the phrase "promise of the Father" meant: "Yea, verily I say unto you I gave unto you a commandment that you should build a house, in the which house I design to endow those whom I have chosen with power from on high; for this is the promise of the Father unto you" (D&C 95:8–9). The Lord instructed the **disciples** further, telling them to look beyond **Judea** to **Samaria**, the location of one of **Jesus'** most successful teaching experiences (John 4:39).

While Matthew and Mark end with the disciples having traveled to **Galilee**, Luke ends and Acts begins with the Lord instructing them to stay in Jerusalem for the promise of the Father to be given. This apparent contradiction in the accounts may simply reveal that the endings of the Gospels reflect a time longer than the forty-day ministry.

As expected, the disciples went to the upper room, the location of which still seems to be implied in Luke's Gospel, to consider how to implement the instructions given in the forty-day ministry (a "**sabbath** day's journey" was about a thousand yards; Josephus, *Antiquities* 20.169). That first apostolic council considered other matters besides a worldwide mission. They were also faced with replacing one of the members of their quorum. Acts 1:14 refers to another meeting as well, one in which Jesus' mother and siblings were present. The reference to Jesus' brothers provides the first indication in the New Testament that Jesus' siblings had come to believe in him (John 7:1–7; 1 Corinthians 15:7).

The Calling of a New Member of the Twelve
Acts 1:15–26

Some time has passed between the forty-day ministry and Peter's call for a council, as Luke notes subtly that the number of members has continued to grow, implying that the new **Church** indeed had a future. Luke then recounts a separate tradition concerning the death of Judas Iscariot, one both similar and different from that of Matthew 27:3–10. The Joseph Smith Translation of Matthew 27:5 harmonizes the accounts.

Peter put forth two requirements for the newly called member of the Twelve: first, the individual had to company "with us all the time that the Lord **Jesus** went in and out among us, beginning from the **baptism** of John, unto that same day that he was taken up from us" (Acts 1:21–22); and second, the individual must "be ordained to be a witness with us of his resurrection" (1:22). The implications of these requirements imply a special witness, which can be gleaned from the phrase "with us," in the sense of "like us." That the individual must be a follower of Jesus from the days of John the Baptist would severely limit the number of potential candidates, and by the end of the first century all potential candidates would have passed on. This requirement, while probably not intended to be interpreted rigidly through all time, may signal the reason why the second generation of Jesus' followers ceased to refer to their leaders as apostles and preferred rather the title of **bishop**. On the other hand, that Jesus had called and trained special witnesses would suggest that he intended to have such in every dispensation.

The Day of Pentecost
ACTS 2:1–13

Pentecost is celebrated seven weeks after **Passover**/Easter Sunday, or fifty days later, which places the event in late spring at the time of the harvest of the first crops of the season, and its celebration is described in the Old Testament (Exodus 23:16; 34:22; Numbers 28:26). The foundational accounts of the beginning of the **Church** in the meridian of time were as important to the Saints of that dispensation as our own beginnings are in our dispensation. This account, which in many ways resembles a First Vision account with parallels to the events that occurred on the day the Kirtland Temple was dedicated, describes the prophetic beginnings of a Christian church. Of particular interest is the number of people who witnessed the event. The verbs of recognition are important also, where the crowd *heard* a "rushing mighty wind, and it filled all the house where they were sitting" (2:2) and they *saw* "cloven tongues like as of fire" (2:3).

The story also advances the role of Galileans in these accounts, a sentiment that likely reveals a continuing distrust of Judean Jews and their opposition to **Jesus**. The list of nations spans much of the known world in the **disciples**' day, although it does not reach as far as Spain or into northern Europe, thus suggesting at least initially that the list is not a stylized portrayal, but rather in many ways a literal listing of those present. However, the mention of countries such as Elam, which had ceased to exist, suggests a symbolic emphasis in the account. The reference to new wine is probably associated with the concept of harvest that Pentecost was intended to celebrate, but certainly not new in the sense of without fermentation as implied in their assumption: "Others mocking said, These men are full of new wine. But Peter . . . lifted up his voice, and said . . . be this known unto you . . . these are not drunken, as ye suppose" (2:13–15).

Peter's Speech on the Day of Pentecost
ACTS 2:14–36

In Peter's odyssey from Galilean fisherman to head of the **Church**, perhaps no single speech more fully represents his growth as president and the sentiments of the earliest members. The speech follows a threefold structure. First, the earliest Christians understood what they were experiencing as a fulfillment of prophecy in a literal way (Joel 2:28–32; compare Joseph Smith–History 1:41). Second, Peter taught that the death of **Jesus** should not be interpreted as a setback, but rather as part of the "determinate counsel and foreknowledge of God" (2:23); and although the Judean plot against Jesus is acknowledged, there is no lingering animosity as Peter quickly returns to the theme of God's plan (2:24–25). Third, the Resurrection and the power of the Resurrection to bring mankind out of "**hell**" and "corruption" have become the message (2:27). Peter's message is that of victory and not defeat, which stands in stark contrast to his earlier admonition to Jesus that he not go to Jerusalem and offer his life in **sacrifice** (Matthew 16:21–23). This threefold approach may represent the core of the gospel message the missionaries carried into **Samaria**, **Galilee**, and beyond.

A modern reader may find the references to David's prophetic psalms unsettling in light of his later actions against Uriah, but Luke fully represents the sentiments of the first century, that David's words were still highly respected (Psalms 16:8–10; 110:1). Although the location of David's tomb is uncertain, it was apparently well known in Peter's day and may have been considered a national treasure (Acts 2:29).

Early Followers
ACTS 2:37–40

In reading these verses, the impression made is that an ancient reader would understand the allusions and implications of these verses, so Luke is able to move quickly to the organization of the **Church** in Jerusalem. He passes over the form of **baptism** and other important details. Although it is unclear where Peter's speech was delivered, it is reasonable to assume that it was given at or very near the **temple** where there would have been *mikva'ot*, or ritual immersion pools. There, in the shadow of the temple, stood several *mikva'ot*, and Peter instructed those who had been "pricked in their heart" (Acts 2:37) to "be baptized" (2:38), thus possibly using the setting to foreshadow how the new **covenant** would reform the old.

Continuing in the Apostles' Doctrine
ACTS 2:41–47

Luke wrote many years after the events described in these verses occurred, and therefore the events are described in past tense. With that perspective, it is important that Luke offer some description of origins for practices with which Christians were generally familiar. Luke moves quickly, and in a single verse details the revelation and implementation of the law of consecration (Acts 2:44). For Luke, the institution of the practice of the law of consecration may have been part of the distant past, an event for which he had only the sketchiest details. Luke also explains that the earliest Christians continued to participate in **temple** activities in Jerusalem while the temple still stood (prior to A.D. 70) *and* that they broke bread from house to house following the practice the Lord had revealed on the night of the **Last Supper**. But perhaps the most profound inference came through Luke's perspective of having written during the last decades of the first century: "And they continued stedfastly in the **apostles'** doctrine and fellowship, and in breaking of bread, and in prayers" (2:42). The early members found safety standing in the doctrine as taught by the apostles, perhaps hinting at one of the causes of **apostasy** as Luke understood it.

A Miracle in the Temple
ACTS 3:1–11

The ninth hour of prayer signaled also the time of the evening **sacrifice** that was made in the temple by the **priests**, and Peter's and John's presence there may reflect both their interest in teaching the gospel to their countrymen and their continuation in following the practices they had consistently observed while **Jesus** was with them. The man who asks Peter and John for **alms** appears to have been well known: "They knew that it was he which sat for alms" (Acts 3:10). He was probably perpetually in that condition, even during Jesus' ministry to the **temple**. At the conclusion of the **miracle**, "all the people ran together unto them in the porch that is called Solomon's, greatly wondering" (3:11). The antecedent of "them" in the 3:11 appears to be Peter and John, who respond in 3:12 as though the crowd has approached them. Luke, with this brief description of the **miracle**, subtly illustrates the growing power of the **disciples** in contrast to the waning power of the temple and its **priests**.

Peter Addresses Those Who Have Seen the Miracle in the Temple
ACTS 3:12–18

Those who assembled to hear Peter's response in light of having witnessed a **miracle** were strongly rebuked by Peter, evidence that the audience was not composed simply of interested onlookers. Peter chose to rebuke them on the matter of **Jesus'** death, perhaps further identifying some members of the crowd as belonging to the group who condemned Jesus (John 18:15, 35) and cried for the release of Barabbas. Peter interpreted Pilate's role as less significant than those who cried for the condemnation of Jesus, and may already represent a trend to see Pilate as a manipulated, incapable governor (Acts 3:13).

The Prophet like Moses
ACTS 3:19–26

A second theme of Peter's discourse was **Jesus'** future fulfillment of the prophecy of the coming of a prophet like Moses (Deuteronomy 18:15–18). When Jesus returns in the "times of restitution of all things" (Acts 3:21), he will also fulfill Moses' prophecy of a prophet that should be heard, "in all things" (3:22). Although Peter does not specifically mention **baptism**, there is optimism in his closing words, encouraging his audience to see Jesus through the prophets and the "**covenant** which God made with our fathers" (3:25).

Apostles Continue in the Example of Jesus
ACTS 4:1–22

Following the pattern that is also present in the Gospel of John, that **miracles** and teaching truth provoke the wicked, the **disciples** here are treated in a manner similar to the way **Jesus** was treated, thus providing evidence that they are following his example. Luke reports that the **priests**, probably meaning those who administered the **sacrifices** in the **temple**, the appointed captain of the temple guard, and the **Sadducees** came together. Although an official inquiry into the matter is implied, more than likely it was mob oriented, given the diverse groups who confronted the **apostles**. The primary concern of that group was that the apostles were teaching the Resurrection, thus suggesting that the opposition may have been primarily

Sadducean (the **Pharisees** purportedly accepted the doctrine of a resurrection). Perhaps Luke's source for this incident was not clear whether this was an official inquiry by the Sanhedrin, which was controlled primarily by Sadducees, or whether it was a mob action.

The disciples spent the night in prison, awaiting a hearing during the day, which Luke reports resulted from Jewish concerns for holding the hearing at night (Acts 4:3). When the hearing reconvened, the confronting group was fundamentally different, and now there were "rulers, and elders, and **scribes**, and Annas the high priest, and Caiaphas, and John, and Alexander, and as many as were of the kindred of the high priest, were gathered together at Jerusalem" (4:5–6), thus making the high priest and those protecting his interests to blame for the arrest and interrogation. Annas was not actually serving as high priest at the time this incident occurred, and perhaps Luke intended to indicate Jonathan ben Ananus or Caiaphas, or perhaps the title stayed with him for life.

Peter was permitted to address those who were concerned about his teachings in the temple. When he did so, he returned to the volatile topic of the interpretation of Psalm 118:22, which Jesus had also addressed shortly after the triumphal entry (Matthew 21:42). Peter testified boldly to the truthfulness of the gospel message *and* the miracle, showing that the disciples were continuing in the example and teachings of Jesus and that they were not perpetuating some new philosophy. The historical foundation for the apostles' doctrine is an important point of emphasis in Luke's account.

The council, or the implied Sanhedrin, convened to settle the matter, deciding that the apostles' witness was too powerful to deny. Luke reports that their official response was to threaten the disciples, which had little effect. This ironic portrayal of the council threatening the disciples because the witness was too great to deny also implies that the witness would be too great for anyone to deny and therefore the threat would be useless.

Details of the Law of Consecration
ACTS 4:31–37

By returning to the subject of the practice of consecration, Luke intentionally shows how the threats recorded in Acts 4:30 resulted in a strengthening of the Christian community. In fact, the "company . . . lifted up their voice to God *with one accord*" and now speaks with a unified voice (Acts 4:23–24; emphasis added). Peter made a full report of their experiences to the assembled Christians who were no doubt concerned about their overnight absence. The threats also have the added benefit of strengthening the fledgling consecrated community.

It is difficult to know exactly how the early Saints practiced the law of consecration, and Luke here reports some details: "Neither was there any among them that lacked: for as many as were possessors of lands or houses sold them, and brought the prices of the things that were sold, and laid them down at the **apostles'** feet: and distribution was made unto every man according as he had need" (4:34–35). The ownership of consecrated properties is not mentioned, and Luke's description could lead to the conclusion that all properties were sold and the proceeds consecrated, but such a landless community would have little hope of long-term survival. The structure, however, seems to have strong parallels to the annual Jewish festivals where the poor were fed from the **sacrifices** made in the **temple**. The focus in Acts 4 is also to meet needs and to take care of those who lack. Joseph (Acts gives the shortened form "Joses") Barnabas is also introduced for the first time in the account as one who lived the law of consecration (4:36).

Ananias and Sapphira
ACTS 5:1–11

Although Luke does not unequivocally mention it, this incident appears to constitute the end of the practice of the law of consecration among the members of the early **Church**. The practice is not mentioned in detail again in the remainder of the New Testament, and by the time Paul wrote

Galatians (Galatians 2:10; c. A.D. 48–50), the poor were being cared for through a general collection. Ananias and Sapphira's duplicity in holding back a portion of the price from selling a possession was likely one of many events that led to the practice being discontinued and may also reveal why the Lord acted so decisively in punishing their disobedience. The practice of the law of consecration was likely limited to the Jerusalem Saints and the ending of it, or at least the problem of corruption here detailed, foreshadows later internal issues that would rend the **Church**.

The Apostles Face Persecution in Jerusalem
ACTS 5:12–42

The reason one account is preserved and another is passed over is often an integral part of interpreting what that account is intended to teach. In Acts 5 a straightforward cause-and-effect story is retold: the **apostles** performed **miracles**, which led to the **Sadducees** imprisoning and threatening them. Luke shows no concern for historical intricacies in the story, such as how the Sadducees were able to wield the power to arrest and harass so freely. Instead, he seems to follow the prophecy of the Gospel of John, in which the Lord told the **disciples**, "Verily, verily, I say unto you, He that believeth on me, the works that I do shall he do also; and greater works than these shall he do; because I go unto my Father" (John 14:12), and then subsequently, "They shall put you out of the **synagogues**: yea, the time cometh, that whosoever killeth you will think that he doeth God service" (John 16:2). Both of these predictions were fulfilled in these events.

The **apostles** were arrested for violating the command they were given in Acts 4:18 to not teach in the name of **Jesus** (Acts 5:25, 28), which would have been a violation of a Sanhedrin edict but probably not punishable under Roman law. Luke adds as a conclusion to this account the intervention of Gamaliel, a moderate Jewish voice and Paul's teacher, where he called for restraint in harassing the **disciples** of Jesus, teaching instead that "if it be of God, ye cannot overthrow it; lest haply ye be found even to fight against God" (5:39), a statement that Luke certainly understood as prophetic. The rebellions of Judas and Theudas (5:36–37) are also referred to by Josephus and can be dated respectively to circa A.D. 6 and circa A.D. 45 (*Antiquities* 18.6; 20.5; *War* 2.8).

Care for the Widows
ACTS 6:1–8

Following the practice of the entire community living the law of consecration, Luke now reports that the "number of the **disciples** was multiplied," but that with this increase in membership, the Greek widows were not being cared for in the same way that the Hebrew widows (probably Greek and **Aramaic** speaking Judeans) were being cared for (Acts 6:1). The "daily ministration" (6:1) appears to be a modified form of the law of consecration, which Paul also mentions in 1 Timothy 5:9. The calling of seven men to serve the widows raises the question of which **priesthood** office they were called to serve in, and although Luke does not specifically mention it in the account, he twice uses the Greek term *diakonia* "service" from which the modern word **deacon** ultimately derives (6:1–2, 4). Philip, who is called here, is also noted later as having the authority to baptize (Acts 8:38). More important perhaps for Luke is the introduction of Stephen into the story, which provides a transition to the introduction of Paul (Acts 7:58).

The Synagogue of the Libertines
ACTS 6:9–11

The King James Version's translation "synagogue of the Libertines" intends to convey the idea that the synagogue in question was a gathering place for freedmen, or former slaves (Acts 6:9). These former slaves could have obtained their freedom through a variety of means; Luke also notes that they were foreigners, which most likely is intended to indicate that they were Greek-speaking Jews whose parents had been taken into captivity and that once they had obtained their freedom they returned to Jerusalem, or their place of origin. Cilicia, the region of Tarsus and the hometown of

Paul, is specifically mentioned. That Paul bore both a Roman name (Paul) and a Hebrew name (Saul) indicates that his family maintained ties with their ancestral faith. His Roman name may also reveal a servile heritage (**Latin**, *paulus*, "short" or "small") or a connection to the influential Roman family bearing the same name, *Paullus*. A dispute arose in that synagogue that led to further persecution of the **disciples**, which may foreshadow the stoning of Stephen and Paul's role as a witness to that event.

Stephen, the First Martyr
ACTS 6:12–7:57

The first seven chapters of Acts cover a brief period, about three years (A.D. 30–33). Heightening the tension in the history, Jewish officials in Jerusalem worry about the emerging **Church** as highlighted in three separate trials before the Sanhedrin with increasingly hostile consequences. The first trial concluded with a stern warning to Peter and John to not "speak at all nor teach in the name of **Jesus**" (Acts 4:18). The second trial ended with the same warning, but Peter and John were also beaten (5:40). Finally, the third trial ended with Stephen being summarily stoned to death (7:57–59). Luke clearly saw Stephen's execution as part of a concentrated effort to stop Jesus' followers from preaching, teaching, and healing in his name—signaling the beginning of a greater persecution that forced many early believers to flee Jerusalem. The central issue that led to Stephen's death was probably his report of having seen God (7:56) and not simply a dislike of his interpretation of scripture.

The last trial before the Sanhedrin began when "certain of the synagogue" stirred up a controversy that resulted in Stephen's arrest and trial before the Sanhedrin (6:9–12). In this setting, Luke presents Stephen's discourse before the council, the longest speech preserved in Acts, which most likely reveals the importance of its message to Luke and the early Church.

In this speech, Stephen criticized the continuing rejection of the Lord's message and messengers. Although it was not an attack on the **Law** or the **temple**, it was nevertheless a strong condemnation of a lack of faith in the

Lord and the **Torah** from the time of Joseph, who was sold into Egypt, until the present period. Stephen charged the Jewish leaders, "Ye stiffnecked and uncircumcised in heart and ears, ye do always resist the **Holy Ghost**: as your fathers did, so do ye. Which of the prophets have not your fathers persecuted?" (7:51–52).

Saul the Persecutor
ACTS 7:58; 8:1–3

Luke introduces Saul, later known as Paul, to his audience in the last verses of chapter 7 and the first three verses of chapter 8. Saul is portrayed as an important figure in the persecution of the Saints in Jerusalem "entering into every house, and haling men and women committed them to prison" (Acts 8:3). He may have been involved in the debate with Stephen in the synagogue in the first place (Acts 6:9–11). We should recall that Saul was from Cilicia (Acts 21:39). He was also present when Stephen was killed (7:58). Later he led a delegation to arrest those who called upon **Jesus'** name in Damascus (9:1–2).

Philip's Ministry
ACTS 8:4–40

In the face of mounting persecution in Jerusalem, many Saints were "scattered abroad," preaching the word in the regions round about the Holy City (Acts 8:4). Luke focused his attention on the activities of Philip, who preached to the **Samaritans, proselytes,** and even a eunuch—all individuals and groups marginalized in first-century Judaism. Later, Luke informs us that he met Philip (Acts 21:8–10), providing strong evidence that Luke used eyewitness sources in preparing his two-part work (Luke 1:2). Peter and John followed in Philip's footsteps in **Samaria,** conferring the **Holy Ghost** on those who had been baptized (8:14–25).

Saul Persecutes the Church

Acts 9:1–9

Luke describes Saul's persecution of the **Church** as though it were a legally sanctioned action, with the caution that he was "breathing out threatenings and slaughter against the **disciples** of the Lord" (Acts 9:1). Although Luke does not specifically mention it, Saul could not legally kill Christians in Damascus or in Jerusalem, which may be hinted at with the verb "breathing" (Greek, *empneōn*). Moreover, Saul sought permission from the high priest in Jerusalem (probably Caiaphas) to harass Damascus Christians. The King James Version uses the term "bound" (9:2), but historically it seems unlikely that Paul would have had the power to arrest and bind anyone. Rather, those Christians whom he found "of this way" would have to willingly submit to their excommunication and any associated punishments (Galatians 1:13).

The vision that Saul saw on the way to harass Christians powerfully changed his direction in life, as he discovered that he must follow the Lord **Jesus Christ**. The persecutor would soon become the persecuted. Saul's vision appears to be different from that of his companions, of whom Luke notes, "And the men which journeyed with him stood speechless, hearing a voice, but seeing no man" (9:7). The story also plainly teaches that Saul had to seek further directions from the leaders of the Church in Damascus, or in other words, Saul was being called into the Church and was not to function as an independent representative of God's power.

Acts preserves a brief outline of how outsiders described Christianity. At the beginning of this chapter, Paul refers to Christianity using the oldest known title: "this way" (9:2). Shortly thereafter, the title "Christian" was applied to what was originally another way to be Jewish (Acts 11:26), and later Christians were referred to as belonging to the "sect of the Nazarenes" (Acts 24:5).

Saul Is Healed
ACTS 9:10–31

The otherwise unknown Ananias likewise had a vision in which he was shown Saul and what he should do for him. Luke's abrupt introduction of Ananias into the account serves to heighten the contrast between the increasingly powerful persecutor and the humble servant of the Lord. The contrast is further emphasized when Ananias asks the Lord concerning Saul, implying that it might be prudent not to heal him (Acts 9:13–14).

The verses following Ananias's discussion with the Lord are key to understanding Paul's later role in the **Church**: Paul was baptized into the Church, thus confirming his vision on the road to Damascus. The restoration of his vision signaled the beginning of his conversion process, but **baptism** was still required for formal entrance into the kingdom, a point that Luke pauses to note. From the time of his conversion forward, roughly fifteen to seventeen years would pass before Paul would again enter the history of the early Church (Galatians 1:18; 2:1).

In a later epistle, Paul also commented on the persecution during his time in Damascus (Acts 9:23–25; 2 Corinthians 11:32–33). The exact reason why Aretas IV Philopatris would have sought his life is uncertain, although it may have been an extension of hostilities between Aretas and Herod Antipas over a border dispute or Herod Antipas's divorce of Aretas's daughter.

Peter's Early Mission
ACTS 9:32–43

Peter's visit to Lydda (modern Lod) near Joppa was the setting for two healing **miracles**. It may be that Luke placed the account of Peter and the healings of Aeneas and Tabitha in proximity to the account of Paul's conversion to illustrate Peter's inspired leadership of the **Church** and to show how closely Peter's own ministry now resembled that of Jesus' during the Lord's mortal ministry. In fact, Tabitha, like Lazarus, had been dead long enough that her body had been washed and prepared for burial, while the healing of Aeneas reminds the reader of the healing at the Pool of Bethesda (John 5:5–9). The mention of "Simon a tanner," a person who was likely well known to the early Saints, may also reveal the source of this story.

Peter, Cornelius, and Caesarea
ACTS 10:1–48

Luke here turns his attention to the spread of the gospel to the wider **Gentile** world. In this case, Peter preaches to and baptizes an uncircumcised Gentile named Cornelius. Paralleling Saul's turnaround, Peter also experienced a complete turnaround in accepting Gentiles into the **Church** (Acts 10:28). The decisive moment came about only after a series of interconnected visions (10:3–6, 10–16), reminding the reader of the earlier visions of Saul and Ananias, which signaled another decisive moment in the history of the early Church (9:3–6, 10–16): Peter's prompting by the Holy Spirit to visit Cornelius (10:19–20) and the unexpected and visible descent of the **Holy Ghost** upon Cornelius and his household (10:44).

It is during this significant gathering at Caesarea that Peter speaks one of the most memorable lines in the New Testament: "Of a truth I perceive that God is no respecter of persons: but in every nation he that feareth him, and worketh righteousness, is accepted with him" (10:34–35). In that same setting Peter also describes **Jesus**' ministry in some of the most beautiful words recorded in the Bible: "That word, I say, ye know, which was published throughout all Judaea, and began from **Galilee**, after the **baptism** which John preached; how God anointed Jesus of Nazareth with the Holy Ghost and with power: who went about doing good, and healing all that were oppressed of the devil; for God was with him" (10:37–38).

Additionally, Luke provides a window into the operation of the early Church in reporting this incident by demonstrating how Church policy and doctrine were established through revelation, including open visions and the promptings of the Holy Ghost. For Luke, it was important that Peter and the Church leaders in Jerusalem approve the decisive step of taking the gospel to the Gentiles, acknowledging that the Lord had accepted those they had previously believed were unacceptable to him. In other words, the gospel was intended for all people.

Moreover, the account showed the important role that "God-fearers" played in the expansion of missionary work among Gentiles. These men, like Cornelius, attached themselves to a synagogue and were prepared for the "good news" through their study of the **Septuagint (LXX)**, fasting, prayer, and good works.

Acknowledging the Lord's Will
ACTS 11:1–18

The history of Peter and Cornelius is repeated in chapter 11, when the senior **apostle** relates his experience in Caesarea to **Church** leaders in Jerusalem. Peter's report is more about the revelation Peter received than about his decision to eat with **Gentiles** (Acts 11:3), marking an important change in the spiritual border that separated Jews and Gentiles in the first century. The situation is resolved when Peter informs the apostles and brethren in Jerusalem about his visions in Joppa (11:5–10); the prompting of the Holy Spirit to travel to Caesarea (11:11–12); Cornelius's vision (11:13–14); and finally, how the **Holy Ghost** fell upon the uncircumcised Gentiles while he preached to them (11:15–17). Luke concludes, "When they heard these things, they held their peace, and glorified God, saying, Then hath God also to the Gentiles granted repentance unto life" (11:18).

Antioch, Barnabas, and Saul
ACTS 11:19–30

Luke turns his attention back to Barnabas and Saul as he describes what happened in Antioch on the Orontes (Acts 11:19–30). Antioch, often identified as Antioch of Syria, was considered the third most important city in the Empire after **Rome** and Alexandria.

In the wake of the continuing persecution in **Judea**, several **disciples** reach "Phenice [Phoenicia], and Cyprus, and Antioch" (11:19).

Additionally, some unknown disciples from Cyprus introduce the good news about the "Lord **Jesus**" (11:20) to the Hellenists (KJV, "Grecians"), most likely Greek-speaking **Gentiles** living in Antioch. Luke continues, "And the hand of the Lord was with them: and a great number believed, and turned unto the Lord" (11:21). Church leaders in Jerusalem send Barnabas, who hailed from Cyprus (located sixty miles off the coast of **Asia** Minor), to continue the work begun by the unknown Cypriot disciples.

Scholars are divided on the chronology of the events described in this chapter. Some assume that Luke might be discussing a period of between two and three years before the famine struck Judea, usually dated between A.D. 45 and 46 (with continuing effects thereafter). More commonly, scholars date the events just weeks or months before the famine, which would mean that Luke is not driven religiously by a strict chronological ordering of his account since the events described in chapter 12 (the martyrdom of James and the death of Herod Agrippa I) are dated to spring through August A.D. 44. In making this suggestion, scholars argue that Luke is interested primarily in ordering his account based on geographical concerns. Certainly, this section describes an important shift in focus of the missionary efforts—away from Jerusalem to the large cities of the Roman world and to the Gentiles.

Luke provides an interesting insertion about Barnabas at this point (11:24) and then continues his account as Barnabas leaves Antioch and travels to Tarsus to find Saul. Barnabas had been much impressed with Saul when he heard him preach in Damascus before taking him to Jerusalem where Barnabas introduced Saul to the **apostles** (9:27). Apparently, he did the same thing here—introduce Saul to the Church at Antioch.

Barnabas and Saul spent a year teaching and preaching in Antioch to great crowds, which must have included Gentiles. They did so here as "Christians" for the first time (11:26. This might represent a specific strategy to reach out to Gentiles who would not understand the previous designation of "the way" (9:2) used by the followers of Jesus (disciples, brothers, sisters, believers, and followers). The new term means "pertaining to or belonging to **Christ**." Interestingly, it is only mentioned in one other place in the New Testament (1 Peter 4:16). Nevertheless, the designation is important as it demonstrates that the disciples were identified separately from other Jews and that such a designation was not based on ethnicity but on faith in and loyalty to Jesus. Eventually, it became the general way to identify those who accepted Jesus of Nazareth as the Christ (**Messiah**).

Luke again inserts a separate account when he introduces a prophet named Agabus who is mentioned later (Acts 21:10). Agabus prophesied of a famine in the Empire in c. A.D. 46 that resulted in a call to action in Antioch to help the "brethren which dwelt in Judea" (11:29), sending relief with Barnabas and Saul (11:30). Following the interlude in chapter 12, Luke focuses his attention on Antioch again, setting the stage for the so-called first mission where Barnabas and Saul covered more than 1,400 miles before retuning back to Antioch.

Herod Agrippa and James
ACTS 12:1–25

For the first time since Herod the Great, a Jewish king ruled in **Judea**, **Galilee**, and **Samaria**. Herod Agrippa I (10 B.C.–A.D. 44) was Herod's grandson and was portrayed by the Jewish historian Josephus as a strictly observant Jew who had remarkable connections and influence in **Rome**. Luke related that at this time, in the spring of A.D. 44 at the time of the Feast of Unleavened Bread (**Passover**), the king summarily executed James and arrested Peter. Surprisingly, given James's prominence in the Gospel of Luke (Peter, James, and John constituted the inner circle of the Twelve), Luke provides little information about James's execution except that he was "killed with the sword" (Acts 12:2), indicating that he was likely beheaded. Immediately Luke turns his attention back to Peter, who had been arrested in the wake of James's execution. After Peter is miraculously released from prison by an angel, he makes his way to the home of "Mary the mother of John, whose surname was Mark" (12:12) where the **Church** met, possibly the site of the **Last Supper** and the meeting where Matthias was called to the Twelve. Here Peter instructs the Saints to tell James, **Jesus'** brother, what has happened. Known as James the Just, he may have been included in the group (Mary Jesus' mother, and with his brethren) mentioned earlier in Acts 1:14. James plays a significant role in the Jerusalem Church thereafter (Acts 15:13–22; 21:18–25).

Peter then "departed, and went into another place" (12:17), signaling the beginning of Peter's absence from Jerusalem for the rest of the account (except for the brief appearance at the Jerusalem Conference in A.D. 49; see Acts 15:7) and from Luke's account.

For some reason, Luke decided to include the story of Herod Agrippa's death in August A.D. 44 at Caesarea. Combining the account in Luke with the account in Josephus, scholars suggest that Agrippa died of poisoning or peritonitis. With his passing, Rome took direct control of the region, quashing Jewish nationalistic hopes for a season.

Barnabas, Saul, and Mark
ACTS 13:1–14:28

In Acts 13 and 14, Luke describes the first mission beyond the eastern Mediterranean seaboard. Again, Luke provides a window into the early **Church's** operations when he describes the mission call and departure of Barnabas, Saul, and Mark from Antioch in Syria (Acts 13:1–40).

The missionaries are called after the **Holy Ghost** has instructed, "Separate me Barnabas and Saul for the work whereunto I have called them" (13:2). They are then set apart by local Church leaders: "And when they had fasted and prayed, and laid their hands on them, they sent them away" (13:3). Luke then gives a fairly detailed account of their travels, first to the island of Cyprus and then on to what today is south central Turkey (Pamphylia, Pisidia, and Galatia). After retracing their steps, Barnabas and Saul, now known as Paul, return to Antioch in Syria where "they rehearsed all that God had done with them, and how he had opened the door of faith unto the **Gentiles**" (14:27).

During this first missionary journey described in Acts, Paul found his voice and established his missionary strategy. First, he typically preached in the synagogue on the **Sabbath** to Jews, **proselytes**, and God-fearers

(13:15–16, 26), eventually attracting the attention of a wider group (13:44), resulting in some Jewish concerns about his message and activity (13:45) and thus forcing him to turn his attention to **Gentiles** (13:46–48).

Additionally, he seems to have taken lead of the mission from Barnabas; note that his name is mentioned first beginning in 13:13, suggesting pre-eminence. Luke also notes John Mark's departure back to Jerusalem at this point without explaining why he deserted the group. A number of suggestions have been advanced, including Mark's possible resentment that Paul took Barnabas's (his cousin's) leadership position; the mission had gone further than expected; and finally, Paul's efforts to preach to the Gentiles. Later, we learn that Paul and Mark likely reconciled (2 Timothy 4:11).

The Jerusalem Conference
ACTS 15:1–35

The Jerusalem Conference is traditionally dated to A.D. 49, a dating that is arrived at through comparative chronological considerations with the tenure of the proconsul Junius Annaeus Gallio who served in Corinth c. A.D. 51–52 (Acts 18:12). The Council of Jerusalem, or the Jerusalem Conference, was convened to settle the disconcerting issue of whether **Gentile** converts should be required to be circumcised (Acts 15:1), an issue that eventually led to "no small dissension and disputation with them" (15:2). A council was convened to settle the issue wherein Paul and Barnabas told of their experiences, where some "**Pharisees** which believed" (15:5) gave their input, and where Peter presided.

Peter had been uniquely prepared through revelation to handle the matter, having been shown in vision the Lord's will concerning the Gentiles (10:9–16). He testified, providing a clear outline of how the **Church** should proceed: "*Put no difference between us and them*, purifying their hearts by faith" (15:9; emphasis added). Luke's account seems to reach a conclusion at the end of Peter's declaration. That conclusion is interrupted by James's summary of the council's decision: "Men and brethren, hearken unto me. . . . my sentence is, that we trouble not them, which from among the Gentiles are turned to God: but that we write unto them, that they abstain from pollutions of idols, and from fornication, and from things strangled, and from blood" (15:13, 19–20). The decision effectively required two things of Gentile converts: first, they were required to follow the kosher requirement to abstain from eating blood, which accounts for the mention of strangulation, blood, and pollutions of idols (the eating of meat that had been used in a pagan sacrifice); second, new converts were required to remain chaste. It is assumed that new male converts would not be required to be circumcised, thus removing the most significant obstacle to Gentile conversions.

The decision of the council was to be announced by Paul and Barnabas through "letters," and the effort to announce the decision accounts for the second missionary journey of Paul (15:30). The announcement of the removal of the burden of **circumcision** was greeted warmly in Antioch, where "they rejoiced for the consolation" (15:31), although for some this decision would have been very difficult to accept because Judaism was more than a religion; it also provided them with a national identity. Therefore, in some instances the line between tradition and law was almost impossible to determine.

Paul and Barnabas Part Ways
Acts 15:36–41

Luke attributes the origin of the contention between Paul and Barnabas to a lingering issue over John's actions on the first missionary journey when John had left them near Perga in **Asia** (Acts 13:13). The two **disciples** separated, with Barnabas returning to Cyprus to announce the council's decision and Paul returning to Cilicia and the northern parts of the first mission to announce the decision of the Jerusalem Council. Although both men remained faithful, the rift between them was significant enough to cause them to part ways for a time.

To Europe

Acts 16:1–40

During the so-called second mission, or better, the Aegean mission journey, described in 15:35–18:32, Paul traveled some twenty-eight hundred miles. In Acts 16, Luke provides the story of another significant expansion in Paul's efforts—this time the crossing of another important physical boundary between **Asia** and Europe.

Paul provides a glimpse into his life on the road in one of his letters to the Corinthian Saints when he details some of the hardships he has endured "in labours more abundant, in stripes above measure, in prisons more frequent, in deaths oft. Of the Jews five times received I forty stripes save one. Thrice was I beaten with rods, once was I stoned, thrice I suffered shipwreck, a night and a day I have been in the deep; in journeyings often, in perils of waters, in perils of robbers, in perils by mine own countrymen, in perils by the heathen, in perils in the city, in perils in the wilderness, in perils in the sea, in perils among false brethren; in weariness and painfulness, in watchings often, in hunger and thirst, in fastings often, in cold and nakedness. Beside those things that are without, that which cometh upon me daily, the care of all the churches" (2 Corinthians 11:23–28).

Beginning with this section, Luke concentrates exclusively on Paul for the rest of his narrative, providing us an important window into his missionary efforts. Regrettably, however, Luke at the same time pulled down the shades on other individuals and events that would be of great interest to the modern student of the early **Church**.

Luke informs his readers that Paul and Silas traveled to "Derbe and Lystra" where they recruited "Timotheus," better known simply as Timothy, to join them (Acts 16:1). Revealing Paul's practical nature, he asked Timothy to submit to **circumcision** "because of the Jews which were in those quarters: for they knew all that his father was a Greek" and his mother was a Jew (16:3). Paul continued his effort in spreading the news of the important apostolic decree from the Jerusalem Conference that **Gentile** converts were not required to submit to circumcision (16:4).

As the missionary team traveled westward, they were "forbidden of the **Holy Ghost** to preach the word in Asia" (16:6). As a result, they decided to head toward Bithynia (the region near the Black Sea), but again the Spirit instructed them to change direction (16:7). One can only imagine the group's perplexity as they traveled for several hundred miles toward some uncertain destination. Eventually they made their way toward Troas—known as Troas Alexandria, which in antiquity was located on the west coast of Asia. If we assume the group was in northern Galatia at the time, it would have taken about six weeks to get to Troas, a journey of nearly five hundred miles. By this time, Paul may have been seeking medical help, which may explain how he met Luke, identified as a physician by Paul (Colossians 4:14).

In Troas, an important event transpired that ended any questions the group may have had about direction. Luke noted: "And a vision appeared to Paul in the night; There stood a man of Macedonia, and prayed him, saying, Come over into Macedonia, and help us" (Acts 16:9). When Luke continues his narrative, he introduces the famous "we" passages. Traditionally understood as an indication that Luke was present when the event in the account occurred, these passages are made obvious as he moves from third-person singular to first-person plural. If this proposition is correct, it would go a long way in explaining how Luke obtained so much information about Paul and perhaps why he focused his narrative on Paul's missionary efforts. Luke continues, "And after he had seen the vision, immediately *we* endeavoured to go into Macedonia, assuredly gathering that the Lord had called *us* for to preach the gospel unto them. Therefore loosing from Troas, *we* came with a straight course to Samothracia, and the next day to Neapolis; and from thence to Philippi, which is the chief city of that part of Macedonia, and a colony: and *we* were in that city abiding certain days" (16:10–12; emphasis added).

Crossing into Europe, Paul immediately looked for an opportunity to establish a church and did so through the conversion of Lydia, "a seller of purple, of the city of Thyatira, which worshipped God" (16:14). Apparently a "God-fearer," she accepted the message and "was baptized, and her household" (16:15). Her larger-than-average home became the house-church in the city. Luke describes another "sign and wonder" when he records an account of an evil spirit being cast out of a young slave woman, "which brought her masters much gain by soothsaying" (16:16). Angry at the loss of their income, her owners forcibly took Paul and Silas (note that the "we" passages end here) to the city leaders who summarily beat and threw them into prison (16:16–24). Paul mentions the incident explicitly in 1 Thessalonians 2:2 and possibly implicitly in 2 Corinthians 11:33.

Describing another miraculous prison escape, Luke reports the conversion of the jailer (16:25–33). When the city magistrates decide to let Paul go, he asks, "They have beaten us openly uncondemned, being Romans, and have cast us into prison; and now do they thrust us out privily [secretly]?" (16:37). The news that they had beaten and imprisoned Roman citizens sent the officials looking for cover because it was illegal to do so without a trial. Sometime later, the missionaries, without Luke, departed from Philippi to continue their missionary journey farther west.

Paul Teaches in Thessalonica and Berea
ACTS 17:1–15

Paul's vision of the man from Macedonia (Acts 16:9) eventually led him into Greece, specifically to the predominantly Greek-speaking city of Thessalonica, "where was a synagogue of the Jews" (17:1). Following the practice of teaching Jews first and **Gentiles** second, Paul taught in the synagogue there, of which from Luke's narrative it appears that there was only one, thus indicating that there was perhaps only a small Jewish community in the city. Paul's core message and the techniques he used are provided: "And Paul, as his manner was, went in unto them, and three sabbath days he *reasoned* with them out of the **scriptures**, opening and alleging, that **Christ** must needs have suffered, and risen again from the dead; and that this **Jesus**, whom I preach unto you, is Christ" (17:2–3; emphasis added).

That Paul focused his message on proving Jesus to be the Christ ("**Messiah**") from the scriptures demonstrates the uniquely Jewish makeup of the audience, which in turn helps interpret Luke's phrase "and of the devout Greeks a great multitude, and of the chief women not a few" (17:4). The "devout Greeks" in this verse must either be assimilated Jews who had become influential in civic affairs or, more likely, Greeks who had converted to Judaism. In either case, they found Paul's reasoned approach to the gospel credible.

In a complaint against Paul and those who had converted, some other Jews of that same synagogue reported that the teaching of the resurrection and exaltation of Jesus Christ constituted the worship of another king (17:7). Luke, who wrote some time after this event had occurred, adds the legal consideration that such a teaching was "contrary to the decrees of **Caesar**" (17:7). **Rome** permitted wide religious freedom, including the worship of national gods, with the requirement that citizens demonstrate allegiance to Rome. Jews could openly worship Jehovah without breaking this "decree," and it may be that Luke has in mind later decrees that specifically outlawed the worship of Jesus Christ, although it is possible that their complaint is simply a perverted attempt to persecute Christians. As a part of this conspiracy, Jason and other brethren were arrested. Luke does not report what charges, if any, were brought against them.

Paul fled the city at the beginning of this slanderous inquiry and traveled to Berea, a city not far to the south of Thessalonica. Luke gives a brief report of Paul's success in Berea, noting that "these were more noble than those in Thessalonica" (17:11). The persecutors of Thessalonica, however, pursue Paul to Berea and Paul is forced to flee again, this time using a ruse—feigning a trip by sea—but then traveling due south to Athens. Silas and Timothy remained behind in Berea, thus indicating that the persecution had focused more on Paul rather than on all those who taught the gospel message.

Paul in Athens
ACTS 17:16–31

Paul's trip to Athens appears to have been necessitated by the persecutions in Berea and Thessalonica rather than by choice. Luke reports Paul's attempt to teach in the synagogue and indicates that he had no success. The most notable event Luke reports is Paul's speech given on Mars Hill, translated as the "Areopagus" in the King James Version. Located in the shadow of the Parthenon, Mars Hill was a place of public assembly and the city's official tribunal, where on this occasion Stoic and Epicurean philosophers, as well as others, met. Luke may have noted only the Stoics and Epicureans for dramatic effect rather than historical, to highlight the difference between Greek intellectual traditions and the sublime truths of the gospel, which are felt rather than grasped solely through reason. In fact, the accounts of Paul's teachings in Thessalonica and Berea may have anticipated Athens when Luke emphasized in those accounts a reasoned approach to teaching the gospel.

Luke's report reveals little tolerance for the Athenian intellectual environment, which in these short verses is referred to as "idolatry" and "superstitious" while the Athenians "spent their time in nothing else, but either to tell, or to hear some new thing" (17:21). In particular, Paul noted the altar "to the Unknown God" (17:23), which is known from other references outside the New Testament as being an altar to the unknowable god or to all gods that are not specifically known by name (Philostratus, *Life of Apollonius of Tyana* 6.3). The Athenians maintained an altar to the gods not known to prevent their inadvertently offending deity in any way. Paul made an object lesson out of the altar, boldly saying to his Athenian listeners, "whom therefore ye ignorantly worship, him declare I unto you" (17:23). Rather than attempt to find commonality with the Athenian plurality of gods, Paul testifies to the singularity of God as well as God's role as Creator in light of Stoic and Epicurean intellectual antimaterialism.

In this famous sermon, Paul demonstrates familiarity with the poet Aratus, whom he quotes, possibly in an effort to find common ground: "For we are also his offspring" (Aratus, *Phenomena* 5). At the center of Paul's teachings, and indeed the most controversial concept in his speech from Mars Hill, was the doctrine of the resurrection, which "some mocked" because it emphasized the eternal nature of the material body, which the Athenian intellectuals could not accept. Paul, however, did gain some converts on that day: "Dionysius the Areopagite, and a woman named Damaris, and others with them" (17:34).

To Corinth
ACTS 18:1–18

Following his effort in Athens, Paul headed to Corinth, a logical choice given its size (about eighty thousand inhabitants) and prominent geographical position on a narrow isthmus that linked Achaia to the Peloponnese. We do not know if Paul traveled by land or sea, but either way it would have taken between two and three days to make the journey from Athens. So far, Paul has been on the road some twenty weeks, having traveled about twenty-two hundred miles from Antioch to Corinth.

Unlike his visits to Philippi, Thessalonica, and Berea, where he had been chased out of town, Paul stayed at least eighteen months, maybe longer, in Corinth (Acts 18:11). This allowed him to establish a routine that Luke has preserved for us—an important description of Paul's ministry in the Roman colony.

At the beginning of the account, Luke introduces his audience to Aquila and Priscilla, Jewish-Christians who had recently arrived from **Rome** in the wake of the expulsion of some Jewish and Christian leaders by Claudius, dated about A.D. 49. Paul, Aquila, and Priscilla discover they share the same occupation; we learn here for the first time that Paul was a leather worker (KJV, "tentmakers"; the tents were likely made of leather [18:3]). The three also have a mutual witness that **Jesus** is the Jewish **Messiah**, and all this provides a basis for an immediate friendship. Eventually they establish a **house-church** in their apartment and become an important missionary team in Corinth and later in Rome.

As was his practice, Paul "reasoned in the synagogue every **sabbath** and persuaded the Jews and the Greeks" (18:4); eventually he pressed the Jews in Corinth, testifying that "**Jesus** was **Christ**" (18:5). When opposition arose and the Jews "opposed themselves, and blasphemed" (18:6), he vowed that "from henceforth I will go unto the Gentiles" and moved his work to a location adjacent to the synagogue. Additionally, Paul baptized Crispus (1 Corinthians 1:14), the chief ruler of the synagogue, bringing into the fold an important Jewish leader (18:8).

Most scholars assume that Paul wrote his famous letters to the Thessalonians from Corinth after receiving reports from Silas and Timothy, who finally met up with Paul again in this important commercial city (18:5). In Corinth, Paul had another vision (18:9). However, this time he is told to stay instead of to depart (18:9). Additionally, the Lord promised Paul that he would be protected and that he had "much people in this city" (18:10).

Eventually, Jewish agitators took Paul to appear before Lucius Iunius Gallio, the Roman proconsul (18:12–17). Fortunately, we are in a position to provide a rather precise date for Paul's stay based on an inscription found at Delphi regarding Gallio, which dates his proconsulship between spring A.D. 51–52. This suggests that Paul was there between A.D. 49–52. This is one of the few dates regarding Paul which has a general consensus among scholars.

The importance of Paul's appearance before Gallio is significant. The Roman government, through Gallio, decided that the Christians had not broken any Roman law and that they remained under the legal protection offered other Jews—they were seen simply as a subgroup within Judaism. This was a landmark decision and most likely the reason why Luke mentions it.

We gain additional information about Paul's stay in Corinth from his own correspondence (1 and 2 Corinthians).

Return to the Aegean Mission
ACTS 18:18–23

Paul's so-called third missionary journey (Acts 18:23–21:15) took him some twenty-seven hundred miles. When he left Cenchrea, one of the two seaports of Corinth—the Aegean side in this case—he took Priscilla and Aquila with him. Additionally, Luke informs his readers that Paul shaved his head in preparation to begin a vow. Most likely it was a Nazarite vow (Numbers 6:1–21), which entailed that a person not cut his hair for a specific period of time. At the conclusion of the period, the person offered the previously unshorn hair as an offering at the Jerusalem **temple**. That Paul continued to worship in forms familiar to other Jews should not surprise anyone. However, there is nothing in the account that can help us fully understand his position on the **Torah** and the temple. Rather, Luke presents a complex picture of Paul's attitudes about the Torah and the temple that does not allow us to pigeonhole Paul into a neat, tidy box.

Luke continues his sketch: "And he came to Ephesus, and left them there: but he himself entered into the synagogue, and reasoned with the Jews. When they desired him to tarry longer time with them, he consented not; But bade them farewell, saying, I must by all means keep this feast that cometh in Jerusalem: but I will return again unto you, if God will. And he sailed from Ephesus. And when he had landed at Caesarea, and gone up, and saluted the **church** [in Jerusalem], he went down to Antioch. And after he had spent some time there, he departed, and went over all the country of Galatia and Phrygia in order, strengthening all the **disciples**" (18:19–23).

What continues to baffle scholars is why Luke leaves us in the dark on the purpose and outcome of his trip to Jerusalem and Antioch; the distance between the two is about 250 miles. Numerous attempts to clarify the significance of these visits and the possible outcomes fail to adequately explain Luke's short report, even if we use Paul's own letters to fill in details. The evidence is so fragmentary that it may be impossible to discover Paul's original intent. This was not Paul's last visit to Jerusalem, and fortunately Luke is more helpful in providing us details to make some sense of Paul's later visit (Acts 20–21).

Apollos
ACTS 18:24–28

In Acts 18, Luke introduces Apollos, an Alexandrian Jew, who arrives in Ephesus. Apollos is described as "an eloquent man, and mighty in the **scriptures** . . . instructed in the way of the Lord; and being fervent in the spirit, he spake and taught diligently the things of the Lord," but "knowing only the **baptism** of John" he had not yet fully come to a proper under-standing of who **Jesus** was and what Jesus offered, including the Holy Spirit (18:24–25). Aquila and Priscilla "took him unto them, and expounded unto him the way of God more perfectly" (18:26). Now armed with a more complete understanding of Jesus' mission, he is sent by the **Church** in Ephesus to Corinth with a letter of recommendation. In Corinth, Apollos preached, "for he mightily convinced the Jews, and that publickly, shewing by the scriptures that Jesus was **Christ**" (18:28). Apollos became an influential teacher in Corinth (1 Corinthians 1–4).

To Ephesus
ACTS 19:1–41

Paul makes his way to Ephesus at the beginning of this section where an account is given of people who had accepted the **baptism** of John. Paul told them, "John verily baptized with the baptism of **repentance**, saying unto the people, that they should believe on him which should come after him, that is, on **Christ Jesus**" (19:4). Many of them were then "baptized in the name of the Lord **Jesus**" and received the **Holy Ghost** (19:5–6), thus implying that their previous baptism was insufficient.

As was his custom, Paul enters the local synagogue in Ephesus and "spake boldly for the space of three months, disputing and persuading the things concerning the kingdom of God" (19:8). Eventually, Paul is forced to find another location in which to teach: "And this continued by the space of two years; so that all they which dwelt in **Asia** heard the word of the Lord Jesus, both Jews and Greeks" (19:10). Paul's ministry of healing continues in Ephesus (19:11–12), an aspect of Paul's work that Luke highlights in some detail throughout the book of Acts (see, for example, 13:9–11; 14:8–10; 16:16–18; 28:8). Luke also preserves a rather humorous story about the "seven sons of one Sceva, a Jew," who attempt to cast out an evil spirit only to have the spirit respond, "Jesus I know, and Paul I know; but who are ye?" At that point, "the man in whom the evil spirit was leaped on them, and overcame them, and prevailed against them, so that they fled out of that house naked and wounded" (19:14–16). We also learn from Luke's narrative that Paul's ultimate goal was to preach in **Rome** (19:21).

Paul's missionary success was so great in Ephesus and elsewhere that Paul "persuaded and turned away much people, saying that they be no gods, which are made with hands" (19:26). Those connected with the **temple** of Diana (known as the Temple of Artemis and one of the seven ancient wonders of the world) were concerned about the economic impact of his ministry and eventually raised a tumult. A large mob gathered in the theater that still stands in Ephesus today, shouting for two hours, "Great is Diana of the Ephesians" (19:34). Eventually the "townclerk" persuaded the crowd to disperse by reminding them that the Romans would consider the assembly illegal and would punish them—**Pax Romana** must be maintained.

Paul Raises Eutychus from the Dead
Acts 20:1–15

Paul's return through Greece and Macedonia would have permitted him occasion to write, and it is possible that while in Greece, where he "abode three months" (Acts 20:5), he may have written his letter to the Roman Saints. As Luke reports, Paul's travel plans had to be adjusted to avoid persecution from the Jews of Greece and Macedonia. Very little is known of his seven missionary companions, except for Timothy.

The mention of breaking bread on "the first day of the week" refers to a Sunday celebration of the sacrament and not to the continued celebration of the Jewish **Sabbath** on Saturday (Acts 20:7). After celebrating the sacrament, Paul spoke long into the night, hinting that this was a farewell discourse. While Paul was speaking, "a certain young man named Eutychus" fell asleep and tumbled through an open window, causing his death (20:9). The young man, whose name means "good fortune," was raised from the dead by Paul. The incident of bringing one back to life establishes a line of priesthood authority from Jesus to Peter to Paul. By recounting this story here, Luke may also be hinting at Paul's position in the **Church** in light of Peter's absence from the story.

Paul's Farewell Discourse
ACTS 20:13–38

Luke again uses the first-person plural "we" in describing Paul's return trip to Jerusalem, thus indicating an eyewitness source or perhaps even Luke's own participation in these events (Acts 20:13). From the list of cities, it is apparent that Paul was making his way toward Miletus, about thirty-five miles south of Ephesus, where he hoped to depart by ship so he could arrive in Jerusalem by **Pentecost** or fifty days after **Passover** (20:16).

Paul's farewell speech, recorded in verses 18–35, is personal and introspective. Paul clearly has the end of his life in sight, discussing his life in past perspective and not from the present looking toward the future only. Some phrases indicate that Paul has had some revelatory experience concerning his own fate: "I might finish my course with joy" (20:24), but you "shall see my face no more" (20:25), "after my departing" (20:29), and "now, brethren, I commend you to God" (20:32). Paul also warns the Saints, "Of your own selves shall men arise, speaking perverse things, to draw away **disciples** after them" (20:30), testifying of the beginning of the internal and eventual **apostasy** that had begun to take shape.

Luke concludes with what constitutes Paul's final farewell scene with the members he had worked with since the time of his early mission into Greece and Macedonia: "And they all wept sore, and fell on Paul's neck, and kissed him, sorrowing most of all for the words which he spake, that they should see his face no more" (20:37–38), conveying not only the sentiments of the Ephesian Saints but probably Luke's own feelings as well. To comfort the Saints, Paul draws upon an otherwise unknown saying of **Jesus**, referred to frequently as an **agrapha** (defined by *Merriam-Webster's Collegiate Dictionary* as "one of the sayings of Jesus not in the canonical Gospels but found in other New Testament or early Christian writings"): "Remember the words of the Lord Jesus, how he said, It is more blessed to give than to receive" (20:35).

The Final Visit to Jerusalem
ACTS 21:1–40

Often identified as the "passion of Paul," the last eight chapters of Acts focus on Paul's final journey to Jerusalem, his two-year incarceration in Caesarea, and his perilous journey to **Rome**. Luke finds an interesting parallel in **Jesus'** last journey to Jerusalem and that of Paul's. The details in both accounts are remarkably similar, including the decision to go to Jerusalem, the hearing before a Jewish council, the appearance before a Roman governor, and the hearing before a Jewish king. This narrative is about one-fourth of the total text in Acts.

The journey continues when Paul and his traveling companions arrive in Tyre, located in modern Lebanon, where they find **disciples** "who said to Paul through the Spirit, that he should not go up to Jerusalem" (Acts 21:4). Nevertheless, Paul is determined to deliver the collection for the poor Saints in Judea to James in the Holy City. That collection appears to have been intended to alleviate the suffering of the Saints in Jerusalem, who had suffered from food shortages under the Emperor Claudius. Luke adds, "And when we had accomplished those days, we departed and went our way; and they all brought us on our way, with wives and children, till we were out of the city: and we kneeled down on the shore, and prayed. And when we had taken our leave one of another, we took ship" (21:5–6).

The next stop on their journey is Ptolemais, modern Acco in northern Israel. After greeting the **Church**, the party travels to Caesarea where they stay with Philip and his daughters (21:8–9). This fortuitous visit with Philip provides Luke another opportunity to gather an eyewitness account of the history of the early days of the Church (Acts 6:1–5; 8:5–13, 26–40).

Agabus, mentioned earlier (11:28), appears in Caesarea to deliver a dire warning: "And when he was come unto us, he took Paul's girdle, and bound his own hands and feet, and said, Thus saith the **Holy Ghost**, So shall the Jews at Jerusalem bind the man that owneth this girdle, and shall deliver him into the hands of the **Gentiles**" (21:11). Those present plead with Paul not to continue on to Jerusalem. "Then Paul answered, What mean ye to weep and to break mine heart? for I am ready not to be bound only, but also to die at Jerusalem for the name of the Lord Jesus. And when he would not be persuaded, we ceased, saying, The will of the Lord be done" (21:13–14).

"After those days" (21:15), Paul and his party traveled to Jerusalem, where Luke reports, "the brethren received us gladly" (21:17). On the following day, they meet with "James; and all the elders were present" (21:18). Again, this important meeting may have provided Luke another opportunity to obtain crucial information about Jesus' birth and early years from Jesus' brother, James (Luke 1–2).

James's report to Paul about the Church provides us remarkable insight into the situation in Jerusalem. First, the Church was strong with "many thousands" of Jewish converts (21:20). Second, these converts were "all zealous of the law" (21:20). Finally, Paul was thought by some Jewish adherents to be an "apostate," one who encouraged other Jews to desert the faith (21:21).

In order to dispel the notion that Paul had abandoned the Lord, the **Torah**, and the **temple**, James asks Paul to prove his piety by going to the temple. He agrees, but during his visit to the temple, some Jews from **Asia** spotted him and "stirred up all the people, and laid hands on him, crying out, Men of Israel, help: This is the man, that teacheth all men every where against the people, and the law, and this place: and further brought Greeks also into the temple, and hath polluted this holy place" (21:27–28). Such a charge, that he had defiled the temple by bringing a Gentile into the sacred precinct, causes a crowd to run together and take Paul outside of the temple in order to kill him. (21:30–31). The question of whether Paul had been set up by going to the temple or if James was used by manipulative instigators is a valid one, and the fact that Paul was arrested for Trophimus's infraction leads to the conclusion that someone with wicked designs had orchestrated the event.

The Roman soldiers, who are watching from the Antonia fortress, which is connected to the Temple Mount on the north side, quickly intervene and rescue Paul from certain death. As the soldiers descend into the court of the Gentiles, the crowd disperses, leaving a roughed-up Paul. The soldiers immediately bind him and lead him to the Antonia Fortress.

As they move to the safety of the fortress, Paul speaks to the Roman chief captain in Greek, who is surprised that Paul speaks Greek (21:37). Paul then asks permission to address the angry crowd. Rather dramatically, Paul motions to the crowd to listen, and when they do, he speaks to them in **Aramaic** (21:40). The next chapter contains his speech.

Paul's Appeal to the People
ACTS 22:1–30

Acts 22 details Paul's personal defense of his ministry and teachings to Judean Jews, which is reported to have been given in "the Hebrew tongue" or, more properly, **Aramaic** (Acts 22:2). Paul's account of his upbringing and training in Jerusalem under the famed **Pharisee** Gamaliel point out the irony of the charges brought against him: Gamaliel was a known moderate and earlier had argued against prosecuting Christians (Acts 5:34–40). Paul testifies of otherwise unknown actions that are also implied in Acts 9:2: "And I persecuted this way unto the death, binding and delivering into prisons both men and women" (22:4). Unless Paul is referring to Stephen in this verse, it is unlikely that he actually killed Christians, and the binding and delivering of Christians to prisons must refer to actions in **Judea** before his trip to Damascus and to Jewish tribunals rather than Roman prisons. In fact, the Romans protect Paul from the Jews.

Paul's account of his vision here matches the earlier account in Acts 9 with some minor differences in detail (the most significant differences have to do with the men who traveled with Paul). It is important to note that the differences in the two stories are less significant than the commonalities, which present an enduring story that did not suffer from a variety of retellings. Some details of the events following his vision are also reported. Specifically, Paul describes a vision in the **temple**, which must have taken place nearly three years after his first vision, (Galatians 1:18) in which Jesus had commanded Paul to teach the gospel to the **Gentiles** (22:21).

The entire speech focuses on revelation as a means of authorization. Having seen and heard the Lord and participated in appropriate priesthood ordinances (22:16), Paul is authorized to teach the gospel. This emphasis on revelation may have been necessary given the status of the **Church** in the decade beginning in A.D. 50 when this event took place and when the apostles had departed from Jerusalem. The people here are not specifically Jews or Christians, but rather a crowd that interprets Paul's teachings as blasphemous by casting off their clothes (their outer cloak) and throwing dust into the air (22:23). It may be that Luke intended to leave the identity of this audience ambiguous because it likely included Christians who continued to oppose Paul.

The chief captain is a Roman military officer (Greek, *xiliarxos*, "captain of six hundred to one thousand men") who ordered that Paul be brought into the "castle" (22:24) or military barracks (Greek, *parembolē*, "barracks" or "camp"). Their intent was to scourge Paul to determine any guilt, but probably more specifically as a punishment for instigating a riot. Paul appeals to an officer below the chief captain (Greek, *hekatontarxon*, "captain of one hundred men"), citing his Roman citizenship and the fact that he should not be scourged as a slave or as a noncitizen would be. The chief captain appears incredulous that Paul is a Roman citizen, and Paul would have been required to produce physical proof of his citizenship in the form of official documents. Following the treatment accorded to citizens, Paul was given the opportunity to confront his accusers the day following this event.

Paul Defends His Ministry to the Council
Acts 23:1–35

Surprisingly, Paul has no one to defend him, thus hinting at a Jewish takeover of the Christian community in Jerusalem or an almost absolute suppression of Christianity in the city. One would expect that the dispute mentioned in these verses would be between Christians and Jews, but Luke reports it rather as a division between **Sadducees** and **Pharisees** (Acts 23:6). Moreover, Ananias is permitted to physically abuse Paul, something that Paul's Roman guards were unwilling to do upon learning that he was a citizen (23:2). Legally it seems that Ananias had no authority over Paul unless Paul willingly submitted himself to Ananias's command. In other words, Paul most likely permitted the questioning reported here.

Unfortunately, no primary sources exist detailing the Sadducees' beliefs, and the mention that they do not believe in the "resurrection, neither angel, nor spirit" (23:8) is left unexplained. Their defense of their belief is so spirited that the inquiry into Paul's teachings takes second place to their dispute over the Resurrection. Luke sees no difficulty in reporting Paul's ruse. Again, it is the Romans who protect Paul, likely indicating that Luke was writing at a time when the Jews were viewed as a greater threat than Roman anti-Christian legislation.

Mentioned only here, Paul's nephew (23:16) had learned of a conspiracy to kill Paul, which he made known to Paul and which led to the news being relayed to his Roman guards. Although the Romans were in control of the legal process of trying Paul, this account makes it apparent that the Jews had learned to manipulate that system for their own purposes (23:14). That the chief captain took the information from Paul's nephew to represent a credible threat shows a contrast between how the Pharisees and Sadducees reacted out of hate while the Romans carefully considered witnesses and acted accordingly. Roughly 470 soldiers accompanied Paul to his place of imprisonment at Caesarea Maritima, unless Luke intended to indicate that the 200 hundred spearmen were the same as the 200 soldiers under the direction of the centurions (23:23).

The chapter concludes with what appears to be a private copy of a letter from Claudius Lysias to the governor (Greek, *hēgemōn*). Claudius's soldiers executed the order given to them and delivered Paul safely to a prison on the Mediterranean coast where the governor of Jerusalem would typically reside. Herod Antipas maintained a palace at Caesarea Maritima, where it is likely that the Roman governors resided when not officiating in matters in Jerusalem. Luke reports that Paul, while in Roman custody, was held in Herod's prison (Greek, *praitōriōn*, "guard" or "residence").

Ananias Brings Charges against Paul
ACTS 24:1–21

Tertullus, a Roman attorney and professional orator and one whom the Jews believed could plead their case better than they, follows the standard practice of extolling the virtues of the Roman governor before making any formal requests. The specific charges brought against Paul are that he is "a pestilent fellow," or more specifically, one who teaches against the Jewish law (Acts 24:5), a leader of a seditious group called the Nazarenes (24:5), and has profaned the **temple** (24:6), probably referring to the event described in Acts 21:28–29.

Following the practice of indulging the conscience of his interrogator before presenting his defense, Paul specifically addresses their accusations, stating that even though the crimes of which he has been accused are only twelve days past (24:11), there are yet no credible witnesses who saw him profane the temple. Moreover, Paul similarly defends himself against the charge that he had instigated a riot by stating that there are no witnesses to such an act. Finally, as to the charge of breaking the law, Paul testifies that he too worships the God of Israel. Paul then offers an explanation of why charges have been brought against him by stating that he believes it is because he teaches the Resurrection (24:15, 17). Paul also offers as evidence that he is not anti-Jewish by declaring that he has in the past delivered "alms to my nation, and offerings" (24:17).

Felix Hopes for a Bribe
ACTS 24:22–27

After hearing the accusations brought against Paul as well as his defense, Felix (procurator of **Judea** A.D. 52–60) holds Paul in custody, hoping to receive money to secure his release. Felix was roundly despised by Judeans, and contemporary accounts of him reveal that he sought bribes on other occasions (Josephus, *Antiquities* 20.162) while other accounts show that rioting had broken out under his tenure (Josephus, *War* 2.270). Felix was replaced by Porcius Festus (procurator of Judea A.D. 59–62), who appears to have been more evenhanded in his treatment of Paul, and Josephus likewise treats him with respect (*Antiquities* 20.8.9–11). Luke's statement that Porcius Festus was willing to show the Jews a favor by keeping Paul imprisoned may also reflect the time that it took Festus to reinterview the witnesses before making any decision in the matter.

Leading Jews Request That Paul Be Tried in Jerusalem
ACTS 25:1–27

After Festus's arrival in the province, the Jews again asked that Paul be sentenced for his supposed crimes. Acts 25:2 contains a textual variant, and although the King James Version reads, "the high priest and the chief of the Jews," it is more likely, based on other surviving New Testament manuscripts, that the text as Luke wrote it read "leading Jews," so that the conspiracy was not necessarily instigated by the high priest himself. Under Festus the charges against Paul were renewed, although with the added claim that Paul was somehow anti-**Caesar** in his teachings. Paul vigorously defended himself against such a claim (25:8). Festus, for whatever reason, asked Paul if he would accept a trial in Jerusalem, which Paul interpreted to be a death sentence.

Paul's request that he be granted the rights of a Roman citizen and be tried by the emperor (Nero, December A.D. 37–June A.D. 68) is clearly stated in Acts, but the legality of such a request is somewhat unclear based on the surviving judiciary evidence. Festus sought Agrippa's advice on the matter, although Marcus Julius Agrippa (also referred to as Herod Agrippa II, king of **Judea** A.D. 52), son of Herod Agrippa, was unlikely to judge favorably on Paul's behalf given the Herodian family's historical anti-Christian actions. Bernice, Agrippa's sister, accompanied him for the hearing (25:13).

We should like to be more informed about Paul's attitudes toward his Roman captors and Agrippa. However, while Festus makes a somewhat lengthy aside on Roman judicial procedure, the reader is left to wonder at the justice of the proceedings. Festus appears to sense this problem and states that it would be difficult to send Paul to **Rome** for trial without specific charges (25:27).

Paul's Testimony before Marcus Julius Agrippa
ACTS 26:1–32

In testifying before Agrippa, Paul chose a different tack in his defense, drawing instead from his past as a faithful **Pharisee** and devout Jew concepts that he believed Agrippa could comprehend (Acts 26:3). Paul even refers to Agrippa as an expert in Jewish matters, suggesting that Paul felt the charges against him pertained solely to matters of Jewish law. Paul's defense is to describe himself as thoroughly Jewish, and to do so he relates his past as a persecutor of Christians. Paul even implies that he was at one time much like his accusers: "having received authority from the chief **priests**" (26:10), he punished Christians who attended their local Jewish **synagogues** (26:11). In other words, Paul at one time saw Christianity through the eyes of the chief priests, or at least through the eyes of a Pharisaic opponent to Christianity. Underlying Paul's defense is his belief that the teaching of the doctrine of the resurrection of the dead has caused the charges to be brought against him, and Paul concedes that he once thought such a belief was incredible (26:8–9).

Paul cites the witness he received while journeying towards Damascus, the implications of which Agrippa would understand but which would be entirely unconvincing to Festus. In recounting his vision and subsequent conversion, Paul passes over his **baptism** and Ananias's healing his blindness, probably in an attempt to avoid the previous accusations that he had been an agitator among the Nazarenes. Instead, in this telling of the story, Paul emphasizes his divine commission to witness to the **Gentiles** (26:17) and therefore his calling as a prophet following Old Testament models. Paul specifically testifies that he had been commanded of God to deliver the message: "That **Christ** should suffer, and that he should be the first that should rise from the dead, and should shew light unto the people, and to the Gentiles" (26:23).

Festus interprets Paul's testimony from the standpoint of a philosophical defense of his beliefs, which he believes is an indication that Paul had lost his mind (26:24). Realizing that his defense was being judged by the wrong ears, Paul again addresses Agrippa, asking how he understands the matter. Agrippa responds famously, "Almost thou persuadest me to be a Christian" (26:28), probably indicating his legal opinion concerning Paul's defense and not necessarily something he feels. In other words, Agrippa agrees that Paul's defense is credible to the point that one might even be persuaded to become a Christian. Agrippa pursues this line of thinking by stating, "This man doeth nothing worthy of death or of bonds. Then said Agrippa unto Festus, This man might have been set at liberty, if he had not appealed unto **Caesar**" (26:31–32). Luke concludes Paul's defense, ironically stating that Paul's own request to be heard by Caesar is what cost him his freedom.

At Sea
ACTS 27:1–12

Luke began Acts by recording **Jesus'** commission to the **disciples**: "But ye shall receive power, after that the **Holy Ghost** is come upon you: and ye shall be witnesses unto me both in Jerusalem, and in all **Judea**, and in **Samaria**, and unto the uttermost part of the earth" (Acts 1:8). Now, in the final chapters, the commission is completed. It began with an account of the earliest days of the **Church** in Jerusalem (1–5), expanded to Judea and Samaria (6–12), and then to Antioch (13–15), and from there to the Aegean (16–20), and now finally the expanding circle is completed when Paul arrives in **Rome** where he preached "the kingdom of God, and teaching those things which concern the Lord Jesus **Christ**, with all confidence, no man forbidding him" (28:31).

In what many believe to be one of the most detailed ancient sea-travel narratives, Luke provides a dramatic and fast-paced story of Paul's departure from Caesarea and his journey to **Rome,** focusing more on natural dangers (the sea and a snake) instead of on human conspiracies to beat, imprison, and kill Paul. Unlike his earlier abbreviated descriptions of Paul's voyages, Luke provides detailed information about ships, cargo, ports, destinations, and winds in this narrative (because the journey is long, and each factor plays a significant role in the drama we are about to read).

The "we" passages begin again as Paul departs Caesarea: "And when it was determined that *we* should sail into Italy, they delivered Paul and certain other prisoners unto one named Julius, a centurion of Augustus' band. And entering into a ship of Adramyttium, *we* launched, meaning to sail by the coasts of **Asia;** one Aristarchus, a Macedonian of Thessalonica, being with *us.* And the next day *we* touched at Sidon. And Julius courteously entreated Paul, and gave him liberty to go unto his friends to refresh himself. And when *we* had launched from thence, *we* sailed under Cyprus, because the winds were contrary. And when *we* had sailed over the sea of Cilicia and Pamphylia, *we* came to Myra, a city of Lycia" (Acts 27:1–5; emphasis added).

One can only wonder where Luke was during Paul's two-year confinement when the "we" passages disappear, only to reappear at this critical moment. Was he conducting research for his two-part work? Interviewing eyewitnesses? Was he visiting places of interest in Jerusalem and on the roads between the Holy City and Joppa and Caesarea? Whatever the explanation may be, beginning in chapter 27, Luke and Paul are apparently together again as they make their way toward Rome. Additionally, Luke informs his readers that Aristarchus from Thessalonica is also present (Colossians 4:10; Philemon 1:24).

Paul was by now a seasoned traveler, both on land and sea. He certainly must have known that the trip to the Roman capital from one of its farthest outposts was not going to be easy. Additionally, he must have wondered about his reception in Rome—a place he had wanted to visit for some time but had not been instrumental in founding any of the **house-churches** there. Rome had been his goal and now the journey had begun.

When the Roman officer "found a ship of Alexandria sailing into Italy" (27:6), Paul and the other prisoners were placed on board. It was most likely a grain ship bound for Rome, which had originated in Alexandria. Egypt had become the breadbasket for Rome with ships plying their way between the two cities on a regular basis.

We soon discover, however, that the trip was taken late in the sailing season (which ran between May 27 and September 14). As a result, we should expect rough seas ahead. Luke's mention of the fast most likely refers to the Day of **Atonement** (Hebrew, *Yom Kippur*) observed between late September and early October. If the journey began in A.D. 59, the celebration was held on October 5, well beyond the season. Nevertheless, traveling was still possible even though the Mediterranean was volatile. However, after November 11 few people dared to make an open sea journey. The few who were willing to risk the treacherous seas did so because of the extraordinary high profit margin that a winter grain delivery would ensure in Rome.

There is an ominous sense right from the beginning that this journey will not be a simple one. Paul was no stranger to the dangers associated with sea travel, as he had been shipwrecked three times already (2 Corinthians 11:25). As an experienced sea traveler himself and with prophetic insight, Paul knows that a storm is on the horizon: "Sirs, I perceive that this voyage will be with hurt and much damage, not only of the lading and ship, but also our lives" (Acts 27:10).

An Angel and a Storm
ACTS 27:13–32

The ship captain, the owner, and the centurion decided to disregard Paul's warning and left the safe harbor of Fair Havens at Crete. As the party made its way to a more commodious harbor, the gentle southwestern soon gave way to "a tempestuous wind" literally "typhonic," a northeaster called Euroclydon (Acts 27:14).

In what is the last mention of a heavenly manifestation in Luke's writings, Luke wrote, "But after long abstinence Paul stood forth in the midst of them, and said, Sirs, ye should have hearkened unto me, and not have

loosed from Crete, and to have gained this harm and loss. And now I exhort you to be of good cheer: for there shall be no loss of any man's life
among you, but of the ship. For there stood by me this night the angel of
God, whose I am, and whom I serve, Saying, Fear not, Paul; thou must be
brought before **Caesar**: and, lo, God hath given thee all them that sail with
thee [276 people were aboard]. Wherefore, sirs, be of good cheer: for I believe God, that it shall be even as it was told me" (27:21–25).

A Shipwreck
ACTS 27:33–44

As the storm continued to grow more violent, nothing the crew did
seemed to make the situation any better. There is simply no place to hide in
a storm at sea. The ship had drifted some five hundred miles when it finally
ran aground and began to break up. At this point, the soldiers decided to
kill the prisoners in order to prevent their escape (Acts 27:42). This should
not surprise us since Roman soldiers were continually in the business of
killing people. In this case, if any prisoner escaped, the soldier would not
simply be demoted in rank; he would be killed instead. Luke wrote, "But
the centurion, willing to save Paul, kept them from their purpose; and commanded that they which could swim should cast themselves first into the
sea, and get to land: and the rest, some on boards, and some on broken
pieces of the ship. And so it came to pass, that they escaped all safe to land"
(27:43–44).

On the Island of Malta
ACTS 28:1–10

The party landed on Malta, a small island some eighteen miles long
and eight miles wide. Here the group met a "barbarous people" (Acts 28:2),
that is, people who did not speak Greek (they spoke Punic). They were
kind, and their first act was to build a bonfire for the party. As Paul "gathered a bundle of sticks, and laid them on the fire, there came a viper out of

the heat, and fastened on his hand" (28:3). Luke provides a vivid description of the incident, and one can easily imagine the irony of the situation. After all Paul had suffered—perils on the road from robbers, beatings
and imprisonments by city officials, death threats from his enemies, ston-
ings from mobs, hunger, sickness, and exposure to extreme heat and cold,
and four shipwrecks—it now appears that a simple snakebite will kill Paul.
Those watching, a superstitious group, assume that Paul is truly guilty of his
crime because, having escaped the sea, he is nevertheless punished—Justice
has her due anyway. Not surprisingly, when Paul does not die from the bite
(28:6), the local inhabitants think Paul is "a god," so Justice has the final
word after all! The word picture Luke provides is memorable—the rain,
cold, fire, and snakebite—an eyewitness account for sure.

Paul continued on the island for another three months, healing people
and finding success as a missionary (28:7–10). Today, Malta is a conservative bastion of Christianity, with churches located throughout the island,
and a bay called St. Paul's reminds us of Paul's visit there so long ago.

On to Rome
ACTS 28:11–22

After three months, the party found "a ship of Alexandria, which
had wintered in the isle, whose sign was Castor and Pollux" (Acts 28:11).
The soldiers loaded the prisoners, most likely in February A.D. 60, to continue their journey to **Rome**. The ship first made landfall at Syracuse
(in modern-day Sicily) and then landed in Rhegium, modern-day Reggio
Calabria. They made their final landfall at Puteoli, modern-day Puzzuoli
located just north of present-day Naples (28:13). In Puteoli, Paul and Luke
found members of the **Church** and tarried for seven days with them. Luke,
in what some have considered a great literary turn of a phrase, continued,
"and so we went toward Rome" (28:14).

The group began the land portion of their journey on the famous
Appian Way—a five- or six-day journey on foot. As the party traveled toward Rome, they encountered two delegations of Church leaders from the

city itself: "And from thence, when the brethren heard of us, they came to meet us as far as Appii forum [about forty-three miles from Rome], and The three taverns [about thirty-three miles from Rome]: whom when Paul saw, he thanked God, and took courage" (28:15). They had read his letter, they had been waiting for his visit, they had welcomed him, and now they accompanied him the rest of the way to Rome itself.

Within a short time, Luke noted, "we came to Rome, the centurion delivered the prisoners to the captain of the guard: but Paul was suffered to dwell by himself with a soldier that kept him" (28:16).

In Rome

ACTS 28:23–31

Luke ends his two-part story in the imperial capital as Paul continues bearing witness of **Jesus Christ** for the next two years. If Luke knew what happened afterward, he chose not to include it. It is possible that Paul's execution was well known and therefore Luke felt no reason to tell about it. Nevertheless, Luke's original purpose and Paul's divine commission were in fact now complete.

When Jesus first called Paul, the Lord said to Ananias, "Go thy way: for [Paul] is a chosen vessel unto me, to bear my name before the **Gentiles**, and kings, and the children of Israel" (Acts 9:15). The hearings before the "children of Israel" (22:1–22; 23:1–10), before the "Gentile governor" (24:1–25:12), and before the Jewish king (25:13–26:32) were in some way the immediate and direct fulfillment. In a wider context, Paul's entire missionary experience was only the day-to-day effort to fulfill this prophecy. The risen Lord also informed Ananias, "For I will shew [Paul] how great things he must suffer for my name's sake" (9:16). In Luke's account and throughout Paul's letters, we get a sense of what sufferings he experienced as "a servant of Jesus Christ, called to be an **apostle**, separated unto the gospel of God" (Romans 1:1).

3

ROMANS

With a few exceptions, Paul's letters are basically organized in the New Testament by length. His letter to the Romans is his longest and therefore is placed first in the Pauline corpus. Paul, as was traditional in the first century, used scribes in composing his letters. In this case the scribe is known—Tertius (Romans 16:22). Scribes likely played a rather significant role in a letter's composition.

Additionally, other voices are heard in some of Paul's letters, suggesting that in some cases it might be better to identify a letter as coming from Paul and other **disciples** (1 Thessalonians 1:1). Ascertaining the authorship of Paul's letters is, therefore, more complex than may sometimes be appreciated. In the case of his epistle to the Romans, Paul appears to be the sole author, and some scholars suggest that Romans may be one of the few letters that was dictated word-for-word. It is best read aloud to get a sense of Paul's speech and cadence.

Unlike his other letters addressed to specific **congregations**, Paul's letter to the Romans was written to a branch of the **Church** he had not established. Written sometime between A.D. 55 and 59, Romans is by far his most influential letter, speaking beyond the immediate context of its composition to generations of Christians.

Greetings and Setting of Romans
ROMANS 1:1–7

Paul followed first-century convention in preparing his letters, except that they were often longer than a standard personal letter. The greeting section usually includes an introduction or salutation and identifies the recipient. In this case, Paul begins by introducing himself: "Paul, a servant of **Jesus Christ**, called to be an **apostle** [one sent by Jesus], separated [as Jeremiah] unto the gospel of God" (Romans 1:1). The fact that he interrupted the introduction by inserting a comment about the gospel of God suggests that Paul wanted to capture the attention of his audience when they heard it read. Generally assumed to be an important statement of faith, possibly adapted or modified by Paul from an earlier source, the epistle to the Romans declares at the outset that the gospel of God is about "his Son Jesus Christ our Lord, which was made of the seed of David according to the flesh; And declared to be the **Son of God** with power, according to the spirit of holiness, by the resurrection from the dead: By whom we have received grace and apostleship, for obedience to the faith among all nations, for his name" (1:3–5). What is significant about Paul's testimony is that Jesus is identified as the Jewish **Messiah** and also the exalted Lord. Additionally, the gospel is characterized as thoroughly Jewish in content ("Which he had promised afore by his prophets in the holy **scriptures**"), but sent to "all nations," that is, to the **Gentiles**. Some have suggested that this represents a summary of the **apostles**' teachings and a summary of Paul's synagogue teachings. Paul may have contributed significantly to early Christian usage of the term *gospel*, a secular Greek word minted fresh in light of the life, death, and resurrection of Jesus of Nazareth.

Returning to a standard opening, Paul addresses this important letter "to all that be in **Rome**, beloved of God, called to be saints" (1:7), adding, "Grace to you and peace from God our Father, and the Lord Jesus Christ" (1:7).

Paul Desires to Preach the Gospel in Rome
ROMANS 1:8–17

In laying the foundation for what he intends to say to the Roman Saints, Paul first applauds them because their "faith is spoken of throughout the whole world," thus indicating that he has heard of their faith though he had not witnessed it firsthand (Romans 1:8). Indeed, Paul explains that he had hoped to travel to **Rome** but had been prevented (1:13). Paul describes being prevented using a passive form of the verb, perhaps intending to infer that God's work had kept him away and not persecution as he mentions using similar language in another epistle (1 Thessalonians 2:18). Paul wanted to extend a spiritual gift (Greek, *charisma*), or perhaps, more literally, he intended to use his God-given gift in establishing the **Church** in Rome (1:11). Hinting at what he would have discussed with the Romans had he been able to see them in person, Paul speaks of the "righteousness of God" (1:17) and the "Jew first, and . . . the Greek" (1:16), both of which receive significant discussion in the epistle.

God's Laws Are Manifest in Creation
ROMANS 1:18–32

In these verses Paul presents an argument based both on his perceptions of the **Gentile** religious experience and the possibility of knowing God through the material world. His first premise is that God punishes "*all* ungodliness and unrighteousness" (Romans 1:18; emphasis added) with the underlying assumption that God's punishment is eventual and not always immediate. The justice of such punishment upon "all" is addressed with the thought that the things of God are made known through his manifestation/presence in the natural world. In other words, God can be perceived in creation, thus testifying that "all" are aware to some degree of God's commands.

Many Gentiles had become confused by God's presence in the material world and began worshipping the material world itself, or, as Paul said, they "became vain in their imaginations, and their foolish heart was darkened" (1:21) and they "changed the glory of the uncorruptible God into an image made like to corruptible man, and to birds, and fourfooted beasts, and creeping things" (1:23). Some sins Paul interprets as directly contradictory to nature or to God's presence in the natural world. Those sins are specifically listed in Romans 1:24–31, which ends with the dramatic statement, "Who knowing the judgment of God, that they which commit such things are worthy of death" (1:32). The final phrase of verse 32 is somewhat cumbersome in Greek and English and attempts to convey the idea that those who break God's commands enjoy seeing others do likewise: "not only do the same, but have pleasure in them that do them [also]" (1:32).

There Is No Respect of Persons with God
ROMANS 2:1–11

The first word of chapter 2 has proven difficult for translators because "therefore" (Greek, *dio*) seems to imply a conclusion drawn from chapter 1 (directed to **Gentiles**) while commentators would prefer to see this material directed at Paul's Jewish audience. The wording, however, appears to be rather straightforward: "Therefore thou art inexcusable, O man, whosoever thou art that judgest" (Romans 2:1; emphasis added). It seems that Paul has both Gentiles and Jews in mind when he addresses the issue of those who judge others but who do not themselves obey the commandments. The most pressing matter, as Paul begins his discussion of foreordination/election, God's chosen people, and teaching the gospel to Gentiles, is to avoid judging other persons when those persons continue in disobedience.

Also of concern to Paul is the issue of how birth within the **covenant** affects judgment. From the language of these verses, it appears that some believed that being born within the covenant is reason enough to suppose that they would be judged favorably while those born outside the covenant would be punished. Paul addresses this fallacy twice, stating, "God . . . will render to every man according to his deeds (2:5–6) and "there is no respect of persons with God" (2:11).

Doers of the Law

ROMANS 2:12–29

For purposes of advancing his larger discourse, Paul now addresses an idealized "Jew" who seeks to define himself as having the revelation of the law of God and is therefore superior to others who do not have the law. This idealized "Jew" (Romans 2:17) is contrasted to the ambiguous "O man" (2:1), which invokes both Jews and **Gentiles**. For both Jew and Gentile, "the doers of the law shall be justified" (2:13) whether that law is known through creation or human teaching (2:13–20). Although Paul's teachings are frequently taken to mean that mankind is saved by grace, the emphasis on works as a fundamental part of the process of gaining salvation is striking. What is perhaps more profound is how living the law fundamentally defines mankind's relationship to God in judgment (2:14–16). Moreover, for Paul, knowledge of the law does little if it does not lead to obedience (2:15). In other words, hearing the word of God must lead to action (2:13) so that we avoid becoming as the blind (those who know the law and do not obey it) leading the blind (those who do not know the law; 2:19).

Paul rails against the idea that birthright or participation in the ordinances of the law (e.g., **circumcision**) can alone provide special status in the eyes of God. By analogy Paul teaches that circumcision is useful only if the law is kept as well (2:25), and circumcision is rendered equivalent to uncircumcision when a person does not obey the "righteousness of the law" (2:26). That is not to say that minor sin negates the ordinances of God, but rather, that obedience to the law is more effectual in pleasing God than possessing a birthright in Israel. Paul ends this section with his most profound thought, namely that inward religion or religion from the heart is greater than external religious trappings: "But he is a Jew, which is one inwardly; and circumcision is that of the heart, in the spirit, and not in the letter; whose praise is not of men, but of God" (2:29).

The Oracles of God

ROMANS 3:1–31

The teaching that internal religion is what matters most to God could lead to the idea that organized religion is unnecessary. Paul foresaw that this question would arise, and argued that the ordinances (here epitomized through **circumcision**) are important, "because that unto them [God's people in all ages] were committed the oracles of God" (Romans 3:2). In other words, God's people receive the blessing of administering the **covenants** of the gospel, for which they are blessed as they bless others.

Paul addresses a second important question, namely, whether the unbelief of some within the covenant in some way makes the "faith of God without effect" (Greek, *pisten tou theou*, "integrity of God"; 3:3) because it may imply that God chose and continues to favor a people among whom some sin. To counter this argument, Paul teaches that if every man were a liar, God would still be God, or as in the example from Psalm 51:4, David declares that even though he had sinned, God was forever just.

The third problem Paul addresses is somewhat difficult to unravel in the King James language because the phrase "if our unrighteousness commend the righteousness of God" (3:5) can also be translated as "if our unrighteousness demonstrates the righteousness of God" (ASV), meaning that if all men sin and God is righteous regardless, then some could interpret our sin as a means of defining who God is. Paul realized that such a question was foolishness "(I speak as a man) God forbid: for then how shall God judge the world?" (3:5–6). Of course this idea is ridiculous to Paul, but he seems to be aware that Christians were being slandered because of their teachings regarding the law of Moses, "(as we be slanderously reported, and as some affirm that we say,) Let us do evil, that good may come? whose damnation is just" (3:8). The new covenant of Christianity proved difficult for some Jews who felt that leaving behind portions of God's former law constituted lawless behavior.

Returning to the issue of the divide between Jewish and **Gentile** Christians, Paul uses a quotation of Psalms 14:1–3 and 53:1 to remind his readers that all have fallen short of the glory of God (3:10). Paul elaborates through a lengthy list of sins the ways in which mankind, but more particularly those who have slandered his message, have sinned. "As it is written, There is none righteous, no, not one" (3:10). As a conclusion to this list of sins, Paul acknowledges that the law judges only those who have it or "who are under the law" and not those (Gentiles) who have not been taught the law (3:19). But Paul also reminds the reader of his previous discussion of natural law as a way that God will judge those outside the law because they are able to discern at least portions of the law through the creation. Bringing Christians into the mix, Paul then states that there are those "by faith of **Jesus Christ** unto all and upon all them that believe: for there is no difference" (3:22). In other words, God will judge those who learn the law through the creation (Gentiles), those who had the oracles of God (Jews), and those who believe on Jesus Christ for salvation (Christians). Indeed, salvation is available to all through Jesus Christ.

The lawlessness ascribed to Christians was of great concern to Paul, and the final verses of the chapter are devoted to a discussion of how God would save them. Drawing upon the language of Mosaic **sacrifices**, which a Jewish audience would understand, Paul declares that "God hath set forth to be a propitiation through faith in his blood, to declare his righteousness for the remission of sins that are past, through the forbearance of God" (3:25). In a way of speaking, the sacrifice of Jesus Christ brought believers into the covenant of God. Because God has literally redeemed all of those who would believe on his name *and* who did not live within the law of Moses, Paul says, "Therefore we conclude that a man is justified by faith without the deeds of the law" (3:28). Paul did not argue for belief without works but rather that God could save the **Gentiles** independently of those parts of the law of Moses that were done away with at Christ's crucifixion and resurrection.

The Faith of Abraham

ROMANS 4:1–25

In typical Jewish fashion, Paul draws upon the scriptural example of Abraham to prove his previous point that God found some faithful apart from the **covenant** revealed through Moses. To demonstrate how righteousness is determined through faith, Paul speaks specifically of the righteousness of Abraham before he received the covenant of **circumcision**, which was a sign of his faith. Specifically, "Abraham *believed* God, and it was counted unto him for righteousness" (Romans 4:3; emphasis added; see also Genesis 15:6). Paul's larger purpose in emphasizing Abraham's belief over his acts of righteousness is to help a Jewish audience understand that **Gentiles** can be saved as well apart from the law of Moses.

Paul sees the covenant of circumcision as a type of the later acceptance of Gentiles because God gave unto Abraham a promise that he would be the father of all those who believed, prior to his receiving the sign of circumcision, thus prefiguring the gospel being taught to the circumcised (Jews) and the uncircumcised (Gentiles).

Using reasoning to explain his teachings, Paul taught that the law defines sin, and therefore where there is no law, "there is no transgression," thus making the law the primary determiner of what constitutes sin (4:15). That does not imply that the law is sinful, but that the law both defines and identifies sin, and thus with such a focus on sin, Paul sees belief in **Jesus** as freedom from this emphasis.

In conclusion, Paul teaches that "it [the reward] is of faith, that it [the reward] might be by grace; to the end the promise might be sure to all the seed; *not to that only which is of the law*, but to that also which is of the faith of Abraham; who is the father of us all" (4:16; emphasis added). Paul goes on to emphasize the challenge of faith, and in a way faith becomes the new law and work of the gospel of Jesus **Christ**. Abraham believed in the unbelievable; "he considered not his own body now dead, when he was about an hundred years old, neither yet the deadness of Sara's womb: he staggered not at the promise of God through unbelief; but was strong in faith, giving glory to God" (4:19–20). Paul's concluding thoughts in this chapter appear aimed at establishing belief as the beginning of action—a belief that leads to powerful works of righteousness and not a declaration of accepted principles only.

The Atonement
Romans 5:1–19

Having established that faith justifies (Greek, *dikaiōthentes*, "being made right") us to enter into God's grace, Paul now addresses the role of tribulation in salvation (Romans 5:1). Rejoicing in the "hope of the glory of God" (5:2), we "glory in tribulations also: knowing that tribulation worketh patience" (5:3). Belief or faith is not an abstract state of existence in which one simply ponders the reality of God; rather, belief opens a door to grace, which in turn leads to the need for patience, experience, hope, and faith (5:3–5).

Following his remarks on being justified by faith, Paul embarks upon the doctrine of the **Atonement**, which he establishes first by pointing to the universality of death and sin, which entered the world "by one man" (5:12). If sin and death entered into the world through a single man, then the remedy to that Fall should also be offered by one man: "Much more then, being now justified by his blood, we shall be saved from wrath through him" (5:9). Paul here teaches of the "atonement" (Greek, *katalaggēn*, "reconciliation") and this is the only place where that word appears in the English King James Version (5:11). However, the Greek word is used elsewhere in the New Testament (Matthew 5:24; 1 Corinthians 7:11; 2 Corinthians 5:18–20).

Some of Paul's language in this chapter is weighed down with technical terminology describing the **justification** of the sinner in light of the disobedience of one man. (5:19). Paul's overarching theme is that the **Atonement** had to be a universal act removing the sins of all mankind and not only the sins of the **covenant** people. In contrast, Adam brought an offense while **Christ** brought an eternal gift (5:15). Following his arguments of chapter 4, Paul now concludes that sin did exist in the world prior to the **Law**, but that the revelation of God's law brought punishment for those sins (5:13). Verse 15 can be rendered more clearly "But the free gift is not like the offense" (authors' translation) because one leads to life and one to death.

The Christ-Centered Life
ROMANS 5:20–6:23

Paul's teaching, "Where sin abounded, grace did much more abound" (Romans 5:20), could be taken to the illogical extreme: "Shall we continue in sin, that grace may abound?" (6:1). Following Paul's line of reasoning, when sin must be reconciled through grace, in its extreme form, one could argue that sinning permits God the opportunity to provide grace and in turn could be interpreted positively. For whatever reasons, Paul specifically mentions this twisted interpretation of his words, and perhaps there were those among his listeners who had already used this type of thinking in their attempts to discredit Paul.

To counter such thinking, Paul taught that true Christians are dead to sin when baptized "into **Jesus Christ**" (6:3) and that **baptism** signals an entry into a new life, "planted together" (6:5) with Christ, and "our old man is crucified with him" (6:6). This newness of life should lead to a newness in commitment to obedience as we seek to be "freed from sin" (6:7).

Furthermore, citing the fact of Christ dying for our sins, Paul points out that Christ died once, implying that our new life should begin only once as well our symbolic death to sin, which should also be a singular occurrence following the pattern of Christ's death (6:8–10). To achieve this goal, Paul immediately addresses the main culprit of sin, namely the lusts of the mortal body. From Paul's perspective, the mortal body wages war against the spiritual mind, trying to subject and perhaps convince the mind to sin. To counter that, Paul encourages us to yield ourselves to God because of the grace given to us freely as a gift.

To conclude this section of his discourse, Paul uses the analogy of the workman who receives wages from his master. Paul teaches, "The wages of sin is death; but the gift of God is eternal life through Jesus Christ our

Lord" (6:23). Comparing the two types of wages, death and eternal life, one wonders why anyone would choose the former. Hinting at how this might occur, Paul mentions briefly the "infirmity of your flesh" (6:19), which implies weakness of the body, or something that might be referred to more broadly as mortal weakness. Paul realized that these mortal weaknesses challenge the Christ-centered mind and attempt to lead it into service to sin.

The Law Brings Us to Christ
ROMANS 7:1–25

Turning his attention to the law and how we are to understand it in light of living a life in the grace of God, Paul uses an analogy of a husband and wife: "For the woman which hath an husband is bound by the law to her husband so long as he liveth; but if the husband be dead, she is loosed from the law of her husband" (Romans 7:2). Paul saw in this relationship a similarity to the new law of the gospel, whereby Jews who were once married to the law of Moses, which has symbolically died or passed away, are now bound by a new **covenant** of marriage to **Jesus Christ**.

Realizing that by referring to the law as "dead" (7:6), Paul might also have unintentionally denigrated the law of Moses, the possibility of which he addresses through the question, "What shall we say then? Is the law sin? God forbid" (7:7). Paul's teaching in Galatians is perhaps more understandable on how he viewed the eternal role of the law of Moses when he said, "Wherefore the law was our schoolmaster to bring us unto Christ, that we might be justified by faith" (Galatians 3:24).

Our fundamental relationship to law is the focus of Romans 7, where Paul discusses at some length how bodily desires and appetites wage war against the commandments. To lay the foundation for this discussion, Paul again reminds his readers that the law defines sin, and once that definition is in place, the desire to sin "wrought in me all manner of concupiscence [lust]" (7:8). Those wicked desires (concupiscence) "deceived me, and by it slew me" (7:11). In other words, Paul realized the very real force and desire to sin, so much so that in comparison to the defining force of law, he had no hope to win that war but would fall short of it because he had given in to sin.

The law, by defining what sin is, is not inherently wicked but rather is a list of requirements aimed at creating a spiritual being: "Wherefore the law is holy, and the commandment holy, and just, and good" (7:12) and "we know that the law is spiritual" (7:14). What Paul appears to be emphasizing is the idea that no mortal can succeed in living the law perfectly and that falling short of perfection, we will all become subject to the law's punishments. Thus, as all mankind fall short, there arises a need for a Redeemer and for grace to forgive the shortcomings.

The final section of this discussion reveals a very personal side of the **apostle** Paul, who here speaks of his own struggle in fighting sin. He describes obedience as suppressing the desires to do evil and doing those things that he hates (7:15). Describing his desire to sin, Paul said, "For I know that in me (that is, in my flesh,) dwelleth no good thing: for to will is present with me; but how to perform that which is good I find not" (7:18). The phrase "for to will" could also be rendered "the desire," referring to the desire to do evil. By acknowledging this internal struggle, Paul accepts that the struggle itself is a tacit acceptance that the "law . . . is good" because we spiritually accept it as a measure of our righteousness (7:16).

Paul does not specifically discuss the struggle of the natural man versus the spiritual man in the same way that King Benjamin does (Mosiah 3:19), but he seems to be addressing the same principle, namely, that the body provides an inherent opposition in all things and that the spirit must bring the unruly body into subjection to the commandments of God: "So then with the mind I myself serve the law of God; but with the flesh the law of sin" (Romans 7:25).

Life in Christia

ROMANS 8:1–17

In contrast to those who live after the law and commandments are those who live in **Jesus Christ** and walk "after the Spirit" (Romans 8:1). Having already addressed the issue that such a life is not lawless (3:8–9; 7:7–22), Paul is free to discuss what a life in **Christ** truly entails. Drawing upon the incarnation and resurrection as types, Paul discusses how the flesh of Jesus (symbolizing the law of carnal commandments) was condemned and symbolically and literally passed away. Carnal or fleshly existence "cannot please God" (8:8), which appears to be aimed at those who would consider the possibility of following the Spirit and pursuing carnal desires. For Paul, it is only either/or and not both: "But ye are not in the flesh, but in the Spirit, if so be that the Spirit of God dwell in you. Now if any man have not the Spirit of Christ, he is none of his" (8:9).

Recalling the Resurrection of Jesus, Paul teaches that here there is a symbol as well so that the Resurrection is symbolic of being raised through the Spirit to a spiritual existence. Living after the Spirit, we "mortify the deeds of the body" (8:13) and "are the sons of God" (8:14). This freedom of life in the Spirit leads to a renewed relationship with the Father, whom we now address personally (Abba) and not formally (Elohim) because we know him (8:15). It may be that for this very reason early Christians preserved the word *Abba* in **Aramaic** because it revealed a very personal relationship with God that was fundamentally different from what had been taught through traditional practice. This new, more intimate relationship with God makes more believable the notion of the righteous being "heirs of God, and joint-heirs with Christ; if so be that we suffer with him, that we may be also glorified together" (8:17).

The Earnest Expectation of the Creature
ROMANS 8:18–39

The spiritual individual yearns for the reality of enjoying an eternal existence with God, which is in direct conflict with the temporal and carnal desire to sin. Much like the mortal body's natural proclivity to sin, the spirit "waiteth for the manifestation of the sons of God" (Romans 8:19) because the creature seeks to be freed from "the bondage of corruption" (8:21). This desire might be described as an inherent desire to do good that permeates all creation and, in fact, underlines the human experience. Paul does not see the entire human family as inherently wicked or evil, but rather at war with itself as the body and spirit struggle against each other. Paul even sees this struggle taking a more cosmic stage when he declares, "For we know that the whole creation groaneth and travaileth in pain together until now" (8:22). Similarly, we "groan within ourselves, waiting for the adoption, to wit, the redemption of our body" (8:23). Time and the degradation of his physical body may have helped Paul appreciate this idea (Paul was near the end of his life when he wrote Romans), but his earlier letters also reveal a similar body-versus-spirit conflict.

To guide us to the realization of the promise of eternal glory, the Holy Spirit leads us on through hope (8:24), a hope that is not seen but rather requires us to have patience to wait for it (8:24–25). Not being able to physically see the realization of God's promises, the Spirit guides us because "we know not what we should pray for as we ought: but the Spirit itself maketh intercession for us with groanings which cannot be uttered" (8:26). The path of salvation is both hoped for and impassable without the help of the Spirit as our guide. For Paul, this profound act of trust and hope on the Spirit is what leads to salvation (8:28).

In this context, Paul considers the issue of foreordination, which seems to imply that God chose a people whom he knew beforehand and who would be able to follow the Spirit to salvation. The New Testament does not distinguish between foreordination and predestination (Greek, *proorizō*, "decide beforehand"), and so it is possible to confuse foreknowledge with predetermined outcomes (predestination). Given the context, however, of life in the Spirit, God called those who would follow his will and who would "be conformed to the image of his Son" (8:29). God's work is described in verse 30 as the **justification** and glorifying of his children. Paul goes on to ask, "If God be for us, who can be against us?" (8:31), which looks back to the beginning of the epistle where Paul discussed the advantage God's followers have in receiving the oracles of God (Romans 3:2).

The Law of Election
ROMANS 9:1–33

In our modern world, where we wish to distinguish what is fair and equal from what discriminates and favors, the doctrine of election may seem strange. Paul, in fact, appears to anticipate that some in his own audience would find the doctrine unpalatable (Romans 9:14). Paul's answers to these concerns, found here in Romans 9, present the overarching theme that God's work is not fully known to man and therefore to question his work based on a single doctrine that appears unfair to our sensibilities would be to exclude God from our lives and keep us from the promises Paul has previously enumerated.

Paul's introduction to this subject is heartfelt, and he wishes that if it were possible he would be "accursed from Christ" (9:3) if it would mean that his fellow Israelites would accept the gospel of **Jesus Christ**. This expression seems to suggest that Jews were turning away from the **covenant** of the gospel in the middle of the first century A.D. when this letter was written.

Paul's first premise is that birth into Israel is not a guarantee of receiving the promises of the gospel (9:6); and to explain this phenomenon, Paul teaches that even though both of Abraham's children were born within the covenant, only one received the promises of the gospel covenant—Isaac (9:7). Again, Paul sees a similar example in Rebecca's twins, one of whom was chosen and one of whom was not, even though both were born within the covenant (9:10–13). These two examples establish that birth is not a sufficient guarantee of foreordination or of a chosen status.

Paul's second premise is that some may consider this example inherently unfair: "What shall we say then? Is there unrighteousness with God? God forbid" (9:14). To answer this, Paul cites Exodus 33:19, in which Moses declared that God "will have mercy on whom I will have mercy, and I will have compassion on whom I will have compassion" (9:15). Furthermore, Paul explicitly states that foreordination is not a matter of personal will or ability ("So then it is not of him that willeth, nor of him that runneth, but of God that sheweth mercy" [9:16]), but is rather a result of God's purposes.

By introducing what appear to be two paradoxes, God's raising up of Pharaoh for his own purposes (9:17) and the potter who makes one vessel of honor and one of dishonor (9:21), Paul has placed the burden of making sense of this upon the reader. Unfortunately, the entire and complete outline of the plan of salvation is not readily knowable to mankind, which makes God's use of Pharaoh to bring about the salvation of the children of Israel appear unfair. Acknowledging this possible conclusion, Paul holds out hope to all who participate in the execution of God's plan: "What if God . . . might make known the riches of his glory on the vessels of mercy, which he had afore prepared unto glory, even us, whom he hath called, not of the Jews only, but also of the **Gentiles**?" (9:22–24).

Paul's third premise is the idea that God will call his own people, here based on the analogy of Pharaoh and the potter, which would prove to be a scandalous proposition to the children of Israel. What Paul appears to be suggesting here is that as did Pharaoh, God is reaching out to Gentiles: "What shall we say then? That the Gentiles, which followed not after righteousness, have attained to righteousness, even the righteousness which is of faith" (9:30). Paul perceives that the very idea that God would save those outside Israel would be a "stumblingstone" (9:32–33), as foreshadowed in the prophecies of Isaiah (Isaiah 8:14; 28:16).

Faith unto Salvation

ROMANS 10:1–21

After having emphasized the role of faith that leads to good works in **Christ**, Paul now turns his attention to the work of teaching and preaching Christ. Speaking of the Jews in the third person plural, Paul now seems to direct his attention to the Jews within the Roman **congregation** of Saints. Zeal without knowledge is criticized (Romans 10:2), and in contrast Paul applauds focused righteousness, or righteousness that is Christ-centered. The duty of the Saints is to preach the gospel of Jesus Christ: "If thou shalt confess with thy mouth the Lord Jesus, and shalt believe in thine heart that God hath raised him from the dead, thou shalt be saved" (10:9). These ideas are not abstractions but a heartfelt and genuine expression of a new-ness of life in the Lord Jesus Christ.

Again in contrast to those who obey without knowledge, Paul empha-sizes belief as the means of salvation so that works no longer become the focus and object of our salvation. He expresses this idea succinctly when he says, "For whosoever shall call upon the name of the Lord shall be saved" (10:13). Without the emphasis upon belief as the defining feature of Christian identity, we would lapse into the law of Moses mentality that God saves only one people through obedience to stringent laws. Now that belief is the focus, "there is not difference between the Jew and the Greek" (10:12), and thus the modern community of believers is defined indepen-dently of birth within Israel.

The blessings to those who preach the gospel are described in the prophecy of Isaiah 52:7: "How beautiful upon the mountains are the feet of him that bringeth good tidings, that publisheth peace" (quoted in Romans 10:15). The teaching of the gospel to all the world and beyond the borders of Israel was foreseen by Moses (Deuteronomy 32:21) and Isaiah (65:1), say-ings that Paul feels were "very bold" (Romans 10:20).

A Remnant Is Preserved

ROMANS 11:1–12

In addressing the question of whether Israel's rejection of the gospel of **Jesus Christ** constitutes their complete falling away, Paul reminds his audience of Israel's troubled past. He recalls an instance when the prophet Elijah (KJV, "Elias") preserved seven thousand men from destruction (Romans 11:4; 1 Kings 19:18). Whether that number seems large or small by comparison to the number of Israelites who had joined themselves to the Christian **Church** is unknown, it is clear that Paul found the comparison startling. Paul refers to the number of Israelites who have followed Jesus as "a remnant" (11:5).

This "remnant" has come to the knowledge of the gospel "by grace" and not by works. And in one of Paul's most succinct statements on grace versus works, he describes how the remnant of Israel has been preserved: "And if by grace, then is it no more of works: otherwise grace is no more grace. But if it be of works, then is it no more grace: otherwise work is no more work" (11:6). Though a remnant had been preserved, a portion of Israel had fallen away through a stumbling block, which Paul sees as fortuitous because it opened the way for salvation to, "come unto the **Gentiles**, for to provoke them [the Jews] to jealousy" (11:11).

Paul Addresses Roman Gentiles

ROMANS 11:13–36

Turning specifically to the **Gentile** members of the **Church** in **Rome**, Paul encourages them to emulate the Jews who were once the **covenant** people. Paul asks them pointedly, "For if the casting away of them be the reconciling of the world, *what shall the receiving of them be, but life from the dead?*" (Romans 11:15; emphasis added). The second part of this question reminds the members that if they receive the gospel, they too will be saved and given life from the dead. To explain how the Church had come to be an admixture of Jewish and Gentile members, Paul refers to an allegory of an olive tree, which may represent his own thinking on the matter, but it has strong similarities to the allegory of the olive tree in Jacob 5 (11:16–19, 21, 23–24).

The fundamental reason for the process of grafting natural and wild branches is "unbelief," and although it is unstated here, the owner of the vineyard intends to keep the olive tree thriving. The current grafting in of wild branches will continue until "the fulness of the Gentiles be come in" (11:25). Israel has only "in part" (11:25) been blinded, and when the fulness of Gentiles comes, "all Israel shall be saved" (11:26). What Paul meant by the "fulness of the Gentiles" is not certain, but in context it appears that there will come a time when Israel will again be gathered with the Gentiles and no longer will she be saved only as a remnant.

In discussing the return of Israel, Paul cites Isaiah 59:20 and 27:9 to teach that "out of Sion the Deliverer" (11:26) shall come, reminding the Gentile Christians that the deliverer of the latter days (Christ) will be of Israelite heritage. Exactly why a deliverer is needed at the coming of the fulness of the Gentiles is not addressed in Romans; however, from Paul's discourse on the matter, it is apparent that he sees it as a troubling time when a deliverer from "ungodliness" will be needed (11:26). Although it may have been painful to admit this, Paul teaches that Israel "are enemies for your sakes: but as touching the election, they are beloved for the fathers' sakes" (11:28).

Paul concludes this section by mentioning the mystery of God in casting away the elect and choosing the Gentiles. Paul suggests that God has done this, "that he might have mercy upon all" (11:32) but that the full extent of God's work is "unsearchable" (11:33). In conclusion to these thoughts, Paul reminds his readers, "Who hath known the mind of the Lord?" (11:34) indicating that his thoughts on the subject may not fully span nor describe the depth and wisdom of God's plan of salvation.

Present Your Bodies a Living Sacrifice
ROMANS 12:1–21

The concept of presenting our bodies as a **sacrifice** unto God draws upon the imagery of the Mosaic animal sacrifices that were still being offered in the Jerusalem **temple** at the time this letter was written. Such sacrifices required unblemished victims, which Paul here encourages the members to become. Paul had previously addressed the idea that life in the Spirit would lead to perfection (Romans 8:1–17).

Acknowledging true human nature, Paul speaks of the issues dividing **Church** members, which he identifies as vanity (12:3), pride (12:4), and the practice of denigrating the spiritual gifts of others (12:6–8). The ideal branch of the Church should be built upon "love . . . without dissimulation" (12:9). Furthermore, Paul encourages the Saints in a number of areas that reflect the problems common in all dispensations of the Church. He calls for love, service to the Lord, diligence, hope, patience in tribulation, prayer, caring for the poor, and hospitality. Paul has no illusions that Christians are free from sin, and these reminders come sharply on the heels of his discussion of how a part of Israel fell away.

Earthly Rulers
ROMANS 13:1–14

Paul lived under Roman rule, a system that has been popularly described as harsh and impersonal, with the overt goal of maintaining peace even if it meant overriding personal freedoms. His comments on government, which come somewhat as an appendage to his discourse on election and the dispensation of the **Gentiles**, should be interpreted in light of the fact that the rulers he was speaking of were not democratic leaders but foreign oligarchs with their own interests and agendas.

That Paul endorsed government is expressly stated in his opening lines of chapter 13: "Let every soul be subject unto the higher powers. For there is no power but of God: the powers that be are ordained of God" (Romans

13:1). The higher powers (Greek, *ezousiais hyperxousais*) are placed in position by God and are "ordained of God," and Paul encourages obedience to civil law in order to maintain civic harmony. The Joseph Smith Translation alters the context of this verse, applying Paul's teaching to the **Church** and its powers. It is possible that both applications were originally intended by Paul. Although Paul does not expressly state it, he seems to suggest that obedience to governments is appropriate as long as those governments "are not a terror to good works" (13:3). Fighting against such authorities only brings punishment and the execution of "wrath upon him that doeth evil" (13:4). The overarching theme appears to be maintaining harmony in civic affairs with government leaders serving as keepers of the peace. Basing his thinking on a saying of **Jesus** in Matthew 22:15–22, in which Jesus said, "Render therefore unto **Caesar** the things which are Caesar's; and unto God the things that are God's" (Matthew 22:21), Paul interprets that saying as "Render therefore to all their dues: tribute to whom tribute is due; custom to whom custom; fear to whom fear; honour to whom honour. Owe no man any thing, but to love one another; for he that loveth another hath fulfilled the law" (Romans 13:7–8).

Alongside civic laws are the commandments of God, which Paul enumerates following the list of the Ten Commandments of Exodus 20:1–17. The harmony achieved from this obedience to government will be short-lived because "now it is high time to awake out of sleep: for now is our salvation nearer than when we believed. *The night is far spent, the day is at hand*" (13:11–12; emphasis added). In light of the approaching doom, Paul encourages obedience and law-abiding behavior. It remains unclear how heavily the context of his remarks has influenced his thinking on these issues.

Kosher Concerns
ROMANS 14:1–23

The Jerusalem Council prohibited the eating of meat that had been previously sacrificed to a pagan deity, the official wording of which reads, "that they [Gentiles] abstain from pollutions of idols, and from fornica-tion, and from things strangled, and from blood" (Acts 15:20). Nearly two decades later, the Saints were still facing internal disputes over lingering questions about the kosher requirements. It seems from Paul's words here that some held to a more stringent reading of the kosher law, whereas oth-ers were more lax in their observance. Unfortunately, Paul does not state whether the issue was over their reading of the Jerusalem Council's decision or whether it extended beyond that decision into other kosher matters as well.

Regardless of specific context, the main issue here is the question of eating certain unkosher foods and the celebration of certain holy days. Certainly at the heart of this division is the question of whether or not Christians should continue to observe all of the statutes of the law of Moses, including kosher laws and holidays, or whether Christians should follow only a very limited set of kosher laws (those given by the Jerusalem Council) and celebrate new holidays (probably those associated with **Jesus'** life). Some Christians had begun to despise others because of what they ate and which holidays (holy days) they celebrated (Romans 14:3, 5).

Paul's first response is to remind the Saints that they should eat with thanksgiving to the Lord and celebrate the Lord in their holidays (14:7–8). He then introduces principles regarding certain religious diets, namely, "that no man put a stumblingblock or an occasion to fall in his brother's way" (14:13). The stumblingblock of verse 13 is a private interpretation of what constitutes a kosher diet. This principle is stated a second time using different wording: "But if thy brother be grieved with thy meat, now walkest thou not charitably. Destroy not him with thy meat, for whom **Christ** died" (14:15).

Although his thinking may be difficult to understand in the modern world, Paul taught that the food itself was not inherently clean or unclean, but it is private interpretation that renders it so (14:14). That is not to say that certain foods are good or bad, but rather with regard to religious di-ets, we observe them for reasons beyond the inherent goodness or badness of the food itself: "*For the kingdom of God is not meat and drink; but righ-teousness, and peace, and joy in the* **Holy Ghost**" (14:17; emphasis added).

Paul concludes by stating that we pursue those things that lead to peace and avoid those things that lead to offense (14:20–21).

The Gospel to the Gentiles
ROMANS 15:1–33

Continuing with his concluding thoughts in chapter 14, Paul summarizes his thinking that the strong in the kingdom should tolerate or "bear the infirmities of the weak" (Romans 15:1). He sees an example in **Christ**, who did likewise, bearing our weaknesses and fulfilling scripture that he would endure the reproaches of men (Psalm 69:9). This simple principle would lead to harmony in the branch and a unity of "one mind and one mouth" (15:6).

Outlining his own work among the **Gentiles**, Paul shows a profound appreciation for those who did not know God but who have come to know God through his mission. He sees both groups of people as mutually indebted to each other, the Gentiles for receiving the word of God and the ministry of **Jesus** Christ through the Jews and the Jews for receiving temporal assistance from the Gentiles (15:27). It had been Paul's policy to teach the gospel where the name of Christ had not been heard (15:20), and therefore he desired to take the gospel to Spain, likely indicating that Christianity had not made it that far west by the middle of the first century A.D. (15:24). Obviously the gospel had already been preached in **Rome**, probably through Peter, and Paul laments that he had been hindered from visiting them previously (15:22).

This letter was probably written at the end of the third missionary journey, when Paul was preparing to travel to Jerusalem to deliver the collection for the poor in that city. Unfortunately, his trip to Jerusalem did not proceed fully as planned, and he was taken to Rome as a prisoner. It is uncertain whether he ever traveled to Spain or left Rome as a free man. He was hopeful in this letter that those things would happen, but his imprisonment in Caesarea Maritima delayed him for several years. The doctrinal part of the letter appears to end at Romans 15:33.

Greetings

ROMANS 16:1–27

Romans is one of the few letters that are virtually universally accepted as a unified letter, with former concerns about chapter 16 having virtually disappeared (some argued that this material originally was addressed to the Saints in Ephesus). This means that the "greeting section" is of tremendous importance in any efforts to reconstruct what the early **Church** membership was like in **Rome**. This long greeting section, the longest in the New Testament, lists twenty-six individuals associated with at least five separate **house-churches** scattered throughout Rome. As was the case in every situation throughout the **Roman Empire**, including Jerusalem, the Saints met in private homes or apartments for their worship meetings. In Romans 16, three house-churches are specifically mentioned: (1) "the church [Greek, *ekklēsias*] that" meets at the house of Priscilla and Aquila (16:3, 5); (2) the house-church of Asyncritus, which included "Phlegon, Hermas, Patrobus, Hermes, and the brethren which are with them" (16:14); and (3) Philologus's house-church, which included "Julia, Nereus, and his sister, and Olympas, and all the saints which are with them" (16:15). Besides these three house-churches, two other pockets of Christians in the city of Rome are identified: (1) the Christians gathered in Aristobulus's household (16:10) and (2) the Christians in Narcissus's household (16:11). There may have been other house-churches in the city since fourteen people named in this list were not specifically identified as belonging to the house-churches already mentioned.

The current **congregations** in Rome today are surprisingly similar to the original ones—they are composed of social and ethnically diverse people. In the first century, many emigrants came from the eastern part of the Empire and were either already members of the **Church** or had joined in Rome.

Paul ends this long letter with a final exhortation (16:17–20), greetings from members of the church in Corinth (16:21–23), and final ending: "The grace of our Lord **Jesus Christ** be with you all. Amen. Now to him that is of power to stablish you according to my gospel, and the preaching of Jesus Christ, according to the revelation of the mystery, which was kept secret since the world began, but now is made manifest, and by the **scriptures** of the prophets, according to the commandment of the everlasting God, made known to all nations for the obedience of faith: to God only wise, be glory through Jesus Christ for ever. Amen" (16:24–27).

4

FIRST CORINTHIANS

Unlike Paul's doctrinally oriented letter to the Romans, 1 Corinthians is a response to problems in the Corinthian branch of the **Church**. Its somewhat fragmented contents can be ascribed to the fact that Paul was answering questions and not preparing a treatise. The letter was written after Paul's first visit to Corinth, which is described in Acts 18:1–18. Paul's stay in the city lasted eighteen months, and it appears from his correspondence that he made many close friends, as well as some enemies, in the city (Acts 18:12). Although not mentioned in Acts, a friend of Paul's—Chloe—wrote to him after his departure detailing events that had taken place since he had left. The time frame is not specified, but it appears that this letter must have been written several months after Paul's departure and therefore sometime near the beginning of his third mission.

Introduction

1 Corinthians 1:1–9

First Corinthians mentions a lost letter (5:9) that was focused on issues pertaining to chastity, and suggests that the problems faced in this letter were not new or surprising to the **apostle**. He wrote with Sosthenes, who is otherwise unknown (a different man with the same name is mentioned in Acts 18:17), although he may be the same person as Crispus in 1 Corinthians 1:14, based on the fact that Acts 18:8 and 17 equate the two names Crispus and Sosthenes.

Corinth was a Roman colony with a Jewish synagogue, some physical remains of which still survive at the archaeological site. Because the name *Corinth* is linguistically connected to the Greek verb meaning "to fornicate," some have speculated that the inhabitants of this city were particularly given to sexual misconduct. Historically, it is unlikely that the inhabitants of Corinth were any worse than other Roman-period Greek cities. The city boasted many important **temples** to the Greek gods as well as monuments to the Caesars.

Paul's introduction to the epistle reveals a certain warmth and particular concern for the well-being of the Saints. In the opening verse Paul refers to being "called to be an apostle" (1:1), and in some early manuscripts the word translated "called" is missing. It is difficult to know with certainty whether the word was removed by later scribes who objected to Paul's apostleship or whether it was added by those who wished to defend it. In either case, this is the earliest reference to Paul's apostleship where it appears he refers to the calling of an apostle rather than being made an apostle (Greek, *apostellō*, "to send out" or "a missionary") through the vision of **Jesus Christ**. The opening verses offer the traditional praise of Jesus Christ, known as a doxology, and of the faith of the Saints.

Chloe's Letter to Paul

1 CORINTHIANS 1:10–31

The spartan introduction to the origin of the problem in the city of Corinth leaves room for doubt regarding what information Chloe initially conveyed to Paul. Through his own acknowledgment, Paul relates that the problems he will address were related to him "of the house of Chloe" (1 Corinthians 1:11). The problem, at least initially, appears to be the rise of factions in the branch, some identifying with Paul, some with Apollos, some with Cephas (Peter), and others with **Christ** (1:12). It should not be inferred from the final reference to **Jesus** Christ that the other factions were anti-Christian, but rather it appears that some claimed special status because their ordinances could be traced back through Paul, Apollos, Cephas, and Jesus (see John 3:22 and JST John 4:1–2 for an example of Jesus per-forming the ordinance of **baptism**).

Paul's specific mention of baptizing in "the name of Paul" (1:13) and the pointed, if not sarcastic, statement, "I thank God that I baptized none of you, but Crispus and Gaius" (1:14), lead to the conclusion that the Saints of Corinth were claiming special status based on who had baptized them or to whom they could trace other **priesthood** ordinances. This factionalism is the first and most serious problem arising out of Chloe's letter, and Paul deals with it succinctly, telling the Saints: "For it is written, I will destroy the wisdom of the wise, and will bring to nothing the understanding of the prudent" (1:19, quoting Isaiah 29:14).

The other matter in Chloe's letter that Paul seems to be addressing is that the divisions seem to have fallen along ethnic lines, between Jews and **Gentiles**. Paul points out that both Greeks and Jews have stumbled over the crucifixion of Jesus, while "the Jews require a sign, and the Greeks seek after wisdom" (1:22). In reality, the unifying power of the gospel resides in Jesus Christ.

Paul's allusion to the folly of human reason seems to imply that he viewed the division among the Saints as petty, childish, and condemnable ("God is stronger than men" [1:25]). Perhaps the emphasis on the folly of human reason and the weak things of the world reveal Paul's opinion that he perceived the formerly Gentile Christians to be the primary instigators of the problem.

We Speak Wisdom among Them That Are Perfect
1 CORINTHIANS 2:1–3:9

In the opening lines Paul describes his previous visit to Corinth in humble terms, declaring that the focus of his ministry is "**Jesus Christ**, and him crucified" (1 Corinthians 2:2). His specific appeal to having declared the gospel in weakness may underlie his questions concerning how the problems in Corinth arose given the simplicity of his message. The problems that arose after his departure, which are dealt with in the later chapters of

1 Corinthians, are far afield from the crucifixion and resurrection of Jesus Christ.

In this chapter, Paul introduces a new concept into his teachings, referring to the teaching of the gospel: "Howbeit we speak wisdom among them that are perfect" (2:6). The word translated as "perfect" (Greek, *teleios*, "whole" or "complete") may be used more broadly here to refer to those who are whole or complete in Christian ordinances, and thus Paul may be differentiating between his public discourses and the "wisdom" that he spoke among those who were ready to receive it. The following verse speaks of "the wisdom of God in a mystery, even the hidden wisdom, which God ordained before the world unto our glory" (2:7), again suggesting a private discourse for members of the **Church**.

This private discourse, Paul surmises, would have led people to accept Jesus, "for had they known it, they would not have crucified the Lord of glory" (2:8). Even though the subject matter of this private discourse is unknown, from Paul's letters it would appear that it was focused on demonstrating the coming of Christ using the prophecies of the Old Testament. Verses 9–16 may allude to such an idea with its quotation of Isaiah 64:4. The Spirit "searcheth all things" (2:10) so that the prophecies become clear to those who listen. These verses probably do not refer to an esoteric Christian teaching but rather to private discourses that developed initially among Jews who believed in Christ and then later became the central focus of Christian teaching. Referring to the natural man who does not receive "the things of the Spirit of God" probably has reference to those who insist on following the traditional interpretations of the Old Testament that were passed on in the Jewish scholastic tradition.

Chapter 3 continues the discussion of public and private teachings using the analogy of milk and meat. The problems transmitted to Paul induce him to say, "Ye are yet carnal: for whereas there is among you envying, and strife, and divisions, are ye not carnal, and walk as men?" (3:3). Judging by the length of this discussion and the pointed rebuke, it is evident that Paul is disappointed in the divisions that have arisen among the Saints since his departure. In remarkably clear language, Paul teaches the proper course of missionary work: "I have planted, Apollos watered; but God gave the increase. So then neither is he that planteth any thing, neither he that watereth; but God that giveth the increase" (3:6–7).

The Foundation of Missionary Work
1 CORINTHIANS 3:10–23

Even though Paul clearly outlined his own role in laying the foundation for others to follow after him in teaching the gospel in Corinth, there is a hint of warning in his words too as he sought to determine how the Saints had so quickly gone astray. The warning is voiced in the following words: "Let every man *take heed how he buildeth* thereupon" (1 Corinthians 3:10; emphasis added).

Paul's singular and generic statements about "if any man" seem to imply that he suspected another person had followed him and taught things that were both inappropriate and destructive. Sometimes this other person is referred to as the "other builder" in scholarly discussions, and Paul asks that the test of time be applied both to his teachings and to those of the other builder. Specifically, he says, "If any man's work abide which he hath built thereupon, he shall receive a reward" (3:14), and Paul suspected that perhaps this other builder might "defile the **temple** of God" (3:17) figuratively. It is possible that some report in Chloe's letter had been given of this man because Paul's rebuke becomes more transparent toward the end of chapter 3, in which he insinuates the other builder thinks himself "wise" when he is really "vain" (3:18–20). Paul concludes by bearing testimony of his own work as well as that of Apollos and of Peter, indicating those who taught truth as he had.

Ministers of Christ
1 CORINTHIANS 4:1–21

Reflecting on his own calling and ministry as an **apostle**, Paul here inserts some of his own thoughts on the struggles and difficulties that he has faced and will face. Because the dissensions in Corinth had enveloped him as well and some had apparently disparaged him publicly, he forgives those who had "judged" him (1 Corinthians 4:3). He then reminds his readers that what he had taught had been given to him by the Lord, and the Lord would judge him and not those who had criticized him (4:4).

Paul's work with Apollos is here confirmed when he speaks of having been an example of knowing "nothing by myself" (4:4) and says: "I have in a figure transferred to myself and to Apollos for your sakes; that ye might learn in us not to think of men above that which is written" (4:6). Revealing the depth of his commitment, Paul lets on that he anticipates his calling will lead to his own death, "For I think that God hath set forth us the apostles last, as it were appointed to death" (4:9), and that his sincerity had been demonstrated through "working with our own hands: being reviled, we bless; being persecuted, we suffer it" (4:12).

To stem the growing division in Corinth, Paul sent Timothy to remind them "of my ways which be in **Christ**" (4:17). One particular teaching that Timothy encourages is that the Saints should "be . . . followers of me" (4:16). The statement, at face value, may appear self-serving and would perhaps be phrased differently in other contexts. However, the depth of the divisions and the fact that Paul was contending against a specific individual help contextualize this statement as a call to cease following the other builder and return to the gospel of **Christ** as Paul taught it.

Question Regarding Marriage
1 CORINTHIANS 5:1–13

From his surviving words, it appears that Paul is alarmed to hear that a male member of the Corinthian branch has married his stepmother. Given early wedding ages and high mortality rates, it would not be uncommon for families to experience situations in which children were not much younger than a stepparent. In this instance, because the issue of divorce is not mentioned, it appears that a man had married his stepmother after his father's death. Chloe's letter contained information about this event, and the members were clearly seeking counsel on how to handle the matter.

Paul's counsel on the matter is "to deliver such an one unto **Satan** for the destruction of the flesh, that the spirit may be saved in the day of the Lord **Jesus**" (1 Corinthians 5:5). Although his answer does not specifically mention excommunication, Paul's clarification in the following verses makes it clear that this is his intent. He speaks of acting in this way because "a little leaven leaveneth the whole lump" (5:6), and he reminds them he had previously written the Saints, telling them "not to company with fornicators" (5:9), again implying that the man should be cut off from the community of Saints. Verse 11 appears to preserve a specific reference to eating with the Saints at sacrament meetings with the specific instruction that the man in question should be excluded from doing so.

Should Christians Take Other Christians to Court?
1 CORINTHIANS 6:1–20

Unfortunately, the specific legal matter behind this question is not stated, making it difficult to find a modern application of Paul's teachings. The most basic summary of this question from Chloe's letter is whether it is appropriate for Christians to take other Christians to court. Paul felt that such a question was ridiculous because exalted Christians will eventually judge the "world" (6:2) and the "angels" (6:3). Moreover, bringing a case to a judge was equivalent to going "to law before the unjust" (6:1). This last comment should not be taken as a criticism of the Roman legal system, but may in fact reflect a saying of **Jesus** where he also refers to civic authorities as unjust (Luke 18:6) without specifically commenting upon the justice of the system in which they worked.

Paul clearly counseled against Christians taking other Christians to court, even to the point where he referred to the question as shameful: "I speak to your shame. Is it so, that there is not a wise man among you? no, not one that shall be able to judge between his brethren?" (6:5). The reason the Saints should judge one another is because they have been made competent by being "washed" (i.e., baptized), "sanctified," and "justified in the name of the Lord Jesus, and by the Spirit of our God" (6:11).

Because Paul treats the issue of kosher concerns extensively at the end of this chapter, it may be that the legal issue at hand had something to do with the Jewish faction of the branch insisting that the **Gentile** faction remain broadly kosher (6:13). Paul goes on to teach concerning the body being a **temple** and that joining that temple "to an harlot," which here symbolizes civic authorities, is utterly ridiculous. If indeed the context for this legal question is a kosher concern, then Paul's statement makes sense: "All things are lawful unto me, but all things are not expedient: all things are lawful for me, but I will not be brought under the power of any" (6:12). In other words, Paul teaches that there are no legal prohibitions about eating any foods under Roman law, but within that setting, "all things are not expedient [that I eat them]."

Questions about Marriage
1 CORINTHIANS 7:1–40

Chloe's letter specifically addressed the issue of celibacy in marriage, asking whether "it is good for a man not to touch a woman" (1 Corinthians 7:1). The question is based on the ascetic ideal, which holds that mortal, physical desires are to be absolutely suppressed in an effort to strengthen the soul. In this instance, the Saints wondered whether married couples ought to live celibate lifestyles even though they had been married. The source of this thinking is not known, and it may simply be a holdover from Roman-period moralistic piety, or it may have its origins in assumptions regarding the marital status of **Jesus** or his **disciples**.

Paul recommends against living a married but celibate lifestyle because it leads to "fornication" (Greek, *porneias*, "sexual misconduct"), although he does counsel that at times the practice may be acceptable as long as it is temporary: "Defraud ye not one the other, except it be with consent for a time, that ye may give yourselves to fasting and prayer; and come together again, that **Satan** tempt you not for your incontinency" (7:5). The Greek word rendered here as "defraud" might be better translated as "do not refuse" (Greek, *apostereite*, "rob" or "deny"), whereas the English word *incontinency* could be better rendered as "celibacy." The first part of Paul's response is based on his own opinion, which he clearly states (7:6).

Scholars who have studied this chapter have raised intriguing questions regarding Paul's marital status because of some of the things said herein. More specifically, in addressing widows, Paul said, "For I would that all men were even as I myself. But every man hath his proper gift of God, one after this manner, and another after that. I say therefore to the unmarried and widows, It is good for them if they abide even as I" (7:7–8). Apparently, Paul may have been unmarried at the time he wrote this epistle, although some commentators have seen the evidence otherwise. For reasons that are not entirely clear, he recommends that widows remain that way, although he does allow for them to marry: "But if they cannot contain, let them marry: for it is better to marry than to burn" (7:9). The suggestion that persons might "burn" if they do not marry refers to the possibility of committing sexual sin rather than some hint at eternal punishment for remarrying.

It appears that Chloe's letter also addressed the problem of marriages in which one spouse was a believing Christian while the other spouse was not. Paul recommended that in such instances they not divorce, because it might be that "the unbelieving husband is sanctified by the wife, and the unbelieving wife is sanctified by the husband" (7:14).

In the middle of this discussion concerning marriage, Paul introduces some of his own thoughts and opinions as well as the reasons why he was making such recommendations. His concern is that the return of the Lord in glory would soon be upon them and that calamities would befall the world. Almost everything he says in the last part of this chapter is colored by his perception of the immediacy of Christ's return. He speaks of the present, saying, "I suppose therefore that this is good for the present distress" (7:26) and "the time is short: it remaineth, that both they that have wives be as though they had none" (7:29), and finally, "for the fashion of this world passeth away" (7:31). Because the Lord would soon return and the world would be enveloped in difficulty ("distress"), Paul counseled the Saints not to seek a change in status (7:18, 21, 26). In reference to his counsel that men and women remain unmarried, he contextualizes his thoughts by adding, "He that is unmarried careth for the things that belong to the

Lord, how he may please the Lord" (7:32), implying that service to the Lord is the most important matter given the present distress. The Joseph Smith Translation also offers the possibility that at least portions of this discussion were given in the context of missionaries, and the recommendation not to marry would apply to them (JST, 1 Corinthians 7:29). If, however, an individual "think that he behaveth himself uncomely toward his virgin, if she pass the flower of her age, and need so require, let him do what he will, he sinneth not: *let them marry*" (7:36; emphasis added), indicating that marriage itself is not being disparaged but rather that Paul feels that in some situations it is preferable to remain unmarried for a time.

Questions Regarding Eating Animals That Had Been Used in Pagan Sacrifices
1 CORINTHIANS 8:1–13

Because the Jerusalem Council declared that Christians should not eat "things strangled" or "blood" (Acts 15:20), it became a particular concern to the Saints that they avoid eating meat that had not been butchered according to kosher practices. More specifically, they wondered whether it was appropriate to eat meat where a portion of the animal had been offered in **sacrifice** at the local shrine of a Greek or Roman god. Interestingly, Paul responds to this question first by teaching that "knowledge puffeth up, but charity edifieth" (1 Corinthians 8:1), suggesting that the arrogance of knowledge is a greater problem than the actual eating of nonkosher meat.

Paul's specific answer is that the gods to whom the animals were sacrificed do not truly exist and therefore our focus on "none other God but one" should direct us in matters of religious conscience (8:4). Paul does acknowledge that there are many "called gods" (8:5), but "to us there is but one God, the Father" (8:6). Whether the final parenthetical phrase of verse 5 is intended to indicate the actual existence of "gods many, and lords many" (8:5) has been the subject of scholarly discussion. However, it would indeed be ironic if in discussing the one and only true God that Paul would affirm the existence of other gods given the historical context of the first

353

century. However, the Prophet Joseph Smith cited this text as part of a discourse in defense of the subject of the plurality of gods (*Words of Joseph Smith*, 378–79).

To confirm his answer that kosher concerns should not lead to divisions within the branch of Saints, Paul taught a foundational principle for religious diets: "Wherefore, if meat make my brother to offend, I will eat no flesh while the world standeth, lest I make my brother to offend" (8:13). Paul's main concern was that he not "wound their [his brother's] weak conscience" (8:12). Summarizing his thoughts, it is apparent that he prefers to judge food concerns on a situational basis rather than make blanket regulations.

Questions Concerning Paul's Apostleship

1 CORINTHIANS 9:1–27

Modern readers were not the first to ask whether Paul was an **apostle** or not. In fact, the question had already arisen during his lifetime. The challenge to Paul's apostleship may have originated in some Christian circles through their definition of the qualifications of an apostle found in Acts 1:15–26, in which the first vacancy in the quorum was filled by a man who had followed **Jesus** from the time of John the Baptist *and* who had seen the risen Lord. Some may have applied those requirements rigidly to all new apostles and, having done so, they would have questioned Paul for not being a follower of Jesus from the time of John the Baptist.

Again, Paul found the question ridiculous and declared boldly his calling as an apostle. One of the specific questions being asked was why, when he visited the city of Corinth, Paul did not act in the same way the other apostles had while there. When speaking of "apostles," it is important to remember that the term meant both a missionary (Greek, *apostellō*, "to send") and someone who held the specific **priesthood** office. In this chapter it appears that Paul is joining the two concepts.

The other apostles, here used in the generic sense as missionaries because it includes both members of the Quorum of the Twelve and others

(Peter and the brothers of the Lord), apparently traveled with their wives when doing missionary work and were fed by the members of the local branch while they stayed with them. Paul responded to these criticisms forcefully: "Mine answer to them that do examine me is this, Have we not power to eat and to drink? Have we not power to lead about a sister, a wife, as well as other apostles, and as the brethren of the Lord, and Cephas? (9:3–5). "We" in these verses is difficult to interpret because it may be that Paul intends to refer to himself and Barnabas (9:6), or he may have in mind the other apostles, namely Peter and the others (9:5). It is obvious that the common practice was for missionaries to be cared for temporally while they visited a city, and in contrast to this practice, Paul worked with his own hands to provide for his needs.

Paul specifically addresses the question of caring for the temporal needs of the missionaries, citing the Old Testament ban on placing a muzzle on the mouth of an ox while it treads out a field of grain (KJV, "corn"; Deuteronomy 25:4). It is clear that Paul endorses the practice of caring for the traveling missionaries, who in this era were likely traveling without purse or scrip. To strengthen his argument, Paul also references the Levites who were fed from the **sacrifices** made in the **temple** (9:13). In Paul's dispensation "hath the Lord ordained *that they which preach the gospel should live of the gospel*" (9:14; emphasis added).

Paul acted differently from some of his peers, making it a practice to earn his own living and to preach "the gospel of **Christ** without charge, that I abuse not my power in the gospel" (9:18). In his concluding remarks to the question about his apostleship, Paul taught famously, "I am made all things to all men" (9:22), implying that he had worked for his own support just as those who had accepted the gospel. If he intended to make this connection, then we may conclude that the early Christian **Church** gained its converts from among the menial laborers or lower class of Roman society. Luke, on the other hand, notes in Acts 17:4 that a number of "chief women" had accepted the gospel message, thus indicating an early stratification of members in the branches.

Unity among the Saints Challenged

1 CORINTHIANS 10:1–33

Continuing his discussion about eating nonkosher food, specifically meat when a portion of the animal had been used in a pagan **sacrifice**, Paul addresses the issue of disunity among the members of the Corinthian branch. Drawing upon the example of Moses passing through the Red Sea, which symbolized a **baptism** for the Israelites, Paul draws out the lesson that they "did all drink the same spiritual drink: for they drank of that spiritual Rock that followed them: and that Rock was **Christ**" (1 Corinthians 10:4). Their experiences, beginning with their baptisms, had brought them together, which is precisely the opposite of what was taking place at that time among the Corinthian Saints.

As an example, Paul also notes that the Lord did not hesitate to punish the wayward Israelites, probably making reference to their worship of the golden calf. The specific problems that Paul mentions are "fornication," trying the Lord's patience (KJV, "tempt"), and murmuring (10:8–10), although when he draws a conclusion he seems to imply that the issue is actually pride: "Wherefore let him that thinketh he standeth take heed lest he fall" (10:12).

Forming part of this discussion are Paul's thoughts on trials and temptations. He certainly understands that trials are the common lot of mankind, but assures the Saints that "God is faithful, who will not suffer you to be tempted above that ye are able; but will with the temptation also make a way to escape, that ye may be able to bear it" (10:13). In English the difference between a trial and temptation is often mentioned in reference to this passage. However, the Greek word used here (*peirasmos*) does not distinguish between a trial and temptation, although the way Paul constructs his thinking indicates that God allows trial to take place while controlling the extent of it, in the manner of the trials that are described in the book of Job. The concern about eating nonkosher meat is the trial in question here, and Paul's answer implies that he believes this particular trial can be overcome, if the Saints become "one bread, and one body" (10:17).

In celebrating the sacrament, early Christians actually celebrated the Lord's **Last Supper** and not only through the breaking of bread and the drinking of wine. They held communal meals to remember the event, and it was at these meals that the division would arise, when someone would bring meat that may have been part of a pagan sacrifice. Paul pointed out the greater problem was eating it at the "Lord's table" and being sinful (10:21). He advised, *"Whatsoever is sold in the shambles, that eat, asking no question for conscience sake:* For the earth is the Lord's, and the fulness thereof" (10:25–26; emphasis added). Verse 27 appears to expand the recommendation to include invitations to dine with those who were not members where the Saints might eat meat that was not kosher. Paul counseled that we act in this way for "conscience sake . . . not thine own, but of the other" (10:28–29). The principle in question, based on the difficult wording of verse 29, appears to be that the Saints should act with consideration of the sensibilities of others, an idea that Paul rhetorically challenges: "For why is my liberty judged of another man's conscience?" (10:29). That rhetorical challenge was intended to lead to his main conclusion: "Do all to the glory of God" (10:31).

Questions Regarding Hair and Also the Sacrament
1 CORINTHIANS 11:1–34

The introductory verse of chapter 11 appears aimed at summarizing the final verse of chapter 10: "Even as I please all men in all things" (1 Corinthians 10:33), therefore, "be ye followers of me" (11:1). Paul's statements concerning the role of women are partly informed by social context, and it is important to note that in his summary of gender roles he draws an analogy that is based on the natural world and his own conclusions, rather than on scripture or the word of the Lord as he has done in other instances. The question he addresses is whether women can take control of meetings, including praying and prophesying. Paul does not object to women doing so but reminds that women are dishonored in doing so when their heads are uncovered, implying that women veiled or covered their heads in early

Christian worship services. If this is indeed the question that Paul is responding to, then it may be that **Gentile** converts saw no reason for women to cover their heads in worship services, while Jewish converts would do so perhaps out of tradition. It appears that Paul defends the practice of women covering their heads and recommends that it be continued.

Paul sees an analogy in nature to this recommendation because women wear their hair long, a symbol of having their heads covered, and men wear their hair comparatively short, symbolizing that they can attend meetings uncovered (11:14). It is difficult to know the full extent of the problem addressed in this chapter, but it appears to extend beyond the simple issue of women worshipping with uncovered heads and likely includes the question of gender roles in conducting meetings.

The chapter concludes with a brief discussion of partaking of the sacrament unworthily, which may indeed be a continuation of the previous discussion, although the links between the two may be difficult to see. Paul refers here to "heresies" (11:19), a word that can be rendered as "factions," which helps make sense of the remainder of the verse: "For there must be also heresies [factions] among you, *that they which are approved may be made manifest* among you" (emphasis added). The purpose of the factions, Paul intimates, is to reveal which side is approved of God. One of the "factions" follows the practice of attending the community meals of the Saints where "one is hungry, and another is drunken" (11:21). The practice of celebrating the Last Supper appears to have evolved into each member bringing his own food ("every one taketh before other his own supper" [11:21]), which caused some who brought no food to go hungry.

To help the Saints understand the origin of the practice and therefore better celebrate its intent, Paul recounted what he knew from oral sources about the **Last Supper**. The focus of their celebrations should be the sacramental emblems and not a lavish meal where some are "drunken." The Last Supper was indeed a meal, but Paul taught that the focus for Christians was the broken bread and the cup. Warning the Saints that unworthily eating of the emblems of the sacrament leads to damnation, Paul teaches that the way in which they had been celebrating the sacrament had led to many "weak" and "sickly" among them. These adjectives appear to describe spiritual weakness or sickness in their original context, but some commentators have suggested a literal interpretation. In conclusion, Paul encourages the Saints to "eat at home" (11:34) previous to coming to partake of the sacrament.

Spiritual Gifts
1 Corinthians 12:1–31

Paul's introduction to the topic of spiritual gifts includes a reminder that there are restraints on what the Spirit will lead a person to say or do, and that inspired utterance is respectful: "No man speaking by the Spirit of God calleth **Jesus** accursed: and that no man can say that Jesus is the Lord, but by the **Holy Ghost**" (1 Corinthians 12:3). Paul continues his discussion of the known gifts of the Spirit by providing a list that follows nearly the same order and language as the gifts of the Spirit found in Moroni 10:8–18 and D&C 46:16–33. What Paul adds to this discussion is a powerful statement suggesting a comparative value of some of the gifts. By analogy, the gifts of the Spirit help the **Church** function as a well-trained body, where every part is both necessary and needful even though some parts of that body are smaller and seemingly less important than others. Paul expresses this feeling by saying, "And the eye cannot say unto the hand, I have no need of thee: nor again the head to the feet, I have no need of you. Nay, much more those members of the body, which seem to be more feeble, are necessary" (12:21–22). In fact, Paul argues that the part of the body that is lacking receives greater honor (12:24), thus playing into the natural human emotion to admire what we do not have.

The Church is structured with the spiritual gifts incorporated into its workings: "And God hath set some in the church, first **apostles**, secondarily prophets, thirdly teachers, after that **miracles**, then gifts of healings, helps, governments, diversities of tongues" (12:28). The Church is built upon the apostles and prophets and administered through the gifts of the Spirit. Paul concludes by encouraging the members to covet (Greek, *zeloute*, "to set one's heart upon") the "best gifts," a division within the gifts that seems to contradict this discussion, but which will prove to expand the discussion in "a more excellent way" (12:31).

The Gifts of Charity and Prophecy
1 CORINTHIANS 13:1–13

The "more excellent way" that Paul refers to at the end of the previous chapter is charity, which in the Pauline epistles is not included as a gift in the same way as it is in Moroni, but rather is the principle upon which the gifts are based. Charity is here translated from the Greek *agapaō* "love" or "concern for another." Without love (KJV, "charity") the gifts are meaningless, and "I am become as sounding brass, or a tinkling cymbal" (1 Corinthians 13:1). Paul here realizes that external acts do not guarantee a heart full of love: "And though I bestow all my goods to feed the poor, and though I give my body to be burned, and have not charity, it profiteth me nothing" (13:3). Charity is indeed the "more excellent way" (12:31).

Reflecting on his own gift, Paul turns his attention to the gift of prophecy, concerning which he says some rather remarkable things. First, Paul teaches that some prophecies will fail, speaking in tongues will eventually cease, and knowledge will vanish (13:8). The prophecies in question are not referred to as false or of a questionable source, but some prophecies will indeed fail, probably due to the agency of man. Second, Paul indicates that "we know in part, and we prophesy in part" (13:9), indicating that a portion of prophecy is knowable through spiritual means, and prophecy fills in the details. In other words, visions provide a framework and prophecy provides the explanation. Paul compares this to being a child: "When I was a child, I spake as a child, I understood as a child, I thought as a child: but when I became a man, I put away childish things" (13:11). Finally, Paul teaches that prophecy is similar to seeing a reflection in a mirror: "Now we see through a glass, darkly" (13:12). The ancient mirror being described here was actually highly polished metal, and although certainly an improvement on some mirrors, it rendered the reflection in a less than perfect way. Even so, understanding prophecy is likened to looking into an ancient mirror where the reflection is certainly transmitted, but the finer details may be lacking.

Tongues and Prophecy Compared
1 CORINTHIANS 14:1–25

Continuing the discussion of spiritual gifts, Paul encourages the members to "follow after charity, and desire spiritual gifts, but rather that ye may prophesy" (1 Corinthians 14:1). Following the Greek, the "but" in the final phrase of the first sentence should be rendered "and," which encourages a person to seek spiritual gifts, *particularly* the gift of prophecy. In contrast to prophesying, it appears that the ability to speak in tongues was much sought after, and Paul devotes considerable time to a discussion of the value of that gift. Speaking in tongues has a distinct purpose, and to summarize Paul's thoughts, it can be concluded that he preferred to see it used when there was someone present to translate (14:9).

Paul relates that he had frequently used the gift of tongues while teaching in Corinth (14:18), and perhaps the Saints' fondness for this particular gift was in emulation of Paul rather than simple fascination. Paul also teaches that the gift of tongues is present in the **Church** as a sign to unbelievers, whereas the gift of prophecy is given for those who already believe (14:22).

Early Worship Services
1 CORINTHIANS 14:26–40

Unfortunately, no exact outline of an early Christian worship service has survived from the first century, and we can only reconstruct them through scattered references. These verses contain what appears to be an admonition to follow certain practices during meetings. The meetings seem to have been Spirit led and Spirit filled, and when they met the meeting could take several forms. Paul mentions the singing of psalms, teaching doctrine, speaking in tongues with an accompanying interpretation, and the discussion of revelations (1 Corinthians 14:26). Paul also teaches, "Let the prophets speak two or three, and let the other judge" (14:29), which is here used in a local sense to refer to the leaders of the branch, who were to lead by prophecy or inspiration. Paul reminds them that whatever they might prophesy, it should be subject to the written word: "And the spirits of the prophets are subject to the prophets" (14:32). Returning again to a theme he had mentioned previously, Paul teaches the importance of following the customs of his day and age, specifically that women should attend meetings to learn and not take the lead in the meetings (14:34–35). Paul's conclusion to this section, "Wherefore, brethren, covet to prophesy, and forbid not to speak with tongues," appears to reflect his understanding of how an ideal meeting should be conducted (14:39).

Paul's Testimony
1 CORINTHIANS 15:1–11

Tying his own testimony to the doctrine and witness of the **apostles**, Paul recounts the known witnesses of the Resurrection, although certainly his list is incomplete (for example, Jesus' appearance to Mary Magdalene and to the **disciples** on the road to Emmaus are missing). His purpose is to describe his own testimony in terms of the apostolic tradition. Departing slightly from the canonical Gospels, Paul reports that the resurrected Lord appeared first to Peter (Cephas) and then to the Twelve (minus Judas, of course). The canonical Gospels do not report a separate vision where Peter saw the Lord. Following his visit to Peter, **Jesus** appeared to about "five hundred brethren at once; of whom the greater part remain unto this present, but some are fallen asleep" (1 Corinthians 15:6). Although we know very little of these five hundred brethren, Paul reports that by the middle of the first century most of them were still alive. Unlike the usage of the term in the modern era, Paul here uses *apostle* in its generic sense of messenger: "After that, he was seen of James; then of all the apostles" (15:7). The "apostles" of this verse are all those who became messengers of the gospel of Jesus **Christ**, a group that included Jesus' brother James. Finally, "he was seen of me also, as of one born out of due time" (15:8), thus linking Paul's vision on the road to Damascus temporally and spiritually to those who had witnessed the Resurrection. It may be that Paul's vision followed very closely the **Passover** appearances recorded at the ends of the Gospels.

Paul's reference to being the "least of the apostles" (15:9) should not necessarily be interpreted as a reference to the office—both because he has just used the term generically and because he seems not to be indicating his status among the Twelve Apostles—but rather as an indication of how little he deserved such an appearance of the Lord. To make certain that the Saints understand that his doctrine has always been the same, Paul concludes this section by saying, "Therefore whether it were I or they, so we preach, and so ye believed" (15:11).

The Resurrection of the Dead

1 CORINTHIANS 15:12–34

Paul's statements concerning the resurrection from the dead have provided a heated discussion since the first centuries after **Christ** died. In the modern era they are interpreted both literally and figuratively as though Paul were making an analogy. The function of the verses is what is most often overlooked in these discussions. Paul seems to feel a certain frustration that his work and the work of others has been interpreted as useless by those who teach that there is no resurrection from the dead. What appears to annoy him most is the idea that vicarious ordinances are useless without a universal resurrection of the dead, as are his own sufferings and trials in teaching the gospel. The ordinances, doctrine, and life experiences of Christians hinge upon the reality of the Resurrection.

One of Paul's most memorable reflections appears in this context when he says, "If in this life only we have hope in Christ, we are of all men most miserable" (1 Corinthians 15:19). In this instance, the idea is not that hope itself is useless, but hope in something that is not real (here pointing to the fallacy of those who teach there is no resurrection) would indeed make us like all men and that most miserable. Arguing from the **scriptures** of the Old Testament, Paul teaches that the universal death brought about through Adam's choice needed to be remedied through a universal resurrection or victory over death.

A nuance in the argument against those who preach against the Resurrection can be seen in Paul's commentary on Psalm 8:6 (1 Corinthians 15:27): "For he hath put all things under his feet. But when he saith all things are put under him, it is manifest that he is excepted, which did put all things under him." The verse says literally that God will subdue all enemies, including death, which some appear to have interpreted to mean also conquering the human body, thus implying that Christ will not have a physical, resurrected body. Against this view, Paul says that God will subdue all enemies and "it is manifest that he [God or Christ] is excepted," thus arguing that the conquering of death did not include ridding Christ's spirit of its mortal tabernacle.

Paul's frustration boils over when he considers his own experiences, which have nearly cost him his life. In a somewhat ironic tone, Paul points to his own sufferings as evidence that he genuinely believes in and hopes for a resurrection: "If after the manner of men I have fought with beasts at Ephesus, what advantageth it me, if the dead rise not? let us eat and drink; for to morrow we die" (15:32). The final phrase, spoken in exasperation, signals that without resurrection, we should simply give up and embrace the futility of life without hope. As a rejoinder, Paul adds that the doctrine of **baptism** for the dead makes little sense without a resurrection: "Else what shall they do which are baptized for the dead, if the dead rise not at all? why are they then baptized for the dead?" (15:29). This important aside is reported in the third-person plural and may refer to the practice being done elsewhere, not among the Corinthians Saints but perhaps in another branch or at an earlier time. The Saints know about the practice and are familiar enough with it that Paul feels he can reference it without further explanation, but this verse remains the only reference to the practice in the Bible, although Zechariah 9:11 may foreshadow the practice.

The Resurrected Body
1 Corinthians 15:35–58

It may be that the final section of the epistle treats a lingering question in the letter from Chloe, or perhaps it is a tangential discussion to the previous conversation about the reality of resurrection. Some have said, "How are the dead raised up? and with what body do they come?" (1 Corinthians 15:35). To answer this, Paul teaches, "All flesh is not the same flesh: but there is one kind of flesh of men, another flesh of beasts, another of fishes, and another of birds. There are also celestial bodies, and bodies terrestrial: but the glory of the celestial is one, and the glory of the terrestrial is another" (15:39–40). Not all mankind will come forth in the same type of resurrected body, and their glory will differ as do the "sun" and "moon" and "stars" (15:41).

After the revelation recorded as Doctrine and Covenants 76 was received in response to the Prophet's inquiry about John 5:29, this verse appeared doctrinally incomplete, and the Prophet Joseph Smith added a reference to telestial glory alongside the references to celestial and terrestrial glory. It may be, however, that Paul revealed as much as he knew on the subject, here arguing for "earthly" (KJV, "terrestrial") and "heavenly" (KJV, "celestial") bodies. In other words, Paul was teaching those who argued against the resurrection that there are earthly bodies, namely the ones we now possess, and there are heavenly bodies as well, namely the glorious bodies we shall receive in the resurrection.

Paul continues, arguing from his understanding of two differing bodies, the earthly and heavenly, the latter of which indeed differs in glory from the former (15:41). Commenting on Genesis 2:7, Paul refers to a first and a last Adam, the first being formed of the ground and symbolic of the earthly body, who was quickened in the Spirit and became a spiritual being (15:45–46). The reference to the last Adam most likely preserves the idea that the continuing influence of Adam in later dispensations (for example, Jude 1:9) is evidence that he continued to live in a spiritual existence. Note that the King James Version italicizes the verb "is," indicating that it is an addition to the text to help it make sense to the reader. The "is," however, is interpretive and seems to disrupt the parallelism of the first part of the verse where "of" works better. In most instances the additional italicized words represent implied Greek words, but in other instances they are interpretations and miss the point (see, for example, John 8:6, "*as though he heard them not*"). That later spiritual existence is described doctrinally: "Now this I say, brethren, that flesh and blood cannot inherit the kingdom of God; neither doth corruption inherit incorruption" (15:50). The use of the word *spiritual* in reference to the resurrected body should be interpreted not as a noncorporeal existence but rather as a way to contrast what is mundane and earthly with what is glorious. Paul's reference to a "mystery" seems to imply that the Lord had revealed to him that some would be caught up in the heavens at the Lord's appearing and would not taste death. He had sought an answer to this question many years previous while writing to the Thessalonian Saints (1 Thessalonians 4:13–18).

Conclusion

1 CORINTHIANS 16:1–24

The Jerusalem Council asked that the Saints give generously to alleviate the effects of a famine that afflicted the region of Jerusalem under the emperor Claudius (c. A.D. 49). Paul here refers to what has become known as the collection for the poor, detailing some of the specific guidelines the Saints had been given: "Now concerning the collection for the saints, as I have given order to the churches of Galatia, even so do ye. Upon the first day of the week let every one of you lay by him in store, as God hath prospered him, that there be no gatherings when I come. And when I come, whomsoever ye shall approve by your letters, them will I send to bring your liberality unto Jerusalem" (1 Corinthians 16:1–3). Paul planned to pick up the money they had gathered when he visited them again on his third missionary journey, when he planned to travel through Macedonia (Philippi and Thessalonica, as well as other cities previously visited).

Paul had hoped to spend the winter in Corinth, perhaps because of its mild climate. The mention of his stay in Ephesus "until **Pentecost**" (16:8) appears to date the writing of this epistle to the end of the second mission or the early part of the third mission. Timothy was not with Paul at the time he wrote, and it appears Timothy was headed to Corinth at the time of writing (16:10). Apollos had also desired to visit them, but Paul had learned that Apollos had other matters on his mind (16:12). Paul's reason for staying at Ephesus is revealed in his hope that there might be an "effectual" missionary door opened to him in the city (16:9). When interpreted in conjunction with an earlier verse, "If after the manner of men I have fought with beasts at Ephesus, what advantageth it me, if the dead rise not?" (15:32), it may be that the missionary door was the result of some spectacular **miracle** wherein Paul was forced to face "wild beasts" in an arena and in which he survived. It is also possible that this verse has a metaphorical interpretation, although Paul used it literally in the context of 1 Corinthians 15.

Paul mentions Stephanas, Fortunatus, and Achaicus, the latter two of which seem to be slave names (16:17). Paul also mentions Aquila and Priscilla, a husband-and-wife missionary team, formerly of **Rome**, who worked in Corinth and now held **Church** meetings in their house (16:19). Paul encourages the Saints to greet one another with "an holy kiss," reflecting the Mediterranean method of greeting and not the western handshake.

In conclusion, Paul adds, "If any man love not the Lord **Jesus Christ**, let him be Anathema Maran-atha" (16:22). The untranslated **Aramaic** phrase "Maran-atha" can be translated as "The Lord has come" or "Come, Lord," and it may have been a popular salutation among early Christians. The phrase may also be interpreted to mean that when someone is declared "anathema," Christians may yearn, "Come, Lord," so that vengeance may be carried out.

5

SECOND CORINTHIANS

Paul's letters to the Corinthians, some of which seem to have been lost, attempted to answer questions and concerns that were in some instances unique to the branch in Corinth. Following a painful visit, not recorded in Acts, Paul wrote his second epistle to the Corinthians hoping to heal the growing chasm that had developed between him and the branch he had founded there. Most likely written in the autumn of A.D. 55 from Ephesus, this letter addresses some of the problems that had recently surfaced, particularly the activity of what might be called the "super apostles" (Greek, *tēn hyperlian apostolōn*) in Corinth (see 2 Corinthians 11:4–6; the King James Version identifies them as "the very chiefest apostles"). However, it is difficult for the modern reader to follow the conversation because we often hear only half of it; many of the arguments made by the Corinthians are not preserved in this letter. Additionally, the letter may also be a collection of separate letters, even copies of some early drafts, making it even more challenging to follow along.

Introduction

2 Corinthians 1:1–11

One reason scholars suggest that 2 Corinthians is a collection of letters is the apparent shifts in tone throughout. For example, Paul is sorrowful (2:1–4), happy (7:13–16), hopeful (1:7, 10), and even outraged (11:13–21). This phenomenon could be explained if the letter had been written over a long period of time, giving Paul an opportunity to receive several reports from Corinth, to which he might logically respond in a variety of ways. Those commentators who think 2 Corinthians must be a collection of letters also believe it may contain between two and five separate letters. A common proposal divides the epistle into three smaller letters: (1) chapters 1–8; (2) chapter 9; (3) chapters 10–13. Other proposals adjust the division slightly. Another proposal suggests that the various letters have been preserved out of order, which has caused scholars to try to rearrange the sequence to make better sense of the dialogue. The puzzle that confronts anyone who is interested in dealing with composition issues is challenging. Unless the original letter(s) is found we will most likely never be unable to answer these questions with any kind of certainty.

Nevertheless, a study of 2 Corinthians can be rewarding. The letter has been described as one of Paul's most intimate, revealing a very personal side, but also shedding additional light on his calling as an apostle of **Jesus Christ**. If Paul's letter to the Galatians reveals anger, and if his letter to the Philippians reveals joy, then this letter reveals deep pain on Paul's part.

Addressed to the "church of God which is at Corinth," Paul's epistle contains one of the most beautiful prayers recorded in his letters: "Blessed be God, even the Father of our Lord Jesus Christ, the Father of mercies, and the God of all comfort; who comforteth us in all our tribulation, that we may be able to comfort them which are in any trouble, by the comfort wherewith we ourselves are comforted of God. For as the sufferings of Christ abound in us, so our consolation also aboundeth by Christ. And whether we be afflicted, it is for your consolation and salvation, which is effectual in the enduring of the same sufferings which we also suffer: or whether we be comforted, it is for your consolation and salvation. And our hope of you is stedfast, knowing, that as ye are partakers of the sufferings, so shall ye be also of the consolation" (1:3–7). Consolation is emphasized throughout the letter (2:7–5:5; 6:4–10; 11:23–12:10; 13:4). In this opening, the idea of comfort is repeated five separate times.

Additionally, Paul begins to explain the meaning of suffering— suffering with Christ. This is one of the earliest attempts to do so in the New Testament. He continues to report how God had saved him from a terrible struggle he had experienced in **Asia** (1:8). Although we do not know the exact nature of the ordeal—whether it was a deadly sickness, violent persecution, or imprisonment—we do know the experience had a profound impact on Paul and reinforced his belief that one must trust only in God (1:9). In fact, his own suffering has brought to his mind a new sense of God's purpose through Jesus Christ—that through his death we share his death, and if we share his death, we also share his resurrection and his glory. Not only will the Saints receive comfort from God, but they will also be victorious with Christ in the future (1:5–7, 9–10).

The letter shifts focus again as Paul explains why he has not visited them as promised and why he wrote the so-called "tearful letter": "For out of much affliction and anguish of heart I wrote unto you with many tears" (2:4). The letter may be lost, or it may be contained in chapters 10 through 13.

Paul's Ministry

2 CORINTHIANS 2:14–5:17

Paul turns his attention to his ministry among the Corinthians and to those who followed in his footsteps. Paul believes that God has accomplished a great work through him and his fellow workers, so his defense is rather strong—suggesting how hurt Paul was at the time and what he thought was at stake in Corinth.

Apparently, a false apostle had come with letters of recommendation—or at least a claim to have received such recommendations (2 Corinthians 3:1). Paul asks the Corinthians about that letter of recommendation and argues, "Ye are our epistle written in our hearts, known and read of all men: Forasmuch as ye are manifestly declared to be the epistle of **Christ** ministered by us, written not with ink, but with the Spirit of the living God; not in tables of stone, but in fleshy tables of the heart" (2 Corinthians 3:2–3). This spiritual confirmation of his ministry stands in contrast to those who carried physical letters of recommendation, commending them as servants of God when they were not.

Paul says that he trusts only in God, through Christ (3:4)—he does not rely upon himself, but he and his co-workers are simply "ministers of the new testament [**covenant**]" (3:6). Further, he argues that the gospel he delivered them was superior to the old covenant (Greek, *diathēkēs*, "testament") because "the letter killeth, but the spirit giveth life" (3:6). Nevertheless, the old covenant, "written and engraven in stones, was glorious" (3:7). If so, then the new covenant is all the more glorious (3:8). The veil that separated ancient Israel from the presence of the Lord was "done away in Christ" (3:14), even though for many the "vail is [still] upon their heart" (3:15). The gospel of Christ brings the Spirit and "where the Spirit of the Lord is, there is liberty" (3:17).

Paul also states, "Therefore seeing we have this ministry, as we have received mercy, we faint not; But have renounced the hidden things of dishonesty, not walking in craftiness, nor handling the word of God deceitfully; but by manifestation of the truth commending ourselves to every man's conscience in the sight of God" (4:1–2). He also testifies of Christ's divinity: "the glorious gospel of Christ, who is the image of God" (4:4). Paul continues, "For we preach not ourselves, but Christ **Jesus** the Lord; and ourselves your servants for Jesus' sake" (4:5). These phrases seem to speak of those who, unlike Paul, were dishonest, crafty, deceitful, proud, and self-promoting.

Being servants, however, has not removed the suffering of this world: "We are troubled on every side, yet not distressed; we are perplexed, but not in despair; Persecuted, but not forsaken; cast down, but not destroyed" (4:8–9). Nevertheless, Paul testifies that the Saints have hope in Christ and in their sufferings: "For which cause we faint not; but though our outward man perish, yet the inward man is renewed day by day. For our light affliction, which is but for a moment, worketh for us a far more exceeding and eternal weight of glory; while we look not at the things which are seen, but at the things which are not seen: for the things which are seen are temporal; but the things which are not seen are eternal. For we know that if our earthly house of this tabernacle were dissolved, we have a building of God, an house not made with hands, eternal in the heavens. For in this we groan, earnestly desiring to be clothed upon with our house which is from heaven: If so be that being clothed we shall not be found naked. For we that

371

are in this tabernacle do groan, being burdened: not for that we would be unclothed, but clothed upon, that mortality might be swallowed up of life. Now he that hath wrought us for the selfsame thing is God, who also hath given unto us the earnest of the Spirit" (4:16–5:5). Paul's hope as expressed in these verses shows a fundamental shift from an expectation of immediate triumph to a hope for otherworldly glory. Affliction is momentary whereas resurrection is endless, insinuating that the immediate recognition his opponents are receiving will be nothing compared to the eventual glory that will be shared by the Saints.

Reconciliation through Christ
2 CORINTHIANS 5:18–21

Paul knows that if any person "be in **Christ**, he is a new creature" (2 Corinthians 5:17), but that is not the natural state of things since all have sinned (Romans 3:23) and are therefore alienated from God. In human relationships, when one spouse hurts or offends the other, the offending party usually seeks reconciliation with the one offended. Often this is accomplished through giving some type of gift, the purpose of which is to placate the offended spouse. In antiquity, pagans did the same through **temple sacrifices**—the sacrifices represented the gifts to the gods. Apparently, even Israel slipped into believing that they could placate God with a multitude of sacrifices and rituals (Isaiah 1:11–15).

On the other hand, Paul knows there is nothing humans can do to effect reconciliation with God. Therefore, Paul testifies that **Jesus** is the representative of God in effecting the reconciliation: "And all things are of God, who hath reconciled us to himself by Jesus Christ, and hath given to us the ministry of reconciliation; to wit, that God was in Christ, reconciling the world unto himself, not imputing their trespasses unto them; and hath committed unto us the word of reconciliation" (5:18–19). In other words, the offended party, in this case God, sent his Son to effect the reconciliation, a rather strange idea that the offended party gives the gifts to the offender so that reconciliation can be accomplished.

Paul adds that the **apostle** is the representative of God in proclaiming it: "Now then we are ambassadors for Christ, as though God did beseech you by us: we pray you in Christ's stead, be ye reconciled to God" (5:20). That is, God extends his invitation to reconciliation through the apostles.

Paul's Labors
2 CORINTHIANS 6:1–7:16

Paul continues to defend his ministry among the Corinthians: "But in all things approving ourselves as the ministers of God, in much patience, in afflictions, in necessities, in distresses, In stripes, in imprisonments, in tumults, in labours, in watchings, in fastings; by pureness, by knowledge, by longsuffering, by kindness, by the **Holy Ghost**, by love unfeigned, By the word of truth, by the power of God, by the armour of righteousness on the right hand and on the left" (6:4–7). Such attributes are the fruits by which we may recognize the servants of God (Matthew 7:16), which are in this list colored by suffering and trial.

Picking up a metaphor very common for the period, Paul tells the Corinthians, "Be ye not unequally yoked together with unbelievers: for what fellowship hath righteousness with unrighteousness? and what communion hath light with darkness?" (6:14). In this advice Paul calls on the Corinthian Saints to separate themselves from the unbelievers and to come together as a faithful people. That unity underlines Paul's counsel seems clear in his injunction to "come out from among them, and be ye separate, saith the Lord, and touch not the unclean thing; and I will receive you" (6:17). The "unclean thing" probably has reference to some aspect of pagan ritual, perhaps animal **sacrifices**, or perhaps figuratively the mindset of division and backbiting. Paul desired the Saints to "cleanse ourselves from all filthiness of the flesh and spirit, perfecting holiness in the fear of God" (7:1).

The Jerusalem Collection
2 CORINTHIANS 8:1–9:15

Paul spent a significant amount of energy in collecting donations from the churches he established for the support of impoverished Saints in Jerusalem (Romans 15:25–32). His efforts in Corinth are noted in both letters (1 Corinthians 16:1–4; 2 Corinthians 8–9). Luke provides a list of **Church** delegates who accompanied Paul to Jerusalem to deliver the collection (Acts 20:4; compare 2 Corinthians 8:23).

The genesis of the project is lost to us. Some suggest that the beginning is directly connected to the decision made at the Jerusalem Conference regarding new **Gentile** converts (Acts 11:27–29; 15:1–20), in which one of the stipulations for the Gentiles, who would not be required to submit to **circumcision**, was to "remember the poor; the same which I also was forward to do" (Galatians 2:10). The giving of **alms** was an important aspect of first-century Judaism and had become a symbol among Christians of **covenant** faithfulness. Whether or not Paul understood this stipulation as simply a continuation of the Jewish tradition of concern for the poor (Exodus 23:10–11; Isaiah 58:6–7, 9–10; Amos 2:6–8; 5:11–12; 8:4–6) or as a specific covenant mandate is difficult, even impossible, to determine based on the fragmentary evidence that has survived from the first-century Church.

At some point Paul began to prepare a monetary collection that he planned to personally deliver to Jerusalem. In many ways this was a radical call to discipleship and a test for the Gentile converts who may have felt marginalized by some Jewish-Christians. It was also unprecedented in its scope—collecting a charitable donation from around the Mediterranean world for a specific group in **Judea**. Additionally, Paul may have hoped to bond members of the Gentile branches to their counterparts in Jerusalem. Certainly, love stood at the center of the collection as Paul urged, "Every man according as he purposeth in his heart, so let him give; not grudgingly, or of necessity: for God loveth a cheerful giver" (2 Corinthians 9:7).

Interestingly, Paul provides one of the earliest allusions to the premortal existence in the New Testament as he argues for the collection. "For ye know," Paul says, "the grace of our Lord **Jesus Christ**, *that, though he was rich*, yet for your sakes he became poor, that ye through his poverty might be rich" (8:9; emphasis added).

Judging by Outward Appearance

2 CORINTHIANS 10:1–18

The letter turns again to defending Paul's apostleship—his authority. Some scholars suggest that this section represents an independent letter about those identified by Paul as "false apostles" (2 Corinthians 11:13). Paul begins this section with a plea: "Now I Paul myself beseech you by the meekness and gentleness of **Christ**" (10:1). One is reminded of **Jesus'** compassionate entreaty: "Come unto me, all ye that labour and are heavy laden, and I will give you rest. Take my yoke upon you, and learn of me; *for I am meek and lowly in heart*: and ye shall find rest unto your souls. For my yoke is easy, and my burden is light" (Matthew 11:28–30; emphasis added).

Paul asks the Corinthians not to consider the "outward appearance" (10:7), and in his doing so, we learn about another accusation the false apostles have brought against Paul: "For his letters, say they, are weighty and powerful; but his bodily presence is weak, and his speech contemptible" (10:10). These accusations are particularly personal in nature and attack what some felt was Paul's weak personal appearance. Paul disparages such thinking, noting that his opponents measure themselves only by one another and not the word of God (10:12), thus giving them a false sense of security and well-being.

Paul's Boasts

2 CORINTHIANS 11:1–12:6

In his battle for the hearts and minds of the Corinthian Saints, Paul notes, "For I am jealous over you with godly jealousy: for I have espoused you to one husband, that I may present you as a chaste virgin to **Christ**"

(2 Corinthians 11:2). In some of the strongest language yet, Paul attacks his enemies: "For if he that cometh preacheth another **Jesus**, whom we have not preached, or if ye receive another spirit, which ye have not received, or another gospel, which ye have not accepted, ye might well bear with him" (11:4).

Paul argues that he is "not a whit behind the very chiefest apostles" (11:5). His missionary strategy in Corinth had been to labor with his own hands (Acts 18:3). Apparently, this offended some in Corinth—believing that Paul, in refusing their hospitality, was rejecting their thoughtful invitations (2 Corinthians 11:7–9). Rhetorically, he asks, "Have I committed an offence in abasing myself that ye might be exalted, because I have preached to you the gospel of God freely?" (11:7). His purpose in pursuing this strategy was to keep himself from the patron-client system typical of first-century society. He says, "And when I was present with you, and wanted, I was chargeable to no man: for that which was lacking to me the brethren which came from Macedonia supplied: and in all things I have kept myself from being burdensome unto you, and so will I keep myself" (11:9).

Paul identifies his critics, as noted above, as "false apostles, deceitful workers, transforming themselves into the apostles of Christ" (11:13). Even though they claim to be Hebrews, Israelites, and the seed of Abraham, Paul says, "so am I" (11:22). Finally, he asks, "Are they ministers of Christ? (I speak as a fool) I am more" (11:23). Paul counters their claim to be ministers of Christ and says they are actually ministers of **Satan** in disguise (11:13–15). The references to false apostles, Israelites, and ministers of Christ all indicate the beginnings of an internal **apostasy** in the early **Church**, where those from within began deceiving the other members. Paul's excoriating language should be interpreted in that light, and his almost complete lack of patience for their heretical views can be understood as an attempt to pluck the buds of apostasy in their beginning stages of growth.

Paul then provides an accounting of the cost of discipleship that he has already paid: "In labours more abundant, in stripes above measure, in prisons more frequent, in deaths oft. Of the Jews five times received I forty stripes save one. Thrice was I beaten with rods, once was I stoned, thrice I suffered shipwreck, a night and a day I have been in the deep; in journeyings often, in perils of waters, in perils of robbers, in perils by mine own countrymen, in perils by the heathen, in perils in the city, in perils in the wilderness, in perils in the sea, in perils among false brethren; in weariness and painfulness, in watchings often, in hunger and thirst, in fastings often, in cold and nakedness. Beside those things that are without, that which cometh upon me daily, the care of all the churches" (11:23–28).

Apparently the false apostles had claimed certain visions and revelations, and Paul feels compelled again to draw a comparison between them and himself: "I knew a man in Christ above fourteen years ago, (whether in the body, I cannot tell; or whether out of the body, I cannot tell: God knoweth;) such an one caught up to the third heaven. And I knew such a man, (whether in the body, or out of the body, I cannot tell: God knoweth;) how that he was caught up into paradise, and heard unspeakable words, which it is not lawful for a man to utter" (12:2–4). Paul clearly intends to relate his own visionary experience, which is made obvious by the continuing first-person references to "I." The implications of what Paul might have seen in the "third heaven," which he could not relate, can be interpreted in two ways: first, assuming that Paul was counting from the bottom up, the third heaven would logically be the celestial realm; and second, personal revelation is sacred, and the fact that his opponents had made claims based on their supposed visions is a sign of their sinfulness.

Although it is impossible to determine exactly what doctrinal differences existed between Paul and these false apostles, Paul's authority was certainly central to his claim of authenticity. This appears also in 1 Corinthians (5:3–5; 7:12, 25, 40; compare 7:10; 14:37–38).

Paul's Thorn in the Flesh
2 CORINTHIANS 12:7–9

As noted above, the false **apostles** criticized Paul over his appearance. He may make reference to this when he writes, "And lest I should be exalted above measure through the abundance of the revelations, there was given to me a thorn [Greek, *skolops*, "thorn" or "splinter"] in the flesh, the messenger of **Satan** to buffet me, lest I should be exalted above measure" (2 Corinthians 12:7). Commentators have long speculated on the nature of the thorn; however, it was most likely a long-term health issue. He notes, "Ye know how through infirmity of the flesh I preached the gospel unto you at the first. And my temptation [test or trial] which was in my flesh ye despised not, nor rejected; but received me as an angel of God, even as **Christ Jesus**. Where is then the blessedness ye spake of? for I bear you record that, if it had been possible, *ye would have plucked out your own eyes, and have given them to me*" (Galatians 4:13–15; emphasis added). This suggests that it may have been a degenerative eye disease—a health concern for anyone living at any time, but which in antiquity it would also have had social implications. In those times people believed that the eyes are the window into the soul and would have seen a remarkable paradox if one who claimed to have seen Jesus could not see very well or that one who claimed to heal could not heal himself.

Whatever the thorn was, Paul had sought the "Lord thrice, that it might depart from me. And he said unto me, My grace is sufficient for thee: for my strength is made perfect in weakness" (2 Corinthians 12:8–9).

Paul Returns to Boasting
2 CORINTHIANS 12:10–13:12

Paul continues boasting in his defense against the attacks by the false **apostles**: "I am become a fool in glorying; ye have compelled me: for I ought to have been commended of you: for in nothing am I behind the very chiefest apostles, though I be nothing" (2 Corinthians 12:11). He reminds them of his own ministry among them: "Truly the signs of an apostle were wrought among you in all patience, in signs, and wonders, and mighty deeds" (12:12).

Paul admits that he is still hesitant to visit them: "For I fear, lest, when I come, I shall not find you such as I would, and that I shall be found unto you such as ye would not: lest there be debates, envyings, wraths, strifes, backbitings, whisperings, swellings, tumults: And lest, when I come again, my God will humble me among you, and that I shall bewail many which have sinned already, and have not repented" (12:20–21). It appears that Paul is uncertain whether his letter will have the desired effect of turning the tide of **apostasy** and indeed believes that his presence in Corinth would only bring debates and backbiting.

Exhortations and Final Benediction
2 CORINTHIANS 13:11–12

Paul concludes his letter with these words: "Finally, brethren, farewell. Be perfect, be of good comfort, be of one mind, live in peace; and the God of love and peace shall be with you. Greet one another with an holy kiss. All the saints salute you. The grace of the Lord **Jesus Christ**, and the love of God, and the communion of the **Holy Ghost**, be with you all. Amen" (2 Corinthians 13:11–14).

Applying the scripture in a nineteenth-century American context, the Joseph Smith Translation adjusts the phrase "Greet one another with an holy kiss" to "Greet one another with an holy *salutation*" (JST, 2 Corinthians 13:12; emphasis added).

6

GALATIANS

There is almost universal agreement that Paul's earliest letters are Galatians, 1 and 2 Thessalonians, and 1 and 2 Corinthians. The exact dating for each is vigorously debated because Paul did not, as is our custom today, date his letters. However, most commentators believe these letters were composed between A.D. 50 and 57.

For a number of reasons, it has been assumed that 1 Thessalonians was the first composed. Recently a number of commentators have suggested that the epistle to the Galatians was actually written first. If Galatians was in fact written before 1 Thessalonians, usually dated about A.D. 50 or 51, then Galatians could have been written as early as A.D. 48—pushing the range of composition earlier by two years. Additionally, such a historical dating of Galatians would mean that it was written before the famous Jerusalem Conference held in A.D. 49 (Acts 15). The implications are significant, reorienting the discussion regarding the crisis in Antioch (Galatians 2:11–14). We will examine the implication of this point below.

Introduction

GALATIANS 1:1–9

Although Paul's audience is not specifically identified beyond the "churches of Galatia" (Galatians 1:2), the unanimous conclusion is that he was writing to **Gentile** Christians living in what is known today as Turkey. Commentators have advanced two propositions. First, they were composed of a mixture of people of Lycaonia, Phrygia, and Pisidia, regions that fell within the Roman province of Galatia. Paul visited this region during his so-called first mission (Acts 13:14–15; 14:1) before the Jerusalem Conference. Second, they were ethnic Galatians who were descendants of immigrants from Gaul (modern France) and who resided in central **Asia** Minor. Although this area is not specifically mentioned, many scholars believe Paul could have visited the "Galatians" during the so-called second mission (Acts 16:6; 18:23) after the Jerusalem Conference.

This letter is by far Paul's most passionate and confrontational letter. Well remembered is Paul's blistering attack: "O foolish Galatians, who hath bewitched you" (Galatians 3:1). Certainly, Paul at other times expresses disappointment in his fellow laborers (2 Timothy 4:10) and with failures in other branches of the Church (2 Corinthians 2:1, 4), but this stands out among all of his letters as the most emotional. He is angry with his opponents and with members of the **Church** who have apparently listened to them.

Throughout the letter, Paul attacks his opponents, charging them with a number of offenses. They have "troubled" the Galatians (1:7; 5:10); "perverted" the "good news" (1:7); they have "bewitched" the Saints (3:1); they have hindered them "that [they] should not obey the truth" (5:7); they do not "keep the law" themselves (6:13); and finally, they want the Galatians to submit to **circumcision** so that "they may glory" in their efforts (6:13).

He reminds the churches that he is "Paul, an **apostle**, (not of men, neither by man, but by **Jesus Christ**, and God the Father, who raised him from the dead)" (1:1). Surprisingly, his greetings are brief in this letter: "Grace be to you and peace from God the Father, and from our Lord Jesus Christ, who gave himself for our sins, that he might deliver us from this present evil world, according to the will of God and our Father: to whom be glory for ever and ever. Amen" (1:3–5). Changing directions suddenly, Paul fails to include his typical thanksgiving section (Romans 1:8–10; 1 Thessalonians 1:2–5; 1 Corinthians 1:4–9; Philippians 1:3–11; Philemon 1:4–7). Instead, he writes, "I marvel that ye are so soon removed from him that called you into the grace of Christ unto another gospel" (Galatians 1:6). He blames the defection on "some that trouble you, and would pervert the gospel of

Christ" (1:7). Paul's comment "ye are so soon removed" may suggest that this letter was written within a very short time after Paul had established churches in Galatia.

What gospel do they offer? Apparently, they do not fault Paul's presentation of the "good news" but argue that it is insufficient. What more is needed to be done? Those who have troubled the Galatians have demanded that they need to submit to circumcision (5:2–3). It had been the sign of the **covenant** between the Lord and Abraham, his descendants, and the strangers among them for generations (Genesis 17:10–14).

One may ask why Paul is worried about this particular issue. What harm could come of this if the Galatians otherwise remain faithful to Christ? Even Paul points out that "for in Jesus Christ neither circumcision availeth any thing, nor uncircumcision" (Galatians 5:6). Nevertheless, Paul says, "But though we, or an angel from heaven, preach any other gospel unto you than that which we have preached unto you, let him be *accursed*" (1:8; emphasis added). Paul emphasizes his accusation: "As we said before, so say I now again, If any man preach any other gospel unto you than that ye have received, let him be *accursed*" (1:9; emphasis added).

Paul's Authority

GALATIANS 1:10–24

Apparently, Paul's opponents challenged his credentials by saying that he had received information about **Jesus** secondhand. Paul counters that claim: "But I certify you, brethren, that the gospel which was preached of me is not after man. For I neither received it of man, neither was I taught it, but by the revelation of Jesus **Christ**" (Galatians 1:11–12). For Paul, his call by the Lord on the road to Damascus was a pivotal event providing him a similar experience as the other **apostles** (1 Corinthians 15:5–8). He explains, "For ye have heard of my conversation in time past in the Jews' religion, how that beyond measure I persecuted the **church** of God, and wasted it: and profited in the Jews' religion above many my equals in mine own nation, being more exceedingly zealous of the traditions of my fathers"

(1:13–14). Paul continues, "But when it pleased God, who separated me from my mother's womb, and called me by his grace, to reveal his Son in me, that I might preach him among the heathen" (1:15–16). An underlying implication of these verses is an emphasis that Paul's authority does not rely upon popular approval of his message. Instead, Paul's authority comes directly from God.

Nevertheless, Paul believes Church leaders in Jerusalem have approved his message and call. He recalls, "Then after three years I went up to Jerusalem to see [Greek, *historēsai*, "to know the history"] Peter, and abode with him fifteen days. But other of the apostles saw I none, save James the Lord's brother" (1:18–19). A simple get-to-know-you opportunity would not have taken fifteen days. Certainly, Paul asked questions of Peter and James about Jesus. There is ample evidence Paul knew many details regarding Jesus' mortal ministry even though Paul chose to focus much of his attention on Jesus as the risen Lord (1 Corinthians 11:23–26; 15:3–4).

James's death is not reported in Acts or in the Pauline epistles, but James, who had a powerful influence in the Jerusalem Church in the earliest period, suffered martyrdom in Jerusalem at the hands of the Sanhedrin. According to Josephus, in A.D. 62 the high priest Ananus murdered James, the brother of Jesus, during a change of governors when Albinus was sent to replace Festus, who had passed away (*Antiquities* 20.9).

A Meeting in Jerusalem
GALATIANS 2:1–3

Continuing the theme that his work is in harmony with **Church** leaders in Jerusalem, Paul then mentions another visit to the Holy City: "Then fourteen years after I went up again to Jerusalem with Barnabas, and took Titus with me also. And I went up by revelation, and communicated unto them that gospel which I preach among the **Gentiles**, but privately to them which were of reputation, lest by any means I should run, or had run, in vain. But neither Titus, who was with me, being a Greek, was compelled to be circumcised" (Galatians 2:1–3).

The debate over dating the epistle to the Galatians focuses on this meeting. Was Paul referring to the famous Jerusalem Conference held in A.D. 49? Or was it an earlier meeting held before that conference? For a rather long time, most commentators believed that Paul referred to the Jerusalem Conference in this brief notation. However, a number of scholars have recently questioned that interpretation, suggesting that a careful comparison of what is recorded in Acts 15 regarding the Jerusalem Conference does not match Paul's description of the meeting here. Therefore, they conclude that Paul must be talking about another meeting—one held prior to the Jerusalem Conference. In this earlier meeting, Paul held that Church leaders had recognized that "the gospel of the uncircumcision was committed unto me" and that "the gospel of the **circumcision** was unto Peter" (2:7). Specifically, Paul states, "And when James, Cephas [Peter's **Aramaic** name], and John, who seemed to be pillars, perceived the grace that was given unto me, they gave to me and Barnabas the right hands of fellowship; that we should go unto the heathen, and they unto the circumcision" (2:9).

Interestingly, nowhere in this letter is the decision of the Jerusalem Conference mentioned. Silence on this point suggests that it had not been made or Paul would have certainly used it to his advantage. Note that when the ruling was made, the **apostles** "wrote letters" (Acts 15:23). Those letters stated, "The apostles and elders and brethren send greeting unto the brethren which are of the Gentiles in Antioch and Syria and Cilicia: Forasmuch as we have heard, that certain which went out from us have troubled you with words, subverting your souls, saying, Ye must be circumcised, and keep the law: to whom we gave no such commandment: It seemed good unto us, being assembled with one accord, to send chosen men unto you with our beloved Barnabas and Paul, men that have hazarded their lives for the name of our Lord **Jesus Christ**. We have sent therefore Judas and Silas, who shall also tell you the same things by mouth. For it seemed good to the **Holy Ghost**, and to us, to lay upon you no greater burden than these necessary things; that ye abstain from meats offered to idols, and from blood, and from things strangled, and from fornication: from which if ye keep yourselves, ye shall do well. Fare ye well" (Acts 15:23–29).

Are those men from James, who arrived in Antioch, the same as "certain which went out from us have troubled you. . . . to whom we gave no such commandment" (Acts 15:24)? The practice seems to have been that Paul would take the letter and read it in the **congregations**: "and when they had gathered the multitude together, they delivered the epistle" (Acts 15:30). Paul had continued this practice for some time: "And they went through the cities, they delivered them the decrees for to keep, that they were ordained of the apostles and elders which were at Jerusalem" (Acts 16:4). One may wonder why Paul did not quote from or at least refer to such an authoritative letter about a formal decision. If Galatians was written before the Jerusalem Conference, the crisis in Antioch makes a lot more sense.

Crisis in Antioch
GALATIANS 2:4–14

Shortly after the Jerusalem meeting, Paul went to Antioch, as did Peter. In this setting, a crisis broke wide open when Paul "withstood [Peter]" face-to-face (Galatians 2:11). Apparently, having approved Paul's mission strategy, Peter ate with the **Gentile** converts in Antioch. However, when a group of emissaries arrived from Jerusalem, claiming to represent James, Peter waffled. These were most likely those who Paul described earlier: "And that because of false brethren unawares brought in, who came in privily to spy out our liberty which we have in **Christ Jesus**, that they might bring us into bondage: to whom we gave place by subjection, no, not for an hour; that the truth of the gospel might continue with you" (2:4–5).

Paul continues, "When they were come, [Peter] withdrew and separated himself, fearing them which were of the **circumcision** [party]" (2:12). Other Jewish-Christians present, including Barnabas, followed Peter's example and also withdrew from eating with the Gentile Christians. This was all too much for Paul, so he confronted Peter in front of the entire group: "If thou, being a Jew, livest after the manner of Gentiles, and not as do the Jews, why compellest thou the Gentiles to live as do the Jews? We who are Jews by nature, and not sinners of the Gentiles, knowing that a man is not justified by the works of the law, but by the faith of Jesus Christ [or "by faith in Jesus Christ"], even we have believed in Jesus Christ, that we might be justified by the faith of Christ, and not by the works of the law: for by the works of the law shall no flesh be justified" (2:14–16).

O Foolish Galatians

GALATIANS 3:1–25

Paul calls the Galatians "foolish" (Galatians 3:1), arguing that they had been "bewitched" into believing that the gospel of **Jesus Christ** was insufficient to save them. He then reminds them of his ministry among them at the very beginning, asking them, "Received ye the Spirit by the works of the law, or by the hearing of faith?" (3:2) Rhetorically, he also asked, "Are ye so foolish? having begun in the Spirit, are ye now made perfect by the flesh? Have ye suffered so many things in vain?" (3:3–4)

Paul then presents a series of arguments based on several scriptural stories in the Old Testament, which indicate that reliance upon the law is inconsistent with faith in Jesus Christ (3:6–18). He then turns his attention to demonstrating the true purpose of the law: "Wherefore then serveth the law?" (3:19). Paul goes on to say, "Wherefore the law was our schoolmaster to bring us unto Christ, that we might be justified by faith. But after that faith is come, we are no longer under a schoolmaster" (3:24–25).

A Gospel Paradox

GALATIANS 3:10–13

Paul then presents what is sometimes identified as a "gospel reversal" or "paradox"—one of the counterintuitive insights about **Christ**'s death. Paul later recalls, "We preach Christ crucified, unto the Jews a stumblingblock, and unto the Greeks foolishness" (1 Corinthians 1:23). Why was it a stumbling block to teach Christ crucified? For Paul and other first-century Jews, the **disciples**' declaration that **Jesus** had been crucified was an oxymoron— the **Messiah** could not be crucified, and a crucified man could not be the

Messiah. For the **law** states, "for he that is hanged is accursed of God" (Deuteronomy 21:23). Apparently, Jewish interpretation of Deuteronomy eliminated any possibility that a righteous man, let alone the Messiah, would be crucified. This may explain Paul's initial bitter opposition to the disciples. However, after meeting Jesus on the road to Damascus, Paul reread the Hebrew Bible through the lens of the Resurrection. Jesus had provided such a lens to the disciples following his death and resurrection (Luke 24:27, 32, 44–47).

What Paul discovered and what he now tells the Galatians is that the Messiah (Christ) had been crucified—had been cursed. However, it was not for his own sins: "Christ hath redeemed us from the curse of the law, *being made a curse for us:* for it is written, Cursed is every one that hangeth on a tree" (Galatians 3:13; emphasis added). The Messiah stood in our place, acting as a proxy for us—"being made a curse for us."

Neither Jew nor Greek
GALATIANS 3:26–29

In what some commentators believe is a negation of first-century Jewish prayer practice, Paul tells the Galatians that in **Christ Jesus** they have become "the children of God by faith in Christ Jesus" (3:26). Apparently, Jewish men were accustomed to praying along the lines of "Praised are you, O Lord, who hath not made me a **Gentile**, Praised are you, O Lord, who did not make me a [slave], and Praised are you, O Lord, who did not make me a woman" (*Menahot*, 1.66). If so, Paul would have offered a prayer like this every day of his life, thanking God that he was inherently different from the supposedly lower classes of creation, until he met the risen Lord on the road to Damascus. Here in Galatians 3, Paul states, "For as many of you as have been baptized into Christ have put on Christ. There is neither Jew nor Greek, there is neither bond nor free, there is neither male nor female: for ye are all one in Christ Jesus. And if ye be Christ's, then are ye Abraham's seed, and heirs according to the promise" (3:27–29).

God Sent Forth His Son
GALATIANS 4:1–7

Paul tells the Saints that **Jesus** was sent by God to be born at exactly the precise moment—not a month or year too early or too late, but "when the fulness of the time was come" (Galatians 4:4).

In a chiasmus (reversing the order of individual points), Paul continues outlining this gospel paradox, emphasizing the reversal of the law that Jesus **Christ** effected:

(1a) God sent his Son, made of a woman

(2a) made [born] under the law

(2b) to redeem them that were under the law

(1b) that we might receive the adoption of sons

Paul concludes, "And because ye are sons, God hath sent forth the Spirit of his Son into your hearts, crying, Abba, Father. Wherefore thou art no more a servant, but a son; and if a son, then an heir of God through Christ" (4:6–7). Here Paul preserves the **Aramaic** word for Father (*Abba*), witnessing the continued influence of Jesus' prayer in Gethsemane (Mark 14:35; Romans 8:15).

The Earlier Days
GALATIANS 4:8–15

Reflecting on the Galatians' **Gentile** upbringing, Paul mentions that they formerly served "them which by nature are no gods" (Galatians 4:8). Their service to pagan deities is in contrast to their service to the "known God" (4:9). Unfortunately, their conversion to belief in the "known God" did not include leaving behind their service to worshipping the "beggarly elements, whereunto ye desire again to be in bondage" (4:9). This service to the elements is further explained as observing "days, and months, and times, and years" (4:10), which may allude to an early dispute concerning the Jewish versus the Christian calendar of holy days or possibly even to some reference to pagan astronomical observations. Paul is afraid that this backsliding into their former ways means that "I have bestowed upon you labour in vain" (4:11). See 2 Corinthians 12:7–9 for a discussion of Paul's thorn in the flesh.

The Joseph Smith Translation adds an interesting reinterpretation of 4:12, rephrasing it as follows: "Brethren, I beseech you to be perfect as I am perfect; for I am persuaded as ye have a knowledge of me, ye have not injured me at all by your sayings." The word *perfect* probably is meant as an intentional parallel to Matthew 5:48, where the Lord speaks of the Father's perfection. In that verse the Greek word (*teleios*) implies completion, which can be applied to a number of contexts such as completion of a mission, complete obedience, or perhaps completion of the ordinances. It is doubtful, based on Paul's other writings, that Paul intended to assert his own mortal perfection, and perhaps he was here recommending his complete obedience or completion of the ordinances of salvation as a model for the Saints to follow.

In Bondage

GALATIANS 4:16–31

In a rather unique reading of the story of Abraham, Sarah, and Hagar, Paul argues that Christians, through the new **covenant**, are born free: "For it is written, that Abraham had two sons, the one by a bondmaid, the other by a freewoman. But he who was of the bondwoman was born after the flesh; but he of the freewoman was by promise. Which things are an allegory: for these are the two covenants; the one from the mount Sinai, which gendereth to bondage, which is Agar. For this Agar is mount Sinai in Arabia, and answereth to Jerusalem which now is, and is in bondage with her children. But Jerusalem which is above is free, which is the mother of us all. . . . Now we, brethren, as Isaac was, are the children of promise. . . . So then, brethren, we are not children of the bondwoman, but of the free" (4:22–31). Reversing the standard logic of his Jewish peers, Paul sees the gospel of **Christ** as leading to freedom and the law as leading to bondage.

Stand Fast in Liberty

GALATIANS 5:1–14

Paul's important and eloquent discussion on liberty and freedom follows: "Stand fast therefore in the liberty wherewith **Christ** hath made us free, and be not entangled again with the yoke of bondage" (Galatians 5:1). He then argues "that if ye be circumcised, Christ shall profit you nothing" (5:2). Further, Paul believes that **circumcision** is the first step down a slippery slope: "For I testify again to every man that is circumcised, that he is a debtor to do the whole law" (5:3). In other words, if you accept circumcision, then you must expect also to obey all 613 **Torah** commandments (mentioned in the **Talmud** and established by Maimonides [A.D. 1135–1204]).

In a reconciliatory tone, Paul tells the Galatians, "I have confidence in you through the Lord, that ye will be none otherwise minded: but he that troubleth you shall bear his judgment, whosoever he be" (5:10). However, it is obvious that Paul is not interested in a civil debate with his opponents—he is only worried about the Saints in Galatia. He presses the issue by arguing that if circumcision counts for something, then his opponents should go all the way and, according to a literal rendering of the Greek text, castrate themselves (5:12). The King James Version softens the rhetoric and uses the translation "to cut off."

Paul returns to his discussion of freedom and liberty: "For, brethren, ye have been called unto liberty; only use not liberty for an occasion to the flesh, but by love serve one another" (5:13). He then reminds them that the "law is fulfilled in one word, even in this; Thou shalt love thy neighbour as thyself" (5:14).

Fruits of the Spirit

GALATIANS 5:16–26

Paul pleads with the Galatians to "walk in the Spirit" (Galatians 5:16). He begins to contrast the works of the Spirit with the works of the flesh by enumerating the works of the flesh in detail: "Adultery, fornication, uncleanness, lasciviousness, idolatry, witchcraft, hatred, variance, emulations, wrath, strife, seditions, heresies, envyings, murders, drunkenness, revellings, and such like" (5:19–21), and he warns that "they which do such things shall not inherit the kingdom of God" (5:21). He then enumerates the "fruits of the Spirit" (5:22). They include love, joy, peace, longsuffering, gentleness, goodness, faith, meekness, and temperance (5:22–23). Some have supposed that after conversion the gifts of the Spirit come naturally. Instead, Paul encourages his readers to seek the gifts, a process that at times is arduous (1 Corinthians 12:31).

Exhortations

GALATIANS 5:26–6:10

Paul brings his letter to an end with several short but powerful exhortations. He indicates that we should not desire "vain glory" by "provoking one another, envying one another" (Galatians 5:26). He also warns the Saints that they should "restore" an errant brother or sister in "the spirit of meekness; considering thyself, lest thou also be tempted" (6:1), believing that **Christ** required us to bear "one another's burdens" (6:2). Harking back to the fruits of the Spirit, Paul says, "For whatsoever a man soweth, that shall he also reap. For he that soweth to his flesh shall of the flesh reap corruption; but he that soweth to the Spirit shall of the Spirit reap life everlasting" (6:7–8). Finally, Paul exhorts, "Let us not be weary in well doing" and "let us do good unto all men, especially unto them who are of the household of faith" (6:9–10).

In Paul's Own Hand

GALATIANS 6:11–18

In this earliest letter, Paul began a practice he would often follow thereafter. As was his custom and tradition in the first century, he dictated his letters to a scribe (Romans 16:22). After finishing the body of the letter,

Paul often took pen and ink and added a short note to the letter just written, providing the recipient with his seal of approval. In this particular case, Paul ends his letter to the Galatians: "Ye see how large a letter I have written unto you with mine own hand. As many as desire to make a fair shew in the flesh, they constrain you to be circumcised; only lest they should suffer persecution for the cross of **Christ**. For neither they themselves who are circumcised keep the law; but desire to have you circumcised, that they may glory in your flesh. But God forbid that I should glory, save in the cross of our Lord **Jesus** Christ, by whom the world is crucified unto me, and I unto the world. For in Christ Jesus neither **circumcision** availeth any thing, nor uncircumcision, but a new creature. And as many as walk according to this rule, peace be on them, and mercy, and upon the Israel of God. From henceforth let no man trouble me: for I bear in my body the marks of the Lord Jesus. Brethren, the grace of our Lord Jesus Christ be with your spirit. Amen" (6:11–18).

7

EPHESIANS

The letter to the Ephesian Saints may be misnamed, a result of the fact that in verse 1 the name of the city, Ephesus, is missing in some of the earliest manuscripts. The letter may have originally been a circular letter written to a specific region of the **Church**, perhaps **Asia**, and later scribes may have added the name from memory of that region or by tradition.

Introduction

EPHESIANS 1:1–2

Tychicus carried the letter to Paul, expecting to receive a report from him, thus indicating that originally there was at least a regional destination in mind (Ephesians 6:21–22). Paul was imprisoned at the time he wrote the letter (6:20), but he was free to communicate with the Saints. The date of Paul's writing of this epistle is notoriously difficult to establish, and many scholars have dated it to the later period of Paul's life based on the subject matter, which is significantly different from Paul's more easily datable early epistles (see, for example, 1 Thessalonians). One of the themes that causes scholars to postulate a late date for this epistle is the growing threat of Christian Gnosticism, a heresy that in its most basic sense emphasized salvation by private and spiritual knowledge of heavenly mysteries. The beginnings of this heresy appear in this letter as well as in Colossians and 1–2 Timothy.

Thanksgiving
EPHESIANS 1:3–23

This epistle contains an extended prayer of thanksgiving (a doxology) for the blessings of God. Some of the language of this section may appear exclusionary, relegating the blessings of salvation to a single people: "Having predestinated us unto the adoption of children by **Jesus Christ** to himself, according to the good pleasure of his will" (Ephesians 1:5). The language of predestination is used here not of a people but in reference to the gathered Saints of God. In other words, God has indeed "predestinated" his Saints for adoption as children. In his doing so, we are thankful (1:6), and we participate and receive the blessings of "redemption through his blood" (1:7).

God, as a result of his choosing a people, has also revealed to them his future plan of salvation, "that in the dispensation of the fulness of times he might gather together in one all things in Christ, both which are in heaven, and which are on earth; even in him" (1:10). Paul triumphs in being included in those who are gathered in, "in whom also *we* have obtained an inheritance" (1:11).

Verses 13 and 14 shift from the first-person plural "us" to the second-person plural "you" in an attempt to call the Saints to action and to remind them of the available promises, namely sealing by the "holy Spirit of promise" (1:13). Even though the verbs are past tense ("trusted," "heard," and "sealed"), they reflect the path the Saints are on: Having trusted and heard, they seek the "holy Spirit of promise." To clarify this latter point, Paul adds, "Which [sealing] is the earnest of our inheritance until the redemption of the purchased possession, unto the praise of his glory" (1:14). The letter reflects hope of redemption and not achieved redemption.

Paul outlines what is still lacking in their quest to be sealed by the Holy Spirit. He prays that they will receive "wisdom and revelation" (1:17) that the "eyes of your understanding being enlightened; that ye may know what is the hope of his calling, and what the riches of the glory of his inheritance in the saints" (1:18). The prayer for revelation precedes Paul's later rebuke for disunity in the branches, thus implying that this prayer was to remedy a lack of the Spirit generally (4:14–32).

The final five verses of the first chapter begin to treat popular Gnostic themes, namely the structure of the heavens and Christ's role in relationship to other heavenly beings. Here, Paul seems to push aside such speculation, testifying of the centrality of Christ regardless of the popular esoteric interests of some in his audience. The themes of principalities (Greek, *archēs*), powers (Greek, *exousias*), might (Greek, *dynameōs*), and dominion (Greek, *kyriōtētos*) are frequently discussed in **Gnostic** documents preserved outside the New Testament and written much later than the canonical books. In those documents, anonymous authors attempted to fit together a detailed cosmogony. Although this growing intellectual tradition became a major threat to the teachings of the **apostles**, Paul remains focused on the positive message rather than offering a specific rebuttal.

Gentiles Become Saints
EPHESIANS 2:1–22

A portion of this letter is addressed directly to those Saints who were **Gentiles** before their conversions. Paul's summary of their lives prior to believing in **Christ** is telling: "*Wherein in time past ye walked* according to the course of this world, *according to the prince of the power of the air*, the spirit that now worketh in the children of disobedience" (Ephesians 2:2; emphasis added). God had called them from this life of idolatry and wickedness, which must have been startling for Jews to observe. Citizenship in a Greek city would have entailed many things that Jews found offensive, and just as Paul does, Jews living beyond **Judea** describe Gentile religiosity and civic life in entirely negative terms. Gentiles needed to be called out of wickedness, while Jews needed to be convinced that **Jesus** was the **Messiah** according to scripture.

Paul refers to this calling out of the world as an act of grace: "For by grace are ye saved through faith; and that not of yourselves: it is the gift of God" (2:8). It would be inappropriate to make this verse a doctrinal statement on the method of salvation for all mankind. For Paul, it described the salvation of Gentiles, which God offered as an act of grace—not a reward for their works, which were sinful prior to their conversions.

Paul teaches that Gentile converts are now joined with Jewish converts in the hope of salvation: "That at that time ye were without Christ, being aliens from the commonwealth of Israel, and strangers from the **covenants** of promise, having no hope, and without God in the world: but now in Christ Jesus ye who sometimes were far off are made nigh by the blood of Christ. For he is our peace, *who hath made both one*, and hath broken down the middle wall of partition between us" (2:12–14; emphasis added). The unity thus achieved is built upon the foundation of "**apostles**" (a term reflecting the New Testament dispensation) and "prophets" (a term that harks back to the Old Testament) so that all are "fellowcitizens with the saints" with "Jesus Christ himself being the chief corner stone" (2:19–20).

In this context, Paul also speaks of abolishing "in his flesh the enmity" that formerly existed between Jews and Gentiles and abolishing "even the law of commandments contained in ordinances," implying a formal end to the ordinances of the law of Moses (2:15). Theologically, the removal of the **law** opened the way for complete unity between Jews and Gentiles, but the full implications of ending the law are not here addressed. The law of the gospel, which can be defined as the doctrine taught by the apostles, is itself a new law. That new law is based on the old law, and therefore interpreting that the end of the old law signifies its complete removal is going too far.

Gentiles Become Fellow-Heirs

EPHESIANS 3:1–21

Acts records a lengthy stay for Paul in Ephesus (Acts 19), which causes some difficulty in interpreting verse 2: "if ye have heard of the dispensation of the grace of God" (3:2). In the epistle, it appears that Paul is not acquainted with the Saints, whereas the extended stay in Acts would seem to contradict this. As noted previously (Ephesians 1:1–2), the name of the city Ephesus was added later to this epistle, and it is likely that the original audience did not know Paul as well as did the Ephesian Saints. This, coupled with an earlier statement, "Wherefore I also, *after I heard of your faith*" (1:15; emphasis added), seems to confirm that Paul was unfamiliar with his audience.

The discussion of the mystery of God (1:9) leads Paul to repeat some of his earlier discussion, again mentioning the salvation of the **Gentiles**: "That the Gentiles should be fellowheirs, and of the same body, and partakers of his promise in **Christ** by the gospel" (3:6).

Paul's hope, as expressed in this chapter, is that all men (Jew and Gentile) shall see that God has reached out to create a new people (3:9–10), that all might "have boldness and access" to the Lord **Jesus** Christ (3:12), and that the Saints would not "faint" at learning of Paul's tribulations (3:13). This threefold prayer encapsulates the gospel Paul taught, namely that the foundation of the new dispensation in Christ was built upon unity, free and open access to God, and the example of the **apostles**. These three things would lead the Saints "to know the love of Christ, which passeth knowledge, that ye might be filled with all the fulness of God" (3:19). This endowment of love is much greater than the **Gnostic** speculation alluded to again in this chapter (3:10) and may represent Paul's way of comparing intellectual conversion with spiritual conversion, the latter being almost beyond description with a concluding hint: "world without end. Amen" (3:21).

The phrase "world without end" is somewhat awkwardly rendered in the King James Version; from the Greek it could be more simply translated, "through all generations of eternity forever, Amen." The word *world* is a holdover from the Douay-Rheims translation (New Testament completed in A.D. 1582) and does not appear in the Greek text, although it does attempt to translate a somewhat redundant phrase. Paul concludes this section by looking forward to the eternity where Christ will rule forever and where Jews and Gentiles will be fellow-heirs of the promises of God (3:6).

For the Perfecting of the Saints
EPHESIANS 4:1–16

Elaborating on his plea for unity among Jews and **Gentiles** in the **Church,** Paul draws on his own experiences as a way to express his sincerity. Contextually, his teachings, "There is one body, and one Spirit . . . one Lord, one faith, one **baptism**, one God and Father of all" (Ephesians 4:4–6), are to be interpreted initially as encouragement to work toward harmony in the branch. Paul here admonishes the Saints to see that there is one body (the Church) and only one baptism providing entry into the Church of God. Gentiles are baptized in the same way that Jews are, which Paul sees as confirmation of "the unity of the Spirit" (4:3).

Paul explains that to maintain that unity, God "gave some, **apostles**; and some, prophets; and some, evangelists; and some, pastors and teachers; for the perfecting of the saints, for the work of the ministry, for the edifying of the body of **Christ**" (4:11–12). This statement is not a comprehensive description of the **priesthood** offices in the first century or in the modern era but instead a general description of the purpose of priesthood and Church government. The offices listed are given to perfect the Saints and to edify the body of Christ. Most of the offices are recognizable because the modern term is the same as the ancient one. The office of "pastor" is that of overseer or **bishop**, while an "evangelist" in its ancient sense is a person who declares the gospel or who evangelizes (Greek, *euangelizō*, "to declare the good news"). In a modern sense, the term "evangelist" could apply to a patriarch as one who declares the good news through a blessing.

Verse 13 is constructed in a way to suggest that the offices of the priesthood are given in mortality *until* (KJV, "till") "we all come in the unity of the faith, and of the knowledge of the **Son of God**, unto a perfect man, unto the measure of the stature of the fulness of Christ" (4:13). This temporal aspect of the priesthood is fundamental to Paul's understanding, with the added explanation that the priesthood also enables us to avoid doctrinal heresies and instead teach "the truth in love" (4:14–15). Eventually the priesthood will lead to the body being "fitly joined together" (4:16; see also

2:21). Probably more than any other author in the New Testament, Paul interprets the priesthood as a temporal entity given to mankind to give life to God's kingdom on earth. This emphasis on the earthly role of the priesthood does not undermine the eternal aspect of priesthood, but only reinforces Paul's point of emphasis that the priesthood helps bring unity to God's kingdom to the earth.

Counsel to Be Faithful
EPHESIANS 4:17–5:20

Paul exhorts those who are newly baptized members of the **Church**, "that ye henceforth walk not as other **Gentiles** walk, in the vanity of their mind" (Ephesians 4:17). His counsel to them is practical, with an emphasis on solving general problems, unlike many of his previous letters where he dealt with very specific issues in the branches. His counsel focuses on the need to create a unified community rather than on issues of individual sin. Many of the principles he teaches are introduced with a logical explanation and compose verses 19 through 32.

Chapter 5 continues the list of items of exhortation, again focusing on what appear in many instances to be obvious points of counsel. The underlying implications of these very general suggestions are that Gentiles had not been raised to think in these ways and that their previous upbringing might actually encourage them to idealize other lifestyles. Using the language of Christ as the replacement **sacrifice** for our sins, Paul asks that the Saints also sacrifice their former lives of sin. Some of the things Paul condemns may be common descriptions of Gentile wickedness of the day, but it is also likely that Paul had some knowledge that these sinful behaviors were rife among the Saints. For example, "For it is a shame even to speak of those things which are done of them in secret" (5:12) appears to be a generalization of Gentile behavior, whereas "And be not drunk with wine, wherein is excess" (5:18) offers specific counsel.

The Word of Wisdom (D&C 89) is a modern revelation given to counter problems facing the Latter-day Saints. In the first century, wine containing alcohol was in common usage, with the alcohol serving to purify otherwise unhealthy water. Paul's prohibition against the use of wine was not intended to prevent the ancient Saints from drinking it altogether; rather, he desired to prevent drunkenness or excessive drinking. In our day and age, when water supplies are clean and filtered, it is not necessary to add alcohol to cleanse it. Elsewhere in the New Testament, drunkenness is also prohibited (Galatians 5:21; 1 Corinthians 6:10; 1 Timothy 3:3).

Husbands and Wives
EPHESIANS 5:21–33

Paul's advice to husbands and wives encourages mutual submission: "submitting yourselves one to another in the fear of God" (Ephesians 5:21); and though Paul also encourages wives to submit to their husbands and children to submit to their fathers, the framework for this advice is mutual care and concern for the other. The structure of a perfect marriage is described in terms of **Christ's** relationship to the Church (5:23). Just as Christ serves as a loving Savior, leading and guiding his children to perfection, so should a man love, lead, and guide his family.

A husband is to "love [his wife], even as Christ also loved the church, and gave himself for it" (5:25), rather than pursue a selfish agenda based on worldly lusts without regard for those entrusted to his care. Eventually Christ will present the Church "not having spot, or wrinkle, or any such thing; but that it should be holy and without blemish" (5:27), which is a model for the family as well.

Paul also instructs fathers to treat their families as well as they would "their own bodies" (5:28). In case it might appear that the counsel is entirely for fathers, Paul also reminds Church members that "we are members of his body, of his flesh, and of his bones" (5:30), implying that spouses share responsibility in the creation of this unspotted family unit. Quoting Genesis 2:24 (5:31), Paul teaches a mystery, namely that Christ's relationship to the Church is a perfect example of a harmonious and righteous marriage.

Counsel to Children and Servants
Ephesians 6:1–9

The previous discussion regarding husbands and wives is now applied to children and servants. The advice to children is based on the commandment of Exodus 20:12 and points out that it is the first with a promise, "that thy days may be long upon the land which the Lord thy God giveth thee," which Paul interprets as a present reality: "That it may be well with thee, and thou mayest live long on the earth" (Ephesians 6:3). Fathers are given counsel on rearing children that they "provoke not your children to wrath: but bring them up in the nurture and admonition of the Lord" (6:4). Because of the large number of slaves and servants in the Roman world and the large number of slaves who converted to Christianity (many of Paul's converts bear slave names), it is natural that Paul address their situation as well. He encourages them to be obedient to their masters, "not with eye-service, as menpleasers; but as the servants of **Christ**" (6:6), implying that they should offer genuine and heartfelt service and not simply go through the external motions of servitude. With an open perspective on the equality of mankind, Paul remarks, "Knowing that your Master also is in heaven; neither is there respect of persons with him" (6:9).

Put on the Whole Armor of God
Ephesians 6:10–24

Paul concludes with language that is again reminiscent of Gnosticism ("against principalities, against powers, against the rulers of the darkness of this world, against spiritual wickedness in high places" [Ephesians 6:12]), suggesting that his counsel has again turned to the intellectual threats the Saints would face. This pseudo-intellectualism (Gnosticism) grew into a major movement within early Christianity and in some instances certainly influenced the doctrine of the **Church** in the second century and later. It became an all-encompassing concern for some of the early patristic writers, and from **Gnostic** records that have survived (see, for example, the late

Gnostic document *The Gospel of Truth*) it is obvious that they had many followers and interested readers. Against this intellectual movement, Paul encouraged the Saints to "put on the whole armour of God" (6:11).

The armor of God is intended to help us ward off the threats of heresy or, perhaps more specifically, losing sight of what is most important—**Christ**—and becoming converted to a worldly interpretation. To aid the Saints in this struggle, Paul teaches simple, life-saving truths that have also a broader application to withstanding the onslaughts of the adversary: "Stand therefore, *having your loins girt about with truth,* and *having on the breastplate of righteousness;* and your *feet shod with the preparation of the gospel of peace;* above all, taking *the shield of faith,* wherewith ye shall be able to quench all the fiery darts of the wicked. And take *the helmet of salvation,* and *the sword of the Spirit,* which is the word of God: *praying always* with all prayer and supplication in the Spirit, and *watching thereunto with all perseverance* and supplication for all saints" (6:14–18; emphasis added). It is telling that Paul does not answer the questions raised by Gnostics in a point-by-point manner but instead counsels obedience in truth and prayer, which in turn will help the faithful discern between truth and error.

Paul closes the epistle by asking that the Saints communicate to him through Tychicus, who would apparently bear the report of their well-being back to Paul wherever he was imprisoned. The mention of "our affairs" reveals that Paul was not alone in his imprisonment, or at least that he had open contact with the branch of the Saints nearby, who may have been known to the recipients of this letter (Ephesians 1:1–2). Paul looks forward to his freedom in the closing lines, hoping that he may again preach the gospel and "open my mouth boldly" (6:19). These hints suggest that wherever he may have been imprisoned at the time of writing, he had not received a condemning sentence, thus suggesting the early part of the imprisonment at Caesarea Maritima, his first weeks or months in **Rome**, or perhaps another unknown imprisonment.

8

PHILIPPIANS

Paul visited Philippi on his second mission, and his work there constitutes the first missionary work in Europe. Philippi was a Roman colony where **Latin** was the official language, although the indigenous residents would also have spoken Greek, the language of Paul. The colony was inhabited by expatriates from Italy, likely former soldiers who had fought in the Roman civil wars of 44 B.C. Luke records that Paul was imprisoned at Philippi, the result of a dispute over Jewish sensitivities (Acts 16:24–30).

Introduction

PHILIPPIANS 1:1–2

Paul and Timothy wrote the letter to the Philippians, which should help to date the letter, but the reference to Paul's imprisonment (Philippians 1:7) and to the "palace" (Greek, *praitorion*, 1:13; see also 4:22) make it difficult to determine precisely when Paul was in Roman imprisonment. The palace refers to the residence of the local Roman official and need not be interpreted as an imprisonment in **Rome**. It is difficult to know whether Paul would follow the usage of the term as it appears in the Gospels, or whether he would have used it in the general sense (Mark 15:16).

The reference to "the bishops and **deacons**" gives the impression that Paul was writing from a place where the **Church** was well established and where there were multiple bishops. By the time of this writing, which is estimated to be around A.D. 60, there were very few known regions of the Church where this would have been possible.

Thanksgiving
PHILIPPIANS 1:3–11

As is his custom in his other epistles, Paul begins the letter with a customary thanksgiving that touches upon his previous work in the city (Philippians 1:4–5) and the Saints' concern for Paul's well-being. The tone of the letter suggests that Paul wished to convey his thanks for providing financial assistance (4:15–18) and to update them on his current situation (1:19–25). Some of the wording suggests a personal and intimate concern for the Saints in Philippi: "How greatly I long after you all in the bowels of **Jesus Christ**" (1:8).

Paul Discusses His Own Death
PHILIPPIANS 1:12–2:5

While imprisoned, Paul had the opportunity to either make a thoroughgoing defense against the charges brought against him or not to answer the charges and suffer the punishment given. It is logical to assume that most would defend themselves against false accusations and to at least attempt to obtain their freedom. But in this instance, Paul reports, "I am in a strait betwixt two" (Philippians 1:23). The charges against Paul had to have been based on some matter of Jewish law or practice because the preaching of the gospel furthered the hostility against him. In fact, when his enemies realized this effect, they endeavored to heighten the tension of the situation: "*And many of the brethren* in the Lord, waxing confident by my bonds, are much more bold to speak the word without fear. *Some indeed preach* **Christ** even of envy and strife; and some also of good will" (1:14–15; emphasis added). Paul ascribes these malicious desires to "the brethren," indicating that the problems he faced arose within the **Church** and not from outsiders interested in doing him harm: "*The one preach Christ* of contention, not sincerely, *supposing to add affliction to my bonds*" (1:16; emphasis added).

Given the choice of defending himself or letting the accusations stand, Paul shares his personal feelings that perhaps dying would be preferable: "For to me to live is Christ, and to die is gain," (1:21) and "having a desire to depart, and to be with Christ; which is far better: nevertheless to abide in the flesh is more needful for you" (1:23–24). There may have been many reasons that Paul considered not defending himself, and in the end he did choose life over an unjust punishment. Unfortunately, we do not know whether his defense was successful, but only that he chose life: "I know that I shall abide and continue with you all for your furtherance and joy of faith" (1:25). His sincere desire to live notwithstanding, apocryphal texts suggest that the **apostle** did eventually suffer martyrdom, probably in **Rome** toward the end of Nero's reign (c. A.D. 64–66).

Paul hopes that despite his incarceration he will receive news from the Philippians, particularly that they have not feared their adversaries (1:28). He even remarks dryly that when their enemies sense fear, they assume that fear is an "evident token of perdition" (1:28). Paul's adversaries are similarly challenged in Joseph Smith's translation of this verse through the change, "And in nothing terrified by your adversaries: *who reject the gospel*, which *bringeth on them destruction; but you who receive the gospel*, salvation, and that of God" (JST changes in italics).

The "consolation of Christ" or the love that he brings is Paul's expressed hope in the opening verses of chapter 5. Paul calls for an end of divisions and strife and expresses the need to live a Zion principle: "Look not every man on his own things, but every man also on the things of others" (2:4). In his later epistles, Paul frequently longs for a Zion community, perhaps because the early **Church's** attempt failed and perhaps also because of the continued divisions in the communities he founded.

An Early Christian Hymn

PHILIPPIANS 2:6–11

The origin of this hymn is unknown, and textually it is very unlikely that Paul is the author. Rather, it appears that Paul has included this hymn in the text of his epistle because of what it expresses about **Jesus Christ**. The hymn probably originated in the Jerusalem or Galilean community of Saints from the first decades after the Resurrection, and it envisions Christ as a co-heir with God the Father. Such hymns were common, and the author of the Gospel of John also included a hymn with commentary in the opening verses of that Gospel (John 1:1–18; Colossians 1:15–20; Hebrews 1:1–4; 1 Timothy 3:16). Some of the language or concepts are derived from Isaiah 53, which appears to have provided a starting point for the author's inspiration. One reason that Paul includes it here in his letter is that it emphasizes the exaltation of Jesus Christ as well as the centrality of Christ in the gospel: "And that every tongue should confess that Jesus Christ is Lord" (Philippians 2:11). Although the hymn is simple, its poetic structure sets it apart from the surrounding context, and it offers profound commentary on the roles of both the Father and Son.

Paul Sends Missionaries to Philippi

PHILIPPIANS 2:12–30

Paul's personal concern for the welfare of the Philippian Saints is expressed in this section as he deliberates sending Timotheus (Philippians 2:19) and Epaphroditus (2:25). Paul has obviously been absent for some time and is pleased to learn the Saints have done well without him and that they have remained true to the faith (2:12–16). Paul's trusted companion Timothy is with him, and Paul hopes to be able to send him soon. His remarks concerning Timothy, "For I have no man likeminded," reveal the apostle's trust in him (2:20). Apparently Timothy was either to assist in Paul's defense ("Him therefore I hope to send presently, so soon as I shall see how it will go with me"; 2:23), or Paul wanted him near when the verdict was given ("if I be offered"; 2:17).

Paul also considered sending Epaphroditus, another traveling companion who is otherwise unknown. Epaphroditus had been sick and unable to visit Philippi to check on the Saints there, and Paul chastised the Philippian Saints because Epaphroditus had supported Paul financially when others would not (2:30).

Paul's Israelite Heritage
PHILIPPIANS 3:1–21

Even though the letter has been almost entirely positive up to this point, Paul apparently is aware of some opposition to the ministry in that city. Specifically, he challenges those who claim Jewish heritage as a basis for their authority, specifically those who require **circumcision** (Philippians 3:3). Paul's words to this group are harsh—"Beware of dogs" (3:2)—and reveal that the disunity he referenced in the first part of the epistle was real. The Greek noun corresponding to "concision" in the phrase "beware of the concision" (3:2) is difficult to translate and means something along the lines of mutilating themselves with reference to circumcision.

Realizing the futility of basing one's authority on heritage, Paul ironically recounts his own to show that he could have done the same when he was with them. Paul specifically mentions his lineage (Benjamin), his school of thought (a **Pharisee**), his righteousness, and his former life as a persecutor of the **Church**. Even though his own heritage is superlative in comparison, Paul remarks, "But what things were gain to me, those I counted loss for **Christ**" and even refers to his past as "dung" (3:7–8), using a word that would have been offensive to some in order to emphasize his point.

What mattered most to Paul was knowing **Jesus** Christ experientially and having "fellowship of his sufferings" (3:10) so that in knowing Jesus he might "attain unto the resurrection of the dead" (3:11). Having considered his own demise, Paul now openly considers the eternal weight of glory that awaits him, hoping to achieve exaltation: *"not as though I had already* *attained, either were already perfect*" (3:12; emphasis added). Even though at this stage Paul has devoted nearly his entire adult life to building up the kingdom and serving as an **apostle** of the Lord Jesus Christ, he still hopes and yearns for a glorious postmortal existence. This hope drives Paul to think of heaven in a real, physical sense, a thought that is underlined in his previous statement that dying would be far better (1:23).

Those who have made claims of authority based on their Israelite heritage are to be marked (3:17) and the members are encouraged to follow Paul's example instead. Those who have been marked will be destroyed, "whose end is destruction" (3:19), while the faithful have their "conversation . . . in heaven; from whence also we look for the Saviour" (3:20). Revealing his own hope in the resurrected body that he would receive in contrast to his own aging body, Paul says, God "shall change our vile body, that it may be fashioned like unto his glorious body, according to the working whereby he is able even to subdue all things unto himself" (3:21). The resurrected body is both glorious and powerful, able to subdue the physical creation as Jesus had done.

Conclusion

PHILIPPIANS 4:1–23

The final chapter is devoted entirely to greetings and updates; Paul addresses four male traveling companions, Euodias, Syntyche, "true yokefellow" (perhaps the name Syzyge), and Clement (Philippians 4:2–3). These fellow laborers are to help care for "those women which laboured with me in the gospel" (4:3), but the names of these women are nowhere given.

The awkward translation "be careful for nothing" (4:6) could be more simply rendered "do not be anxious about anything" (NIV 4:6) and in everything be prayerful. Paul's reflection on what the hearts of Christians ought to be set upon provides the foundation for Article of Faith 13. This thought forms a bookend to the beginning of the epistle where Paul longs for harmony among the Saints and an end to divisions, which he realizes may only be achieved in the hereafter.

Paul also thanks the Philippian Saints for providing financial assistance to him: "Now at the last your care of me hath flourished again; wherein ye were also careful, but ye lacked opportunity" (4:10). It is not known why they stopped providing for him, and it may be that his intent was to thank them for providing for him again and for being willing to provide for him when they lacked the opportunity to do so. Regarding the physical/temporal setbacks he had experienced, Paul shrugs them off, saying, "I have learned, in whatsoever state I am, therewith to be content" (4:11), thus forgiving the Philippians for any suffering that resulted from a lack of assistance. Verse 15 provides one piece of information that is not found elsewhere in the New Testament, namely that Paul's mission into Greece was financed, at least in part, by the Philippian branch of the **Church** (4:15–16).

The letter concludes with a typical note about those who joined with Paul in sending the epistle, as well as the intriguing mention of "**Caesar's** household" (4:22). Oftentimes this reference is used to place the letter in **Rome**, even within the imperial palace of Nero. This view, however, is challenged by the fact that this generic reference may just as easily refer to a local governor's palace and not specifically to the residence of the emperor in Rome. Some of those living within Caesar's palace, which would include workers and slaves, had joined the Christian faith and now joined with Paul in saluting the Philippian Saints.

9

COLOSSIANS

Paul's letter to the Saints at Colossae is an important source in helping us understand his situation around A.D. 60 and the continuing revelation regarding **Jesus Christ**—who he is and what he has done.

The letter to the Colossians was most likely written before A.D. 61 because there is no reference to the catastrophic earthquake that destroyed many towns and cities, including Colossae, in the Lycus Valley in that year. It is uncertain whether Colossae was rebuilt after the disaster. There is a clear indication in the letter itself that Paul was in prison when he wrote (Colossians 4:3, 10, 18). If indeed Colossians was written during Paul's Roman imprisonment, which the book of Acts indicates as taking place between A.D. 60 and 62, then he would have had about a year to write this letter before receiving word concerning the effects of the destructive earthquake.

Introduction

COLOSSIANS 1:1–14

Paul's missionary strategy included establishing a mission center and then sending the good news from the center to the region round about through co-workers. In this instance, Paul established a mission center at Ephesus in **Asia** and then sent co-workers to the major cities of the Lycus Valley, including Laodicea, Hierapolis, and Colossae. Apparently, Paul sent "Epaphras our dear fellowservant" to begin the work in Colossae (1:7). In this letter, Paul reveals that the Saints in Colossae, as those at Laodicea, had "not seen my face in the flesh" (2:1).

As was customary, Paul and Timothy begin this letter with a standard greeting (1:1–2). Addressed to the "saints and faithful brethren in Christ" at Colossae, this epistle has Paul commenting on his calling as an **"apostle** of Jesus Christ by the will of God." Timothy, on the other hand, is identified simply as "our brother" (1:1).

Paul and Timothy's prayer of thanksgiving (1:3–8) informs us of the beginning of the work in Colossae by Epaphras, whose efforts brought "forth fruit" (1:6). Nevertheless, Paul and Timothy were worried about the situation in Colossae and had been praying for the Saints (1:9). The letter also reveals that there were some problems in the branch, although not as significant perhaps as those in Galatia (2:8–23).

A Hymn to Christ

COLOSSIANS 1:15–20

Continuing the Jewish tradition of singing praise to the Lord, the **disciples** of **Jesus** incorporated such hymns in their gatherings (Matthew 26:30). Later in the letter, Paul and Timothy admonish the Colossians to "let the word of **Christ** dwell in you richly in all wisdom; teaching and admonishing one another in *psalms and hymns and spiritual songs, singing* with grace in your hearts to the Lord. And whatsoever ye do in word or deed, do all in the name of the Lord Jesus, *giving thanks* to God and the Father by him (3:16–17; emphasis added).

Fortunately, at least five early Christian hymns have survived from the first century (John 1:1–18; Philippians 2:6–11; Colossians 1:15–20; Hebrews 1:1–4; 1 Timothy 3:16), providing us an important window into the earliest Christian sacrament meetings. For example, the hymn preserved in Colossians focuses on Jesus as "the firstborn of every creature" (1:15); "the firstborn from the dead" (1:18); who "is the image of the invisible God" (1:15); through whom "all things [were] created" (1:16) and "by him all things consist" (1:17). "He is the head of the body, the **church**" (1:18). The hymn reveals that "it pleased the Father that in him should all fulness dwell" (1:19). Finally, the unknown author of this hymn says that God has worked to "reconcile all things unto himself" through Jesus Christ (1:20).

In this breathtaking vision of Jesus Christ, Paul and Timothy reveal much about how the early Christians understood the risen Lord's place in the cosmos. However, neither Paul nor Timothy believe that they are passing on new insights about Jesus Christ to the Saints in Colossae. They believe this vision of the exalted Lord is consistent with what they have already taught: "As *you have therefore received* Christ Jesus the Lord, so walk ye in him: rooted and built up in him, and stablished in the faith, *as ye have been taught*, abounding herein with thanksgiving" (2:6–7; emphasis added).

The Risen Lord

COLOSSIANS 1:21–2:23

Paul reminds the Saints at Colossae that they have been "alienated and enemies," but now are "reconciled" (Colossians 1:21). However, they needed to "continue in the faith grounded and settled, and be not moved away from the hope of the gospel" (1:23). Following his thinking in Romans, Paul seems to hint that all creation also testifies of God's plan, it being manifest to all, but in this case "preached to every creature which is under heaven" (1:23; Romans 1:18–25).

In this section, Paul continues to focus on the blessings of the gospel, "which hath been hid from ages and generations" (1:26). In particular, Paul is interested in reminding them of the central role of **Jesus Christ**, "That their hearts might be comforted, being knit together in love, and unto all riches of the full assurance of understanding, to the acknowledgement of the mystery of God, and of the Father, and of Christ; in whom are hid all the treasures of wisdom and knowledge" (2:2–3).

412

Issues at Hand

COLOSSIANS 2:8–23

Paul and Timothy warn and encourage the Saints in Colossae to "beware lest any man spoil you through philosophy and vain deceit, after the tradition of men, after the rudiments of the world, and not after **Christ**" (Colossians 2:8). They add, "For in [Christ] dwelleth all the fulness of the Godhead bodily. And ye are complete in him, which is the head of all principality and power" (2:9–10). Paul and Timothy assure them that they have been "buried with him in **baptism**, wherein also ye are risen with him through the faith of the operation of God, who hath raised him from the dead" (2:12).

It is important to know, as noted on several occasions within the letter, that God has forgiven them, through **Jesus** Christ, of all their sins (Colossians 1:14, 20, 22). To emphasize this reality, Paul and Timothy use a metaphor of a condemned man who carries a placard listing his crimes to the site of execution. When the prisoner arrives at the site, the soldiers take the sign and nail it to the cross (Mark 15:26). In this context, Paul and Timothy say that Jesus has "forgiven you all trespasses; blotting out the handwriting of ordinances that was against us, which was contrary to us, and took it out of the way, *nailing it to his cross*" (2:13–14; emphasis added).

Paul and Timothy then turn their attention specifically to the issues at hand. For a number of years, commentators have focused their attention on the material in this section in an effort to identify why Paul and Timothy wrote the letter in the first place; we know that they were concerned and had prayed for the Saints (1:9). New Testament scholars have often referred to the crisis as the "Colossian heresy." Interestingly, there have been more than forty different proposals set forth to explain the threat. However, given that the letter lacks the strong condemnations found in Galatians and 2 Corinthians 10–13, some commentators have called for a reexamination of the text in context of what is known about first-century religious practice in **Asia** Minor. There have been remarkable advances through archeological and textual discoveries during the past few decades that have illuminated the world of the New Testament in ways never conceived before by scholars. Given the current state of affairs, many commentators have rejected earlier attempts to identify the "Colossian heresy," suggesting instead that the Saints, who are continually praised in the letter, are under pressure from an outside source—most likely a local Jewish synagogue where some of the Jewish-Christians and God-fearers had worshipped. In this case, the older established institution attempted to marginalize the Saints by mocking their faith. To counter this attack, Paul and Timothy urge the Saints, "Let no man therefore judge you in meat, or in drink, or in respect of an holyday, or of the new moon, or of the **sabbath** days" (2:16). This hostile group is teaching the "commandments and doctrines of men" (2:22), which immediately brings to mind Jesus' own teaching regarding the tradition of the elders (Mark 7:7). The description of "philosophy" presented in this section fits within the typical Jewish concerns of the first century. It should be recalled that Josephus and other Jewish writers used the term *philosophy* to describe Judaism. The worry about what one eats, drinks, and touches (2:21) is typical of Jewish concerns about ritual purity and food laws that govern life. Paul and Timothy's mention of **circumcision** also adds weight to the argument (2:11). The only real challenge to this reconstruction is the KJV phrase, "worshipping of angels" (2:18). Obviously, observant Jews did not worship angels—they were a strictly monotheistic religion; however, some translators have suggested that the phrase should be translated "worship rendered by angels," suggesting that what is envisioned here is the desire to worship with the angels in heaven—something not totally foreign to Jewish thought in the first century.

Exhortations

COLOSSIANS 3:1–17

Paul and Timothy exhort the Saints at Colossae to "seek those things which are above" (Colossians 3:1). The theme of putting off the "dead" man and woman continues throughout this section (3:10). They encourage their readers to "mortify therefore your members which are upon the earth; fornication, uncleanness, inordinate affection, evil concupiscence, and covetousness, which is idolatry" (3:5) and add, "But now ye also *put off* all these; anger, wrath, malice, blasphemy, filthy communication out of your mouth. Lie not one to another, seeing that ye have put off the old man with his deeds (3:8–9; emphasis added). At this point Paul and Timothy promote their efforts to "put on therefore, as the elect of God, holy and beloved, bowels of mercies, kindness, humbleness of mind, meekness, longsuffering; Forbearing one another, and forgiving one another, if any man have a quarrel against any: even as **Christ** forgave you, so also do ye. And above all these things put on charity, which is the bond of perfectness" (3:12–14).

Household Rules

COLOSSIANS 3:18–4:1

In this section we find one of the earliest examples of a so-called Christian household code, or rules governing a Christian home. Some scholars posit that the code may have been added later or at least adapted by a second-generation Christian scribe. Unless the original letter or a very early copy of Colossians is found, such speculation is just that, speculation. Nevertheless, it may be of interest to consider such a proposal as we study the instructions.

Here Paul and Timothy ask wives to "submit yourselves unto your own husbands" (3:18); husbands are enjoined to "love your wives" (3:19); and children are commanded to "obey your parents in all things" (3:20). However, fathers (and mothers) are also commanded to "provoke not your children to anger" (3:21).

In one of the most morally challenging aspects of the household code, Paul and Timothy command slaves (*doulos* in Greek, which is often translated "servant" in the KJV) to "obey in all things your masters according to the flesh" (3:22). Even with the command to slave owners to "give unto your servants that which is just and equal; knowing that ye also have a Master in heaven" (4:1), the injunction seems anti-gospel to the modern reader. Additionally, Paul and Timothy's apparent support for slavery has troubled many Christians for centuries. Used to justify slavery in the Americas by pro slavery preachers, teachers, and practitioners, this passage is fraught with difficulties of interpretation and remains difficult to understand.

Slavery was a fundamental and integral aspect of ancient society. It was ubiquitous; every culture, society, and civilization practiced some form of it in the past. Unlike American slavery, ancient slavery was not based on ethnicity and in many cases was not a lifelong experience. This does not minimize the harshness of the institution, which obviously was abusive in most respects. Nevertheless, modern readers must attempt to look beyond the American experience and understand the context of Paul and Timothy's teachings on the subject. As reflected in their references to wives and children, they believed that slaves formed part of the **Church** and were full participants in the blessing of the "good news." As we should recall, Paul and Timothy previously argued, "Where there is neither Greek nor Jew, **circumcision** nor uncircumcision, Barbarian, Scythian, *bond nor free:* but **Christ** is all, and in all" (3:11; emphasis added; compare Galatians 3:28). Paul and Timothy are infusing into the common understanding of household order a new Christian spirit or ethic as they emphasize the part the Lord plays in all relationships (3:18, 20, 22, 23, 24, 4:1).

Greetings and Salutations
COLOSSIANS 4:1–17

Paul continues his exhortations to the Colossian Saints by reminding them of his own circumstances: "Withal praying also for us, that God would open unto us a door of utterance, to speak the mystery of **Christ,** *for which I am also in bonds* (Colossians 4:3; emphasis added). This has led many commentators to assume that Paul was in prison and, given the probable time period when Paul wrote this letter, that he was incarcerated in **Rome.** Two additional evidences that support this thesis are found at the end of the letter. First, among those with Paul was "Aristarchus my *fellowprisoner*" (4:10; emphasis added), and second, Paul pleaded with the Colossians to "Remember *my bonds* [chains]" (4:18; emphasis added).

The main purpose for this closing was to inform the Colossians that he had sent his letter with Tychicus ("beloved brother," "faithful minister," and "fellowservant in the Lord") and Onesimus ("faithful and beloved brother, who is one of you"). Paul added that they will "make known unto you all things which are done here" (4:7, 9). Additionally, the mention of Onesimus, who is the subject of Paul's letter to Philemon, suggests that both letters were written about the same time.

Paul then passes along greetings from several people who are with him in Rome—people Paul would assume they knew. They include Aristarchus (noted above), Mark (the son of Mary, Barnabas's sister), **Jesus** (identified as Justus), Epaphras, who has "great zeal for you, and them that are in Laodicea, and them in Hierapolis. Luke, the beloved physician and Demas, greet you" (4:13–14).

Paul also asks the Colossians to "salute the brethren which are in Laodicea, and Nymphas, and the **church** which is in his house" (4:15). Additionally, he wants them to exchange letters (4:16). Apparently Paul had written a letter to Laodicea, now lost. In one final request, Paul asks Archippus to fulfill his assignment of the Lord (4:17). Modern readers are left to wonder what the assignment was and whether or not Archippus ever completed his task.

Paul's Own Hand

COLOSSIANS 4:18

As was often his custom from the beginning (Galatians 6:11–18), Paul would finish dictating his letter to a secretary and then take pen to papyrus to add a personal, handwritten note: "The salutation by the hand of me Paul. Remember my bonds. Grace be with you. Amen" (Colossians 4:18).

10

FIRST THESSALONIANS

The short first letter to the Thessalonians is perhaps the earliest surviving Christian writing (Galatians and James are also very early) and predates the Gospels by perhaps as much as two decades or more.

Introduction

1 THESSALONIANS 1:1

The early date of writing makes this epistle quite important in understanding the growth of the earliest Christian branches. Paul has already made converts in Macedonia and here reflects on his visit to Thessalonica while on his second mission. Timothy and Silas/Silvanus are with Paul, suggesting that perhaps this letter was written from Corinth (1 Thessalonians 3:1–2).

Most of this letter is written to express thanksgiving for the grace of God in accepting **Gentiles** into the fold, "Knowing, brethren beloved, your election of God" (1:4), although the latter portion deals with a question relating to the timing of the Second Coming of the Lord. Paul's positive demeanor is in sharp contrast to the hostility shown to Paul while he served in Thessalonica and reveals Paul's enduring hope of eventually achieving a positive outcome (Acts 17:1–14).

Thanksgiving

1 THESSALONIANS 1:2–10

Following Greco-Roman letter-writing conventions, Paul includes in his introduction an expression of thanks. Often this would be expressed directly to the recipient, but here he thanks God for the good that has occurred in Thessalonica. Paul mentions specifically that the Saints "became followers of us, and of the Lord" (1 Thessalonians 1:6), suggesting that their early teaching in the city focused on creating a unique Christian ethic. The people's reception of the gospel led to "much affliction," which, following the description provided in the book of Acts, was instigated by the Jews in the city. The opening lines also show that the Saints had an earnest expectation for the return of **Jesus Christ**: "And to wait for his Son from heaven" (1:10).

Saints Experience Persecution

1 THESSALONIANS 2:1–20

Referring to his imprisonment and beating at Philippi (Acts 16:19–24), Paul helps the Saints see that those who accept the gospel of **Jesus Christ** are persecuted. The believers' own experiences at the hands of the Jews in the city are akin to what Paul experienced in Philippi. This persecution is all the more startling because they taught the gospel without "guile" (1 Thessalonians 2:3) and without the use of "flattering words" (2:5). Paul here downplays the threat felt by the Jewish community, who likely saw the conversions to Christianity as cutting into their membership. Instead, Paul sees this as an inexplicable contradiction because they did not seek for glory but were sincere in their desire to help teach the truth, "So being affectionately desirous of you, we were willing to have imparted unto you, not the gospel of God only, but also our own souls, because ye were dear unto us" (2:8).

While in the city, Paul worked for his own support, which he specifically mentions, most likely as a sign of his sincerity ("we would not be chargeable unto any of you" [2:9]). He did receive financial assistance from other branches, and it is certain that he was not opposed to receiving help (Philippians 4:15–16). Moreover, Paul felt that his conduct in the city had been such that no one would want to harm him (2:10). These factors caused him to question why the Saints were then being persecuted.

That persecution had come at the hands of their "own countrymen" (2:14), which could mean either Jews or **Gentiles**. Acts indicates that the persecution originated in the Jewish community in the city, whereas the letter is addressed to Gentiles. The punctuation of the sentence describing their persecution is important to understanding what Paul intended to say: "For ye also have suffered like things of your own countrymen, even as they have of the Jews: who both killed the Lord Jesus, and their own prophets, and have persecuted us" (2:14–15). A colon or a comma following "Jews" creates a nonrestrictive clause indicating that all Jews persecuted the Lord; the absence of a comma or colon following "Jews" indicates a restrictive clause and thus Paul's intent to focus only on the Jews who killed the Lord. From the context, it seems that Paul was restricting his criticism and thus intended to say that the persecution the Saints in Thessalonica received was similar to what a few Jews did to the Lord Jesus.

Paul Sends Timothy to Thessalonica
1 THESSALONIANS 3:1–13

Because conditions were so dire when Paul left Thessalonica, he worried that subsequent to his departure, the Saints would experience persecution and then fall away. While at Athens (1 Thessalonians 3:1), Paul sent his trusted missionary companion Timothy back to the city to obtain a report. For some reason, Timothy was safe in the city but Paul was not (Acts 17:14). Before Paul wrote this epistle, he had received word back that the Saints had endured these persecutions faithfully (3:7).

The Gospel Paul Taught

1 Thessalonians 4:1–12

A brief outline of Paul's teachings can be found in this chapter, where he warns against fornication, against defrauding Christian brothers, against lust and wicked desires, while encouraging readers to aspire to holiness. In conjunction with these gospel principles, Paul also admonishes the Saints to follow the popular wisdom of the day: "And that ye study to be quiet, and to do your own business, and to work with your own hands, as we commanded you" (1 Thessalonians 4:11).

A Question Concerning the Second Coming

1 Thessalonians 4:13–18

Paul here addresses a concern about the timing of the Second Coming and how it would affect the deceased. In his response, Paul also reveals his own expectation that he would be alive to see the return of the Lord in glory, although the Joseph Smith Translation does change the wording in a way that suggests Paul did not expect to live until the Second Coming (1 Thessalonians 4:15, 17). The precise question Paul answers is unfortunately not preserved or even summarized clearly, but the concern appears to be whether the living would precede the dead in the resurrection or vice versa at the time of the Lord's return. Paul responds saying, "Them also which sleep [are dead] in **Jesus** will God bring with him" (4:14), thus indicating that the dead will descend with Jesus at his return. And then those "which are alive and remain unto the coming of the Lord shall not prevent them which are asleep" (4:15). In other words, the living will not precede (KJV, "prevent") the dead in the Resurrection, but rather will follow them. Paul includes himself among the living, saying, "We which are alive and remain" (4:15). The return of the Lord shall be signaled with a trump, and "then *we which are alive and remain* shall be caught up together with them in the clouds, to meet the Lord in the air: and so shall we ever be with the Lord" (4:17; emphasis added). The Joseph Smith Translation clarifies this verse to read: "Then *they who* are alive, shall be caught up together into the clouds *with them who remain*, to meet the Lord in the air; and so shall we be ever with the Lord" (4:17). Paul's response shows that he expected their kindred dead to return with the Lord and that the dead would not have to wait while the winding-down scenes of the earth's end unfolded. In concluding this chapter, Paul admonishes the Saints to "comfort one another with these words" (4:18), suggesting that the Thessalonian Saints had sought an answer to this question.

Conclusion
1 THESSALONIANS 5:1–28

Drawing a lesson from the preceding question on the timing of the Second Coming, Paul concludes by admonishing the Saints to be prepared at all times and in all seasons because "the day of the Lord so cometh as a thief in the night" (1 Thessalonians 5:2). The children of darkness will be caught off guard in the day of the Lord's return, but simple obedience will help the Saints, or the "children of light," be prepared (5:5). That Paul would discuss the return of the Lord so extensively in his earliest surviving epistle, and indeed in perhaps the earliest surviving Christian document, suggests that even after two decades, interest in the Lord's return was still high. Christians asked questions on this subject and sought answers on fairly detailed matters.

Using language similar to that of Ephesians 6:13–18, Paul encourages the Saints to put on the armor of God to prepare them for the time of the Lord's return (5:8). Specifically, Paul admonishes Church members to live in harmony one with another and to cherish those who labor as leaders among the branch (5:12). They are also supposed to warn the "unruly," suggesting that the Saints had experienced the same problems that are common to the **Church** in all dispensations. The Saints were to seek for the Spirit and "despise not prophesyings" (5:20), proving or testing "all things" (5:21) according to the words that Paul had delivered.

11

SECOND THESSALONIANS

The content of the second epistle sent to the Thessalonians by Paul, together with Silas/Silvanus and Timothy, is similar to the first, suggesting that the date of writing is very close to the time when the first Thessalonian epistle was written.

Introduction

2 THESSALONIANS 1:1

Second Thessalonians is a response to a report Paul had received, probably from Timothy. Paul suspected that someone had forged a letter in his name (2 Thessalonians 2:3), the contents of which appear to have had something to do with the timing of the Second Coming. Because Paul's first epistle to Thessalonica dealt with the subject of the time of the Second Coming, it may be that this was of perennial concern to the Saints there and that rampant speculation had led to the dispute discussed in chapter 2.

Thanksgiving

2 THESSALONIANS 1:2–12

Typical of his other epistles, Paul here begins his letter with words of thanksgiving, although this section also includes a warning to those who have troubled the Saints. Having heard of the faith of the Saints and the challenges they are facing, Paul writes, "Seeing it is a righteous thing with

God to recompense tribulation to them that trouble you" (2 Thessalonians 1:6). That Paul would include such a statement in his letter to the Saints suggests either that he felt such a reminder would comfort them or that some members had been caught up in the doctrinal dispute.

In structuring his thanksgiving, Paul reveals what had not been recorded elsewhere, namely that God would return in "flaming fire" and punish those who do not obey the gospel of **Jesus Christ** (1:8). Their punishment is described as "everlasting" (1:9), and hints at a larger contextualized understanding of the doctrine of the Second Coming. It is apparent that Paul's thanksgiving quickly gives way to frustration that someone would pervert the doctrine that he had taught while he was there and in his first epistle to the Thessalonians.

Events Related to the Second Coming
2 THESSALONIANS 2:1–17

At the heart of Paul's second epistle to the Thessalonian Saints is this section treating the issue of the timing of the Lord's return in glory and exploring the events that will precede it. Whether he had seen the letter or simply heard of one, Paul warns the Saints to be careful when receiving any letters "as from us" (2 Thessalonians 2:2). However the false information was disseminated, Paul considers the information deceptive (2:3). To set matters right, he tells his readers that the day of the Lord's coming will not occur until after there is an **apostasy** (Greek, *apostasia*, "mutiny" or "rebellion"). The King James Version places the phrase *"that day shall not come"* in italics, but the word *day* is the only word that should technically appear in italics. (Words in italics in the King James Version are words that either are supplied by the translators to make sense of the Greek or Hebrew text or are implied in the Greek or Hebrew but not actually written.)

Paul turns his attention to events that will precede the Lord's return, particularly the revealing of the son of perdition. Verses 3 and 4 constitute a single sentence, which reads in part, "the son of perdition; who opposeth and exalteth himself above all that is called God, or that is worshipped;

so that he as God sitteth in the **temple** of God, shewing himself that he is God" (2:3–4). Speaking of the revelation, or more technically the fall of the son of perdition, Paul speaks of him as a man of sin sitting in a temple of the Lord and pretending (KJV, "shewing") that he is God. Anciently the Jews recognized the desecration of the Jerusalem temple under Antiochus IV Epiphanes and the Roman general Titus as a desolating sacrilege. Paul here seems to be describing a similar future event, which others have seen as a modern natural disaster.

Paul's purpose in mentioning this matter is to forewarn the Saints in a way that they would be able to prepare for the Lord's return: "Remember ye not, that, when I was yet with you, I told you these things? And now ye know what withholdeth [remains] that he might be revealed in his time" (2:5–6). This event is one of the things that remains to be fulfilled prior to the Lord's return. Even though the sack of the Jerusalem temple was yet a future event when Paul wrote this epistle, it is not that event he had in mind because he also predicted an **apostasy** or rebellion that would precede the event he described, which would preclude the sack of the temple by the Romans in A.D. 70.

In the following verses, Paul also gives his interpretation of the timing of the event, telling his readers that "the mystery of iniquity doth already work" (2:7; see also JST, 2:7), indicating that he sensed the event was coming soon. Paul also noted his belief that **Satan** would come with power, signs and lying, suggesting that he had seen events that he chose not to relate in this epistle (JST, 2:9). For those who reject the Lord in the day of his return, Paul hints that "God shall send them strong delusion, that they should believe a lie" (2:11), although the "lie" here mentioned is not explained.

Paul's concluding verses in this section are intended to comfort those who had been troubled by those who had become caught up in speculation regarding the Second Coming. Rather than list events in a way that would help the Saints understand their progress toward that great event, Paul teaches them to focus on the gospel, standing fast in the traditions that he had taught, and the "everlasting consolation" that the Lord **Jesus Christ** gives (2:16).

Conclusion

2 THESSALONIANS 3:1–18

This short letter was written to answer one question, and now Paul swiftly concludes by giving thanks and admonishing the Saints to live faithfully. Paul continues to express concern over the persecution the Saints in Thessalonica were facing (2 Thessalonians 3:2–3), which appears to have been a consistent concern in that city (1 Thessalonians 2:1–20). Paul also encourages the Saints to be "patient waiting for **Christ**" (3:5), thus following up on his more detailed answer to their question with a subtle rejoinder that they wait instead of focus on the details of that event.

Although he does not specifically state it, Paul's advice in verse 6 implies that various doctrinal concerns have arisen as a result of the behavior of some of the members who are "disorderly" and who walk "not after the tradition which he received of us" (3:6). The singular "he" may imply that Paul had in mind a single individual, though he is not named. The **apostle** also encourages the Saints to work with their own hands (3:8), to earn their own living (3:8), to do things in an orderly way (3:10), to avoid being "busybodies" (3:11), and to do their work "with quietness" as they eke out their existence (3:12). This advice may be intended to describe a person opposite to the one Paul had in mind in verse 6 and to help the Saints see that this individual is leading them astray. His actions are probably here described in a negative way. As a word of warning, Paul counsels the Saints to "have no company with him, that he may be ashamed" (3:14).

Paul closes with a "salutation of Paul with mine own hand, which is the token in every epistle: so I write" (3:17), which is probably intended to refer to a scribal feature that would enable the Saints to distinguish his letter from forgeries. The nature of the scribal feature or signature that he had in mind is not known.

12

FIRST TIMOTHY

The three letters recorded in 1 and 2 Timothy and Titus are written to individuals and are known as the Pastoral Epistles because they deal with issues associated with caring for the **Church**, particularly the offices of **bishop** and **deacon**. Many scholars have questioned the authenticity of these three epistles, and indeed Paul does discuss matters in them that are not dealt with in his previous epistles. As with many academic theories, there is no way to either prove or disprove the authenticity of the epistles. Following the tradition of the Church from earliest times, there is no compelling reason to dismiss these epistles as forgeries, while at the same time it is wise to recognize that they do address matters that are not found in the other Pauline letters.

Introduction

1 TIMOTHY 1:1–3

In the opening lines of 1 Timothy, Paul addresses Timothy, his "own son in the faith," and recalls a time when Paul had encouraged him to stay in Ephesus (1 Timothy 1:2–3). The exact moment in Paul's ministry that this verse describes is not known, although it could come from a time after Luke concludes the narrative of Acts or from another moment in Paul's life that simply was not documented. Because Paul instructs Timothy on how to call a bishop, it is likely that Timothy was in a position in **Asia** Minor that required him to oversee the governance of the **Church** there. The office of bishop is not new in these epistles, although the description seems to imply that bishops are being newly called (3:1–11). Paul also specifically mentions Gnosticism in the epistle, the only explicit mention of this heresy in the New Testament, which may indeed be used to help date these epistles to the last years of Paul's ministry (6:20). For the modern reader, the letters are invaluable in helping us understand how Paul and others sought to lead a church on the verge of **apostasy**, while at the same time seeking to reconcile popular customs of the day with the tenets of the gospel.

Paul's Counsel to Timothy
1 TIMOTHY 1:4–20

In light of the personal **apostasy** of Hymenaeus and Alexander, Paul counsels Timothy to remain true and faithful, even though some have been excommunicated, or "delivered unto **Satan**" (1 Timothy 1:20). Paul's counsel takes a minor detour in verses 5 through 17, in which Paul recounts his own days of unbelief. The matter at hand, and perhaps by implication the nature of the apostasy of Hymenaeus and Alexander, is that "some" have endeavored to bring the **Church** back to the Jewish law, "desiring to be teachers of the law" (1:6–7). For those who live in the Spirit of the Lord, this back-stepping is unthinkable, and Paul teaches that the law is meant to correct the "ungodly" (1:9). Realizing that Paul had openly taught of the freedom associated with living the gospel (Romans 3:19–25), it is not surprising that he would say, "*Knowing this, that the law is not made for a righteous man*, but for the lawless and disobedient, for the ungodly and for sinners, for unholy and profane, for murderers of fathers and murderers of mothers, for manslayers, for whoremongers, for them that defile themselves with mankind, for menstealers, for liars, for perjured persons, and if there be any other thing that is contrary to sound doctrine" (1:9–10; emphasis added).

Paul's own thoughts on his life as a persecutor are different from what he had said previously. Now he is willing to call himself a "blasphemer," which blasphemy he committed "ignorantly in unbelief" (1:13).

In connection with being a blasphemer, Paul also counts himself among the "sinners; of whom I am chief" (1:15). When he speaks of being a sinner, he must have meant sinning against the gospel or the Lord **Jesus Christ**, a conclusion that he had not arrived at previously. In Philippians, he had referred to his life before his conversion as "blameless" (Philippians 3:6). The final three verses of the chapter return to Paul's counsel to Timothy to remain true and to avoid the "shipwreck" associated with losing the faith (1:19).

Responsibilities of Christians
1 Timothy 2:1–15

Continuing his exhortation to Timothy, Paul here counsels him in civic and religious matters. Paul specifically counsels Timothy to pray "for kings, and for all that are in authority" (1 Timothy 2:2) and enjoins the Saints to pray everywhere without doubting (2:8). Further, Paul counsels the women that they "adorn themselves in modest apparel" (2:9) and not "usurp authority over the man" (2:12).

Some of Paul's advice reflects the customs of his day, which he seeks to clarify using scriptural precedent. The custom in question is braided hair for women, which Paul recommends Christian women not wear because of cultural associations in the first century A.D. Also at issue is the wearing of costly jewelry (2:9). The matter, however, does not seem to be limited to wearing certain types of clothing that Paul deems offensive, but rather the usurpation of authority. Whether this was a widespread phenomenon or a specific heresy associated with the branches where Timothy presided is not known, but it is certain that Paul connects the challenge to authority with clothing and thus hints that the issue is not entirely a cultural bias.

The Offices of Bishop and Deacon
1 TIMOTHY 3:1–16

The office of a **bishop** (Greek, *episkopos*, "overseer") had already been established prior to the writing of 1 Timothy, as had the office of **deacon** (Greek, *diakonos*, "servant"). The instructions given regarding these two **priesthood** offices are probably intended for Timothy's sake because he had recently been placed in a position to oversee those who would be called as bishops and deacons. The modern dispensation of the fulness of times enjoys the unique position of gathering in aspects of previous dispensations so that in a way it is like every other dispensation, but no previous dispensation is exactly like it. With respect to the offices of the priesthood, the New Testament provides very little evidence that all of the modern offices of the priesthood were known in the meridian of time (or that they were strictly analogous to latter-day designations), although many are named (Matthew 10:2; Luke 10:1; Ephesians 4:11; 1 Timothy 2:7). That Paul here focuses only on the offices of bishop and deacon may suggest that the early **Church** was already losing some of the breadth it had previously enjoyed and that priesthood offices had been narrowed to that of bishop, elder, and deacon.

This idea is further hinted at in the requirements given for bishops and deacons, which appear relatively simple: "Not given to wine, no striker, not greedy of filthy lucre; but patient, not a brawler, not covetous" (3:3). Interestingly, Paul also tells Timothy that the bishops cannot be novices, a word signifying new converts to the faith. This would indicate that by the time 1 Timothy was written, there were enough members who were not considered novices to make this requirement helpful and meaningful.

The requirements for deacons are very similar to those of bishops, although deacons are permitted to be new converts or novices, suggesting this might have been a preparatory office. Another significant difference between the two sets of requirements is that the bishop is required to have a positive relationship with civic leaders because he represents the Church: "Moreover he must have a good report of them which are without; lest he fall into reproach and the snare of the devil" (3:7). On the other hand, deacons are responsible for teaching: "holding the mystery of the faith in a pure conscience" (3:9).

The final two verses of chapter 3 openly discuss the mystery of **Christ**, using language that is formulaic, suggesting that these ideas had formed into a formal confession of faith in the Lord: "God was manifest in the flesh, justified in the Spirit, seen of angels, preached unto the **Gentiles**, believed on in the world, received up into glory" (3:16).

The Rebellion of the Saints
1 TIMOTHY 4:1–16

As in his other epistles, Paul here warns Timothy of a departure from the faith using the Greek verb *apostēsontai*, "they shall apostasize." This **apostasy** originates within the **Church**—"some shall depart from the faith" (1 Timothy 4:1)—but does not explicitly state that all the faithful shall fall away. Their apostasy will have its origins in ascetic interests and practices: "Forbidding to marry, and commanding to abstain from meats, which God hath created to be received with thanksgiving of them which believe and know the truth" (4:3). Asceticism, the belief that denying the mortal body of certain pleasures and necessities would lead to a stronger spiritual identity, was a major force in the Church in the late apostolic and later periods. Paul here interprets emphasis on ascetic concerns as a leading cause of apostasy.

In the first century, the Greek ideal of a perfect physical body was widespread, and athleticism, much like today, was highly regarded. Many cities housed gymnasia where wealthy and privileged men could exercise. Paul rebuffs those who become consumed with the pursuit of physical perfection: "For bodily exercise profiteth little: but godliness is profitable unto all things, having promise of the life that now is, and of that which is to come" (4:8). The phrase translated as "bodily exercise" (Greek, *somatikē gymnasia*) can also refer to physical discipline, and in this context it appears that Paul's focus is rather on ascetic concerns and not on physical exercise per se.

The pursuit of physical discipline is problematic to Paul because it interferes with weightier matters, and here he counsels Timothy to "give attendance to reading, to exhortation, to doctrine" (4:13). In context then, it appears that Paul's main interest in this chapter is to exhort Timothy to give precedence to spiritual matters over physical pursuits. In particular, Timothy is to pursue his spiritual gifts, namely "prophecy, with the laying on of the hands of the presbytery" (4:14). The word translated as "presbytery" refers to the elders (Greek, *presbyterion*, "council of elders").

Temporal Concerns in the Church
1 TIMOTHY 5:1–25

The practice of the early **Church** in its first few generations was to assume financial care for the widowed sisters. This chapter is devoted almost entirely to discussing the care of the widows and who should be permitted to join their ranks. Some of the requirements for entry into the ranks of the widows who would be cared for by the Church are that they will have reared their children in a manner that is "acceptable before God" (1 Timothy 5:4), that they have no one else to care for them (5:8), that they are older than sixty years (5:9), and that they themselves have cared for the Saints by washing feet and relieving the afflicted (5:10). These detailed instructions suggest that Paul was attempting to limit the number of widows admitted, likely because their ranks had swollen to the point that it was becoming a burden on the members to care for them.

Paul does counsel the younger widows to remarry and to raise families (5:14), and the somewhat difficult wording of verses 11 and 12 suggests that Paul forbade the younger widows to join the ranks of the cared-for widows because they might eventually desire to marry ("begun to wax wanton against **Christ**" [5:11]) and then would marry and deny the promises they had made when they entered the ranks of the cared-for widows "because they have cast off their first faith" (5:12). This had already occurred in a few instances, and Paul sought to avoid this problem in the future: "For some are already turned aside after **Satan**" (5:15). The renouncing of their promises upon joining the ranks of the widows appears to have coincided with renouncing their faith in **Jesus** Christ.

The ministering elders are also to be cared for by the members of the Church, based on the Old Testament precedent that "thou shalt not muzzle the ox that treadeth out the corn. And, The labourer is worthy of his reward" (1 Timothy 5:18; Deuteronomy 25:4). That Paul would admonish the Saints to provide financially for these elders suggests that these men served full time in their callings.

In a passing comment, Paul also encourages the Saints to "drink no longer water, but use a little wine for thy stomach's sake and thine often infirmities" (5:23). This counsel follows the understanding of the day that a city's health was often tied to the quality of its main water source, and wine, or, more precisely, alcohol, was effective in purifying water. Plain water was frequently dangerous, and wine was much safer to drink in many instances.

Counsel on Servants and Riches

1 TIMOTHY 6:1–21

Although the precise number or proportion of servants (slaves) who converted to Christianity is not known, many scholars believe that the number was substantial. Servants are counseled to honor their masters even in situations where both the master and servant are converted Christians (1 Timothy 6:1–3). Those who teach against this submissive attitude are compared to the "proud, knowing nothing, but doting about questions and strifes of words, whereof cometh envy, strife, railings, evil surmisings, perverse disputings of men of corrupt minds, and destitute of the truth, supposing that gain is godliness: from such withdraw thyself" (6:4–5). Such strong counsel shows that Paul intended to single out those who taught differently.

Paul also counsels Timothy on riches: "But they that will be rich fall into temptation and a snare, and into many foolish and hurtful lusts, which drown men in destruction and perdition. For the love of money is the root of all evil: which while some coveted after, they have erred from the faith, and pierced themselves through with many sorrows" (6:9–10). It is generally assumed that Christian communities were composed primarily of the poor, but this counsel on riches suggests that there might have been some wealthy Christians as well. The division between rich and poor was significant enough to lead to problems within the **Church**, and Paul here counsels against the "love of money," which afflicts the poor and rich equally. Paul differentiates also between being rich and the sin of being rich by emphasizing the problem of being "highminded" and trusting in "uncertain riches" (6:17). Because the counsel on riches follows so closely the counsel on caring for the widows and the hint that caring for them had begun to be a burden on the Saints, it is likely that underlining the counsel on riches is the frustration that the Saints could afford to care for the widows and traveling elders but would not do so.

Calling on Timothy to remain steadfast and faithful, Paul encourages him to avoid Gnosticism, "avoiding profane and vain babblings, and oppositions of science falsely so called" (6:20). Science in this verse translates the Greek *gnōseōs*, "knowledge" or "esoteric knowledge." At the time the King James Version was translated, early Christian Gnosticism was known as a movement within Christianity, but recognizing it as a distinct and unique religion was still foreign. Today, Gnosticism is considered to be a distinct and sometimes separate religious tradition, and Paul's counsel in verse 20 to avoid Gnosticism demonstrates that some of the Saints had become caught up in the pursuit of esoteric knowledge, which is also associated with "profane and vain babblings," or speaking nonsense, an outsider's apt description of **Gnostic** teachings. Paul taught that Gnosticism grew from within the Church, "which some professing have erred concerning the faith" (6:21).

13

SECOND TIMOTHY

This private letter from Paul to Timothy is one of the three Pastoral Epistles, so named because they deal with pastoral care of the **Church**.

Introduction

2 TIMOTHY 1:1–6

Unlike 1 Timothy, in 2 Timothy there is a clear perspective of retrospection on Paul's ministry (see, for example, 2 Timothy 3:10–11). Paul is imprisoned, probably in **Rome**, or at least some time after Paul had already been to Rome (2 Timothy 1:17). The final chapter takes the form of a last will and testament as Paul recounts who has remained faithful to him and those who have departed. Although troubling, Paul's reference to Titus may imply that the latter has fallen away: "For Demas hath forsaken me, having loved this present world, and is departed unto Thessalonica; Crescens to Galatia, Titus unto Dalmatia. Only Luke is with me" (4:10–11). The question in this verse is whether the verb *forsaken* governs the prepositional phrases, which can be interpreted both positively and negatively. The wording suggests that Demas, Crescens, and Titus have forsaken Paul and each had departed into a different region of the **Roman Empire**. If this is correct, then Paul's letter to Titus must predate this epistle.

Paul makes reference to a number of individuals by name in this epistle, including Timothy's mother (Eunice) and grandmother (Lois). He mentions the **apostasy** of Demas, Crescens, Phygellus, Hermogenes, Titus,

Hymenaeus, Philetus, and Alexander. In a positive vein, Paul mentions his faithful missionary companions, Trophimus, Tychicus, Luke, Mark, and probably Carpus, as well as Prisca and Aquila and the household of Onesiphorus. Eubulus, Pudens, Linus, and Claudia send their greetings with Paul at the end of the letter. The prevalence of so many named individuals in the letter suggests that 2 Timothy was received when Timothy was staying in a city where Paul was well acquainted with the members of the Church.

Counsel to Stand Fast in the Faith
2 TIMOTHY 1:7–18

This reminder to remain faithful, not in the "spirit of fear," but in the "testimony of our Lord" (2 Timothy 1:7–8) hints at Paul's concern for Timothy's welfare in light of the onslaught of dissensions in the **Church**. Both 1 and 2 Timothy offer counsel to Timothy to remain strong, and in this epistle Paul's imprisonment and afflictions are given as further evidence that one can withstand the pressure of **apostasy** and rebellion. The otherwise unknown Onesiphorus has cared for Paul during his afflictions, and this letter is written as much to thank Onesiphorus and others as it is to help Timothy see that there are yet faithful individuals who have not forsaken the Lord.

Avoid Foolish and Unlearned Questions
2 TIMOTHY 2:1–26

The verses in this chapter preserve almost cryptic references to such earlier Pauline themes as salvation by grace, ascetic mastery, election, sharing in the Lord's sufferings, and avoiding contention based on what is described as "profane and vain babblings" (2 Timothy 2:16). The chapter can in some sense be described as a summary of Pauline teachings, condensed in a way that they recall his earlier epistles.

Some of the more difficult phrases in English are actually quite clear in

Greek. In verse 4, Paul draws an analogy to the soldier who worries about pleasing his commander at the expense of his own needs. Verse 5 mentions the athlete whose crown is legitimate only if he plays by the rules. Timothy is encouraged to do as the soldier did, caring only for the things of the Lord, and as the athlete did, to follow the law of the gospel so that he may win the crown of eternal life. Paul's imprisonment becomes a matter of importance only inasmuch as it exemplifies to the elect his willingness to follow the Lord at all costs (2:10). The "elect's sakes" (2:10) refers to the Jews who have not wholeheartedly converted to **Christ** but for whom Paul strives to be an example.

The problems in the region where Timothy resides are certainly of a doctrinal nature, and Paul mentions striving about words and "profane and vain babblings," which led to the fall of Hymenaeus and Philetus (2:14–17). These discussions were likely centered on esoteric or mystical interpretations of scripture, which led to the fall of some. Paul counsels against entering into such potentially destructive discussions. One specific matter that became a focus of these doctrinal controversies was the name of Christ, probably debating the variety of Old Testament names that refer to him and some supposed mystical meanings (2:19). Speculation concerning things that do not advance the gospel of **Jesus** Christ is compared to asking "foolish and unlearned questions" (2:23).

Perilous Times

2 TIMOTHY 3:1–17

The immediate shift to a discussion of the **last days** may be an effort to show that doctrinal heresy is not new and that in fact the future holds trials that far exceed doctrinal heresies alone. It may also be that Paul refers to the last days in this context because the Saints understood their own day as part of the decline that would lead to the eventual return of the Lord. In other words, their difficulties were akin to the difficulties that would be experienced in the last days.

Paul's list of sins associated with the "perilous times" (2 Timothy 3:1) is detailed, extensive, and fairly self-explanatory. The "incontinent" are those who have no self-control or who are out of control in their personal relationships (3:3). The wicked of the last days are similar to those who "creep into houses, and lead captive silly women laden with sins, led away with divers lusts" (3:6), a statement that must have had some cultural context to give it sense. Certainly Paul did not intend to blame "silly women" for the problems of those perilous times. Rather, it may be a social reference that has lost its meaning in the modern era.

At the heart of the problem is "learning, and never able to come to the knowledge of the truth" (3:7), indicating an intellectual heresy as well as a physical sin. The apocryphal story of Jannes and Jambres, the names given to the **priests** of Pharaoh who withstood Moses, provides an analogy for those who reject the prophet in the last days despite signs and **miracles** (3:8). Paul implies that persecution is the lot for those who stand firm in the faith in those days (3:10–11).

Paul's conclusion to his warning on the last days includes a reference to "the holy **scriptures**" (3:15), which must be a reference to the Old Testament because the New Testament had not been written and gathered by the time 2 Timothy was written. "All scripture" (3:16) implies the Old Testament and those writings such as the Gospels and Paul's epistles that were newly inspired by God. Paul encouraged Timothy to use those as well for "doctrine, for reproof, for correction, for instruction in righteousness: that the man of God may be perfect, throughly furnished unto all good works" (3:16–17).

Paul's Hope of Exaltation
2 TIMOTHY 4:1–8

No longer expecting that his appeals would result in his release or that those accusing him would somehow accept his defense, Paul openly discusses his own demise. At the time of writing, he expects that it will come soon, but at this point in his life death has no sting, and he is willing to die. Paul testifies that he looks forward to exaltation and not back to the wrongs that he has suffered during his lifetime. In fact, he expects to be exalted and hope appears to have been replaced by knowledge: "For I am now ready to be offered, and the time of my departure is at hand. I have fought a good fight, I have finished my course, I have kept the faith: *henceforth there is laid up for me a crown of righteousness*, which the Lord, the righteous judge, shall give me at that day: and not to me only, but unto all them also that love his appearing" (2 Timothy 4:6–8; emphasis added).

Conclusion
2 TIMOTHY 4:9–22

Because 2 Timothy seems to imply the falling away of Demas and perhaps others (4:10), as well as Paul's expectation that he himself would soon die, this chapter may preserve Paul's last recorded words. The chapter laments the loss of several co-workers but also celebrates the faith of Luke and Mark, both of whom wrote Gospels. While imprisoned, Paul longs for his cloak, books, and "especially the parchments," which probably refers to writings about **Jesus** and appear from this verse to be gathered in sheet form (4:13). The parchments may also refer to Paul's own writings that he wished to work on while imprisoned.

The departure of so many is troubling, particularly the actions of the otherwise unknown "Alexander the coppersmith" (4:14). In context, the evil done to Paul by Alexander must be understood in terms of his trial and condemnation, but Paul only mentions the source and not the details of the matter. As the Lord had done at his crucifixion, Paul prays that those who forsake him will be forgiven (4:16). Prisca and Aquila, with whom he labored in Corinth remained faithful to the end of Paul's life, as did Erastus, who is mentioned also in Romans 16:23. Trophimus had grown too ill to travel, and Paul left him at Miletus to recover (4:20). It may be that Paul intended Timothy to understand that Trophimus was left at Miletus while Paul traveled to **Rome** to face his death, or that he had been left there some time ago when both were still free. The individuals of verses 20 and 21 are otherwise unknown co-workers of Paul.

14

TITUS

Titus accompanied Paul during his missionary journeys. Little is known of Titus other than he was of Greek descent and Paul was particularly fond of him. Similar to Timothy, Titus seems to have been in a position where he oversaw the calling of bishops during a time when Paul was imprisoned or otherwise unable to attend to local matters himself (1:5–7).

Introduction

TITUS 1:1–5

Titus was in Crete (Titus 1:5) when the letter to him was written, and he was given the responsibility to establish the fledgling **Church** there. Paul hopes that Titus will visit him in Nicopolis (3:12), and he seems free to send and receive visitors.

The letter is one of the three Pastoral Epistles (with 1 and 2 Timothy), and is very similar in form to 1 Timothy in its instructions on the calling of **bishop**. Of particular concern in this short private letter is the issue of heresy, and Paul's concluding advice is for Titus to avoid heresy. The language he uses to describe the heresy is semi-**Gnostic**, suggesting perhaps that the letter was written at a time when Gnosticism was in its infancy. Titus was instructed to set the Church in Crete "in order" (1:5), possibly because of some rift there. The calling of "elders in every city" was intended to remedy the problem (1:5).

The Office of a Bishop
TITUS 1:6–16

Following a similar discussion in 1 Timothy 3:1–7, Paul here lists the requirements of someone who is to be ordained to the office of a **bishop**. One significant difference in the two lists is the mention of "holding fast the faithful word as he hath been taught, that he may be able by sound doctrine both to exhort and to convince the gainsayers" (Titus 1:9), suggesting that this particular consideration was necessary because of the growing threat of heresy in the branches. The threat of heresy is specifically mentioned as originating among the Jewish members, "specially they of the **circumcision**" (1:10), who taught the word for money with the intent to lead away the Saints. That **Gentile** Christians were also caught up in the heresy is made obvious through the following reference: "One of themselves, even a prophet [a Greek philosopher] of their own, said, The Cretians are alway liars, evil beasts, slow bellies" (1:12). The statement "All Cretans are liars" is known as the Epimenides Paradox; it challenges the reader to consider whether the speaker spoke the truth in calling all Cretans liars or lied in making such a claim. Paul sees in this statement an analogy to the way the members had become embroiled in discussions of words: "Jewish fables" (1:14) and "foolish questions, and genealogies, and contentions" (3:9).

Private Counsel to Timothy
TITUS 2:1–3:8

Counseling Timothy on a number of issues associated with maintaining harmony in the branches of the **Church**, Paul here advises him on family matters relating to the elderly (Titus 2:1–2), to parents (2:4–5), to youth (2:6), and to slaves (2:9). Giving Titus what amounts to practical advice, Paul concludes the chapter with a summary of his thoughts on how the Church might exist in harmony. The issues Paul addresses appear to be matters of opinion and not actual sin. Paul desires the Saints to live in consideration of the truth that God has brought salvation to the entire human family that all might be saved through the process of denying themselves all "ungodliness and worldly lusts" (2:12). For Paul, the gospel is here very practical at its foundation, and at its core promotes sober, righteous, godly living (2:12). The doctrine that underlines this practical foundation is that **Jesus Christ** "gave himself for us, that he might redeem us from all iniquity, and purify unto himself a peculiar people, zealous of good works" (2:14). The gospel of Jesus Christ, then, is hope of ultimate salvation through the grace of Jesus Christ.

Some of the good works that Paul encourages are to obey governments and "to speak evil of no man, to be no brawlers, but gentle, shewing all meekness unto all men" (3:2). Paul emphasizes that the gospel of Jesus Christ came "not by works of righteousness," a euphemism for living the law of Moses, but rather by "mercy he saved us" (3:5). Paul's thoughts here should not be interpreted to imply that Jesus somehow did not live the law, but rather that Jesus did not reemphasize salvation through renewed obedience to the law of Moses specifically, but rather through his grace and acceptance of all people everywhere who would believe on him. This kind of belief leads to good works, which Paul is hesitant to specify because they could be interpreted as a new law by which we might judge ourselves.

Avoid Foolish Questions
TITUS 3:9–15

Without sufficient documentation, it is always difficult to know the historical situation that led to specific counsel from a **Church** leader, but in this instance it appears that Paul's mention of "genealogies" and "strivings about the law" (3:9), as well as the label of "heretick" (3:10), imply a distinct doctrinal heresy rather than a general condition of malaise. The heresy was likely a budding interest in esoteric doctrines and a quest to understand the angelic hierarchy of heaven ("genealogies," which were a matter of intense interest for Gnostics). Such matters are not important for Church members to know, and Titus is encouraged to cut them off after the "second admonition" (3:10).

Tychicus is known from Paul's other letters (Ephesians 6:21; Colossians 4:7), while Artemas and Zenas are not (Titus 3:12–13). Apollos labored in Corinth and is mentioned by Paul in his letters (1 Corinthians 1:12; 4:6; Acts 19:1). The mention of Zenas's occupation may imply that Paul hoped for aid in preparing for his defense, although the remainder of the letter does not confirm or undermine this suggestion. The abrupt ending indicates that Paul hoped to see Titus soon and to receive a full report from him orally.

15

PHILEMON

A short private letter to an individual, Philemon, this letter is a plea for the merciful treatment of a runaway slave.

Introduction and Plea to Philemon
PHILEMON 1:1–25

From the surviving lines of this letter, it appears that Paul, while imprisoned (Philemon 1:1), met a slave named Onesimus (Greek, "useful") whose master Paul knew. The nature of Onesimus's crime is not specified, but it seems reasonable to assume that theft was involved: "If he hath wronged thee, or oweth thee ought, put that on mine account" (1:18). Because Paul refers to Onesimus as his "son," it may be that Paul was involved in the man's conversion (see, for example, Titus 1:4). Paul has certainly grown fond of Onesimus, and the letter is written on his behalf. Because the exact imprisonment is not known, this letter cannot be dated with any accuracy, although Paul does refer to himself as "the aged," which is the only time he refers to himself in that way (1:9).

Paul seems to have known Philemon quite well, and in this epistle he is somewhat lighthearted, making a play on Onesimus' name. Onesimus ("useful") "was not useful to you, but now is useful to you" (1:11; authors' translation). Paul is willing to repay any debt Onesimus owes, but he also reminds Philemon, "Albeit I do not say to thee how *thou owest unto me even thine own self* besides" (1:19; emphasis added). How long Paul was in prison with Onesimus is not known, but Paul had grown so fond of him that he desired Onesimus to stay with him in prison and minister to him, although he knew that Onesimus should return to his master (1:13–14).

Paul seems to expect his release soon, and he asks that Philemon prepare him a place to stay after his release (1:22). Epaphras is also imprisoned with Paul, and Mark, Aristarchus, Demas, and Luke are in contact with him. The recipients at the beginning of the epistle (1:2) are not known except for a passing reference to Archippus in Colossians 4:17. Philemon was a member of the **Church** that met in Archippus's house, which was a fairly common practice in the first decades of Christianity. This private letter was preserved because it could be traced back to Paul, rather than for its doctrinal content, as with the other Pauline epistles.

16

HEBREWS

The King James Version of the Bible identifies the book of Hebrews as "The Epistle of Paul the **Apostle** to the Hebrews," borrowing the title from the **Latin** Vulgate. This was an unfortunate decision because the oldest and best Greek manuscripts simply state, "To the Hebrews."

Introduction

Hebrews 1:1–3

The identity of the writer of Hebrews has been debated from the earliest period of Christianity. Nevertheless, from the King James Version identification, many people associate the book with Paul, even though it is placed after the Pauline corpus, which is generally arranged by length, from the longest (Romans) to the shortest (Philemon). The book itself seems to rule out Paul as an author: "How shall we escape, if we neglect so great salvation; which at the *first began to be spoken by the Lord, and was confirmed unto us by them that heard him*" (Hebrews 2:3; emphasis added). The author suggests that he is not an eyewitness of the Lord in the same sense that Peter, James, John, and Paul claimed to be. Paul testified time and time again that he received the gospel from the Lord himself, whom he had both heard and seen (Galatians 1:1; 1 Corinthians 15:8).

If not Paul, then who? A likely candidate may be his co-worker Apollos (Acts 18:24–28). The recipients, who may have been Jewish-Christians in **Rome** (2 Corinthians 11:22), knew the writer and Timothy (Hebrews

13:22–23). It should be recalled that Timothy was known in Rome (Romans 16:21). The book appears to have been accepted originally on its content instead of any claims to apostolic authority, though Timothy and Apollos appear to have been apostolic delegates to several important branches of the Church, including Corinth and Ephesus. Commentators have noted that Apollos may have been a pupil of Philo of Alexandria, who was well-known for his rhetorical and philosophical skills. Additionally, Luke described Apollos as being an "eloquent" man. The book contains eloquent Hellenistic Greek, with traces of Classical Greek phrases and sophisticated rhetorical and philosophical arguments that may comport well with Apollos's background and experience. Hebrews is universally considered the best Greek in the New Testament and appears to be superior in every way, including vocabulary and sentence structure, to any of Paul's letters. The book contains nearly five thousand Greek words, of which nearly seventy are found nowhere else in the New Testament and another ten are found nowhere in any Greek text before this period, suggesting the author was a well-educated person with a rich vocabulary. The author skillfully uses the **Septuagint (LXX)** quoting it more than thirty times with an additional forty allusions. Interestingly, he often cites a version similar to codex A (Alexandrinus), whereas Paul generally quotes a version similar to codex B (Vaticanus).

The date of the writing of Hebrews has also been fiercely debated and is directly tied to the question of authorship. However, given that the author does not mention the destruction of the **temple**, it seems likely that Hebrews was written sometime before the catastrophic events overtook the Holy City of Jerusalem in A.D. 70, as the book seems to presuppose continuing daily **sacrifices** in the temple in Jerusalem. The silence on the demise of the temple is deafening. Additionally, internal evidence may suggest that it was written right after Nero's brief but violent attack on the **Church** in Rome at about the same time 1 and 2 Peter and Mark were written from Rome. There is a sense that even though the attack on the Saints is recently over, there remains the possibility of danger in the near future.

In the end, as did the early Church, we may want to focus more on the message of Hebrews than on the messenger. Certainly, we live without knowing the authorship of other books in the Bible, such as 1 and 2 Kings, and yet we still enjoy reading the stories contained in them—drawing out applications as we study these remarkable inspired and canonized books.

There are several important themes that flow through the book. However, there appears to be one overriding purpose: The writer wants to warn the original audience that the consequences of returning to Jewish worship (feast days, sacrifices, and tabernacle/temple) will have devastating effects on the vitality of the Church. To persuade his readers to remain faithful to **Jesus Christ**, the author explains the cosmic significance of Jesus Christ. Although there is historical information about Jesus' mortal mission with allusions to his birth, **baptism**, temptations, and death, the author is much more interested in what his suffering, death, and resurrection signifies for his readers.

To counter any possible draw that the holy days and rituals (including sacrifice) of first-century Judaism might have upon the people, he uses nearly thirty comparisons. For example, the author argues that Jesus' sacrifice was superior to the sacrifices offered at the Jerusalem temple and that through Jesus Christ, God established a new **covenant** as prophesied in the Old Testament. Paradoxically, the author of Hebrews uses the Jewish **scriptures** extensively to demonstrate that the law of Moses is insufficient to save them completely—forever. Finally, the author is also interested in Jesus as Savior (Greek, *sōtēria*), as the word appears more times in Hebrews than in any other in writing in the New Testament.

The book of Hebrews does not begin as a traditional letter; there is no introduction, greeting, or prayer, but appears to be more like a sermon with a letter attached to it (Hebrews 13:22–25). The author writes, "And I beseech you, brethren, suffer the *word of exhortation*" (13:22; emphasis added). As has been noted on several occasions, this is exactly the same term used for a sermon in Acts: "And after the reading of the law and the prophets the rulers of the synagogue sent unto them, saying Ye men and brethren, if you have any *word of exhortation* for the people say on" (Acts 13:15; emphasis added). Most likely, this sermon was to be read aloud to the Jewish-Christians (Hebrews) in **Rome**.

The book may contain an early Christian hymn fragment imbedded in the first long Greek sentence, divided into four verses in English trans-lations (Hebrews 1:1–4). It is difficult to discern the hymn, but it likely includes the material partially found in verses 2 and 3: "God, who at sundry times and in divers manners spake in time past unto the fathers by the prophets, hath in these **last days** spoken unto us by his Son, *whom he hath appointed heir of all things, by whom also he made the worlds; who being the brightness of his glory, and the express image of his person, and upholding all things by the word of his power, when he had by himself purged our sins, sat down on the right hand of the Majesty on high;* being made so much better than the angels, as he hath by inheritance obtained a more excellent name than they" (1:1–4; emphasis added; see other hymn fragments in John 1:1–18; Philippians 2:6–11; Colossians 1:15–20; 1 Timothy 3:16).

The hymn emphasizes that God has revealed himself completely, ul-timately, and definitively in Jesus Christ who was "appointed heir to all things." This idea is somewhat paradoxical because in antiquity the son became heir only after the father's death. In this case, the author states that the Son became the heir after his own death. The hymn further emphasizes that Jesus created and upholds the world as the Father's agent. Jesus is also described as being in the "express image" (Greek, *charaktēr*) of the Father. (*Charaktēr* is the impression left by a signet ring on wax or the coin after being stamped.) Having given himself through death, Jesus now sits exalted on the "right hand" of God (1:3; compare Acts 2:32–33).

The Preeminence of Christ

HEBREWS 1:5–3:6

The author of Hebrews declares that **Christ** is superior to the angels, "as he hath by inheritance obtained a more excellent name than they" (Hebrews 1:4). Here the author begins to quote extensively from the Old Testament: "Thou art my Son, this day have I begotten thee" and "I will be to him a Father, and he shall be to me a Son" (1:5; compare Psalm 2:7). It seems obvious that the intended audience was thoroughly conversant with the Old Testament (Jewish-Christians, or possibly God-fearers at least).

Interestingly, the longest quotation from the Old Testament found any-where in the New Testament also appears in Hebrews (8:8–11; compare Jeremiah 31:31–34).

Thoughtful New Testament students recognize that many Old Testament quotations found in the book do not often match the same pas-sages in the current Old Testament. As noted above, the reason for the dif-ference is that the author of Hebrews regularly quoted from the **Septuagint** (**LXX**) whereas the current King James Version Old Testament, like other modern English translation, is based on the Hebrew Old Testament.

In what has been described as the clearest New Testament example of **Jesus** being identified as God, the author of the book of Hebrews employs words from Psalms to show that Jesus was addressed in a way no angel had ever been addressed: "But unto the Son he saith, Thy throne, O God, is for ever and ever: a sceptre of righteousness is the sceptre of thy kingdom. Thou hast loved righteousness, and hated iniquity; therefore God, even thy God, hath anointed thee with the oil of gladness above thy fellows" (1:8–9; compare Psalm 45:7–8).

The writer's point in this section is that Jesus stands above all others and that God has "put in subjection the world to come" to Jesus (2:5, 8). It is important to note, as many commentators have done, that the Father is an active agent throughout the book of Hebrews (see 3:11 where he swears an oath; 11:4 where he testifies; 6:13 where he makes promises; 11:8 where he calls; 11:16 where he is not ashamed; 12:26 where he moves and shakes all things). This is a striking observation given the dominant role Jesus (the Son) plays throughout the New Testament.

Hebrews preserves the now-famous phrase that Jesus had become "the captain of their salvation perfect through sufferings" (2:10). Note that the author does not say that Jesus was exalted without suffering, but that he was exalted "through suffering." Because Jesus was "made like unto his breth-ren," he is a "merciful and faithful high priest in things pertaining to God, to make reconciliation for the sins of the people. For in that he himself hath suffered being tempted, he is able to succour them that are tempted" (2:17–18).

Additionally, the author emphasizes the relationship between "[him] that sanctifieth" and "[them] who are sanctified" (2:11). He says they "are all of one [family]" (2:11) and are the "children" of God (2:13). This is a remarkable insight, provided here for the first time in Hebrews. Additionally, Jesus is identified as the sanctifier; as noted earlier, sanctification comes by the shedding of blood—specifically the blood of Jesus Christ (9:13; 10:10; 13:12). The author further emphasizes that the Saints have been sanctified (10:10, 29) and are being sanctified (2:10; 10:14). He admonishes them to continue so they can become holy, for only through sanctification can they "see the Lord" (12:14).

The author returns to Christ's preeminence, adding to the list of glorious titles for Christ that Jesus was also superior to Moses: "Consider the *Apostle* and *High Priest* of our profession, Christ Jesus. . . . For this man was counted worthy of more glory than Moses" (3:1, 3; emphasis added). Here the author of Hebrews also introduces one of his favorite words: *heavenly* (3:1). He also speaks of the "heavenly gift" (6:4), "heavenly things" (8:5), heavenly country (11:16), and "heavenly Jerusalem" (12:22).

God's Rest

HEBREWS 3:1–4:13

An important theme in the book of Hebrews is divine rest. The author recalls the story of ancient Israel: "Harden not your hearts, as in the provocation, in the day of temptation in the wilderness: When your fathers tempted me, proved me, and saw my works forty years. Wherefore I was grieved with that generation, and said, They do alway err in their heart; and they have not known my ways. So I sware in my wrath, They shall not enter into my rest" (Hebrews 3:8–11). Because ancient Israel had an "evil heart of unbelief" (3:12, 19; 4:6, 11) and hardened their hearts (3:13, 15; 4:7), they did not receive the rest they had been promised—to enter into the promised land. The Doctrine and Covenants further clarifies the ultimate meaning of rest, "which rest is the fulness of his glory" (D&C 84:24).

Jesus as High Priest

HEBREWS 4:14–10:39

In this rather long section, the author of Hebrews introduces another of his favorite words: *eternal*. He states: "And being made perfect, [**Jesus**] became the author of eternal salvation unto all them that obey him" (Hebrews 5:9). He also speaks of eternal judgment (6:2); eternal redemption (9:12); eternal Spirit (9:14); eternal inheritance (9:15); and an eternal **covenant** [KJV, "everlasting"] (13:20). However, the main focus of this section is the portrayal of Jesus as high priest (4:14; 5:5, 10; 6:20; 7:26; 8:1; 9:11; 10:21), an idea already alluded to earlier in Hebrews (2:17; 3:1).

The author of Hebrews suggests that the ancient tabernacle served as an ideal type and shadow of what God planned to execute through his Son Jesus **Christ**. The author assumes that his audience is familiar with the ordinances and holy days associated with worship in the ancient Mosaic tabernacle. He states, "Seeing then that we have a great high priest, that is passed into the heavens, Jesus the **Son of God**, let us hold fast our profession" (4:14). In speaking of Jesus as a "great high priest," the author of Hebrews most likely had reference to ancient **temple** worship and the parting of the veil by the high priest on the Day of **Atonement** (Hebrew, *Yom Kippur*). When the high priest entered into the Holy of Holies on this most holy day, he moved from the Holy Place into the Holy of Holies through the veil of the temple. Likewise, Jesus, who is the "great high priest," entered into the heavenly Holy of Holies when he "passed into the heavens."

The author also stresses Jesus' compassion toward humanity: "For we have not an high priest which cannot be touched with the feeling of our infirmities; but was in all points tempted like as we are, yet without sin. Let us therefore come boldly unto the throne of grace, that we may obtain mercy, and find grace to help in time of need" (4:15–16). That Jesus Christ was the great high priest did not diminish his capacity to understand his people in the least, but throughout his time in mortality, he participated in the human drama of life.

The author of Hebrews says that "no man taketh this [**priesthood**] honour unto himself, but he that is called of God, as was Aaron" (5:4) and then explains that God called Jesus as high priest: "So also Christ glorified not himself to be made an high priest; but he that said unto him, Thou art my Son, to day have I begotten thee. As he saith also in another place, Thou art a priest for ever after the order of Melchisedec" (5:5–6; compare Psalm 110:4). The use of Psalm 110 is unique in Hebrews. The author continues, "Though he were a Son, yet learned he obedience by the things which he suffered; and being made perfect, he became the author of eternal salvation unto all them that obey him; *called of God an high priest* after the order of Melchisedec" (5:8–10; emphasis added).

The King James Version text indicates that Jesus suffered in Gethsemane: "Who in the days of his flesh, when he had offered up prayers and supplications with strong crying and tears unto him that was able to save him from death, and was heard in that he feared" (5:7), while the Joseph Smith Translation focuses attention on Melchizedek (JST, 5:7–8). However, what is said of Melchizedek can also be said of Jesus Christ, since Melchizedek was a type and shadow of Christ.

In an important discussion, the author then outlines six basic principles that should be thoroughly understood by mature Saints—not "babes," but those ready to feast on "strong meat" (5:12–14): first, "**repentance** from dead works" (6:1); second, "faith toward God" (6:1); third, "baptisms" (6:2); fourth, "laying on of hands" (6:2); fifth, the "resurrection of the dead" (6:2); and finally, "eternal judgment" (6:2).

The author turns full face into the wind to deal with his immediate and urgent concern—the reason for preparing the epistle to the Hebrews in the first place (6:4–8; 10:26–31). Hebrews contains a dire warning against **apostasy**—that is, abandoning faith in Jesus. The Jewish-Christians, in the wake of the recent Neronian persecution, may have considered returning to the relative safety of the Jewish synagogue. No matter what the actual historical setting might have been, the book of Hebrews argues that it is "impossible" for anyone who has truly become a Saint to return from the dark abyss of complete apostasy—the consequences of which are terrible to consider (10:26–31).

For the author, a true Saint is someone who is "enlightened," who has "tasted the heavenly gift," and who is a partaker "of the **Holy Ghost**" (6:4). In word and deed, they have "tasted the good word of God" and the "powers of the world to come" (6:5). When such a person apostatizes, he crucifies Jesus afresh, putting him "to an open shame" (6:6). They have received the "rain" from God, but instead of bearing fruit, they bear "thorns" and "briers" and will be rejected, cursed, and ultimately burned (6:7–8).

The writer tells the Saints that they can count on blessings from God because of "two immutable things" (6:18): first, it is "impossible for God to lie" (6:18); and second, God "confirmed [promises] by an oath" (6:17). All of which should give them "a strong consolation, who have fled for refuge to lay hold upon the hope set before us: which hope we have as an anchor of the soul, both sure and steadfast, and which entereth into that within the veil; whither the forerunner is for us entered, even Jesus" (6:18–20).

In this subsection, the author of Hebrews explains the significance of Jesus being a high priest after the order of Melchizedek (7:1–2): "For this Melchisedec, king of Salem, priest of the most high God, who met Abraham returning from the slaughter of the kings, and blessed him" (7:1). According to the Joseph Smith Translation it is the priesthood that is "without father, without mother, without descent, having neither beginning of days, nor end of life; but made like unto the **Son of God**; abideth a priest continually" (7:3). The author argues, "Now consider how great this man was, unto whom even the patriarch Abraham gave the tenth of the spoils" (7:4). He reasons, "And as I may so say, Levi also, who receiveth tithes, payed tithes in Abraham. For he was yet in the loins of his father, when Melchisedec met him" (7:9–10).

In a slightly different argument, the author further states, "If therefore perfection were by the Levitical priesthood, (for under it the people received the law,) what further need was there that another priest should rise after the order of Melchisedec, and not be called after the order of Aaron? For the priesthood being changed, there is made of necessity a change also of the law" (7:11–12).

Because Jesus Christ, as a high priest after the order of Melchizedek, makes continuous intercession, the endless replacement of levitical **priests** is no longer necessary (7:23–25). The author of Hebrews adds an important observation at this point, providing an unforgettable insight: that Jesus Christ "is able also to save them to the uttermost [Greek, *eis to panteles*] that come unto God by him" (7:25). The King James Version provides an adequate translation, but it is more precisely translated "completely," "fully," or "perfectly." That is, forever and for all time.

Ultimately, Jesus is supreme because he offered one last and eternal **sacrifice** in our behalf: "Who needeth not daily, as those high priests, to offer up sacrifice, first for his own sins, and then for the people's: for this he did once, when he offered up himself" (7:27).

The book of Hebrews indicates that the new covenant instituted through Jesus Christ is not only new but also better than the old covenant. Jesus has "obtained a more excellent ministry, by how much also he is the mediator of a better covenant, which was established upon better promises. For if that first covenant had been faultless, then should no place have been sought for the second" (8:6–7).

Adding to his witness, the author of Hebrews compares the sacrifice of Jesus in the heavenly tabernacle to the sacrifices offered in the "worldly" tabernacle on the Day of Atonement. First, he provides a word-picture of the ancient Mosaic tabernacle (9:2–5). In this "worldly" tabernacle, the priests went into the holy place (9:6), but only the high priest went into the Holy of Holies: "But into the second went the high priest alone once every year, not without blood, *which he offered for himself*, and for the errors of the people" (9:7; emphasis added). The author continues his analogy: "But Christ being come an high priest of good things to come, by a greater and more perfect tabernacle, not made with hands, that is to say, not of this building; Neither by the blood of goats and calves, but by his own blood he entered in once into the holy place, having obtained eternal redemption for us" (9:11–12).

As a result, the author testifies, Jesus became "the mediator of the new testament, that by means of death, for the redemption of the transgressions that were under the first testament, they which are called might receive the promise of eternal inheritance. For where a testament is, there must also of necessity be the death of the testator" (9:15–16).

Interestingly, the writer says that "the law" is a "shadow of good things to come" (10:1).

A Cloud of Witnesses
HEBREWS 11:1–12:1

The author of Hebrews next turns his attention to providing a list of former Saints who had lived their lives as a testimony of their faith: "the substance of things hoped for, the evidence of things not seen" (Hebrews 11:1). The list includes most of the recognizable heroes and heroines from the Old Testament, including Abel, Enoch, Noah, Abraham, and Sara. The author states, "These all died in faith, not having received the promises, but having seen them afar off . . . and confessed that they were strangers and pilgrims on the earth" (11:13). It is interesting to note that all of these are dead—no living example is given. The author explains that through their faith they survived death, disappointment, and a host of other challenges. However, they have "obtained a good report through faith, [but] received not the promise" (11:39). The author had access to additional information not currently found in the Old Testament about many of these people. Josephus, who wrote at the end of the first century, was able to also collect and record stories about Israel's past that are not found in today's Bible.

In a passage that has become important to the Latter-day Saints, the author says, "God having provided some better thing for us, that they without us should not be made perfect "(11:40; compare D&C 128:15). The author then declares, "Wherefore seeing we also are compassed about with *so great a cloud of witnesses,* let us lay aside every weight, and the sin which doth so easily beset us, and let us run with patience the race that is set before us" (12:1; emphasis added).

The Power of Suffering

HEBREWS 12:2–11

The book of Hebrews admonishes the Saints to look "unto **Jesus** the author and finisher of our faith; who for the joy that was set before him endured the cross, despising the shame, and is set down at the right hand of the throne of God. For consider him that endured such contradiction of sinners against himself, lest ye be wearied and faint in your minds" (Hebrews 12:2–3). The writer adds his thoughts on the power of suffering, which includes a further exhortation to stand firm in the face of trials: "And ye have forgotten the exhortation which speaketh unto you as unto children, My son, despise not thou the chastening of the Lord, nor faint when thou art rebuked of him" (12:5; compare Proverbs 3:11). This sentiment is reiterated a few verses later when the author writes, "For whom the Lord loveth he chasteneth, and scourgeth every son whom he receiveth" (12:6). Again, it appears that suffering and trials are of great concern, and the author seems to be encouraging the Saints to stand in the faith under the Neronian persecution (12:11).

In the end, suffering, like so many other gospel principles, is a paradox. Suffering can be a punishment from a just God. However, it can, as noted above, be a means of teaching and training and should be seen as an indication that God loves us and claims us as his sons and daughters. The opposite is also true: "If ye be without chastisement . . . then are ye bastards, and not sons" (12:8).

The Old and New Covenants

HEBREWS 12:12–29

To compare and contrast the two **covenants,** the old and the new, the author of Hebrews compares the old to Mount Zion that could not be approached while Moses was speaking with God. The Israelites were permitted to hear the voice of the Lord, but Moses remained their mediator (Hebrews 12:12–21). In contrast, the new covenant offers a personal audience with the Lord in the "city of the living God" (12:22) and the privilege of encountering "God the Judge of all" (12:23). This new covenant with its associated privileges far outstrips the promises of the old and becomes in Hebrews the object of faith, with the reminder that in living the new covenant we are receiving "a kingdom which cannot be moved, let us have grace, whereby we may serve God acceptably with reverence and godly fear: for our God is a consuming fire" (12:28–29). The reference to God as "a consuming fire" reminds us of Deuteronomy: "For the Lord thy God is a consuming fire, even a jealous God" (Deuteronomy 4:24)

Admonitions

HEBREWS 13:1–13

As the sermon draws to its conclusion, the author of Hebrews admonishes the Saints to "let brotherly love continue" and to not be "forgetful to entertain strangers: for thereby some have entertained angels unawares" (Hebrews 13:1–2). Those listening are asked to "remember them that are in bonds, as bound with them; and them which suffer adversity, as being yourselves also in the body" (13:3). However, the Saints should not fear since the Lord has promised, "I will never leave thee, nor forsake thee" (13:5). As a result, the Saints respond, "The Lord is my helper, and I will not fear what man shall do unto me" (13:6).

The author of Hebrews specifically enjoins the Saints to take heed of the teachings of their leaders (13:7). Additionally, they are instructed to "obey them that have the rule over you, and submit yourselves: for they watch for your souls, as they that must give account, that they may do it with joy, and not with grief: for that is unprofitable for you" (13:17). In what is considered a brilliant insight, the writer assures the Saints that they can learn from the past because **Jesus** is "the same yesterday, today, and forever" (13:8).

Closing

HEBREWS 13:18–25

This section ends as a typical first-century letter with an appropriate prayer, blessings, and personal greetings to members of the **congregation**. The blessing reminds the reader of the central role of **Jesus Christ**: "Now the God of peace, that brought again from the dead our Lord Jesus, that great shepherd of the sheep, through the blood of the everlasting **covenant**, make you perfect in every good work to do his will, working in you that which is wellpleasing in his sight, through Jesus Christ; to whom be glory for ever and ever. Amen" (Hebrews 13:20–21).

Finally, the author informs the congregation of "brother Timothy," who has recently been set free (13:23). He adds, "Salute all them that have the rule over you, and all the saints. They of Italy salute you. Grace be with you all. Amen" (13:24–25).

17

JAMES

The epistle of James begins with a clear statement of authorship and purpose: "James, a servant of God and of the Lord **Jesus Christ**, to the twelve tribes which are scattered abroad, greeting" (James 1:1). James is almost universally recognized as Jesus' brother (Mark 6:3). He was active in Jerusalem from around A.D. 40 until A.D. 62, when he suffered martyrdom. Tradition ascribes to him the office of **bishop** of the Jerusalem **Church**, and Acts 15:13 places him in a pivotal position in the Jerusalem Conference of A.D. 49. James is called an **apostle** in the sense of being one of those who saw the risen Lord and who bore testimony of it (Galatians 1:19; 1 Corinthians 15:7), although he was never associated with the Quorum of the Twelve Apostles in the New Testament. Historically speaking, James's role was to oversee affairs in Jerusalem, and he was particularly influential after the apostles had departed from the city (Acts 21:18).

Introduction

JAMES 1:1

That the letter is addressed to the "twelve tribes" suggests a very early notion that the religion of Jesus, which would later be called Christianity, was in reality the new law to all the tribes. Later, as Christians and Jews began to distance themselves from one another, this address would make little sense, when Christianity's origins from the ten tribes was no longer a matter of emphasis. In fact the opening lines mention "God *and* the Lord

460

Jesus Christ" (1:1; emphasis added), again showing a very early association with God the Father and Jesus Christ, helping Jewish-Christians and perhaps Jews associate the two as equal.

Some scholars dispute the authenticity of this letter because of its excellent Greek and evident awareness of Hellenistic forms of thought. This challenge is based on the assumption that a Jew raised in rural Nazareth would have had little training outside the **law**, and his awareness of Greek culture and ideas would necessarily be very limited. This viewpoint seems to overlook the evidence that James lived much of his adult life in Jerusalem where Hellenistic culture was widely known. It is also possible that James used scribes to help him in writing Greek and in refining his thoughts for Jewish-Christians who had grown up in Greek cities.

The letter is largely a collection of aphorisms, or short statements emphasizing principles and truths. For this reason the letter may at times appear disjointed. It is not a discussion of a problem, as is the case in many of the Pauline epistles, but rather it gives advice for living life as a Christian in a world where faith and piety were under siege. The author also seems to know of a version of the Sermon on the Mount that is different from that contained in the Gospel of Matthew (James 4:11–12; 5:12).

If Any Lack Wisdom

JAMES 1:2–27

This chapter contains nine aphorisms or injunctions to be faithful. They are: (1) "The trying of your faith worketh patience" (James 1:3); (2) "If any of you lack wisdom, let him ask of God" (1:5); (3) "A double minded man is unstable in all his ways" (1:8); (4) "Blessed is the man that endureth temptation" (1:12); (5) "God cannot be tempted with evil, neither tempteth he any man" (1:13); (6) "Every good gift and every perfect gift is from above" (1:17); (7) "Let every man be swift to hear, slow to speak, slow to wrath" (1:19); (8) "But be ye doers of the word, and not hearers only" (1:22); and (9) "Pure religion and undefiled before God and the Father is this,

To visit the fatherless and widows in their affliction, and to keep himself unspotted from the world" (1:27).

These injunctions reveal a very practical side of Christianity and avoid the sectarian debates that Paul faced wherein he sought to settle doctrinal disputes between Jewish and **Gentile** Christians. Because this epistle does not address those later issues, it may be that it was written very early, at a time when those issues had not yet arisen. James's injunction to seek wisdom offers an ironic opening statement: "If any of you lack wisdom." James may have seen the growth of Christianity as reliant upon the Saints' willingness to seek for wisdom and to live in harmony. The injunctions in this chapter form an anthology of gospel principles in the beginning years of Christianity.

God Is No Respecter of Persons
JAMES 2:1–13

In a somewhat surprising reversal, James here encourages Christians to eschew preferential treatment of the rich. In the modern world, this teaching may not seem surprising in the least, but in the first century, when so many people were cared for through a wealthy patron, and where it may have been necessary to have a wealthy patron in order to provide financially for a family, it would seem odd that James would not encourage Christians to seek for a kind and wealthy patron. This counsel may represent one of the issues that Christians, and perhaps Jewish-Christians in particular, had with the Roman world. The inability of an individual to experience any upward social mobility may have been seen as contrary to the gospel, in which all are considered equal.

Some of the terminology of this section implies that legal action had been taken against Christians, and, in fact, James asks, "Do not rich men oppress you, and draw you before the judgment seats?" (James 2:6). This reference seems to imply Jewish opposition, where "judgment seats" implies a Jewish council rather than being brought before a Roman governor. If this is the case, then the concluding verses of this section are a reminder that sinning against any portion of the **law** makes a person guilty of the entire law, "for whosoever shall keep the whole law, and yet offend in one point, he is guilty of all" (2:10). The burden of being subject to the entire punishment of the law is overcome in **Christ**, where we "shall be judged by the law of liberty" (2:12) in contrast to those who have oppressed the Saints and will suffer under the weight of the entire law.

Faith and Works

JAMES 2:14–26

Some scholars have detected an overt anti-Pauline stance in these verses, which emphasize work as the means of salvation rather than belief or faith. This view seems to miss the different emphases in the two texts. James appears to be challenging a Jewish mentality that focuses narrowly on the belief "in one God" and known as the Shema (the text of which is recorded in Deuteronomy 6:4). Paul, on the other hand, seems to intend that **Gentiles** are not required to become subject to the entire law of Moses but instead can be saved through faith as Abraham had been before the revelation of the **law** to Moses. The distinction is that James's teachings seem to envision a problem similar to that of **Jesus'** ministry where religious concerns impeded one from caring for the needy (Mark 7:11–13).

James uses a reasoned approach, asking questions to induce the reader to think through the issues and arrive at the practical solution: "What doth it profit" and "wilt thou know . . . that faith without works is dead?" (James 2:14, 20). Interestingly, James does not connect the issues of faith and works with salvation or exaltation, but rather with judgment: "Was not Abraham our father justified" and "was not Rahab the harlot justified by works?" (2:21, 25). One way of understanding these verses is to consider them in light of the real-life problem faced in Acts 6:1–4, in which the Greek widows complained that the Hebrew widows were being better cared for. James's counsel is designed to create unity in the faith and to avoid laying a foundation of a faith that emphasizes proper belief only as a means of salvation.

A Very Small Helm

JAMES 3:1–18

In chapter 3, James returns to exhorting the Saints through aphorisms, much as he did in chapter 1. In chapter 3, James warns against "many masters" and giving offense with the "tongue" which "is a little member and boasteth great things" (James 3:1, 5). The injunction to avoid having many masters should probably not be interpreted to mean avoiding having divided loyalties, but rather seeking for personal mastery that leads to ascetic attitudes or attitudes that exalt bodily perfection over personal righteousness. Indeed, the ascetic attitude even teaches that denial of physical appetites is the primary means of obtaining spiritual knowledge. The Joseph Smith Translation appears to understand it in this way as well: "Strive not for the mastery" (JST, 3:1).

The tongue, which is understood as a window to the soul or heart, is recognized as the cause of a "world of iniquity" (3:6). What stands behind this counsel is not entirely clear, other than a concern that backbiting leads to unrest and unruliness in the branch. Most of this chapter focuses on problems caused by the tongue and offers a number of memorable comparisons. In fact, one of the comparisons resembles one of **Jesus'** sayings from the Sermon on the Mount (3:10–12 and Matthew 7:16–20). The final verses of the chapter focus on the pursuit of wisdom, which cannot be obtained through "strife" (3:14). Wisdom is "pure, then peaceable, gentle, easy to be intreated" (3:17), which is in contrast to the noisy, haphazard, difficult world in which the Saints live. James appears to be attempting to create a distinct contrast between the ways of the world and the way of wisdom.

Submit Yourselves to God

JAMES 4:1–17

Verse 1, in the King James translation, indicates that James is speaking of wars, but in reality the language indicates an internal struggle and quarrels among the Saints. The beginning of the verse can equally be rendered,

"Where do quarrels and conflicts come from?" (authors' translation), which James answers with another question: "Come they not hence, even of your lusts that war in your members?" (James 4:1). At issue is the internal struggle the Saints experience as carnal desires make war against the desire to live righteously. James's solution to this struggle is to "submit yourselves therefore to God. Resist the devil, and he will flee from you" (4:7). James's answer to resisting the desires of the flesh is a matter of having a friendship with God and renouncing the world, explained in terms of being friends with the world, which is said to be "enmity with God" (4:4).

The other practical matter that James discusses is the temptation to judge one another, which is countered through humility. James probably has in mind Christians judging other Christians, although it is possible that if this letter dates from the early A.D. 40s, the matter might actually be Christians judging Jews who failed to convert to the gospel. Judging is a foolish endeavor because life "is even a vapour that appeareth for a little time, and then vanisheth away" (4:14), implying that those who judge others will soon be judged by the Lord in eternity. These verses have a strong parallel in the Sermon on the Mount in Matthew 7:1–5, and James encourages Christians not to view the world myopically but instead to live life according to the Lord's will.

Conclusion

JAMES 5:1–20

Turning attention to the rich again, the opening verses of the final chapter address the rich directly and convict them of oppressing the poor and needy. The injunction to remember the poor reminds the reader of the parable of the rich man and Lazarus as well as **Jesus'** teaching to the rich young man (Luke 16:19–31; Matthew 19:21). These teachings may be the earliest surviving application of Jesus' teachings that were eventually recorded in the canonical Gospels. In this context, James represents a very early effort to understand Jesus' teachings and to apply them to new contexts, thus attesting to James's change of heart (John 7:3, 5) and to how revered Jesus' words became almost immediately after his death.

Following the logical progression of the final chapter, James next turns his attention to the Saints who are suffering under the weight of persecution. The connection that James seems to be making is that the "rich" are in part responsible for this oppression. In his teachings, James cites the prophets "for an example of suffering affliction, and of patience" (5:10). In fact, one of the most memorable aphorisms in the epistle of James is "we count them happy which endure" (5:11).

Beginning with an almost verbatim quotation from the Sermon on the Mount in verse 12 (Matthew 5:33–34), James concludes the epistle by touching upon some matters of general concern to the Saints. The final matters he covers are blessing the sick and afflicted, anointing with oil, prayer, and helping those who have fallen away from the faith. The letter does not end in typical fashion with salutations and a personal note from the author. These final items appear almost as an afterthought, matters that are mentioned but not explained in depth.

The matter of prayer does receive greater attention, and James certainly encourages personal, private prayer as a means of accessing the blessings of heaven. Private prayer was in many ways different from the established public prayers of the Jews of Jesus' day, and this contrast is emphasized by drawing upon the example of Elijah, whose prayer brought about a famine (5:17). The example reminds the reader the prophet Elijah had the power to close heaven and also to return the rains and bring forth the bounty of the earth again. In light of the hardships the Saints had experienced at the hands of the rich, this final point may contain a hint of warning (5:1–7).

18

FIRST PETER

This letter opens with a salutation: "Peter, an **apostle** of **Jesus Christ**, to the strangers scattered throughout Pontus, Galatia, Cappadocia, **Asia**, and Bithynia, Elect according to the foreknowledge of God the Father, through sanctification of the Spirit, unto obedience and sprinkling of the blood of Jesus Christ: Grace unto you, and peace, be multiplied" (1 Peter 1:1–2). This identifies 1 Peter as a circular letter destined for several **congregations** scattered throughout five Roman provinces (Acts 15:23–29; Colossians 4:16; Revelation 1–3).

Interestingly, the authorship and destination of the letter was never questioned in antiquity, and 1 Peter is one of only two letters from the general epistles section of the New Testament whose authorship and authority were never question by the early **Church** (1 John is the other).

However, commentators today debate issues relating to audience, rather than destination, and to authorship. Many scholars believe the original audience (the "strangers" of verse 1) was **Gentile** Christians. Additionally, some commentators argue that Peter could not have written the letter based on a number of internal issues, which we will discuss after a brief discussion of audience.

Introduction

1 PETER 1:1–12

First Peter was addressed to the "elect sojourners of the Diaspora" in five regions. Paul had begun missionary work in Asia and Galatia but had been forbidden by the Spirit "to go into Bithynia" (Acts 16:7). We know very little about the spread of the "good news" into Pontus, Cappadocia, and Bithynia except for a brief reference about Jews from these regions visiting Jerusalem on the day of **Pentecost** when Peter preached (Acts 2:9). It is certainly possible that the audience was recent Gentile converts. However, there are some very good reasons to consider that the audience was Jewish-Christians living in a hostile Gentile world. They are described as residents in foreign lands (*parepidēmoi*), as aliens or strangers (*paroikias, paroikous*) in 1:17; 2:11, and as the elect (*eklektois*) in 1:2; 2:4, 9. It has been pointed out that the **covenant** curse (Deuteronomy 28:63–68) indicated that Israel would be spread throughout the nations if they failed to obey the stipulations of the covenant. Peter may refer to the prophetic promises to Israel of a return, "who prophesied of the grace that should come unto you" (1:10).

The language noted above was typical for describing the exiles following the fall of Jerusalem in 597 B.C. It should be acknowledged that in many instances the early Christians, such as Paul, appropriated Jewish terms and ideas and applied such terms and ideas to Gentile converts. Nevertheless, in 1 Peter, Gentile Christians are not addressed; there is no Jewish-Christian versus Gentile Christian debate, discussion, or reference. In fact, the original audience is described as living in Gentile nations where they are aliens, or strangers.

The call to return to the Lord in 1 Peter fits very well with the prophetic tradition of the Old Testament. Peter states, "But as he which hath called you is holy, so be ye holy in all manner of conversation; because it is written, Be ye holy; for I am holy" (1:15–16; compare Leviticus 11:44–45; 19:2). Additionally, Peter tells the Saints, "But ye are a chosen generation, a royal **priesthood**, an holy nation, a peculiar people" (1 Peter 2:9) reminding us of Exodus 19:6.

Authorship issues have been raised because the letter is written in excellent Greek with some of the best Greek prose in the New Testament. Additionally, commentators have identified numerous quotes and allusions from the **Septuagint (LXX)**, suggesting someone rather familiar with the Greek translation of the Old Testament. There are as many as twenty direct quotations, including citations from Leviticus, Isaiah, Psalms, Hosea, and Proverbs, making this letter rather Jewish in character.

Basically, many commentators have suggested that a Galilean fisherman, described as "unlearned or ignorant" (Greek, *agrammatoi*) in Acts 4:13, could not have produced such a letter. This description may have fit Peter around A.D. 30, but this letter was most likely written in the 60s—more than thirty years later. By this time, Peter had traveled extensively around the eastern Mediterranean and certainly would have become rather proficient in Greek by the time this letter was written. Additionally, the letter indicates that Peter wrote the letter "by [Greek, *dia*] Silvanus" (5:12), suggesting possible help, which is likely reflected in the final form of the letter. Silvanus (also known as Silas) had coauthored letters with Paul before (1 Thessalonians 1:1 and 2 Thessalonians 1:1) and had been instructed earlier to deliver a circular letter from James, Peter, and other Church leaders after the Jerusalem Conference (Acts 15:22–29).

Two other arguments against Petrine authorship focus on the lack of direct references to the mortal ministry of Jesus and that much of the letter seems to reflect a Pauline point of view.

Recently, some scholars have discovered twelve possible references that correlate with Jesus' own teachings (see, for example, see 1 Peter 1:6; 4:13 and Matthew 5:12), demonstrating that the author was indeed familiar with them. Moreover, many have cogently demonstrated that Peter and Paul, similar to other first-century Saints, shared a common point of emphasis in teaching about Jesus (1 Corinthians 11:23; 15:3) and a common view about Israel and the expanding Gentile mission after the Jerusalem Conference in A.D. 49.

The place of composition is often discussed. The author indicates that he is in Babylon, a possible code word for **Rome** (Revelation 17:5). There is a strong tradition, without any alternative proposition, that Peter suffered martyrdom in Rome under Nero in A.D. 64, which tradition is preserved in the apocryphal *Acts of Peter*. Many of the details are most likely legendary, but few commentators reject the basic story that Peter was in Rome and died there during the time of Nero. The letter continues with a typical Jewish blessing known as the *Berakah* or "blessing of God" (1:3–12).

A Holy People
1 PETER 1:13–2:10

The letter turns to the renewal the Saints have experienced—redeemed through "the precious blood of **Christ**, as of a lamb without blemish and without spot" (1:19); who was "foreordained before the foundation of the world" (1:20). Peter reminded his audience that they have been "born again, not of corruptible seed, but of incorruptible, by the word of God" (1:23). He further states that this was "the gospel . . . preached unto you" (1:25).

God's purpose in announcing the good news was to build "up a spiritual house," that is a **temple** (2:5). The "**priesthood**" would "offer up spiritual **sacrifices**" in that temple (2:5). As a result of their call, the Saints "should shew forth the praises of him who hath called you out of darkness into his marvellous light" (2:9). Pursuing a slightly different emphasis, Peter teaches that Christ is the "chief corner stone" (2:6), using a word that can be translated also as "keystone." In Ephesians, Paul had taught that Christ was the foundation of the kingdom (Ephesians 2:20). The underlying difference resides in the point of emphasis, where Peter sees **Jesus** and the gospel as the crowing achievement of God's saving work from the beginning of time, while Paul struggles to build a new kingdom on a new foundation, namely **Christ** and his gospel.

Examples among the Gentiles
1 PETER 2:11–3:17

In this section, Peter asks the Saints to live good lives "among the **Gentiles**" (1 Peter 2:12). In particular, they are to "submit . . . to every ordinance of man for the Lord's sake: whether it be to the king, as supreme; Or unto governors, as unto them that are sent by him for the punishment of evildoers, and for the praise of them that do well" (2:13–14).

First Peter contains another version of a household code (Colossians 3:18–22). Interestingly, this adaptation began with slaves: "Servants, be subject to your masters with all fear; not only to the good and gentle, but also to the forward" (2:18). Apparently, Christian slaves were unfairly abused and beaten by their Gentile masters (2:19–20). Peter uses **Christ**, "who did no sin" (2:19–22), as the example of one who was abused and beaten unfairly.

In what is an excursion from the topic but nevertheless a fundamental truth of the gospel, Peter reminds the Saints that **Jesus** carried "our sins in his own body on the tree" and that we are healed by his "stripes" (2:24). This is the most explicit use in the New Testament of the Suffering Servant prophecy from Isaiah (Isaiah 53; compare Acts 3–4; 8:32–35).

Peter returns to the household code when he enjoins women to "be in subjection to your own husbands," especially nonbelieving husbands (3:1). It should be remembered that traditional culture demanded that wives and slaves follow their husband and master. If the husband or slave owner accepted a religious faith, the wife or slave should accept the same faith (Acts 10:2; 16:14–15). In such a context, wives and slaves would have been vulnerable to criticism and abuse for having become Christians. These passages may reveal the composition of the **Church** in the regions at this time—principally composed of slaves and women.

Peter finally turns to the men: "Likewise, ye husbands, dwell with them according to knowledge, giving honour unto the wife, as unto the weaker vessel [Greek, *skeuei*], and as being heirs together of the grace of life; that your prayers be not hindered" (3:7). The mention of a "weaker vessel," as in pottery, refers mainly to physical capacity and strength and not necessarily moral, intellectual, or spiritual capacity. In fact, in the verses just before this one, women are seen as possibly having great spiritual insight (3:1–2). Again, like Paul, Peter adapts traditional household codes with a new Christian ethic. Here for example, he asks husbands to give their wives "honour" since they are "heirs together of the grace of life" (3:7), suggesting the kind of equity Paul notes in Galatians 3:27–29.

Peter later adds, "Likewise, ye younger, submit yourselves unto the elder. Yea, all of you be subject one to another, and be clothed with humility: for God resisteth the proud, and giveth grace to the humble. Humble yourselves therefore under the mighty hand of God, that he may exalt you in due time" (5:5–6). In so doing, Peter pleads with the Saints to cast "all your care upon him; for he careth for you" (5:7).

This section ends, "Finally, be ye all of one mind, having compassion one of another, love as brethren, be pitiful, be courteous: Not rendering evil for evil, or railing for railing: but contrariwise blessing; knowing that ye are thereunto called, that ye should inherit a blessing" (3:8–9). In summary, Peter tells the Saints that in doing good they stand as an example to the Gentiles, giving "an answer to every man that asketh you a reason of the hope that is in you with meekness and fear: Having a good conscience; that, whereas they speak evil of you, as of evildoers, they may be ashamed that falsely accuse your good conversation in Christ. For it is better, if the will of God be so, that ye suffer for well doing, than for evil doing" (3:15–17).

The phrase "asketh you a reason" (Greek, *aitounti hymas logon*) has been described as coming from a judicial context, suggesting that some of the Saints had been interrogated. First Peter assumes that the Saints are living in a hostile world where local persecution may have included appearances before magistrates questioning slaves and wives about their decision to depart from traditional household order (4:15–16).

Christ's Continuing Ministry
1 PETER 3:18–22

Although the Gospels are silent about what transpired on Saturday after **Jesus**' death, Peter reveals that **Christ** "went and preached unto the spirits in prison" (1 Peter 3:18–22). He adds, "Who shall give account to him that is ready to judge the quick and the dead. For for this cause was the gospel preached also to them that are dead, that they might be judged according to men in the flesh, but live according to God in the spirit" (4:5–6), revealing that the early Saints knew more about Jesus' continuing ministry in the world of the spirits than the Gospels reveal.

Christ Suffered
1 Peter 4:1–5:11

As he had done before (2:18–25), Peter reflects on **Christ's** suffering, indicating that **Jesus** is a model for true believers: "Arm yourselves likewise with the same mind" (4:1). He adds, "Beloved, think it not strange concerning the fiery trial which is to try you, as though some strange thing happened unto you: But rejoice, inasmuch as ye are partakers of Christ's sufferings; that, when his glory shall be revealed, ye may be glad also with exceeding joy" (4:12–13).

The term *Christian* (Greek, *christianous*) appears only three times in the New Testament (Acts 11:26; 26:28; 1 Peter 4:16). Peter states, "Yet if any man suffer as a Christian, let him not be ashamed" (4:16). This statement implies that Christians had become models of suffering nobly, so that Peter could encourage the Saints to "suffer as a Christian" normally would. It may be that by the time 1 Peter was written, the Saints had already experienced significant local persecution.

The theme of suffering continues to the end of the letter. As he concludes his letter, Peter admonishes the "elders which are among you" to "feed the flock of God" (5:1–2). This reminds us of Peter's own special commission (John 21:15–17).

Final Greeting
1 Peter 5:12–14

Peter ends his letter with a final greeting and blessing: "By Silvanus, a faithful brother unto you, as I suppose, I have written briefly, exhorting, and testifying that this is the true grace of God wherein ye stand. The **church** that is at Babylon, elected together with you, saluteth you; and so doth Marcus my son. Greet ye one another with a kiss of charity. Peace be with you all that are in **Christ Jesus**. Amen" (5:12–14). In this greeting, Peter mentions Marcus (Mark), his "son." This designation is universally regarded as a metaphor. Traditionally, Marcus is identified as John Mark, mentioned at various times throughout the second half of the New Testament (Acts 12:11–12, 25; 15:37, 39; Colossians 4:10; Philemon 1:24; 2 Timothy 4:11).

In the end, Peter's letter to the scattered Saints in **Asia** Minor reminds them that the "God of all grace" has "called us unto his eternal glory by Christ Jesus, after that ye have suffered a while, make you perfect, stablish, strengthen, settle you" (5:10).

19

SECOND PETER

Sometimes identified as a farewell speech, 2 Peter is an important New Testament text that reveals some of the internal struggles of the first-century **Church** and preserves one of Peter's last testimonies before his death in **Rome**.

Introduction

2 PETER 1:1–2

The author of 2 Peter introduces himself as "Simon Peter, a servant and an **apostle** of **Jesus Christ**" (2 Peter 1:1). No one in the early Church would have wondered who was intended because Peter was the most recognizable **disciple** of Jesus. The author of 2 Peter provides a second personal reference in the opening chapter: "For he received from God the Father honour and glory, when there came such a voice to him from the excellent glory, This is my beloved Son, in whom I am well pleased. And this voice which came from heaven we heard, when we were with him in the holy mount" (1:17–18). This is an obvious reference to the Mount of Transfiguration, an incident in which Peter played a significant role (Matthew 17:1–9). The third personal reference suggests that this is a follow-up letter to 1 Peter: "This second epistle, beloved, I now write unto you; in both which I stir up your pure minds by way of remembrance" (2 Peter 3:1).

Despite the presence of these personal identifications and reflections, questions regarding authorship of this letter were raised in antiquity and continue to be debated today, even among conservative New Testament scholars. Nevertheless, a number of commentators continue to argue that 2 Peter was written by the apostle and most likely was produced in Rome sometime just before his death in A.D. 64 (1:12–15). Latter-day Saints generally accept this traditional understanding. However, scholars have increasingly challenged this assumption and have suggested several alternative explanations for authorship. One argument suggests that 2 Peter is the last book produced in the New Testament, written many years after Peter's death, and should properly be identified as the "Testament of Peter." Testament literature is an important ancient genre presenting the purported final teachings or sayings of a famous person. Based on similar types of material found in the Old Testament (Genesis 49 and Deuteronomy 33), testament literature was well-known during the Hellenistic and Roman periods. The most famous Jewish example is the Testament of the Twelve Patriarchs (dated from the second century B.C.). Additional examples from this period were discovered in Cave 4 at **Qumran (Dead Sea Scrolls)**, including the Testaments of Naphtali, Judah, Joseph, and the **Aramaic** Levi text.

Finally, another option suggested is a middle position between the two noted above. In this scenario, 2 Peter is a "Testament of Peter" that contains authentic Petrine material (1:13–18).

Despite disagreements over authorship, scholars generally concur on several important points regarding the message and purpose of the letter, including the existence of a striking parallel between 2 Peter and Jude. There are some twenty-five direct parallels with Jude, found between 2:1 and 3:3. Universally, commentators suggest that Peter copied material from Jude. This should not surprise anyone since there are numerous examples of such borrowing in antiquity, including Matthew and Luke's use of Mark (Peter's memoirs). In this case Peter, for good reason, chooses to quote from the Lord's brother, adapting Jude's material to suit his needs and purpose. The changes include Peter's omitting Jude's allusion to the story from the Assumption of Moses (Jude 1:9) and the quotation from 1 Enoch (Jude 1:14–15).

Second Peter opens, as one would expect, with a personal greeting, referencing both the sender (Simon Peter) and the audience: "To them that have obtained like precious faith with us through the righteousness of God and our Saviour Jesus Christ" (1:1). The literal reference to "our God and Saviour Jesus Christ" is the clearest example of Jesus being identified as God in the New Testament. A blessing naturally follows. In this case, Peter writes, "Grace and peace be multiplied unto you through the knowledge of God, and of Jesus our Lord" (1:2).

Godliness
2 Peter 1:3–11

An important focus of Peter's letter is a discussion on godliness. He reveals the "exceeding great and precious promises" of the Lord (1:4), which includes being "partakers of the divine nature" (1:4). To obtain the divine nature, the Saints need to build upon the traits that bring about such a change of their personal nature, including faith, virtue, knowledge, temperance, patience, brotherly kindness, and charity (1:5–7). Peter believes that individuals either grow toward godliness or return to their former lives—metaphorically portrayed as returning to their "vomit" or "mire" (2:22).

Peter then notes, "For if these things be in you, and abound, they make you that ye shall neither be barren nor unfruitful in the knowledge of our Lord **Jesus Christ**" (1:8).

In what may be, for Latter-day Saints, one of the most famous sections in this letter, Peter tells the Saints that if they do not acquire these traits, they are "blind" and cannot "see afar off" (1:9). "Wherefore the rather," Peter exhorts, "give diligence to make your calling and election sure" (1:10). Having one's calling and election made sure means that a person "shall never fall" (1:10) and that "an entrance shall be ministered . . . into the everlasting kingdom of our Lord and Saviour Jesus Christ" (1:11).

Peter's Last Testament

2 PETER 1:12–21

In a section that includes several first-person references (1:12, 13, 14, 15), Peter states that it is important for him to "put you always in remembrance of these things" so that the Saints will "be established in the present truth" (1:12). He writes, "Knowing that shortly I must put off this my tabernacle, even as our Lord **Jesus Christ** hath shewed me" (1:14; compare John 21:18–19), suggesting a final witness or testimony.

Peter then reflects personally on his upcoming demise, sharing with the Saints his fortitude to face his end with faith and confidence: "For we have not followed cunningly devised fables, when we made known unto you the power and coming of our Lord Jesus Christ, but were eyewitnesses of his majesty. For he received from God the Father honour and glory, when there came such a voice to him from the excellent glory, This is my beloved Son, in whom I am well pleased. And this voice which came from heaven we heard, when we were with him in the holy mount. We have also a more sure word of prophecy; whereunto ye do well that ye take heed, as unto a light that shineth in a dark place, until the day dawn, and the day star arise in your hearts" (1:16–19).

Interestingly, at the end of his last will and testament Peter also addresses the issue of private interpretation of scripture. Perhaps his reason for doing so is to remind the reader that reliance upon the **Holy Ghost** is what has made him confident when facing death: "No prophecy of the scripture is of any private interpretation" because "the prophecy came not in old time by the will of man: but holy men of God spake as they were moved by the Holy Ghost" (1:20–21).

Warning against False Teachers

2 PETER 2:1–22

At this point Peter turns his attention to the second of the two important themes in the letter—the coming of false teachers who will be characterized by "pernicious ways" (2 Peter 2:2). The early Saints were threatened by various forces, including social, political, and religious (1:4; 2:8, 20), which come from "among you" (2:1). There are numerous warnings about false teachers in other books of the New Testament, suggesting that many others saw the threat of **apostasy** as originating within Christian communities (see, for example, Matthew 24:4–5; Acts 20:29–30; 2 Thessalonians 2:1–4; 2 Timothy 3:1–8).

These false teachers will "secretly" introduce "damnable heresies." Peter warns the Saints that God did not spare those who turned away from Him in the past (2:4–8). In this, Peter testifies that God's judgment is certain. He had intervened in human history in the past (2:5; 3:3–5) and will do so in the future (3:7, 10–12). However, God's judgment punishes the wicked and at the same time vindicates the righteous (2:9).

Using a series of powerful metaphors that originate from the epistle of Jude, Peter says that the promises of the false teachers are just that—false promises. For example, they are like "wells without water" (2:17).

In the end, Peter argues that the Saints, having been redeemed, should not return to "the pollutions of the world." He infers that if they have not been truly redeemed—changed in their very nature—then they will likely be "entangled" again. He highlights this point by recalling two well-known sayings (2:22). The first comes from the Old Testament, referring to a dog returning to his own vomit (Proverbs 26:11; see also 3 Nephi 7:8); the second from a non-Biblical source and found in Semitic and Greek traditions: "the sow that was washed to her wallowing in the mire" (2 Peter 2:22; see also 3 Nephi 7:8).

False Teachings

2 PETER 3:1–10

In the next section, Peter outlines some of the counterfeit teachings being espoused, including the rejection of a belief in **Christ's** Second Coming (2 Peter 3:4). He argues that the "Lord is not slack concerning his promise" (3:9). Peter also declares that the promise of Christ's return is not based on fables (1:16). He adds that those who perceive that the Lord is delaying his return base their assumption on limited human perspective (3:8). Finally, Peter indicates that the extended period of time from the present until the Second Coming gives more people a chance to hear the "good news" and respond to it (3:9).

Exhortation and Conclusion
2 PETER 3:11–18

Peter turns to a small but significant observation at this point: "And account that the longsuffering of our Lord is salvation; even as our beloved brother *Paul* also according to the wisdom given unto him hath written unto you; as also *in all his epistles*, speaking in them of these things; in which are some things hard to be understood, which they that are unlearned and unstable wrest, as they do also the other **scriptures**, unto their own destruction" (3:15–16; emphasis added). Surprisingly, Peter mentions a collection of Pauline letters that were well-known at the time and that were read and studied as though they were equal to scripture. Naturally, the question arises about when such a collection could have begun to circulate.

Peter's final exhortation includes this admonition: "Ye therefore, beloved, seeing ye know these things before, beware lest ye also, being led away with the error of the wicked, fall from your own stedfastness" (3:17). He concludes with a final doxology: "To him be glory both now and for ever. Amen" (3:18).

20

FIRST JOHN

The three short epistles attributed to the **apostle** John are placed by
length in the New Testament alongside the letters of Peter, James, Jude, and
the author of Hebrews.

Introduction

1 JOHN

Although they bear the name *John*, the author refers to himself as the
"elder" (2 John 1:1), and tradition ascribes the letters to John, the "beloved"
disciple of the Lord. These letters are extremely difficult to date in relationship to the other writings attributed to John (the Gospel of John and
Revelation), but there are some historical matters that may help determine
a rough estimate of when they were written. First, 1 John 1:1–5 discusses
some of the same themes as John 1:1–18, although the former appears to
be a rough draft of the latter. Second, the epistles of John seem to be concerned with a heresy known later as Docetism, which arose toward the
close of the apostolic era in the last decades of the first century A.D. Third,
both the Gospel of John and the epistles of John deal with similar issues
such as light and darkness, the Word, witnesses, and obeying **Jesus'** commandment to love one another.

Of particular interest to the author is the group of Christians who
"went out from us" (1 John 2:19) and who fell away into personal apostasy. Their heresy is associated with denying the physical ministry of Jesus

Christ: "Every spirit that confesseth not that Jesus Christ is come in the flesh is not of God" (4:3). Another prevalent issue of these epistles, and one that John may have addressed because their teachings had to do with claiming perfection or sinlessness, is that "if we say that we have not sinned, we make him a liar, and his word is not in us" (1:10). The two ideas are actually quite similar because those who deny the existence of the mortality of Jesus Christ are also inclined to deny the importance of the eternal nature of the mortal body. If in their thinking the mortal body is unnecessary or not eternal, then sins committed in the mortal body would not be considered sins at all, but rather infractions against our fallen nature and of no eternal consequence. Certainly this logic is twisted, but scholars have identified this trend in other **noncanonical** texts as well, and generally this belief is referred to in the modern era as Docetism (Greek, *dokeō*, "to seem," or "to appear"). This heresy appears to have its beginnings in the latter half of the first century, and represents an intellectual threat to Christianity as Greek converts wrestled with the troubling concepts of the corporality of God and an eternal material existence.

The language of these three epistles is sharp and critical of certain beliefs, not because the author is prone to writing in this style but rather because the heresy facing the Saints is so widespread. There is no way to convincingly place the three letters in chronological order because they are included in the New Testament only by length. The designations of first, second, and third are modern conventions. For this reason, it is difficult to know whether this letter was successful in suppressing the heresy or whether the heresy blossomed further after the letters were sent.

The Word of Life
1 JOHN 1:1–10

The opening lines of the epistle have several formal similarities to the prologue of the Gospel of John (John 1:1–10), with the emphasis on handling and seeing the resurrected Lord. The author is clearly drawing upon experience in relating a personal witness of the Lord that contradicts what some have taught to the contrary. The prologue of the epistle is written in the first-person plural (we) and may reveal the author's desire to provide a wider apostolic witness ("we" representing the testimony of the eleven **disciples** who saw the Lord after his Resurrection).

The author was given a message to teach "that God is light" (1:5), which is a contrast to the old ideal that God is law and can be followed only through the written word. Because God is light, we must follow him openly, in a way that others can see us, and together with others who likewise follow the Lord. This idea is given in contrast to those who teach that they follow the Lord, but whose actions are secret and hidden from the world or the Saints. John desires his readers to know that all have sinned and that perfection is not attainable without the "blood of **Jesus Christ**" (1:7).

Safety in the Ordinances
1 JOHN 2:1–29

The beginning of this chapter consistently touches upon the idea that a person cannot break the commandments and at the same time claim to walk in the light. The two ideas are simply not compatible. This convoluted idea, that one can break the commandments and somehow believe that one is still following God, is associated with the spirit of the anti-Christ (1 John 2:18). Although the anti-Christ is associated with the **last days**, John reports that there are "even now . . . many antichrists" (2:18).

One way to avoid being caught up in the spirit of heresy is to immerse oneself in the safety of prophecy and the ordinances: "an unction from the Holy One, and ye know all things" (2:20). The word translated as "unction" (Greek, *chrisma*, "anointing") might refer to **baptism** and the gift of the Holy Spirit or another ordinance where the Saints were anointed. The anointing specifically led the Saints: "the same anointing teacheth you of all things" (2:27), which favors the interpretation that the anointing was the giving of the Holy Spirit (John 14:26). John also encouraged the Saints, telling them, "Ye know all things," which should be interpreted in light of the preceding verses that draw upon the prophecy of the anti-Christ. John specifically comforts the Saints, telling them that they already knew the anti-Christ would come. Trusting in prophecy therefore is a stay against falling into heresy.

The Glory of the Resurrection Leads to Hope
1 JOHN 3:1–24

Having seen the resurrected body of the Lord, John offers insight into the glory of the resurrected body, stating that "it doth not yet appear what we shall be" (3:2), or in other words we do not now appear in the same form as we shall be when we are resurrected. In hope, we look forward to receiving a glorious resurrected body: "When he shall appear, we shall be like him; for we shall see him as he is" (3:2). This hope in a glorious resurrection leads us into a life of obedience, which provides the framework for the discussion of chapter 3. The devil, in contrast, offers nothing similar to the eternal glory of the son.

The signs of those who follow **Christ** and who believe in him are being hated by the world (3:13), loving one another (3:14), caring for the poor or needy (3:17), and receiving answers to prayer (3:22). This practical approach to religion is a sharp contrast to the intellectualized religion being disparaged throughout the epistle, where the emphasis is on esoteric understanding of the eternal nature of the mortal body. Although not specifically stated, John's emphasis can be summarized as giving priority to charity over knowledge.

Test the Spirits
1 JOHN 4:1–21

Heresy is easy to identify when it is dressed differently and comes with an identifying label. The Lord warned, however, that some will come among the Saints who dress and act like sheep but who are inwardly not sheep (Matthew 7:15). This chapter revisits the issue of trying "the spirits whether they are of God" (1 John 4:1), where "spirits" should be interpreted in the context of the spirit of discernment and not in an angelic sense. At issue are those who teach one thing but are not of God (4:3).

At least one line in this chapter appears to be an interpolation: "No man hath seen God at any time" (4:12), which is qualified in the Joseph Smith Translation through the addition of "except them who believe." Certainly he was familiar with the Old Testament revelations and his own personal witness of the Lord. It may be, however, that John was attempting to teach that we are not led by sight but rather by the Spirit, which seems to be the major teaching of this chapter (4:13).

The goal of the mortal experience is expressed here in a single verse: "That we may have boldness in the day of judgment: because as he is, so are we in this world" (4:17), which is achieved through love. We find unity with God, and indeed similarity with God, when we love one another even as he loved us (John 3:16). In a very real way, loving one another provides a way to test the spirits, because "if a man say, I love God, and hateth his brother, he is a liar: for he that loveth not his brother whom he hath seen, how can he love God whom he hath not seen?" (4:20).

Conclusion

1 JOHN 5:1–21

This chapter contains one of the most significant scribal interpolations in the New Testament and is referred to in scholarly literature as the Johannine Comma—a single verse inserted parenthetically between two existing verses. The verse in question, "For there are three that bear record in heaven, the Father, the Word, and the **Holy Ghost**: and these three are one" (5:7) was added to the New Testament at a much later date and was probably first introduced via a fourth-century A.D. **Latin** homily (the *Liber Apologeticus*). It survives in the King James Version because the translators relied on Erasmus's third Greek edition of the Textus Receptus, which also contains the interpolation. The verse appears to be a late addition to support the growing concern to scripturally support the doctrine of the Trinity.

Knowing the Lord can be achieved through at least three distinct means: "the Spirit [Holy Ghost], and the water [**baptism**], and the blood [the **Atonement**]" (5:8). Following John's earlier points of emphasis in this epistle, this chapter again seeks to create a foundation of faith in **Jesus Christ** that is informed by the Spirit and the ordinances of the gospel. This discussion is constantly in contrast to the positions of those who "went out from us" (2:19). Encouraging his readers to ask of God and to try the spirits, John assures them, "And this is the confidence that we have in him, that, if we ask any thing according to his will, he heareth us" (5:14).

21

SECOND JOHN

The short epistle known as 2 John is private correspondence between John and the "elect lady" whose identity is otherwise unknown, although she may be a personification of the **Church** (2 John 1:1).

Introduction

2 JOHN

The letter congratulates those who have stood firm in light of growing **apostasy** and discord. Similar to the message of 1 John, this epistle confronts the issue of those who deny the physical body of **Jesus Christ**. John hopes to visit the branch, which probably meets in the home of the "elect lady." This letter encourages the Saints to exclude those who deny Christ from their meetings.

Love One Another

2 JOHN 1:1–13

After a conventional salutation, John recalls the commandment that the Lord spoke on the night of the **Last Supper** (John 13:34–35) that the disciples should "love one another" (2 John 1:5). This spirit of love will lead to walking in the commandments (1:6), which will in turn help the Saints avoid falling prey to the enticements of the deceivers (1:7). This doctrine is to be used as a test to exclude the deceivers: "If there come any unto you, and bring not this doctrine, receive him not into your house" (1:10).

22

THIRD JOHN

Similar in content to 2 John, the short epistle of 3 John is written to the otherwise unknown Gaius, for whom John wishes prosperity and good health.

Introduction

3 JOHN

Gaius is commended for showing hospitality to the Saints and is warned that some individuals have turned away from the faith, namely one Diotrephes (3 John 1:9). The letter promises that John will come to Gaius to set in order the affairs of the **Church**, and it is likely that Gaius owns the home where the fledgling branch meets.

Gaius a True Christian

3 JOHN 1:1–14

This short letter is partially a note of thanksgiving for Gaius's charitable actions and partially a promise to reestablish the **Church** after Diotrephes has turned away. Gaius, who bears a Greek name, is congratulated for caring for the brethren, particularly for those who were "strangers" to Gaius (3 John 1:5). These brethren have reported back to John that they were cared for and offered support by Gaius ("taking nothing of the **Gentiles**"; 1:7).

In contrast to Gaius, Diotrephes would not offer hospitality to John and "receiveth us not" (1:9), which John intends to deal with when he comes. Diotrephes's offense lies not only in his failure to accept John but also in loving his position of "preeminence" (1:9). Moreover, Diotrephes has spoken against John, "prating against us with malicious words: and not content therewith, neither doth he himself receive the brethren, and forbiddeth them that would, and casteth them out of the church" (1:10), which implies that he was attempting to take unrighteous control of the branch.

Demetrius, on the other hand, has remained faithful, and John's congratulations on his actions may be intended to allay fears that he had likewise fallen into **apostasy**. John concludes by promising to visit and resolve any lingering issues.

23

JUDE

The short epistle from Jude rounds out a collection of letters that spans from Hebrews to Jude in the New Testament and that have been organized according to the length of the epistle.

Introduction

JUDE 1:1

Jude refers to himself in this epistle as the "servant of **Jesus Christ**, and brother of James" (Jude 1:1), which is almost certainly in reference to the brothers of Jesus by those names. In Mark 6:3 the brothers of Jesus are named—"James, and Joses, and of Juda, and Simon," where Juda is the same name as the author of this epistle. Some recent commentators have suggested that the epistle of Jude was authored by the **apostle** Thomas. This suggestion is based on the apostle Thomas's Syrian name, Judas Didymos Thomas, but the evidence for this name dates from the third century A.D. (in the Acts of Thomas) and cannot be traced back earlier to the first century when the epistle was written. It is, however, somewhat of a surprise that the author does not make any reference to his filial relationship to Jesus.

The contents of this short epistle, or, more accurately, circular letter, detail a serious division in the **Church** that Jude condemns from the position of a local Church leader. His rebuke is pointed and warns its readers to beware of the punishments of the Lord if they persist in sin. The structure of the letter takes the form of a history of God's actions in punishing sinners with the implication that God will also eventually punish all sinners, including those spoken of in this letter. To make this point, the epistle of Jude draws upon some sources that are not part of the Christian or Jewish Canon (such as the Assumption of Moses and the Book of Enoch). These extracanonical books receive authoritative status in the epistle of Jude.

Warning to Those Who Sin

Jude 1:1–25

Jude begins this epistle by recounting how the Lord punished three classes of sinners: those who were led out of Egypt but who did not forsake their sins, the third of the host of heaven who followed **Satan**, and the inhabitants of Sodom and Gomorrah. This survey is intentional, to "put you in remembrance, though ye once knew this" (Jude 1:5). From verse 4, it is apparent that the problem facing the Saints is internal **apostasy**, and that some "men crept in unawares." Jude associates these "men" with those who were punished in Sodom and Gomorrah and those who sinned after leaving Egypt. His warning is strong concerning those "who were before of old ordained to this condemnation, ungodly men, turning the grace of our God into lasciviousness, and denying the only Lord God, and our Lord **Jesus Christ**" (1:4).

An account of Michael disputing with the devil over the body of Moses is recorded here but nowhere else in the Old or New Testaments. The incident is used to make a logical deduction, namely that when Michael contended with the devil and was in position to rebuke him, he "durst not bring against him a railing accusation" (1:9), or, in other words, he showed restraint even though he was right and the devil was wrong. Jude's conclusion is that sometimes the Lord shows restraint in punishing the wicked, but eventually the wicked are punished. The implications of this statement are that the wicked among the Saints should not interpret their present state to mean that the Lord will not eventually punish them.

Jude moves from the doctrine of divine restraint to a more detailed

MAKING SENSE OF THE NEW TESTAMENT

comparison of the sins being committed by a select group of Saints. He compares their actions to those of Cain, Balaam, and Core (1:11; see Numbers 16). He even suggests that these sinners are defiling the sacrament meetings or the celebration of the **Last Supper** using a technical term to indicate the common meal Christians celebrate in remembrance of the Lord's last meal with his **disciples**: "These are spots in your *feasts of charity*" (1:12; emphasis added). These comparisons make it difficult to pinpoint the exact nature of the sin being committed because the comparisons are so broad and varied. Perhaps more importantly, Jude wanted his readers to know how sorely displeased the Lord was with their actions.

Eventually the wicked will receive their due recompense when "Enoch also, the seventh from Adam . . . cometh with ten thousands of his saints" (1:14), an event not described in the Old Testament or the book of Moses. This fearsome resurrected army will not give way to any mortal army. The severity of the language and the sharp warning suggest that this letter is an important piece of evidence in the history of the Apostasy and shows the inroads that the wicked had made already by the end of the first century.

Jude concludes with a reminder that safety is to be found in "the words which were spoken before of the apostles of our Lord Jesus Christ" (1:17), particularly in regard to their prophecies that there would arise "mockers" in the **last days**. These mockers would come from the ranks of **Church** members (1:18–19), but Jude nonetheless encourages the Saints to build up the kingdom and to look to Jesus Christ for mercy. Jude concludes the epistle in hope that the righteous will succeed in "making a difference" (1:22), even though some have fallen away. In an interesting note, Jude also makes reference to those who were increasingly righteous in the face of the schism, hating even the thought of sin. This further distancing between the wicked and righteous may be one more way that Jude suggests that the Lord is identifying those who are ready for punishment.

24

REVELATION

The author of the book of Revelation refers to himself by name—John—and tradition identifies this John with the author of the Gospel of John and the three epistles bearing his name. The letters, the Gospel, and the Apocalypse share common themes and concepts, but very little in the way of style and organization, most likely a result of different purposes for writing and different audiences. Although there is a fairly entrenched scholarly discussion concerning the dating of the three compilations, it is nearly impossible to firmly assign a relative date to any of the writings. Scholars have assigned a date for the book of Revelation anywhere between Nero's reign (A.D. 54–68) and the latter part of Domitian's reign (A.D. 81–96). Because the number 666 seems to be a coded form of Nero's name (see discussion for Revelation 13:18), it is possible that the book had its origin during his reign when obscuring anti-Nero rhetoric would make sense (Revelation 13:1–18). Some scholars interpret the coded name as also making sense in Domitian's reign, where Domitian is understood to be a Neronic archetype. This later dating may account for the finished form of the book and addition of the introductory letter, while the original revelation may have been recorded earlier.

The revelation contained in the book is actually composed of an introductory letter to seven churches in **Asia** (Revelation 1:1–3:22) and the revelation proper, which constitutes the remainder of the book. The opening verse refers to the book as the *apokalypsis* of **Jesus Christ**, or the revelation of what has been hidden away. John also refers to "the **Lord's day**," and therefore Sunday instead of the Jewish **Sabbath** (1:10).

This book is unlike any other writing in the New Testament and has its closest affinities with the **noncanonical** writing entitled the *Shepherd of Hermas*. The book of Revelation defined the genre of apocalypse and represents a significant shift in early Christian expectation when the Saints began to hope in a triumphant return of the Lord to help shift the momentum back in the battle against the evil forces of the world. In other words, Christians began to hope for another world and eternal existence rather than for peace and safety here on the earth. This book preserves a revelatory answer to those struggling Christians, declaring triumphantly, "Blessed are the dead which die in the Lord from henceforth: Yea, saith the Spirit, that they may rest from their labours; and their works do follow them" (14:13).

The revelation has frequently been interpreted in a linear way, beginning with a fixed point in time and progressing toward another point in the future. Consequently, the book is often understood as predictive of events that will occur if the reader can only find a reference point and then interpret forward and backward from that point. Although there are many other ways to interpret the book, one very productive way of reading it is to see in it a series of cycles containing seven events. In this way of thinking, there are seven churches, and seven dispensations, and seven trumpets, and seven vials poured out on the inhabitants of the earth, which describe the same events in a cyclical way. The vials and trumpets describe the same plagues and punishments that are poured out in every dispensation. In other words, the earth progresses through a series of cycles that are repeated—righteousness, **apostasy**, punishment, and renewal.

If the book is understood cyclically, then the signs and wonders are descriptive rather than predictive, and the book then becomes a message of hope for those who experience turbulent times. Many have read the book of Revelation and sought for clues to understand modern events. Finding safety through physical resistance is not emphasized in the book; rather, John finds hope and safety through dying in the Lord. The Doctrine and Covenants also includes a clarifying statement on how the structure of the book follows a dispensational pattern (D&C 77:6). Some commentators have interpreted Doctrine and Covenants 77:7 to exclude a cyclical interpretation: "Q. What are we to understand by the seven seals with which it was sealed? A. We are to understand that the first seal contains the things of the first thousand years, and the second also of the second thousand years, and so on until the seventh." It is also possible to see that the events of the thousand-year periods cyclically recur and that the seven dispensations provide context for understanding the events of each individual period.

The Opening

REVELATION 1:1–3

In what has been described as an expanded title, John announces the "Revelation of **Jesus Christ**, which God gave unto him, to shew unto his servants things which must shortly come to pass; and he sent and signified it by his angel unto his servant John" (Revelation 1:1). John declares that he has recorded "all things that he saw" (1:2). This is the first of some fifty-five times the verb *saw* is used in Revelation, emphasizing John as a seer—one who "sees."

Although we generally think of the Sermon on the Mount when the word *beatitude* is mentioned, the New Testament actually contains more than thirty beatitudes. One of those is found here: "Blessed [Greek, *markarios*] is he that readeth, and they that hear the words of this prophecy, and keep those things which are written therein" (1:3). This is the first of seven beatitudes found in the book of Revelation (14:13; 16:15; 19:9; 20:6; 22:7, 14). This particular beatitude emphasizes that the book is to be read aloud, heard by those who receive it, and that they should keep the commandments contained therein. The Joseph Smith Translation adds that reading and hearing are insufficient without understanding (1:3).

The Salutation

REVELATION 1:4–8

The customary first-century letter salutation follows: "John to the seven churches which are in **Asia**" (Revelation 1:4). What we will discover shortly is that the book of Revelation contains seven independent letters that have become parts of one large letter (Revelation 22:19). John introduces an important three-part pattern in his letters to the seven churches: "Grace be unto you, and peace, from him [1] *which is*, and [2] *which was*, and [3] *which is to come*" (1:4; emphasis added). This pattern is replicated throughout the book.

The Joseph Smith Translation provides the identity of the seven spirits: they are the "*seven servants who are over* the seven churches in Asia" (1:4). John identifies **Jesus Christ** as (1) the faithful witness (*ho martys ho pistos*), that is, the one who was faithful in death; (2) the first begotten of the dead, that is, the one who was raised from the dead; (3) and the prince [Greek, *archōn*, "ruler"] of the kings of the earth, the one who was exalted to the right hand of God (1:5). This is followed by another three-part pattern where Jesus is identified as the one who (1) "loved *us*"; (2) "washed *us* from our sins"; and (3) "made *us* kings and **priests** unto God" (1:5–6; emphasis added). The first-person plural most likely emphasizes the fact that Jesus' role as Savior and Redeemer is ongoing for all those who believe and follow him—not just the Saints in the seven cities mentioned. The reference to "kings and priests" reminds us of Exodus 19:6 (see also Revelation 20:6 and 1 Peter 2:5, 9). As noted above, Jesus is identified as he (1) which is, (2) which was, and (3) which is to come (1:8). Finally, Jesus announces that he is "the Almighty [Greek, *pantokratōr*, "powerful over all"]," the first of nine such designations in Revelation (1:8). In addition to this opening vision of Jesus Christ, the book of Revelation provides three other visions of the Lord (5:1–4; 19:11–21; 22:13–20), each of which is unique in perspective. These four visions combine to give the reader a distinct perspective on the risen Lord that is not fully depicted in the canonical Gospels.

The Command

REVELATION 1:9–20

John found himself on the Aegean island of Patmos, some forty-five miles southwest of Ephesus off the coast of the Roman province of **Asia** (Revelation 1:9). He was there "for the word of God, and for the testimony of **Jesus Christ**" (1:9). There has been some uncertainty about what John intended with this statement. Traditionally, commentators have suggested that John may have been banished to the small (four by seven miles) rocky island. There is no evidence that it was a Roman penal colony; it may simply have been the place to which John was sent to get him out of the way. Another possibility is that John went to the island voluntarily to preach the gospel.

The vision came to John on the "**Lord's day**" (1:10). He heard a loud voice (as a trumpet) saying, "I am Alpha and Omega," the first and last letters of the Greek alphabet, signifying the beginning and the ending. The voice commanded John to write what he was to see and send it to the seven churches located in modern western Turkey: Ephesus, Smyrna, Pergamos, Thyatira, Sardis, Philadelphia, and Laodicea (1:11).

The vision that follows could remind the Saints of Isaiah's vision of the Lord in the Jerusalem **temple** (Isaiah 6:1–13).

The Individual Letters

REVELATION 2:1–3:22

It has been noted that the promises to the faithful in this section are deeply rooted in **temple** worship, both ancient and modern. Prefaced with the phrase "he that hath an ear, let him hear what the Spirit saith unto the churches" (Revelation 2:7), the promises will be realized for those who overcome—those who have conquered through the blood of the Lamb.

The Lord commends the Ephesians for their patience and for rejecting false **apostles**, including the enigmatic and otherwise unknown "Nicolaitans." As will be the case in all of the seven letters, the Saints at

Ephesus are warned, "He that hath an ear, let him hear what the Spirit saith unto the churches" (2:7). In so doing, the Lord promises, "I give to eat of the tree of life, which is in the midst of the paradise of God" (2:7).

The Lord warns the Saints in Smyrna, envisioning local persecution by **Gentiles** and Jews, that "the devil shall cast some of you into prison." However, if they are "faithful unto death," the Lord will give them "a crown of life" (2:10). Additionally, they will "not be hurt of the second death" if they "hear what the Spirit saith unto the churches" (2:11).

The Altar of Zeus, now on view at the Pergamum Museum in Berlin, is thought to have been **"Satan's** seat" mentioned in the Lord's warning to Pergamos (2:13). Antipas, one of the local Saints, had already been martyred. Some members of the **Church** held the "doctrine of Balaam" and the doctrine of the "Nicolaitans." Although we cannot ascertain the exact nature of the doctrine noted in this passage, the Lord commands them to **repent**. If they have ears to hear they are promised, "I give to eat of the hidden manna [see John 6], and will give him a white stone, and in the stone a new name written, which no man knoweth saving he that receiveth it" (2:17; compare D&C 130:10–12).

In what is the longest of the seven letters, John addresses "the church in Thyatira" (2:18). The Lord describes himself as "the **Son of God**, who hath his eyes like unto a flame of fire, and his feet are like fine brass" (2:18). The Saints are commended for their works, charity, service, faith, and patience. Nevertheless, the Lord says, "I have a few things against thee, because thou sufferest that woman Jezebel, which calleth herself a prophetess, to teach and to seduce my servants to commit fornication, and to eat things sacrificed unto idols" (2:20). The faithful, however, are promised "power over the nations" (2:26) as they "rule [the nations] with a rod of iron" (2:27). Finally, they are promised "the morning star," often associated with Venus when it appears in the east, though here it is most likely a symbol of **Jesus Christ** (2:28).

The Church at Sardis is warned to "be watchful, and strengthen the things which remain, that are ready to die: for I have not found thy works perfect before God" (3:2), and the Lord commands them to repent (3:3). However, there are those who "have not defiled their garments," and as a result they will "walk with me in white: for they are worthy" and will "be clothed in white raiment" (3:4–5). For him who has ears to listen, the Lord will "not blot out his name out of the book of life" and "I will confess his name before my Father" (3:5; compare Matthew 10:33; 2 Timothy 2:12; 2 Nephi 9:41; D&C 45:3–5).

The Lord tells the Church in Philadelphia, "I know thy works: behold, I have set before thee an open door, and no man can shut it: for thou hast a little strength, and hast kept my word, and hast not denied my name" (3:8). The Saints also received a promise: "Him that overcometh will I make a pillar in the temple of my God, and he shall go no more out: . . . and I will write upon him my new name," signifying that he or she belongs to God (3:12; compare Revelation 7:1–3).

To the Laodiceans the Lord says, "Thou art neither cold nor hot . . . So then because thou art lukewarm, and neither cold nor hot, I will spue thee out of my mouth" (3:15–16). The implication of the warning to the Church of the Laodiceans is that the Church there must have been relatively well off. However, the members there do not recognize that they are in fact "wretched, and miserable, and poor, and blind, and naked" (3:17). They are counseled "to buy of me gold tried in the fire, that thou mayest be rich; and white raiment, that thou mayest be clothed, and that the shame of thy nakedness do not appear; and anoint thine eyes with eyesalve, that thou mayest see" (3:18). In one of the most memorable word pictures in the Bible, the Lord describes himself: "Behold, I stand at the door, and knock: if any man hear my voice, and open the door, I will come in to him, and will sup with him, and he with me" (3:20). Finally, the Lord promises that to those who overcome "will I grant to sit with me in my throne, even as I also overcame, and am set down with my Father in his throne" (3:21). Enthronement is an important aspect of ancient kingship; however, in the book of Revelation we have another gospel reversal. Paradoxically, the subjects of the kingdom are to be enthroned with Christ to reign forever and ever (1:6; 2:26–27; 5:10; 20:4, 6; 22:1, 3, 5; compare Matthew 19:28).

Elders in Heaven

REVELATION 4:1–11

After writing the letters to the seven churches, John is shown a vision of a gathering in heaven where God sits surrounded by twenty-four elders. This vision sets the stage for the remainder of the book because actions emanate outward from this group where God is seated and in control. There is no turmoil or worry here, and so with peace prevailing, God proceeds to do his work.

It is often overlooked that the Roman world in which John lived was made primarily of stone. There were stone streets and buildings as well as stone monuments and even stone utensils. When John saw heaven, it was a glorified image of his stone world, and every description that he gives of the heavenly realm is punctuated by a description of the precious building stones. In other words, heaven is a reflection of earthly existence, only more glorious and finely wrought. Furthermore, earth is administered through God's commands, which are interpreted as "lightnings and thunderings and voices" (Revelation 4:5).

John also sees four beasts in front of the throne that have a resemblance to earthly things—a lion, a calf, a man, and an eagle. Each of the beasts is able to fly and see while at the same time declaring the holiness of the "Lord God Almighty" (4:8). The Prophet Joseph Smith sought an explanation of these four beasts, which function as messengers in the vision. He taught, "They are figurative expressions, used by the Revelator, John, in describing heaven, the paradise of God, the happiness of man, and of beasts, and of creeping things, and of the fowls of the air; that which is spiritual being in the likeness of that which is temporal; and that which is temporal in the likeness of that which is spiritual; the spirit of man in the likeness of his person, as also the spirit of the beast, and every other creature which God has created" (D&C 77:2). Following the overall focus of chapter 4, the beasts represent God's care and administration for all aspects of his creation on the "sea of glass" (4:6), a representation of "the earth, in its sanctified, immortal, and eternal state" (D&C 77:1).

The Lamb

REVELATION 5:1–14

John's vision of the heavenly throne room continues. He sees God sitting upon his throne, holding a scroll with seven seals upon it (interestingly, the scroll is written on both sides). The only one worthy to open the sealed document is the "Lion of the tribe of Judah," who is also the "root" that is the descendant of King David (Isaiah 11:1). Paradoxically, the lion turns out to be a "lamb," the first of some twenty-nine references to **Jesus** as lamb in the book of Revelation. In what can only be considered a gospel reversal, the **messianic** king does not slay the wicked but is himself "slain" (4:6). He is at the same time the fulfillment of the *tamid*, or burnt offering (Exodus 29:38–46; Numbers 28:3–8), the **Passover** Lamb (Exodus 12:1–20; Numbers 9:2–5; Deuteronomy 16:1–8), and the Suffering Servant (Isaiah 53:7). Together they represent Jesus' death (John 1:29; 1 Corinthians 5:7).

Those present "fell down before the Lamb" and sang "a new song" (5:8–9). The worship of the Lamb here is the most vivid description of it in the New Testament (Philippians 2:9–11; Hebrews 1:6). John identifies three reasons the Lamb is worshipped: the Lamb is (1) worthy, (2) slain, (3) and redeems us by his "blood." Continuing, John expands his vision of salvation and worship. Redemption comes to "every kindred, and tongue, and people, and nation" (5:9). As "kings and **priests**," the Saints are promised that they will "reign on the earth" (5:10). The vision of heavenly worship continues with shouts of acclamation: "Worthy is the Lamb that was slain to receive power, and riches, and wisdom, and strength, and honour, and glory, and blessing" and "blessing, and honour, and glory, and power, be unto him that sitteth upon the throne, and unto the Lamb for ever and ever" (5:12–13).

The Opening of the Book with Seven Seals

REVELATION 6:1–17

The Prophet Joseph Smith taught, "We are to understand that the first seal contains the things of the first thousand years, and the second also of the second thousand years, and so on until the seventh" (D&C 77:7). Following this revelation, John moves quickly through the events of the first four seals and pauses for a moment on events associated with his own seal—the fifth—in which he sees the martyred Saints (Revelation 6:9). The colors of the horses and the description of the events largely emphasize the calamities of each dispensation rather than the times of righteousness. War seems to be a dominant theme. The prices given in verse 6 are famine prices.

The author moves swiftly to the sixth seal, where the revelation will pause to describe events in greater detail. At the opening of the sixth seal, heaven speaks in the form of an earthquake, a metaphor John uses for the warning voice of God (Revelation 4:5). The earth departs as a scroll and other calamities attend the opening of the sixth seal. Because early Christians wrote on scrolls, it is natural that they would describe the record of the earth as being written on a scroll, whereas we in modern times might refer to it as a book. When John speaks of heaven being "rolled together" as a scroll, we might say "shut like a book." The image represents the beginning of a new chapter of the story and not a destructive action. The Joseph Smith Translation tells us that with this new chapter, "the heavens opened as a scroll is opened when it is rolled together; and every mountain, and island, was moved out of its place" (JST, Revelation 6:14), and many, including kings and great men, "hid themselves in the dens and in the rocks of the mountains" (Revelation 7:15). This new chapter is the "great day of his wrath" (6:17). Following the cyclical interpretation of the book, it is helpful to note that John sees himself as part of the larger cycle of events but also places himself in the vision at a specific time (the fifth seal). That past, however, still interprets the present; and what lies ahead of the fifth seal is still in the future. A cyclical interpretation does not diminish a linear progression in the book but rather shows how history occurs in cycles—in this case a cycle of punishment, judgment, and salvation, much in the same way the Book of Mormon emphasizes a cycle of pride.

Who Is Able to Stand?

REVELATION 7:1–17

In this section, John "saw" the angels intervene to protect the Saints (Revelation 7:1–4). They are sealed: "And I heard the number of them which were sealed [indicating that they belong to God]: and there were sealed an hundred and forty and four thousand of all the tribes of the children of Israel" (7:4; see also D&C 77:11). The vision expanded to include "a great multitude, which no man could number, of all nations, and kindreds, and people, and tongues" (7:9). The earlier question, "For the great day of his wrath is come; and who shall be able to stand?" (6:17) is now answered. They "stood before the throne, and before the Lamb, clothed with white robes, and palms in their hands" (7:9) because they have come "out of great tribulation, and have washed their robes, and made them white in the blood of the Lamb" (7:14). Here is another important gospel reversal: washing in blood makes one's garments white! The result is that they are "before the throne of God, and serve him day and night in his **temple**" (7:15). They are blessed beyond measure in what has often been described as one of the most beautiful images of heaven: they are not hungry or thirsty, because the shepherding "Lamb which is in the midst of the throne shall feed them, and shall lead them unto living fountains of waters" (7:17). Ultimately, God "shall wipe away all tears from their eyes" through the slaughtered Lamb (7:17).

The First Four Angels

REVELATION 8:1–9

Chapter 8 recounts the opening of the seventh seal, and thus the beginning of the end. At the opening of the seventh seal, seven angels come forward with seven trumpets, and before any destruction is unleashed upon the earth the prayers of the Saints are heard, thus giving context for what will occur thereafter. The content of that prayer is not indicated, but drawing upon the previous metaphor for the voice of God, the inhabitants of the earth hear "voices, and thunderings, and lightnings, and an earthquake" (8:5). The implication is that God is warning his Saints in preparation for what will take place.

The seven plagues to be poured out upon the earth are (1) "hail and fire mingled with blood" (8:7); (2) "a great mountain burning with fire was cast into the sea" (8:8); (3) "a great star [falling] from heaven" (8:10); (4) "the third part of the sun was smitten, and the third part of the moon, and the third part of the stars" (8:12); (5) "a star falls from heaven unto the earth" (9:1); (6) a prophetic warning to **repent**; and (7) and the testimony of the elders. As it was with the seven horsemen, John's attention is on the sixth and seventh angels, spending only nine verses on the first four seals.

Following John's emphasis on descriptive rather than predictive signs, the plagues describe natural calamities that affect trees and grass, the sea, rivers, and the stars (8:7–13). Because John does not provide any specific instructions on how the reader is to react to these signs, it is likely that his purpose is to help the faithful see that the Lord speaks with the thunder, lightning, and natural disasters. The chapter is addressed to the faithful and does not provide a warning to the wicked.

In verse 11 the star that pollutes the waters is referred to by name, "Wormwood" (Greek, *apsinthos*, "wormwood" or "apsinthe"; 8:11). If John has a specific person or event in mind, the reader is left to seek further prophetic explanation to understand the intended point of reference. This star has a parallel to the fall of **Satan**, which also resulted in the casting out of a third part of the host of heaven. Here the fall of Wormwood results in "the third part of the waters" (8:11) becoming bitter or poisonous. Some commentators have sought to identify a specific event in the reference to Wormwood. Such an identification, however, must rely on further reve- lation because John's purpose is wholly descriptive. No actions are required upon seeing Wormwood.

The Fifth Angel
REVELATION 9:1–12

After the description of events associated with the first four angels, the events following the sounding of the fifth angel's trumpet result in a calamity upon the earth (Revelation 9:1–4). The fifth angel holds the key to the bottomless pit, which is described as a prison holding menacing creatures that are akin to locusts and scorpions (9:2–3). These creatures come up out of the pit through a veil of smoke. John paints a vivid word picture of these creatures and describes their shape as being "like unto horses" (9:7), and they wear crowns on their heads like "men" (9:7). These "men" wear their hair as that of "women" (9:8). Then John proceeds to describe their teeth, breastplates, and the sound of their movement, which was "as the sound of many horses running to battle" (9:9).

This detailed description is the first in the book of Revelation of any of the plagues and is interpreted as one of the three "woes" (9:11–12). Figuratively, this army is not mortal, coming from the "bottomless pit," but at the end of the chapter the king who leads them is identified as "Abaddon" (Hebrew) and "Apollyon" (Greek), both symbolic names that connect the figurative with the temporal (9:11). John seems to indicate a mortal king and army with the following verse, or at least a mortal reaction to a symbolic event: "And in those days shall men seek death, and shall not find it; and shall desire to die, and death shall flee from them" (9:6), and the earth will be tormented for five months (9:5), suggesting a limited time rather than an enduring plague. Interestingly, in this chapter the verbs detailing the reaction to the fifth angel suggest a very human response, where men "seek death" and "desire to die" (9:6).

The Sixth Angel
REVELATION 9:13–21

As he did with the events following the trumpet of the fifth angel, John treats the events of the sixth trumpet in great detail. Again, there is a specific duration of time given amounting to a little over a year and may be a figurative reference rather than an exact prediction of time. The angels unleash the river Euphrates, which is symbolic of a mortal army: "The horsemen were two hundred thousand thousand: and I heard the number of them" (9:16), a number that John does not estimate but gives precisely. The army is also described in gruesome detail. John's use of symbolic or figurative language implies that the army was unlike anything he had seen before. Even though this terrible army inflicts death upon mankind, some "yet repented not," evoking further calamities. The fifth and sixth trumpets sound to signal the unleashing of a mortal army.

Another Angel in Heaven
REVELATION 10:1–11

Chapter 10 interrupts the seven angels to report "another mighty angel," who brings a positive message, likely an encouragement to **repent** because many yet remain hard-hearted: "The rest of the men which were not killed by these plagues yet repented not of the works of their hands" (Revelation 9:20). The heavenly interruption is signaled again by thunderous voices (10:4) and the accomplishment of God's "mystery . . . as he hath declared to his servants the prophets" (10:7). John is shown a "little book" (10:9), which he is instructed to eat. The book represents a mission that the prophet is given, which "was in my mouth sweet as honey: and as soon as I had eaten it, my belly was bitter" (10:10; D&C 77:14). That mission, given the context of chapter 10, is bitter because the plagues do not result in the **repentance** of mankind, and by implication the testimony of the prophet likewise does not result in repentance by the wicked. This chapter has conceptual parallels to Isaiah 6:5–13, in which Isaiah was given a bitter mission to "make the heart of this people fat, and make their ears heavy, and shut their eyes" (Isaiah 6:10).

The Two Prophets

REVELATION 11:1–14

When John is given a "reed like unto a rod" (11:1) to measure the **temple**, the implication is that the temple is being restored. A similar situation occurs in Zechariah 2:5–9, and John only measures the holiest precincts and the altar but not the outer court of the Gentiles, "for it is given unto the Gentiles" (11:2). The idea is that the holiest area of the temple is preserved from being defiled, whereas the outer, and public, court is overrun for "forty and two months" (11:2). The time allotted for the Gentiles to run freely in the outer court is limited, while the number of months is also mentioned in Daniel 7:25 and 12:7. This symbolic time of three and a half years is important because it allows the reader to see that the destruction will not last indefinitely.

Two prophets will minister in Jerusalem at the same time as the Gentiles shall overrun the court of the temple. The duration of their ministry is the same as the "forty and two months" (1,260 days = 42 months of 30 days). These two prophets are also spoken of in Zechariah 4:1–14 and Isaiah 51:19–20 (as quoted in 2 Nephi 8:19–20), where they are referred to as "two sons." In the context of this chapter, the ministry of the two sons proceeds outward from the holiest part of the temple, and as they go forth into the wicked city of Jerusalem (11:1–7), the two prophets are killed. They have the power to save themselves from death and to smite their enemies (11:5), but in the end, when they have finished their mission, they are martyred (11:8).

Upon hearing of their deaths, "the people and kindreds and tongues and nations," a euphemism for the entire world, celebrate the cessation of prophetic warning against their actions (11:9). However, the two prophets are resurrected after lying in the street for three and a half days, a number that is not exactly equivalent to but perhaps reminiscent of the time the Lord spent in the tomb (Matthew 12:40). The visible resurrection of the two prophets serves as a reminder and warning that their testimony was of the Lord. A "great earthquake," a figurative statement that is used in the book of Revelation to signify the voice of God, attends their **ascension** into heaven. Given the number of the slain—seven thousand—and its size relative to the population of Jerusalem both in John's day and in the modern era, it is likely that the author intends to emphasize the prophetic warning and not the catastrophic calamity that would befall Jerusalem. If the two prophets are sent as a sign of warning, then the majority of the people are given ample time to accept it, even though the two prophets are killed. John refers to this event as the "second woe" (11:14). This event, which may indeed depict a singular future event, also fits well into the cyclical interpretation, in which the Holy of Holies of the temple is protected from defilement, prophetic voices go unheeded, and the Resurrection of **Christ** remedy the rejection his prophets have received.

The Seventh Angel
REVELATION 11:15–19

Chapter 11 returns to the sounding of the seventh and final trumpet, signaling what the reader has come to expect will be another plague, but instead this time the trumpet signals the testimony of twenty-four elders (Revelation 11:16). In light of the prophetic warning issued by the two prophets who shall minister in Jerusalem, the inhabitants of the earth need time to accept or reject their witness. The testimony of these twenty-four elders is not well received, and in reaction to it "the nations were angry" (11:18). The elders call upon God to judge the nations and "give reward unto thy servants the prophets" (11:18; see Psalm 82). The concluding testimony of this chapter is the voice of God emanating from the holiest place of the **temple**: "And there were lightnings, and voices, and thunderings, and an earthquake, and great hail" (11:19).

The Rise of the Dragon

REVELATION 12:1–17

If the book of Revelation is a linear description of the **last days**, then this chapter begins with a flashback to the fall of **Satan** and his war, which was initiated in the premortal realm and has spilled over to the war that is being waged on the earth. If the book is to be understood as a cyclical description of earth's existence, then this chapter begins a new cycle describing evil that will help the reader understand why mankind refuses to **repent** and come to the Lord. The two figures entering into battle are diametrically opposed to each other: "a woman clothed with the sun" (12:1) and a "great red dragon" (12:3). The woman is unarmed, unless her glory is her weapon to defend herself against the dragon. The woman represents the **Church**, and the dragon represents the devil, the original enemy of God's kingdom (JST, 12:7–9). In John's day, the need for a savior was taught in contrast to abiding the Jewish law, which emphasized salvation through obedience to the commandments. The Jews needed a physical deliverer, but Christianity—the Church—helped reemphasize the need for the spiritual Savior in that increasingly legalized perspective (Romans 3:20–28; 7:1–8). The woman brings forth the child that will save mankind, or, in other words, the woman brought forth the realization that salvation began with the birth of a child and not with the revelation of the law. Some commentators have seen the child as the political kingdom born from the Church in the latter days. Indeed, Revelation 12:2 in the Joseph Smith Translation could be interpreted in that way. However, because the child rules "with a rod of iron" (12:5), a metaphor for the gospel (1 Nephi 11:25), it is also possible that John here envisions the world as rejecting gospel rule, resulting in the gospel being taken from the earth.

When the woman flees "into the wilderness" (Revelation 12:5) to hide from the dragon, she stays in hiding for 1,260 days, the same amount of time that the two prophets will minister in Jerusalem (11:3; see JST Revelation 12:5, which changes "days" to "years.") This specific time frame is probably figurative, representing a limited time. In the same way that

Michael battled Satan in the premortal existence, he now continues that battle here on the earth. Eventually Satan was cast out of heaven, and his anger for having been cast out has provoked him to continue his struggle against good here.

The war between Michael and Satan is won not through strength of arms or innovation but rather through testimony and "the blood of the Lamb" (12:11)—not, however, before the dragon pursues the Church (the woman) into the wilderness. The woman is forced into hiding and is given assistance through "two wings of a great eagle" to help her in her flight (12:14). While in the wilderness the woman is nourished for "a time, and times, and half a time" (12:14), again a reference to a forty-two months or a "a year, two years, and a half." Thus the prophets minister for forty-two months, and the woman is pursued for forty-two months.

The Identity of the Dragon
REVELATION 13:1–18

John's detour from discussing the plagues of the latter days continues in this chapter as the identity of the beast is considered. Using descriptive language to paint a recognizable picture of the beast, the author first looks at an event that has predictive value for the reader. A beast raises its head "out of the sea" (Revelation 13:1) and is wounded, perhaps prior to raising its head out of the water (13:3). The reader can see that the beast has dominion over many kingdoms, which are figuratively described as seven heads and ten horns. That wound "was healed" (13:3), the passive verb form suggesting that an agent was needed, and it is probable that the dragon (13:2) healed the beast in an act of deception. The beast, just as the animals in heaven before it (Revelation 4:7), is described in figurative language suggesting the ability to move swiftly (a leopard) and surely (a bear) and with power (a lion). Because of the healing **miracle**, "they worshipped the dragon" (13:4), where "they" refers to the inhabitants of the earth and not the righteous.

The result of the widespread acceptance of the beast causes him to speak blasphemy and to come out against God more openly, in a way revealing his true identity more fully. The ministry of the beast endures for forty-two months, the same amount of time that the two prophets minister in Jerusalem and the same duration that the **Church** hides in the wilderness.

John does not relate the fall of the first beast here, but verse 11 discusses "another beast" that has "two horns like a lamb" but that "spake as a dragon" (13:11; see also Matthew 7:15). The description of being like a lamb appears to be John's way of expressing the deceptive guise of the second beast and the possibility that it may literally be one of **Christ**'s followers. The second beast is actually the prophet of the first beast, or the dragon, because he performs false miracles (13:13) and attempts to enforce faith in the first beast (13:14). His attempt to grow faith in the first beast extends to creating an image/statue that figuratively comes to life. All those who refuse to worship the image of the beast are to "be killed" (13:15), whereas those who worship the image receive a mark in their right hand or their forehead.

Thus far it appears that John's description of the beast is representative of events that John has seen in vision. The final verse provides a clue to the identity of the beast: "Here is wisdom. Let him that hath understanding count the number of the beast: for it is the number of a man; and his number is Six hundred threescore and six" (13:18). The number 666 has led to many speculative interpretations, and in the first centuries after Christ, some Christians thought that John was speaking of the Roman emperor Nero. By taking the name **Caesar** Neron (the Greek rendering) and writing it using the Hebrew alphabet and then counting the value of those letters (the alphabet in Hebrew and Greek is used for numbers, for example alpha=1, beta=2, etc.), the reader winds up with the number 666. In **Latin**-speaking areas of the Church, the manuscripts record the number in 13:18 as 616, which is the number equivalent of Caesar Nero in Latin. It is not clear whether John intended to encode Nero's name or not; but in the event that he did, he may have been expressing his understanding that the beast of the latter days would be wicked in some of the ways that Nero was.

Interestingly, following a cyclical understanding of the book, where literal events are depicted, the chapters spanning the two prophets in

Jerusalem, the war in heaven, the beast that rises up to fight the Saints, and the Lamb on Mount Zion describe the gospel plan in its cyclical entirety: Prophets warn the wicked and prepare the righteous as Satan carries out his war here on the earth through his servants (the many-headed beast), while the Redeemer atones for this calamity, bringing creation back into harmony with God's will.

The Lamb on Mount Zion
REVELATION 14:1–20

Chapter 14 shifts the story back to the epic of salvation and away from the punishments of the wicked and the deceptive ministry of the dragon. Here, **Christ** stands triumphantly on Mount Zion with the "hundred forty and four thousand" (Revelation 14:1), who also have a mark on their foreheads. In contrast to the mark of the beast (13:16–17), this mark signifies those who are saved through the name of the **Son of God**. These individuals also sing "a new song" (14:3), which is known only to them. They are depicted in celebration while the wicked are coerced to worship the beast. John calls these righteous souls "virgins" (14:4), although it is unlikely that he intends this to be understood as encouragement to live a life of celibacy. Rather, they are unspotted from the world and are pure, symbolized figuratively though the concept of virginity. They also stand as a contrast to those who have followed the whore of all the earth (17:1).

The 144,000 are "without fault before the throne of God" (14:5), and the reference to another angel flying "in the midst of heaven, having the everlasting gospel to preach," connects the work of the 144,000 with the spread of the gospel to counter the ministry of the beast (14:6). Contextually, the author places the ministry of the 144,000 alongside that of the other angel, who has the gospel to preach and who declares that "the hour of his judgment is come" (14:7). These latter-day ministers also carry a voice of prophetic warning against those who follow the beast, telling them that undiluted punishment will be poured out upon the wicked (14:10).

This positive interlude does not indicate a cessation of hostilities, and

John hints that some will suffer martyrdom during this period: "Blessed are the dead which die in the Lord from henceforth" (14:13). Three angels (14:15, 17–18) come out of the **temple**, two with sickles and one declaring the time for the harvest to begin. The angel who comes out "from the altar" (14:18) reminds the reader of the martyrs who cry from beneath the altar (Revelation 6:9–11); perhaps the connection is intentional to suggest that the cry of the martyrs has led to the beginning of the harvest. The harvest here has negative overtones as the "angel thrust in his sickle" (14:19) and cast the gathered vines into the winepress which "was trodden without the city, *and blood came out of the winepress,* even unto the horse bridles, by the space of a thousand and six hundred furlongs" (14:20; emphasis added).

The Seven Angels
REVELATION 15:1–8

Chapter 15 returns to the cycle of destruction inflicted upon the inhabitants of the earth and documents in figurative language the calamities of the latter days. The victory of the 144,000 and the Lamb on Mount Zion is declared in the opening verses of this chapter as an introduction preceding widespread calamity. The 144,000 sing a new song of victory and salvation (D&C 84:89; 133:56). Immediately following their song, the seven angels go forth to inflict "seven plagues" (15:6), which are symbolically poured out from vials. Returning to the cyclical structure of the book, the events described in this chapter both prophesy of the **last days** and also depict a reality of every dispensation, where some are saved from every tribe. Certainly John wants the reader to understand the future component of the revelation but also to appreciate that his understanding is based on the cycle of similar events from all previous dispensations.

The Seven Plagues

Revelation 16:1–21

Like the destruction following the seven trumpets, these seven plagues result largely in the destruction of the physical world. In them, the earth, sea, rivers, sun, and air are smitten, each resulting in a catastrophe upon mankind. The figurative plagues may be literal in some sense, but the author provides few details and instead seems to focus on purpose, thus giving the reader a slightly different point of emphasis.

The first plague results in the smiting of those who wear the "mark of the beast" (Revelation 16:2), while the second results in the death of "every living soul" in the sea (16:3). The third angel smites the fresh water (16:4), the fourth angel smites the sun (16:8), the fifth angel smites the physical "seat of the beast" (16:10), and the sixth angel smites the Euphrates, causing it to dry up (16:12). All of these plagues are punishments for those who will not **repent**, and there is as much emphasis on the kind of suffering as there is on identifying the exact plague. For example, one plague is so painful that those who experience it "*gnawed their tongues for pain*, and blasphemed the God of heaven because of their pains and their sores, and repented not of their deeds" (16:10–11; emphasis added).

The seventh plague comes shortly after the gathering of armies at Armageddon or the mountain of Megiddo. When the armies of the Lamb and the 144,000 (the righteous preserved in the book, the sealed from each tribe) are gathered against the followers of the beast, the seventh angel "poured out his vial into the air; and there came a great voice out of the **temple** of heaven, from the throne, saying, *It is done*" (16:17; emphasis added). This declaration is made by "voices, and thunders, and lightnings; and there was a great earthquake" (16:18). The seventh plague is overwhelming to mankind, bringing a hailstorm in which the hailstones weigh roughly one talent each, or a little over fifty-five pounds. The first plagues follow closely the order and descriptions of the previous plagues in the book, and here John again seems to emphasize the struggle and not the linear predictive value of reading their descriptions.

The Identity of the Woman and the Beast
Revelation 17:1–18

John is given an interpretation of some portions of the vision, which he also shares with his readers. Following the struggle between good and evil (Revelation 16:17), John reveals some specific details regarding the beast and its rider, although surprisingly the beast has had no rider up to this point in the vision. The rider is negatively depicted, being called "the great whore that sitteth upon many waters" (17:1), with a mark on her forehead, "the mother of harlots" (17:5), and she is "drunken with the blood of the saints" (17:6). The idea John seems to convey is one of sexual impurity, the figurative master of the beast. This provocative image may signal John's understanding that immorality and unchaste behavior are at the heart of the fight against God's kingdom.

Verses 7 through 18 provide a more detailed description of the beast with seven heads and ten horns. The seven heads of the beast represent seven mountains that are ruled by the unchaste woman. This figurative representation may have been a veiled reference to **Rome**, the city of seven hills. If that identification is correct, then it should be understood figuratively as representing the seat of corruption in John's day and not as a specific prophecy of Rome's involvement in the future. The horns of the beast represent kings that are controlled by the woman who sits on the seven hills and probably represent kingdoms ruled by Rome, although even here the number ten appears figurative. In the end, the ten kings will rebel against the woman and overthrow her (17:16), John's purpose being to describe her fall as the result of inner conflict and dissension. The reference to "the beast that was, and is not, even he is the eighth, and is of the seven, and goeth into perdition" (17:11) is too vague to be interpreted with any confidence.

The Fall of Babylon
REVELATION 18:1–24

This entire chapter is devoted to a description of the fall of Babylon, where the wicked have "lived deliciously" but have now been cast down. The book of Revelation has up until this point used many figurative expressions of time such as a "half an hour" (Revelation 8:1) and forty-two months, and the author now tells the reader that the plagues of the book come upon Babylon "in one day" (18:8), again suggesting that the references to time are largely figurative and meant to convey a sense of limited duration.

The fall of Babylon is described in economic terms: "For no man buyeth their merchandise any more" (18:11), and with her fall, precious things disappear from the market: "Thou shalt find them no more at all" (18:14). Such an emphasis on markets may represent John's desire to convey the truth that the beast is not simply a figurative image; instead, it is an entity that is driven by commerce and riches. The pursuit of riches may indeed be one of the many reasons the beast fights against the Saints of God. John evokes the powerful image of a millstone being hurled into the sea, recalling Jesus' teaching that "whosoever shall offend one of these little ones that believe in me, it is better for him that a millstone were hanged about his neck, and he were cast into the sea" (Mark 9:42).

The Marriage of the Lamb
REVELATION 19:1–21

As the vision begins to draw to a close, the author returns to the twenty-four elders seated around the throne of God (Revelation 4:4), who now praise the Lord because of his work of salvation. Although there was no disorder in heaven, John's returning to the subject of the elders in heaven and their shouts of "Alleluia" (19:1) demonstrate that the plan of God has been carried out successfully. The righteous dead form a significant number in heaven, "a great multitude, and as the voice of many waters, and as the voice of mighty thunderings" (19:6) and speak with the voice of God, implying unity with him.

The scene is one of rejoicing, using the figurative language of a wedding celebration in which the Lamb of God is married to the **Church**, which marriage is personified in verse 8. The Lord and his Church were already wed in a spiritual sense, but the formalized wedding described here depicts the **ascension** of the Saints to a position of equality with the Lamb. This stunning gift is an ideal that John seeks to convey through a series of contrasting descriptions of wickedness and righteousness. For instance, the clothing of the bride—"fine linen, clean and white" (19:8)—is in sharp contrast to the gaudy, colorful, and extravagant clothing of the harlot (17:4).

John relates his attempt to worship the angel who acted as his guide. He is rebuffed in the attempt but taught that the "testimony of **Jesus** is the spirit of prophecy" (19:10). The implication of this interchange is that the eyes may at times deceive but that the testimony of Jesus leads to a correct understanding of things as they really are. John returns the reader's attention to the "white horse" and its rider, who is now the **Son of God** or "Faithful and True" (19:11). The earlier white horseman had come at a time of war (6:2), which set the stage for the triumphant ride of "The Word of God" (19:13).

The final battle, in which the Son of God faces off against the powers of the devil, is not described in terms that suggest a mortal struggle between men. Instead, the Son smites his enemies with the word of his mouth (19:21), and his vesture is already bloodied even before the battle begins, suggesting that he has already overcome the foe.

The First Resurrection

REVELATION 20:1–15

At the beginning of the millennial reign of **Christ** on the earth, God will bind **Satan** for "a thousand years" (Revelation 20:2), which in the context of the book of Revelation comes as a welcome relief after the plagues that have been poured out upon the inhabitants of the earth. God is in control of the binding of Satan, and here it appears as a physical binding and not simply as Satan's departure because the children of men are no longer willing to follow him. Shortly after or even coinciding with the binding of Satan is the "first resurrection" (20:5) wherein the righteous shall come forth and reign with Christ on the earth for a thousand years. John does not specify whether those who will come forward in the first resurrection will belong to one kingdom only but rather that they are all those who successfully resisted taking upon themselves the mark of the beast.

John pauses only briefly to describe the millennial reign, devoting only six verses to the subject. His interest appears to be centered on the absolute fall of Satan and not the temporary binding of the devil for a thousand years. At the end of the thousand years, the devil again gathers his forces under the symbolic names of "Gog and Magog" (20:7–9; see also D&C 88:111–116). This massive army, whose numbers are "as the sand of the sea," surrounds "the camp of the saints about, and the beloved city [Jerusalem]" (20:9). The gathering of this army, though its numbers are "as the sand of the sea," is of little consequence, for it is quickly dispatched by "fire [that] came down from God out of heaven, and devoured them. And the devil that deceived them was cast into the lake of fire and brimstone, where the beast and the false prophet are, and shall be tormented day and night for ever and ever" (20:9–10).

Using the image of "books" (Greek, *biblia*), John foretells how the mortal experience will lay the foundation for exaltation. The judgment from the "books, according to their works" (20:12) is by implication a judgment of mortality, which in light of the prevailing wickedness described in the book of Revelation will go poorly for some. They will suffer a "second death" (20:14), in contrast to those who will enjoy eternal life and exaltation. The warning that the wicked will be cast into the lake of fire describes figuratively what will be experienced emotionally and spiritually.

The New Jerusalem

REVELATION 21:1–22:5

After the victory of the Lamb, the "new heaven and new earth" (Revelation 21:1) are adorned with the descent of a "new Jerusalem" (21:2). Heaven and earth are "new" in the sense that they are rejuvenated or refreshed, but, particularly with regard to heaven, they are not re-created or refashioned. The city is also new in the sense that it now exists as God has intended it, with God himself dwelling with them in a joyous reunion where there are no more tears or death (21:3–4). God is both the beginning and the end, "Alpha and Omega" (21:6), the first and last letters of the Greek alphabet, and also structurally in this book in which a vision of God is interwoven into the beginning of the revelation as well as its conclusion (2:2, 8, 12, 18; 3:1, 7, 14).

The description of the New Jerusalem is largely figurative, with its twelve gates and illumination by the glory of God. No fire burns in the city. The frequent use of the number twelve may be an intentional reference to a city that is founded on the teachings of the Twelve **Apostles** of the Lamb. The city is built on "twelve foundations" which have the names of the apostles written on them (21:14). The city is a perfect cube, each side measuring twelve thousand stadia (KJV, "furlongs"), reminding the reader of the twelve thousand sealed from every tribe. The city is built of precious stones, some of which were used in the ephod of Aaron (Exodus 28:17–21; 39:10–14; Ezekiel 28:13). Although the purpose of numbering the stones is unclear, the depiction of God's kingdom being made out of precious stones reminds the reader that John is describing a glorified and exalted version of an ancient city in his day that was similarly made of stone, albeit common stone.

The purpose of the **temple**, to come into the presence of God, is realized on the new earth because God is physically present with the righteous. John notes somewhat surprisingly, "*And I saw no temple therein:* for the Lord God Almighty and the Lamb are the temple of it" (21:22; emphasis added). The mention of the tree of life brings the reader visually back to the Garden of Eden and Nephi's vision (1 Nephi 11:1–28). Mankind can now safely partake of the fruit of the tree of life without being barred from doing so by the cherubim (Revelation 22:1–5).

John's Concluding Testimony
REVELATION 22:6–21

The book of Revelation closes with a purpose statement for the book, telling the reader that the blessed are those who keep the "sayings of the prophecy of this book" (22:7). Keeping the sayings of the book implies being prepared and focused on the Lamb of God, believing that he can save despite what appear to be overwhelming odds. The book does not enumerate commandments, but rather it advocates belief in the idea that God is powerful enough to save us.

John also warns that "the time is at hand" (22:10), which has been true in every dispensation. The time of the Lord's coming may be many years off, but that should not be used to undermine the central ideas of the book, namely that wickedness opposes everything good and wholesome and that only God can save us. That day is always here.

John also seems to have understood that his writings would not fare well over time, and that some would attempt to manipulate the words of his prophecy. He warns any who would add to or take away from the words written in "this book" (22:18). John wrote several centuries before there was an official canon of books comprising the New Testament (usually dated to c. A.D. 367), and therefore his warning can only be interpreted as a reference to the prophecy contained in the book of Revelation. If the revelation of John were intended to serve as a warning, then tampering with it would circumvent both his testimony and warning to the Saints to be prepared.

The book ends with a first-person testimony of the Lord: "I **Jesus** have sent mine angel to testify unto you" (22:16). He extends the promise to all humanity—the same promise he offered to the woman at the well in **Samaria**: "And whosoever will, let him take the water of life freely" (22:17; John 4:10–15).

Epilogue

THE NEW TESTAMENT AND THE RESTORATION

Joseph Smith read a passage in the New Testament that changed his life—and the world. He recalled, "I was one day reading the Epistle of James, first chapter and fifth verse, which reads: *If any of you lack wisdom, let him ask of God, that giveth to all men liberally, and upbraideth not; and it shall be given him*" (Joseph Smith–History 1:11). He continued, "Never did any passage of scripture come with more power to the heart of man than this did at this time to mine. It seemed to enter with great force into every feeling of my heart. I reflected on it again and again, knowing that if any person needed wisdom from God, I did; for how to act I did not know, and unless I could get more wisdom than I then had, I would never know; for the teachers of religion of the different sects understood the same passages of scripture so differently as to destroy all confidence in settling the question by an appeal to the Bible" (Joseph Smith–History 1:12).

Fortunately, Joseph followed what was surely divine inspiration and knelt in a grove of trees near his home in Palmyra, New York, seeking the God of the Bible. In that sacred place he met the Father and his Son, the risen Jesus Christ. They spoke to him—and their words have spread throughout the world as missionaries have taken the good news of the restored gospel of Jesus Christ to the inhabitants of the world.

With Joseph's remarkable First Vision, the Restoration began in 1820. Throughout his work and ministry, the New Testament continued to play a significant role in the unfolding of the glorious gospel revealed again by a modern witness of Jesus Christ. As Joseph translated the Book of Mormon, phrases, direct quotes, images, and examples from the New Testament filled its pages, providing a familiar environment for those Christians who read it (see, for example, 3 Nephi 12–14; compare with Matthew 5–7). The Prophet and other Church leaders and members often quoted and taught from the New Testament, drawing important lessons from this sacred book of scripture. New Testament words, phrases, and allusions naturally fell from their lips, and the same is true today. We sing hymns based on various New Testament passages, and our lessons and talks are infused with New Testament language, doctrine, and stories. We continue to quote from and study this remarkable book as an inspired witness of the Father, the Son, and the Holy Ghost.

Joseph Smith never felt a contradiction between believing in the New Testament and accepting new revelation. He understood that a belief and trust in the New Testament impelled one to accept continuing revelation through the Holy Ghost. Indeed, he often testified that he was restoring the ancient New Testament faith—the principles, practices, and doctrine origi- nally taught by Jesus Christ and his apostles in the first century (Articles of Faith 1, 3, 4, 5, 6, and 13).

While the New Testament is a priceless record of the original Church of Jesus Christ, many of its teachings, practices, and principles are clarified, explained, and confirmed in Restoration scripture and in Joseph Smith's prophetic teachings and sermons. Modern prophets and apostles continue to provide authoritative doctrinal interpretations and inspired applications to teachings and stories from the New Testament. These leaders minister to the Church for the very same reasons the apostle Paul described: "For the perfecting of the saints, for the work of the ministry, for the edifying of the body of Christ: till we all come in the unity of the faith, and of the knowledge of the Son of God, unto a perfect man, unto the measure of the stature of the fulness of Christ: that we henceforth be no more children, tossed to and fro, and carried about with every wind of doctrine, by the sleight of men, and cunning craftiness, whereby they lie in wait to deceive" (Ephesians 4:12–14).

Joseph Smith did not believe that the Bible contained all of God's word. Instead, he understood that the Lord was revealing through him things "kept hid from before the foundation of the world, things that pertain to the dispensation of the fulness of times" (D&C 124:41). Significantly, neither did he believe that everything had been revealed to him (Articles of Faith 9). Hence the continuing need for modern prophets and apostles—those divinely called leaders to whom God reveals his will.

Joseph Smith and his successors taught and testified that modern revelation should become the lens through which one reads the New Testament and that the Restoration provided new insights about God's eternal plan that were only hinted at in the Bible. Therefore, the New Testament was a springboard for Joseph Smith to announce the Lord's mind and will concerning his plan to save and exalt his children (see, for example, D&C 76:11–19 and 138:6–11). The Prophet did not believe he was reading anything new into the book, but instead was simply drawing the true meaning out of the Bible as he taught members of the Church the restored gospel he had received from the Lord (Joseph Smith–History 1:73–74).

One of the most significant blessings of the Restoration was the Prophet's inspired translation of the Bible, both the Old and New Testaments. This work, which he once described as a "branch of my calling," was one of the important ways the Lord taught his young prophet the fulness of the gospel (*History of the Church*, 1:238). Through the Holy Spirit, he tutored Joseph as he carefully read the Bible. The Joseph Smith Translation not only provided a text but also facilitated additional revelation, insights, and teachings regarding the New Testament. The influence of the Joseph Smith Translation continues to affect the modern Church as we become more familiar with it and use it in our efforts to study the scriptures and learn the doctrines of Jesus Christ.

Modern prophets have testified to the importance and value of the Bible, both the Old and New Testaments. They continue to draw inspiration from the stories preserved in it. The Prophet Joseph Smith said, "I believe in this sacred volume. In it the 'Mormon' faith is to be found. We teach nothing but what the Bible teaches. We believe nothing, but what is to be found in this book" (*History of the Church*, 4:78; see also Ehat and Cook, *Words of Joseph Smith*, 33).

Elder James E. Talmage wrote: "The Church of Jesus Christ of

Latter-day Saints accepts the Holy Bible as the foremost of her standard works, first among the books which have been proclaimed as her written guides in faith and doctrine. In the respect and sanctity with which the Latter-day Saints regard the Bible they are of like profession with Christian denominations in general" (*Articles of Faith*, 236).

Elder Bruce R. McConkie testified: "There are no words to describe the power of a single book. . . . During all this long period the Bible did more to mellow the souls of men, more to keep such light and truth alive as was then found on earth, more to prepare men for a day when new revelation would come than any other book" ("The Book of Mormon—Its Eternal Destiny," August 18, 1978).

Elder Neal A. Maxwell noted: "In the New Testament and its four Gospels, each with its unique emphasis, the portrait of the living and mortal Messiah is painted powerfully. All of it was done not merely to provide an assemblage of aphorisms, but for the primary purpose described by John: 'But these are written, that ye might believe that Jesus is the Christ, the Son of God; and that believing ye might have life through his name' (John 20:31)" ("The New Testament—A Matchless Portrait of the Savior," 21).

President Boyd K. Packer taught: "In the New Testament course, you learn of the birth and ministry of Jesus the Christ and his divine sonship. You learn about ordinances, about baptism by immersion for the remission of sins. You read of the call of the Twelve and follow their ministry. You learn of the fatherhood of God. You learn of the Holy Ghost, the Comforter, and personal revelation. You relive the days of the Betrayal and the Crucifixion, and learn transcendent truths of the Atonement and the Resurrection. You learn of love and law and why a Redeemer. From the four Gospels to the book of Revelation, the teachings of the Master and of His Apostles—the Lord Jesus Christ's gospel—are opened to you" ("Library of the Lord," 38).

President Thomas S. Monson often draws from the New Testament as he teaches the Saints to live better lives as we serve one another and follow Jesus' example. His inspiring address in the January 2008 *Ensign*, "The Master Bridge Builder," declares that "Jesus Christ was the supreme architect and builder of bridges for you, for me, for all humankind. He has built the bridges over which we must cross if we are to reach our heavenly home" (6). Drawing from compelling New Testament stories, he describes how Jesus "grew, and waxed strong in spirit, filled with wisdom: and the grace of God was upon him" (Luke 2:40), and that he "went about doing good" (Acts 10:38). President Monson urges us to joyfully cross the bridges of obedience, service, and prayer the Savior built for us while reminding his followers that "inasmuch as ye have done it unto one of the least of these my brethren, ye have done it unto me" (Matthew 25:40). This living prophet of God recognizes the power of New Testament scripture to lift and shape the lives of each of God's children.

Who can doubt that the influence of the New Testament is immeasurable? Billions of people have been drawn closer to the Lord through this remarkable collection of inspired writings, and millions of them have been prepared to receive the fulness of the restored gospel because of their faith in and devotion to the New Testament.

One of the greatest miracles of the Restoration lies in how it helps us reconstruct the world of the Bible, particularly as it reveals the "plain and precious" truths and ordinances lost through centuries of apostasy and darkness but revealed again in our own day through a latter-day seer (1 Nephi 13:28). As one of the great explicators of the gospel of Jesus Christ, the New Testament's vital place in the canon of scripture can never be underestimated or even fully appreciated. The more we study its precepts in the light of the restored gospel, the closer we will draw to the Source of all truth.

GLOSSARY

Agrapha. Means "not written" and refers to the words of Jesus that are recorded outside of the canonical Gospels. For example, Luke preserves an agrapha of Jesus transmitted through Paul: "Remember the words of the Lord Jesus, how he said, It is more blessed to give than to receive" (Acts 20:35).

Alms. Jews were commanded to pay a tithe to provide for the poor, referred to in the modern era as the *Maaser Ani*. The biblical injunction to care for the poor through giving alms (Greek, *dikaiosunē*, "righteousness") is expressed clearly in Deuteronomy 14:28 and 26:12.

Aramaic. See **Languages.**

Ascension. The Ascension is the term used to describe Jesus being taken up into heaven after he was resurrected. Jesus ascended to heaven immediately after his first post-Resurrection appearances (Luke 24:50–51) and following his forty-day ministry (Acts 1:9–12).

Asia. The Roman province of Asia was governed by a proconsul whose duties were primarily to oversee judiciary matters in the province. During the reign of Augustus, some cities in Asia were given greater autonomy and were permitted to largely govern themselves. The Roman province of Asia covered most of what is today western Turkey.

Apostle. See **Disciple/Disciples.**

Apostasy. The Greek term *apostasia* refers to an inner rebellion or abandonment. The word is formed from the preposition *apo*, "away," and the verb *histēmi*, "to stand." The term, as used in the New Testament, describes those who stood away or apart from the apostles. The New Testament authors teach of two types of apostasy: individual and corporate.

Atonement. In the New Testament, the English word *atonement* is used to

527

translate the Greek word *katallagē*. *Atonement* appears only once in English in the New Testament (Romans 5:11), although the Greek word and the corresponding English verb form *reconciling* appear frequently (Romans 11:15; 2 Corinthians 5:19; Acts 12:12; 1 Corinthians 7:11). The root word in Greek has the meaning of reconciling two things, generally someone to someone else.

Baptism. The word appears already in the New Testament as a technical term describing the ordinance administered by John the Baptist, although a near context in the Old Testament is difficult to identify. The Greek verb (*baptizō*) was used originally to describe plunging something under water or sinking a ship. The Hebrew/Aramaic word for baptism is not known, although the contemporary practice of ritual washing in *mikva'ot* is similar.

Benedictus. A song of thanksgiving attributed to Zacharias (Luke 1:68–79).

Bishop. Derived from the Greek root *episkopos* "overseer" or "guardian," the office of bishop is mentioned in the letters of Paul and Peter (see, for example, Philippians 1:1; 1 Timothy 3:1; 1 Peter 2:25). The increase in the influence of the office of bishop occurs after the New Testament period, where the apostles remain in authority.

Caesar. See **Rome**.

Church, house-church, congregation. The church (Greek, *ekklēsia*, "assembly") replaced the local synagogue. Church buildings are not attested in the first decades of Christianity, where members met in the homes of individuals (see, for example, 1 Corinthians 16:19). Christians chose to describe the gathering and not the edifice, although modern translations frequently use the modern designation *church* (from the Greek, *kyria*, "the Lord's").

Christ. See **Messiah**.

Circumcision. The practice of circumcision was required of all Jewish males as a sign of their obedience to the law of Moses (Genesis 17:12). The practice divided the early Christian community when some Jewish-Christians attempted to enforce the practice upon Gentiles who converted to the Lord (Acts 15:1–31).

Congregation. See **Church**.

Covenant. A covenant describes any promise between God and man in which obedience to the covenant leads to promised rewards or blessings. Jesus used the word *covenant* in describing the Atonement and spoke of a new testament of his blood (Matthew 26:28). *Testament* used in this way actually translates the Greek *diathēkē*, "last will and testament." The New Testament and the Atonement of Christ were understood as covenants in the proper sense as a promise that requires faithfulness.

Deacons. The office of a deacon (Greek, *diakonos*, "servant") occurs only in the letters of Paul (see, for example, Philippians 1:1; 1 Timothy 3:10). Those called to the office of deacon were to assist the bishop in his duties and were adult males, not young men.

Dead Sea Scrolls. The Dead Sea Scrolls were discovered in eleven caves near the Jewish sectarian community of Qumran near the Dead Sea. The texts were discovered between 1947 and 1956 and included portions of every book of the Bible with the exception of Esther. The scrolls provide valuable evidence for understanding Judaism at the time of Jesus, but unfortunately Christians are not mentioned in any of the scrolls.

Dedication. See **Jewish Holy Days.**

Demons. In New Testament times, demons were viewed as existing in the void between the divine and human realms. Jesus was accused of healing by the power of the prince of the demons, Beelzebub (Matthew 12:24). In 1 Timothy 4:1, false teaching is described as demonic teaching (KJV, "doctrines of devils"). Spirit possession in the New Testament is often assumed to be the result of demonic forces.

Disciple/Disciples. The New Testament authors recognized several levels of discipleship. Among Jesus' followers were those who were singled out as disciples (see, for example, Matthew 5:1) and those who were sent out as apostles. From among the latter group, twelve were ordained. Some of Jesus' disciples lost faith (John 6:66), but the Twelve Apostles remained faithful, with the exception of Judas Iscariot. *Apostle* has both a regular and a technical meaning. The Greek word *apostolos*, "messenger," can refer to a missionary or to someone who holds the office of apostle.

Elder/Elders. The term *elder* (Greek, *presbyteros*) is used negatively in the Gospels but positively in the writings after the Acts of the Apostles (see, for example, Titus 1:5). *Elder*, in its technical sense in the Gospels, refers to the governing body of priests of a synagogue or of the Sanhedrin. It is not a designation of religious affiliation, such as Pharisee or Sadducee. John, the apostle and author of 2 and 3 John, refers to himself as an "elder" (2 John 1:1; 3 John 1:1). The term *elder* is not used in the Gospel of John.

Essenes. The Essenes may have been the compilers of the Dead Sea Scroll library, although this association has been called into question. Josephus mentions the Essenes, who were probably a religious movement similar to the Pharisees and Sadducees (*Jewish War* 2.119).

Faith. Used to translate the Greek word *pistis*, the English word *faith* occurs numerous times in the New Testament. *Pistis* implies not only believing in the unseen but also in trusting in something or someone or having confidence that events will end in a certain way. Hebrews interprets *pistis* as faith in "things hoped for, the evidence of things not seen" (Hebrews 11:1), which moves away from an abstract interpretation to thinking of faith as the force leading to action.

Fasting. In Jesus' day, some Jews may have fasted twice a week (Luke 18:12), although the duration of their fasts is not known. Fasting is frequently mentioned in both the Old and New Testaments. Jesus encouraged fasting privately (Matthew 6:16–18) while some Pharisees questioned Jesus because the disciples did not fast frequently enough (Matthew 9:14–15). Jesus taught that the ability to cast out spirits may be linked to fasting (Mark 9:29).

Feasts. See **Jewish Holy Days**.

Galilee. The region surrounding the Sea of Galilee and north of Jerusalem by about eighty miles. During Jesus' lifetime Herod Antipas (c. 4 B.C.–A.D. 39) ruled Galilee. Herod the Great began construction on a major Hellenistic city in Galilee—Sepphoris—prior to Jesus' birth. Herod Antipas moved the capital from Sepphoris to his new city, Tiberias. Galilee was composed largely of small agriculturally connected villages. Galilean hamlets and towns figure predominantly in the Gospels—Capernaum, Nazareth, Magdala, Cana, Chorazin, and Nain.

Gentile/Gentiles. The modern English word *Gentile* translates the Greek word *ethnos*, "people" or "nations," and was used to describe all of the classes of people who were not descendants of Abraham. The term is typically not used in a negative way in the New Testament.

Gifts. Korban or "gift" offerings describe anything that is offered in sacrifice to God, particularly the animal sacrifices offered daily in the temple. The Lord commanded that such sacrifices be offered, but in New Testament times Jesus criticized the practice of giving gifts when it interfered with offering care to family members (Mark 7:11).

Gnostics. A sect or movement within mainstream Christianity that emphasized salvation through esoteric knowledge (Greek, *gnōsis*, "knowledge"). Paul spoke against Gnostic trends in 1 Timothy 6:20, and the beginnings of a Gnostic movement can be seen in the letter to Ephesus. Many of the writings discovered at Nag Hammadi (A.D. 1945) in Egypt were originally written by Gnostic Christians.

God-fearers. Gentiles who followed the Jewish law to some degree but who were unwilling to become full proselytes and undergo circumcision.

Gospel. In Greek, the term *gospel* means "good news" and was used as a technical term to describe the teachings of Jesus and the message of salvation by the time the Gospels were written.

Gospel of Judas. A Gnostic Gospel written in the second century A.D. that alleges to provide Judas Iscariot's viewpoint on the death and resurrection of Jesus. The document does not provide any reliable information about Judas or Jesus but does provide important details about the development of Gnosticism after the close of the New Testament era.

Hell (Gehenna). Written as *geena* in Greek, which is an attempt to convey the Aramaic *gehena* or "valley of Hinnom." The word appears frequently in the Gospels as a description of hell (see, for example, Matthew 5:22) and probably has reference to the ancient valley of Hinnom near the southern wall of Jerusalem where trash was burned. In Jesus' day this practice had ceased, but the image of eternal burning and filth had endured.

Herodians. The precise identity of the Herodians is unknown, and interpretations of who they are and what they did range from a political party to a faction of the Pharisees. They appear on two occasions in the New Testament (Mark 3:6; 8:15) where they are coupled with the Pharisees. They seem to be powerless in the Gospels and opposed to Jesus, representing the historical likelihood that they were nothing more than Herod Antipas's informants.

High Priests. See **Priesthood.**

Holy Ghost. The appellation or title "Holy Ghost" occurs for the first time in the New Testament, although the Old Testament speaks of the Spirit frequently. The phrase should more properly be translated as the "Holy Spirit"; the word translated *spirit* is the same used to describe the departing spirit of the deceased in the New Testament (John 19:30). John is the only author to mention that its administration was limited (John 7:39), and the Gospel authors frequently refer to the Holy Spirit being present for the major events of Jesus' life.

House Church. See **Church.**

Jesus. Jesus' proper name was *Yeshua* and is normally translated into English as *Joshua*. However, because the name was first translated into Greek, we commonly use the Greek form of the name (i.e., Jesus) instead.

Jewish Holy Days. The most important Jewish festivals were *Pesach* (Passover), *Rosh Hashanah* (the New Year's celebration), *Yom Kippur* (the Day of Atonement), *Sukkot* (Feast of Tabernacles), *Shavuot* (Weeks of Pentecost), *Shabbat* (Sabbath), and *Hanukkah* (Feast of Dedication). Christians still recognize a number of these festivals and celebrate them in different forms. Jesus' frequent trips to Jerusalem in the Gospel of John follow the celebration of Passover in the Holy City. In fact, Jesus' three-year ministry is also calculated using the number of Passover celebrations he attended. Paul also traveled to Jerusalem on several occasions to celebrate these annual feasts.

Jewish Scriptures. There were several popular divisions among Jews of Jesus' day regarding what constituted scripture. All Jews regarded the Law as binding (the Torah/the five books of Moses); others also accepted the Prophets as binding. It appears from Josephus that there was a division between the Pharisees and Sadducees regarding which books of scripture should be accepted as authoritative. Some scholars have taken this to mean that the Sadducees accepted only the Torah while Pharisees accepted the Torah, Prophets, and Writings (Luke 24:44). In addition, the Pharisees also accepted oral tradition. Such a division between the sects may indeed be too strong. The real issue behind the division was ritual purity and how purity was interpreted. By the time of Jesus, the Jewish canon was not formalized but in practice was essentially closed. Jews of his day, particularly those living outside of Judea, used a Greek translation of the scriptures known as the Septuagint and abbreviated as LXX. The Gospel authors sometimes show traces of having used the LXX when they composed their Gospels. For example, Matthew 21:5, which mentions an "ass, and a colt the foal of an ass" preserves an LXX confusion of having two animals instead of one.

Judea. The region west of the Dead Sea surrounding Jerusalem. Pilate and other Roman governors ruled this area after Herod the Great's son Archelaus (ruled 4 B.C.–A.D. 6) was removed because of incompetence. Herod the Great had originally intended for his son to rule Judea, but Caesar Augustus removed Archelaus because he had cruelly oppressed the people of Judea.

Justification. The English word *justification* is derived from Latin roots meaning "to make just or right according to law." In the New Testament the Greek word is actually translated *righteousness* (see, for example, Romans 4:25).

Languages. All of the books of the New Testament were composed in Greek, although the quality of Greek ranges from relatively low Greek such as the book of Revelation and fairly eloquent Greek in the book of Hebrews. The Greek of the New Testament is *koine*, whereas classical Greek authors such as Plato used Attic Greek. It is unlikely that Jesus spoke a significant amount of Greek, and the phrases that are preserved in an untranslated form in the New Testament and that were spoke by Jesus are preserved in Aramaic. Biblical Hebrew had largely fallen into disuse in the New Testament period, and the common language of the day was Aramaic. The scriptures were written in Hebrew and may have been translated into Aramaic in the Targum, but evidence for this is slim in the first century.

Last Days. Usually the term refers to the Eschaton, or the end of the present world order (John 7:37). The word *Eschaton* is typically used to refer to the absolute end of something or the furthest point of comparison. This word was used by New Testament authors to translate Jesus' teachings on the last days of the world.

Last Supper. The Last Supper of Jesus is described in the Synoptic Gospels (Matthew, Mark, and Luke) as a Passover meal; in the Gospel of John it is not. The meal and the ordinance of the sacrament, which was revealed at that time, were celebrated by early Christians (1 Corinthians 11:24; Jude 1:12). Traditionally the meal is thought to have taken place on Thursday evening before the Sunday of the Resurrection (now known as Easter Sunday).

Latin. The common language of Rome. Some inscriptions in Jesus' day were written in Aramaic, Greek, and Latin (John 19:20). It is doubtful that many Jews were extensively familiar with spoken Latin.

Law. See **Torah.**

Leper. See **Leprosy.**

Leprosy. Archaeologists have recently countered the long-standing assumption that leprosy was unknown in the first century A.D. Excavations of first-century tombs have revealed the existence of Hansen's disease (commonly referred to as leprosy). The Old Testament classifies a number of skin ailments as leprosy, and thus New Testament authors would have considered not only persons afflicted with Hansen's disease as leprous but also those afflicted with severe skin ailments.

Levirate Marriage. Deuteronomy 25:5–10 commands that a brother marry his deceased brother's spouse in the event that the brother had no children prior to his death. This practice of raising a family with a brother's widowed spouse is referred to as levirate marriage.

Lord's Day. See **Sabbath.**

LXX. See **Jewish Scriptures.**

Magnificat. The Magnificat is a song or ode that is sung or chanted liturgically as part of Christian worship services, and the modern title describes Mary as blessed or literally magnificent, although the term is not mentioned in the New Testament. The song has similarities to Hannah's song (1 Samuel 2:1–10) when she praised the Lord for being given a son; the text is found in Luke 1:46–55.

Messiah, messianic, Christ. For Christians the Messiah is the Savior of mankind, and for Jews the Messiah is a deliverer of the Jewish people. Although the Messiah was not viewed as a divine personage, nevertheless many Jews in Jesus' day looked for a messiah to deliver them. Jesus did not meet any of the popular messianic expectations of his day, such as the deliverer who would throw off Roman occupation. Instead, he offered a contrasting interpretation of a messiah who would suffer. The title *Christ* is the Greek translation of the Hebrew word *Messiah* and both mean "anointed." In Jesus' lifetime, *Christ* functioned as a title and not a name, and Paul clearly understood it this way: "Unto the church of God which is at Corinth, to them that are sanctified in Christ Jesus" (1 Corinthians 1:2).

Miracles, signs. The Gospels frequently use two words in reference to Jesus' miracles. The Greek word *dynamis* refers to an act of power or a supernatural power that demonstrates Jesus' control over the physical world (Mark 9:39). The other word translated as "miracle" is *sēmeion* and refers to a sign or portent. In the Gospel of John, Jesus' miracles are referred to as signs, signaling to the reader that we are to come to faith in Jesus through the signs he has provided us. This is in light of the fact that the Holy Spirit had been withdrawn (John 7:39). The Synoptic authors may have wished to convey the idea that Jesus had come in power as evidenced through his acts of power or "miracles."

Mishnah. A written collection of oral tradition, religious practices, and laws, the Mishnah is an important source for reconstructing rabbinic Judaism during the first two centuries of the Christian era. The writings contained in the Mishnah are a record of oral traditions that were written down in the first two decades of the third century A.D. and tell us more about Judaism after Christianity began than about Judaism at the time of Jesus. We must be cautious using the Mishnah, which represents a Pharisaic viewpoint, in reconstructing New Testament Jewish practice and belief. The Mishnah is actually a division of the Talmud, a collection of rabbinic writings that also includes the Gemara. The Mishnah contains the legal codes of the rabbis and the Gemara preserves a discussion of how the legal codes and other matters should be interpreted.

New Testament. The title "New Testament" is comparative with respect to the "Old Testament." Neither collection is referred to using these titles by their authors: the titles developed much later when the books of the two testaments were canonized. Jesus spoke to his disciples of the new testament of his blood (Mark 14:24), and Paul also speaks of being ministers of the new testament (2 Corinthians 3:6; Hebrews 9:15). The word translated as "testament" is better translated as "covenant."

Noncanonical writings. Those writings excluded from the New Testament because of concerns about forgery, doctrine, or other matters are classed together as the noncanonical writings. These writings are now numerous, numbering into the hundreds. They did not circulate as a collection of texts in any meaningful way; instead, they were used in various communities throughout the Mediterranean region. The noncanonical texts are similar in form to and postdate the New Testament texts and preserve pseudepigraphical epistles, gospels, apocalypses, and exhortations.

Parables. Speaking in parables was not unique to Jesus, but his reason for doing so may have been the following: "Therefore speak I to them in parables: because they seeing see not; and hearing they hear not, neither do they understand" (Matthew 13:13). The word translated as "parable" in the New Testament refers to any type of figurative or symbolic speech and can refer more broadly to a saying or story that has a context beyond the immediate point of comparison readily identifiable. Matthew taught that Jesus shifted to speaking in parables after the opposition against him escalated, but Mark and Luke contain parables throughout the ministry.

Passover. See **Jewish Holy Days.**

Pax Romana. Translated as "Roman peace," the idea of the Pax Romana is that Rome, despite overrunning neighboring states and countries, brought peace to the world. Some seemed to openly embrace the ideal, while others chaffed at foreign domination.

Pentecost. See **Jewish Holy Days**.

Pharisees. One of the three principal Jewish philosophies identified by Josephus— Pharisees, Sadducees, and Essenes. It appears that the Pharisees held sway with the people while Sadducees were popular among the ruling aristocracy. In many ways Jesus' teachings are similar to those of the Pharisees, although there were certainly matters where their views clashed. The constant debates between Jesus and the Pharisees may represent the efforts of some interested followers to understand specifically how Jesus' teachings differed from Pharisaic viewpoints. Paul was a trained Pharisee, and some Pharisees attended the Jerusalem Conference (A.D. 49) to voice their opinions on Church matters (Acts 15:5). After Jesus died, the Zealots, who were closely associated with the Pharisees, coalesced as a major militant faction opposing Roman occupation.

Priests. See **Priesthood**.

Priesthood. At the time of Jesus, priests descended through Levi cared for all aspects of temple worship/ordinances, particularly carrying out the daily and celebratory sacrifices. From the time of David onward, the priests were divided into twenty-four courses, or divisions (1 Chronicles 24:7–23), and strict requirements were in place to determine that only the pure were permitted to officiate in the priesthood. The office of high priest at the time of Jesus was filled by appointment that sometimes followed family lines but was not required to do so. Rome held the sacred vestments of the high priest in safekeeping, and many Jews felt that this action was a violation against their religion. Zacharias was a Levite of the course of Abia. As far as history permits us to say, none of Jesus' disciples were priests or of priestly families. Pharisees and Sadducees were not priestly movements but religious traditions or philosophies.

Prophets. See **Jewish Scriptures**.

Proselytes. See **God-fearers**.

Publicans. In the Roman system, the opportunity to collect taxes was auctioned off, and those whose bids were accepted collected the amount of their bid plus whatever amount they could collect over it, which was their profit. Although the New Testament treats all publicans as tax collectors, they also helped supply the Roman armies and helped collect funds for building projects. Publicans were frequently despised and may have been excommunicated from their local synagogues for supporting the Roman occupation of Judea and Galilee.

Qumran. See **Dead Sea Scrolls.**

Rabbi. The first historical usage of the title *rabbi* occurs in the New Testament, which itself refers most simply to a teacher of the law. Very little is known about how a person became a rabbi in the first century, and assumptions about who the rabbis were are based on much later sources such as the Mishnah. Jesus was a rabbi in the sense that he was a teacher, but not in the sense that he would have followed any courses for rabbinic training. Paul was trained in the rabbinic tradition, but it is unclear whether the title was in use in his day in the way it is used today.

Repent, repentance. The concept of repentance in the New Testament is conveyed through the Greek word *metanoeō*, a word that means to "change one's mind." This might also be understood as a change of heart. John the Baptist began teaching a gospel of repentance, calling on Jews to have a change of mind and to accept baptism, a rite that was up to that point associated with conversion into Judaism.

Roman Empire. See **Rome.**

Rome. Jesus was born during the reign of the emperor Augustus (31 B.C.–19 August A.D. 14) and taught under the emperor Tiberius (A.D. 14–A.D. 37). The reigns of Augustus and Tiberius were relatively peaceful times in Judea and Galilee, as Rome was able to suppress the constant threat of revolts and the incursion of eastern armies into Judea and Galilee. Jewish opinions regarding Rome are difficult to assess and are probably much more complex than anecdotal evidence could describe. In a number of instances, the Gospels seem to imply that the people viewed Rome negatively, a position that Jesus' enemies tried to use against him (Matthew 22:15–22). For the most part, the Herodian family was of more immediate influence on the affairs of Jesus and his disciples.

Sabbath. Jews celebrated the Sabbath beginning at sundown on Friday evening and ending at sundown on Saturday evening, with the largest portion of the Sabbath falling on what is called Saturday today. Christians almost immediately began celebrating the day of the Resurrection—Sunday—in remembrance of the Lord's triumphant day. John, who wrote the book of Revelation, refers to Sunday as "the Lord's day" already in the first century (Revelation 1:10).

Sacrifice. See **Temple**.

Sadducees. Tracing their authority to Zadok (1 Chronicles 6:4–8), a priest at the time of Solomon, the Sadducees are probably best described as a religious philosophy rather than a religion in the modern sense. Our surviving sources are biased against the Sadducees, whom they see as a manipulative, authoritative sect influenced primarily by concerns for cleanliness and holiness. Unlike the Pharisees, the Sadducees do not appear to be a proselytizing movement and constituted a small, wealthy elite, numbering considerably less than the Pharisees and Essenes. Historically they ceased to exist not long after the fall of the Jerusalem temple (A.D. 70), suggesting that their authority may have been tied to that edifice.

Samaria. See **Samaritans**.

Samaritans. Jesus' excursion into Samaria brought him into contact with a woman who seems to personify the religious bias of the Samaritans towards Jews. In the fourth century B.C., the Samaritans had constructed a temple on Mount Gerizim. Samaritans saw themselves as the true Israel, the one that God established after the Jews were carried captive into Babylon. Jews, on the other hand, felt that Samaritan claims were illegitimate and excluded them from participating in temple services in Jerusalem. During Jesus' day Jews and Samaritans existed alongside one another with shared antipathy.

Satan. The New Testament largely transliterates the older terms for the devil, such as *satanas*, "the adversary." The term *devil* derives from *diabolos*, "slanderer." The authors of the New Testament offer very little to our overall understanding of his role as adversary or slanderer and instead focus largely on the schisms originating among members.

Scribes. In the New Testament, the scribes are presented as a unified group with a distinct perspective on issues, which may overrepresent the historical evidence. They sometimes appear affiliated with the Pharisees, and this connection may reveal that by using the term *scribes*, the evangelists intended to indicate local bureaucrats with connections to the synagogue. Their presence in Judea, however, indicates that they may have been lower level government officials who carried out the tasks of documenting civic affairs. Their opposition to Jesus may therefore represent a larger concern that Jesus' teachings were interpreted to be antigovernment.

Scriptures. See **Jewish Scriptures**.

Septuagint (LXX). See **Jewish Scriptures**.

Son of David. This title has messianic overtones, hinting that the Son of David would restore Israel to its former glory. Jesus never specifically referred to himself as the Son of David, although others thought of him in this way.

Son of God. The title *Son of God* can refer to the sons of God who become such through obedience to the gospel (John 1:12) and also to the Son of God, Jesus Christ (John 1:34). The title itself conveys the idea of being chosen and was not simply a divine title for the Messiah, but rather an indication of Jesus' special relationship with the Father. Satan challenged Jesus, calling him the Son of God (Luke 4:9). The title is used widely in the New Testament and almost always refers to Jesus in the role of God's chosen Son.

Son of man. The title *Son of man* is one of the most hotly debated issues in New Testament scholarship, partly because of its Old Testament antecedents and partly because the title can be interpreted broadly to mean any son of a man. Jesus does not specifically indicate what he intended by referring to himself as the Son of man. The Restoration in one context expands the meaning of the term *Son of man* (Moses 6:57). Certainly Jesus knew that he was the Son of Man of Holiness, or the Son of the Father, but the usage in the Synoptic Gospels shows how the term provided a way for Jesus to delay opposition to his ministry, so that he taught the mission of the Son of man in the third person and then eventually made the connection that he was the Son of man. His inner circle of followers may have known the connection from the beginning, but outsiders were likely unaware of the association until later in his ministry.

Synagogue. From the Greek word meaning "place of assembly," the synagogue represented a place for local meetings and study of the Hebrew Bible. Synagogues feature prominently in the Gospel narratives, and Jesus healed in them as well as read the scriptures in them. Synagogues were led by an *archisynagogos*, a position that may have been passed on through lineage. The term *elders* may refer to local synagogue leaders in some instances (Luke 7:3). Only later did the Pharisees gain control of the synagogues, and in Jesus' day rabbis did not lead the synagogues. In fact, the synagogue may have been led in some cases by the most influential local Jewish elder, who may have also been from a priestly family. Weddings were held in the synagogue, and the youth were educated there.

Synoptic. Based on the Greek word meaning to "see together" or to "see the same thing," the adjective *synoptic* refers to the Gospels of Matthew, Mark, and

Luke, who share roughly 90 percent of the same material in very similar and sometimes identical language.

Talmud. See **Mishnah.**

Targum. See **Jewish Scriptures.**

Temple. The Jewish temple in Jerusalem was destroyed at the end of the Roman attack on the city in A.D. 70. Titus's men literally tore down the walls of the temple in dramatic fashion in an attempt to disrupt the heartbeat of the Jewish faith. Despite Peter's and John's attendance at the temple (Acts 3:1), Christians did not perform ordinances in the Jewish temple. Instead, in the earliest years in the city, Christians appear to have attended the call to prayer (Acts 3:1) and Paul fulfilled a Nazarite vow there (Acts 21:23–30). The site lay in ruins for years and the emperor Hadrian began to build a city—the Aelia Capitolina—that included plans for the Temple Mount.

For most Jews the temple was the focus of religious worship, and animal sacrifice, prayer, and singing were performed there. The yearly calendar was punctuated by various religious festivals, which drew thousands of people to Jerusalem from all over the Jewish diaspora. The temple was internationally renowned and drew Gentile visitors as well.

Torah. The first five books of the Old Testament constitute the Torah, or "teachings." The Torah is frequently referred to as the "Law," but a more accurate translation of the word *Torah* would be "instructions." In Jesus' day, the Torah was translated into Greek and possibly Aramaic and was considered binding for all sects of Jews (Pharisees, Sadducees, Essenes). For Jesus and his disciples the Torah was accepted as authoritative, and in debates Jesus taught from the Torah with the assumption that his hearers would accept it as binding upon them.

Traditions. See **Pharisees.**

Zealots. See **Pharisees.**

BIBLIOGRAPHY

The following provides sources consulted and also those recommended for additional reference.

Ancient Sources

Aratus. *The Phenomena and Diosemeia of Aratus.* Whitefish, Mont: Kessinger Publishing, 2010.

Eusebius. *The Ecclesiastical History of Eusebius Pamphilus.* New York: Stanford and Swords, 1850.

Irenaeus. *Against Heresies.* Oxford: J. Parker, 1872.

Josephus. *Jewish Antiquities.* Translated by H. St. J. Thackeray. 9 vols. Cambridge: Harvard University Press, 1998–2001.

———. *The Jewish War.* Translated by H. St. J. Thackeray. 3 vols. Cambridge: Harvard University Press, 1997.

———. *The Life of Flavius Josephus.* Radford, Va.: Wilder Publications, 2009.

Philostratus. *The Life of Apollonius of Tyana.* New York: Macmillan, 1912.

Pliny the Elder. *Natural History.* Edited by H. Rackham. Cambridge: Harvard University Press, 1969.

Suetonius. *Lives of the Caesars.* Translated by Catharine Edwards. New York: Oxford University Press, 2000.

Tacitus. *The Annals, Books XIII–XVI.* Translated by J. Jackson. Cambridge: Harvard University Press, 1969.

Tertullian. *The Prescription Against Heretics.* Whitefish, Mont.: Kessinger Publishing, LLC, 2010.

Latter-day Saint Works

Brown, S. Kent. *Mary and Elisabeth: Noble Daughters of God*. American Fork: Covenant Communications, 2004.

Brown, S. Kent, and Richard Neitzel Holzapfel. *The Lost Five Hundred Years: What Happened between the Old and New Testaments*. Salt Lake City: Deseret Book, 2006.

Ehat, Andrew F., and Lyndon W. Cook. *Words of Joseph Smith*. Salt Lake City: Deseret Book, 2009.

Hall, John F. *New Testament Witnesses of Christ*. American Fork: Covenant Communications, 2002.

Hall, John F., and John W. Welch, eds. *Masada and the World of the New Testament*. Provo, Utah: Brigham Young University Studies, 1997.

Holland, Jeffrey R. "The Other Prodigal." *Ensign*, May 2002, 62–64.

Holzapfel, Richard Neitzel, Eric C. Huntsman, and Thomas A. Wayment. *Jesus Christ and the World of the New Testament*. Salt Lake City: Deseret Book, 2006.

Holzapfel, Richard Neitzel, and Thomas A. Wayment, eds. *The Life and Teachings of Jesus Christ*. 3 vols. Salt Lake City: Deseret Book, 2003–6.

———. *The Life and Teachings of the New Testament Apostles*. Salt Lake City: Deseret Book, 2010.

Kimball, Spencer W. *Peter, My Brother*. Brigham Young University Speeches of the Year. Provo, Utah, 13 July 1971.

Maxwell, Neal A. "The New Testament—A Matchless Portrait of the Savior." *Ensign*, December 1986, 20.

McConkie, Bruce R. "The Book of Mormon—Its Eternal Destiny." Address to Church Educational System Religious Educators Symposium, August 18, 1978.

Monson, Thomas S. "The Master Bridge Builder." *Ensign*, January 2008, 4–9.

Ogden, D. Kelly. *Where Jesus Walked: The Land and Culture of New Testament Times*. Salt Lake City: Deseret Book, 1991.

Packer, Boyd K. "The Library of the Lord." *Ensign*, May 1990, 36.

Parry, Donald W., and Jay A. Parry. *Symbols and Shadows: Unlocking a Deeper Understanding of the Atonement*. Salt Lake City: Deseret Book, 2009.

Smith, Joseph. *History of the Church*. Edited by B. H. Roberts. 7 vols. 2d ed. rev. Salt Lake City: The Church of Jesus Christ of Latter-day Saints, 1932–51.

———. *Messenger and Advocate*, December 1835, 225.

———. *Teachings of the Prophet Joseph Smith*. Selected by Joseph Fielding Smith. Salt Lake City: Deseret News Press, 1938.

Talmage, James E. *Jesus the Christ*. Salt Lake City: The Church of Jesus Christ of Latter-day Saints, 1916.

———. *The Articles of Faith*. Salt Lake City: The Church of Jesus Christ of Latter-day Saints, 1924.

Wayment, Thomas A. *From Persecutor to Apostle: A Biography of Paul*. Salt Lake City: Deseret Book, 2006.

———, ed. *The Complete Joseph Smith Translation of the New Testament: A Side-by-Side Comparison with the King James Version*. Salt Lake City: Deseret Book, 2005.

Welch, John W. *The Sermon on the Mount in Light of the Temple*. Burlington, Vt.: Ashgate, 2009.

Welch, John W., and John F. Hall. *Charting the New Testament*. Provo, Utah: FARMS, 2002.

General Works

Barker, Margaret. *Temple Themes in Christian Worship*. London and New York: T&T Clark, 2008.

Bauckham, Richard. *Jesus and the Eyewitnesses: The Gospels as Eyewitness Testimony*. Grand Rapids, Mich.: Eerdmans, 2006.

Bock, Darrell L. *Jesus according to Scripture*. Grand Rapids, Mich.: Baker Academic, 2002.

Brown, Raymond E. *An Introduction to the New Testament*. New York: Doubleday, 1997.

———. *The Death of the Messiah: From Gethsemane to the Grave, a Commentary on the Passion Narratives in the Four Gospels*. 2 vols. New York: Doubleday, 1994.

Brown, Raymond E., Joseph A. Fitzmyer, and Roland E. Murphy. *The New Jerome Biblical Commentary*. Englewood Cliffs, N.J.: Prentice Hall, 1990.

Bruce, F. F. *The International Bible Commentary with the New International Version*. Grand Rapids, Mich.: Zondervan, 1986.

Burridge, Richard A. *What Are the Gospels? A Comparison with Graeco-Roman Biography*. Grand Rapids, Mich.: Eerdmans, 2004.

Crossan, John Dominic, and Jonathan L. Reed. *Excavating Jesus: Beneath the Stones, behind the Texts*. New York: HarperSanFrancisco, 2001.

———. *In Search of Paul*. New York: HarperSanFrancisco, 2004.

Dunn, James D. G. *Christianity in the Making: Beginning from Jerusalem.* Grand Rapids, Mich.: Eerdmans, 2009.

———. *Christianity in the Making: Jesus Remembered.* Grand Rapids, Mich.: Eerdmans, 2009.

———. *The Theology of Paul the Apostle.* Grand Rapids, Mich.: Eerdmans, 1998.

Dunn, James D. G., and John W. Rogerson. *Eerdmans Commentary on the Bible.* Grand Rapids, Mich.: Eerdmans, 2003.

Ehrman, Bart D. *The New Testament: A Historical Introduction to the Early Christian Writings.* New York: Oxford University Press, 2008.

———. *Misquoting Jesus: The Story behind Who Changed the Bible and Why.* New York: HarperSanFrancisco, 2005.

Elliot, Elisabeth. *Through Gates of Splendor.* Carol Stream, Ill.: Tyndale House, 1986.

Evans, Craig A. *Fabricating Jesus: How Modern Scholars Distort the Gospels.* Downers Grove, Ill.: InterVarsity Press, 2006.

Fee, Gordon D., and Douglas Stuart. *How to Read the Bible for All It's Worth: A Guide to Understanding the Bible.* 3d ed. Grand Rapids, Mich.: Zondervan, 2003.

———. *How to Read the Bible Book by Book: A Guided Tour.* Grand Rapids, Mich.: Zondervan, 2002.

Freedman, David Noel, ed. *Eerdman's Dictionary of the Bible.* Grand Rapids, Mich.: Eerdmans, 2000.

Harris, Stephen L. *The New Testament: A Student's Introduction.* 4th ed. Boston: McGraw Hill, 2002.

Harvey, A. E. *A Companion to the New Testament.* Cambridge: Cambridge University Press, 1970.

Hunt, Arthur S., and Edgar, C. C. *Select Papyri.* New York: G. P. Putnam's Sons, 1932

Keefer, Kyle. *The New Testament as Literature: A Very Short Introduction.* New York: Oxford University Press, 2008.

Lane, William L. *The Gospel according to Mark: The English Text with Introduction, Exposition, and Notes.* Grand Rapids, Mich.: Eerdmans, 1974.

Malina, Bruce J., and Richard L. Rohrbaugh. *Social-Science Commentary on the Synoptic Gospels.* 2d ed. Minneapolis: Fortress Press, 2003.

Metzger, Bruce M., and Michael D. Coogan, eds. *The Oxford Companion to the Bible.* New York: Oxford University Press, 1993.

Murphy-O'Connor, Jerome. *The Holy Land: An Oxford Archaeological Guide*. New York: Oxford University Press, 2008.

The New Interpreter's Bible. 12 vols. Nashville, Tenn.: Abingdon Press, 1994.

Powell, Mark Allan. *Introducing the New Testament: A Historical, Literary, and Theological Survey*. Grand Rapids, Mich.: Baker Academic, 2009.

Witherington, Ben, III. *Grace in Galatia: A Commentary on Paul's Letter to the Galatians*. Grand Rapids, Mich.: Eerdmans, 1998.

———. *Letters and Homilies for Jewish Christian: A Socio-Rhetorical Commentary on Hebrews, James and Jude*. Downer's Grove, Ill.: InterVarsity, 2007.

———. *Matthew*. Vol. 19 of *Smyth & Helwys Bible Commentary*. Macon, Ga.: Smyth & Helwys, 2006.

———. *The New Testament Story*. Grand Rapids, Mich.: Eerdmans, 2004.

———. *New Testament History: A Narrative Account*. Grand Rapids, Mich.: Baker Academic, 2001.

———. *The Paul Quest: The Renewed Search for the Jew of Tarsus*. Downers Grove, Ill.: InterVarsity Press, 1998.

Wright, N. T. *Matthew for Everyone, Part One and Part Two*. Louisville, Ky.: Westminster John Knox Press, 2004.

———. *Mark for Everyone*. Louisville, Ky.: Westminster John Knox Press, 2004.

———. *Luke for Everyone*. Louisville, Ky.: Westminster John Knox Press, 2004.

———. *John for Everyone, Part One and Part Two*. Louisville, Ky.: Westminster John Knox Press, 2004.

———. *Acts for Everyone, Part One and Part Two*. Louisville, Ky.: Westminster John Knox Press, 2004.

———. *Paul for Everyone: Galatians and Thessalonians*. Louisville, Ky.: Westminster John Knox Press, 2004.

———. *Paul for Everyone: 1 Corinthians*. Louisville, Ky.: Westminster John Knox Press, 2004.

———. *Paul for Everyone: 2 Corinthians*. Louisville, Ky.: Westminster John Knox Press, 2004.

INDEX OF STORIES
IN THE GOSPELS

The following chart identifies the content of passages in the Gospels in the order in which they are discussed in this volume.

Event	Matthew	Mark	Luke	John
The Beginning of the Gospel of Jesus Christ	1:1	1:1	1:1–4	1:1–18
Genealogies of Jesus	1:2–17		3:23–38	
Zacharias and Elisabeth			1:5–25	
Joseph and Mary	1:18–25		1:26–39	
The Magnificat			1:39–56	
Zacharias Reveals John's and Jesus' Roles in God's Plan			1:57–80	
The Taxation by Caesar Augustus (Octavian)			2:1–7	
The Shepherds and Wise Men Adore Jesus	2:1–12		2:8–18	

EVENT	MATTHEW	MARK	LUKE	JOHN
The Circumcision and Naming of Jesus	1:25		2:21	
The Flight to Egypt, Herod Slays Infants in and near Bethlehem	2:1–23			
Passover in Jerusalem When Jesus Was Twelve Years of Age			2:41–52	
The Beginning of the Ministry of John the Baptist	3:1–12	1:1–8	3:1–18	1:19–34
The Baptism of Jesus and the Beginning of His Ministry	3:13–17	1:9–11	3:21–22	1:32–34
Jesus' Temptations	4:1–11	1:12–13	4:1–13	
THE GALILEAN MINISTRY				
John Is Imprisoned	4:12	1:14	3:19–20	
Jesus' Ministry Prior to Gathering His Disciples	4:12–17; 23–25		4:14–15	
Early Disciples	4:18–22	1:14–20	5:4–11	1:35–51
Jesus' Ministry in Nazareth			4:16–30	
The Wedding at Cana				2:1–11
The Ministry at Capernaum		1:21–28	4:31–37	2:12

Event	Matthew	Mark	Luke	John
Raising the Widow's Son at Nain			7:11–17	
Simon Peter's Mother-in-Law	8:14–15	1:29–31	4:38–39	
Early Miracles in Galilee	4:23–25; 8:14–15	1:7–12; 32–45	4:40–44	
Jesus Teaches from a Boat on the Sea of Galilee			5:1–3	
THE EARLY JUDEAN MINISTRY				
The Cleansing of the Temple				2:13–25
Nicodemus				3:1–21
Jesus Baptizes in Aenon near Salim and Appeals to John's Followers				3:22–36
JESUS RETURNS TO GALILEE				
Jesus Departs from Judea	4:12, 17	1:14–15	4:14–15	4:1–3, 43–45
Samaria and the Woman at the Well				4:4–42
The Setting for the Sermon on the Mount	5:1–2		6:17–19	
The Beatitudes	5:3–12		6:20–26	
The Salt of the Earth	5:13–16	9:50	8:16–18; 11:33–36; 14:34–35	

Event	Matthew	Mark	Luke	John
The Law Is Fulfilled	5:17–20			
The Five Laws	5:21–48		6:27–36	
Public Forms of Worship and the Lord's Prayer	6:1–18		11:2–4	
Treasure in Earth	6:19–34		11:34–36; 12:22–34; 16:9–13	
Judgment	7:1–5		6:37–39, 41–42	
Sacred Things	7:6–12		11:9–13	
The Way	7:13–14		13:23–24	
Opposition from Within	7:15–27		6:43–49; 13:25–30	
Jesus Teaches with Authority	7:28–29			
MIRACLES IN GALILEE				
The Healing of a Man with Leprosy	8:1–4	1:40–45	5:12–16	
The Healing of the Centurion's Servant/ Nobleman's Son	8:5–13		7:1–10	4:46–54
The Son of Man Has Nowhere to Lay His Head	8:18–22		9:57–62	
Calming the Storm on the Sea of Galilee	8:23–27	4:35–41	8:22–25	

Event	Matthew	Mark	Luke	John
Jesus Casts Out Devils That Enter Swine	8:28–34	5:1–20	8:26–40	
The Healing at Capernaum	9:1–8	2:1–12	5:17–26	
Matthew the Tax Collector	9:9–13	2:13–17	5:27–32	
The Question about Fasting	9:14–17	2:18–22	5:33–39	
The Raising of Jairus's Daughter	9:18–19, 23–26	5:21–24, 35–43	8:41–42, 49–56	
A Woman Touches Jesus' Garment and Is Healed	9:20–22	5:25–34	8:43–48	
The Blind Are Healed	9:27–31; 20:29–34	10:46–52	18:35–43	
First Accusation of Healing by the Power of the Prince of Devils	9:32–34		11:14–15	
Jesus Preaches in Unnamed Galilean Cities	9:35–38	6:6	8:1–3	
The Calling of the Twelve	10:1–4	3:13–19	6:12–16	
The Mission of the Twelve Apostles	10:5–42	6:7–13	9:1–6; 12:2–9, 11–12, 49–53; 14:25–28	

Event	Matthew	Mark	Luke	John
Follow-Up Mission in the Cities of the Apostolic Mission	11:1		10:1	
John the Baptist Sends Followers to Jesus	11:2–6		7:18–23	
Jesus' Testimony of John	11:7–19		7:24–35; 16:16–17	
Jesus' Disciples Pluck Wheat on the Sabbath	12:1–9	2:23–28	6:1–11	
Jesus Heals a Man with a Withered Hand	12:10–15	3:1–6	6:6–11	
Isaiah's Servant Song	12:16–21			
Jesus Is Accused of Healing by the Power of Beelzebub	12:22–30	3:20–27	11:14–20	
Blasphemy against the Holy Ghost	12:31–37	3:28–30	12:10	
Jesus' Mother and Brothers Seek Him	12:46–50	3:31–35	8:19–21	
Why Jesus Taught in Parables	13:1–2; 10–17, 34–35	4:1–2, 10–13, 33–34	8:4, 9–10; 10:23–24	
The Parable of the Sower	13:3–9, 18–23	4:3–9, 14–20	8:5–8, 11–15	
The Candle under a Bushel		4:21–25	8:16–18	

EVENT	MATTHEW	MARK	LUKE	JOHN
The Wheat and the Tares	13:24–30, 36–43	4:26–29		
The Mustard Seed	13:31–32	4:30–32	13:18–19	
The Leaven	13:33		13:20–21	
The Treasure in a Field	13:44			
The Pearl of Great Price	13:45–46			
The Net Cast into the Sea	13:47–50			
The Householder	13:51–52			
The Second Rejection in Nazareth	13:53–58	6:1–6		
Report on the Death of John the Baptist	14:3–12	6:17–29		
Herod and Jesus	14:1–2	6:14–16	9:7–9	
The Feeding of the Five Thousand	14:13–21	6:30–44	9:10–17	6:1–14
Jesus Walks on Water	14:22–33	6:45–52		6:15–21
The Bread of Life Discourse				6:22–71
Jesus Teaches Again in Galilee				7:1
Jesus' Return to Gennesaret	14:34–36	6:53–56		

Event	Matthew	Mark	Luke	John
What Comes Out of a Man Defiles	15:1–20	7:1–23		
The Gentile Woman's Daughter	15:21–28	7:24–30		
Healings	15:29–31	7:31–37		
Jesus Feeds the Four Thousand	15:32–39	8:1–9		
Pharisees and Sadducees Ask for a Sign	16:1–4	8:10–13	12:54–57	
Jesus Teaches the Disciples about the Pharisees	16:5–12	8:14–21	12:1	
The Healing at Bethsaida		8:22–26		
"Whom Say Men That I Am?"	16:13–20	8:27–30	9:18–22	
Jesus Rebukes Peter	16:21–23	8:31–33		
On Taking Up a Cross	16:24–28	8:34–38; 9:1	9:23–27	
The Mount of Transfiguration	17:1–13	9:2–13	9:28–36	
Jesus Heals a Boy Possessed	17:14–21	9:14–29	9:37–42; 17:4–6	
Jesus Prophesies of His Death and Resurrection	17:22–23	9:30–32	9:43–45	
A Question about Taxation	17:24–27			

Event	Matthew	Mark	Luke	John
Who Is Greater?	18:1–6	9:33–37	9:46–48	
Woe to Those Who Offend	18:7–11	9:42–50	14:34–35; 17:1–2	
The Other Healer	10:42	9:38–41	9:49–50	
The Parable of the Lost Sheep	18:12–14		15:1–7	
The Parable of the Lost Coin			15:8–10	
The Parable of the Prodigal Sons			15:11–32	
Reproving a Brother	18:15–22		17:3	
Unprofitable Servants			17:7–10	
The Parable of the Unmerciful Servant	18:23–35			
Jesus and the Feast of Tabernacles				7:2–9
Jesus Departs from Galilee	19:1		9:51	
Jesus Sends Missionaries to Samaria			9:52–56	
The Calling of the Seventy			10:1	
The Mission of the Seventy			10:2–12	

EVENT	MATTHEW	MARK	LUKE	JOHN
Jesus Upbraids Capernaum, Bethsaida, and Chorazin	11:20–24		10:13–16	
The Seventy Return			10:17–20	
Jesus Gives Thanks	11:25–30		10:21–22	
The Parable of the Good Samaritan			10:25–37	
Mary and Martha			10:38–42	
The Friend at Midnight			11:5–8	
Keep the Word			11:27–28	
Coveting			12:13–21	
The Parable of the Barren Fig Tree			13:1–5	
A Woman Is Healed on the Sabbath			13:10–17	
Jesus Turns toward Jerusalem			13:22	
Jesus Comments on Herod Antipas			13:31–33	
Counting the Costs of Discipleship			14:28–33	
The Parable of the Unjust Steward			16:1–8	
Lazarus and the Rich Man			16:19–31	

Event	Matthew	Mark	Luke	John
Ten Men with Leprosy			17:11–19	
The Unjust Judge			18:1–8	
Perea	19:1–2	10:1		
The Feast of Tabernacles				7:10–13
Discourse on Jesus' Mission				7:14–30
The Spirit Testifies				7:37–53
The Woman Taken in Adultery				8:1–11
The Light of the World				8:12–59
A Blind Man Is Healed				9:1–41
The Parable of the Good Shepherd				10:1–21
The Question about Divorce	19:3–12	10:2–12		
Suffer the Little Children	19:13–15	10:13–16	18:15–17	
The Rich Young Ruler	19:16–26	10:17–27	18:18–27	
The Twelve to Rule Israel	19:27–30	10:28–31	18:28–30; 22:28–30	
The Parable of the Laborers in the Vineyard	20:1–16			

Event	Matthew	Mark	Luke	John
The Feast of Dedication				10:22–39
John's Followers Believe				10:40–42
Lazarus Dies				11:1–7
Lazarus Is Raised				11:8–53
On Being Great	20:20–28	10:35–45	22:24–27	
Two Blind Men Are Healed	20:29–34	10:46–52	18:35–43	
Zacchaeus			19:1–10	
Jesus Travels to Ephraim				11:54
Jerusalem at Passover				11:55–57; 12:1
Conspiracy to Kill Lazarus				12:9–11
Prophetic Preparation for the Triumphal Entry	21:1–6	11:1–6	19:28–34	
The Triumphal Entry	21:7–11	11:7–11	19:35–40	12:12–18
Pharisees Disapprove			19:39–40	12:19
Jesus Weeps over Jerusalem			19:41–44	
Greeks Wish to See Jesus				12:20–22
Jesus Is Sent by the Father				12:23–50

EVENT	MATTHEW	MARK	LUKE	JOHN
Jesus Cleanses the Temple	21:12–16	11:15–19	19:45–48	
Jesus Is Curses the Barren Fig Tree	21:17–22	11:12–14, 20–26	13:6–9	
Priests Challenge Jesus		11:27–33	20:1–8	
Prophecy of Death and Resurrection	20:17–19	10:32–34	18:31–34	
The Parable of the Two Sons	21:28–32			
The Parable of the Wicked Husbandmen	21:33–36	12:1–12	20:9–20	
The Parable of the King's Son	22:1–14		14:15–24	
On Paying Tribute to Caesar	22:15–22	12:13–17	20:21–26	
Seven Husbands	22:23–33	12:18–27	20:27–38	
The Great Commandment	22:34–40	12:28–34	10:25–37	
Two Pharisees Are Silenced	22:41–46	12:35–37	20:41–44	
The Widow's Mite		12:41–44	21:1–4	
A Denunciation of Hypocrisy	23:1–36	12:38–40	11:37–54; 18:9–14; 20:45–47	
Jesus Laments over Jerusalem	23:37–39		13:34–35	

EVENT	MATTHEW	MARK	LUKE	JOHN
Signs of the Second Coming	24:1–51	13:1–37	12:35–48; 17:20–37; 21:5–38	
The Parable of the Ten Virgins	25:1–13			
The Parable of the Talents/Pounds	25:14–30		19:11–27	
The Parable of the Sheep and Goats	25:31–46			
Prophecy of the Crucifixion	26:1–2			
Caiaphas's Palace	26:3–5	14:1–2		
The Feast with Simon the Pharisee	26:6	14:3	7:36	
The Anointing of Jesus	26:7–13	14:4–9	7:37–50	12:1–9
Judas's Conspiracy	26:14–16	14:10–11	22:3–6	
The First Day of Unleavened Bread	26:17–19	14:12–16	22:7–13	
The Passover Meal	26:20	14:17	22:13–14	13:1–2
The Prophecy of Betrayal	26:21–24	14:18–21	22:21–23	13:18–22
Judas Is Identified	26:25			13:23–30
The Sacrament Is Instituted	26:26–29	14:22–25	22:15–20	
Peter's Protest				13:2–12
Jesus Is an Example				13:13–17

EVENT	MATTHEW	MARK	LUKE	JOHN
A New Commandment				13:31–35
Jesus Comforts the Disciples				14:1–15
Another Comforter				14:16–31
The True Vine				15:1–8
Love One Another				15:9–17
Hatred of the World				15:18–27
Warning to the Apostles				16:1–6
The Comforter				16:7–16
Opposition				16:17–30
The Flock to Be Scattered	26:31–32	14:27–28		16:31–33
The Great Intercessory Prayer				17:1–26
The Mount of Olives	26:30	14:26	22:39	18:1
When You Are Converted			22:31–32	
Before the Cock Crows	26:33–35	14:29–31	22:33–34	13:36–38
Reckoned among the Transgressors			22:35–38	
Jesus' Prayer in Gethsemane	26:36–46	14:32–42	22:40–46	18:1
Judas's Betrayal	26:47–50	14:43–46	22:47–48	18:2–3
"I AM"				18:4–9

Event	Matthew	Mark	Luke	John
Peter Defends Jesus with a Sword	26:51–54	14:47	22:49–53	18:10–11
The Disciples Flee	26:56	14:50		
Jesus Is Arrested	26:55–57	14:46–52	22:52–54	18:1–3, 12–13
The Hearing before the Chief Priests	26:57–68	14:53–65	22:54, 63–71	18:12–15, 19–24
Peter's Denial	26:69–75	14:66–72	22:55–62	18:15–18, 25–27
Soldiers Mock Jesus	26:67–68	14:65	22:63–65	18:22
The Transfer to Pilate	27:2	15:1	23:1	18:28
The Hearing before Pilate	27:11–14	15:1–5	23:1–6	18:28–38
Judas's Death	27:3–10			
The Hearing before Herod			23:7–10	
Herod and Men Mock Jesus			23:11–12	
The Return to Pilate	27:15–26	15:6–15	23:13–23	
Barabbas Is Released	27:15–21, 26	15:6–15	23:18–25	18:39–40
Pilate Washes His Hands	27:24–25		23:22	19:4
Jesus Is Scourged and Mocked	27:27–31	15:15–20		19:1–12
Golgotha	27:32–34	15:20–23	23:26–31	19:13–17
The Crucifixion	27:25–44	15:24–33	23:32–43	19:18–22

EVENT	MATTHEW	MARK	LUKE	JOHN
The Soldiers Cast Lots	27:35	15:24	23:34	19:23–24
The Sign on the Cross	27:37	15:26	23:38	19:19–22
John Is Charged to Take Care of Jesus' Mother				19:25–27
Jesus' Last Words	27:46	15:34	23:34, 43, 46	19:26–28, 30
The Death of Jesus	27:45–50	15:33–37	23:46	19:28–30
Jesus' Side Is Pierced				19:31–34
The Veil of the Temple Is Rent	27:51–53	15:38	23:45	
The Scriptures Are Fulfilled				19:35–37
Watchers near the Cross	27:54–56	15:39–41	23:47–49	
Jesus' Burial	27:57–61	15:42–47	23:50–56	19:38–42
The Tomb Is Sealed	27:62–66			
Women Disciples Visit the Tomb	28:1–2		24:1–2	
Peter and Another Disciple Go to the Tomb			24:12, 24	20:3–10
Mary Magdalene Witnesses the Resurrected Lord				20:11–17

EVENT	MATTHEW	MARK	LUKE	JOHN
Disciples Disbelieve Reports of Jesus' Resurrection		16:10–11	24:9–11	20:18
The Two Marys	28:1	16:1–4	23:55; 24:3, 10	20:1–2
"He Is Risen"	28:2–8	16:5–8	24:4–8	
The Women Meet Jesus	28:9–10	16:9		
Officials Bribe Soldiers	28:11–15			
Two Disciples		16:12–13	24:13–35	
Jesus Appears to His Disciples		16:14	24:36–49	20:19–23
Thomas Disbelieves				20:24–25
Jesus Appears Again to His Disciples				20:26–29
John's Closing Testimony				20:30–31
The Disciples in Galilee				21:1–19
Peter Inquires Concerning the Fate of John the Beloved				21:20–22
Testimony about John				21:23–25
The Great Commission	28:16–20	16:15–18		
Jesus' Ascension and Proclamation		16:19–20	24:50–53	

INDEX